THE LAW AND PRACTICE OF ADMIRALTY MATTERS

THE LAW AND PRACTICE OF ADMIRALTY MATTERS

SECOND EDITION

SARAH C. DERRINGTON
Professor and Dean of Law, The University of Queensland, Brisbane

JAMES M. TURNER QC
Quadrant Chambers, Quadrant House, London

OXFORD
UNIVERSITY PRESS

OXFORD
UNIVERSITY PRESS

Great Clarendon Street, Oxford, OX2 6DP,
United Kingdom

Oxford University Press is a department of the University of Oxford.
It furthers the University's objective of excellence in research, scholarship,
and education by publishing worldwide. Oxford is a registered trade mark of
Oxford University Press in the UK and in certain other countries

First Edition published in 2007
Second Edition published in 2016
Impression: 1

Published in the United States of America by Oxford University Press
198 Madison Avenue, New York, NY 10016, United States of America

British Library Cataloguing in Publication Data
Data available

Library of Congress Control Number: 2015954361

ISBN 978–0–19–872955–6

Printed and bound by
CPI Group (UK) Ltd, Croydon, CR0 4YY

FOREWORD

There is both a domestic and an international aspect to Admiralty matters. The domestic aspect focuses upon the domestic law of the court of the country exercising its Admiralty jurisdiction. The international aspect reflects the circumstance that the courts of most trading nations with a coastline possess an Admiralty jurisdiction and in exercising that jurisdiction deal with problems which must occur in all such courts. It is common for admiralty textbooks to focus on the domestic law of Admiralty with which the writer is concerned. The particular value of this admiralty textbook is that its distinguished English and Australian authors reflect the international aspect of Admiralty matters by drawing upon the Admiralty law not only of England and Australia but also, in particular, of Canada, New Zealand, South Africa, Hong Kong, and Singapore. This is, or should be, of particular value to the advocates who practise in Admiralty courts and to the courts themselves. Whenever a problem of Admiralty law arises which does not appear to be covered by a clear and binding precedent (and perhaps even when it does appear to be so covered) the Admiralty court, in whatever country, will or should be assisted by knowing how the problem has been approached or solved by other courts exercising an Admiralty jurisdiction.

Three examples will suffice. The first comes from the process of sale, an essential component of the *in rem* jurisdiction. Some claimants *in rem*, usually mortgagees of vessels, would prefer, for understandable reasons of economy, practicality, and convenience, to obtain an order for the sale of a vessel under arrest to a buyer of their own choosing, rather than to the successful bidder following upon an appraisal of the vessel's value by the Admiralty Marshal or his equivalent. This problem has recently been encountered in the Admiralty courts of England, Singapore, Hong Kong and Canada. Happily the Admiralty courts of those countries have agreed that in general the sale of a vessel should be in the hands of the Admiralty Marshal rather than in the hands of the claimant *in rem* (see Chapter 7 of *Admiralty Matters*). The second example concerns international conventions governing such matters as arrest and limitation of liability. They will inevitably give rise to similar problems in different jurisdictions (for example, the question whether a limitation fund can be constituted by a letter of undertaking from a P&I Club: see the *Atlantik Confidence* [2014] EWCA Civ 217, [2014] 1 WLR 3883). In that context it is essential, or at any rate desirable, that the Admiralty courts applying those conventions know how other Admiralty courts have resolved the same or similar problems (see Chapter 10 of *Admiralty Matters* concerning limitation of liability).

The third example concerns insolvency. When a shipowning company becomes insolvent there is often a tension between the jurisdiction of the Admiralty court which has arrested, or is asked to arrest, one or more of the company's vessels and the jurisdiction of the companies court which is managing the distribution of the assets of the insolvent company. A domestic example of such tension arose in *In re Aro Co Ltd* [1980] Ch 196. The most recent international example of such tension is the *Sanko Mineral* [2014] EWHC 3927 (Admlty), [2015] 1 Lloyd's Rep 247. In the light of the Cross Border Insolvency Regulations 2006, pursuant to which foreign insolvency proceedings may be recognized as the 'foreign main proceedings', these international tensions are likely to be more frequent. It is therefore appropriate and helpful that *Admiralty Matters* has a section in Chapter 8 on insolvency issues.

I consider that these examples illustrate the value of the authors' emphasis in *Admiralty Matters* on the international or comparative aspect of admiralty law and practice. I commend this book to all advocates in Admiralty matters.

The Hon Mr Justice Teare
Admiralty Judge
Royal Courts of Justice
September 2015

PREFACE TO THE SECOND EDITION

Ten years since we first suggested that Admiralty continues to matter, we have been challenged in this edition of the work to assimilate the jurisprudence that has emerged over that decade in the jurisdictions whose law and practice we consider, as well as the revisions to their statutes or rules. If it is possible to identify a single theme that runs through this work, it is perhaps a comforting convergence of many of the important principles of admiralty law amongst these legal systems. Of course, exceptions remain, notably in the acceptance or otherwise of the House of Lords' still-controversial decision in *The Indian Grace (No 2)* and in the very recent Australian decision in *The Sam Hawk*, rejecting *The Halcyon Isle* approach to maritime liens.

Our aspiration in this work continues to be to provide, for those engaged in or coming to grips with admiralty matters, a useful guide to and insight into the theories, principles, and procedures which underpin the law applied to commercial disputes within the jurisdiction of the admiralty courts. We hope that practitioners will find useful the identification and exploration of areas of similarity and difference in the admiralty laws of England, Australia, Canada, Hong Kong, New Zealand, Singapore, and South Africa. Above all else, we hope that this work will be a fertile source of food for thought in the ongoing development of the Admiralty jurisdiction.

We are very grateful for the support and assistance we have received from many people in the course of writing. In particular we would like to thank the team at OUP, especially Alexander Johnson, Rachel Mullaly, and Emma Taylor, and Ms Mahalakshmi Kathirreshan of Newgen Knowledge Works Pvt Ltd, above all for accommodating changes wrought by the important Court of Appeal decision in *The Stolt Kestrel* [2015] EWCA Civ 1035, well after submission of the manuscript. We would also like to express particular thanks to our dedicated team of research assistants, all of whom have been persuaded to study or practise admiralty law in greater or lesser measure: Rosemary Gibson (now of Thynne + Macartney), Nicholas Derrington (now of the Queensland Bar), and Georgia Williams and Leo Rees-Murphy (students at the University of Queensland). We are humbled by and grateful to The Hon Mr Justice Teare for his generous Foreword. Unavoidably, all errors and omissions remain ours alone.

We have attempted to state the law as at 15 October 2015.

SCD, Brisbane

JMT, London

PREFACE TO THE FIRST EDITION

So, *Admiralty Matters*, does it? Well yes, actually, it does. Although the rich *in rem* diet enjoyed by Sir Anthony Clarke MR in his youth may have given way over the years to more balanced, more *in personam*, fare for his successors at the Admiralty Bar, the law of Admiralty has neither stood still nor lost its relevance in the modern commercial context; nor yet have he and the other distinguished Admiralty judges of recent and more distant times resolved all of the many and varied issues which beset their jurisdiction. Indeed, the relative infrequency with which those issues nowadays trouble the courts—and the often very large sums involved when they do—make a work such as this more rather than less *à point*, as the 'great education' in matters Admiralty, served up by the future Lord Brandon to the present Master of the Rolls and Lord Chief Justice, is no longer on the menu for today's practitioner.

Our aspiration in this work is to provide, for those engaged in or coming to grips with admiralty matters, a useful guide to and insight into the theories, principles, and procedures which underpin the law applied to commercial disputes within the jurisdiction of the Admiralty courts. Above all else, we hope that this work will be a fertile source of food for thought in the ongoing development of the Admiralty jurisdiction. To that end, and although of necessity the work concentrates upon English law, we have sought to include developments, practice, and jurisprudence in other jurisdictions whose admiralty law is derived from that of England, namely Australia, Canada, Hong Kong, New Zealand, Singapore, and South Africa.

We are very grateful for the support and assistance we have received from many people in the course of writing. In particular we would like to thank the team at Oxford University Press, especially Wendy Lynch and Faye Judges; Justis.com for providing us with some of the materials in the appendices; the staff of the Walter Harrison Law Library at the University of Queensland for their unfailing assistance in obtaining materials; Graham Lopes SC of the South African Bar for his insights into South African arrest and attachment; Ian Koh of Drew & Napier, Singapore for procuring copyright permissions at very short notice; The Hon Mr Justice Teare, particularly for his comments on an earlier draft of the Limitation chapter, and Sir Anthony Clarke MR for his generous Foreword (and for the educational experience which appearing in front of him has always been). We owe a great deal of thanks to The Hon Justice James Allsop of the Federal Court of Australia and Professor Ross Grantham of the T C Beirne School of Law at the University of Queensland, both of whom read and commented constructively on various versions of the manuscript. Unavoidably, all errors and omissions remain ours alone.

Finally, we express our love and gratitude to our families who have endured this project to the detriment of family life. Sarah dedicates this book to her husband Roger, without whose constant support and encouragement she could not have embarked upon the task, and to her children, Nicholas, Stephanie, and Emilie, who know far more about Admiralty law than is necessary for any childhood. James dedicates the book to his wife Franca, who would have much preferred it if he had not embarked upon it at all, but without whose selfless devotion to their four children over the interminable summer holiday he would certainly never have finished it.

We have attempted to state the law as at 31 July 2006.

SCD, Brisbane
JMT, London

CONTENTS—SUMMARY

TABLE OF CONTENTS

TABLE OF CASES

Notes: Cases beginning with 'Re'/'In Re' are indexed under the first significant word which follows, as are those beginning with 'The'; definite articles in languages other than English are treated as indexable words.

References are by paragraph (or footnote) number; chapter numbers appear in **bold**, paragraph numbers in plain. Footnote numbers are in italic and preceded by *n*. **App** = Appendix.

Po, The [1991] 2 Lloyd's Rep 206 . . . . 1.*n2*, 6.32
Podmore v Aquatours Pty Ltd [1984] 1 NSWLR 111 . . . . 10.190
Point Breeze, The [1928] P 135 . . . . 6.53, 6.70
Pointer Apitong, The [1991] 2 HKC 503 . . . . 4.32, 4.33, 4.37, 4.38
Polar Shipping Inc v Plan Marine AG (The Bugaz) 31 August 1997, M Stranex, *Shipping Cases of South Africa* (3rd edn, 2000) D1 . . . . 5.75
Polish Steam Ship Co v Atlantic Maritime Co [1985] 1 QB 41, [1984] 2 Lloyd's Rep 37 . . . . 10.184
Polo II, The [1977] 2 Lloyd's Rep 115 . . . . 7.19, 7.21
Polpen Shipping Company Ltd v Commercial Union Assurance Company Ltd [1943] KB 161 . . . . 2.72
Port of Geelong Authority v The Ship The Bass Reefer (1992) 37 FCR 374, (1992) 109 ALR 505 . . . . 5.72, 5.80, 5.*n139*
Porto Seguro Companhia de Seguros Gerais v Belcan SA [1997] 3 SCR 1278 . . . . 9.38, 9.44
President of India v La Pintada Compania [1985] AC 104, [1984] 3 WLR 10, [1984] 2 All ER 773, [1984] 2 Lloyd's Rep 9 . . . . 6.46
Prince George, The (1837) 3 Hag Adm 376, 166 ER 449 . . . . 4.34
Profit Country Enterprises Ltd v Sea-Land Service Inc [1998] HKCU 2060 . . . . 10.107
Programmed Total Marine Services Pty Ltd v The Ship 'Hako Fortress' [2012] FCA 805, (2012) 293 ALR 139 . . . . 5.72
PST Energy 7 Shipping LLC v OW Bunker Malta Ltd, 'The Res Cogitans' [2015] EWHC 2022 (Comm) 4.*nn202–203*

Qenos Pty Ltd v The Ship APL Sydney [2009] FCA 1090, (2009) 187 FCR 282 . . . . 10.69, 10.74, 10.120
Q's Estate, In re [1999] 1 Lloyd's Rep 931 . . . . 11.44
Queen of the South, The [1968] P 449, [1968] 1 Lloyd's Rep 182 . . . . 1.*n5*, 5.*n157*

R v Forty Nine Casks of Brandy (1836) Hag Adm 257 . . . . 3.13
R v Goodwin [2005] EWCA Crim 3184, [2006] 1 WLR 546 . . . . 2.69, 2.*n174*, 2.*n187*, 2.*nn189–190*, 2.*n198*
R v Judge of City of London Court [1892] 1 QB 273 . . . . 4.25, 5.41
Rail Equipment Leasing Pty Ltd v CV Scheepvaartonderneming Emmagracht [2008] NSWSC 850 . . . . 4.*n83*
Rajah, The (1872) LR 3 A & E 539 . . . . 10.*n170*
Rama, The [1996] 2 Lloyd's Rep 281 . . . . 4.18–4.19, 4.22
Ran, The [1922] P 80 . . . . 10.*n179*
Rana, The (1921) 8 Ll L Rep 369 . . . . 8.09
Rangitata, The [1998] FCA 244 . . . . 7.*n118*
RD Summers Fisheries CC v Viking Fishing Co Pty Ltd (MFV Logan Ora) (1999) 4 SA 1081 . . . . 7.79
Readhead, Phillip & Ors v Admiralty Marshal, Western Australia District Registry [1998] FCA 1173 . . . . 7.69–7.70
Reef Shipping Co Ltd v The Fua Kavenga [1987] 1 NZLR 550 . . . . 2.*n231*, 5.47
Regalia, The (1884) 5 Asp 338 . . . . 3.08
Reina, The (No 2) [1963] 2 Lloyd's Rep 513 . . . . 8.09
Reiter Petroleum Inc v The Ship 'Sam Hawk' [2015] FCA 1005 . . . . . 4.54, 4.*n35*, 4.*n188*, 4.*n202*
Rena K, The [1979] 1 QB 377, [1978] 3 WLR 431, [1979] 1 All ER 397, [1978] 1 Lloyd's Rep 545 . . . . 2.07, 2.33, 2.*n74*, 5.*n268*, 11.47, 11.51–11.54
Republic of India v India Steamship Co Ltd (The Indian Grace) (No 2) [1997] UKHL 40, [1998] AC 878, [1997] 3 WLR 818, [1997] 4 All ER 380, [1998] 1 Lloyd's Rep 1 . . . . 1.13, 2.27, 2.29–2.31, 2.33–2.51, 2.57, 2.60, 2.*n3*, 2.*n7*, 2.*n163*, 4.54, 5.15, 6.35, 6.*n141*, 6.*n180*, 6.*n185*, 11.52–11.53
Res Cogitans, The see *PST Energy 7 Shipping LLC v OW Bunker Malta Ltd*
Resource I, Re [2000] 3 HKLRD 49 . . . . 5.*n35*

TABLE OF LEGISLATION

Note: References are by paragraph (or footnote) number; chapter numbers appear in **bold**, paragraph numbers in plain. Footnote numbers are in italic and preceded by *n*. **App** = Appendix.

UK LEGISLATION

Statutes

Statutory Instruments

INTERNATIONAL LEGISLATION

EU LEGISLATION

Treaties and Conventions

Regulations

NATIONAL LEGISLATION

Australia

Canada

Hong Kong

New Zealand

Singapore

1

INTRODUCTION

Admiralty jurisdiction in England and Wales dates back to the early Middle Ages. **1.01** Nowadays, however, it is derived in the first instance from the provisions of the Senior Courts Act (SCA) 1981[1] and encompasses both *in rem* and *in personam* actions. Some of those provisions give effect to the International Convention on the Unification of Certain Rules relating to the Arrest of Seagoing Ships 1952 (the Arrest Convention) and so are to be construed in its light.[2] A new International Convention on the Arrest of Ships was adopted on 12 March 1999 (the Arrest Convention 1999). It entered into force on 14 September 2014, the date by which ten States had expressed their consent to be bound by it. At the date of writing, only eleven States have become party to the Arrest Convention 1999,[3] none of which are the subject of this work.

The Admiralty jurisdiction of the High Court is defined in s 20(1) of the SCA **1.02** 1981. This sets out four broad areas of jurisdiction: (i) maritime claims, whose common feature[4] is that they may be brought *in rem*; (ii) claims which may only

[1] Previously, the Supreme Court Act 1981, renamed the 'Senior Courts Act 1981' pursuant to s 59(5) and para 1(1) of pt 1 of sch 11 to the Constitutional Reform Act 2005.

[2] *The Eschersheim* [1976] 1 WLR 430, 436, [1976] 1 All ER 920, 924, [1976] 2 Lloyd's Rep 1, 6 per Lord Diplock. It has been held that the Arrest Convention has been incorporated directly into English municipal law through the 1968 EC Jurisdiction Convention and the Civil Jurisdiction and Judgments Act 1982 (*The Nordglimt* [1988] QB 183, 195, [1988] 2 WLR 338, 349, [1988] 2 All ER 531, 541 [1987] 2 Lloyd's Rep 470, 478), but the scepticism expressed by Clarke J in *The Tjaskemolen* ([1997] 2 Lloyd's Rep 476, 478) appears justified and it is respectfully suggested that Hobhouse J's view does not reflect the law. See also per Lloyd LJ in *The Po* [1991] 2 Lloyd's Rep 206, 211.

[3] Albania, Algeria, Benin, Bulgaria, Congo, Ecuador, Estonia, Latvia, Liberia, Spain, and the Syrian Arab Republic.

[4] With the sole exception of an action for damage received by a ship (s 20(2)(d)).

be brought *in personam* (collision, limitation, and Merchant Shipping Act actions); (iii) the residual jurisdiction; and (iv) the procedural jurisdiction. That jurisdiction is exercised by the Admiralty Court by virtue of s 62(2) of the SCA 1981.

A. Jurisdictional Overview

Maritime claims

1.03 Section 20(1)(a) provides for the Admiralty Court to have jurisdiction to hear and determine any of the 18 'questions and claims' listed in sub-section (2). That list reflects, with some additions, the list of maritime claims contained in art 1(1) of the Arrest Convention. It is a 'closed' list; in other words, unless it can be established that a particular claim falls squarely within one of the heads listed, the Court will not have Admiralty jurisdiction in respect of that claim.

1.04 Maritime claims themselves subdivide into what the helpful Australian nomenclature categorizes as 'proprietary claims', 'maritime liens (and "other charges")', and 'general maritime claims'.

Claims enforceable only *in personam*

1.05 Section 20(1)(b) of the SCA 1981 confers jurisdiction in relation to any of the proceedings mentioned in sub-section (3), ie, applications under the Merchant Shipping Act 1995 (MSA), certain actions arising out of or relating to collisions, and actions to limit liability under the MSA. The jurisdiction granted by this provision is exercisable only *in personam*, but that does not of course prevent the bringing of proceedings *in rem* where their subject matter is covered by, eg, the paragraphs referred to in s 21(4) as well as by s 20(1)(b).

The residual jurisdiction

1.06 Under s 20(1)(c), sometimes described as the 'sweeping-up' provision,[5] the Court retains any other Admiralty jurisdiction which it had immediately before the commencement of the SCA 1981—and, by extension, any which it had before the Judicature Acts.[6]

1.07 It is not clear whether this section preserves not only the Admiralty jurisdiction *per se* but also the power to exercise that jurisdiction *in rem*.[7] It is submitted, however, that whilst the earlier *jurisdiction* is expressly preserved by the SCA 1981, nothing in that

[5] See, eg, per Brandon J in *The Queen of the South* [1968] P 449, 455 *et seq*, [1968] 1 Lloyd's Rep 182, 188.
[6] Administration of Justice Act 1956, s 1(1).
[7] *The Antonis P Lemos* [1984] 2 WLR 825, 831, [1984] 2 All ER 353, [1984] 1 Lloyd's Rep 464.

Act makes any reference to the *mode of exercise* of that jurisdiction and the specific provisions of s 21 relating to the mode of exercise of jurisdiction are exhaustive.

There is, however, at least one modern authority to the contrary, albeit this precise point was not argued; in *The Despina GK*,[8] Sheen J followed the decision of Sir Robert Phillimore in *The City of Mecca*[9] to enforce a foreign judgment *in rem* by means of action *in rem*. However, it is respectfully doubted that this doctrine can be good law,[10] and there is much to be said against it in practical and policy terms.[11] If, of course, *The Despina GK* does not represent the law, then it can afford no support for the view that s 20(1)(c) preserves the mode of exercise as well as the jurisdiction of the pre-Judicature Acts Admiralty Court. **1.08**

Procedural jurisdiction

Finally, s 20(1)(d) of the SCA 1981 grants to the Admiralty Court any other jurisdiction connected with ships or aircraft which is (i) vested in the High Court; (ii) assigned by Rules of Court made or coming into effect after the commencement of the Act to the Queen's Bench Division; and (iii) directed by those Rules to be exercised by the Admiralty Court. Obvious examples of this are applications under the Merchant Shipping Acts,[12] which are directed by CPR 61.2(1)(a)(iv) to be started in the Admiralty Court. **1.09**

B. The Action *In Rem* Introduced

Although actions in most instances can and in some cases must be brought in the Admiralty Court *in personam*, the defining feature of the Admiralty jurisdiction of England and Wales—and those of the other countries considered in this work—is the action *in rem*. **1.10**

---

[8] *The Despina GK* [1983] QB 214, [1982] 2 Lloyd's Rep 555.

[9] *The City of Mecca* (1879) 5 PD 28; the 'mode of exercise' point was taken before Sir Robert, at p 32, and dealt with by him unconvincingly at p 33 on the basis that 'it is my duty to place the English Court in the position of the Portuguese Court after its sentence has been given against the defendants'. The decision was overruled on the facts by the Court of Appeal, (1881) 6 PD 106, further investigation having established that Portugal had abolished or did not recognize actions *in rem*. The potential for the doctrine to operate in a discriminatory fashion—and thus contrary to fundamental principles of the European legal order—is plain to see.

[10] For the reasons considered in paras 6.50 and following below.

[11] It is not difficult to imagine, for example, a need for expert evidence in order to determine whether or not the particular foreign judgment is properly to be characterized as *in rem* or not; indeed, by whose law is the characterization of a judgment as *in rem* or *in personam* to be assessed? Does the doctrine operate following a change of ownership after judgment or in respect of claims which the enforcing court would not but the originating court did recognize as giving rise to a right to proceed *in rem*? See also n 9 for the potential for the doctrine to operate in a discriminatory fashion.

[12] Eg, under s 61 of the 1995 Act.

1.11 The action *in rem* enables property, most usually a ship, to be arrested to compel the provision of security and, if security is not forthcoming, to enable the Admiralty Court to sell the vessel free of all encumbrances to satisfy the claims against the ship.

1.12 The action *in rem* is an odd beast, and not merely because it is one of very few uses of Latin to have survived the anglicizing fervour of the reforms of English civil procedure in the 1990s.[13] That linguistic survival has a neat symbolism to it, however, in that the story of the Admiralty action *in rem*, inseparable from that of the Admiralty Court itself, is one of survival. By the early nineteenth century the Common Law Courts, jealous and suspicious of the Admiralty Court's civilian jurisdiction,[14] had reduced it to a rump to which they could mount no sustainable claim. The action *in rem* and the maritime lien to which it gave effect defined and thus preserved that jurisdiction[15]—before it was finally secured and its ambit extended by the Admiralty Court Acts of 1840 and 1861.[16]

1.13 The action *in rem* evolved in an earlier time, and its evolution was far from complete when it was overlaid with the encrustations of the first of four reforming statutes,[17] followed by the implementation in English law of the Arrest Convention[18] and the changes wrought by what is now CPR Part 61, not to mention 165 years of often-conflicting jurisprudence. Small wonder, perhaps, if the House of Lords itself 'appears to have misunderstood the true nature of the action *in rem*'[19] in the leading case of *The Indian Grace (No 2)*,[20] a question considered further below.[21]

---

[13] Claims *in personam* were no more to be so called (in the English Court at least); §12.1 of the Practice Direction to CPR Part 61, under the heading 'Other Claims', states that 'This section applies to Admiralty claims which, before the coming into force of Part 61, would have been called claims *in personam*.' This work continues to use '*in personam*' in preference to 'formerly known as *in personam*' or (which is worse) 'other claims'. The courts have done the same: note the wry comment of Tomlinson LJ in *The Stolt Kestrel* [2015] EWCA Civ 1035, [13].

[14] And of its practitioners, doctors of civil law—at a time when the common law was not thought an appropriate subject for academic study. The jurisdiction of the civilian courts was not confined to Admiralty, but included matters then subject to canon law, most significantly probate and divorce. Although the members of 'Doctors' Commons' (the civilian equivalent of the Inns of Court, ridiculed by Dickens in *Sketches by Boz* and *David Copperfield*) lost much of their monopoly in 1857 and dissolved their institution shortly afterwards, the legacy of the jurisdiction lingered on well into the twentieth century in the form of the Probate, Admiralty and Divorce Division. For further reading, start with J H Baker, *An Introduction to English Legal History* (4th edn, 2002) and continue with F L Wiswall Jr, *The Development of Admiralty Jurisdiction and Practice since 1800—An English Study with American Comparisons* (1975).

[15] *The Bold Buccleugh* (1851) 7 Moo PC 267, 13 ER 884; *The Banco* [1971] P 137.

[16] For more detailed accounts of the history of the Admiralty jurisdiction, see Prichard and Yale (eds), *Hale & Fleetwood on Admiralty Jurisdiction* (1992, Selden Society) , and *Wiswall* n 14 above.

[17] The Admiralty Court Acts of 1840 and 1861, the Administration of Justice Act 1920, and the Supreme Court of Judicature (Consolidation) Act 1925, to say nothing of the Judicature Acts.

[18] Which has itself gone through two editions: the Administration of Justice Act 1956 and the Supreme Court Act 1981, which was renamed the 'Senior Courts Act 1981' pursuant to s 59(5) and para 1(1) of pt 1 of sch 11 to the Constitutional Reform Act 2005.

[19] B Davenport QC, 'End of an Old Admiralty Belief' (1998) 114 LQR 169.

[20] *The Indian Grace (No 2)* [1997] UKHL 40, [1998] AC 878, [1997] 3 WLR 818, [1997] 4 All ER 380, [1998] 1 Lloyd's Rep 1.

[21] In Chapter 2.

It is no easy matter, in such circumstances, to go beyond an adjectival analysis[22] and to formulate a theory which explains all the peculiarities of the action *in rem*. In recent years, the focus of the debate in this connection has been between the so-called 'personification' and 'procedural' theories of the action *in rem*, neither of which is wholly satisfactory. In order to see whether the formulation of such a theory is not only possible but helpful, it is necessary first to identify and consider the characteristics of the action *in rem*. These characteristics are examined in Chapter 2 and the interaction between the maritime lien and the statutory action *in rem* is explored. **1.14**

C. Issues of Procedure and Dispute Resolution

Once it has been determined that a claim is susceptible to the jurisdiction of the Admiralty Court, the processes which are peculiar to the Admiralty jurisdiction are triggered. There is no particular mystique about the practice and procedure of the Admiralty Court. Claims in Admiralty are usually commercial disputes between commercial parties, and the practice and procedure of the Admiralty Court is intended to facilitate the resolution of disputes in a timely and cost-effective manner. Nonetheless, the availability of the arrest process for many Admiralty claims, and the particular procedures applicable to collision and limitation actions, single out the practices and procedures of the Admiralty Court for special treatment. **1.15**

In addition to the procedures provided by the Admiralty Court for the resolution of maritime disputes, arbitration has long been favoured as a dispute resolution mechanism by parties to a maritime dispute. The procedures of the Admiralty Court are, in many respects, anathema to the arbitral process. However, the arrest of a ship is a common method of securing claims which are subject to arbitration agreements. The practices and procedures of the Admiralty Court remain relevant to those involved in arbitration and the interplay between the two processes must be understood. **1.16**

D. A Comparative Overview

It is trite to observe that the nature of maritime trade means that most disputes which arise within the Admiralty jurisdiction involve parties domiciled in different jurisdictions and transactions governed by the laws of States other than that in which the claim is litigated or arbitrated. This work does not attempt to deal with all or even many of the private international law issues which arise in **1.17**

[22] For an example of which, see D C Jackson, *Enforcement of Maritime Claims* (4th edn, 2005) para 17.43.

the context of maritime law; the reader is referred instead to the leading texts on conflicts of laws.[23] Nor does it attempt to provide a complete analysis of the impact of European procedural law on the exercise of Admiralty jurisdiction, although it is referred to where necessary.[24] It does, however, seek to highlight significant features of the Admiralty jurisdiction in those countries whose jurisdiction is derived from English law and which have a vibrant and evolving Admiralty jurisdiction. In many respects, the Admiralty law of these countries differs little from English law and the comparative overview may be useful in shedding light on the equivalent English provision. In other respects, however, the law has taken a dramatically different turn and the comparative overview may serve to highlight any juridical advantage to a claimant or defendant in potential alternative fora.[25] It may also inform future debate (should there be any) regarding the uniformity of Admiralty law and procedure around the common law world. As Scott LJ said in *The Tolten*:[26]

> ... it is to the interest of maritime commerce that [British admiralty law] should not unnecessarily diverge [from the general law of the sea amongst Western nations]. If there is doubt about some rule or principle of our national law and one solution of the doubt would conform to the general law and the other would produce divergence, the traditional view of our admiralty judges is in favour of the solution which will promote uniformity. For this there are two good reasons, first because that course will probably be the true reading of our legal development and, secondly, because uniformity of sea law throughout the world is so important for the welfare of maritime commerce that to aim at it is a right judicial principle ...

1.18 The jurisdictions considered in this work, apart from that of England and Wales, are Australia, Canada, Hong Kong, New Zealand, Singapore, and South Africa.[27]

1.19 Unlike the United Kingdom, Australia has not ratified the Arrest Convention. However, the Admiralty Act 1988 (Cth) is largely consistent with its provisions. Until 1988, Australia's Admiralty jurisdiction was governed by the Colonial Courts of Admiralty Act 1890 (UK) which limited Australia's jurisdiction to matters within the Admiralty jurisdiction in England in 1890. The Law Reform

---

23 Notably *Dicey, Morris & Collins on the Conflict of Laws* (15th edn, 2015).

24 A detailed analysis of European law in the Admiralty context is offered by D C Jackson, *Enforcement of Maritime Claims* (4th edn, 2005) Chapters 3–8. This analysis remains valuable, but it should be noted that European procedural law has moved on with the advent of the recast Brussels I Regulation (EU) 1215/2012, which entered into force on 10 January 2015.

25 It can pay to shop around, even if, as Lord Denning famously put it in *The Atlantic Star* [1973] 1 QB 364, 382: "You may call this 'forum-shopping' if you please, but if the forum is England, it is a good place to shop in, both for the quality of the goods and the speed of service."

26 *The Tolten* [1946] P 135, 142, (1946) 79 Ll L Rep 349, 352.

27 The relevant portions of the UK statutes are included as appendices to this work, as are the web addresses for the legislation from each non-UK jurisdiction conferring admiralty jurisdiction. A selection of cases and materials (the scope of which varies from jurisdiction to jurisdiction) may be accessed free of charge on the internet from the 'Legal Information Institute' of each (including England and Wales), links to which may be found at the foot of the homepage at <http:// www.worldlii.org>.

Commission prepared an extensive report and a draft bill, the aim of which was said to be to strike a balance between following the English legislation (the SCA of 1981) and seeking to clarify and simplify the law.[28] Admiralty jurisdiction is exercised concurrently by the Federal Court of Australia and the State Courts (within the limits of their monetary jurisdiction), although only the Federal and superior State Courts have *in rem* jurisdiction.

Similarly, Canada has not ratified the Arrest Convention but has adopted some of its provisions into Canadian domestic law, notably the concept of sister-ship arrest.[29] The history of Admiralty jurisdiction in Canada is more colourful than the Australian history although, in 1891, the jurisdiction of the two countries was largely identical.[30] In 1891, Canada passed the Admiralty Act 1891 which gave the Canadian Exchequer Court the same Admiralty jurisdiction as the High Court of England. Ultimately, in 1971, the Federal Court Act was passed which established the Federal Court of Canada as the Admiralty Court for Canada, although the jurisdiction is also exercised concurrently by the provincial courts.[31] The Admiralty jurisdiction of the Federal Court of Canada finds its most recent manifestation in the Federal Courts Act 1985.[32] **1.20**

Hong Kong ratified the Arrest Convention on 29 March 1963, which continues to apply to the Hong Kong Special Administrative Region after 1 July 1997. The Admiralty jurisdiction of the Supreme Court of Hong Kong originally derived from the Colonial Courts of Admiralty Act 1890 which, by s 16, came into force in Hong Kong on 1 July 1891. By art 3 of the Admiralty Jurisdiction (Hong Kong) Order 1985, s 21 of the Supreme Court Act 1981 was extended to Hong Kong.[33] Since 1989, the High Court of Hong Kong's Admiralty jurisdiction has been prescribed in the High Court Ordinance. The provisions of the 1952 Convention are given effect to by ss 12A and B of the High Court Ordinance (Cap 4). **1.21**

New Zealand has also not ratified the Arrest Convention but, like Australia, has given effect to most of its provisions in the Admiralty Act 1973. Admiralty jurisdiction in New Zealand is exercised by both the High Court and the District Courts. The Admiralty Act 1973 grants unlimited Admiralty jurisdiction *in rem* and *in personam* to the High Court but, as in Australia, the District Courts are limited to *in personam* jurisdiction (within the limits of their monetary jurisdiction).[34] **1.22**

---

28 Civil Admiralty Jurisdiction, ALRC No 33, (1986).

29 Federal Courts Act RSC 1985, c.F-7, ss 22 and 43; Supreme Court Act RSBC 1996 c.443.

30 A detailed description of the history of Canadian Admiralty jurisdiction can be found in E Gold, A Chircop, and H Kindred, *Essentials of Canadian Maritime Law* (2003) Chapter 3.

31 Federal Court Act SC 1971 c.1.

32 Federal Courts Act RSC 1985 c.F-7.

33 *Kingstar Shipping Ltd v Owners of the Ship 'Rolita' (The Rolita)* [1989] 1 HKC 160; [1989] 1 HKLR 394 (Court of Appeal).

34 Admiralty Act 1973, s 3(1)(b).

1.23 Likewise, Singapore has not ratified the Arrest Convention but it is largely given effect to in the High Court (Admiralty Jurisdiction) Act, which confers Admiralty jurisdiction on the High Court of Singapore.[35]

1.24 South Africa has not ratified the Arrest Convention and, in the Admiralty Jurisdiction Regulation Act 105 of 1983, has adopted a much broader Admiralty jurisdiction than is provided for in the Arrest Convention. The Act confers Admiralty jurisdiction in two ways. First, in relation to any matter in respect of which a court of admiralty of the Republic referred to in the Colonial Courts of Admiralty Act 1890 (UK) had jurisdiction immediately before the commencement of the Act (in 1983), the court is to apply the law which the High Court of Justice of the United Kingdom in the exercise of its Admiralty jurisdiction would have applied at the time of commencement. Secondly, in respect of any other matter, the court is to apply Roman–Dutch Law as applicable in the Republic.[36]

---

[35] Chapter 123, 15 January 1962 as amended.

[36] Admiralty Jurisdiction Regulation Act 105 of 1983, s 6: for a commentary on the difficulties with the statutory formulation of Admiralty jurisdiction in South Africa see M Wagener, 'South African Admiralty and its English Origins—Will it Jump or must it be Pushed?' (2005) 36 *Journal of Maritime Law and Commerce* 61.

2

THE NATURE AND SCOPE OF THE MODERN ADMIRALTY ACTION

A. Introduction

The Admiralty jurisdiction of the High Court, assigned by s 62(2) of the Senior Courts Act 1981 to the Admiralty Court,[1] is delineated in s 20(1) of that Act as follows: **2.01**

(a) jurisdiction to hear and determine any of the questions and claims mentioned in sub-s (2) (maritime claims);

(b) jurisdiction in relation to any of the proceedings mentioned in sub-s (3) (purely *in personam* claims);

(c) any other Admiralty jurisdiction which it had immediately before the commencement of this Act (the residual jurisdiction);[2] and

[1] Along with the High Court's prize jurisdiction, derived in the first instance from s 27 of the 1981 Act. We do not consider the arcane subject of prize in this work.

[2] This sub-section preserves any jurisdiction which existed prior to 1 November 1875 and will be relevant only to the extent that Admiralty jurisdiction at that time exceeded that now expressed in

(d) any other jurisdiction connected with ships or aircraft vested in the High Court and assigned for the time being by rules of court to the Queen's Bench Division and directed by them to be exercised by the Admiralty Court (the procedural jurisdiction).

2.02 In setting out the scope of Admiralty jurisdiction, the Senior Courts Act 1981 distinguishes between actions *in rem* and *in personam*. Thus s 21(1) provides that, subject to s 22, an action *in personam* may be brought in the High Court in all cases within its Admiralty jurisdiction. The facility to proceed *in rem*, on the other hand, is limited to maritime claims, and the identity of the property against and the circumstances in which the action may be brought varies between different groups within that heading.

2.03 The differences between proceeding *in rem* and *in personam* go beyond the merely formal: the former mode of exercise of the Admiralty jurisdiction carries with it opportunities, within the same procedural wrapper, to found jurisdiction to try, and to obtain security for and even satisfaction of, a claim. Such opportunities are not readily to be found elsewhere in English civil litigation. Quite how far these differences extend is, and has for well over a century been, a matter of debate. In the era of European cross-border cooperation in matters of civil and commercial litigation (and of the statute which accompanied it, the Civil Jurisdiction and Judgments Act 1982), that debate has become acute. Although they are of course insulated by geography from the immediacy of much of that debate, the other Admiralty jurisdictions considered in this work are also affected by it.

2.04 In this chapter, the Admiralty Court's contemporary jurisdiction, both *in rem* and *in personam*, is outlined with a view not merely to elucidating it in practical terms, but to contributing to the core issue in the debate referred to above, namely the true nature of the action *in rem*.

B. The Modern Action *In Rem*

Preliminary observations

2.05 Uniquely among English process, the claim form in an action *in rem* may be served on a thing, usually a ship. The circumstances in which such an action will lie are considered in detail in Chapters 3 to 5, but for present purposes they may be noted to fall broadly into three categories:

(1) proprietary claims, including claims by mortgagees;
(2) claims giving rise to a maritime lien (and other charges); and
(3) general maritime claims (commonly known as statutory claims *in rem*).

the Senior Courts Act 1981. It is not contended that the Senior Courts Act 1981 itself has narrowed the scope of Admiralty jurisdiction.

There is some overlap between these categories, in particular between the second and third, but that is for present purposes of no consequence. More relevant is the well-known ability of maritime liens to survive a change in the ownership of the ship to which they attach, an attribute which clouds the debate about the nature of the action *in rem*. **2.06**

The characteristics of the action *in rem*

The characteristic incidents of an action *in rem* are presently understood[3] to include the following. **2.07**

(1) Once a claim form *in rem* has been issued, a change in ownership in the vessel will be ineffective to prevent the action proceeding against it,[4] an effect known colloquially as the 'statutory lien'.[5]
(2) In the absence of statutory permission, an action *in rem* lies only against the vessel in connection with which the claim arises.[6]
(3) If the owners of the ship appear and defend the action (or at any rate submit to the jurisdiction of the court), the action proceeds thereafter as if it had also been commenced *in personam*,[7] with the result that if the *res* itself proves

---

[3] Or at any rate had been so understood prior to the House of Lords' ruling in *Republic of India v India Steamship Co Ltd (The Indian Grace) (No 2)* [1997] UKHL 40, [1998] AC 878, [1997] 3 WLR 818, [1997] 4 All ER 380, [1998] 1 Lloyd's Rep 1. One of the unsatisfactory features of that decision is that precisely because these features were not considered in the leading speech, it is unclear whether and if so how they are compatible with Lord Steyn's view of the action *in rem*—and thus whether all or any of these hitherto well-established attributes will survive. This section proceeds upon the working assumption that they will; more detailed prognosis for each is considered later in this chapter.

[4] *The Monica S* [1968] P 741, [1968] 2 WLR 431, [1967] 3 All ER 740, [1967] 2 Lloyd's Rep 113.

[5] '... the expression "statutory lien" is a convenient one if it is used to mean no more than an irrevocably accrued statutory right of action in rem', ibid 768G, 453, 758, 130.

[6] *The Beldis* [1936] P 51, (1935) 53 Ll L Rep 255. Although in the 17th and 18th centuries both the defendant and any of his property had been liable to arrest in proceedings in the Admiralty Court, the restraint of its jurisdiction by the common law courts and the resultant development of the notion of the maritime lien resulted in a restriction on the right of arrest to the ship in connection with which the cause of action arose, a restriction which persisted after the expansion of the Court's jurisdiction under the Admiralty Court Acts 1840 and 1861. Sister-ship arrest was thus unavailable in England and Wales until the International Convention on the Unification of Certain Rules relating to the Arrest of Sea-going Ships 1952 (the Arrest Convention) and its subsequent authorization by the predecessor to s 21(4) of the Senior Courts Act 1981 (previously, the Supreme Court Act 1981).

[7] *The Dictator* [1892] P 304; *The Gemma* [1899] P 285; *The Dupleix* [1912] P 8; *The Banco* [1971] P 137, 151; *The August 8* [1983] 2 AC 450 PC. This rule has, apparently, been abrogated in South Africa (by Admiralty Rule 8(3)), where appearance in an action *in rem* will not render the vessel's owner 'liable *in personam*, save as to costs, merely by reason of having given such notice and having defended the action *in rem*': *The Argun* 2004 (1) SA 1 (SCA); *SA Boatyards CC v The Lady Rose* 1991 (3) SA 711 (CPD); *MV Zlatni Piasatzi: Frozen Foods International v Kudu Holdings* 1997 (2) SA 569 (CPD). The apparent clarity of the rule is, however, complicated by the continued operation in South Africa of English law (para 1.24 above). Hare has expressed the view that *The Dictator* would continue to apply to any dispute involving a cause of action within the original colonial jurisdiction of the South African admiralty courts, whereas it would not apply to any novel cause of action

insufficient to meet the claimant's claim, the owners' other assets will be available for enforcement purposes.[8]

(4) Conversely, if the owners do not appear, the claimant is limited to such of the realizable value of the *res* which is available once those whose claims rank in priority have been satisfied.[9] Any balance may be recovered in a subsequent action *in personam*.[10]

(5) Participation in *in rem* proceedings is not confined to the claimant and to the owners of the *res*; others may intervene in the proceedings in order to assert or protect their own rights or the priority accorded to them. Such participation neither requires nor brings with it any personal liability to the claimant.[11]

(6) A cause of action *in rem* does not merge in a judgment *in personam*.[12]

(7) The claimant in an action *in rem* may procure the issue of a warrant of arrest, after judgment as well as before judgment.[13]

(8) Once arrested, the ship may be sold by the court, in which event all outstanding claims which could be brought by action *in rem* against her are transferred to the fund in court.[14]

2.08 Identification of these characteristics of the action *in rem*, however, goes only so far in illuminating its fundamental nature—which, as alluded to earlier, remains unsettled. To that end, its functions and availability are considered next, before proceeding to contrast those claims which give rise to maritime liens with those in respect of which statute has granted the right to proceed *in rem*.

---

created post-1983 (J Hare, *Shipping Law & Admiralty Jurisdiction in South Africa* (2nd edn, 2009) para 1-9). This view does not appear to have been argued in the cases cited above, one of which involved a cause of action which was certainly within the colonial jurisdiction. The better view would therefore seem to be that the *in personam* liability of the owner is unaffected by the *in rem* proceedings or his participation in them.

In an analysis of the current nature of the *in rem* action in South Africa, Hofmeyr considered that the effect of *The Alina II* (2011) (6) SA 206 (SCA) was that the Admiralty Rules and the Admiralty Act did not mark a departure from English law: English law, including the decision in *The Indian Grace (No 2)* and all of its uncertainties, is regrettably now the law in South Africa (G Hofmeyr, *Admiralty Jurisdiction Law and Practice in South Africa* (2nd edn, 2012) [III.1]–[III.31].

[8] *The Dictator* [1892] P 304; *The Gemma* [1899] P 285; *The Dupleix* [1912] P 8.

[9] *The Banco* [1971] P 137, 151.

[10] *Nelson v Couch* (1863) CB (NS) 99, 143 ER 721, 33 LJ (CP) 46, 48, cited in *The Joannis Vatis (No 2)* [1922] P 213, 222.

[11] *The Nordglimt* [1988] 1 QB 183, 200–201, [1988] 2 WLR 338, 354, [1987] 2 Lloyd's Rep 470, 482.

[12] *The Cella* (1888) 13 PD 82, 85; *The Rena K* [1979] 1 QB 377, 405–406, [1978] 3 WLR 431, [1979] 1 All ER 397, 416, [1978] 1 Lloyd's Rep 545.

[13] Civil Procedure Rules (CPR) 61.5(1), overruling—in relation to judgment creditors—*The Alletta* [1974] 1 Lloyd's Rep 40 in favour of *The Daien Maru No 18* [1986] 1 Lloyd's Rep 387 (High Court of Singapore).See further paras 6.47 and following.

[14] *Corps v Owners of the Paddle Steamer 'Queen of the South'* [1968] P 449, [1968] 1 Lloyd's Rep 182; *The Leoborg (No 2)* [1963] 2 Lloyd's Rep 441; *The Silia* [1981] 2 Lloyd's Rep 534.

The functions of the action *in rem*

The action *in rem* can be described as a method of enforcing specified proprietary interests in relation to assets against others, including those having interests in those assets and against those having only personal claims against the owner.[15] This adjectival description of the process is reflected to some degree in the threefold function of the arrest of the ship or other property, usually cargo or freight, in the action *in rem*. **2.09**

(1) Most importantly, the action ensures that the claimant's claim is secured by placing the property under judicial detention pending determination of the claim by the Admiralty Court.[16]
(2) If the claimant is ultimately successful, the judgment is enforceable against the arrested property, the security given in its place, or the fund produced by its judicial sale.
(3) It may, at any rate in the European context, provide a basis for subject-matter jurisdiction.[17]

The action *in rem* often also has the effect of securing the appearance of the owner of the ship or other property.

The categories of *in rem* claims

Section 20(2) provides a list of maritime claims which reflects art 1(1) of the Arrest Convention 1952, and which may be divided into the four main categories of claim falling within the Admiralty *in rem* jurisdiction. **2.10**

'Proprietary' maritime claims

Section 21(2) provides that an action *in rem* may be brought in relation to the matters set out in s 20(2) paras (a), (b), (c), or (s).[18] These are, respectively: **2.11**

(a) claims relating to the ownership and possession of a ship, or any of its shares;
(b) questions arising between co-owners as to possession, employment, or earnings of the ship;
(c) claims in respect of mortgages or charges on the ship or any share therein; and
(d) claims for the forfeiture and condemnation of a ship or any goods, or for the restoration of the ship or goods following seizure or for droits of admiralty.

---

[15] D C Jackson, *Enforcement of Maritime Claims* (4th edn, 2005) para 17.43.

[16] The claim may also be determined by arbitration or by the court of another country. In relation to the former, see para 11.43 below; as to the latter, see s 26 of the Civil Jurisdiction and Judgments Act 1982 and, for a recent example, *The Uranus* [2015] EWHC 1269 (Admlty), [2015] 2 Lloyd's Rep 175.

[17] Cf *The Deichland* [1990] 1 QB 361, [1989] 2 All ER 1066, [1989] 2 Lloyd's Rep 113. See para 6.32 below.

[18] Considered in more detail in Chapter 3.

Maritime liens

2.12 Section 21(3) provides that an action *in rem* may be brought in any case in which there is a maritime lien or other charge on any ship, aircraft, or other property for the amount claimed.[19] These are all represented (or substantially overlap with other claims listed) in s 20(2).

General maritime claims

2.13 Section 21(4) permits any of the claims mentioned in sub-ss (e) to (r) of s 20(2)[20] to be brought *in rem* where the personal liability of the owner, charterer, or person in possession or control of the ship can be established at the time when the cause of action arose and such person is the beneficial owner of the 'wrongdoing ship' or of another ship, or the demise charterer of the 'wrongdoing ship'. These are the statutory actions *in rem*.[21]

Some claims relating to aircraft

2.14 Section 21(5) permits an action *in rem* to be brought on a claim in the nature of towage or pilotage in respect of an aircraft if, at the time when the action is brought, the aircraft is beneficially owned by the person who would be liable on the claim in an action *in personam*.

It will be seen that the only claim listed in s 20(2) for which an action *in rem* cannot be brought is that for damage received by a ship.[22]

Maritime liens and statutory actions *in rem*

2.15 The Senior Courts Act 1981 defines[23] the scope of the action *in rem* in relation to the claims mentioned in s 20(2) (e) to (r), as being the general maritime claims where an *in personam* liability must be shown in order for the action to be brought *in rem*, a condition not required in relation to the proprietary claims mentioned in s 20(2) (a) to (c) or (s);[24] nor is such a linkage required in relation to claims giving rise to a maritime lien.[25] The effect of s 21 is that all *in rem* actions, once commenced by issue of the claim form, touch the named ship by creating or giving effect to a property interest in it. In the case of the proprietary claims and those giving rise to a maritime lien, that interest was already in existence prior to issue of the

[19] See para 2.17 and, more generally, Chapter 4 below.
[20] See para 2.23 and Chapter 5 below.
[21] More properly called 'statutory rights of action *in rem*' and not to be confused with the 'statutory lien' which arises once the right of action has been exercised: per Hewson J in *The St Merriel* [1963] P 247, 253, [1963] 1 Lloyd's Rep 63, 68, and Brandon J in *The Monica S* [1968] P 741, 768, [1968] 2 WLR 431, [1967] 3 All ER 740, [1967] 2 Lloyd's Rep 113, 130.
[22] s 20(2) (d). Of course, where that damage was done *by* a ship, it will be possible to proceed *in rem*.
[23] By s 21(4).
[24] s 21(2).
[25] s 21(3).

in rem process; in the case of the general maritime claims, however, the property interest[26] is created by the process itself.[27]

Does this difference shed any light on the nature of the *in rem* process itself? In order to investigate that question, it is necessary first to consider in outline the nature of the maritime lien and then the development of the statutory right of action *in rem*. **2.16**

Maritime liens

The Senior Courts Act 1981 does not define a maritime lien and it is necessary to refer to judicial authority for that purpose. The classic description of the maritime lien is that it is: **2.17**

> ... a claim or privilege upon a thing to be carried into effect by legal process ... wherever a lien or claim is given upon the thing, then the Admiralty forces it by a proceeding *in rem*, and indeed is the only Court competent to enforce it ... A maritime lien is the foundation of the proceeding *in rem*, a process to make perfect a right inchoate from the moment the lien attaches; and whilst it must be admitted that where such a lien exists, a proceeding *in rem* is the proper course, it will be found to be equally true, that in all cases where a proceeding *in rem* may be had, there a maritime lien exists ... This claim or privilege travels with the thing into whosesoever possession it may come. It is inchoate from the moment the claim or privilege attaches, and when carried into effect by legal process, by a proceeding *in rem*, relates back to the period when it first attached.[28]

The decision of the Privy Council in *The Bold Buccleugh* clearly articulated the theory of the maritime lien as it existed in England and identified the following as its characteristics:[29] **2.18**

(1) it does not include or require possession;
(2) the lien adheres to the *res* notwithstanding that the *res* has been sold to a *bona fide* purchaser;
(3) it is inchoate from the moment when the claim attaches and when carried into effect by legal process it relates back to the time when it first attached;
(4) the legal process in question is an action *in rem* and hence a maritime lien can only be enforced in Admiralty; conversely, wherever a proceeding *in rem* is the proper course, there a maritime lien exists.

It may also be noted that Sir John Jervis expressly rejected the submission that the action *in rem* was 'merely to compel an appearance'.[30]

---

[26] ie, that referred to in para 2.07(1) above.

[27] See, to similar effect, D C Jackson, *Enforcement of Maritime Claims* (4th edn, 2005) para 17.36.

[28] *Harmer v Bell, The Bold Buccleugh* (1851) 7 Moo PC 267, 284–285, 13 ER 884, 890–891, and for similar definitions see *The Two Ellens* (1872) LR 4 PC 161, 169; *The Ripon City* [1897] P 226, 242; *The Tervaete* [1922] P 259, 273; *The Tolten* [1946] P 135, 150.

[29] *The Bold Buccleugh* (1851) 7 Moo PC 267, 283–285, 13 ER 884, 890–891.

[30] Ibid 283, 890.

2.19 To similar effect in *The Two Ellens*, Mellish LJ explained the creation and manner of extinguishment of a maritime lien in this way:

> A Maritime lien ... adheres to the ship from the time that the facts happened which gave the Maritime lien, and then continues binding on the Ship until it is discharged, either by being satisfied or from the laches of the owner, or in any other way by which, by law, it may be discharged. It commences and there it continues binding on the Ship until it comes to an end.[31]

2.20 The following categories of claim give rise to a maritime lien:[32]

(1) damage done by a ship;
(2) salvage;
(3) seamen's wages;
(4) bottomry and respondentia;
(5) master's wages and disbursements.

The first four liens are creations of the Admiralty Court. The last category was created by statute.[33]

2.21 Whilst judicial definitions of maritime liens abound, justification for their creation is elusive. However, it may be noted that those whose claims fall into the categories of maritime lien have provided fundamental services to the ship or are victims of a maritime wrong which must be compensated. The fact that ships were highly mobile and could flee the jurisdiction of the court, coupled with the additional fact that their owners could continue to incur liabilities to the detriment of existing creditors, may have resulted in special protection being given to those who fell within the various categories mentioned. That special protection took the form of the artifice of the maritime lien, which survived transfers of ownership, and was given effect to by the action *in rem*.

2.22 With respect to the relationship between the maritime lien and the action *in rem*, maritime law historians note[34] that there is scarcely any trace in the records of the Admiralty Court in the sixteenth century that the action *in rem* was justified on the basis of the proprietary interest recognized under a maritime lien. The explanation for this is probably that at that time, the jurisdiction of the High Court of Admiralty was exercised by attaching both property and person of the defendant. There was therefore little or no need to justify the exercise of *in rem* jurisdiction by reference to such considerations. As the prohibitions of the common law courts took effect, however, the jurisdiction *in personam* declined and the need to justify

---

[31] *The 'Two Ellens'* (1872) LR 4 PC 161, 169.

[32] These are discussed in more detail in Chapter 4.

[33] See the various manifestations of the Merchant Shipping Act: 1854, s 191; 1894, s 167; 1970, s 18; 1995, s 41.

[34] M J Prichard and D E C Yale (eds), *Hale & Fleetwood on Admiralty Jurisdiction* (1992, Selden Society) xlvi.

the exercise of jurisdiction *in rem* increased. This process had evolved by the nineteenth century to the position that the court's jurisdiction was coterminous with the maritime lien and the action *in rem* which enforced it. This would explain Sir John Jervis' suggestion that 'wherever a proceeding *in rem* is the proper course, there a maritime lien exists',[35] a statement which should be understood as one of (slightly out of date)[36] fact rather than of principle.

Statutory actions in rem

It has been argued that, in contrast to a maritime lien, a statutory action *in rem* is purely procedural, its function being to confer on a claimant having a certain type of maritime claim the right to arrest the vessel as security for that claim.[37] The argument that the new statutory rights to proceed *in rem* had created new classes of maritime lien foundered with the House of Lords' decision in *The Henrich Björn*,[38] the premise underlying that decision being that the statutes which had expanded the range of matters which could be brought in Admiralty were essentially procedural in nature, even if those statutes had various substantive effects on the rights of the parties. In *The Henrich Björn*, Lord Bramwell, in speaking of the Admiralty Court Act 1861, said that it 'gave, as it says, jurisdiction and jurisdiction only'.[39] This view persisted into the twentieth century, with Brandon J in *The Monica S* noting that 'a statutory right of action *in rem* is a procedural right, [although] it does in practice enable claimants to be paid claims out of the proceeds of ships which they might not otherwise be able to enforce at all'.[40] **2.23**

Thus the effect of the statutory action *in rem* differs from a maritime lien in that: **2.24**

(1) it does not create any right in or against the ship at any time prior to the commencement of proceedings;[41]
(2) unless already carried into effect by the commencement of proceedings *in rem*, the right created by the statutory action *in rem* does not survive a *bona fide* change of ownership;[42]

---

[35] Para 2.17 above. This had already ceased to be the position by the time that he uttered it, as a result of the Admiralty Court Act 1840 and Merchant Shipping Act 1844 (*Bankers Trust International Ltd v Todd Shipyards Corporation* (*The Halcyon Isle* [1981] AC 221, 232)), although it was not finally resolved that the new actions *in rem* did not carry with them a maritime lien until *The Henrich Björn* (1886) 11 App Cas 270.

[36] Fn 35 above.

[37] W Tetley, 'Arrest, Attachment and Related Maritime Law Procedures' (1999) 73 *Tulane Law Review* 1895, 1910.

[38] *The Henrich Björn* (1886) 11 App Cas 270.

[39] Ibid 283; see also *The Mary Ann* (1865) LR 1 A & E 8; *The Pieve Superiore* (1874) LR 5 PC 482.

[40] *The Monica S* [1968] P 741, 768, [1968] 2 WLR 431, 453, [1967] 3 All ER 740, 758, [1967] 2 Lloyd's Rep 113, 130.

[41] Ibid.

[42] Ibid.

(3) in determining the priority of competing claims, whereas a claim secured by maritime lien takes priority over a mortgage, a statutory action *in rem* ranks after both maritime liens and mortgages.[43]

2.25 The fact remains, however, that issue of the *in rem* claim form[44] protects the claimant against subsequent changes in ownership of the ship. In this respect it is difficult to contend that its effect is anything other than substantive.[45] Of course, it may be countered that the same could be said of the effect of issue of a claim form on the running of a limitation period, which may itself be substantive and not merely procedural in nature. That is so, but the prolongation, for the duration of the validity of the claim form, of a prescription period affects only the rights of the claimant and defendant. It is unlikely, in the usual course of things, to impact directly upon the rights of third parties—which is, of course, precisely the effect which the issue of *in rem* process may have.

C. The Competing Theories of the Nature of the Action *In Rem*

2.26 In an attempt to explain how the action *in rem* operates in the context of maritime liens on the one hand and statutory actions *in rem* on the other, it is common to point to two competing theories: the personification theory and the procedural theory. It should be said at once that—as an explanation of the *in rem* process—neither is entirely satisfactory and that history and authority can be cited in support of both.

The personification theory

2.27 According to Lord Steyn, the 'personification theory' was developed 'as a means of defending and extending the jurisdiction of the High Court of Admiralty',[46] in the days before the Admiralty Court 1840, against the encroachments of the common law courts and their writs of prohibition. As formulated by Lord Steyn in *The Indian Grace (No 2)*, this theory would seem to hold that the vessel is a quasi-juristic person, since:

> The ship was regarded as both the source and limit of liability. The ship herself was the 'wrongdoer'.[47]

---

[43] The question of the priority of competing claims is considered in Chapter 8.

[44] Valid in the first instance for twelve months (CPR 61.3(5)(b)), rather than the usual four months (CPR 7.5(1)).

[45] Cf Brandon J in *The Monica S* [1968] P 741, 769A, [1968] 2 WLR 431, 453, [1967] 3 All ER 740, 758, [1967] 2 Lloyd's Rep 113, 130.

[46] *The Indian Grace (No 2)* [1997] UKHL 40, [1998] AC 878, 907, [1997] 3 WLR 818, 823, [1997] 4 All ER 380, 385, [1998] 1 Lloyd's Rep 1, 6.

[47] Ibid. It is not clear whether and if so from what Lord Steyn was quoting.

The picture is in fact not quite so simple, in that there are cases to be found on either side of the question whether the personal liability of the shipowner had to be engaged before an action *in rem* could be brought against his ship. Dr Lushington himself, later an exponent of the view that it did not,[48] expressed himself at an earlier time in the following terms:

> In all causes of action which may arise from circumstances occurring during the ownership of the persons whose ship is proceeded against, I apprehend that no suit could ever be maintained against a ship where the owners were not themselves personally liable, or where their personal liability had not been given up, as in bottomry bonds, by taking a lien on the vessel. The liability of the ship and the responsibility of the owners in such cases are convertible terms; the ship is not liable if the owners are not responsible, and vice versa, no responsibility can attach upon the owners if the ship is exempt and not liable to be proceeded against.[49]

Whatever the uncertainties about the pedigree of the personification theory in English law, there is no doubt that the theory is dominant in the United States[50] where, in *Tucker v Alexandroff*, it was explained in terms which find no echo in the jurisprudence of the High Court of Admiralty:[51] **2.28**

> Prior to her launching she is mere congeries of wood and iron—an ordinary piece of personal property ... In the baptism of launching she receives her name, and from the moment her keel touches the water she is transformed, and becomes a subject of admiralty jurisdiction. She acquires a personality of her own; becomes competent to contract, and is individually liable for her obligations, upon which she may sue in the name of her owner, and be sued in her own name.[52]

---

48 *The Ticonderoga* (1856) Swab 215, 166 ER 1103; *The Ruby Queen* (1861) Lush 266, 167 ER 119; *The Edwin* (1864) B & L 281, 167 ER 365. In none of those cases, however, did Dr Lushington ascribe *personality* to the ship, and the defence of compulsory pilotage (expressly adverted to by Dr Lushington in *The Ticonderoga* at 217–218, 1104), which exonerated an owner (and his ship) from damage caused by the negligence of a compulsory pilot, is of course inconsistent with the personification theory.

49 *The Druid* (1842) 1 W Rob 391, 399, 166 ER 619, 622. To identical effect, Brett LJ in *The Parlement Belge* (1880) 5 PD 197, 218:

> In a claim made in respect of a collision the property is not treated as the delinquent per se. Though the ship has been in collision and has caused injury by reason of the negligence or want of skill of those in charge of her, yet she cannot be made the means of compensation if those in charge of her were not the servants of her then owner, as ... if she was in charge of a compulsory pilot. This is conclusive to shew that the liability to compensate must be fixed not merely on the property but also on the owner through the property.

50 It is quite possible that the stark competition between the procedural and personification theories has its origins more in transatlantic differences than in differences of approach between the civilians and the common lawyers: see *The Ripon City* [1897] P 226, 240, where the respective proponents of the rival theories are recorded as 'O.W. Holmes J., of Boston' and 'Mr. Marsden'.

51 Jackson (n 15 above), p 257 fn 6, cites seven authorities from the 'eighteenth century (and earlier)' which he says 'stress the liability of the ship as distinct from the owners'. All but one of those cases were decided in the common law courts, most relate to bottomry (as to which, see para 4.47 below), and none is in terms resembling those used in *Tucker v Alexandroff*.

52 *Tucker v Alexandroff* (1902) 183 US 424, 438.

2.29 Thus according to the personification theory as Lord Steyn defined it, the ship itself is amenable to *in rem* proceedings which create substantive or near-substantive rights over it, without the need for any concurrent *in personam* liability on the part of the shipowner. As such, a judgment *in rem* does not merge with a judgment *in personam* and can only be enforced against the value of the *res*; if the value of the claim exceeds the value of the *res*, the claimant is unable to recover the shortfall from the owners without fresh proceedings against them.

The procedural theory

2.30 Against the personification theory, with its obvious weakness in the unreality of viewing a ship in animate terms, is ranged the procedural theory, said to have achieved prominence[53] in Sir Francis Jeune P's judgment in *The Dictator*.[54] It is not easy to discern, either from Jeune P's judgment, nor even from Lord Steyn's speech, of what the procedural theory is supposed to consist. Lord Steyn quotes[55] from the following passage of Jeune P's judgment:[56]

> It may well be that, if the owners do not appear, the action only enforces the lien on the res, but that, when they do, the action in rem not only determines the amount of the liability, and in default of payment enforces it on the res, but is also a means of enforcing against the appearing owners, if they could have been made personally liable in the Admiralty Court, the complete claim of the plaintiff so far as the owners are liable to meet it.[57]

According to Lord Steyn, in the very next sentence of his speech, 'This was the procedural theory which subsequently became dominant'. Yet, with respect, it is no easy matter to discern any theory in this passage in Jeune P's judgment, let alone one which would hold the owner of a ship party to an action *in rem before* he had entered an appearance; the question at issue in that case was whether, *following* appearance, the owner of the *res* could be held liable for more than the amount of bail originally posted.[58] Nowhere in his judgment did he suggest that the owners could be so treated if they did not appear. Indeed, he continued in the very next sentence of his judgment:

> It appears to be consonant with common sense that if the owners have had no personal notice, and are not … before the Court, the effect of its judgment should be limited to the res in its hand …

53 Or, as Lord Steyn put it at [1998] AC 878, 908: 'The breakthrough came in *The Dictator*.'
54 *The Dictator* [1892] P 304.
55 At [1998] AC 878, 908.
56 At [1892] P 304, 320.
57 The underlined words are omitted from Lord Steyn's speech.
58 *The Dictator* [1892] P 304, 310. It was held that the owner who entered an appearance could be so liable, and it was on this that the decision was approved and followed by the Court of Appeal in *The Gemma* [1899] P 285 and by Sir Samuel Evans P in *The Dupleix* [1912] P 8.

These minor difficulties aside, it seems safe to assume that by 'the procedural theory', Lord Steyn had in mind the notion that: **2.31**

> ... an action in rem was not based upon the wrongdoing of the ship personified as an offender but was a means of bringing the owner of the ship to meet his personal liability by seizing his property.[59]

There is some support for that notion in *The Dictator*, although it is limited to a passing reference to Godolphin, a late seventeenth century author, who is said to have spoken of the arrest of property in such terms,[60] and to the comment that 'arrest of property merely to enforce appearance became rare or obsolete'.[61] Those passages of the judgment must anyway be set against Jeune P's citation[62] of the Privy Council decision in *The Bold Buccleugh*:[63] **2.32**

> ... disapproving the decision of Dr. Lushington in *The Volant* and *The Johann Friederich* that the arrest of the res operated only to compel appearance in a manner analogous to the procedure in foreign attachment, and to furnish security for prompt and immediate payment ...

which he did 'not think ... militates against [the] view' that the defendant, by appearing personally, introduces his personal liability.[64] Insofar as it is possible to discern any view on the part of Jeune P as to the function of the arrest process (which was until some years after the Judicature Acts indistinguishable from the action *in rem*),[65] it is that its 'main object ... was to secure that bail should be given to satisfy the judgment',[66] and that as it evolved during the period that the maritime lien developed, 'arrest [as] the distinctive feature of the action in rem [had] primarily for its object the satisfaction of the creditor out of the property seized'.[67] This of course makes perfect sense when it is borne in mind that until 1861 the Admiralty Court's means of executing its decrees were limited to sale of the *res* in its possession and 'monition' of a defendant or his bail to pay the amount decreed, an order enforceable only by attachment (ie, imprisonment) for contempt,[68] though it

[59] For which proposition he cited (at 908, 825, 387, 7) no less an authority than Scrutton LJ in *The Tervaete* [1922] P 259, 270. In that case, Scrutton LJ stated that in his 'view' the proposition was 'established', even though when, as Scrutton KC in *The Burns* [1907] P 137, he had advanced the very same proposition, it had been rejected in terms by Fletcher Moulton LJ (at 148). Scrutton LJ repeated his view in *The Jupiter* [1924] P 236, 243.

[60] *The Dictator* [1892] P 304, 312.

[61] Ibid 313.

[62] Ibid 320.

[63] *The Bold Buccleugh* (1859) 7 Moo PC 267, 13 ER 884, para 2.17 above.

[64] *The Dictator* [1892] P 304, 319–320.

[65] *The Monica S* [1968] P 741, 749G–750F, [1968] 2 WLR 431, 437, [1967] 3 All ER 740, 746, [1967] 2 Lloyd's Rep 113, 119.

[66] *The Dictator* [1892] P 304, 311.

[67] Ibid 313.

[68] For an example, see *The Triune* (1834) 3 Hag Adm 114, 166 ER 348. It was not until the Admiralty Court Act 1861 that the enforcement machinery of the common law courts was made available to the Admiralty Court.

is some distance removed from the procedural theory espoused by Lord Steyn (or, at any rate, Scrutton LJ).

2.33 Indeed, it can be argued with some force that the procedural theory itself tends to the conclusion that an action *in rem* is against the ship.[69] Moreover, the characterization of the action *in rem* as a purely procedural device encounters some difficulties in explaining various features of the Admiralty jurisdiction.

(1) It does not explain the 'statutory lien' identified by Brandon J in *The Monica S*,[70] a case not apparently cited to the House of Lords in *The Indian Grace (No 2)*. As Clarke J asked rhetorically in his judgment at first instance in *The Indian Grace (No 2)*,[71] which owner does the issue and service of a writ *in rem* make a party to the proceedings when there has been a change in ownership between issue and service?[72] The same question would arise where the owner ceased to exist during the same interval.[73]

(2) It cannot account for the circumstance[74] that a cause of action *in rem* does not merge in a judgment *in personam* but remains available to the person who has it so long as and to the extent that such judgment remains unsatisfied.[75]

(3) It cannot explain why a maritime claimant should not be able to enter default judgment against the persons liable *in personam* rather than being restricted to the value of the *res*, nor why he should before the 1956 Act have been unable to arrest sister-ships.[76]

(4) It simply ignores the amenability of the process to other parties interested in the ship,[77] and—perhaps most tellingly—that in its origin as the procedural adjunct to the maritime lien, it was and is readily contemplated that the

69 This is the conclusion of Allsop J in *Comandate Marine Corporation v Pan Australia Shipping Pty Ltd* [2008] 1 Lloyd's Rep 119, [2006] 157 FCR 45, [120].

70 *The Monica S* [1968] P 741, [1968] 2 WLR 431, [1967] 3 All ER 740, [1967] 2 Lloyd's Rep 113; para 2.07(1) above.

71 With which Allsop J agreed in *Comandate Marine Corporation v Pan Australia Shipping Pty Ltd* [2008] 1 Lloyd's Rep 119, [2006] 157 FCR 45, [105].

72 *The Indian Grace (No 2)* [1994] 2 Lloyd's Rep 331, 355.

73 As occurred in *The Blue Bridge* [2010] HKCFI 87, [2010] 2 HKLRD 285. The Court's conclusion was that the dissolution of the owner did not invalidate the *in rem* proceedings, so that judgment in default could validly be given against the ship. The Court's reasoning at [31]–[33], consisting of a short series of negative propositions, is attenuated. It neither engages nor disagrees with Lord Steyn's analysis.

74 Described by Lord Steyn as 'ancient and strange' at [1998] AC 878, 911–912, and apparently (and, if so, wrongly) thought by him to be confined to cases involving maritime liens; as Young J pointed out in *The Irina Zharkikh and Ksenia Zharkikh* [2001] 2 NZLR 801, 2 Lloyd's Rep 319, [90], two of the leading cases on the point involved only a statutory right of action *in rem*: *The Cella* (1888) 13 PD 82, 85; *The Rena K* [1979] 1 QB 377, 405–406, [1978] 3 WLR 431, [1979] 1 All ER 397, 416, [1978] 1 Lloyd's Rep 545.

75 *The Rena K* [1979] QB 377, 405.

76 *The Beldis* [1936] P 51.

77 Para 2.07(5) above.

owner of the vessel might very well not be the person liable *in personam*,[78] a feature reflected today in s 21(3) of the Senior Courts Act 1981, but simply 'put to one side' by Lord Steyn.[79]

In short, the procedural theory 'is not an all-embracing theory explaining all aspects of the action *in rem*'.[80]

Moreover, if the action *in rem* were *simply* a means of bringing the true person liable before the court, it would have breached (in spirit at least)[81] art 3.2 of the former[82] European Judgments Regulation,[83] which prohibited (through Annex 1) the founding of jurisdiction on the seizure by the claimant of property within the United Kingdom.[84] It is submitted that there is much in the observation that:

> ... it is probably an over-simplification to regard the action [*in rem*] merely as a procedural device to compel the owner or other interested party to enter an appearance ...[85]

The conclusion reached by the House of Lords in *The Indian Grace (No 2)* is in short at odds with a century's understanding of the nature of the action *in rem* that such an action is confined to the *res* unless and until an owner liable *in personam* chooses **2.34**

[78] In the case of bottomry, it was apparently recognized that the owner was *not* liable on the bottomry bond. However it seems improbable, had the device of the bottomry bond not been available, that the relevant lacuna would not have been filled by another, such as agency of necessity.

[79] *The Indian Grace (No 2)* [1997] UKHL 40, [1998] AC 878, 908, [1997] 3 WLR 818, 824, [1997] 4 All ER 380, 386, [1998] 1 Lloyd's Rep 1, 7. See now *The Stolt Kestrel* [2015] EWCA Civ 1035, [67].

[80] *Comandate Marine Corporation v Pan Australia Shipping Pty Ltd* [2008] 1 Lloyd's Rep 119; [2006] 157 FCR 45, [75], referring to the *Australian Law Reform Commission Report* (No 33).

[81] In that a saving is made for (among other matters) jurisdiction founded by arrest pursuant to the Arrest Convention by art 71 of the Regulation (art 57.1 of the Brussels and Lugano Conventions): *The Anna H* [1995] 1 Lloyd's Rep 11.

[82] The recast Brussels I Regulation (EU) 1215/2012 has now taken its place, applying to proceedings commenced on or after 10 January 2015. There is no direct equivalent to art 3.2 of the former Judgments Regulation in the recast Brussels I Regulation.

[83] Council Regulation (EC) 44/2001 (generally known as the 'Judgments Regulation' or the 'Brussels I Regulation'). Art 3.2 of the Judgments Regulation was derived from art 3 of the Brussels and Lugano Conventions. See further Chapter 6, n 50.

[84] Note in this connection Hobhouse LJ's reasoning in *The Anna H* [1995] 1 Lloyd's Rep 11, 19–20 that the rule that appearance on the merits exposes the shipowner to liability *in personam* was itself a breach of art 3, on the basis that such jurisdiction was outside the protection of art 71 (57). There is to date no reported instance of this argument being deployed in order to limit a party's exposure to the value of the arrested *res*.

[85] Per Scott J in *SA Boatyards CC v The Lady Rose* 1991 (3) SA 711 (CPD). As noted above (n 7), by reason of Admiralty Rule 8(3), an owner's appearance in an action *in rem* in South Africa does not expose him to *in personam* liability (other than in relation to costs). It is instructive to note that, by contrast with arrest in *in rem* proceedings, South African procedure also permits *attachment*, the effect of which is that—if another ground of jurisdiction exists—service *in personam* may be effected by attaching any item of the defendant's property, such as a ship; in order to lift the attachment, security for the full amount of the claim is given. It is, at any rate in South Africa, this process which harks back to the common law (and Admiralty Court) attachments to compel appearance, not arrest.

to appear. In the latter case, the action proceeds both *in rem* and *in personam*.[86] In Lord Steyn's view all this has been swept away:

> The role of fictions in the development of the law has been likened to the use of scaffolding in the construction of a building. The scaffolding is necessary but after the building has been erected scaffolding serves only to obscure the building … The idea that a ship can be a defendant in legal proceedings was always a fiction. But before the Judicature Acts this fiction helped to defend and enlarge Admiralty jurisdiction in the form of an action *in rem*. With the passing of the Judicature Acts that purpose was effectively spent … The fiction was discarded.[87]

It is respectfully submitted that this comment betrays a number of misconceptions. In order to explore them, it is necessary to look more closely still at the House of Lords' decision in *The Indian Grace (No 2)*.

The Indian Grace (No 2)

2.35 *The Indian Grace (No 2)* concerned a cargo of munitions on a voyage from Sweden to Cochin in India. A fire broke out during the voyage and, ultimately, a claim was lodged for heat damage and crushing to the cargo caused when other cargo in the hold was swollen by the water pumped in to extinguish the fire. The plaintiffs notified the defendant of two separate claims: one for a claim for total loss of the cargo and the second for short delivery based on the loss of cargo jettisoned after the fire. On 1 January 1988, the plaintiffs commenced an action in the subordinate judge court in Cochin in relation to the claim for the jettisoned cargo. On 25 August 1989, while the Indian proceedings were still pending, the plaintiffs commenced an action by a writ *in rem* in the English High Court in respect of damage to the cargo caused by heat. The Indian court gave judgment for the plaintiffs on 16 December 1989 and the writ *in rem* was served on the sister-ship to the Indian Grace, the Indian Endurance, on 24 May 1990.

2.36 The precise question before the House of Lords was whether the English Admiralty action *in rem* was brought against the same parties as those to the Indian action *in personam*. This question arose in the context of s 34 of the Civil Jurisdiction and Judgments Act 1982, which provides:

> No proceeding may be brought by a person in England and Wales or Northern Ireland on a cause of action in respect of which a judgment has been given in his favour in proceedings between the same parties or their privies in a court in another part of the United Kingdom or in a court of an overseas country, unless

[86] *The Dictator* [1892] P 304; *The Gemma* [1899] P 285; *The Burns* [1907] P 137; *The Dupleix* [1912] P 8; *The Joannis Vatis (No 2)* [1922] P 213; *The Beldis* [1936] P 51; *The Banco* [1971] P 137; *The August 8* [1983] 2 AC 450; *The Nordglimt* [1988] 1 QB 183; *The Maciej Rataj* [1992] 2 Lloyd's Rep 552; *The Anna H* [1995] 1 Lloyd's Rep 11; *The Indian Grace (No 2)* [1994] 2 Lloyd's Rep 331 (per Clarke J).

[87] *The Indian Grace (No 2)* [1997] UKHL 40, [1998] AC 878, 913, [1997] 3 WLR 818, [1997] 4 All ER 380, 391, [1998] 1 Lloyd's Rep 1, 10.

that judgment is not enforceable or entitled to recognition in England and Wales or, as the case may be, in Northern Ireland.[88]

If the Indian proceedings were 'between the same parties' as the English *in rem* proceedings, then s 34 operated as an absolute bar to the latter proceedings.

The context in which the question arose in *The Indian Grace (No 2)* led the Court of Appeal of Singapore, in *Kuo Fen Ching v Dauphin Offshore Engineering & Trading Pte Ltd*,[89] to distinguish the House of Lords' decision on the ground that it was based on the doctrine of *res judicata* and s 34 of the Civil Jurisdictions and Judgments Act, and to dismiss the discussion which it contains of the nature of the action *in rem* as 'theoretical expositions on the nature of *in rem* actions [which] did not constitute the ratio'.[90] Whilst it is possible to argue that the decision in the *Indian Grace (No 2)* is confined to the context of the Civil Jurisdictions and Judgments Act, it is respectfully submitted that the decision has rather broader implications and that for that reason Lord Steyn's reasoning merits closer examination than the Singapore Court of Appeal was prepared to afford it. **2.37**

Lord Steyn advanced three reasons for his conclusion that, for the purposes of s 34, an action *in rem* is an action against the owners from the moment that the Admiralty Court is seised with jurisdiction, viz, from the moment of service of the writ: **2.38**

(1) the dominance of the procedural theory as an explanation of the action *in rem*;
(2) the effect of the sovereign immunity cases;
(3) further developments of the law by the Privy Council in *The August 8*,[91] by the Court of Appeal in *The Deichland*,[92] and by the European Court of Justice in *The Maciej Rataj*.[93]

It is respectfully submitted that none of these reasons withstands scrutiny.

Lord Steyn's reliance on the procedural theory was based on the judgment of Sir Francis Jeune P in *The Dictator*. However, nowhere in *The Dictator* is it said that an action *in rem* was, in substance, an action *in personam* before the appearance of the owners. On the contrary, Jeune P held that the full amount of judgment in such an action could be enforced against the owners once they had entered an appearance **2.39**

[88] The purpose of this provision was to rectify the anomaly that whereas a cause of action merges with an English judgment on that cause of action, the same is not true of a foreign judgment, with the result that, at common law, it was open to the beneficiary of a foreign judgment either to bring his action afresh in the English Court, or to sue upon the foreign judgment.

[89] *Kuo Fen Ching v Dauphin Offshore Engineering & Trading Pte Ltd* [1999] 3 SLR 721.

[90] Ibid para 24. See to similar effect *The Stolt Kestrel* [2015] EWCA Civ 1035, [66]–[68].

[91] *The August 8* [1983] 2 AC 450.

[92] *The Deichland* [1990] 1 QB 361, [1989] 2 All ER 1066, [1989] 2 Lloyd's Rep 113.

[93] *The Maciej Rataj* [1995] 1 Lloyd's Rep 302.

and thereby submitted to the jurisdiction of the court. If they did not enter an appearance, judgment could only be obtained *in rem*.[94]

2.40 Lord Steyn sought to support[95] what he described as the 'decline' of the personification theory by reference to four other factors:

(1) the expansion of the Admiralty Court's jurisdiction to encompass the new statutory claims *in rem*, claims which, by their very nature, did not give rise to maritime liens and made it less easy to personify the ship as the real defendant;
(2) the procedural changes wrought in the aftermath of the Judicature Acts;
(3) the impossibility, until the Judicature Acts, of combining an action *in rem* with one *in personam*;
(4) the fact that appellate judges, who tended to be common lawyers, took 'the robust view that a ship is an inanimate thing', whereas first instance judges of the Admiralty Court, 'steeped in Admiralty history with its civilian roots, tended to be more sympathetic to the personification theory'.

2.41 Lord Steyn is of course quite right as to his first point; namely, that the new statutory rights of action *in rem* did not require a maritime lien.[96] Indeed, statutory rights of action *in rem* were and are posited upon the personal liability of the shipowner at the time that the process is initiated. His insight into the minds of the Victorian judiciary, his fourth observation, may also be right, although it does not, with respect, provide a firm basis for debate—and it is not unfair to note in this connection that Sir John Jervis, who in *The Bold Buccleugh* rejected in terms the notion 'that the arrest of the vessel is only a means of compelling the appearance of the owners',[97] was a common lawyer and no civilian.[98] He is on shakier ground, moreover, with respect to his second and third points.

2.42 As to procedure, it is simply incorrect that 'before 1873 actions *in rem* were commenced by a form of writ which did not name the owners of the ship as defendants'.[99]

---

[94] Indeed, as Tomlinson LJ pointed out in *The Stolt Kestrel* [2015] EWCA Civ 1035, [60]: 'The identity of the personal defendant to an in rem claim … if there is to be one, is not known until there is an acknowledgment of service …'. See also [12] and [15] in the same judgment.

[95] *The Indian Grace (No 2)* [1997] UKHL 40, [1998] AC 878, 907–908, [1997] 3 WLR 818, 823–824, [1997] 4 All ER 380, 385–386, [1998] 1 Lloyd's Rep 1, 6–7.

[96] Although, as he also points out, that fact was not finally established until a decade after the Judicature Acts, in the *The Henrich Björn* (1886) 11 App Cas 270.

[97] *The Bold Buccleugh* (1851) 7 Moo PC 267, 282, 13 ER 884, 889.

[98] Indeed, it seems that the idea that an action *in rem* was one in which no personal liability on the part of the owner was involved may have been held at least as strongly by common lawyers as it was by civilians. Note in this connection the reasoning of Lord Selborne LC in *The Vera Cruz* (1884) 10 App Case 59, 67: 'Every word of that legislation ... points to a common law action, points to a personal liability and a personal right to recover, and is absolutely at variance with the notion of a proceeding in rem.'

[99] *The Indian Grace (No 2)* [1997] UKHL 40, [1998] AC 878, 907, [1997] 3 WLR 818, 823, [1997] 4 All ER 380, 385, [1998] 1 Lloyd's Rep 1, 6.

The use of writs in the Admiralty Court did not commence until after the Judicature Act 1875. Until then, the initiating process was the warrant of arrest itself.[100] Whilst it is correct that the warrant did not name the owners as defendants, it did call upon the master and those interested in the ship to appear and defend the action.[101] In that regard, no very great change was effected by the new procedure. The writ in use at the time of *The Dictator* was 'directed "to the owners and parties interested" in the *res*, not to specified defendants'.[102] Lord Steyn's remark, that Jeune P 'expressly rejected' an 'argument that the procedural changes brought about no change in substance',[103] is mysterious. Although the point was made in argument, it is nowhere referred to in the judgment; the procedural changes discussed at pp 312–313 are limited to those which took place in the seventeenth century and the Judge mentioned no statute after the Admiralty Court Act 1861. Indeed, the whole tenor of the judgment in *The Dictator* was that Jeune P was going no further than Lord Stowell had gone in *The Dundee*.[104] The same point undermines Lord Steyn's view[105] that it was the 'procedural change [which] influenced the reasoning of judges in subsequent important decisions'. True it is that Atkin LJ was impressed by the form of the process in *The Tervaete*,[106] *The Jupiter*,[107] and, as Lord Atkin, in *The Cristina*,[108] and that his comments are echoed by Lord

100 F L Wiswall, *The Development of Admiralty Jurisdiction and Practice since 1800—an English study with American comparisons* (1970), 12; *The Monica S* [1968] P 741, 749–750, [1968] 2 WLR 431, 437, [1967] 3 All ER 740, 746, [1967] 2 Lloyd's Rep 113, 119.

101 Wiswall, n 100 above, 12; for an example, see *The Neptune* (1834) 3 Hag Adm 129, 132, 166 ER 348, 355.

102 Sir Walter Phillimore, *arguendo, The Dictator* [1892] 304, 307.

103 *The Indian Grace (No 2)* [1997] UKHL 40, [1998] AC 878, 907, [1997] 3 WLR 818, 823, [1997] 4 All ER 380, 385, [1998] 1 Lloyd's Rep 1, 6.

104 (1823) 1 Hag Adm 109, 166 ER 39. Wiswall criticizes that conclusion (n 100 above, Chapter 6), arguing that intervention even by an owner was only to protect his interest in the *res* and no more. He may or may not be correct as a matter of history (as Lord Steyn noted in *The Indian Grace (No 2)* [1997] UKHL 40, [1998] AC 878, 908, [1997] 3 WLR 818, 824–825, [1997] 4 All ER 380, 387, [1998] 1 Lloyd's Rep 1, 7; Marsden reached a rather different view in 1897 (see n 50 above)), but *The Dictator* has been held to be correct as to history and as to law for over a century, and it is now almost certainly too late to reopen the question—and it must moreover be very doubtful that a clear answer would emerge if it were; it is apparent from *The Dictator* itself, let alone from the contrary conclusions of Marsden and Wiswall, that such evidence as there is on the topic does not speak with one voice.

105 *The Indian Grace (No 2)* [1997] UKHL 40, [1998] AC 878, 908, [1997] 3 WLR 818, 824–825, [1997] 4 All ER 380, 387, [1998] 1 Lloyd's Rep 1, 7.

106 *The Tervaete* [1922] P 259, 274: 'The action in rem is an action in which the owners of the ship are named as parties to the proceedings and in which, according to our procedure, if they appear … they will be made liable personally for the full damage regardless of the value of the res. The owner, therefore, in such an action is directly impleaded.'

107 *The Jupiter* [1924] P 236, 244: '… the plaintiffs issued their writ in rem against the steamship *Jupiter* and all persons claiming any right or interest in the said steamship… Therefore it is plain to my mind that this writ, so addressed to these persons and commanding them within eight days after the service of the writ to cause an appearance to be entered, is a writ by which the British Courts purport to exercise jurisdiction over a sovereign independent state [the owners].'

108 *The Cristina* [1938] AC 485, 492: 'In these days it is unusual to name defendants: when the defendants are described as "the owners of a vessel" they can be at once identified. When persons

Wright in the last case,[109] but it is very difficult to identify what in substance the relevant change might be supposed to be—and it is submitted that there was none. Put another way, it is impossible to see how the reasoning of Lords Atkin and Wright would have been different had they had before them the old form of warrant rather than the post-Judicature Acts form of writ *in rem*. Moreover, neither Lord Atkin nor Lord Wright[110] challenged the orthodoxy that—whether or not they were impleaded by the form of the writ—the owners did not become *party* to the proceedings until they entered an appearance.[111]

2.43 As to the possibility of combining actions *in rem* with actions *in personam* within the same proceedings in the Admiralty Court, this was no more or less possible after the Judicature Acts than it was before (or, come to that, is now),[112] at any rate if the analysis of Jeune P in *The Dictator* is correct—as the earlier decisions in *The Triune*[113] and *The Dundee*[114] suggest.[115] This suggests that Lord Steyn was incorrect if he considered that *The Dictator* marked a new departure when he said:[116]

are not entitled the defendants but in the body of the writ are cited to appear as persons claiming an interest ... I incline to hold that ... they are by the very terms of the writ impleaded.'

[109] Ibid 505: 'The defendants cited are "all persons claiming an interest in the *Cristina*", a description which precisely covers ... the Spanish Government ...; under the modern and statutory form of a writ *in rem*, a defendant who appears becomes subject to liability *in personam*. Thus the writ *in rem* becomes in effect a writ *in personam*. This emphasizes the view that the writ directly impleads the Spanish Government.'

[110] Nor even Scrutton LJ.

[111] This distinction impressed Clarke J at first instance in *The Indian Grace (No 2)* [1994] 2 Lloyd's Rep 331, 335. See further N Teare QC, 'The Admiralty action *in rem* and the House of Lords', [1998] LMCLQ 33, 40 esp at n 47, approved by the Court of Appeal in *The Stolt Kestrel* [2015] EWCA Civ 1035, [70]. And see *Comandate Marine Corporation v Pan Australia Shipping Pty Ltd* [2008] 1 Lloyd's Rep 119, [2006] 157 FCR 45, [121], where Allsop J also points out the comment of Lord Esher MR in *The Longford* (1888) 14 PD 34, 37 that '... the most that can be collected from [*The Parlement Belge*] ... is that an action *in rem* is not the same as an action *in personam*, though it may indirectly affect the owners of or persons interested in the ship'.

[112] *Practice Direction (Admiralty: Writ)* [1979] 1 WLR 426, [1979] 2 All ER 155. *Practice Direction (Admiralty Court: Practice)* [1996] 1 WLR 127: 'If it is desired to commence proceedings both *in rem* and *in personam* separate [claim forms] must be issued ...'. Failure to observe this stricture lay at the heart of *The Stolt Kestrel* [2015] EWCA Civ 1035.

[113] *The Triune* (1834) 3 Hag Adm 114, 166 ER 348, in which the owner, who had intervened in the action, was ordered ('monished') to pay the difference between the amount realized from the sale of the *res* and the total due to the claimant.

[114] *The Dundee* (1823) 1 Hag Adm 109, 120, 166 ER 39, 43–44 (*obiter*). The issue in that case was whether fishing tackle on board the defendant vessel was liable to 'contribute', as an appurtenance, to the sum to which the defendant owner was entitled to limit his liability. Lord Stowell's remark that the 'ancient general law exacted a full compensation out of all the property of the owners of the guilty ship' was prefatory to his introduction of the statutes of limitation.

[115] Although—as Wiswall points out (above n 100)—the line of decisions of Dr Lushington in *The Hope* (1840) 1 Wm Rob 154, 166 ER 531, *The Volant* (1842) 1 Wm Rob 383, 166 ER 616, and *The Kalamazoo* (1851) 15 Jur 885 is against it. However, Jeune P dealt with these cases and found other decisions of Dr Lushington to support his view: *The Aline* (1839) 1 Wm Rob 111, 166 ER 514 and *The Zephyr* (1864) 11 LT (NS) 351. It is now too late to say that his analysis was wrong: see to similar effect n 104 above.

[116] *The Indian Grace (No 2)* [1997] UKHL 40, [1998] AC 878, 907, [1997] 3 WLR 818, 823, [1997] 4 All ER 380, 385, [1998] 1 Lloyd's Rep 1, 6.

> Since *The Dictator* was decided in 1892 the law has been that once the owners enter an appearance … there are two parallel actions: an action in personam and an action in rem…

On analysis, therefore, of the four factors relied upon by Lord Steyn it is only the introduction of the statutory rights of action *in rem* which supports the notion of contextual changes leading to a decline in the personification theory. Yet if consideration of maritime liens is to be 'put to one side',[117] this is a slender basis indeed for his view that the 'fiction' that an action *in rem* is against the ship was 'effectively spent'[118] with the passing of the Judicature Acts and thereafter 'discarded'.[119] **2.44**

The second basis for Lord Steyn's conclusion was said to arise from what are known as the 'sovereign immunity' cases,[120] which held consistently that an action *in rem* against a vessel owned by a foreign sovereign impleaded the foreign sovereign. Lord Steyn concluded from that proposition that the sovereign must be a party to the action *in rem*,[121] but that is not, with respect, borne out by those authorities.[122] In *The Christina*, for example, Lord Wright referred to the decisions in *The Dictator*, *The Gemma*, and *The Dupleix* and noted that the modern writ *in rem* was 'directed against the ship' and stated that 'under the modern and statutory form of the writ *in rem*, a defendant who appears becomes subject to liability *in personam*. Thus, the writ *in rem* becomes in effect also a writ *in personam*.'[123] **2.45**

Lord Steyn also drew support for his conclusion from what he described as 'further developments' in the law. He referred to a passage of Lord Brandon's judgment in *The August 8*,[124] in which he explained that once a defendant to an Admiralty action *in rem* has entered an appearance in such action, he has submitted himself personally to the jurisdiction of the English Admiralty Court and the result is that, from then on, the action continues against him not only as an action *in rem* but also as an action *in personam*.[125] That this had been understood to be the case since at least the decision of Jeune P in *The Dictator*[126] is not in doubt, **2.46**

---

[117] Para 2.33 above.

[118] The notion that the form of action can be regarded as 'a historical irrelevance'—at any rate where actions on maritime liens are concerned—is itself aptly characterized by A Briggs (author) and P Rees (ed), *Civil Jurisdiction & Judgments* (6th edn, 2015) para 7.79, n 690, as 'unreal'.

[119] Para 2.34 above.

[120] *The Tervaete* [1922] P 259, *The Jupiter* [1924] P 236 and *The Cristina* [1938] AC 485, and *The Parlement Belge* (1880) 5 PD 197, in which the Court of Appeal held that sovereign immunity from civil suit extended to the public property of the state or sovereign. It went on (217–218) to reject the argument that an action *in rem* against the sovereign's ship did not indirectly implead the sovereign.

[121] *The Indian Grace (No 2)* [1997] UKHL 40, [1998] AC 878, 909, [1997] 3 WLR 818, 825, [1997] 4 All ER 380, 387–388, [1998] 1 Lloyd's Rep 1, 8.

[122] See para 2.42 and, in particular, n 108 above.

[123] *The Christina* [1938] AC 485, 504–505.

[124] *The August 8* [1982] 2 AC 450.

[125] *The Indian Grace (No 2)* [1997] UKHL 40, [1998] AC 878, 909–910, [1997] 3 WLR 818, 826, [1997] 4 All ER 380, 388, [1998] 1 Lloyd's Rep 1, 8.

[126] *The Dictator* [1892] P 304.

however, and the passage does not with respect advance Lord Steyn's reasoning.[127] More important, according to Lord Steyn, was the decision in *The Deichland*[128] in which the Court of Appeal held that the owner of a vessel who is served with proceedings *in rem* is 'sued' for the purposes of art 2, sch 1 of the Civil Jurisdiction and Judgments Act 1982. As Nigel Teare QC pointed out,[129] there is no indication in the judgment of the Court of Appeal of any intention to depart from the analysis of the action *in rem* expounded in *The Dictator*. The Court of Appeal acknowledged that the Admiralty action *in rem* has special characteristics but held that this could not affect the substance of the matter where the court was faced with an international Convention designed to regulate the international jurisdiction of national courts.[130] Indeed, in recent years it has become entirely routine to ascribe 'autonomous meanings' to many of the terms of art in EU legislation such as the Brussels and Lugano Conventions, ie, meanings divorced from the preconceptions inherent in national legal principles.[131] But it is, with respect, flawed reasoning to import those autonomous meanings into domestic English law and to graft them onto established English legal principle.[132] For the same reason, Lord Steyn's reliance upon the decision of the European Court of Justice in *The Maciej Rataj*[133] is misplaced. In that case it was held that actions *in rem* and *in personam* were between the same parties for the purposes of art 21 of the Brussels Convention. However, the European Court expressly—and consistently with its adoption of autonomous meanings for many of the terms deployed in the Conventions and Regulation—disavowed any intention to comment on the nature of the action *in rem* in English law and held that the article had to be interpreted independently of any such considerations.[134]

2.47 In the Australian case of *Comandate Marine Corporation v Pan Australia Shipping Pty Ltd*, Allsop J, with whom Finkelstein J concurred, was critical of Lord Steyn's reasoning, noting that:

> ...the law of Australia is that an action *in rem*, at least prior to the unconditional appearance of a relevant person, is an action against the ship, not the owner or

[127] It is possible that Lord Steyn attributed particular weight to the words 'against him', used by Lord Brandon in connection with the action continuing both *in rem* and *in personam*, but it is respectfully submitted that Nigel Teare QC was correct ('The Admiralty action *in rem* and the House of Lords', [1998] LMCLQ 33, 40) that that is to attribute to those words a significance which they cannot bear.

[128] *The Deichland* [1990] 1 QB 361, [1989] 2 All ER 1066, [1989] 2 Lloyd's Rep 113.

[129] N Teare QC, 'The Admiralty action *in rem* and the House of Lords', [1998] LMCLQ 33, 40.

[130] *The Deichland* [1990] 1 QB 361, 374, [1989] 2 All ER 1066, 1074, [1989] 2 Lloyd's Rep 113, 119; see also *The Anna H* [1995] 1 Lloyd's Rep 11.

[131] *Canada Trust v Stolzenberg (No 2)* [2002] 1 AC 1, 15–16.

[132] To similar effect, A Briggs and Rees, n 118 above. See also *The Stolt Kestrel* [2015] EWCA Civ 1035, [64].

[133] *The Maciej Rataj* [1999] QB 515, [1995] 1 Lloyd's Rep 302.

[134] Ibid 535–536, [47]–[48], 308–309, [47]–[48]. See in this connection *The Stolt Kestrel* [2015] EWCA Civ 1035, [67].

> demise charterer of the ship... After the appearance, it continues as an action *in rem* and also as if it were an action *in personam* against the relevant person who appears.[135]

The issue before the Full Federal Court was whether, by the commencement of an action *in rem* against a vessel to enforce a claim for breach of a time charter, the claimant could be considered to have waived or abandoned its right to enforce the arbitration agreement contained in the charterparty. If *The Indian Grace (No 2)* represents the law generally in relation to the nature of the action *in rem*, then the commencement of the action *in rem* by the demise charterer was the equivalent of the commencement of *in personam* proceedings against the charterers, and not merely the commencement of the action against the ship. It would follow that the demise charterer had adopted a position which was inconsistent with its right to insist on arbitration in accordance with the terms of the charterparty and had waived or abandoned that right.[136]

Such a line of argument, according to the Federal Court of Australia, highlights the difficulties which flow from the decision of the House of Lords and, in particular, its failure to deal with critical aspects of the nature of the action *in rem*, in particular the 'put[ting] to one side' by Lord Steyn of the reconciliation of the nature of the maritime lien in the context of an explanation of the nature of the action *in rem*.[137]

Allsop J pointed out that assimilating judgments resulting from actions *in rem* and *in personam* would debilitate the utility of the action *in rem*: 'To treat it as the equivalent of the *in personam* claim risks making it a dangerous lottery, thereby diminishing its practical value'.[138] A claimant who commences *in rem* proceedings could be seriously disadvantaged if the owner does not appear. That is because Lord Steyn's reasoning effectively precludes the claimant from commencing subsequent *in personam* proceedings, even if it were unable to recover the full amount of its claim in the *in rem* proceedings. It also creates an opportunity for the party liable for the maritime claim 'to collude with others to undermine entirely the worth of the underlying cause of action'.[139] **2.48**

[135] [2008] 1 Lloyd's Rep 119; [2006] 157 FCR 45, [128]. *Comandate* has been followed subsequently, including in *Geraldton Port Authority v The Ship 'Kim Heng 1888' (No 2)* [2012] FCA 353, where McKerracher J held that the plaintiff, who had first commenced *in rem* proceedings, was not precluded from later commencing *in personam* proceedings even though the *in rem* proceedings were time-barred.

[136] Sarah C Derrington, 'The Continuing Utility of the Action *in rem*' (2007) 123 LQR 358. Strictly speaking, Allsop J's analysis of *The Indian Grace (No 2)* was *obiter*: even on the assumption that the *in rem* and *in personam* claims were the same, he rejected the underlying contention that there had been an election between mutually inconsistent rights (see at [60] and [96]).

[137] Ibid. See to identical effect *The Stolt Kestrel* [2015] EWCA Civ 1035, [67].

[138] [2008] 1 Lloyd's Rep 119; [2006] 157 FCR 45, [118].

[139] Ibid. Justice Rares echoed the criticisms of Allsop J in a judicial speech, 'Admiralty Law—the Flying Dutchman of Cross-border Insolvency' (FCA) [2009] FedJSchol 22.

2.49 An additional difficulty with *The Indian Grace (No 2)*, as noted by Rares J of the Australian Federal Court,[140] goes to jurisdiction: the mere arrest of a ship does not effect the exercise of jurisdiction over the owner personally. Ordinarily, the rules of private international law require a person to be effectively served (with a writ or claim form) in order for the court's jurisdiction to be enlivened. Although a shipowner may feel compelled to enter an appearance after his ship has been arrested *in rem*, he need not do so and may indeed elect not to appear so as to avoid becoming personally liable. Thus, says Rares J:

> The unsatisfactory consequence of *The Indian Grace* is that it fails to provide a coherent relationship between its putative joinder of the owner by the service of the proceedings in rem in the arrest of the ship and the patent absence of any personal submission to the jurisdiction by a non-appearing owner. That owner can thus enjoy all of the benefits of a judgment in rem but eschew the detriment of any personal liability for any difference in value between the judgment sum and what the res realises when sold ...[141]

2.50 There does not appear to have been any subsequent decision in which Lord Steyn's analysis of the nature of the *in rem* action has been unequivocally adopted and endorsed. In *Owners of the Stolt Kestrel v Owners of the Niyazi S*, the High Court of England and Wales declined to decide whether or not an *in rem* action is an action against the owner.[142]

2.51 It is submitted, in conclusion, that the reasoning of the House of Lords in *The Indian Grace (No 2)* is unsound. That is not to say, however, that the personification theory should after all have triumphed.[143] Rather, that the resolution of the debate as to the true nature of the action *in rem* into a competition between these two supposedly competing theories has itself obscured rather than illuminated the true nature of the action *in rem*. It is submitted that the House did not need to depart so radically (or perhaps at all) from English precedent in order to reach the conclusion,[144] that:

> It is now possible to say that for the purposes of section 34 an action in rem is an action against the owners from the moment that the Admiralty Court is seized with jurisdiction. The jurisdiction of the Admiralty Court is invoked by the

---

[140] Ibid. See also The Hon Justice James Allsop, 'Admiralty Jurisdiction—Some Basic Considerations and Some Recent Australian Cases' (FCA) [2007] FedJSchol 5, 18 April 2007.

[141] The Hon Justice Steven Rares, 'Admiralty law—the Flying Dutchman of Cross-border Insolvency' (FCA) [2009] FedJSchol 22 [39].

[142] [2014] EWHC 1731; [2014] 2 Lloyd's Rep 483, 488 (Mr Justice Hamblen). The Court of Appeal in the same case felt compelled to confine *The Indian Grace (No 2)* to a decision on s 34 of the 1982 Act: *The Stolt Kestrel* [2015] EWCA Civ 1035, [66]–[68]. See n 73 above, in relation to the Hong Kong decision in *The Blue Bridge*.

[143] As the late Brian Davenport QC remarked, 'End of an Old Admiralty Belief', (1998) 114 LQR 169, '... the fiction was always difficult to understand, if not faintly absurd'.

[144] *The Indian Grace (No 2)* [1997] UKHL 40, [1998] AC 878, 913, [1997] 3 WLR 818, 829, [1997] 4 All ER 380, 391, [1998] 1 Lloyd's Rep 1, 10.

service of a writ ... From that moment the owners are parties to the proceedings in rem.[145]

The basis for that submission is set out in the next section, an attempt to identify the 'true nature of the action in rem', which 'the House of Lords appears to have misunderstood'.[146]

D. The 'True Nature' of the Modern Action *In Rem*

The action *in rem* is best understood as being instrumental in the bringing of the maritime claim. Three of its features may be cited in support of this characterization: that it may found jurisdiction, that it may bring the owners of (or others interested in) the *res* before the court, and—most tellingly for present purposes—that it has the dual effect of creating or giving effect to a positive security interest and enabling the enforcement of that interest through the arrest process and consequent judicial sale. Thus it cannot be viewed simply as a matter of procedure, because the effect of commencing the action *in rem* is to create (or, in the case of claims giving rise to maritime liens, give effect to) what are in effect substantive rights over the *res*, thus altering the relationship which exists between the parties to the underlying claim (or, at least, between the claimant and the owner of the *res*),[147] and affecting others with similar rights or with personal claims against the owner of the *res*. These rights arise not (or not simply) as a reflection of some preexisting proprietary interest held by the claimant, but as a means of facilitating and securing the claimant's claims. This is far removed from the *res* being party to proceedings; English law recognizes that a thing can be subject to a right, but it goes too far to say that an inanimate object can be a party to legal proceedings, even if it is the object of them. **2.52**

In order to understand the instrumental nature of the action *in rem* more fully, it is necessary first to consider the substantive rights which exist between the parties to the underlying claims which may be brought as actions *in rem*. These are the claims listed in s 20(2), with the exception of paragraph (d). As has already been observed, these claims can be divided into three categories. The first category of claims encompasses those referred to in this work as 'proprietary maritime claims', namely those referred to in ss 20(2) (a), (b), (c), and (s). These relate to claims concerning ownership, possession, mortgages, forfeiture, or restoration of a seized ship and are the closest to those understood at common law to be *in rem*. The **2.53**

145 A conclusion with which, as Brian Davenport remarked ('End of an Old Admiralty Belief', (1998) 114 LQR 169, 171): 'The traditionalist would agree, subject to that moment being the moment the owners accept service and the *in rem* nature of the action continuing alongside the newly acquired *in personam* character.'

146 Ibid 169.

147 *The Monica S* [1968] P 741, 769, [1968] 2 WLR 431, 453, [1967] 3 All ER 740, 758, [1967] 2 Lloyd's Rep 113, 130.

proprietary interest which founds the claim arises otherwise than from the process of the action *in rem* itself and this led Professor Jackson to comment that, in relation to this group of claims, the action *in rem* fulfils a predominantly procedural role.[148] That will no doubt be so in many, if not the great majority of cases; for example, a claim on a mortgage is itself proprietary and the rights conferred by it will necessarily have a high priority in any ultimate distribution. Nonetheless, the effect of the action *in rem* is to create a security interest, distinct from and additional to any pre-existing security interest,[149] and facilitates the enforcement of that interest through arrest and judicial sale.

2.54 The second category of claims comprises those which give rise to maritime liens. It is unnecessary in respect of these claims to look beyond *The Bold Buccleugh* in order to appreciate the intimate connection between the inchoate right over the *res* which arises at the same time as the cause of action, and the procedural means of giving effect to that right.[150] Of course, it is fair to say that the underlying cause of action will in almost every case[151] be personal, and to that extent the action *in rem* may operate to bring the 'true' defendant to court, but that incidental benefit sheds no light on the relationship between the right and the *in rem* process which gives effect to it. First, if the 'true' defendant is still amenable to process (whether *qua* owner of the *res* or personally), then whether *in rem* or *in personam* proceedings are used to bring him to court—and, if the former, whether they are brought under s 21(2) or 21(4) of the 1981 Act—is a matter of indifference; secondly, claims giving rise to maritime liens rank in priority to all others; thirdly, the *in rem* process will still give effect to the right when the 'true' defendant is no longer the owner of the *res*.

2.55 The third category is that encompassed in s 20(2) (e)–(r), the general maritime claims, in relation to which the personal liability of the shipowner is a prerequisite to the issue of *in rem* process. By providing that these causes of action can be brought *in rem*, Parliament endowed the maritime claimant with a proprietary right, arising on the issue of the *in rem* process and attached to his claim. The proprietary right so created is not, of course, substantive[152]—any more than is the maritime lien—in the sense that neither can exist outside the scope of the *in rem* process. Moreover, unlike the maritime lien, it does not arise at the time of the events giving rise to the claim, but only at the later date of the commencement of proceedings. Like the maritime lien, however, it is a security interest which cannot be defeated by subsequent change of ownership in the *res*, which can be enforced by the arrest procedure, and which

148 D C Jackson, *Enforcement of Maritime Claims* (4th edn, 2005) para 19.17.

149 A sale of the vessel may defeat a proprietary right just as effectively (if not as readily) as a personal one.

150 Paras 2.17 and 2.18 above.

151 The exception being bottomry, but note—in addition to the obsolescence of bottomry—n 78 above.

152 But see *The Monica S* [1968] P 741, 768D–769D, [1968] 2 WLR 431, 453, [1967] 3 All ER 740, 758, [1967] 2 Lloyd's Rep 113, 129–130.

grants priority to the maritime claimant over those with purely personal claims falling outside s 20(2). It is a procedural proprietary right created by Parliament in order to facilitate the bringing of a certain class of claim.

This 'instrumental' view of the action *in rem* resonates with certain of the *dicta* of Jeune P in *The Dictator*:[153] **2.56**

> ... arrest of property over which a lien could be enforced became more common as the idea of a pre-existing maritime lien developed, and arrest of property, in order to assert, for the creditor, that legal nexus over the proprietary interest of his debtor[154] ... grew up. The result was that arrest became the distinctive feature of the action in rem, such arrest having primarily for its object the satisfaction of the creditor out of the property seized.[155]

It also fits with the view expressed by the Court of Appeal (the constitution of which included the future Lords Brightman and Brandon) in *In re Aro Co Ltd*[156] that:

> The usual object of suing in rem is to obtain security. The plaintiff becomes entitled upon the institution of his suit to the arrest and detention of the subject matter ... pending adjudication, and on adjudication in his favour to a sale and satisfaction of his judgment out of the net proceeds thereof, subject to other claims ranking in priority to or pari passu with his own.

Thus it is submitted that it is possible to reconcile the conclusion reached by the House of Lords in *The Indian Grace (No 2)* with the prior jurisprudence. In considering whether the Indian action *in personam* was between the same parties as the English action *in rem*, it is necessary to bear in mind that the role of the *in rem* character of the latter proceedings can only be to give effect to the security interest, whether of a maritime lien or (as in that case) of a statutory action *in rem*. Pursuant to s 21(4), the right to proceed *in rem* in respect of a general maritime claim, and therefore to create a security interest to attach to it, depends upon liability *in personam*. If the person with the underlying substantive liability on which the action *in rem* is premised is the same as the person against whom *in personam* proceedings have been commenced elsewhere, then it is possible to say that the proceedings are against the same party. However, simply saying that the action *in rem* is against the shipowner from the moment of service will not determine that issue. At the moment of service, all that can be said with certainty is that the security interest in the ship is created; the person with the underlying substantive liability may well differ depending upon how that substantive liability arose and **2.57**

[153] *The Dictator* [1892] P 304, 313.

[154] Though of course not necessarily just of his debtor: note Atkin LJ's acid remark on this topic in *The Tervaete* [1922] P 259, 275.

[155] To identical effect, Dr Lushington in *The Aline* (1839) 1 Wm Rob 111, 117; 166 ER 514, 517: 'In these Courts ... the proceedings are *in rem* (a mode of remedy not originally given as the measure of the damage, but as the best security for indemnity that could be obtained, as the owner might be beyond the reach of the law) ...'.

[156] *In re Aro Co Ltd* [1980] Ch 196, 207. And see *The Stolt Kestrel* [2015] EWCA Civ 1035, [12].

whether there has been change in the ownership of the vessel since the relevant security interest came into being.

2.58 But if the shipowner *is* party to the action from the moment of service, then what of the rule that—in the event of his non-appearance—only the *res* may be taken in execution of the claim? The answer must be that the legitimate compass of an action solely *in rem* is restricted to the *res* by its instrumental nature and cannot engage the wider credit of the underlying debtor (even if he is still the owner of the vessel) in the absence of appearance.[157] It may be noted in this connection that, as a matter of procedure, before it will grant judgment in default of acknowledgement of service the court requires proof to its satisfaction of the *claim*, not of the liability of the owner of the ship at the time of service.[158]

2.59 The same rationale will explain the doctrine that a cause of action *in rem* will not merge with a judgment *in personam* and vice versa. However, in practical terms it is not possible to bring subsequent *in rem* proceedings, other than (i) where a maritime lien is concerned, or (ii) where *in rem* proceedings have already been issued. That is because it could no longer be contended, prior and as a prerequisite to issue of the *in rem* process, that the owner of the ship is 'the person who would *be* liable … *in personam*' in respect of the particular maritime claim, precisely because that claim has merged in the *in personam* judgment. Where, however, the relevant security interest (ie, the statutory or maritime lien) has already come into being, it is difficult to see why that interest should be defeated by any doctrine of merger,[159] or any difficulty which may arise procedurally in determining how judgment *in rem* can be entered so that the fund can be distributed.[160]

2.60 This view of the action *in rem* does not, however, provide an answer to s 34 of the Civil Jurisdiction and Judgments Act 1982. Staughton LJ addressed the topic thus in *The Indian Grace (No 2)*:[161]

> Can it be that by section 34 Parliament has, in a case where the first of two actions is brought in a foreign court (but not if it was brought in England and Wales or Northern Ireland), abolished the well-established rule that a judgment in personam is no bar to an action in rem and vice versa? If so, it is hard to see the rhyme or reason of it. We are however convinced that section 34 must have been intended, like articles 2 and 21 of the Convention, to prevent the same cause of action being tried

[157] For essentially the same reason, *in rem* proceedings will readily accommodate intervention by parties who are *not* liable *in personam*, but who are nevertheless interested in it, such as purchasers and mortgagees.

[158] CPR 61.9(3)(iii).

[159] Mocatta J's decision to the contrary in *The Alletta* [1974] 1 Lloyd's Rep 40 notwithstanding. That decision is unsound, and the decision of Thean J in *The Daien Maru No 18* [1986] 1 Lloyd's Rep 387 (Sing Ct) to be preferred. See further para 6.53 below.

[160] A topic considered further in para 6.56 below.

[161] *The Indian Grace (No 2)* [1998] AC 878, 896.

> twice over between those who are, in reality, the same parties. Where the owners of the vessel served in an Admiralty action in rem are the same person as would be liable in an action in personam, that test is satisfied …

It is respectfully submitted that Staughton LJ's reasoning, quoted and not dissented from by Lord Steyn,[162] is correct. The result, of course, is twofold. The first is that s 34 is capable of working real injustice, in that where for example an undefended judgment *in rem* does not give a complete (or perhaps any) remedy to the claimant—because (for whatever reason) the available fund is insufficient—no further action *in personam* will be possible.[163] The second is the anomaly that if judgment *in personam* is entered after (i) the accrual of the relevant security interest (ie, the statutory or maritime lien), and (ii) a change of ownership, an action *in rem* will still be possible, since it will not be between the same parties as the action *in personam*.[164] It could be argued that the position is different in cases of maritime liens, where the relevant sale takes place after the judgment *in personam*, and that the effect of s 34 is that the maritime lien itself is defeated in its still-inchoate state, but it is hard to see why it should be, since that is not what s 34 purports to do. Section 34 is a procedural defence and no more. On the other hand, if the sale of the vessel takes place after both the judgment *in personam* and the commencement of the *in rem* action, then Lord Steyn's expansive construction of the word 'brought' to include 'continue'[165] may present a more difficult obstacle, since if the proceedings should not have been 'brought' (in the sense of 'continued') between the *in personam* judgment and the sale, how could they be 'brought' (in that sense) after the sale. One answer may be that the (*ex hypothesi*[166] inchoate) bar to the proceedings falls away again as soon as the parties to the proceedings *in rem* are no longer the same.

[162] *The Indian Grace (No 2)* [1997] UKHL 40, [1998] AC 878, 911–912, [1997] 3 WLR 818, 827–828, [1997] 4 All ER 380, 389–390, [1998] 1 Lloyd's Rep 1, 9–10.

[163] The capacity for this rule to work real injustice is plain and was specifically noted by the Full Federal Court of Australia in *Comandate Marine Corporation v Pan Australia Shipping Pty Ltd* [2008] 1 Lloyd's Rep 119; [2006] 157 FCR 45, [118] discussed above. It is plainer still if its operation in conjunction with the South African rule (above, n 7) is borne in mind: even in a case in which the defendant appears and defends an action *in rem*, under South African law the owner is only exposed to the value of the *res* in an action *in rem* (and costs). Unlike the position in South Africa, however, the effect of s 34 is forever to preclude a further action *in personam*, should the claimant bring subsequent *in personam* proceedings in England. The injustice of the rule could only be avoided if it were held that an owner was not 'party' to the South African *in rem* proceedings; but if that were so, the same would have to be true of an owner whose ship was served but who did not appear in English *in rem* proceedings.

[164] To similar effect, N Teare QC, 'The Admiralty Action *in rem* and the House of Lords', [1998] LMCLQ 33, 39. The argument considered by Lord Steyn (*The Indian Grace (No 2)* [1997] UKHL 40, [1998] AC 878, 912, [1997] 3 WLR 818, 828, [1997] 4 All ER 380, 390, [1998] 1 Lloyd's Rep 1, 10) that 'the anomaly disappears in fact' (and on which he 'expressed no considered view') does not meet this point.

[165] Ibid.

[166] If the point had already been taken and ruled upon, then the action would have been dismissed, rather than stayed, and could not be revived within the same proceedings.

2.61 If the above, instrumental, analysis of the nature of the action *in rem* is correct, then there is no need to distinguish between the actions involving maritime liens and those brought pursuant to a statutory right *in rem*,[167] nor any need to rely on either the personification or the procedural theory, for the purpose of explaining the nature of the action *in rem*. It must be acknowledged, however, that that analysis is predicated upon the continued survival in law of all the features of the action *in rem* outlined in paragraph 2.07 above.[168]

E. Overview of the Mode of Exercise of Admiralty Jurisdiction

2.62 Section 21 of the Senior Courts Act 1981 is concerned with the manner in which the Admiralty jurisdiction of the High Court may be exercised, be it *in rem* or *in personam*. Section 21(1) provides that, subject to certain restrictions which apply to claims relating to collisions,[169] an action *in personam* may be brought in the High Court in all cases within the Admiralty jurisdiction of that court. Section 21(2)–(5) specifies the claims which may also be brought *in rem*. In most circumstances claims falling within the Admiralty jurisdiction may be commenced either *in rem* or *in personam*.

2.63 Those claims which may also be brought *in rem* extend to three types of claims:

(1) claims which can only be brought against the particular ship in relation to which the claim arose, being claims based upon a maritime lien or charge or claims of a proprietary nature;
(2) claims which can be brought against either the particular ship in relation to which the claim arose or against some other ship where certain conditions in relation to *in personam* liability are met (so-called 'sister-ships'); and
(3) claims which can be brought against a particular aircraft in relation to which the claim arose.

2.64 If the claim relates to the enforcement of a maritime lien or charge, the action *in rem* can only be brought against the particular ship to which the lien or charge attaches. However, the nature of the claims which give rise to maritime liens is such that a claim *in rem* may also be brought in relation to the underlying claim against a sister-ship. The priority consequences will, of course, differ.[170]

[167] To similar effect, D C Jackson, *Enforcement of Maritime Claims* (4th edn, 2005) para 17.40. For a contrary view, see M West, 'Arbitrations, Admiralty Actions *in rem* and the Arrest of Ships in the Hong Kong SAR: in the Twilight of *The Indian Grace (No 2)*' [2002] LMCLQ 259.

[168] As to which, note the remarks of Brandon J in *The Conoco Britannia* [1972] 2 QB 543, 555D–G, [1972] 2 WLR 1352, [1972] 2 All ER 238, 245f–j, [1972] 1 Lloyd's Rep. 342, 348 col 1.

[169] As to which, see Chapter 9.

[170] As to which, see Chapter 8.

The circumstances in which a claim may be brought *in rem* ('an *in rem* claim') reflect the original foundation of Admiralty jurisdiction on the existence of a maritime lien. The *leitmotif* connecting the *in rem* claims is that they must arise in connection with a ship (or other property which can be the subject of an admiralty action *in rem*). Apart from ships, the property which has been able to be the subject of an action *in rem* in English law on the basis that it attracts a maritime lien includes cargo,[171] freight,[172] and, in the case of salvage, flotsam, jetsam, lagan, derelict, and wreck. By contrast, the 1952 Arrest Convention only permits the arrest of a 'ship'. **2.65**

The meaning of 'ship'

Section 24(1) of the Senior Courts Act 1981 defines a 'ship' to include, unless the context otherwise requires, 'any description of vessel used in navigation', and, subject to certain limitations, hovercraft. Hovercraft aside, the definition of a 'ship' thus has two limbs: it must be a vessel and it must be used in navigation. **2.66**

'Vessel'

In *Steedman v Schofield*,[173] Sheen J observed that, 'in common parlance, "vessel" was a word used to refer to craft larger than rowing boats, which included every description of watercraft used or capable of being used as a means of transportation on water'.[174] In that case, it was held that a jet ski did not fall within the definition of a vessel. **2.67**

The 'ship' includes all its equipment and appurtenances, including those which have been removed for maintenance and/or safekeeping.[175] In the context of the predecessor to the Supreme Court Act 1981,[176] Sheen J held that the word 'ship' in the Administration of Justice Act 1956 includes all the property aboard the ship other than that which is owned by someone other than the owner of the ship. It therefore included the bunkers on board, unless it could be shown that they were the property of the charterer.[177]

---

[171] *The Willem III* (1871) LR 3 A & E 487; *The Gas Float Whitton No 2* [1897] AC 337.

[172] *The Orpheus* (1871) LR 3 A & E 308; *The Salacia* (1862) Lush 545; *The Andalina* (1886) 12 PD 1; *The Castlegate* [1893] AC 38; *The Kaletan* (1914) 30 TLR 572.

[173] *Steedman v Schofield* [1992] 2 Lloyd's Rep 163.

[174] Ibid 166; cited with apparent approval in *R v Goodwin* [2005] EWCA Crim 3184, [2006] 1 WLR 546.

[175] *The Alexander* (1811) 1 Dods 282; *The Honshu Gloria* [1986] 2 Lloyd's Rep 67; *The Pan Oak* [1992] 2 Lloyd's Rep 36; *The Eurosun and Eurostar* [1993] 1 Lloyd's Rep 106.

[176] Now the Senior Courts Act 1981.

[177] *The Silia* [1981] 2 Lloyd's Rep 534; see also *The Honshu Gloria* [1988] 2 Lloyd's Rep 67; *The Pan Oak* [1992] 2 Lloyd's Rep 36; *The Eurosun and Eurostar* [1993] 1 Lloyd's Rep 106.

'Used in navigation'

2.68 More critical than whether a particular craft meets the description of a 'vessel' is the purpose for which it is used. Structures which are designed and constructed for the purpose of carrying out specific activities on water and which are capable of movement across the water have been held to be 'vessels' used in navigation even though they lack some of the characteristics normally associated with a ship. Such structures have been held to include a backhoe dredger,[178] jack-up drilling rigs,[179] a hopper barge,[180] dumb barges with rudders,[181] barges with sails,[182] and a 'flotel'.[183]

2.69 The meaning of 'used in navigation' was considered by the Court of Criminal Appeal in the context of a charge arising under s 58(2)(a) of the Merchant Shipping Act (MSA).[184] The Court held that the phrase is confined to vessels which are used to make ordered progression over the water from one place to another[185] and excludes from the definition of 'ship or vessel' craft that are simply used for having fun on the water without the object of going anywhere.[186] Thus, for example, jet skis—with which the Court was concerned[187]—are clearly used for having fun on the water and not for 'navigating' it.[188] Not without some trepidation, this approach is respectfully questioned. Few would doubt, for example, that sailing yachts or power boats are ships, at any rate for the purposes of ss 20 to 24 of the Senior Courts Act 1981,[189] yet it is hard to see why they are not in the same 'messing about in boats' category as jet skis.[190]

---

[178] *The Von Rocks* [1998] 2 Lloyd's Rep 198.

[179] *Clark v Perks (No 2)* [2001] EWCA Civ 1228, [2001] 2 Lloyd's Rep 431.

[180] *The Mac* (1882) 7 PD 126.

[181] *The Mudlark* [1911] P 116; *The Harlow* [1922] P 175.

[182] *St John Pilot Commissioners v Cumberland Railway and Coal Co* [1910] AC 208.

[183] *Addison v Denholm Ship Management* [1997] ICR 770.

[184] *R v Goodwin* [2005] EWCA Crim 3184, [2006] 1 WLR 546.

[185] A description which would apply, eg, to a chain ferry, a craft whose repeated progression across the same short expanse of water would not naturally be described as 'navigation'.

[186] *R v Goodwin* [2005] EWCA Crim 3184, [2006] 1 WLR 546, [33].

[187] The particular craft was of a different type from that considered by Sheen J in *Steedman v Schofield* [1992] 2 Lloyd's Rep 163. *Steedman* concerned the type which can only be mounted once the craft is underway; in *Goodwin* the craft was of the wet-bike variety, on which the rider and passenger(s) can sit even when it is stationary. The Court of Criminal Appeal accepted (at para 17) that the latter craft fell within the first part of the statutory definition—'every description of vessel'— which the craft in *Steedman* did not.

[188] Cf *Gibbs v Mercantile Mutual Insurance (Australia) Ltd* [2003] HCA 39; (2003) 214 CLR 604 where, in the context of the Marine Insurance Act 1909 (Cth), the High Court of Australia held that the use of a run-about skiboat could amount to 'navigation of the sea' within the meaning of the definition of 'maritime perils' in that Act.

[189] This was of course not the statutory context with which the Court of Appeal was concerned—and Lord Phillips CJ was at pains to emphasize that in which the question arose in that case: see paras 18 and 32. Notwithstanding, therefore, that the same expression is used in both Acts, perhaps the difference in statutory context means that different results may obtain depending upon which is invoked.

[190] A point made *obiter* by Keane J in the Irish case *The Von Rocks* [1998] 2 Lloyd's Rep 198, 207–208; although this passage was quoted by the Lord Chief Justice at para 23 of his judgment in *R v Goodwin*, he did not address the difficulty which it throws up.

However, the House of Lords refused permission to appeal[191] and so the Court of Appeal's decision will represent the law (at any rate of England and Wales) for the foreseeable future.

More recently, in *Michael v Musgrave*[192] (a decision of the Admiralty Registrar) the question arose as to whether or not a rigid inflatable boat (RIB) was a 'ship' within the meaning of the Athens Convention. The Athens Convention defines 'ship' as 'only a seagoing vessel, excluding an air-cushion vehicle'.[193] The Court considered that a ship 'may include any vessel used in navigation and … this means capable of being used in navigation whether or not she is actually being used in navigation at the relevant time'.[194] As the RIB was 'intended to be used in navigation and was capable of being navigated' in the *Goodwin* sense, she was a vessel for the purposes of the Merchant Shipping Legislation.[195] **2.70**

Further, the concept of navigation presupposes that the waters being traversed are 'navigable waters'. In *The Mayor of Southport v Morriss*[196] it was held that a launch used for the purpose of carrying passengers on pleasure trips around an artificial lake half a mile long by 180 yards wide was not being 'used in navigation', having regard to the size of the sheet of water on which it was being used;[197] nor were sailing dinghies being used on a reservoir 'for pleasure purposes by people who were messing about in boats'.[198] Conversely, the waters of a canal have been held to be navigable.[199] **2.71**

In addition to the jet skis in *Steedman* and *Goodwin*, structures which have been held not to be ships include a gas float shaped like a boat but moored in tidal waters as an aid to navigation,[200] a pontoon with a crane mounted on it,[201] a flying boat,[202] and a seaplane.[203] **2.72**

---

[191] *R v Goodwin* [2005] EWCA Crim 3184, [2006] 1 WLR 780.

[192] *Michael v Musgrave (trading as Ynys Ribs) (The 'Sea Eagle')* [2011] EWHC 1438, [2012] 2 Lloyd's Rep37.

[193] Convention relating to the Carriage of Passengers and their Luggage by Sea (Athens Convention), art 1(3).

[194] Jervis Kay QC gave *obiter* examples of vessels that are capable of being used in navigation but may not have been used in that capacity for some time, such as HMS *Victory*, HMS *Warrior*, and vessels moored in the Thames and used as restaurants. In Jervis Kay QC's view, those vessels remain 'ships', unlike other structures such as gas floats and floating stages: [2012] 2 Lloyd's Rep 37, 44. That view may be doubted, eg, if the vessel's engine or rudder have been removed.

[195] *Michael v Musgrave (trading as Ynys Ribs) (The 'Sea Eagle')* [2012] 2 Lloyd's Rep37, 44. The second question was whether the RIB was a 'seagoing' ship, with the Court concluding that she was: [2012] 2 Lloyd's Rep 37, 44–45, [31]–[33].

[196] *The Mayor of Southport v Morriss* [1893] 1 QB 359.

[197] Ibid 361.

[198] *Curtis v Wild* [1991] 4 All ER 172, a decision which seemed questionable until *Goodwin*.

[199] *Weeks v Ross* [1913] 2 KB 229.

[200] *Wells v The Gas Float Whitton No 2* [1897] AC 397; *The Upcerne* [1912] P 160.

[201] *Merchant's Marine Insurance v North of England P&I Association* (1926) 26 Ll L Rep 201.

[202] *Polpen Shipping Company Ltd v Commercial Union Assurance Company Ltd* [1943] KB 161.

[203] *Watson v RCA Victor* (1934) 50 Ll L Rep 77.

2.73 Hong Kong,[204] New Zealand,[205] and Singapore[206] each define 'ship' in the same manner as in the Senior Courts Act 1981.

2.74 The Australian legislation also adopts a similar definition but expressly includes a barge, lighter, or other floating vessel, a hovercraft, an offshore industry mobile unit, and a vessel that has sunk or is stranded and the remains of such a vessel. It expressly excludes from the definition a seaplane, an inland waterways vessel, and a vessel under construction that has not been launched.[207] The Full Federal Court of Australia has expressly endorsed Sheen J's definition of 'ship' in *The Silia*.[208]

2.75 The Canadian legislation defines a 'ship' to mean 'any vessel or craft designed, used, capable of being used solely or partly for navigation, without regard to method or lack of propulsion and includes (a) a ship in the process of construction from the time that it is capable of floating, and (b) a ship that has been stranded, wrecked or sunk and any part of a ship that has broken up'.[209] The Canadian definition, therefore, embraces a far greater number of structures than would be encompassed by the legislation of comparable jurisdictions. In *Cyber Sea Technologies Inc v Underwater Harvester Remotely Operated Vehicle*, the Federal Court of Canada held that a submersible was in all probability a ship.[210]

2.76 The South African legislation does not utilize the test of 'navigation'. Rather, it simply defines a 'ship' to mean 'any vessel used or capable of being used on the sea or internal waters, and includes any hovercraft, powerboat, yacht, fishing boat, submarine vessel, barge, crane barge, floating crane, floating dock, oil or other floating rig, floating mooring installation or similar floating installation, whether self-propelled or not'.[211] Section 1(1)(k) Admiralty Jurisdiction Regulation Act 105 of 1983 extends the Admiralty jurisdiction by including as a maritime claim, 'any claim arising out of the Wreck and Salvage Act 1996'. It is also suggested that Admiralty jurisdiction in respect of wreck may exist in terms of s 1(1)(ee) of the Act.[212]

The meaning of 'property'

2.77 Sections 21(2) and (3) permit an action *in rem* to be brought against the ship or property in connection with which the claim arises. There is, however, no definition in the Senior Courts Act 1981 of 'property' as it is used in those

[204] *High Court Ordinance* s 12E(1).
[205] Admiralty Act 1973, s 2.
[206] High Court (Admiralty Jurisdiction) Act, s 2 (although there is no mention of hovercraft).
[207] Admiralty Act 1988, s 3(1).
[208] *Scandinavian Bunkering AS v The Bunkers on Board the Ship FV Taruman* [2006] FCAFC 75, (2006) 151 FCR 126.
[209] Federal Courts Act, s 2(1).
[210] *Cyber Sea Technologies Inc v Underwater Harvester Remotely Operated Vehicle* [2002] FCT 794.
[211] Admiralty Jurisdiction Regulation Act 105 of 1983, s 1(1).
[212] G Hofmeyr, *Admiralty Jurisdiction Law and Practice in South Africa* (2nd edn, 2012) [III.112].

sub-sections.[213] Historically, the only 'property' liable to arrest is the ship, cargo,[214] or freight in connection with which the claim arises, and there is no suggestion that the Senior Courts Act 1981 widens the scope of the type of property which might be subject to the action *in rem*. Indeed, the Arrest Convention limits the arrest process to the ship alone.

The absence of any modern authority on the meaning of 'property' in the context of arrest may be explained on either or both of two bases. First, that there is no particular difficulty with the concept of property in the context of the action *in rem*. Secondly, that in practice the arrest of property other than ships is comparatively rare. **2.78**

Again, Hong Kong,[215] New Zealand,[216] and Singapore[217] adopt the same approach as the United Kingdom. **2.79**

The Canadian legislation does not define the term in any specific sense[218] but it has been held that 'it must be possible to say that it is the use of this ship or the carriage of this cargo that justifies the action *in rem* brought against the property arrested'.[219] **2.80**

Australia also chose not to define the concept of 'property' except to the extent of providing that an action *in rem* can be commenced against the proceeds of sale that have been paid into court under the Act.[220] The Full Federal Court of Australia has confirmed that bunkers fall within the definition of 'ship' and cannot therefore be 'other property' for the purposes of arrest.[221] It is respectfully questioned whether the reasoning adopted by the Full Federal Court does indeed have the effect of precluding for all purposes the arrest of bunkers within the Australian admiralty jurisdiction. The Court endorsed the definition of 'ship' stated by Sheen J in *The Silia*[222] and adopted by the Australian Law Reform Commission as the basis of the definition of 'ship' in the *Admiralty Act*: namely, that 'in the context of an action *in rem* the word "ship" includes all the property aboard the ship other than that which **2.81**

---

213 PD61 §3.6 indicates that 'property' may consist of freight but is otherwise silent as to the meaning of 'property'.

214 'Cargo' does not include the personal effects of the master, crew, or passengers: *The Willem III* (1871) LR 3 A & E 487.

215 High Court Ordinance, s 12B(2) and (3).

216 Admiralty Act 1973, s 5(1) and (2).

217 High Court (Admiralty Jurisdiction) Act, s 4(2) and (3).

218 Federal Courts Act, s 2(1) provides a broad generic definition of 'property'.

219 *Paramount Enterprises International Inc v An Xin Jiang* [2001] 2 FC 551, 553 (Federal Court of Appeal), followed in *Kremikovtzi Trade v Phoenix Bulk Carriers Ltd* [2006] FCA 1 (Federal Court of Appeal).

220 ALRC No 33, 1986 para 110; Admiralty Act 1988 s 24.

221 *Scandinavian Bunkering AS v The Bunkers on Board the Ship FV Taruman* [2006] FCAFC 75, (2006) 151 FCR 126, cited more recently in *Daebo Shipping Co Ltd v The Ship 'Go Star'* (2012) 207 FCR 220; [2012] FCAFC 156 and *Elbe Shipping SA v The Ship 'Global Peace'* (2006) 154 FCR 439; [2006] FCA 954.

222 *The Silia* [1981] 2 Lloyd's Rep 534.

is owned by someone other than the owner of the ship'.[223] There was no suggestion in the *FV Taruman* that the bunkers were owned by anyone other than the owner of the vessel. The Court therefore did not have to consider whether, had the bunkers been owned by a charterer, they would still not have been amenable to arrest in any circumstances. However, the circumstances in which bunkers might be susceptible to arrest under the provisions of the *Admiralty Act* as 'other property' will be few and far between given the nexus that must exist between the maritime claim which arises under s 4(3) of the Act and the right to proceed *in rem*.[224]

2.82 The South African legislation specifically defines the property against which an action *in rem* may be commenced.[225]

F. Claims Enforceable Only *In Personam*

2.83 Not every claim within the Admiralty jurisdiction of the High Court can be commenced *in rem*.[226] The right to bring an action *in rem* is not available for the following claims:

(1) claims for damage received by a ship;
(2) limitation claims;
(3) applications under the Merchant Shipping Acts.

These heads of claim are considered in turn below.

Damage received by a ship

2.84 The words 'damage received by a ship' are broad words, construed broadly.[227]

[223] Civil Admiralty Jurisdiction, ALRC No 33 (1986) para 107.

[224] It is suggested that those circumstances will be limited to those relating to salvage (s 4(3)(g)), general average (s 4(3)(h)), and to the enforcement of an award relating to such a claim (s 4(3)(u)) or to interest on such a claim (s 4(3)(w)); see also *Metall und Rohstoff Shipping v the Owners of Bunkers on Board the ship MV 'Genco Leader'* [2005] FCAFC 162, (2005) 145 FCR 145.

[225] Admiralty Jurisdiction Regulation Act 105 of 1983, s 3(5) provides: 'An action *in rem* shall be instituted by the arrest within the area of jurisdiction of the court concerned of property of one or more of the following categories against or in respect of which the claim lies—

(a) the ship, with or without its equipment, furniture, stores or bunkers;
(b) the whole or any part of the equipment, furniture, stores or bunkers;
(c) the whole or any part of the cargo;
(d) the freight;
(e) any container, if the claim arises out of or relates to the use of that container in or on a ship or the carriage of goods by sea or by water otherwise in that container;
(f) a fund.'

[226] Nor is every claim connected with a ship within the Admiralty jurisdiction, the obvious example (in English law at least) being a claim for breach of a ship sale agreement.

[227] *Mersey Docks & Harbour Board v Turner (The Zeta)* [1893] AC 468, 477 and 485; see also *Bouygues Offshore v The Owner of the M/T Tigr Ultisol Transport Contractors Ltd* [1996] 2 Lloyd's Rep 153 (Supreme Court of South Africa).

2.85 The Arrest Convention confers no right of arrest in respect of a claim for damage received by a ship. Such a right was provided for in s 3(4)(e) of the Administration of Justice Act 1956, but as Lord Diplock pointed out in *The Eschersheim*,[228] damage received by a ship, if it gives rise to any claim against a ship at all, gives rise to a claim against the ship that caused the damage not the ship that received it. In such a claim, the owners of the damaged ship cannot invoke the Admiralty jurisdiction by an action *in rem* against their own ship. Any claim to arrest some other ship must be founded on another head of jurisdiction.

2.86 The error in the Administration of Justice Act 1956 of providing for a right to bring an action *in rem* for damage received by a ship was not repeated in the Senior Courts Act 1981. It is also omitted from the Australian and Hong Kong legislation,[229] but it remains possible (in theory at least) to bring an action *in rem* for damage received by a ship, subject to proof of *in personam* liability, in Canada,[230] New Zealand,[231] Singapore,[232] and South Africa.[233]

Limitation claims

2.87 The mode of exercise of Admiralty jurisdiction in relation to limitation claims is governed by the Civil Procedure Rules (CPR) and is discussed in Chapter 10.

Applications under the Merchant Shipping Acts

2.88 Applications under the Merchant Shipping Acts may arise in relation to a variety of circumstances including those under the provisions relating to mortgages and registration of ships, the provisions relating to the payment of wages, and the provisions relating to various environmental conventions. There will clearly be some overlap with the *in rem* jurisdiction in relation to some of these categories. However, unless the claim falls specifically within one of the enumerated paragraphs of s 20(2), the application remains solely within the *in personam* jurisdiction of the court.[234]

---

[228] *The Eschersheim* [1976] 1 WLR 430, 439–440, [1976] 1 All ER 920, 927–928, [1976] 2 Lloyd's Rep 1, 9.

[229] Indeed, in *The Asian Atlas* [2008] HKLRD 461; [2008] HKEC 693, the Hong Kong Court of Appeal set aside *in rem* proceedings commenced by the owner of a subsurface launchway against the owners of a vessel. The vessel had sustained damage after it collided with the launchway. The Court based its decision partly on the fact that it was the vessel itself and not the launchway that had sustained the damage.

[230] Federal Courts Act 1985, s 22(2)(e) and Federal Courts Rules, r 477(1).

[231] Admiralty Act 1973, ss 4(1)(e) and 5(2)(b); see also *Reef Shipping Co Ltd v The Fua Kavenga* [1987] 1 NZLR 550.

[232] High Court (Admiralty Jurisdiction) Act, ss 3(1)(e) and 4.

[233] Admiralty Jurisdiction Regulation Act 105 of 1983, ss1(1)(e) and 3(4).

[234] CPR Rule 61.2(1)(a)(iv) provides that all claims under the MSA 1995 must be started in the Admiralty Court.

3

PROPRIETARY MARITIME CLAIMS

A. The Jurisdictional Foundation for Proprietary Maritime Claims

3.01 The Senior Courts Act 1981 provides that a claim may be brought as an action *in rem* against the ship or property to which the claim relates in any of the following cases:[1]

(a) any claim to the possession or ownership of a ship or to the ownership of any share therein;[2]
(b) any question arising between the co-owners of a ship as to possession, employment, or earnings of that ship;[3]
(c) any claim in respect of a mortgage of or a charge on a ship or any share therein;[4] and
(d) any claim for the forfeiture or condemnation of a ship or goods which are being or have been carried, or have been attempted to be carried, in a ship, or for the restoration of a ship or any such goods after seizure, or for droits of Admiralty.[5]

[1] s 21(2).
[2] s 20(2)(a).
[3] s 20(2)(b).
[4] s 20(2)(c).
[5] s 20(2)(s).

3.02 The types of claims encompassed by this section, discussed in more detail below, are concerned with questions of property and possession, and may be regarded as proprietary, or quasi-proprietary, in character. As such, the dispute is about the ship or property itself as opposed to merely being a dispute arising out of the utilization of the ship. Consistently with art 3(1) of the Arrest Convention, the right to proceed *in rem* is restricted to the ship or property and no action *in rem* lies against a sister-ship in respect of these types of claims.

Claims to ownership or possession (section 20(2)(a))

3.03 This head of claim[6] reflects paras (o) and (p) of art 1(1) of the Arrest Convention; the Senior Courts Act 1981 omits the specific reference in the Convention to disputes as to the 'title' to any ship, but there is no material distinction between 'title to' and 'ownership of'. This conclusion is supported by the French text of the Convention which refers simply to '*la propriété contestée d'un navire*'.[7]

3.04 All questions relating to the possession of a ship, both legal and equitable,[8] whatever the nationality of the ship, or the domicile or residence of the owner,[9] are within the ambit of the jurisdiction. Thus, there is jurisdiction in respect of possession of a ship, including a foreign ship, wrongfully taken on the high seas.[10] Consistently with the view of the nature of the action *in rem* expressed in Chapter 2, a claim for specific performance or some other equitable remedy is no bar to proceeding *in rem*.[11] Thus, the court has power to grant a declaration that the claimant is the legal owner of the ship and is entitled to be so registered,[12] to rectify the register of a British ship where an incorrect entry has been made,[13] and to order delivery up of a certificate of registry of a British ship.[14]

3.05 Consistently with the proprietary basis of this head of jurisdiction, a claim for damages arising out of a breach of a contract for the sale of the vessel is not within the jurisdiction conferred by this sub-paragraph. In such a case, there is no claim to

6 s 20(2)(a) makes provision for 'claims to ownership or possession of a ship or a share in a ship'.

7 F Berlingieri, *Arrest of Ships* (5th edn, 2011) 4.09.

8 *Foong Tai & Co v Buchheister & Co* [1908] AC 458, 467–468.

9 s 20(7)(a); in the absence of any substantial connection to England a claim relating to title to a foreign vessel is likely to be vulnerable to being stayed on the grounds of *forum non conveniens, The Lakhta* [1992] 2 Lloyd's Rep 269.

10 *Baxter v Blanshard* (1823) 23 Dow & Ry KB 177, 107 ER 374; *The Pitt* (1824) 1 Hag Adm 240, 166 ER 86; *The Beatrice* (1866) 36 LJ Adm 9; *The Annette: The Dora* [1919] P 105.

11 *The Conoco Britannia* [1972] 2 QB 543, 554–555; *The Owners of the Ship Shin Kobe Maru v Empire Shipping Company Inc* (1994) 181 CLR 404 (High Court of Australia); *Antares Shipping Corp v The Capricorn* [1977] 2 SCR 422, (1980) 111 DLR (3d) 289 (Supreme Court of Canada).

12 *The Bineta* [1966] 2 Lloyd's Rep 419.

13 *The Rose* (1873) LR 4 A & E 6; *Brond v Brommhall* [1906] 1 KB 571; *The Ocean Enterprise* [1997] 1 Lloyd's Rep 449.

14 *The Frances* (1820) 2 Dods 420; *The St Olaf* (1877) 2 PD 113.

ownership or possession; in fact the converse is being claimed.[15] Nor does a claim against the shipowner by one of its minority shareholders for damages for breach of the company's articles of association by selling the ship fall within section 20(2)(a) or (b). That is because such a claim cannot be characterized as a claim to the ownership of the vessel within sub-section (2)(a); and the co-ownership required by sub-section (2)(b) is of the vessel and not of the owning company.[16]

3.06 Pursuant to para 6 of sch 1 to the Merchant Shipping Act 1995 (MSA), the court may make an order prohibiting for a specified time any dealing with a ship or a share therein. The right to apply for such an order extends only to a person with a proprietary interest in the ship, or at least to a person having a claim against the ship which could lead to such an interest, and does not include a mere personal creditor.[17]

Questions arising between co-owners (section 20(2)(b))

3.07 This head[18] reflects art 1(1)(p) of the Arrest Convention and to some extent overlaps with the previous paragraph. As between co-owners, claims under this head include the arcane and little-seen suits for possession, actions of restraint, and actions of co-ownership. The jurisdiction also includes the power to settle any account outstanding and unsettled between the parties in relation to the ship and to direct that the ship, or any share, be sold, or to make any other order that the court thinks fit.[19]

3.08 The minority interests in a ship may bring an action for restraint in circumstances where, without consent, the majority is about to send the ship on a voyage. The minority may take out a warrant of arrest and have the ship detained until security is given for its safe return.[20] As soon as the security is given, the ship may sail and it does so wholly at the risk of and for the profit of the majority.[21] The question may arise as to whether the security is only required to cover the ship's safe return to the jurisdiction or whether it can be required to cover return to a particular port. The better view appears to be that it will only be required for the safe return to the jurisdiction.[22]

---

[15] *The Pal Marinos* (Admiralty Court, 5 August 1991, unreported); a similar construction was adopted by the Supreme Court of Tasmania in *Paul Allison & APAI Pty Ltd v The Ship Greshanne* (1996) 6 Tas R 137, (1996) 125 FLR 342.

[16] *The Uranus* [2015] EWHC 1269 (Admlty), [54] and [57], [2015] 2 Lloyd's Rep 175.

[17] *The Mikado* [1992] 1 Lloyd's Rep 163; *The Siben* [1994] 2 Lloyd's Rep 420.

[18] s 20(2)(b) makes provision for claims involving 'Questions arising between co-owners as to possession, employment or earnings'.

[19] s 20(4); *The Vanessa Ann* [1985] 1 Lloyd's Rep 549.

[20] *The Apollo* (1824) 1 Hag Adm 306.

[21] Ibid 311.

[22] *The Margaret* (1829) 2 Hag Adm 275; *The Regalia* (1884) 5 Asp 338; *The Robert Dickinson* (1884) 5 Asp 341; *The Vivienne* (1887) 6 Asp 178, cf *The Cawdor* [1900] P 47.

A suit for possession is effectively an action for restraint in reverse. Where the majority interest in a ship wishes to send the ship on a voyage but is unable to do so because the minority refuses to release possession, the majority may arrest the ship. Upon providing security for the ship's safe return in an amount sufficient to cover the minority's interest, the majority will be given possession and the ship may sail. **3.09**

Claims in respect of a mortgage or charge (section 20(2)(c))

This head of jurisdiction[23] reflects art 1(1)(q) of the Arrest Convention. It relates to all mortgages and charges, whether registered or not and whether legal or equitable, and includes all mortgages and charges created under foreign law.[24] **3.10**

It has been held that the word 'charge' in this context means a charge upon the ship as used in the Merchant Shipping Act 1894.[25] Thus, it embraces charges that can be considered *ejusdem generis* with a maritime lien. A possessory lien, however, which does not encompass rights of ownership, is thus excluded.[26] This is consistent with the text of art 1(1)(q) of the Arrest Convention, which refers to claims arising out of 'a mortgage or hypothecation' of a ship. **3.11**

Claims for the forfeiture or condemnation of a ship or goods (section 20(2)(s))

This head of jurisdiction[27] provides for Admiralty jurisdiction to be exercised in cases where a ship or goods is condemned or forfeited. It has no equivalent provision in the Arrest Convention but is not inconsistent with art 2 of that Convention which preserves the rights or powers vested in any government under existing domestic laws to arrest or detain vessels within its jurisdiction. Droits of Admiralty are peculiar to the English Admiralty context (see below) and, in most cases, matters of forfeiture and condemnation arise between the State and an individual, and are not the subject of civil proceedings in Admiralty. There are numerous statutory provisions which may lead to the condemnation or forfeiture of a ship or goods, particularly under Customs and Excise legislation, environmental protection legislation, and port state control requirements. **3.12**

---

[23] s 20(2)(c) makes provision for 'Claims in respect of a mortgage of or a charge on a ship or any share in a ship'.

[24] s 20(7)(c): for a detailed treatment of the law relating to ship mortgages see Nigel Meeson QC and John Kimbell, *Admiralty Jurisdiction and Practice* (4th edn, 2011) Chapter 10.

[25] *The St Merriel* [1963] P 247, [1963] 2 WLR 488, [1963] 1 All ER 537, [1963] 1 Lloyd's Rep 63; *The Acrux* [1965] P 391, [1965] 3 WLR 80, [1965] 2 All ER 323, [1965] 1 Lloyd's Rep 565.

[26] Ibid.

[27] s 20(2)(s) makes provision for 'Claims for the forfeiture or condemnation of a ship or goods which are being or have been carried, or have been attempted to be carried, in a ship, or for the restoration of a ship or any such goods after seizure, or for droits of Admiralty'.

3.13 Droits of Admiralty encompass certain claims for the return of property or for salvage for recovering property found as wreck at sea, which were perquisites of the Crown and generally were assigned to the Admiral.[28] These claims included wreck at sea, pirate goods, and royal fish.[29] Wreck, in this sense, included jetsam (shipwreck and cargo and deck gear jettisoned to lighten the vessel), whether found as flotsam (floating on the surface) or as lagan (sunken but buoyed for retrieval), and derelicts (abandoned vessels).[30]

B. The Approach to Proprietary Claims in Other Jurisdictions

3.14 The mode of exercise of Admiralty jurisdiction in relation to claims for possession, ownership, mortgages, and the like prescribed in the Supreme Court Act 1981 largely accords with the approach in some other common law countries; Hong Kong,[31] New Zealand,[32] and Singapore[33] all confine the right to proceed *in rem* in respect of questions and claims relating to possession, ownership, co-ownership, mortgages, forfeiture, and condemnation to the particular ship or property in respect of which the questions or claims arose. Australia, Canada, and South Africa, however, have adopted a different approach.

3.15 In Australia, the Admiralty Act 1988 divides claims that are the subject of Admiralty jurisdiction into proprietary maritime claims and general maritime claims.[34] Section 16 confers the right to proceed *in rem* 'on a proprietary maritime claim concerning a ship or other property'.[35] Such claims can only be brought against the particular ship or property to which the claim relates.[36]

3.16 The High Court of Australia has held that s 4(2)(a) and (b) of the 1988 Act, which confers jurisdiction in relation to claims 'relating to ... possession ... [and] ... ownership', is wide enough to encompass a claim that a third party is or has been entitled to become the owner of the property in question;[37] the words 'relating to' are to be contrasted with the more narrowly drawn wording in s 20(2)(a) of the

---

[28] *R v Forty Nine Casks of Brandy* (1836) Hag Adm 257, 280.

[29] *Lord Warden of the Cinque Ports v The King in His Office of Admiralty* (1831) 2 Hag Adm 438, 439–440; 166 ER 304 refers to 'all royal fishes, such as sturgeons, grampuses, whales, porpoises, dolphins, riggs and generally all other fishes of very large bulk or fatness'.

[30] Part IX, Chapter II of the MSA 1995 now contains mandatory procedures relating to wreck.

[31] *High Court Ordinance*, s 12B(2).

[32] Admiralty Act 1973, s 5(2)(a).

[33] High Court (Admiralty Jurisdiction) Act, s 4(2).

[34] Admiralty Act 1988 (Cth), s 4(1).

[35] The definition of a proprietary maritime claim is to be found in s 4(2) of the 1988 Act.

[36] Admiralty Act 1988, s 19.

[37] *Owners of Shin Kobe Maru v Empire Shipping Co Inc* [1994] HCA 54, [22], (1994) 181 CLR 404, 418; followed in *Beluga Shipping GmbH & Co Ks 'Beluga Fantastic' v Headway Shipping Ltd* (No 2) [2008] FCA 1770, [12], (2008) 251 ALR 620, [12].

Supreme Court Act 1981, which confers jurisdiction in relation to claims 'to the possession or ownership' of a ship or property.

The High Court went on to hold that the *in personam* nature of the primary relief sought, namely specific performance, did not prevent the bringing of an action *in rem* pursuant to s 4(2)(a) or (b).[38] Although not necessary for its decision, the Court also expressed the opinion that it was wrong to approach the Act on the basis that it is concerned only with title and ownership at common law and not with equitable interests.[39] **3.17**

The scope of the wording 'relating to' was considered by the Federal Court of Australia in an action seeking a declaration that no agreement to purchase a vessel had been made and the return of monies paid into a solicitor's trust account pending the making of an agreement to purchase the ship. Finkelstein J held[40] that there was a 'reasonably direct connection' between the claim and the ownership of the vessel—in that the claim depended upon whether there was a valid sale pursuant to which ownership of the ship had passed to the plaintiff—and that the claim was therefore one 'relating to title to, or ownership of, a ship or a share in a ship'.[41] **3.18**

Australia did not include in its Admiralty Act a provision equivalent to s 20(2)(s) of the Senior Courts Act 1981. It was considered that there was no need to confer Admiralty jurisdiction in respect of the droits of Admiralty as the category was a 'virtually vestigial' residual jurisdiction.[42] Issues relating to wreck are dealt with primarily by the Navigation Act 2012 (Cth), although some provisions relating to the removal of wrecks and derelicts can also be found in various pieces of State legislation.[43] Similarly, it was considered that questions relating to forfeiture, which is in any event a penal jurisdiction rather than one belonging within the scope of civil admiralty jurisdiction, were best left to the relevant pieces of legislation dealing with forfeiture.[44] There has never been any provision in Australian legislation relating to royal fish. **3.19**

Section 22 of the Federal Courts Act of Canada grants jurisdiction in all cases in which a claim for relief is made or a remedy sought under Canadian maritime law or any other law of Canada relating to any matter coming within the class of subject of navigation and shipping, except to the extent that jurisdiction has been **3.20**

---

38 *Owners of Shin Kobe Maru v Empire Shipping Co Inc* [1994] HCA 54, [35], (1994) 181 CLR 404, 422.

39 Ibid [37], 423.

40 Deriving support for his approach from the House of Lords' decision (and the speech of Lord Keith in particular) in *Gatoil International Inc v Arkwright-Boston Manufacturers Mutual Insurance Co* [1985] AC 255.

41 *Caravelle Investments Ltd v Martaban Ltd* (1999) 95 FCR 85.

42 Civil Admiralty Jurisdiction, ALRC No 33 (1986) para 51.

43 Navigation Act 2012 (Cth), ss 227–239.

44 eg, Fisheries Acts of each State and Territory; Shipping Registration Act 1981 (Cth); the various State and Territory Acts relating to marine safety and marine pollution.

otherwise specifically assigned. A non-exclusive list of maritime claims is provided in s 22(2)(a)–(s).[45] Nonetheless maritime jurisdiction is expressly conferred in relation to claims with respect to title, possession, or ownership of a ship (or the proceeds of sale of a ship), or part interests in them;[46] questions arising between co-owners of a ship with respect to its possession, employment, or earnings;[47] and claims in respect of mortgages or hypothecations of, or charges on, a ship or part interests in them.[48] By s 22(3), this jurisdiction applies regardless of the nationality or registration of the ship (or aircraft), the residence or domicile of her owners, or the place where the cause of action arose or its governing law.

3.21 The jurisdiction conferred pursuant to these paragraphs may be exercised *in personam*[49] or *in rem*[50] and, in contrast to the position in England, Australia, Hong Kong, New Zealand, and Singapore, it may be exercised *in rem* against any ship which, at the time when the action is brought, is beneficially owned by the person who is the owner of the ship that is the subject of the action.[51]

3.22 In *Antares Shipping Corp v The Capricorn*,[52] the Supreme Court of Canada held that the words 'any claim as to title, possession or ownership of a ship'[53] extended to a claim for specific performance. By extension, the Federal Court sitting in admiralty could order damages for breach of a contract for the sale of a ship in lieu of specific performance.[54] Similarly, where a seller is entitled to rescind the contract or to exercise an unpaid seller's lien, he would then have a claim for ownership or possession. The Canadian position is thus closer to the Australian than the English ambit of this head of jurisdiction.

3.23 There is no separate head of jurisdiction in the Federal Courts Act in relation to forfeiture, condemnation, or seizure, or in relation to droits of Admiralty. The Canadian definition of maritime claims is, however, inclusive and does not purport to provide an exhaustive list. It is thus likely that any such claims which might arise and which are not governed by specific legislation[55] would fall within the Federal Court's maritime jurisdiction.

---

[45] A detailed treatment of the Canadian position is contained in W Tetley, *Maritime Liens and Claims* (2nd edn,1998).

[46] Federal Courts Act, s 22(2)(a).

[47] Federal Courts Act, s 22(2)(b).

[48] Federal Courts Act, s 22(2)(c).

[49] Federal Courts Act, s 43(1).

[50] Federal Courts Act, s 43(2).

[51] Federal Courts Act, s 43(8); this sub-section is discussed in more detail at para 5.19.

[52] *Antares Shipping Corp v The Capricorn* [1977] 2 SCR 422, (1979) 111 DLR (3d) 289; *Gleason v The Ship Dawn Light* (1997) 223 NR 155.

[53] Federal Courts Act, s 22(2)(a) RSC 1970.

[54] *Beauchamp v Coastal Corporation* [1984] 1 FC 833.

[55] Examples of such specific legislation include the Canada Shipping Act 2001, the Fisheries Act 1985, the Coastal Fisheries Protection Act 1985, and the Customs Act 1985.

Like the Canadian approach, s 2(1) of the South African Admiralty Jurisdiction Regulation Act 105 of 1983 confers admiralty jurisdiction in relation to 'any maritime claim'. A list of maritime claims is contained in s 1(1)(a)–(ff) of the Act and jurisdiction extends to 'any other matter which by virtue of its nature or subject matter is a marine or maritime matter, the meaning of the expression marine or maritime matter not being limited by reason of the matters set forth in the preceding paragraphs'.[56] Nevertheless, claims arising out of or relating to ownership, possession, employment or earnings, mortgages and charges, and bottomry and respondentia are specifically made the subject of admiralty jurisdiction.[57] Such claims may be enforced *in personam*[58] or *in rem*, provided that the claimant has a maritime lien over the property to be arrested or the owner would be liable on the action *in personam*.[59] With the exception of claims relating to any mortgage, hypothecation, right of retention, pledge or other charge on or of a ship, and any bottomry or respondentia bond, any maritime claim, including those relating to possession and ownership as mentioned in s 1(1)(a)–(c), may be brought *in rem* against a ship other than the ship in respect of which the claim arises (an 'associated ship').[60] **3.24**

Jurisdiction, which may be enforced *in personam* and *in rem*, also exists in relation to any claim arising out of or relating to the forfeiture of any ship or any goods carried therein or the restoration of any ship or any such goods forfeited.[61] There is, however, no head of jurisdiction with respect to droits of Admiralty except to the extent that s 6 preserves the pre-existing English Admiralty jurisdiction. **3.25**

---

56 Admiralty Jurisdiction Regulation Act 105 of 1983, s 1(1)(ee).

57 Admiralty Jurisdiction Regulation Act 105 of 1983, s 1(1)(a)–(d).

58 Admiralty Jurisdiction Regulation Act 105 of 1983, s 3(1) and (2).

59 Admiralty Jurisdiction Regulation Act 105 of 1983, s 3(4); except where the owner is seeking to vindicate possession of his own ship, in which case he does not have the underlying personal liability required but can still proceed *in rem*, *The Great Eagle* 1992 (2) SA 87.

60 Admiralty Jurisdiction Regulation Act 105 of 1983, s 3(6).

61 Admiralty Jurisdiction Regulation Act 105 of 1983 s 1(v); see Chapter 1, para 1.24.

4

MARITIME LIENS (AND 'OTHER CHARGES')

A. Introduction

4.01 Although confidently described by Sir John Jervis in *The Bold Buccleugh*[1] as 'simple and intelligible', the law of maritime liens is in significant respects far from straightforward. Difficulties arise, as Brandon J put it in *The Halcyon Skies*,[2] 'because of the history of Admiralty jurisdiction', and remain potentially significant over 165 years after Parliament first intervened to ease the jurisdictional pressure on the High Court of Admiralty. This is despite the availability for all practical purposes of statutory rights *in rem* in all cases in which maritime liens arise, because:

(1) there are two key and uncontested features of the maritime lien:
   (i) claims attracting such a lien are accorded a high ranking when it comes to the distribution of a fund inadequate to meet all the claims against it; and

[1] *The Bold Buccleugh* (1859) 7 Moo PC 267, 285, 13 ER 884, 891. See above, para 2.17, for his classic formulation of the law of maritime lien.

[2] *The Halcyon Skies* [1977] QB 14, 27.

(ii) such a lien survives a change of ownership;

(2) whether a particular claim attracts a maritime lien may therefore be critical to whether recovery is possible, in full or at all;

(3) the list of maritime liens[3] is closed and could only be extended by statute (something which has not happened for well over a century). With the exception of the single statutory extension,[4] the list begins and ends with claims which were within the jurisdiction of the High Court of Admiralty in the early years of the nineteenth century;

(4) it is not always easy to tell whether a particular claim was or was not within that jurisdiction.

The essential difficulty in this connection is that maritime liens evolved hand-in-hand with (but lagging in evolutionary terms slightly behind) the action *in rem*, as a response to the jurisdictional predations of the common law courts and their writs of prohibition—and that evolution was far from complete by the time of the Admiralty Court Act 1840, which confirmed and extended the Admiralty Court's jurisdiction. Thus, for example, as late as 1842, although by that time very many collision cases had been brought and decided in the Admiralty Court, Dr Lushington himself thought it: **4.02**

> ... obvious that a ship may be liable where the owners would not be personally responsible, as, for instance, in cases of lien upon a ship for seamen's wages or bottomry bonds, *when the lien has been acquired before the existing owners made their purchase...* [But only that] it might possibly be that an innocent purchaser may be liable to have his ship arrested and sold for the payment of damages in a case where the former owners would have been responsible, and the damage[5] was occasioned before the purchase was made; *but upon this point I give no opinion whatever.*[6] [Emphasis supplied]

Indeed, it was not until the decision in *The Bold Buccleugh* itself that the existence of the 'damage lien' was finally established.

Uncertainty as to the precise ambit of the maritime lien and the claims which give rise to one was in some respects enhanced rather than resolved by the Acts of 1840 and 1861. One such uncertainty was whether the newly bestowed (or, in some cases, **4.03**

[3] Para 4.06 below.

[4] The lien for master's disbursements: n 9 below.

[5] It is plain that he must have had damage done by a ship in mind (a) because such were the facts of the case before him, and (b) because none of the other claims giving rise to a maritime lien are damages claims.

[6] *The Druid* (1842) 1 W Rob 391, 398–399, 166 ER 619, 622. Dr Lushington vacillated on this topic. Although he did not use the word 'lien', his reasoning in the case of *The Aline* (1839) 1 W Rob 111, 166 ER 514 was consistent with damage giving rise to a lien (and that plainly is how the reporter of that case, who did use the word 'lien', understood him). In *The Volant* (1842) 1 W Rob 383, 387, 166 ER 616, 618, decided a few months after *The Druid*, Dr Lushington expressed the clear view that damage did not give rise to a lien. By the time that he decided *The Bold Buccleugh* at 'instance', however, this had given way to confidence that a lien did arise (1850) 3 W Rob 220, 229, 166 ER 944, 948.

re-conferred) grounds of jurisdiction, such as in relation to claims by 'necessaries-men', themselves gave rise to maritime liens. As noted above,[7] it was not until nearly half a century after the introduction of that ground of jurisdiction[8] that that question was finally resolved in the negative, by the decision of the House of Lords in *The Henrich Björn*.[9] Similar uncertainty arose in relation to pre-existing grounds of jurisdiction whose geographical scope was widened by the Acts to include causes of action arising within the body of a county, where previously the jurisdiction of the Court had been confined to matters arising on the high seas. However, *dicta* in *The Sara* and *The Henrich Björn* encouraged the view that maritime liens did attach to claims within the Court's pre-existing, but geographically widened jurisdiction, and—provided of course that the cause of action existed at all[10]—no particular difficulty appears to have arisen in that regard.[11]

4.04 However, difficulties have continued to arise[12] or remain unresolved[13] even today. The 'vital distinction' drawn by Brandon J in *The Halcyon Skies* was that whereas:

> ... no maritime liens had been created in respect of claims covered by the extended jurisdiction conferred on the court by the Acts of 1840 and 1861 ... in relation, and only in relation, to claims covered by new, as distinct from enlarged jurisdiction ... where existing jurisdiction had been enlarged, maritime liens recognised in respect of claims under the existing jurisdiction should be regarded as extending also to claims of a similar kind under the enlarged jurisdiction.[14]

This distinction, helpful in itself, is a broad one and does not on its own assist the resolution of marginal cases, such as whether a claim for personal injuries is—or is sufficiently similar to—one for 'damage done by a ship' for it to attract a maritime lien. Nor is an answer necessarily to be gleaned from the cases, whether decided before or after the Admiralty Court Acts. That is because:

(1) as will be seen below in relation to personal injury claims, the cases do not always speak with one voice;
(2) the fact that claims of a certain type were not or were only infrequently brought in the Admiralty Court before 1840 (or later) does not necessarily mean that that Court did not (in its own eyes) have jurisdiction to consider them;[15]

---

[7] Para 2.23.

[8] By s 6 of the 1840 Act.

[9] *The Henrich Björn* (1886) 11 App Cas 270. To similar effect in relation to claims for master's disbursements, *Hamilton v Baker, The Sara* (1889) 14 App Cas 209, a decision overturned by Parliament by s 1 of the Merchant Shipping Act 1889, subsequently s 167(2) of the 1894 Act and s 18 of the 1970 Act, now s 41 of the 1995 Act.

[10] Cf *The Goring* [1988] AC 831, [1988] 1 Lloyd's Rep 397: no cause of action for salvage in non-tidal waters.

[11] *The Halcyon Skies* [1977] QB 14, 28–29.

[12] As in the precise scope of the wages lien: *The Halcyon Skies* [1977] QB 14, *The Turiddu* [1999] 2 Lloyd's Rep 401.

[13] As to whether a claim for personal injury gives rise to a maritime lien (paras 4.23 and following).

[14] *The Halcyon Skies* [1977] QB 14, 30.

[15] Cf *The Sylph* (1867) LR 2 A&E 24, 27–28.

(3) times change; claims now recognized as falling within the ambit of the wages lien, for instance,[16] would have been wholly foreign to Lord Stowell and Dr Lushington.[17]

Resolution of these difficulties is not straightforward and to attempt to formulate a theory which would provide the answer in every case is unlikely to be of more assistance than Brandon J's 'vital distinction' and would be rather less reliable. Moreover, their significance in terms of day-to-day practicality should not be exaggerated: the question whether a claim for personal injuries gives rise to a maritime lien has, after all, not arisen squarely for decision in the 145 years since the 1861 Act bestowed (or confirmed) jurisdiction for damage done by a ship. **4.05**

B. The Regime Applicable to the Enforcement of Maritime Liens

Preliminary considerations

An action *in rem* may be brought against a ship, aircraft, or other property in any case where there is a maritime lien or other charge on it for the amount claimed.[18] Although the law relating to maritime liens also applies to hovercraft,[19] an aircraft cannot be subject to a maritime lien,[20] although it can be subject to an 'other charge'. Maritime liens are not defined in the Senior Courts Act 1981 but are generally accepted[21] to arise only in relation to: **4.06**

(1) claims for damage done by a ship;
(2) claims for salvage;
(3) claims for seamen's wages;
(4) claims for master's wages and disbursements;
(5) claims relating to bottomry and respondentia.

---

[16] As in the pension contributions at issue in *The Halcyon Skies*.

[17] The two giants of the Admiralty Court in, respectively, the early and the middle decades of the nineteenth century.

[18] s 21(3): a detailed treatment of the English law of maritime liens is contained in D R Thomas, *Maritime Liens* (1980). Save in respect of salvage (as to which see para 4.28 below), the property to which a maritime lien can attach is restricted in the absence of statutory intervention (as in the case of hovercraft) to ships, their cargo, and freight. See generally Thomas ibid, §§37–42.

[19] Hovercraft Act 1968, s 2(2) and (3).

[20] Save of course as cargo carried by sea. There is nothing in the language of the Civil Aviation Acts, nor of the Senior Courts Act 1981 or its predecessors to extend the law of *lien* (as distinct from the law of salvage) over aircraft; compare the explicit wording used in relation to hovercraft. To contrary effect, however, D R Thomas, n 18 above, §§12(2), 38, 287–288.

[21] In Canada, the right to proceed *in rem* following a change of ownership also exists in relation to claims for pilotage, general average contribution, dock charges, harbour dues, and canal tolls: s 43(3) Federal Courts Act. These are sometimes referred to as 'quasi-maritime liens' in that although they survive a change in ownership, they rank only as statutory actions *in rem*: W Tetley QC, 'Arrest, Attachment & Related Maritime Law Procedures' [1999] 73 *Tulane Law Review* 1895, 1921.

·d above, all the claims which may be the subject of a maritime lien, with ›lete exception of respondentia, are also claims listed in s 20(2) which may ;ht *in rem*. There is, therefore, an overlap between maritime liens and some ...ory actions *in rem*. However, for the reasons set out above the scope of the claim which attracts a maritime lien will generally be narrower than that which gives rise to a statutory action *in rem*; that is because (absent specific legislative intervention) only those claims which were recognized historically as giving rise to a maritime lien continue to do so. Thus a cause of action founded, eg, on a modern statute, will probably not give rise to a maritime lien, although a statutory right to arrest (and, from commencement of the action, associated statutory lien) may exist. It is therefore always necessary to consider whether the cause of action giving rise to the claim is one within the scope of what, historically, would have been recognized as giving rise to a maritime lien. So, for example, in *Seward v The Vera Cruz*,[22] the House of Lords held that a claim arising under the Fatal Accidents Act 1846 could not be pursued by an action *in rem* for damage done by a ship on the basis that the Act was 'legislation for the general case and not for particular injury by ships'. Whilst it is clear that such a claim could now be pursued *in rem* under the provisions of the Senior Courts Act 1981, it would almost certainly not attract a maritime lien.[23] As Fisher J of the High Court of New Zealand observed in *Fournier v the Ship Margaret Z*, jurisdiction is not to be confused with lien status.[24] This chapter concerns only those claims which attract maritime liens.

4.08 The notion of an 'other charge' embraces charges in the nature of mortgages or those contained within shipping legislation which can be considered a charge *ejusdem generis* with a maritime lien. It does not include a possessory lien.[25] This approach has been followed by the High Court of Singapore, which has declined to interpret the equivalent provisions of the Singapore law[26] any more widely than has been done by the English courts.[27]

4.09 Maritime liens are generally recognized in the various jurisdictions as giving the right to proceed *in rem*. Canada, Hong Kong, New Zealand, Singapore, and South Africa adopt a similar approach to that in England and Wales, in that maritime liens are not defined by statute, their scope within the particular jurisdiction being left to the general law, but it is nevertheless provided that the

[22] *The Vera Cruz (No 2)* (1884) 10 App Cas 59, 67.

[23] D C Jackson, *Enforcement of Maritime Claims* (4th edn, 2005) 2.75–2.76. Similarly, whilst damage may be 'done by a ship' in the context of an oil spill, any claim arising out of such an occurrence founded on causes of action created by statutes such as the Merchant Shipping (Oil Pollution) Act 1971 (now Chapter III of Part VI of the *Merchant Shipping Act* 1995) will not attract a maritime lien.

[24] *Fournier v The Ship Margaret Z* [1999] 3 NZLR 111, 121.

[25] *The St Merriel* [1963] P 247, [1963] 2 WLR 488, [1963] 1 All ER 537, [1963] 1 Lloyd's Rep 63; *The Acrux* [1965] P 391, [1965] 3 WLR 80, [1965] 2 All ER 323, [1965] 1 Lloyd's Rep 565.

[26] High Court (Admiralty Jurisdiction) Act (Cap 123), s 4(3).

[27] *The Ocean Jade* [1991] 1 SLR 583; *The Bunga Melati 5* [2011] SGHC 195.

jurisdiction of the relevant court may be invoked *in rem* in any case in which there is a maritime lien.[28]

However, whereas in England and Wales, Hong Kong, New Zealand, and Singapore the right to proceed *in rem* on a maritime lien is restricted to the particular ship in respect of which the lien arises, South Africa permits an action *in rem* to be brought against an associated ship in a claim relating to or arising out of a maritime lien provided that there has been no change in ownership.[29] The Canadian legislation also appears, *prima facie*, to permit an action *in rem* based on a maritime lien to be brought against a sister-ship.[30] The courts have concluded in two cases, however, albeit in the context of foreign maritime liens, that such a lien is 'not portable to sister-ships'.[31] It remains to be seen whether this reasoning will be applied to maritime liens generally, but it is submitted that in principle it should be. Although of course it is a matter for national parliaments to decide, it is anathema to the origin and (insofar as it is possible to articulate it) to the concept of the maritime lien for it to be enforceable against a sister-ship. **4.10**

The Australian legislation defines 'maritime liens' and provides an indicative list which encompasses salvage, damage done by a ship, wages of the master, or of a member of the crew, of a ship or master's disbursements.[32] The Act makes explicit by s 6 that it does not have the effect of creating new maritime liens, charges, or causes of action which would not have existed if the Act had not been passed. Thus the definition, on its face, extends only to the traditional maritime liens recognized in English law; although reference to bottomry and respondentia has been omitted.[33] Whilst not precluding any rare case of bottomry or respondentia being embraced within s 15, the indicative nature of the list has also given rise to arguments that additional liens ought to be embraced within s 15, such as one arising from the commission of a tort on the high seas. Without determining the question, Allsop J has observed that the restrictive approach to maritime liens in Anglo-Australian law places formidable obstacles in the way of recognizing new maritime liens.[34] **4.11**

---

[28] Federal Courts Act s 43(2) (Canada); High Court Ordinance, s 12B(3) (Hong Kong); Admiralty Act 1973, s 5(1) (New Zealand); High Court (Admiralty Jurisdiction) Act, s 4(3) (Singapore); Admiralty Jurisdiction Regulation Act 105 of 1983, s 3(4)(a) (South Africa).

[29] Admiralty Jurisdiction Regulation Act 105 of 1983, s 3(6) and (7); the only matters excluded from associated ship arrest are claims arising out of or relating to any mortgage, hypothecation, right of retention, pledge, or other charge on or of a ship, and any bottomry or respondentia bond.

[30] Federal Courts Act s 43(8).

[31] *Fraser Shipyard and Industrial Centre Ltd v Expedient Maritime Co (The Atlantis Two)* (1999) 170 FTR 1; *Holt Cargo Systems Inc v ABC Containerline NV (The Brussel)* (2000) 185 FTR 145.

[32] Admiralty Act 1988, s 15.

[33] Civil Admiralty Jurisdiction, ALRC No 33 (1986) para 122.

[34] *Elbe Shipping SA v The Ship 'Global Peace'* (2006) 154 FCR 439, 470, [130]; [2006] FCA 954, [130] citing *The Acrux; Bankers Trust International v Todd Shipyards Corp (The Halcyon Isle)* [1981] AC 221; and *Fournier v The Ship Margaret Z* [1999] 3 NZLR 111, [22]–[23].

The further issue which would arise in relation to hitherto unrecognized maritime liens is when the existence of any such lien is to be determined, the claim to a maritime lien having been made to establish jurisdiction. Allsop J concluded that it is necessary, at the point of ruling upon jurisdiction, to decide whether or not by Australian law (including its rules of private international law) what is asserted in the proceeding can found a maritime lien, noting that such an approach accords with comparative practice in other jurisdictions.[35]

The transfer or assignment of maritime liens

4.12 The nature of a maritime lien as a personal privilege attaching to the *res* has led generally to the understanding that a maritime lien, except that attaching to a bottomry bond, is incapable of assignment.[36] That general understanding has arisen, however, in the context of voluntary payments by other creditors, usually of the wages of the crew. The issue becomes important when a third party takes over the obligations to pay the master or the crew or perhaps the salvor, and wishes to assert the same priority in respect of the fund as that held by the crew or other party. It is said to be the 'traditional rule' that a lien over crew wages is not transferable[37] unless sanctioned by the court.[38] In *The Petone*,[39] Hill J observed that 'the weight of authority is strongly against the doctrine that the man who has paid off the privileged claimant stands in the shoes of the privileged claimant and has his lien, whether it be regarded as a general doctrine or applied to wages only'.[40] Hewson J accepted this authority, which had never previously been challenged, in *The Leoborg (No 2)*.[41] Neither of these cases was, however, concerned directly with the question of whether the lien could be transferred by contractual assignment or indeed by subrogation.

4.13 The point was considered by the Court of First Instance in Hong Kong in *The Sparti*,[42] but a determination of the point was not necessary for the decision. Waung J observed that the decision in *The Petone*[43] left little room for the contention that

[35] Ibid 471, [134]–[135]. See also *Reiter Petroleum Inc v The Ship 'Sam Hawk'* [2015] FCA 1005, [74].

[36] See D C Jackson, *Enforcement of Maritime Claims* (4th edn, 2005) 18.74–18.90 for a detailed discussion of the transferability of maritime liens.

[37] *The Petone* [1917] P 198.

[38] *The Cornelia Henrietta* (1866) LR 1 A & E 51; *The James W Elwell* [1921] P 351; *The Leoborg (No 2)* [1964] 1 Lloyd's Rep 380; *The Berostar* [1970] 2 Lloyd's Rep 403; *The Vasilia* [1972] 1 Lloyd's Rep 51.

[39] *The Petone* [1917] P 198.

[40] That weight of authority included *The William F Safford* (1860) Lush 69, 167 ER 37; *The Wasp* (1867) LR 1 A & E 367; *The St Lawrence* (1880) 5 PD 250; *The Tagus* [1903] P 44, none of which dealt directly with the question of whether or not a maritime lien could be assigned or transferred. See also *The Anonymous* (1696) Fort. 230 and *The James W Elwell* [1921] P 351, which do address the question of subrogation, and the approach adopted by the Court of Appeal in *The Turiddu* [1999] 2 Lloyd's Rep 401, in order to circumvent the problem.

[41] *The Leoborg (No 2)* [1964] 1 Lloyd's Rep 380.

[42] *The Sparti* [2000] 3 HKC 323.

[43] *The Petone* [1917] P 198.

a maritime lien could be acquired or transferred by contractual assignment, and that the objection in respect of contractual assignment was stronger than that which might be raised against subrogation, which at least had the merit that the person subrogated had paid off the wages and stood in equity in the shoes of the crew. The judge took comfort from the series of decisions in other Commonwealth jurisdictions which also seemed to be against the proposition that maritime liens were assignable.[44]

More recently, in *Shipping Co Ltd v The Owners and/or Demise Charterers of the Ship or Vessel 'King Coal'*,[45] the High Court in Hong Kong concluded that even if (without deciding) the statutory right *in rem* was assignable, the words in s 12A(2)(n) referred to 'any claim by a master or member of the crew'. These clear words were said to limit the court's jurisdiction to claims for wages 'brought by the master or a member of the crew' and did not extend to claims brought by an assignee.[46] If correct, this would seem to deprive an assignee of any practical ability to enforce an assigned maritime lien, thus limiting the utility of the assignment and of the lien itself.

The same view has been adopted in South Africa.[47]

Were the point to require decision, it would be necessary to consider whether a maritime lien is a chose in action capable of assignment, either at law or in equity. The High Court of Singapore seems to consider that maritime liens can be characterized in such a way. Chan Sek Keong J observed *obiter* in *Soon Aik Marine & Engineering Pte Ltd v Hoesheng* that: **4.14**

> The legal assignment of choses generally has been permitted by statute since the *Judicature Act* 1873. Unless there is binding authority against such assignment, there would seem to be no public policy consideration against the assignment of wages of the master and the crew, and with it the maritime lien.[48]

Whilst expressly declining to determine the question of assignability, the judge held that a claim by the Central Provident Fund Board for the recovery of Central Provident

[44] *The Offi Gloria* [1993] 3 NZLR 576 (High Court of New Zealand); *The Samuel Marshall* [1924] Ex CR 53; *The Aragon* [1943] Ex CR 41 (Exchequer Court of Canada); *The Alarisa* [1996] 2 FC 883 (Federal Court of Canada).

[45] [2013] Lloyd's Rep Plus 55; [2012] HKCFI 2013.

[46] Ibid [13].

[47] *The Argun (No 2)* 2003 (3) SA 149. Cf *Windrush Intercontinental SA v UACC Bergshav Tankers AS* [2015] ZAKZDHC 30, High Court of South Africa, where Olsen J remarked *obiter* that he doubted a maritime lien for wages was not assignable: [63]. See also s 11(8) of the Admiralty Jurisdiction Regulation Act 105 of 1983, which provides that a person who has paid an amount owing under a lien is entitled to 'all the rights, privileges and preferences' of the lienee and effectively steps into the shoes of the lienee: *Mak Mediterranee Sarl v The Fund Constituting the Proceeds of the Judicial Sale of the M C Thunder (S D Arch interested party)* 1994 (3) SA 599 (C) at 607H–608B. The benefits of this provision were recently found to extend even to the sole shareholder of the owner of a vessel: *Maree NO v Fund Constituted from the Proceeds of the Sale of the MV 'Madagascar'* [2010] ZAKZDHC 6.

[48] *Soon Aik Marine & Engineering Pte Ltd v Hoesheng* [1987] 1 SLR 247.

Fund (CPF) contributions due to certain members of the crew from the owners of the vessel was a claim for 'wages' and thus the Board was entitled to a maritime lien. The Court distinguished the decisions in *The Acrux*[49] and *The Fairport*[50] and held that, on the facts of the present case, the Board as trustee had effectively stepped into the shoes of those seamen for whom CPF contributions were payable. Thus, the claim of the Board was in substance the claim of the members of the crew within the wording of s 3(1)(n) of the High Court (Admiralty Jurisdiction) Act 1961.

4.15 In Canada, too, the traditional rule appears to have been sidestepped. In *The Metaxas v The Galaxias (No 2)*,[51] several Greek seamen were stranded as a result of the seizure and sale of their ship. It was held that where a seamen's benevolent organization under authority of statute pays the repatriation costs of stranded sailors in Canada, it is clearly in keeping with current policy that such a payment be given the protection of a maritime lien or its equivalent.[52] The decision does not go so far as to recognize the assignability of a maritime lien but achieves a similar result nonetheless.

In the Australian case of *Ship Haku Endeavour v Programmed Total Marine Services Pty Ltd*,[53] the issue arose as to whether a labour service provider, PTMS, had a maritime lien with respect to the master and crew's wages. PTMS had contracted with the charterers to provide goods and services, in the form of a master and crew, to various vessels. PTMS paid the wages and then sought to recover the amounts paid from the charterers on the basis that PTMS had a maritime lien with respect to those wages under the principle of subrogation. The Full Federal Court of Australia considered the previous line of authority, including *The Petone*, and concluded that PTMS did not have any equitable right of subrogation. That was because, first, the lien is extinguished as soon as the wages are paid and, second, PTMS was the principal debtor in respect of the wages in that it had entered into contracts of employment with each of the crew to perform the services. In paying their wages, PTMS was simply discharging its own obligations.[54] Justice Siopis considered, albeit *obiter*, that the fact the maritime lien was discharged on the payment of the wages would not in itself be an obstacle to subrogation, if it were otherwise available.[55] It was not necessary for the Court to consider whether the lien was capable of assignment.[56]

4.16 The principles relating to the assignability of choses in action were described by Lord Roskill in *Trendtex Trading Corporation v Credit Suisse*[57] in these terms:

---

49 *The Acrux* [1965] P 391, [1965] 3 WLR 80, [1965] 2 All ER 323, [1965] 1 Lloyd's Rep 565.
50 *The Fairport* [1965] 2 Lloyd's Rep 183.
51 *Metaxas v The Galaxias (No 2)* [1989] 1 FC 386 (TD).
52 Ibid 407.
53 (2013) 211 FCR 369, [2013] FCAFC 21.
54 Ibid 394, [88].
55 Ibid 373, [3].
56 Ibid 399 [105].
57 *Trendtex Trading Corporation v Credit Suisse* [1982] AC 679, 703, [1981] 3 WLR 766, 779, [1981] 3 All ER 520, 530.

> The court should look at the totality of the transaction ... If the assignment is of a property right or interest and the cause of action is ancillary to that right or interest or if the assignee had a genuine commercial interest in taking the assignment and in enforcing it for his own benefit ... [the assignment will be valid].

In English law, the position is clear that a maritime lien is non-assignable.[58] However, it is difficult to see why, at an abstract level, this should be so. If a maritime lien arises as a security interest as a result of—and ancillary to—the underlying cause of action, why should not the maritime lien be assignable if the underlying cause of action is assignable?[59] Applying the principles in *Trendtex Trading Corporation v Credit Suisse*,[60] the assignability of a maritime lien ought to be determined by reference to the question whether the assignee has a property interest or a genuine commercial interest in the cause of action, rather than by reference to any supposed characteristic of the security interest to which it gives rise. However, the *sui generis* nature of the maritime lien[61] makes it less likely than it might otherwise be that a rationalization of the law along the lines suggested will be achieved.

C. The Maritime Liens Recognized in English Law

Claims for damage done by a ship

The rationale for the existence of a maritime lien arising out of a claim for damage done by a ship was explained by Lord Watson in *Currie v M'Knight*: 4.17

> ... it is a reasonable and salutary rule that when a ship is so carelessly navigated as to occasion injury to other vessels which are free from blame, the owners of the injured craft should have a remedy against the corpus of the offending ship and should not be restricted to a personal claim against her owners, who may have no substantial interest in her and may be without the means of making due compensation.[62]

In *The Rama*, Clarke J identified the three criteria which must be satisfied in English law for 'damage done by a ship' to give rise to a maritime lien: 4.18

(1) the damage must be caused by something done by those engaged in the navigation or management of the ship in a physical sense; and
(2) the ship must be the actual or noxious instrument by which the damage is done; and

---

[58] For an example and analysis of the authorities, see *The Turiddu* [1999] 2 Lloyd's Rep 401.

[59] So much is recognized by art 10 of the International Convention on Maritime Liens and Mortgages 1993 (to which none of the jurisdictions considered in this work is party): 'The assignment of or subrogation to a claim secured by a maritime lien set out in Article 4 entails the simultaneous assignment of or subrogation to such maritime lien.'

[60] *Trendtex Trading Corporation v Credit Suisse*, n 57 above.

[61] See further below in relation to the treatment of foreign maritime liens.

[62] *Currie v M'Knight* [1897] AC 97, 106.

(3) the damage must be sustained by a person or property external to the ship.[63]

These criteria are considered in turn below.

Damage done by those engaged in the navigation or management

4.19 The first criterion is an extension of the conclusion reached in *The Eschersheim* where Lord Diplock referred only to damage caused by those engaged in the 'navigation' of the ship.[64] Clarke J considered that Lord Diplock was not considering the precise meaning of navigation and so it appeared to him that the test would be satisfied if the damage was caused as a result of the navigation or management of the ship, provided that the expression 'navigation or management' is understood in a physical sense.[65] In *The Eschersheim*, the decision to beach the vessel under tow, which subsequently broke up in the wind and waves, was not a navigational decision but rather a management decision, and thus Clarke J's formulation involves no extension of principle, it being anyway implicit in the decision of the House of Lords.

4.20 In addition, the lien will attach only in so far as the claim is established through proof of fault of the owners or persons lawfully in possession of the ship.[66] Where a maritime lien has been created by a collision, it is available to the injured party even if those directly responsible for the collision were servants of demise charterers and not of the true owners.[67] Traditionally it has been held that the lien will not attach if those lawfully in charge are there compulsorily, as, for example, in the case of compulsory pilots[68] because they were not engaged at the instigation of the owners and so were not in a position to subject the ship to the risk of attachment of a lien. It is submitted in view of the courts' approach to liability where a compulsory pilot is on board[69] that the abolition of the defence of compulsory pilotage[70] will result in the lien arising in such circumstances. This would not amount to the creation of a new lien, since all that has occurred is that the obstacle to it arising has been removed. If as a matter of principle a lien will attach in circumstances where

[63] *The Rama* [1996] 2 Lloyd's Rep 281, 293.

[64] *The Eschersheim* [1976] 1 WLR 430, [1976] 1 All ER 920, [1976] 2 Lloyd's Rep 1.

[65] *The Rama* [1996] 2 Lloyd's Rep 281, 293.

[66] *The Ripon City* [1897] P 226.

[67] *The Father Thames* [1979] 2 Lloyd's Rep 364, 370 per Sheen J; *The Great Loyalty* [1982–1983] 1 SLR 287 (Singapore High Court).

[68] *The Parlement Belge* (1880) 5 PD 197; *The Tervaete* [1922] P 259, 270; (1922) 12 Ll L Rep 252, 254 per Scrutton LJ; *Townsville Harbour Board v Scottish Shire Line Ltd* (1914) 18 CLR 306 (High Court of Australia).

[69] *Esso Petroleum Co Ltd v Hall Russell & Co* [1989] 1 AC 643; *The Cavendish* [1993] 2 Lloyd's Rep 292 (note Clarke J's conclusion at p 300 that the pilot is deemed the servant of the shipowner during pilotage) and, in the Australian context, *Braverus Maritime Inc v Port Kembla Coal Terminal Ltd* [2005] FCAFC 256, (2005) 148 FCR 68 (Full Federal Court of Australia).

[70] Pilotage Act 1987, s 16. The abolition of the defence was achieved by s 15 of the Pilotage Act 1913. In the Australian context, see s 326 of the Navigation Act 2012, which replicated the effect of s 410B of the Navigation Act 1912 (repealed).

damage is done by the ship which is caused by those in control of the navigation of the ship, then there seems no longer to be any justifiable reason for denying the existence of the lien simply because the pilot advising the master in the navigation of the vessel was there compulsorily.

The ship as the noxious instrument

It is essential that the ship (or a part of it)[71] to which the maritime lien attaches is the actual instrument by which the damage was done, although the lien is not limited to collisions between ships.[72] So, for example, where a tug collides with a ship which then leaks oil causing damage, the tug is the noxious instrument which has caused the damage and an action *in rem* cannot be brought against the other ship. In *The Eschersheim*, the House of Lords held that, although a borderline case, the casting-off of the tow by the tug meant that the tug was the active cause of the damage or the instrument of mischief.[73] Loss or damage resulting from a vessel having to leave a fishing ground due to the dangerous navigation of another ship has also been held to be 'damage done by a ship'.[74] By contrast, where a chief officer fell down into a hold because the hatchway was negligently covered only with a tarpaulin, the ship could not be said to be the active cause of the damage, nor was the damage done by those in charge of the ship with the ship as the noxious instrument.[75] In *Currie v M'Knight*,[76] the House of Lords held that the cutting of the cables of another vessel in order to free the ship was not an act of the ship. **4.21**

Other jurisdictions have generally adopted the above approach and have endorsed Lord Diplock's analysis in *The Eschersheim* of the phrase 'damage done by a ship'. In *Administrator of the Ship-Source Oil Pollution Fund v British Columbia (Minister of Finance)*, the Federal Court of Canada noted that the sinking of a ship resulting in pollution of surrounding water may arguably be damage 'caused by a ship' within the meaning of s 22(2)(d) of the *Federal Courts Act*.[77] In *The Asian Atlas*,[78] the Hong Kong Court of Appeal set aside *in rem* proceedings commenced by the owner of a subsurface launchway against the owners of a vessel, partly because it was the vessel herself and not the launchway that had sustained the damage. In *Elbe Shipping SA v Giant Marine Shipping SA*,[79] the Australian Federal Court considered, without deciding the point, that

[71] *The Minerva* (1933) 46 Ll L Rep 212, [1933] P 224; *The Norwhale* [1975] QB 589, [1975] 2 WLR 829, [1975] 2 All ER 501, [1975] 1 Lloyd's Rep 610.
[72] *The Vera Cruz (No 2)* (1885) 9 PD 96.
[73] *The Eschersheim* [1976] 1 WLR 430, [1976] 1 All ER 920, [1976] 2 Lloyd's Rep 1.
[74] *The Dagmara and AmaAntxine* [1988] 1 Lloyd's Rep 431.
[75] *The Theta* [1894] P 280.
[76] *Currie v M'Knight* [1897] AC 97.
[77] [2012] FC 725, [34].
[78] [2008] HKLRD 461; [2008] HKEC 693.
[79] [2008] FCA 1135, [17].

damage caused by a tug involved in a berthing operation may not be damage 'done by' a vessel.

Damage external to the ship

4.22 Objects which may be damaged are not limited to ships, but include, for example, piers and landing stages.[80] A different answer to the question whether the injured person or property must be external to the ship, as Clarke J held in *The Rama*,[81] was reached by the High Court of New Zealand in *Fournier v The Ship Margaret Z*.[82] In that case Fisher J held, consistently with Australian authority,[83] that the chief limits of the lien are now to be found in the requirement that the damage be 'done by the ship' rather than the location of the accident. The Judge made the following observations about the lien for damage done by a ship.

(a) A maritime lien will normally be available where damage is caused by the crew's active operation of the ship or its gear in a manner giving rise to substantive liability.
(b) The ship or its gear must play a significant role in the chain of causation leading to the damage: it is insufficient that the damage could not have occurred but for the existence of the ship or its gear.
(c) The damage in question can be injury to the person.
(d) The damage can be suffered in or on a ship.
(e) Members of the ship's crew qualify as eligible claimants.
(f) The activity is not confined to the navigation of the ship in the usual sense but must involve the active use of the ship or its gear for one of the purposes for which they were designed or installed.
(g) Because the damage must be caused by the active operation of the ship or its gear, injury suffered due to the plaintiff's encounter with a static condition does not apply.
(h) For the same reason, damage caused by the action of one or more individuals on the ship does not qualify unless it was effected through the active operation of the ship or its gear.[84]

Thus the laws of England and Wales on the one hand and of Australia and New Zealand on the other are presently out of step on this point.

---

80 *The Veritas* [1901] P 304.

81 *The Rama* [1996] 2 Lloyd's Rep 281, 293.

82 *Fournier v The Ship Margaret Z* [1999] 3 NZLR 111.

83 *Union Steamship Co of NZ Ltd v Ferguson* (1960) 119 CLR 191; *Nagrint v The Regis* (1939) 61 CLR 688. For a discussion of whether Australian law recognizes a maritime lien over cargo for a tort on the high seas, see *Rail Equipment Leasing Pty Ltd v CV Scheepvaartonderneming Emmagracht* [2008] NSWSC 850. Without deciding the point, the Supreme Court of New South Wales doubted whether s 15 of the Admiralty Act 1988 could found a lien for damage caused to a ship.

84 *Fournier v The Ship Margaret Z* [1999] 3 NZLR 111, 125.

Claims for personal injury and death

A further difference may exist[85] in relation to whether a maritime lien exists for personal injury claims, as to which there is a divergence of opinion,[86] or for fatal accident claims, as to which the divergence of opinion is more muted.[87] The essence of the enquiry is whether such claims were within the jurisdiction exercised by the High Court of Admiralty immediately prior to the Acts of 1840 and 1861. That is because, by that time, the jurisdiction of the Court had been confined to those claims which gave rise to maritime liens, which were of course actionable only *in rem*. Although, in ancient times, the Court clearly had exercised an *in personam* jurisdiction in relation to personal injury claims, that jurisdiction had presumably long since been lost to the common law courts, as the Court did not prior to 1861 exercise any such jurisdiction *in rem*.[88] It is not therefore surprising that Sir Robert Phillimore in *The Sylph* 'should ... have hesitated to entertain this suit,[89] having regard solely to the old law of this Court ...',[90] but in concluding that the Admiralty Court did have jurisdiction, chose to base his conclusion instead on the (relatively) new jurisdiction granted by s 7 of the 1861 Act.[91] **4.23**

There ensued a further jurisdictional struggle between the Admiralty Court and the common law courts. The focus of that struggle was not whether a claim for personal injuries gave rise to a maritime lien, but whether it fell within the phrase 'damage done by a ship' in s 7 of the 1861 Act.[92] This does not lend clarity to the **4.24**

---

[85] If it does, then it exists in relation to Canadian and South African law also. The Canadian law, in s 43(3) of the Federal Courts Act draws a distinction between claims 'for damage or for loss of life or personal injury caused by a ship ...' (s 22(2)(d)), which do not require that the owner of the ship 'that is the subject of the action' was the owner when the cause of action arose, and claims 'for loss of life or personal injury occurring in connection with the operation of the ship ...'(s 22(2)(g)), which do require such a nexus. The former type of claim is recognized as a maritime lien in Canadian law and the latter as giving rise only to a statutory action *in rem*: E Gold et al, *Essentials of Canadian Maritime Law* (2003) 293. The existence of a lien for loss of life or personal injury caused by a ship appears to be unaffected by the fact that liability for such claims is now based on statute pursuant to the Marine Liability Act SC 2001, c6; see also *Ordon Estate v Grail* [1998] 3 SCR 437 as to the applicable law in a maritime tort context. In South Africa, loss of life claims are defined as maritime claims in their own right but do not give rise to a maritime lien: J Hare, *Shipping Law & Admiralty Jurisdiction in South Africa* (2nd edn, 2009) §2-1.7.

[86] Price, in *The Law of Maritime Liens* (1940) 42, thought that there was not; D R Thomas, in *Maritime Liens* (1980) para 220, was certain that there was (although, as Jackson points out, the authority which he cites at n 28 in support of that proposition, *The Tolten* [1946] P 135, is a particularly weak one); D C Jackson, in *Enforcement of Maritime Claims* (4th edn, 2005) 2.69–2.72, is in favour of the latter view, though more cautiously so than was Thomas.

[87] D R Thomas, *Maritime Liens* (1980) para 220; D C Jackson, *Enforcement of Maritime Claims* (4th edn, 2005) §§2.73–2.76.

[88] *The Sylph* (1867) LR 2 A&E 24, 27–28. Such jurisdiction as it had continued to exercise appears to have been limited to cases against masters for alleged maltreatment of crew or passengers, as in *The Centurion* (1823) 1 Hag Adm 161, 166 ER 58, *The Agincourt* (1824) 1 Hag Adm 271, 166 ER 96, and *The Ruckers* (1801) 4 C Rob 73, 165 ER 539.

[89] A claim for personal injuries sustained by a diver caught by the paddle-wheel of a steamer.

[90] *The Sylph* (1867) LR 2 A&E 24, 28.

[91] A decision which he followed and the Privy Council upheld in *The Beta* (1869) LR 2 PC 447.

[92] It was widely assumed following the Privy Council decision in *The Bold Buccleugh* that any claim within the Admiralty Court's jurisdiction, statutory or otherwise, attracted a maritime lien.

issue, not least because it was for some time not even certain that the Court had had a non-statutory jurisdiction in respect of *damage*, as distinct from its undoubted jurisdiction over *collision*. In a number of cases, Dr Lushington appears to have been clearly of the view that it did not;[93] but in his very short judgment in *The Sarah*[94] he took an altogether more expansive view of the Court's jurisdiction:

> The Court has original jurisdiction, because the matter complained of is a tort committed on the high seas. It is not necessary to refer to any statute;[95] and it is immaterial whether the vessel doing the damage was a sea-going vessel …

It was this view which found favour with the House of Lords in *The Zeta*,[96] and has held sway ever since,[97] although it does not on its own decide the existence of a maritime lien.[98]

4.25 The position is clouded further because the claim in several of the cases was not for personal injuries, but for wrongful death, a cause of action introduced by statute some time before the 1861 Act.[99] In *The Guldfaxe*,[100] *The Explorer*,[101] and *The Franconia*,[102] it was held that such a claim was within s 7, albeit *The Franconia* evenly divided a four-strong Court of Appeal, as a result of which the judgment at first instance stood. Against those decisions of the Admiralty Court must be set *Smith v Brown*,[103] in which a writ of prohibition was issued against such a claim proceeding in the Admiralty Court. The majority of the Court of Queen's Bench, expressing itself in wide terms, specifically dissented from the decision of the Privy Council in *The Beta*,[104] remarking that:[105]

See, for example, the argument in *The Beta* (1869) LR 2 PC 447, 449: 'Were this Tribunal to hold that such jurisdiction existed, it would create a lien on every Ship into whosesoever hands it might come: *The Bold Buccleugh* …'.

93 *The Ida* (1860) Lush 6, 9, 167 ER 3, 5 'The Court, it must be remembered, has never exercised a general jurisdiction over damage, but over causes of collision only …'. *The Robert Pow* (1863) Br & Lush 99, 101–102, 167 ER 313, 315: '… this damage was occasioned by the negligence of those on board the tug … But on the other hand, there was no collision of any kind between the two vessels … It is admitted that save by virtue of [the Acts of 1840 and 1861] the Court has no … jurisdiction …'. It was held that the Court did not have jurisdiction under either Act: '… damage … means damage done by collision'. Although Dr Lushington had changed his mind by the time he decided *The Uhla* (1867), noted on p 29 of the report of *The Sylph*, that appears to have been as to the meaning of s 7, not as to the pre-existing jurisdiction of the Court.

94 *The Sarah* (1862) Lush 549, 167 ER 248.

95 Nor, apparently to any authority.

96 *Mersey Docks &Harbour Board v Turner (The Zeta)* [1893] AC 468, 481.

97 *The Ripon City* [1897] P 226, 242; *The Tojo Maru* [1972] AC 242, 296.

98 *The Zeta* itself was a claim brought *in personam* against the owner of a dock for damage to a ship. In *The Ripon City*, however, Gorell Barnes J identified (*loc cit*) 'damage' as one of the classes in which the law 'now recognises maritime liens'.

99 Lord Campbell's Act (9 & 10 Vict c 93), also known as the Fatal Accidents Act 1846.

100 *The Guldfaxe* (1868) LR 2 A&E 325.

101 *The Explorer* (1870) LR 3 A&E 289.

102 *The Franconia* (1877) 2 PD 163.

103 *Smith v Brown* (1871) LR 6 QB 729.

104 Above, n 90.

105 *Smith v Brown* (1871) LR 6 QB 729, 731–732.

> Whatever may have been the pretensions of the Court of Admiralty in ancient times to jurisdiction in the matter of personal injuries arising on the high seas ... it is admitted that, as regards personal injuries caused by collision, no such jurisdiction, independently of recent statutes, has existed in modern times ...[106]

The 'decision and reasoning and observations' in *Smith v Brown* were subsequently approved in strong terms by the Court of Common Pleas in *Simpson v Blues*,[107] a decision on a different point which in turn was disapproved in *The Alina*,[108] itself a case viewed with suspicion by Lord Esher MR in *R v Judge of City of London Court*.[109]

When *The Vera Cruz* came before the House of Lords,[110] no mention was made of the question of jurisdiction over personal injuries claims,[111] save in passing by Lord Blackburn, the erstwhile minority[112] in *Smith v Brown*: **4.26**

> ... if the question now raised had been whether personal damage to a man who lived was within that 7th section of the [1861 Act], I should have had, as I then had, some doubt about the matter, and it would have carried me so far that if that had been the question now raised I certainly should have wished to hear the case argued out to the end before giving an opinion upon it one way or the other.[113]

The decision of the House of Lords in *The Vera Cruz* was predicated not on the idea that newly created causes of action could not have been within the pre-1840 jurisdiction of the Admiralty Court,[114] but on the consideration that the particular cause of action was so plainly one for the common law courts that had Parliament intended when it enacted the 1861 Act that the Admiralty Court should have jurisdiction over it, it would have made that explicit. This was not just jurisdictional jealousy; at that time contributory negligence was a complete defence at common law, but not in collision cases in Admiralty—so the venue of the action could materially affect the rights of the parties.[115]

---

[106] An observation borne out by the account given by Sir Robert Phillimore in *The Sylph* (above, n 90).

[107] *Simpson v Blues* (1872) LR 7 CP 290, 300.

[108] *The Alina* (1880) 5 ExD 227.

[109] *R v Judge of City of London Court* [1892] 1 QB 273, 290–291.

[110] *Seward v Owners of the Vera Cruz* (1884) 10 App Cas 59.

[111] However, both Brett MR and Fry LJ had taken the view in the Court of Appeal that personal injury claims did come within the phrase 'damage done by a ship': *The Vera Cruz (No 2)* (1884) 9 PD 96, 99, 101.

[112] Bizarrely, although he did not dissent from the conclusion reached by the majority, neither was he prepared to concur with it.

[113] *Seward v Owners of the Vera Cruz* (1884) 10 App Cas 59, 72. Bruce J reached a similar view *obiter* in *The Theta* [1894] P 280. In *Mersey Docks & Harbour Board v Turner (The Zeta)* [1893] AC 468, 478, Lord Herschell LC commented that:

> It is not necessary to trouble your Lordships with all the cases. It is enough to say that the proposition that the Act of 1861 applies to damage done by a ship to persons and things other than ships has been well established by many authorities, the correctness of which I see no reason to question. He was not referred to *Smith v Brown*.

[114] In that regard, it is clearly not *in pari materia* with the decisions in *The Henrich Björn* (1886) 11 App Cas 270 and *The Sara* (1889) 14 App Cas 209.

[115] *Smith v Brown* (1871) LR 6 QB 729, 733.

4.27 The law as to the meaning to the phrase 'damage done by a ship' was subsequently changed (or clarified) by legislative intervention to include claims arising out of death and personal injury.[116] As set out above, however, there was by then already a substantial weight of authority (albeit much of it *obiter*) for the proposition that personal injury was encompassed within the phrase;[117] there was likewise authority for the proposition that 'damage' was one of the classes of case attracting the operation of a maritime lien;[118] and for a broad non-statutory jurisdiction of the Admiralty Court over torts committed on the high seas.[119] These factors point towards a maritime lien arising in relation to personal injury claims and it may be argued that the statutes[120] put beyond doubt that there should be no differentiation between different forms of damage arising from the same tortious act,[121] in which case the lien should extend to fatal accident claims also.[122] Some support for this approach may be gleaned from Brandon J's judgment in *The Halcyon Skies*,[123] where he held:

> ... that the effect of section 10 of the Admiralty Court Act 1861 was, first, to give the court all the same jurisdiction over wages claims arising out of special contracts as it had previously had over wages claims arising out of ordinary mariners' contracts, including claims in damages for wrongful dismissal; and, secondly, to extend the maritime lien which had been recognized as existing in respect of the latter claims to the former claims.

The same reasoning may be applied to argue that s 7 of the 1861 Act, with s 5 of the 1911 Act, extended the maritime lien which had been recognized in respect of 'damage done by a ship' to cases of personal injury and death;[124] in other words, that this was not 'new' but merely 'extended' jurisdiction. Against this view, however, it remains the case that the High Court of Admiralty did not prior to 1861 exercise an *in rem* jurisdiction in relation to personal injury and death. That factor alone leaves open the argument that no maritime lien can arise in relation to such claims.[125]

---

[116] *The Sylph* (1867) LR 2 A&E 24: s 5 of the Maritime Conventions Act 1911, replaced by s 22(2) of the Supreme Court of Judicature (Consolidation) Act 1925. The provision was not repeated, however, in s 1 of the Administration of Justice Act 1956, which introduced for the first time (in line with the Arrest Convention) a separate head for 'loss of life or personal injury'.

[117] *The Sylph* (1867) LR 2 A&E 24; *The Franconia* (1877) 2 PD 163, 173; *The Beta* (1869) LR 2 PC 447; *The Zeta* [1893] AC 468, 478; *The Theta* [1894] P 280; and *The Vera Cruz (No 2)* (1884) 9 PD 96, 99, with only *Smith v Brown* (1871) LR 6 QB 729 and half of the stalemated Court of Appeal in *The Franconia* firmly against the proposition.

[118] *The Ripon City* [1897] P 226, 242.

[119] *The Zeta* [1893] AC 468.

[120] Above, n 116.

[121] D C Jackson, *Enforcement of Maritime Claims* (4th edn, 2005) §2.72.

[122] Ibid §2.74.

[123] *The Halcyon Skies* [1977] QB 14, 31.

[124] This argument would have to tackle the absence of any successor to s 5 after 1956.

[125] As Jackson recognizes in *Enforcement of Maritime Claims* (4th edn, 2005) §2.71.

Claims for salvage

A claim for salvage gives rise to a maritime lien.[126] Such a claim arises where a person without any particular relation to a ship in distress proffers useful service[127] and gives it as a volunteer or adventurer without any pre-existing covenant connecting him with the duty of employing himself for the preservation of the ship.[128] At common law, there are four necessary elements for a salvage claim: **4.28**

(1) that the subject matter of the claim is property capable of being salved;
(2) that the property was in danger;
(3) that the salvage services were rendered voluntarily;
(4) that the salvage services were successful.

The second and third of these requirements require no comment in this context.[129] As to the first requirement, in addition to a ship, objects of salvage in a maritime context are apparel, hovercraft, cargo, derelict, flotsam, jetsam and lagan, freight at risk, life from ships, and wreck.[130] Apart from life, the objects of salvage also form the assets to which the maritime lien attaches. Aircraft may also be the subject of salvage, although not subject to a maritime lien.[131] As to the fourth requirement, it is a precondition of the right to a salvage reward at common law that there has been success.[132] This is the basis of the 'no-cure-no-pay' principle on which the principles of salvage at common law are founded. The salvage award is paid out of the property salved. Thus if nothing is saved there can be no reward. It is this feature of salvage which exemplifies the lien. The lien can only attach to a ship or property; if none is salved, then there is nothing to which the lien can attach. **4.29**

The simplicity of the picture has been confused somewhat by the advent of the International Convention on Salvage 1989, as enacted in the Merchant Shipping Act 1995 (MSA).[133] The law in respect of the conventional salvage award is effectively preserved, with some enhancements, in art 13 of the Convention. Article 14, however, introduced the possibility for a salvor to recover valuable remuneration even in the absence of what is termed by the Convention 'a useful result'. In essence, art 14 rewards a salvor (i) where his efforts have had a positive result in **4.30**

---

[126] *The Two Friends* (1799) 1 C Rob 271.
[127] *The Unique Mariner (No 2)* [1979] 1 Lloyd's Rep 37.
[128] *The Neptune* (1824) 1 Hag Adm 227, 236 per Lord Stowell.
[129] Save to note in passing that a claim under a contract for the provision of salvage services would have been unknown to the High Court of Admiralty, yet such claims plainly attract a maritime lien where the other criteria exist. For further guidance, the reader is referred to the standard works on salvage: John Reeder QC, *Brice on Maritime Law of Salvage* (5th edn, 2012); F D Rose, *Kennedy & Rose: The Law of Salvage* (8th edn, 2013).
[130] *The Gas Float Whitton (No 2)* [1896] P 42, 63; Hovercraft Act 1968 and Hovercraft (Application of Enactments) Order 1972 (SI No 971), art 8; Part IX Merchant Shipping Act 1995).
[131] Civil Aviation Act 1982, s 87.
[132] *The San Onofre* [1925] AC 246, 262; *The Tojo Maru* [1972] AC 242, 293.
[133] s 224 and sch 11.

environmental terms and (ii) to the extent that an award under art 14 would exceed one made under art 13. Since art 20 provides that 'Nothing in this Convention shall affect the salvor's maritime lien under any international convention or national law', no maritime lien will arise to secure a claim under art 14, although an amendment to s 20(2)(j) of the Senior Courts Act 1981 has extended the availability of the statutory action *in rem* to such claims.[134]

Claims for seamen's wages

4.31 Like the lien for damage done by a ship and the lien for salvage, the principle on which the lien for seamen's wages is premised puts the ship itself at the centre of the enquiry as to whether or not the lien arises in the context of a particular claim. That enquiry is directed at whether the seamen's claim arises from service given to the ship.

4.32 Before 1861, a distinction was drawn between a sailor's ordinary contract with the master, which was presumed to be on the credit of the ship, and a special or unusual contract which was said to be on the personal credit of the owners. Wages payable under the former gave rise to a lien but those payable under the latter did not.[135] In 1861, the distinction was abolished by s 10 of the Admiralty Court Act by providing that the Court had jurisdiction over 'any claim by a seaman of any ship for wages earned by him on board the ship, whether the same be due under a special contract or otherwise, and also over any claim by the master of any ship for wages earned by him on board the ship and for disbursements made by him on account of the ship'. This section was re-enacted by s 22(1)(a)(vii) of the Supreme Court of Judicature (Consolidation) Act 1925 and then replaced by s 1(1)(o) of the Administration of Justice Act 1956, which provided that the Court had jurisdiction in respect of 'any claim by a master or member of the crew of a ship for wages …', thus removing the reference to the wages having been earned 'on board the ship' and substituting the phrase 'member of the crew' for the term 'seaman'. Section 1(1)(o) of the 1956 Act was, in turn, replaced with the current provision in s 20(2)(o) of the Senior Courts Act 1981, which provides the modern statutory basis for the jurisdiction of the Admiralty Court in respect of seamen's wages. That jurisdiction applies both to a claim for wages in debt and in damages.[136] Whilst s 20(2)(o) is concerned only with founding jurisdiction rather than describing the circumstances in which the lien exists, it has been held that

[134] It has become common in practice for parties to Lloyd's Open Form of Salvage Contract to contract out of art 14 and to replace its provisions with a contract known as 'SCOPIC'. A claim for SCOPIC remuneration would similarly attract no maritime lien, although it is probably within s 20(2)(j) as a 'contract for or in relation to salvage services'. See further below, Chapter 5, para 5.52.

[135] *The Sara* (1889) 14 App Cas 209, 215–216.

[136] *The Halcyon Skies* [1977] QB 14, [1976] 1 Lloyd's Rep 461; *United States Trust Company of New York v Master and Crew of the Ship Ionian Mariner* (1997) 77 FCR 563, (1997) 149 ALR 200 (Full Federal Court of Australia).

there is no difference between the maritime lien for wages and the wages referred to in s 20(2)(o) of the Senior Courts Act 1981.[137]

The entitlement of a seaman to a lien over the vessel on which he has served in respect of his unpaid wages can be traced back to 1597.[138] The rationale for the existence of the lien was explained by Lord Stowell in *The Juliana* in these terms: **4.33**

> The common mariner is easy and careless, illiterate and unthinking; he has no resources in his own intelligence and experience in habits of business as can enable him to take accurate measures of postponed payments, with proper estimates of profits and losses …
>
> The owner contracts with a certainty of receiving his freight at all hazards … But the mariner goes to sea upon the single security of the freight. His labours and perils have nothing else to trust to. Freight is the mother, and the only mother of wages; if that goes, everything goes. He has no stepfather, if I may so say, in the character of insurer, to supply the loss.[139]

Whilst such a paternalistic view is anathema to modern contracts of service, the courts nonetheless adopt a liberal approach to the concept of wages based upon a determination to do what is fair and just in order to secure to the seaman what he has earned by service to and on the ship.[140]

Meaning of 'seamen'

'Seamen' are defined to 'include every person (except masters and pilots) employed or engaged in any capacity on board any ship.'[141] In line with the liberal approach taken by the courts in construing the ambit of the lien for wages, those who have been entitled to a lien for wages include: **4.34**

(1) medical practitioners on board a ship;[142]
(2) pursers;[143]
(3) a steward in charge of a bar.[144]

Service not contract

The lien for seamen's wages is created by service to the ship and not by the contract of employment,[145] since the latter gives rise only to a personal liability on behalf of **4.35**

---

[137] *The Halcyon Skies* [1977] QB 14, [1976] 1 Lloyd's Rep 461; *The Ever Success* [1999] 1 Lloyd's Rep 824; *The Pointer Apitong* [1991] 2 HKC 503 (High Court of Hong Kong).

[138] *Johnson v The Black Eagle*: Marsden, Select Pleas in the Admiralty, Vol II, lxxiv.

[139] *The Juliana* (1822) 2 Dods 503, 509–510, 165 ER 1560, 1562–1563.

[140] *The Tacoma City* [1991] 1 Lloyd's Rep 330; *United States Trust Company of New York v Master and Crew of the Ship Ionian Mariner* (1997) 149 ALR 200 (Full Federal Court of Australia); *Patrick Stevedoring No 2 Pty Ltd v Turakina* [1998] FCA 457 (Federal Court of Australia); *The Pointer Apitong* [1991] 2 HKC 503 (High Court of Hong Kong).

[141] MSA, s 313(1).

[142] *The Prince George* (1837) 3 Hag Adm 376, 166 ER 449; statutory recognition is now accorded to medical practitioners on board through s 47 of the MSA.

[143] *The Prince George* (1837) 3 Hag Adm 376, 166 ER 449.

[144] *Thompson v H & W Nelson* [1913] 2 KB 523.

[145] *The Castlegate* [1893] AC 38, 52 and 55; *The Turiddu* [1999] 2 Lloyd's Rep 401.

the ship's owner or manager. This is the feature which underlies the lien for wages and by reference to which it is determined whether or not a particular type of payment or emolument does or does not fall within the ambit of the lien. In *The Arosa Star*, the Court noted that it:

> ... must keep up-to-date and have regard to the changed and changing conditions of seamen's employment. I suppose that ... as a consequence of changed conditions and modern conceptions of welfare, most seamen are engaged on special contracts which provide for notice of termination of service, paid leave, sick leave, bonuses, and so on, which can be and are properly regarded as additions to wages, additions which the mariner can 'be fairly said to have earned by his services'.[146]

4.36 Whilst the wages earned must be in respect of services to the ship, it does not follow that the crew must be on board to render that service. Crew members who are engaged prior to the sailing of a vessel and who perform the ordinary functions of the crew during such a period are entitled to a lien in respect of their wages for that service.[147] A seaman who acts as a member of the crew, even though not authorized to do so, is entitled to a maritime lien for his wages provided that he did not know that he was not entitled to board the vessel or to carry out the work.[148] The bringing of a claim for wages does not terminate the contract of service and disentitle the seaman to maintain a claim for subsequent wages.[149] A claim for wages must be brought by the master or crew to whom the wages are due and cannot be brought by an assignee.[150] An assignee may bring an *in personam* action but has no right to arrest the vessel.[151]

Scope of 'wages'

4.37 Section 313(1) of the MSA provides that 'wages includes emoluments'. 'Emoluments' were those allowances payable directly to a seaman, such as victualling allowances and bonuses.[152] Subsequently, the notion of 'wages' has been extended to include all payments and allowances which have been obtained in the course of a seaman's duty as recompense for the execution of his duty. These have included:

(1) paid leave, sick leave, and bonuses;[153]
(2) repatriation costs;[154]

---

146 *The Arosa Star* [1959] 2 Lloyd's Rep 396, 402.
147 *The Ever Success* [1999] 1 Lloyd's Rep 824.
148 *Wells v Osman* (1704) 2 Ld Ray 1044, 92 ER 193; *The Edwin* (1864) B & L 281, 167 ER 365; *The Ferret* (1883) 8 App Cas 329; *The Ever Success* [1999] 1 Lloyd's Rep 824.
149 *The Fairport (No 2)* [1967] P 167, [1966] 2 Lloyd's Rep 7, overruling *The Carolina* (1875) 3 Asp MLC 141.
150 *The King Coal* [2013] 2 HKLRD 620.
151 *The Fearless I* [2013] 5 HKLRD 48.
152 *The Tergeste* [1903] P 26; *The Elmville (No 2)* [1904] P 422.
153 *The Arosa Star* [1959] 2 Lloyd's Rep 396, 403.
154 *The Westport No 4* [1968] 2 Lloyd's Rep 559; *The Immacolata Concezione* (1884) 9 PD 37; *Karelrybflot AO v Udovenko* [2000] 2 NZLR 24 (New Zealand Court of Appeal): permissible even following frustration of the contract of employment.

(3) union dues;[155]
(4) damages for wrongful dismissal;[156]
(5) damages for breach of contract by the shipowner in failing to pay employee contributions to a pension fund for the benefit of seamen;[157]
(6) contractual contributions to insurance;[158]
(7) an allotted share of a crew member's wages directed by him to be paid through a third party to an address in his home country;[159]
(8) wages earned by a seaman who remains on board under instruction from the owner following the arrest of the vessel.[160]

Wages may also include future wages.[161]

Not wages

By contrast, the following claims have been held not to attract a maritime lien, either on the basis that they do not reflect claims for service already rendered to the ship but rather represent future claims, or alternatively, on the basis that they do not reflect service to the particular ship sought to be made the subject of the *in rem* action: **4.38**

(1) unpaid insurance contributions not referable to any contract under which the seamen were engaged;[162]
(2) severance payments, on the basis that a severance payment is not payable for 'service to a ship', but is 'compensation' for losing employment and is not part of the emoluments of employment; it is not paid for services rendered because the services are no longer required and the essence of a severance payment is a reward for long service payable as compensation for having had the service cut short;[163]
(3) a lump sum pension or future periodical pension payments upon retirement are unlikely to fall within the concept of 'wages' for which a lien would be

155 *The Westport No 4* [1968] 2 Lloyd's Rep 559.

156 *The Blessing* (1878) 3 PD 35; *The Ferret* (1883) 8 App Cas 329; *The Halcyon Skies* [1977] QB 14; [1976] 1 Lloyd's Rep 461; *The Pointer Apitong* [1991] 2 HKC 503 (where an unemployment indemnity was said to be akin to damages for wrongful dismissal).

157 *The Halcyon Skies* [1977] QB 14, [1976] 1 Lloyd's Rep 461.

158 *The Arosa Star* [1959] 2 Lloyd's Rep 396; *The Arosa Kulm* (No 2) [1960] 1 Lloyd's Rep 97; *The Fairport* [1965] 2 Lloyd's Rep 183 (but not those paid compulsorily under statute); *Soon Aik Marine & Engineering Pte Ltd v Hoesheng* [1987] 1 SLR 247 (High Court of Singapore).

159 *The Turiddu* [1999] 2 Lloyd's Rep 401.

160 *Wallace v The Proceeds of the Ship Otago* [1981] 2 NZLR 740 (High Court of New Zealand).

161 *Windrush Intercontinental SA v UACC Bergshav Tankers AS* [2015] ZAKZDHC 30. The unusual circumstances in that case involved a claim for wages by members of a crew held hostage by Somali pirates.

162 *The Acrux* [1965] P 391, [1965] 3 WLR 80, [1965] 2 All ER 323, [1965] 1 Lloyd's Rep 565; *The Fairport* [1965] 2 Lloyd's Rep 183.

163 *The Tacoma City* [1991] 1 Lloyd's Rep 330; *The Pointer Apitong* [1991] 2 HKC 503 (High Court of Hong Kong).

recognized, on the basis that they are not referable to current service by the seaman;[164]

(4) a claim for wages in lieu of notice referable not to a particular ship but to employment with a group of shipping companies which led to service on various ships;[165] and

(5) a claim for damages for wrongful dismissal in circumstances where the crew member's contract of employment required him to serve on a number of ships.[166]

4.39 Although it is clear that the lien exists independently of any contract and is for service done to (or for) the ship, wages are always quantified in accordance with the terms of the contract in fact in existence, rather than pursuant to a quantum meruit.[167]

4.40 By virtue of s 28 of the *Maritime Transport Act* 1994 (New Zealand), members of the crew of a ship are prohibited from contracting out of their right to a maritime lien in respect of wages.[168]

Claims for master's wages and disbursements

4.41 The liens for master's wages and disbursements were first given statutory recognition by s 16 of the Merchant Shipping Act 1844. That section provided that the master had the same lien for his remuneration as a seaman had for his wages. That section was reproduced in s 191 of the Merchant Shipping Act 1854, s 167(1) of the Merchant Shipping Act 1894, and s 18 of the Merchant Shipping Act 1970, and has its modern manifestation in s 41 of the MSA, which provides:

> The master of a ship shall have the same lien for his remuneration, and all disbursements or liabilities properly made or incurred by him on account of the ship, as a seaman has for his wages.

This does not appear to be the position in Canada. Section 48 of the Federal Courts Act does not use the phrase 'maritime lien', but distinguishes between those claims which do and those which do not require 'the ship ... that is the subject of the action [to be] beneficially owned by the person who was the beneficial owner at the time when the cause of action arose'. Claims for master's disbursements fall in the former category.

---

164 *The Tacoma City* [1991] 1 Lloyd's Rep 330.

165 Ibid; but cf the New Zealand approach in *Mobil Oil New Zealand Ltd v The Ship Rangiora (No 2)* [2000] 1 NZLR 82 (High Court of New Zealand) where redundancy compensation was included within the concept of 'wages'.

166 *Canadian Imperial Bank of Commerce v Le Chêne No 1* [2004] 1 FCR 120 (Federal Court of Canada).

167 *The Ever Success* [1999] 1 Lloyd's Rep 824.

168 *The ANL Progress* [2003] 1 Lloyd's Rep 423.

Meaning of 'master'

A 'master' is defined to include 'every person (except a pilot) having command or charge of a ship and, in relation to a fishing vessel, means the skipper'.[169] **4.42**

A master whose contract provides for termination upon arrest of the ship but who remains on board the vessel, is entitled to have added to his wages and to have covered by his maritime lien his wages and subsistence money up to the time when his employment as master is in fact determined.[170] **4.43**

Meaning of 'disbursements'

'Disbursements' are those made by the master for which he makes himself personally liable and which are necessary for the purpose of the navigation in the sense that they are required immediately and cannot be delayed until the owner can meet them.[171] 'Liabilities' encompass payments properly incurred on account of the ship in the ordinary course of the master's employment,[172] the rationale being that the master will necessarily incur liabilities in the course of a voyage which he will be obliged to satisfy without having first had the opportunity to obtain instructions from the owner. **4.44**

The Canada Shipping Act 2001 provides that the master and crew of a Canadian vessel have a maritime lien 'for claims that arise in respect of their employment on the vessel, including in respect of wages and costs of repatriation'.[173] The Act further provides that the master of a Canadian vessel has a maritime lien 'for claims that arise in respect of disbursements made or liabilities incurred by the master for necessaries on account of the vessel'.[174] The master and crew may bring an *in rem* action against the vessel in respect of any such liens and those claims will rank only behind claims pertaining to the costs of the arrest and judicial sale of the vessel and claims for salvage.[175] These provisions, which came into force on 1 July 2007, appear to have clarified the apparent conflict that had existed between the Canada Shipping Act RSC 1985 (now repealed) and the Federal Courts Act s 22(2)(p). In the Federal Courts Act, s 22(2)(p) lists the master's, charterer's, agent's, and shipper's disbursements as claims which can be defeated by a transfer of title, thus suggesting no more than a statutory action *in rem* for these types of claims. By contrast, the Canada Shipping Act RSC 1985 provided that the master **4.45**

169 MSA, s 313(1).

170 *The James W Elwell* [1921] P 351; *The Ever Success* [1999] 1 Lloyd's Rep 824; *Wallace v The Proceeds of the Ship Otago* [1981] 2 NZLR 740 (High Court of New Zealand).

171 *The Orienta* [1895] P 49, 55; *Doris v The Ferdinand* (1998) 155 FTR 236 (Federal Court of Canada): principal and interest repayments by the chief executive officer for the loans of the shipowning company and interest charges on his personal lines of credit used for business and family expenses not disbursements within the ambit of a master's lien for disbursements.

172 *The Ripon City* [1897] P 226, 233.

173 Canada Shipping Act 2001, s 86. This section came into force on 1 July 2007: s 334, note.

174 Ibid.

175 Ibid.

'has the same rights, liens and remedies for the recovery of disbursements or liabilities properly made or incurred by him on account of the ship as a master has for the recovery of his wages'.[176]

Necessaries

4.46 In 2010, Canadian law was amended to grant a limited maritime lien in respect of necessaries and services supplied to a foreign vessel. The purpose of the provision was to level the playing field between Canadian suppliers and their American counterparts.[177] A person carrying on business in Canada has a maritime lien against a foreign vessel, enforceable by an action *in rem*, for claims that arise in respect of goods, materials, or services supplied to the vessel, including stevedoring and lighterage, or that arise out of a contract for the repair or equipping of the vessel.[178] This provision has been found not to extend to those engaged in the construction of a ship.[179] In order to enjoy the benefit of the section, the stevedoring or lighterage services must have been requested by the owner of the vessel or a person acting on the owner's behalf.[180]

Bottomry and respondentia

4.47 Historically, the commercial instruments of bottomry and respondentia[181] enabled a master in the course of a voyage to procure a loan or advance of credit against the security of the ship or cargo. Bottomry bonds were explained by Lord Stowell in *The Atlas* to be:[182]

> ... contracts in the nature of mortgages of a ship on which the owner borrows money to enable him to fit out the ship, or to purchase a cargo for the voyage proposed, and pledges the keel or bottom of the ship, *pars pro toto*, as security for repayment. It is moreover stipulated, that if the ship is lost in the course of the voyage, by any of the perils enumerated in the contract, the lender also shall lose his money; but if the ship shall arrive safe, then he shall be paid back his principal, and also the interest agreed upon ...

4.48 Respondentia bonds were to similar effect but pledged only the cargo rather than the keel of the ship.[183] Both kinds of bond gave rise to a maritime lien and there was

[176] Canada Shipping Act RSC 1985, s 212(2).

[177] *House of Commons Debates* 40th Parliament, 2nd session 18 (25 February 2009) cited in *Norwegian Bunkers AS v Boone Star Owners Inc* [2014] FC 1200 [77]. See also *Comfact Corp v The 'Hull 717'* [2012] FC 1161, [27]–[31]; 355 DLR (4th) 107.

[178] Maritime Liability Act 2001 SC, s 139.

[179] *Comfact Corp v The 'Hull 717'* [2012] FC 1161, (2012) 355 DLR (4th) 107.

[180] Maritime Liability Act 2001 SC, s 139(2.1). See also *World Fuel Services Corp v The Nordems* [2010] FC 332; 366 FTR 188 (Eng); 186 ACWS (3d) 962; *Comfact Corp v The 'Hull 717'* [2012] FC 1161, (2012) 355 DLR (4th) 107.

[181] Examples of each are included as appendices to D R Thomas, *Maritime Liens* (1980).

[182] *The Atlas* (1827) 2 Hag Adm 48, 53, 166 ER 162, 164.

[183] *The Cargo ex Sultan* (1859) Swab 504, 166 ER 1235.

no *in personam* liability of the owner or master. Hence they could only be enforced by an action *in rem*.[184] Bottomry and respondentia bonds are now obsolete and unlikely to be encountered in modern practice.[185]

D. Foreign Maritime Liens

4.49 In English law, a maritime claim is classified as giving rise to a maritime lien which is enforceable by an action *in rem* in the High Court only where the events on which the claim is founded would have given rise to a maritime lien in English law if those events had occurred within the territorial jurisdiction of the English courts.[186] In *The Halcyon Isle*, a majority of the Privy Council on an appeal from the Court of Appeal of Singapore accepted that a maritime lien in English law is procedural or remedial in nature. Accordingly, the question whether a particular class of claim gives rise to a maritime lien or not was to be determined by English law as the *lex fori*.[187] This view has been accepted and followed in Australia,[188] New Zealand,[189] Singapore,[190] and South Africa.[191] The English Admiralty Court has not yet had occasion to consider directly the point that arose for decision by the

[184] *The Ripon City* [1897] P 226, 245.

[185] *The Conet* [1965] 1 WLR 479, [1965] 1 All ER 946, [1965] 1 Lloyd's Rep 195, appears to be the last reference in the authorities to an outstanding bottomry bond.

[186] *The Milford* (1858) Swab 362, 166 ER 1167; *The Tagus* [1903] P 44; *The Colorado* [1923] P 102; *The Acrux* [1965] P 391; *Bankers Trust International Ltd v Todd Shipyards Corp (The Halcyon Isle)* [1981] AC 221.

[187] *Bankers Trust International Ltd v Todd Shipyards Corp (The Halcyon Isle)* [1981] AC 221, cited in *Ocean Connect UK Ltd v Angara Maritime Ltd* [2010] EWCA Civ 1050, [2011] 1 All ER (Comm) 193, [2011] 1 Lloyd's Rep 399, [2010] 2 CLC 448.

[188] *Morelines Maritime Agency Ltd v Skulptor Vuchetich* (1996) 62 FCR 602. For a discussion of the Australian approach and the need to reconsider *The Halcyon Isle* in light of the decision in *John Pfeiffer Pty Ltd v Rogerson* (2000) 203 CLR 503, see Justice Steven Rares, 'Maritime Liens, *renvoi* and conflicts of law: the far from *Halcyon Isle*' [2014] LMCLQ 183. But see now *The Sam Hawk* (para 4.54 below), in which the opposite view was taken by the Australian Federal Court.

[189] *The Ship Bett Ott v General Bills Ltd* [1992] 1 NZLR 655: for a critique of this decision in the New Zealand context see Paul Myburgh, 'Recognition and Priority of Foreign Ship Mortgages' [1992] LMCLQ 155; *ABC Shipbrokers v The Ship Offi Gloria* [1993] 3 NZLR 576; *Fournier v The Ship Margaret Z* [1999] 3 NZLR 111. But note the veiled criticism levelled at *The Bett Ott* by the New Zealand High Court in *The Ship 'Blaze'* [2007] 2 NZLR 271, where Baragwanath J appeared to accept the 'consensus opinion' that 'the Court of Appeal erred in applying simply domestic law criteria and failing to apply the law of the state of registration as the operative (New Zealand) conflict of laws norm': at 280, [46].

[190] *The Ocean Jade* [1991] 1 SLR 583; *The Ohm Mariana Ex Peony* [1992] 2 SLR 623; *The Andres Bonifacio* [1993] 3 SLR 521.

[191] *Transol Bunker BV v MV Adrico Unity* 1989 (4) SA 325; *Brady-Hamilton Stevedore Co v MV Kalantiao* 1989 (4) SA 355: for critiques of these decisions in the South African context see H Staniland, 'Foreign Maritime Liens not to be Recognized in South Africa' [1991] LMCLQ 491 and 'Should Foreign Maritime Liens be Recognized?' [1991] *South African Law Journal* 293; H Booysen, 'The Recognition of Foreign Maritime Liens in South African Law: A Final Word by the Appellate Division' (1991) 40 *International and Comparative Law Quarterly* 151.

Privy Council in *The Halcyon Isle*. In *The Goring*,[192] the Privy Council's decision was cited with apparent approval but the point did not arise.

4.50 The Canadian courts have taken a different approach, however, and treat the maritime lien as a substantive right, as did the minority in *The Halcyon Isle*. On this view, the right is proprietary in character and, therefore, the attachment of a lien to the *res* has the effect of detracting from the full ownership of the vessel;[193] for this reason the lien is governed by the *lex causae* that generated it.[194] The recognition of foreign maritime liens in Canada is based on a public policy in support of maritime liens wherever and however they are generated and is consistent with the broad jurisdiction conferred on the Canadian courts in relation to maritime matters.[195] Although the existence of the lien will be determined by the foreign law which is said to give rise to the lien, the priority that it is accorded in any ranking process remains to be determined by the law of the forum.[196]

4.51 The Canadian approach has much to commend it and there are without doubt weaknesses in the majority approach in *The Halcyon Isle* (which the minority was not slow to point out),[197] its most objectionable feature being the triumph of procedure over substance. The essence of the majority opinion was that since effect could only be given to the proprietary right conferred by the maritime lien if the lienee could proceed *in rem*, and since the right to proceed *in rem* was a matter of jurisdiction, therefore it was for the *lex fori* to decide both whether the particular cause of action attracted a maritime lien and the priority to be accorded to it in a distribution of the fund in court.[198] Thus, forty years after Lord Atkin's famous remark that '[w]hen these ghosts of the past stand in the path of justice clanking their mediæval

---

192 *The Goring* [1987] QB 687.

193 The view of Gorell Barnes J in *The Ripon City* [1897] P 226, 242, quoted with approval by Scott LJ in *The Tolten* [1946] P 135, 145, but doubted (to say the least) by Lord Diplock in *The Halcyon Isle* [1981] AC 221, 233, who pointed out, with some force, that it:

> ... is inaccurate if it is to be regarded as suggesting that the owner of a ship, once it has become the subject of a maritime lien, can no longer create a charge on the whole property in the ship which will rank in priority to the existing lien. This he can do—as for instance by entering into a salvage contract or by signing on a crew.

It is respectfully submitted that whilst the effect of the detraction may be contingent upon subsequent events, nevertheless the general notion of detraction is helpful and correct.

194 *The Strandhill v W Hodder Inc* [1926] SCR 680; *Todd Shipyards Corp v Altema Compania Maritima SA (The Ioannis Daskalelis)* [1974] SCR 1248; *Marlex Petroleum Inc v The Ship Har Rai* [1984] 4 DLR (4th) 739, 744; *Fraser Shipyard & Industrial Centre Ltd v Expedient Maritime Co* (*The Atlantis Two*) (1999) 170 FTR 57; *J P Morgan Chase Bank v The Ship Lanner* [2006] FC 409.

195 Federal Courts Act ss 22 (1) and (2); E Gold, A Chircop, and H Kindred, *Essentials of Canadian Maritime Law* (2003) 269ff; W Tetley QC, 'Enforcement in Canada of Liens for Necessaries Furnished in the United States' [1989] 20 *Journal of Maritime Law and Commerce* 75.

196 This approach is largely consistent with art 6 of the International Convention on Maritime Liens and Mortgages 1993 which entered into force on 5 September 2004 (although none of the jurisdictions considered in this work is a party to it).

197 See, eg, Lord Diplock's foray into the minds of the New York necessaries men at [1981] AC 221, 231E–G, and the rebuttal by Lords Salmon and Scarman at 247B–D.

198 See, eg, at [1981] AC 221, 234F–H and 235C–E.

chains the proper course for the judge is to pass through them undeterred',[199] the parties' substantive rights were resolved by reference to the form of the action. Even if Lord Diplock's analysis was correct as a matter of history, as an exposition of legal principle it is in some respects disappointing.

There is force in the view that the question whether the particular claim attracts the protection of a maritime lien should be resolved in accordance with the *lex causae*. Moreover, contrary to the approach taken in the Privy Council, but consistently with that adopted in Canada, there seems no sound reason why the issue of priority should not be decoupled from the question whether the particular claim does or does not attract a maritime lien; the former question is quintessentially one for the forum, the latter is, or at any rate is far closer to being, a matter of substance. If the question of priorities in the Admiralty Court is ultimately subject to the Court's discretion,[200] then it need not follow from the fact that a particular claim is held to attract a maritime lien under its *lex causae* that it should be accorded the same priority in a distribution as claims recognized by the *lex fori* as doing so. **4.52**

Pending review by the Supreme Court, however, history and policy dictate that the perception of the maritime lien as an amalgam of security right and procedural device will continue to prevail in the English courts. In practical terms, there is much to be said for that approach, if the maritime lien is properly to be understood as a security interest in the vessel. That is because the creation and passing of interests in goods usually depends not on the *lex causae* but on the *lex rei sitae*, and the determination of the *situs* of a ship is itself not straightforward.[201] There is, plainly enough, ample scope for complex conflicts of laws problems to arise,[202] even in the case of a simple bunker supply contract[203] governed by the law of country A with the bunkers actually stemmed in country B (and the vessel arrested in country C), when not all of the countries involved may have any concept of maritime lien or even vessel arrest. Intractable and thus expensive problems of this nature are avoided—and predictability assured—by the *lex fori* approach.[204] **4.53**

The recent Australian decision in *The Sam Hawk*,[205] in which the Judge held that *The Halcyon Isle* does not represent Australian law, exemplifies these issues. The **4.54**

[199] *United Australia Ltd v Barclays Bank* [1941] AC 1, 29.

[200] *The Ruta* [2000] 1 WLR 2068, [2001] 1 All ER 450, [2000] 1 Lloyd's Rep 359; see also Chapter 8 below.

[201] See *Dicey, Morris & Collins*, (15th edn, 2014), paras 22-058–22-059.

[202] See *The Res Cogitans* [2015] EWHC 2022 (Comm) and *The Sam Hawk* (para 4.54 below) for real-world examples.

[203] Which would be far from common in practice. Bunkers are often supplied by a chain of contracts, which may well not all have the same governing law. (See, eg, *PST Energy 7 Shipping LLC v OW Bunker Malta Ltd, 'The Res Cogitans'* [2015] EWHC 2022 (Comm), [4]–[6].) Which contract would determine the *lex causae* for the purpose of establishing whether or not the supply attracted a maritime lien?

[204] See *The Sam Hawk* (para 4.54 below).

[205] *Reiter Petroleum Inc v The Ship 'Sam Hawk'* [2015] FCA 1005.

ship was arrested in Australia for unpaid bunkers. The bunkers had been supplied in Turkey to the Hong Kong-registered vessel pursuant to an order placed by Egyptian time charterers with a Canadian bunker supplier and sub-contracted to a Turkish supplier; the contract between charterers and head supplier was governed by Canadian law but applied Florida law to the creation of a maritime lien. Without holding which, if any, of these various potential connecting factors would determine the existence or otherwise of a maritime lien, the Judge held for jurisdictional purposes that this was a claim 'on a maritime lien', albeit that Australian law does not ascribe a maritime lien to such claims. The decision turned to some extent on the Australian divide between procedure and substance, which is not in all respects the same in English law,[206] as well as the Australian rejection of *The Indian Grace (No 2)*.[207]

4.55 Finally, it should be noted that it is at least arguable that the approach of the majority in *The Halcyon Isle* is no longer good law even in England. That is because of the Rome I and Rome II Regulations.[208] Under art 12(c) of the Rome I Regulation (on the law applicable to contractual obligations), the *lex causae* (as identified by the Regulation) governs 'within the limits of the powers conferred on the court by its procedural law, the consequences of a total or partial breach of obligations, including the assessment of damages ...'. Similarly, by art 15 of the Rome II Regulation (on the law applicable to non-contractual obligations), the *lex causae* (as identified by the Regulation) governs–

(c) the existence, the nature and the assessment of damage or the remedy claimed;
(d) within the limits of powers conferred on the court by its procedural law, the measures which a court may take to prevent or terminate injury or damage or to ensure the provision of compensation ...

The language of both these provisions is wide enough to encompass the existence of a maritime, or, indeed, a statutory, lien. To date, however, the point has not been taken.

[206] *John Pfeiffer Pty Ltd v Rogerson* (2000) 203 CLR 503 and *Regie Nationale des Usines Renault SA v Zhang* (2002) 210 CLR 491, [75]. Compare *Harding v Wealands* [2006] UKHL 32, [2007] 2 AC 1, [2006] 3 WLR 83, [2006] 4 All ER 1.

[207] In *Comandate Marine Corporation v Pan Australia Shipping Pty Ltd* [2008] 1 Lloyd's Rep 119, [2006] 157 FCR 45. See generally Chapter 2, esp at para 2.47. The scope of the decision in *The Indian Grace (No 2)* now appears much reduced in England as well, following the decision of the Court of Appeal in *The Stolt Kestrel* [2015] EWCA Civ 1035, which saw the House of Lords decision as confined to the effect of s 34 CJJA 1982..

[208] Respectively: Regulation (EC) No 593/2008 (on the law applicable to contractual obligations) and Regulation (EC) 864/2007 (on the law applicable to non-contractual obligations). See generally the standard works on conflicts of laws and specialist texts such as McParland, *The Rome I Regulation on the Law Applicable to Contractual Obligations* (OUP, 2015).

5

GENERAL MARITIME CLAIMS

A. The Scope of the General Maritime Claims

Section 20(1)(a) of the Senior Courts Act (SCA) 1981 provides for the Admiralty Court to have jurisdiction to hear and determine any of the 18 'questions and claims' listed in subs (2). That list reflects, with some additions, the list of maritime claims contained in art 1(1) of the Arrest Convention. It is a 'closed' list: in other words, unless it can be established that a particular claim falls squarely within one of the heads listed, the Court will not have admiralty jurisdiction in respect of that claim. **5.01**

As mentioned in the introductory chapter, it has been held that the scope of the provisions of the SCA 1981 must be construed in light of the Arrest Convention.[1] **5.02**

[1] *The Eschersheim* [1976] 1 WLR 430, 436, [1976] 1 All ER 920, 924, [1976] 2 Lloyd's Rep 1, 6 per Lord Diplock.

However, in determining whether or not a particular claim is within the scope of s 20(2), that proposition is not quite as straightforward as it might at first glance appear. As Lord Brandon explained in *The River Rima*,[2] although the provisions of s 20(2) were derived from s 1(1) of the Administration of Justice Act 1956, which was in turn derived from art 1(1) of the Arrest Convention, art 1(1) was itself based on s 22(1)(a) of the Supreme Court of Judicature (Consolidation) Act 1925; the *travaux préparatoires* to the Arrest Convention make clear that the intention was to adopt the English list of claims as the basis for the list of 'maritime claims' in the Convention.[3] Consequently, it may in an extreme case be necessary to examine which claims fall within s 22(1)(a) of the 1925 Act in order to understand their modern manifestation in s 20(2) of the SCA 1981.

5.03 A similar 'closed list' approach is utilized in Australia,[4] Hong Kong,[5] New Zealand,[6] and Singapore.[7] In Australia, however, provision has been made in the Admiralty Act 1988 for the extension of Admiralty jurisdiction through what is termed the 'associated jurisdiction'. By section 12:

> The jurisdiction that a court has under this Act extends to jurisdiction in respect of Admiralty and maritime jurisdiction not otherwise within its jurisdiction that is associated with a matter in which the jurisdiction of the Court under this Act is invoked.

For s 12 to operate there must already be a matter before the court which is within the closed list of the court's jurisdiction; that is because the associated jurisdiction arises where there is 'a matter in which the jurisdiction of the court under this Act is invoked'.[8]

5.04 The position is, however, different in Canada and South Africa, where a much more liberal approach to the conferral of Admiralty jurisdiction is taken. Section 22 of the Federal Courts Act of Canada grants jurisdiction in all cases in which a claim for relief is made or a remedy sought under Canadian maritime law or any other law of Canada relating to any matter coming within the class of subject of navigation and shipping, except to the extent that jurisdiction has been otherwise specifically assigned. A non-exclusive list of maritime claims is provided in s 22(2)(a)–(s).[9]

---

[2] *The River Rima* [1988] 2 Lloyd's Rep 193.

[3] Page 274 of the *travaux préparatoires*, cited in F Berlingieri, *Arrest of Ships* (5th edn, 2011) 3.01.

[4] Admiralty Act 1988, s 4.

[5] High Court Ordinance, s 12A.

[6] Admiralty Act 1973, s 4.

[7] High Court (Admiralty Jurisdiction) Act, s 3.

[8] For more detailed treatment of the associated jurisdiction see D Cremean, 'Admiralty Jurisdiction in Associated Matters' (2000) *Australian Law Journal* 474, Justice James Allsop, 'Federal Jurisdiction & the Jurisdiction of the Federal Court of Australia in 2002' (2002) 23 *Australian Bar Review* 29, and D Cremean, *Admiralty Jurisdiction and Practice—Australia, New Zealand, Singapore, Hong Kong and Malaysia* (4th edn, 2015) 119–122.

[9] A detailed treatment of the Canadian position is contained in W Tetley, *Maritime Liens and Claims* (2nd edn, 1998).

Similarly, s 2(1) of the South African Admiralty Jurisdiction Regulation Act 105 of 1983 confers Admiralty jurisdiction in relation to 'any maritime claim'. A list of maritime claims is contained in s 1(1)(a)–(ff) of the Act and jurisdiction extends to 'any other matter which by virtue of its nature or subject matter is a marine or maritime matter, the meaning of the expression marine or maritime matter not being limited by reason of the matters set forth in the preceding paragraphs'.[10]

Under s 21(4) of the SCA 1981, the Admiralty Court has jurisdiction to entertain an action *in rem* in respect of any claim mentioned in s 20(2)(e)–(r), both against the ship in connection with which the claim arose (which for ease of reference is referred to below as 'the wrongdoing ship'), and against so-called sister-ships. The cornerstone of this jurisdiction is the *in personam* liability of the owner of the ship against which the action is commenced.[11] There is of course an overlap between the claims which give rise to a maritime lien and the provisions of s 21(2)(e), (j), (n), and (p), which permit statutory *in rem* actions in relation to the same, or similar, claims. Thus, a claimant can pursue claims for damage, salvage, wages, or disbursements either against the particular ship in relation to which the claim arose or against a sister-ship. In the latter case, however, the claim will rank in priority only as a statutory action *in rem* and not as a maritime lien—and the right to arrest will not survive a change in ownership prior to the issue of the claim form. **5.05**

B. The Conditions Relating to *In Personam* Liability

Section 21(4) of the SCA 1981 is the successor to s 3(4) of the Administration of Justice Act (UK) 1956. Its function is to specify the required connecting factors between the ship in connection with which the claim arose ('the wrongdoing ship'), the person liable in respect of that claim, and the vessel against which an action *in rem* can be brought. In permitting the arrest of sister-ships, it gives effect to the United Kingdom's ratification of the Arrest Convention, which introduced sister-ship arrest to common law jurisdictions for the first time. **5.06**

In broad terms, s 21(4) requires: **5.07**

(1) the cause of action to have arisen in connection with a ship (the wrongdoing ship);
(2) a particular connection between the person who would be liable on the claim in an action *in personam* (known as the 'relevant person') and the wrongdoing ship; and

[10] Admiralty Jurisdiction Regulation Act 105 of 1983, s 1(1)(ee).

[11] For that reason (and there may be others), it is submitted that logically no action can lie *in rem* for a declaration of non-liability. It is notable that, despite the vogue for such actions in the EU sphere as a means of forum shopping, none appears yet to have been attempted *in rem* (although the question has certainly arisen in practice).

(3) a particular (but different) connection between the relevant person and the ship-to-be-arrested.

These elements are explored in more detail below.

5.08 Hong Kong[12] and Singapore[13] have legislation identical, or virtually identical, to the English provision.

5.09 In Australia, the Admiralty Act 1988 also, but perhaps more clearly, differentiates between, on the one hand, claims which can be commenced only against the wrongdoing ship, ie, those based on a maritime lien[14] and proprietary claims,[15] and, on the other, 'general maritime claims',[16] which can be commenced either against the wrongdoing ship[17] or against a sister-ship (or 'surrogate ship', to use the language of the 1988 Act).[18] There is a real difference between the 1988 Act and the SCA 1981, however, in that, in addition to ships, it is possible to bring a general maritime claim against 'other property', although only where the cause of action concerns that property; there is, in other words, no 'sister-property' arrest.[19] A second point of difference is that the Australian Act eschews the term 'beneficial owner'; the expression 'owner' is used in relation to both the first and second mentioned ships in each of the sections.

5.10 In New Zealand, s 5 of the Admiralty Act 1973 is drawn in terms not dissimilar to s 21(2)–(4) of the SCA 1981, with the exception that sister-ship arrest may be effected not just against ships *owned by* the relevant person, but also against those demise chartered to him.[20] This has the effect of giving New Zealand a particularly wide sister-ship regime.

5.11 The Canadian Federal Courts Act has a formula different from the SCA 1981 for connecting the right to proceed *in rem* to the owner of the ship. This is considered below. As with the Australian regime, *in rem* jurisdiction is not confined to a ship but may extend to aircraft and 'other property'. Nevertheless, it is critical to the foundation of *in rem* jurisdiction that the claim in fact arose in connection with a ship, aircraft, or other property. In *Roberts v The Elva M No II*,[21] a claim *in rem* was

---

[12] High Court Ordinance, s 12B(4).
[13] High Court (Admiralty Jurisdiction) Act, s 4(4).
[14] Admiralty Act 1988, s 15.
[15] Admiralty Act 1988, s 16.
[16] As listed in s 4(3) of the Admiralty Act 1988.
[17] Admiralty Act 1988, ss 17 and 18.
[18] Admiralty Act 1988, s 19.
[19] Admiralty Act 1988, s 17; although the circumstances in which an action might be commenced against 'other property' appear to be restricted to those relating to salvage, general average, to the enforcement of an award relating to such a claim, or for interest on such a claim following the decision of the Full Federal Court of Australia in *Scandinavian Bunkering AS v The Bunkers on Board the Ship FV Taruman* [2006] FCAFC 75, (2006) 151 FCR 126.
[20] Admiralty Act 1973, s 5(2)(b)(ii).
[21] *Roberts v The Elva M No II* [2003] BCD Civ J 15247, 16 BCLR (4d) 189.

brought in relation to a dispute arising out of a joint venture for fishing between the plaintiff and the defendant, who was the owner of the vessel. It was held that the fishing licences were privileges granted to persons not to vessels and so no action *in rem* could be maintained. In addition, the Canadian sister-ship arrest regime is much less liberal than in comparable jurisdictions. Again, this is considered further below.

The South African legislation permits a maritime claim to be enforced by an action *in rem:* **5.12**

(1) if the claimant has a maritime lien over the property to be arrested; or
(2) if the owner of the property to be arrested would be liable to the claimant in an action *in personam* in respect of the cause of action concerned.[22]

Sister-ship or 'Associated Ship' arrest, as it is called, is permitted in relation to all maritime claims except those relating to or arising out of a mortgage, hypotheque, right of retention, pledge, or other charge on a ship, or any bottomry or respondentia bond.[23] The associated ship regime is considered further below.

The 'relevant person'

The 'relevant person' is key to the exercise of the court's jurisdiction over a general maritime claim. If the same person: **5.13**

(1) would be liable on the claim *in personam*;
(2) was, at the time when the cause of action arose, the owner or charterer of, or in possession or control of the wrongdoing ship; and
(3) is, at the time when the action is brought, the beneficial owner or demise charterer of that ship *or* the beneficial owner of any other ship,

then the claimant may found his claim as of right by bringing *in rem* proceedings against the wrongdoing ship or a sister-ship—and the court has no discretion to prevent him from doing so.[24]

In Canada, the link between the relevant person and the requisite ships in relation to general maritime claims[25] is not that that person would have been liable *in personam*, but that: **5.14**

> ... at the time of the commencement of the action, the ship, aircraft or other property that is the subject of the action is beneficially owned by the person who was the beneficial owner at the time when the cause of action arose.[26]

---

22 Admiralty Jurisdiction Regulation Act 105 of 1983, s 3(4).
23 Ibid s 3(6).
24 *The Varna* [1993] 2 Lloyd's Rep 253; *The Yuta Bondarovskaya* [1998] 2 Lloyd's Rep 357.
25 Unlike the position in England and Wales, master's disbursements fall into this category, but the linkage is not required in relation to claims for pilotage, general average contribution, dock charges, harbour dues, and canal tolls.
26 s 43(3) of the Federal Courts Act.

Subject to that, s 43(8) of the Federal Courts Act permits *in rem* jurisdiction to be exercised '... against any ship that, at the time the action is brought, is owned by the beneficial owner of the ship that is the subject of the action'.

The meaning of the phrase 'would be liable ... *in personam*'

5.15 Thus the right to commence an action *in rem* for one of the claims listed in s 20(2)(e)–(r) depends upon (alleged) underlying personal liability on the part of the owner, charterer, or person in possession or control of the ship at the time when the cause of action arose. The words 'would be liable on the claim *in personam*' refer to the person who would be liable if the action were to succeed; it is not necessary to establish, in order to found jurisdiction, that that person is in fact liable on the claim.[27] It has been held in Australia that if judgment has been entered against a defendant in an action *in personam*, then he is the person who would be liable on the claim, not merely hypothetically but as a matter of record, and accordingly he is the 'relevant person' within the meaning of the section.[28] It seems doubtful that that decision would be followed in England and Wales, following the decision of the House of Lords in *The Indian Grace (No 2)*.[29]

The concept of 'ownership'

5.16 In determining the scope of the jurisdiction to arrest a ship under s 21(4), a distinction is drawn between the 'owner' of the ship at the time when the cause of action arose and the 'beneficial owner' of the same ship, or in the case of sister-ship arrest some other ship, at the time when the action is commenced. The significance of this distinction was discussed by Lord Donaldson of Lymington MR in *The Evpo Agnic*,[30] in which he rejected an attempt to 'lift the veil' between two single-ship companies in related management if not ownership, and held that the word 'owner' meant registered owner. This approach has been followed in Hong Kong, where the High Court has held that, barring exceptional circumstances, a vessel's registration is 'virtually conclusive as to her legal and beneficial ownership'.[31]

[27] *The St Elefterio* [1957] P 179, 186, [1957] 1 Lloyd's Rep 283, 287; *The Moschanthy* [1971] 1 Lloyd's Rep 37; *The I Congreso del Partido* [1978] QB 500, [1977] 1 Lloyd's Rep 536; *The Yuta Bondarovskaya* [1998] 2 Lloyd's Rep 357; *Owners of Iran Amanat v KMP Coastal Oil Pte Ltd* (1999) 196 CLR 130 (High Court of Australia); *Reef Shipping Co Ltd v The Ship Fua Kavenga* [1987] 1 NZLR 550 (High Court of New Zealand).

[28] *Ocean Industries Pty Ltd v The Owners of the Ship MV Steven C* [1994] 1 Qd R 69 (Supreme Court of Queensland).

[29] *The Indian Grace (No 2)* [1997] UKHL 40, [1998] AC 878, [1997] 3 WLR 818, [1997] 4 All ER 380, [1998] 1 Lloyd's Rep 1. That is because the relevant person would no longer 'be' liable on an action *in personam*: although he might once have been so liable, that liability has merged with and been replaced by liability to meet the judgment against him. See, generally, Chapter 2 and, specifically, para 2.59 above.

[30] *The Evpo Agnic* [1988] 1 WLR 1090, 1095–1096, [1988] 3 All ER 810, 814–815, [1988] 2 Lloyd's Rep 411, 414–415; followed in *The Tian Sheng No 8* [2000] 2 Lloyd's Rep 430 (Hong Kong Court of Final Appeal).

[31] *The Almojil* [2014] 4 HKLRD 313.

The drawback to the conclusion reached by Lord Donaldson is that, if applied literally, the true owner of a vessel who had not registered his ownership before the cause of action arose might escape the operation of the section (and thus, if he were not otherwise amenable to suit, liability). In this connection it is instructive to consider the remarks of Thean J of the Singapore Court of Appeal in *The Ohm Mariana ex Peony* when considering s 4(4) of the High Court (Admiralty Jurisdiction) Act, which is in similar terms to s 21(4):[32] 5.17

> We are unable to accept the construction that the word 'owner' ... means the 'registered owner'. First, registration of a ship does not determine and is not conclusive as to the true ownership of the ship. It is *prima facie* evidence that the registered owner is the owner of a ship. Secondly, although the word 'owner' ... can be contrasted with the words 'beneficially owned' in paras (a) and (b), there is nothing to suggest that the word 'owner' should be restricted only to 'registered owner'. It can be validly read and construed more widely than 'registered owner'. Thirdly, it is significant to note that the person who would be liable *in personam* and against whose ship an action *in rem* may be brought is not confined merely to the 'owner' of the ship in question but extends to other categories of person, namely, charterer or person in possession or control of the ship. Each of these categories has a substantive, and not merely a formal or nominal, role in relation to the ship in question. In the context of these words, the word 'owner' cannot be construed to mean only the 'registered owner'. If this narrow construction is adopted, the consequence would be that no action *in rem* would lie against an offending ship whose owner having bought it fails or refuses to register it in his name. Take, for instance, the case of a person who has just bought a registered ship and for some reason has delayed registration of the transaction. If in the meantime the ship incurs a liability ... then on this narrow construction, an action *in rem* could never be brought against the ship in respect of that claim on or after the registration of the transaction.

The difficulty contemplated by the Singapore Court of Appeal arose in the Australian case of *The Cape Moreton*[33] in which the issue for the Full Court of the Federal Court was whether, if a party is in fact registered as owner on an international ship register, that of itself is sufficient to satisfy the criterion of 'owner' in ss 17, 18, and 19 of the Admiralty Act 1988, irrespective of the beneficial ownership of the ship. The Court did not follow the approach of Lord Donaldson[34] and held that the correct test is whether the relevant person answers the description 5.18

[32] *The Ohm Mariana ex Peony* [1993] 2 SLR 698, 710. This case was subsequently cited with approval by the High Court of Singapore in *The Catur Samudra* [2010] SGHC 18 [58]–[59]; [2010] 1 Lloyd's Rep 305, 314 [58]–[59], and was also discussed in *The Eternal Strength* [2006] SGHC 12, [31]–[37] in relation to the operation of s 4(4) of the High Court (Admiralty Jurisdiction) Act. For further analysis of s 4(4) see *The Bunga Melati 5* [2011] SGHC 195, the outcome of which the Court of Appeal reversed on appeal while largely agreeing with the High Court Judge's jurisdictional analysis of s 4(4): *The Bunga Melati 5* [2012] SGCA 46 [90] and following.

[33] *Tisand Pty Ltd v The Owners of the Ship MV 'Cape Moreton' (ex Freya) (The Cape Moreton)* [2005] FCAFC 68, (2005) 143 FCR 43.

[34] See further *Malaysia Shipyard and Engineering Sdn Bhd v 'Iron Shortland' as surrogate for the ship 'Newcastle Pride'* (1995) 59 FCR 535; *Kent v SS Maria Luisa (No 2)* (2003) 130 FCR 12; *Safezone Pty Ltd v The Ship 'Island Sun'* [2004] FCA 1797, (2004) 215 ALR 690.

of 'the owner' in a proprietary sense in all the circumstances, and thus it will not necessarily be sufficient to found jurisdiction to proceed *in rem* under the Act to establish that the relevant person is entered on any international register of ships.[35] On the rare occasion where an action *in rem* is commenced in the interim period during which English law recognizes that the property in the ship is vested in a different person from the registered owner, it is submitted that the reasoning in *The Cape Moreton*[36] should be preferred to that in *The Evpo Agnic*,[37] not least because the point did not arise on the facts of the case before the Court of Appeal.

5.19 In Canada, the wording 'owner of the ship' in s 43(8) of the Federal Courts Act, which permits sister-ship arrest, has also been construed as meaning the registered owner, although the court reached this conclusion on the basis of the Canadian legislation and without reference to *The Evpo Agnic*.[38] In *Looiersgracht (Ssangyong Australia) Pty Ltd v The Ship Looiersgracht*,[39] it was held that ownership of a part interest in two ships was not by itself sufficient to constitute the ships as sister-ships. The total interest in both ships must be the same. Similarly, in Australia it has been held that co-ownership by the relevant person or persons is not sufficient to engage the right in s 19 of the Admiralty Act 1988 to proceed against a surrogate ship.[40]

5.20 Indeed, an owner of a ship under s 19(b) is a person who enjoys a right of dominion and ultimate title over the ship: mere influence or control over it, even the substantial or high degree of control a parent company may have over a ship owned by its one-ship subsidiary, is insufficient.[41]

5.21 Particular difficulties may arise in relation to ships still under construction, where ordinarily title does not pass under the shipbuilding contract and the ship is not registered until delivery. Arguably, the disgruntled purchaser of vessel A could bring *in rem* proceedings against vessel B, under construction at the same shipyard, even though the latter vessel was being built for a different purchaser. One objection to this (depending on the terms on which vessel A was built) might be that, at the time the cause of action arose, the purchaser and not the shipyard owned the ship, because no relevant term was breached until delivery.

Another objection, upheld in Australia by reference to the test of ownership laid down in *The Cape Moreton*, might be that the 'owner' of the ship will be the

[35] *The Cape Moreton* [2005] FCAFC 68, (2005) 143 FCR 43, 65 [92]; a similar approach has been adopted in Singapore: *The Temaesk Eagle* [1999] 4 SLR 250 and in Hong Kong: *Re Resource I* [2000] 3 HKLRD 49; *The Blue Bridge* [2003] 1 HKC 325.

[36] *The Cape Moreton* [2005] FCAFC 68; (2005) 143 FCR 43.

[37] *The Evpo Agnic* [1988] 1 WLR 1090, [1988] 3 All ER 810, [1988] 2 Lloyd's Rep 411.

[38] *The Ryan Leet* (1997) 135 FTR 67.

[39] *Looiersgracht (Ssangyong Australia) Pty Ltd v The Ship Looiersgracht* (1994) 85 FTR 265.

[40] *The Ship 'Gem of Safaga' v Euroceanica (UK) Ltd* [2010] FCAFC 14, (2010) 182 FCR 27.

[41] *Shagang Shipping Co Ltd v Ship 'Bulk Peace' as Surrogate for Ship 'Dong-a Astrea'* [2014] FCAFC 48, (2014) 314 ALR 230. This is in line with the earlier English decision in *The Maritime Trader* [1981] 2 Lloyd's Rep 153.

purchaser rather than the shipbuilder where the purchaser would, at the time the writ is issued, be entitled to specific performance of the shipbuilder's obligation to deliver the vessel.[42] Both arguments will be strongly fact-sensitive.[43] Moreover, any 'ownership' constituted by the availability of specific performance would be beneficial and not legal. In English terms, therefore, that would suffice at most for the purposes of the connection to be established at the time the action is commenced and not the 'ownership' required when the cause of action arose.

The meaning of 'charterer'

The right to commence an action *in rem* in respect of a general maritime claim is not limited to cases where the relevant person in relation to the 'wrongdoing ship' was its owner at the time that the cause of action arose, but extends to cases where the relevant liability is that of the charterer.[44] The term 'charterer' is not construed narrowly, but includes a time charterer,[45] a voyage charterer,[46] and a slot charterer.[47] It has been held that the combination of the words 'owner or charterer of, or in possession or control of the ship' highlights the fact that it is necessary to look at the status of the relevant person at the time when the cause of action arose. Thus, whilst the liability may arise out of a charter, and therefore may concern the defendant's character as charterer of the vessel, nevertheless it must be shown that he was in fact the charterer at the time when the cause of action arose. If the charter has terminated when the cause of action arises, that party can no longer be said to be the charterer.[48] Further, it is not open for a court to find that a party other than the charterer was 'in control of' the ship at the relevant time, even if that other party had some 'say in the operation of the vessel', unless the charter **5.22**

[42] *Virtu Fast Ferries Ltd v The Ship 'Cape Leveque'* [2015] FCA 324, affirmed on appeal, on different, essentially 'no breach', grounds: [2015] FCAFC 58. The factors supporting the conclusion at first instance were these: when the writ was issued the construction of the vessel was 96% complete; and there was a clause in the contract for vessel B prohibiting the builder from registering the vessel (a patrol boat) in its own name at any time: [31]. For further discussion, see Emma Park, 'When is a ship not a ship? *The Cape Leveque* and the limits of surrogate ship arrest' (2015) 6 *Shipping & Trade Law* 1.

[43] Compare, eg, the court's refusal, in *FC Yachts v Splash Holdings* (2007) 289 DLR (4th) 167 (Federal Court of Canada), to allow a shipyard to arrest the ship that it was building before title had passed. See para 5.26 below.

[44] This is not so in Canada: see above, para 5.19.

[45] *The Span Terza* [1982] 1 Lloyd's Rep 225; *The Permina 108* [1975–1977] 1 SLR 221, [1978] 1 Lloyd's Rep 311 (Court of Appeal of Singapore); *The Sextum* [1982] 2 Lloyd's Rep 532; *The Djatianom* [1982] HKLR 427 (High Court of Hong Kong); *The Fua Kavenga* [1987] 1 NZLR 550 (High Court of New Zealand).

[46] *The Tychy* [1999] 2 Lloyd's Rep 11; *Laemthong International Lines Co Ltd v BPS Shipping Ltd* (1997) 190 CLR 181 (High Court of Australia).

[47] A party who has the right to use a specified part of the cargo carrying capacity of a vessel on a particular voyage: *The Tychy* [1999] 2 Lloyd's Rep 11; *The Halla Liberty* [2000] 1 HKC 659 (High Court of Hong Kong). See also the commentary on *The Tychy*; B Davenport, 'Slot Charters', (2000) 116 LQR 36.

[48] *Aluflet SA v Vinave Empresa de Navegacao Maritima LDA (The Faial)* [2000] 1 Lloyd's Rep 473.

is a sham or the corporate veil is lifted so that some other party is held to be the contracting charterer.[49]

The meaning of 'demise charterer'

5.23 The essential characteristic of a demise charter is that it constitutes a contract of hire of the ship, under which possession of the ship passes to the charterer, the master of the ship being the servant of the charterer not of the owner.[50] Ordinarily, a demise charter contemplates an agreement between an owner and a demise charterer, but the expression is not restricted to relationships created by private agreement and will include a person who has possession of the vessel with the consent of the owner and who both manages and employs the crew on his own account.[51]

The meaning of 'beneficial owner'

5.24 The words 'beneficial owner' in s 21 refer to title rather than possession of the ship.[52] In *I Congreso del Partido*, Robert Goff J held that the words 'beneficially owned' in the then applicable section of the Administration of Justice Act 1956 referred only to cases of equitable ownership, whether or not accompanied by legal ownership, and were not wide enough to include cases of possession or control without ownership, however full and complete such possession and control might be.[53] As Colman J observed in *The Kommunar (No 2)*,[54] it is fundamental to the requirements of s 21(4) that the beneficial owner (or demise charterer) of the vessel to be proceeded against *in rem* should also (i) be the person who would be liable *in personam* and (ii) have been the owner or charterer of or in possession or control of the vessel in connection with which the claim is brought at the time when the cause of action arose. If the beneficial owner of the vessel proceeded against *in rem* is not the same person as the relevant person having the required connection with the vessel which is the subject matter of the claim, the proceedings *in rem* cannot be pursued.

49 *The Decurion* [2013] 2 HKLRD 930.

50 *The I Congreso del Partido* [1978] QB 500, 539, [1978] 1 All ER 1169, 1201, [1977] 1 Lloyd's Rep 536, 561.

51 *The Guiseppe di Vittorio* [1998] 1 Lloyd's Rep 136; *Patrick Stevedores (No 2) Pty Ltd v MV Turakina* (1998) 154 ALR 666 (Federal Court of Australia); *CMC (Australia) Pty Ltd v Ship Socofl Stream* (1999) 95 FCR 403 (Federal Court of Australia).

52 *The St Merriel* [1963] P 247, [1963] 1 All ER 537; *The I Congreso del Partido* [1978] QB 500, [1978] 1 All ER 1169, [1977] 1 Lloyd's Rep 536; *Colombo Drydocks Ltd v The Ship Om Al-Quora* [1990] 1 NZLR 608 (High Court of New Zealand); *The Permina 3001* [1979] 1 Lloyd's Rep 327 (Singapore Court of Appeal).

53 *I Congreso del Partido* [1978] QB 500, 542, [1978] 1 All ER 1169, 1203–1204, [1977] 1 Lloyd's Rep 536, 563.

54 *Centro Latino Americano de Commercio Exterior SA v The Owners of the Ship Kommunar (No 2)* [1997] 1 Lloyd's Rep 8; *Sovrybflot v the Ship Efim Gorbenko* [1996] 2 NZLR 727 (High Court of New Zealand).

The concept of 'beneficial ownership' will also arise for consideration in circumstances where the owner of the ship is the subject of winding-up proceedings.[55] The question to be determined is whether it can be said that, upon the commencement of the winding-up, beneficial ownership in the ship is transferred to the liquidators such that there can no longer be said to be parity of ownership at the time when the cause of action arose and at the time when the proceedings *in rem* are commenced. There is English authority[56] which suggests that beneficial ownership in a company's assets is transferred to the liquidator. If that is the correct reading of that authority, then it is submitted that it requires reconsideration, at any rate in the admiralty context, and that the preferable view is that expressed by the High Court of Australia[57] and followed at first instance by the High Court of Hong Kong.[58] However, it is submitted that the better reading of both the English and the Australian decisions is that of the Hong Kong Court of Appeal,[59] ie, that they are to be understood in their particular context (revenue law) and shed no light on the position in admiralty procedure. **5.25**

In the Canadian case of *FC Yachts v Splash Holdings*,[60] the plaintiff shipbuilder, who was building two yachts for the defendant, arrested one of them in order to secure a claim against the defendant buyer and mortgagee for failure to keep up payments on the other. As the yacht construction agreement specifically provided that the builder held title during construction and that title passed on delivery, the defendant mortgagee was not the beneficial owner within the meaning of s 43(3) of the Federal Courts Act and the warrant of arrest was set aside. **5.26**

The lifting of the corporate veil

One consequence of the sister-ship provisions introduced by the Arrest Convention was the practice, which continues today, of shipowners registering 'one ship' companies to circumvent its effect.[61] Each ship in a fleet is typically registered in the name of a separate company so that the requirement that the sister-ship be owned at the time of commencement of the action by the party who, at the time of the cause of action arose, owned the wrongdoing ship, can never be satisfied. There is nothing wrong with such an arrangement in principle.[62] **5.27**

55 See Chapter 8.

56 *Ayerst v C & K (Construction) Ltd* [1976] AC 167, [1975] 2 All ER 537.

57 *Commissioner of Taxation v Linter Textiles Australia Ltd (in Liquidation)* [2005] HCA 20, (2005) 220 CLR 592.

58 *International Transportation Service Inc v The Convenience Container* [2006] 902 HKCU 1; [2006] 2 Lloyd's Rep 556 (Hong Kong Court of First Instance). See further at paras 8.68 and following below.

59 *International Transportation Service Inc v The Convenience Container* [2007] HKCA 306, [2007] 3 HKLRD 575, [2007] 4 HKC 484, [55]–[83], [117]–[119], [168].

60 *FC Yachts v Splash Holdings* (2007) 289 DLR (4th) 167 (Federal Court of Canada).

61 South African Law Commission, Report on the Review of the Law of Admiralty, 1982, para 7.3.

62 *The Evpo Agnic* [1988] 1 WLR 1090, 1097, [1988] 3 All ER 810, 815, [1988] 2 Lloyd's Rep 411, 415.

5.28 In England, the question of lifting the corporate veil has arisen in two situations. The first arose because the statutory right to proceed *in rem* does not survive a change in ownership.[63] In *The Aventicum*,[64] it was argued that the court should disregard a change in ownership where the new owner was a company forming part of the same group as the previous owner; the argument failed on the facts.[65] The second situation concerned the arrest of a ship owned by a subsidiary of the company which was the relevant person. In *The Maritime Trader*,[66] the ship was owned by a company, MTS, a wholly owned subsidiary of MTO. Sheen J held that the ship was not beneficially owned by MTO and, therefore, could not be arrested to secure a claim against MTO:

> ... the starting point is the fundamental principle of company law that a shareholder has no property legal or equitable in the assets of the company ... From that starting point there is no way in which it can be said that the Maritime Trader was 'beneficially owned as respects all the shares therein' by MTO unless the corporate veil can be lifted. I would not hesitate to lift that veil if the evidence suggested that it obscured from view a mask of fraud rather than the true face of the corporation.[67]

5.29 A quite different approach to the challenges created by the one ship company was taken by South Africa. In enacting s 3(7)(a) of the Admiralty Jurisdiction Regulation Act 105 of 1983, South Africa chose to confront the consequences of one ship companies by adopting the concept of an 'associated ship' where the link between the ships can be established by common control rather than merely by common ownership. The effect of this provision is that the corporate veil of company ownership of ships is disregarded as a matter of course. Whereas at common law, a court will not pierce the corporate veil unless it is proved that the corporate structure is a mere façade involving an element of fraud or improper conduct, or that there is failure to maintain the separate identity of the company from that of its shareholders, in the case of the statutory veil piercing provisions

---

[63] s 21(4).

[64] *The Aventicum* [1978] 1 Lloyd's Rep 184; see also *The Rung Ra Do* [1994] 3 HKC 621 (High Court of Hong Kong).

[65] See also *The Helene Roth* [1980] 2 WLR 549; *The Enfield* [1982] 2 MLJ 106; *The Saudi Prince* [1982] 2 Lloyd's Rep 255, a successful challenge to a purported change of ownership. For another, see *The Tjaskemolen* [1997] 2 Lloyd's Rep 465; although the case relied upon by Clarke J, *Creasey v Breechwood Motors Ltd* [1992] BCC 638, was itself disapproved of by the Court of Appeal in *Ord v Belhaven Pubs Ltd* [1998] BCC 607, the principle that a sham transaction performed to hide assets from creditors may be ignored by the courts has not been: see the discussion of this line of cases in *Linsen International Ltd v Humpuss Sea Transport Pte Ltd* [2011] EWHC 2339 (Comm); [2012] Bus LR 1649; [2011] 2 Lloyd's Rep 663.

[66] *The Maritime Trader* [1981] 2 Lloyd's Rep 153.

[67] Ibid 157; followed by the Supreme Court of Hong Kong in *The Neptune* [1986] HKLR 345 and *The Kum Susan Ho* [1982] 1 HKC 289, and by the High Court of Singapore in *The Catur Samudra* [2010] SGHC 18; [2010] 1 Lloyd's Rep 305. See also, to substantially similar effect, *The Evpo Agnic* [1988] 1 WLR 1090, [1988] 3 All ER 810, [1988] 2 Lloyd's Rep 411.

of the Admiralty Jurisdiction Regulation Act, these matters are simply presumed once common control is established.[68]

The South African cases, therefore, are not concerned with 'beneficial ownership', but with 'control' as it is used in s 3(7) of the Admiralty Jurisdiction Regulation Act. In *EE Sharp & Sons v MV Nefeli*,[69] when considering the original text of the legislation prior to its amendment in 1992, King AJ said: **5.30**

> In my view this relates to overall control, such as is exercisable for instance by a majority shareholder or his nominee, of the assets and destiny of the company; it does not refer to its day-to-day management and administration. There must be managing agents in all the major ports of the world who in a sense control innumerable merchant ships owned by different interests and quite independent of each other. It could never have been the intention of the Legislature that such vessels could be arrested as 'associated ships'.[70]

It was held, however, that where all the companies concerned had the same 'president/director' and the same 'director/secretary', and the former had the power to 'sign and act on behalf of the corporation and with his signature to bind the corporation', the power to control the companies was vested in the same person.

Subsequent to the amendments, the focus of the South African courts has been on identifying who is controlling the company in contrast to controlling or owning the shares in the company, as was the position under the original definition.[71] Of course, evidence of common ownership of shares will still be relevant because it may indicate common control between the companies. It is insufficient merely to show that there is a common directorship of shipowning companies in order to establish grounds for associated ship arrest.[72] Similarly, where the formal owner of the shares in a shipowning company is a trustee, it will be necessary to demonstrate that actual ownership of the shares lay with the trustees.[73] **5.31**

In *MV Heavy Metal: Belfry Marien Ltd v Palm Base Maritime SDN BDN*,[74] the majority upheld the arrest of an 'associated' ship which was owned by a company whose majority registered shareholder and sole director was a Mr Lemonaris. At the relevant time, he had also been the registered majority shareholder and **5.32**

---

[68] G Bradfield, 'Guilt by Association in South African Maritime Law' [2005] LMCLQ 234, 240; and for a detailed treatment see G Hofmeyr, *Admiralty Jurisdiction—Law & Practice in South Africa* (2nd edn, 2012) IX and J Hare, *Shipping Law & Admiralty Jurisdiction in South Africa* (2nd edn, 2009) §2–2.6.

[69] *EE Sharp & Sons v MV Nefeli* 1984 (3) SA 325.

[70] Ibid 326–327.

[71] *National Iranian Tanker Co v MV Pericles GC* 1995(1) SA 475 (A) 485B; cf *Transgroup Shipping SA (Pty) Ltd v Owners of MV Kyoju Maru* 1984 (4) SA 210 (D&CLD).

[72] *Owners of the Sandokan v Liverpool and London Steamship Protection and Indemnity Association Ltd* 2001 (3) SA 824.

[73] *Shipper D'Singapore Pte Ltd v Amer Whitney* 28 September 2000, M Stranex, *Shipping Cases of South Africa* (3rd edn, 2000) C86.

[74] *MV Heavy Metal: Belfry Marien Ltd v Palm Base Maritime SDN BDN* 1999 (3) SA 1083.

sole director of the company which owned the wrongdoing ship. Mr Lemonaris asserted that he was merely the nominee shareholder for different 'beneficial' or actual holders of the shares in each of the shipowning companies, but refused to disclose the identity of the person on whose behalf he held the shares. In construing the phrase 'the power, directly or indirectly, to control' in s 3(7)(b)(ii), the majority of the Supreme Court of Appeal held that the section identifies two sources of possible control, direct and indirect. It equated 'direct control' with *de jure* control of the company, namely the control exercised by the registered majority shareholder as the person who, according to the register of the company, controls its destiny. 'Indirect control' meant *de facto* control of the company, namely the power to control a company that would be wielded through someone who had direct control of the company, as would be the case with the beneficial or actual owner holding shares in a company through a nominee. If the same person exercised *de jure* power to control both the company owning the wrongdoing ship and the company owning the arrested ship, the statutory nexus between the two ships would be established. If *de jure* control resided in different hands, it would be open to the arresting party to establish that the same person, or entity, was in *de facto* control. That would also establish the statutory nexus between the ships. On this interpretation of the section, the Court held that the facts established that Mr Lemonaris was the party in direct control of both companies at the relevant time. Mr Lemonaris' refusal to identify those who he asserted to be in indirect control of the company did not matter because the use of the word 'or' in the phrase 'directly or indirectly, to control' meant that the arresting party could rely on either form of control.[75]

5.33 *MV Heavy Metal* was followed in *Sino West Shipping Co Ltd v NYK-Hinode Line Ltd.*[76] In the latter case, Mr Wang was the sole registered shareholder in Smoothie Goodie Limited, which in turn held 100% of the shareholding in Sino West Shipping Company Limited, the owner of the arrested ship. It followed that Mr Wang had the power 'directly to control both companies by voting the majority of the shares in their shareholders meetings'. Whether or not he chose to exercise this power was immaterial.[77]

By contrast, in *Louis Dreyfus Armateurs SNC v Tor Shipping Limited*,[78] the Court held that the applicant, which owned 50% of the shareholding of another company, could not be said to be in control of the shareholding of the company.[79]

[75] See criticism of this interpretation of the section in G Bradfield, 'Guilt by Association in South African Maritime Law' [2005] LMCLQ 234, 246–248.

[76] [2013] ZAKZDHC 7 (8 March 2013).

[77] Ibid [77]–[78].

[78] *Louis Dreyfus Armateurs SNC v Tor Shipping Limited* 2006 (3) SA 441 (D).

[79] The Court also remarked *obiter* that where two companies each hold 50% of the shareholding, it is likely that neither of them has control of the company either directly or indirectly: Ibid 454–455 [55].

In Canada, the position is not dissimilar to that in South Africa. In *Norcan Electrical Systems Inc v Feeding Systems A/S*,[80] it was held that: 5.34

> … in addition to extending the rights of claimants to claim against ships under common beneficial ownership another purpose of the legislation is to allow those having claims against the wrongdoing ship to attach the assets of the *de facto* economic power behind that ship.

Thus a claim which arose in relation to vessels owned by a Chilean subsidiary could be brought against those owned by the Canadian parent company.[81]

C. The Individual General Maritime Claims

There are three features which are central to the jurisdiction to bring an action *in rem* for any of the claims listed in s 20(2)(e)–(r). The first is the link between the claim and the ship in relation to which cause of action arose; in all cases, if that link does not exist, then nor does jurisdiction. The second is the establishment of personal liability in respect of the claim. The third is that the claim itself must fall within one of the categories listed. 5.35

Damage done by a ship

This head of claim corresponds to art 1(1)(a) of the Arrest Convention.[82] It is equivalent to that giving rise to the maritime lien for damage except to the extent that the maritime lien does not extend to certain statutory and judicial developments to the head of damage. As already discussed in relation to the maritime lien for damage,[83] the damage must be the direct result of something done in the course of navigation of the ship and the ship (or part of it)[84] must be the actual instrument by which the damage was done.[85] There does not, however, need to be physical contact between the ship and the damaged thing or person.[86] There is equivalent 5.36

80 *Norcan Electrical Systems Inc v Feeding Systems A/S* (2003) 235 FTR 237 [23].

81 In this respect, a different conclusion was reached to that in *Hollandsche Aannaming Maatschappij v Ryan Leet (The)* (1997) 135 FTR 67, in which it was held that the meaning of 'owner' in s 48(3) FCA was registered owner.

82 s 20(2)(e). 'Any claim for damage done by a ship.'

83 Above, Chapter 4, paras 4.18 and following.

84 *The Minerva* [1933] P 224, (1933) 46 Ll L Rep 212.

85 *The Asian Atlas* [2008] 3 HKLRD 461.

86 *The Dagmara and Ama Antxine* [1988] 1 Lloyd's Rep 431; *The Jade* [1976] 2 Lloyd's Rep 1, 8; *The Miraflores and The Abadesa* [1967] 1 AC 826; *The Industrie* [1871] LR 3 A & E 303, 40 Law J Rep (NS) Adm 26. More questionable is *The Chr Knudsen* [1932] P 153, (1932) 43 Ll L Rep 423 (barge held to 'damage' dock in which sunk), doubted in *The Millie* [1940] P 1, 10–11, (1939) 64 Ll L Rep 318, 322.

jurisdiction in Australia,[87] Canada,[88] Hong Kong,[89] New Zealand,[90] Singapore,[91] and South Africa.[92]

5.37 In addition to the more traditional claims for damage done by ships, there are various statutory provisions giving effect to international conventions directed at claims for environmental damage, or for the costs of avoiding such damage, which create novel causes of action relating to damage caused by ships. As these causes of action are new, they almost certainly do not give rise to maritime liens but only to statutory actions *in rem*.[93]

Loss of life or personal injury

5.38 This paragraph,[94] although much lengthier and more prescriptive, corresponds with art 1(1)(b) of the Arrest Convention. It is conceivable that there might be claims within the broader wording of the Convention which did not meet the formula of s 20(2)(f), but this is unlikely in practice. The wording avoids the difficulty which obtains in relation to para (e), in that the ship does not have to be the instrument of the mischief which causes the death[95] or personal injury. The provision, therefore, covers claims for injuries sustained on board. However, assuming that a maritime lien is available for personal injury claims,[96] no lien will attach unless the damage has in fact been done by the ship. This paragraph does not, in other words, extend the ambit of the maritime lien for damage done by a ship. There is

---

[87] Admiralty Act 1988, s 4(3)(a).

[88] Federal Courts Act, s 22(2)(d). This provision is more widely drawn, however, and extends to 'loss of life or personal injury caused by a ship either in collision or otherwise'.

[89] High Court Ordinance s 12A(2)(e).

[90] Admiralty Act 1973, s 4(1)(d).

[91] High Court (Admiralty Jurisdiction) Act, s 3(1)(d).

[92] Admiralty Jurisdiction Regulation Act 105 of 1983 ss 1(1)(e) and (z).

[93] Note in this connection that s 20(5) of the Senior Courts Act 1981 expressly extends sub-s 20(2)(e) to claims under Chapters III and IV of Part VI of the MSA. These chapters of the Act enact the International Convention on Civil Liability for Oil Pollution Damage 1992 and the International Oil Pollution Compensation Fund 1984. Together, these Conventions provide a uniform set of international rules and procedures for determining and limiting liability and provide compensation to those who have suffered damage caused by the escape or discharge of oil from ships. For further reading on the topic of liability for pollution from ships, see E Gold, *Gard Handbook on Protection of the Marine Environment* (3rd edn, 2006).

[94] s 20(2)(f)—

> Any claim for loss of life or personal injury sustained in consequence of any defect in a ship, her apparel or equipment, or in consequence of the wrongful act, neglect or default of
> (i) the owners, charterers or persons in possession or control of a ship; or
> (ii) the master or crew of a ship, or any other person for whose wrongful acts, neglects or defaults the owners, charterers or persons in possession or control of a ship are responsible, being an act, neglect or default in the navigation or management of a ship, in the loading, carriage or discharge of goods on, in or from a ship, or in the embarkation of persons on, in or from the ship.

[95] In English law, an action for loss of life lies only within the terms of the Fatal Accidents Act 1976 or the Law Reform (Miscellaneous Provisions) Act 1934.

[96] See the discussion in Chapter 4 at paras 4.23 and following.

an equivalent head of jurisdiction in Australia,[97] Canada,[98] Hong Kong,[99] New Zealand,[100] Singapore,[101] and South Africa.[102]

5.39 It may be noted in passing that a ship is defined as 'equipment' for the purpose of defects in it being deemed to be attributable to the 'negligence' of the shipowner by virtue of the Employers' Liability (Defective Equipment) Act 1969. Thus, at any rate where English law applies,[103] a shipowner will be liable in negligence to a seaman who suffers injury or loss of life due to the unseaworthiness of the vessel.[104]

5.40 The Singaporean provision[105] has been construed broadly to include claims for statutory or contractual compensation payable irrespective of fault.[106] The Court of Appeal construed the phrase 'any claim for loss of life or personal injury' to mean 'any claim arising out of loss of life or personal injury', and observed that such a construction was consistent with the broad and liberal construction which had been given to the provisions of the SCA 1981 in conferring Admiralty jurisdiction.[107] Consequently, it was held, the claim for a contractual annuity payable from the date of the accident for the rest of the plaintiff's life was a claim properly brought within s 3(1)(f). It is submitted that even the broadest construction of the provision would require the particular claim to be brought within the wording 'sustained in consequence of any defect in a ship or in her apparel or equipment', as the paragraph otherwise requires 'wrongful act, neglect or default'. As to the claim for an annuity, whilst such a claim is not naturally within the wording 'for personal injury', it would be odd if an injured party's claim were restricted to those heads of damage which fell within that wording, leaving him to pursue the balance of his claims elsewhere.

Loss of or damage to goods carried in a ship

5.41 Paragraph (g)[108] permits cargo owners to arrest the ship in which the lost or damaged goods were carried in an action *in rem* against the owners of the carrying vessel.[109] The reference to 'baggage' in art 1(1)(f) of the Arrest Convention is

97 Admiralty Act 1988, s 4(3)(c) and (d).
98 Federal Courts Act, s 22(2)(g).
99 High Court Ordinance s 12A(2)(f).
100 Admiralty Act 1973, s 4(1)(f).
101 High Court (Admiralty Jurisdiction) Act, s 3(1)(f). But see para 5.40.
102 Admiralty Jurisdiction Regulation Act 105 of 1983, s 1(1)(f).
103 A question regulated by the Private International Law (Miscellaneous Provisions) Act 1995.
104 *The Derbyshire* [1988] AC 276.
105 s 3(1)(f) of the High Court (Admiralty Jurisdiction) Act, which is in near-identical terms to s 20(2)(f) of the 1981 Act.
106 *Zarkovic Stanko v Owners of the Ship Mara* [2000] 4 SLR 156 (Court of Appeal); *The Trade Fair* [1994] 3 SLR 827 (Court of Appeal).
107 Citing *The Antonis P Lemos* [1985] AC 711.
108 s 20(2)(g). 'Any claim for loss of or damage to goods carried in a ship.'
109 *The Eschersheim* [1975] 1 WLR 83, 92, [1974] 2 Lloyd's Rep 188, 194.

maintained by s 24(1) of the SCA 1981, which defines 'goods' to include 'baggage', thus overturning the decision in *R v The Judge of the City of London Court*.[110] However, in *The Eschersheim*, Brandon J at first instance held that this paragraph did not extend to the 'belongings of those who are on board the ship not as passengers or travellers but as crew'.[111] His decision on this point was not considered by the Court of Appeal or House of Lords.

In a more recent Scots case, Lord Emslie considered, *obiter*, that live tuna transported in sea cages (and possibly the cages themselves) were likely 'goods carried in a ship'[112] within the meaning of s 47(2)(f) of the Administration of Justice Act 1956.[113] It is submitted that this broad interpretation of 'goods carried in a ship', which drew support from the French wording of the 1952 Arrest Convention ('par un navire') goes too far; the position is already covered by s 20(2)(e). If correct, however, it should equally apply to claims under s 20(2)(g).

5.42 The provision in s 20(2)(g) is not limited to any particular legal basis of claim[114] and there would seem to be no reason for excluding economic loss claims from its scope.

5.43 There is an equivalent head of jurisdiction in Australia,[115] Canada (which includes passengers' baggage and personal effects),[116] Hong Kong,[117] New Zealand,[118] Singapore,[119] and South Africa. The South African provision includes the baggage and personal belongings of the master, officer, or seamen of the ship and also extends to goods which 'ought to have been carried in a ship'.[120]

Agreements relating to the carriage of goods in or to the use or hire of a ship

5.44 Section 20(2)(h) combines in one paragraph the maritime claims listed in art 1(1)(d) and (e) of the Arrest Convention. Consequently, those claims which are within the scope of paragraph (h) fall into two limbs:[121]

(1) those arising out of an agreement relating to the carriage of goods in a ship; and

---

110 *R v The Judge of the City of London Court* (1883) 12 QBD 115.

111 *The Eschersheim* [1975] 1 WLR 83, 92, [1974] 2 Lloyd's Rep 188, 194.

112 *Fish & Fish Ltd v Sea Shepherd UK* [2011] CSOH 122.

113 This section, the Scots equivalent to s 20(2)(g) SCA 1981, refers to 'loss of, or damage to, goods carried in any ship'.

114 *The Tesaba* [1982] 1 Lloyd's Rep 397 (although the claim in that case is now within the statutory definition contained in the Merchant Shipping Act since the Salvage and Pollution Act 1994).

115 Admiralty Act 1988, s 4(3)(e).

116 Federal Courts Act s 22(2)(h).

117 High Court Ordinance s 12A(2)(g).

118 Admiralty Act 1973, s 4(1)(g).

119 High Court (Admiralty Jurisdiction) Act, s 3(1)(g).

120 Admiralty Jurisdiction Regulation Act 105 of 1983, s 1(1)(g).

121 s 20(2)(h). 'Any claim arising out of any agreement relating to the carriage of goods in a ship or to the use or hire of a ship.'

(2) those arising out of an agreement relating to the use or hire of a ship.

There are equivalent heads of jurisdiction in Australia,[122] Canada,[123] Hong Kong,[124] New Zealand,[125] Singapore,[126] and South Africa.[127]

Nature of remedy sought irrelevant

The type of claim which falls within the scope of para (h) is not limited by reference to the remedy sought. Therefore, it may be based in contract[128] or in tort,[129] or it may be a claim for indemnity or contribution either as a head of damage[130] or under the Civil Liability (Contribution) Act 1978.[131] It may also include a claim for consequential loss.[132] However, the 'subject' of the cause of action must be the ship or cargo. Thus, an allegation in the nature of wrongful interference by a shipowner in the charter of another ship would not be within the *in rem* jurisdiction. **5.45**

Meaning of 'arising out of' and 'relating to'

Claims under s 20(2)(h) must arise out of an agreement. The phrase 'arising out of' connotes the wider expression 'connected with' rather than the narrower expression 'arising under'.[133] Lord Brandon gave four reasons for adopting this construction. The first was that a domestic statute designed to give effect to an international convention should generally be given a broad and liberal construction. Secondly, there is a clear indication in the arrangement and wording of art 1(1) of the Arrest Convention that the expression 'arising out of' is there used in the wider of the two meanings of which it is capable. Thirdly, the rearrangement of the wording of art 1(1) in its equivalent provision of the SCA 1981 cannot have been intended to narrow the Convention meaning. Fourthly, earlier authorities support the broader interpretation.[134] Thus, a claim can fall within para (h) in circumstances where the claim is not brought under the agreement and in circumstances where the agreement was not one concluded between the claimant and the defendant. In the *Antonis P Lemos*,[135] the House of Lords upheld the decision that both the voyage charter and the time trip charter were 'agreements relating to the carriage of goods **5.46**

[122] Admiralty Act 1988, s 4(3)(f).
[123] Federal Courts Act, s 22(2)(f) and (i).
[124] High Court Ordinance s 12A(2)(h).
[125] Admiralty Act 1973, s 4(1)(h).
[126] High Court (Admiralty Jurisdiction) Act, s 3(1)(h).
[127] Admiralty Jurisdiction Regulation Act 105 of 1983, s 1(1) (g), (h), (i), and (j).
[128] *The Conoco Britannia* [1972] 2 QB 543, [1972] 1 Lloyd's Rep 342; *The Bineta* [1966] 2 Lloyd's Rep 419.
[129] *The Antonis P Lemos* [1985] AC 711, [1985] 1 Lloyds' Rep 283; *The Alexandrea* [2002] 3 SLR 56.
[130] *The Eschersheim* [1976] 1 WLR 339, 361, [1976] 1 Lloyd's Rep 81, 96–97 (CA).
[131] *The Hamburg Star* [1994] 1 Lloyd's Rep 399.
[132] Ibid.
[133] *The Antonis P Lemos* [1985] AC 711, [1985] 1 Lloyds' Rep 283.
[134] Ibid 726, 287, citing *The St Elefterio* [1957] P 179 and *The Sennar* [1981] 1 Lloyd's Rep 295.
[135] *The Antonis P Lemos* [1985] AC 711, [1985] 1 Lloyds' Rep 283.

in a ship' out of which the claim by the sub-charterer arose, bringing it within the ambit of para (h).

5.47 Further, the agreement out of which the claim arises must relate to the carriage of goods by a ship or the use or hire of a ship. Whilst the words 'relating to' convey a meaning wider than that which would be conveyed by the use of the word 'for', a narrow meaning is given to the phrase,[136] and there must be some reasonably direct connection with an agreement relating to the carriage of goods in a ship or with the use or hire of a ship;[137] the claim must arise from the terms of the agreement between the parties and not from any collateral or incidental agreement. The degree of connection between the claim and the agreement which is sufficient to found jurisdiction is ascertained by asking whether, giving the English language its ordinary and natural meaning, the claim arises out of the agreement.[138] The following claims have been held to be sufficiently directly connected with the carriage of goods in a ship or with the use or hire of a ship:

(1) An agreement for the cancellation of a contract for the carriage of goods in a ship or for the cancellation of a contract for the use or hire of a ship.[139]
(2) A claim by the owners of containers against shipowners to whom they have leased the containers for the purpose of enabling goods to be carried by sea in the defendant's ships, provided that the claim relates to a particular ship or ships.[140]
(3) A claim in respect of a surety contract which depended upon the outcome of the claimant's claim in respect of a charterparty.[141]
(4) A claim resulting from an alleged breach of an alleged agreement of the nature required, in this case a charter-back agreement.[142]
(5) A claim based on a guarantee of the charterer's full performance of its obligations under the charter, where the guarantee was expressed to be 'entered into on the faith of the said charterparty and not otherwise'.[143]

---

[136] *The Antonis P Lemos* [1985] AC 711, 730, [1985] 1 Lloyd's Rep 283, 289; *The Bumbesti* [2000] QB 559, [2000] 2 WLR 533, [2000] 2 All ER 692, [1999] 2 Lloyd's Rep 481; *The Catur Samudra* [2010] 1 Lloyd's Rep 305, 311, [39].

[137] *Gatoil International Inc v Arkwright-Boston Manufacturers Mutual Insurance Co* [1985] 1 AC 255, 270, [1985] 1 Lloyd's Rep 181, 187 per Lord Keith; *Paramount Enterprises International Inc v An Xin Jiang* [2001] 2 FC 551; *Kremikovtzi Trade v Phoenix Bulk Carriers Ltd* [2006] FCA 1 (Federal Court of Appeal of Canada); *The Fan Yun 123* [2006] 295 HKCU 1 (High Court of the Hong Kong Special Administrative Region).

[138] *Petrofina SA v AOT Ltd (the Maersk Nimrod)* [1992] 1 QB 571, 582, [1992] 2 WLR 266, 277, [1991] 3 All ER 161, 171, [1991] 1 Lloyd's Rep 269, 276; see also *The Tesaba* [1982] Lloyd's Rep 397.

[139] *Gatoil International Inc v Arkwright-Boston Manufacturers Mutual Insurance Co* [1985] 1 AC 255, 270, [1985] 1 Lloyd's Rep 181, 187 per Lord Keith; followed in *Port of Geelong Authority v the Ship The Bass Reefer* (1992) 37 FCR 374, (1992) 109 ALR 505 (Federal Court of Australia).

[140] *The Sonia S* [1983] 2 Lloyd's Rep 63 per Sheen J; cf *The River Rima* [1988] 2 Lloyd's Rep 193.

[141] In *National Bank Leasing v Merlac Marine Inc* (1992) 52 FTR 153 (Federal Court of Canada); see also *Monk Corp v Island Fertilizers Ltd* [1991] 1 SCR 779 (Federal Court of Canada); *Scandia Shipping Agencies Inc v Ship Alam Veracruz* (1997) 148 FTR 164 (Federal Court of Canada). It is submitted, however, that the English Court would look askance at such a claim.

[142] *The Rolita* [1989] 1 HKC 160 (Hong Kong Court of Appeal).

[143] *Reef Shipping Co Ltd v The Ship Fua Kavenga* [1987] 1 NZLR 550 (High Court of New Zealand). But note this case was not followed in *The Catur Samudra* [2010] 1 Lloyd's Rep 305, 311, [39] (High Court of Singapore), discussed below.

(6) A claim for the tort of malicious or injurious falsehood in circumstances where the carriers, pursuant to a charterparty, issued a clean bill of lading and then contradicted themselves in a subsequent letter; the claim 'arose out of' and was 'connected with' the clean bill of lading, read with the charterparty and the subsequent letter.[144]
(7) A joint venture involving the use of an identifiable ship, provided there is some reasonably direct connection with the use of the vessel and the joint venture.[145]

By contrast, the following claims have been held not to fall under this head of jurisdiction: **5.48**

(1) A contract which contemplates the use or operation of vessels to be identified in due course, including vessels engaged under a conference agreement or in a joint service; such a contract is not one relating to the use or hire of or to the carriage of goods in any particular ship or ships.[146]
(2) A contract of insurance on goods.[147]
(3) An agreement for the sale of a ship.[148]
(4) A claim by a seller for demurrage pursuant to the terms of a CIF contract; that contract was independent of, and therefore insufficiently connected with, the charterparty—which was relevant only to demurrage rates.[149]
(5) A claim relating to delay during loading; the agreement in question was 'merely an engagement to deliver coals to a particular place'.[150]
(6) A claim on an arbitration award; the claim arose out of the agreement to refer the disputes arising under the charterparty to arbitration, which agreement was at least one step removed from the 'use or hire' of the ship[151] as an arbitration agreement is distinct from its host contract.[152]
(7) A claim on an undertaking to permit execution on property pursuant to a settlement agreement following an arbitral award and its subsequent conversion

144 *The Indriani* [1995] 3 SLR 381 (Court of Appeal of Singapore).
145 *The Inai Selasih* [2005] 4 SLR 1 (High Court of Singapore).
146 *The Lloyd Pacifico* [1995] 1 Lloyd's Rep 54, 57.
147 *Gatoil International Inc v Arkwright-Boston Manufacturers Mutual Insurance Co* [1985] 1 AC 255, [1985] 1 Lloyd's Rep 181.
148 *Re Pal Marinos* (5 August 1991) per May J; *SOS Maritime Brokers v The Ship Dana Star* [1996] 2 NZLR 482 (High Court of New Zealand) (a claim for commission arising out of a sale contract).
149 *Petrofina SA v AOT Ltd (The Maersk Nimrod)* [1992] 1 QB 571, [1992] 2 WLR 266, [1991] 3 All ER 161, [1991] 1 Lloyd's Rep 269.
150 *The Zeus* (1888) 13 PD 188, 190; *Gatoil International Inc v Arkwright-Boston Manufacturers Mutual Insurance Co* [1985] 1 AC 255, 270, [1985] 1 Lloyd's Rep 181, 187.
151 *The Bumbesti* [2000] QB 559, [2000] 2 WLR 533, [2000] 2 All ER 692, [1999] 2 Lloyd's Rep 481; *The Beldis* [1936] P 51, (1936) Ll L Rep 255: but see, *contra*, *Bremer Oeltransport GmbH v Drewry* [1933] 1 KB 753, (1933) 45 Ll L Rep 133; *The Saint Anna* [1983] 1 WLR 895, [1983] 1 Lloyd's Rep 637.
152 *Heyman v Darwins Ltd* [1942] AC 356, (1941) 72 Ll L Rep 65; *Harbour Assurance (UK) Ltd v Kansa General International Assurance Co Ltd* [1993] QB 701, [1993] 1 Lloyd's Rep 455; *Arbitration Act* 1996, s 7.

to a judgment of the Court; there were legal acts intervening between the charterparty and the defendant's undertaking, with the result that the latter was independent of and in no way related to the former.[153]

(8) A claim under a guarantee securing the performance of the charterer's obligation under a bareboat charterparty. The guarantee was not an agreement which itself related to the use or hire of the vessel; the sole purpose of the guarantee was for a third party to provide financial protection to the owner against the risk of default by the charterer.[154]

5.49 In Canada, it is possible, where the claim arises from an alleged breach of a contract of affreightment, to arrest the cargo under s 43(2) of the Federal Courts Act 1985, provided an 'identifiability' test is satisfied, ie, whether the cargo to be proceeded against is the cargo designated in the contract of affreightment alleged to be breached.[155]

5.50 Where services involving the use of a ship are only an incident of an agreement relating mainly to matters outside the Admiralty jurisdiction, it is possible to sever those parts of the agreement unrelated to the Admiralty jurisdiction to enable a claim to be brought within para (h) in relation to that part of the agreement which related to the use of the ship.[156] In *Petrofina SA v AOT Ltd*, Phillips J (as he then was) posited as an example a contract for the provision of services to a North Sea oil rig, some of which might involve the use of vessels, others the use of helicopters, and others still, no maritime element at all:

> In such a case I see no reason in principle why a claim arising out of that part of the contract involving the use of a vessel should not be brought within the Admiralty jurisdiction. On the contrary, it would seem illogical that the existence of Admiralty jurisdiction should turn on whether there was between the parties a single agreement dealing comprehensively with all the services to be provided or a series of agreements each dealing with a separate type of service.[157]

---

[153] *Ordina Shipmanagement Co Ltd & Ashton Shipping Ltd v United Med Lines Inc (The Sheringham)* (2000) 199 FTR 258: see also *Pakistan National Shipping Corp v Canada* (1991) 50 FTR 24; *Transports Insurance Co Inc v Ship Ondine* (1982) 138 DLR (3d) 745; *Intermunicipal Realty & Development Corp v Gore Mutual Insurance Co* [1978] 2 FC 691 and compare the South African approach in *The Mineral Ordaz* 20 April 1999, M Stranex, *Shipping Cases of South Africa* (3rd edn, 2000) D41, where the Court distinguished the English decisions in *The Beldis* [1936] P 51 and *The St Anna* [1983] 1 WLR 895 on the basis that any uncertainty which might have existed in the South African law arising out of those English decisions had been cured by the enactment of s 1(1)(aa) of the Act, which specifically makes any judgment or maritime award relating to a maritime claim a separate head of *in rem* jurisdiction. In considering the settlement agreement, as opposed to any award or judgment, Pillay J held that he was unable to see how the settlement could destroy the underlying maritime character or nature of the claim, and that the claim was therefore one arising out of the charterparty within sub-para (j).

[154] *The Catur Samudra* [2010] 1 Lloyd's Rep 305, 310–311, [35] (High Court of Singapore).

[155] *Kremikovtzi Trade v Phoenix Bulk Carriers Ltd* (2007) 278 DLR (4th) 628, [2007] 1 SCR 588, overruling, in laconic fashion, the earlier Federal Court of Appeal decision in *Paramount Enterprises International Inc v An Xin Jiang* [2001] 2 FC 551, (2000) 198 DLR (4th) 719.

[156] *Petrofina SA v AOT Ltd (the Maersk Nimrod)* [1992] 1 QB 571, [1991] 1 Lloyd's Rep 269.

[157] Ibid 577–578, 273; see also *The Queen of the South* [1968] 1 Lloyd's Rep 182.

5.51 There is no reason in principle why containers cannot be 'goods', but an agreement for the hire of containers for use on a ship is not within this provision,[158] but raises other problems where they are supplied to a shipowner for the carriage of goods; these are discussed further in paras 5.68 and following below.

Salvage

5.52 In departing significantly from the 'no cure no pay' principle which applied to traditional claims for salvage,[159] the Salvage Convention 1989 allows claims to be brought which fall outside what was traditionally considered 'salvage'. The SCA 1981 has ensured that the broader range of claims available under the Salvage Convention, such as claims under art 14, can be enforced in admiralty, although as mentioned above,[160] it is most unlikely that these broader claims, unlike a conventional claim for salvage under art 13, will attract a maritime lien. The corresponding provision in the Arrest Convention refers only to claims arising out of 'salvage' and so the reference in s 20(2)(j) broadens the scope of this head of claim. The English provision thus anticipates the widening of the head of claim by the 1999 Arrest Convention.[161]

5.53 The Salvage Convention is not the only source of claims which might broadly be described as 'in the nature of salvage'. In response to some of the shortcomings of art 14 of the Convention, industry evolved the SCOPIC clause.[162] It is submitted that a claim for SCOPIC remuneration is sufficiently 'in the nature of salvage' for it to be the subject of an action *in rem* in England: after all, the duty of the salvage contractor under clause 10 of SCOPIC is to exercise its 'best endeavours to salve the vessel and property thereon'—the same, in other words, as its duty under the Lloyd's Open Form of Salvage Agreement. Similar considerations are capable of applying to industry standard forms, such as WRECKHIRE 2010, at any rate where the services to be rendered under them include salvage.

---

[158] *Gatoil International Inc v Arkwright-Boston Manufacturers Mutual Insurance Co* [1985] AC 255, 263, 271, [1985] 1 All ER 129, 131, 137, [1985] 1 Lloyd's Rep 181, 183, 188, overruling *The Sonia S* [1983] 2 Lloyd's Rep 63. Note, however, that in *The River Rima* [1988] 1 WLR 758, [1988] 2 All ER 641, [1988] 2 Lloyd's Rep 193, Lord Brandon accepted that containers were 'goods' within the meaning of sub-para (m) (necessaries).

[159] S 20(2)(j):

> Any claim—
> (i) under the Salvage Convention 1989
> (ii) under any contract for or in relation to salvage services, or
> (iii) in the nature of salvage not falling within (i) or (ii) above;
> or any corresponding claim in connection with an aircraft.

As to whether this wording is wide enough to encompass claims made against salvors, see n 168 below.

[160] Chapter 4, para 4.30.

[161] 1999 Arrest Convention, art 1(1)(c).

[162] Chapter 4, n 134.

5.54 As in England, Hong Kong[163] and South Africa[164] have widened the scope of their Admiralty jurisdiction to extend to the new claims arising under the Salvage Convention 1989; the Hong Kong provision is in the same terms as that in the SCA 1981, and so it is submitted that SCOPIC claims fall within that provision also. The South African provision, however, is more specifically linked to the Salvage Convention and too narrowly drawn to encompass a claim for SCOPIC remuneration.

5.55 The Australian wording, 'relating to salvage',[165] and that of Singapore,[166] 'in the nature of salvage', is also probably wide enough to encompass a claim under art 14 of the Convention or pursuant to a SCOPIC clause. It is submitted that the same can be said of s 4(1)(i) of the Admiralty Act 1973 (New Zealand), which requires the claim to be 'in the nature of salvage'. Against this, however, it may be argued that the general reference to Part XVII of the Maritime Transport Act 1994 appears to be designed to include specific issues of life salvage and salvage of cargo, apparel, or wreck, and that it does not unequivocally signal an extension of the traditional salvage head of jurisdiction to encompass the entire salvage Convention regime, let alone SCOPIC.

5.56 In Canada, by contrast, the claim must be 'for salvage' in order to fall within the relevant provision of s 22.[167] It is submitted that this wording does not extend to claims under art 14 of the Salvage Convention or for SCOPIC remuneration.

5.57 In Singapore, consistently with the broad approach which it has taken generally with respect to the scope of Admiralty jurisdiction, the High Court has construed the phrase 'any claim in the nature of salvage' as meaning 'any claim arising out of salvage'.[168] In *Alexander G Tsavliris & Sons Maritime Co v Keppel*

---

163 High Court Ordinance s 12A(2)(i).

164 Admiralty Jurisdiction Regulation Act 105 of 1983, s 1(1)(k): 'salvage, including salvage relating to any aircraft and the sharing or apportionment of salvage and any right in respect of property salved or which would, but for the negligence of or default of the salvor or a person who attempted to salve it, have been salved, and any claim arising out of the Wreck and Salvage Act 1996'. The Wreck and Salvage Act 1996 gives the force of law to the International Convention on Salvage 1989. Sub-section (k) was substituted by s 25 of the Wreck and Salvage Act (No 94 of 1996) which entered into force on 1 February 1997.

165 The Admiralty Act 1988, s 4(3)(g) uses the phrase 'relating to salvage' which may well be wide enough to encompass claims under the Salvage Convention. Query whether this extends to claims against salvors: cf n 168 below.

166 High Court (Admiralty Jurisdiction) Act s 3(1)(l). This is particularly so in the case of Singapore, given the broad approach adopted by its Courts in relation to these provisions: *The Trade Fair* [1994] 3 SLR 827; *Zarkovic Stanko v Owners of the Ship Mara* [2000] 4 SLR 156.

167 Federal Courts Act, s 22 (2)(j), 'any claim for salvage'.

168 This construction would appear to extend to claims by property owners against negligent salvors. If it does, then the law of Singapore may be out of step with that of England: see the Court of Appeal in *The Eschersheim* [1976] 1 WLR 339, 346, 353, 359; [1976] 1 All ER 441, 446, 452, 458; [1976] 1 Lloyd's Rep 81, 89, 90, 95. Where, however, such a claim arises under a contract for the provision of salvage services, it may now be arguable that such a claim is within the wording 'any claim ... under any contract for ... salvage services'.

Corp Ltd,[169] it held that an agreement to refer to arbitration in London the assessment of the salvage remuneration payable to the salvors arose out of the salvage of the Atlas Pride and that the award of the arbitrator was the result of that reference. Therefore, an action to enforce the award was properly within Admiralty jurisdiction under s 3(1)(l).

In *Transnet Ltd v Mbashi*,[170] the High Court of South Africa was required to determine whether services performed by the port authority, Transnet Ltd, were provided voluntarily as required by the provisions of the Salvage Convention so as to entitle them to a salvage reward or special compensation within the meaning of arts 13 and 14. Pursuant to s 11(d) of the Wreck and Salvage Act 1996, Transnet was empowered to raise or destroy any sunken, stranded, or abandoned ship or wreck within the area owned by the company. Levinsohn J, influenced by the decision in *The Gregerso*,[171] held that Transnet's powers were not circumscribed by the Act and its activities could not be said to lack the character of voluntariness. It was, therefore, entitled to a salvage award which was enforceable *in rem* under sub-para (k). **5.58**

Towage and pilotage

These two heads of claim correspond to arts (1)(i) and (j) of the Arrest Convention, which permit claims 'arising out of' towage[172] or pilotage.[173] Subsections 20(2)(k) and (l) are, therefore, broader in scope, as they extend to claims 'in the nature of' towage or pilotage. In the case of towage, this wording has been held to include escort services rendered by a tug without making fast.[174] Claims for damage caused to the tow by the action of the tug will not fall under this head of jurisdiction but will qualify under (e), (h), or both.[175] Where the tow's negligence prevents performance of the towage contract, the tug owner's claim for damages would likewise not fall within (k),[176] although again it is difficult to see why it should not qualify under (h). **5.59**

Section 21(5) extends the *in rem* jurisdiction to claims in the nature of towage or pilotage in respect of an aircraft if, at the time when the action is commenced, it is **5.60**

169 [1995] 2 SLR 113.

170 *Transnet Ltd v Mbashi* (*The Mbashi*) [2002] 2 Lloyd's Rep 602. Cf *Transnet Ltd t/a National Ports Authority v The MV Cleopatra Dream and Another* (163/10) [2011] ZASCA 12; [2011] 3 All SA 279 (SCA); 2011 (5) SA 613 (SCA) (11 March 2011), where it was held that the local authority did not perform salvage services as a volunteer.

171 *The Gregerso* [1973] QB 274, [1971] 1 All ER 961, [1971] 1 Lloyd's Rep 220.

172 s 20(2)(k). 'Any claim in the nature of towage in respect of a ship or an aircraft.'

173 s 20(2)(l). 'Any claim in the nature of pilotage in respect of a ship or an aircraft.'

174 *The Leoborg* [1962] 2 Lloyd's Rep 146. For a more detailed consideration of this head of jurisdiction, see Simon Rainey QC, *The Law of Tug and Tow and Offshore Contracts*, (3rd edn, 2011) Chapter 13.

175 See *The Isca* (1886) 12 PD 34 and *The Conoco Britannia* [1972] 2 QB 543, [1972] 2 WLR 1352, [1972] 2 All ER 238, [1972] 1 Lloyd's Rep 342, a claim for a contractual indemnity under a towage contract.

176 *The Valsesia* [1927] P 115.

beneficially owned by the person who would be liable *in personam*. 'Towage' and 'pilotage' in relation to aircraft are restricted to towage and pilotage whilst the aircraft is waterborne.[177]

5.61 Hong Kong[178] and Singapore[179] have enacted identical provisions.

5.62 Australia makes provision for *in rem* jurisdiction in relation to claims in the nature of towage or pilotage in respect of a ship,[180] but has not extended its Admiralty jurisdiction to aircraft.

5.63 Whilst New Zealand has included aircraft within its Admiralty jurisdiction under this head of jurisdiction,[181] the Admiralty Act 1973 does not include a provision equivalent to s 21(5) of the SCA 1981. It would therefore seem that claims for towage or pilotage against aircraft in New Zealand can only be brought *in personam*.

5.64 Canada provides for jurisdiction in relation to any claim for towage or pilotage in respect of a ship[182] or of an aircraft but only if the aircraft is waterborne.[183]

5.65 South Africa includes a claim relating to 'towage or pilotage' within its list of maritime claims which can be enforced *in rem*.[184] The South African provisions do not extend to aircraft.

Necessaries

5.66 'Necessaries'[185] was the term used[186] until the 1956 Act replaced it with more general wording taken from the Arrest Convention. The words 'in respect of' are given their ordinary and plain meaning, and 'are certainly no narrower than the claims which were formerly described as claims for necessaries'.[187] Those necessaries themselves are no longer restricted to those supplied to a foreign ship.[188] What is now

[177] Senior Courts Act 1981, s 24(1).

[178] High Court Ordinance s 12A(2)(j) and (k) and 12B(5).

[179] High Court (Admiralty Jurisdiction) Act, s 3(1)(j) and (k) and 4(5).

[180] Admiralty Act 1988, s 4(3)(j) and (k): *Elbe Shipping SA v The Ship Global Peace* [2006] FCA 954, (2006) 154 FCR 439 (Federal Court of Australia).

[181] Admiralty Act 1973, s 4(1)(j) and (k).

[182] *Joint Stock Society Oceangeotechnology v Ship 1201* [1994] 2 FC 265, (1994) 72 FTR 211.

[183] Federal Courts Act, s 22(2)(k) and (l).

[184] Admiralty Jurisdiction Regulation Act 105 of 1983, s 1(1)(l).

[185] s 20(2)(m). 'Any claim in respect of goods or materials supplied to a ship for her operation or maintenance.'

[186] In s 6 of the 1840 Act, s 10 of the 1861 Act, and s 22 (1)(a)(vii) of the Supreme Court of Judicature (Consolidation) Act 1925.

[187] *The Fairport (No 5)* [1967] 2 Lloyd's Rep 162, 163; *The Kommunar* [1977] 1 Lloyd's Rep 1, 5; *The Edinburgh Castle* [1999] 2 Lloyd's Rep 362; *The Sydney Sunset* [2001] FCA 210 (Federal Court of Australia); *Patrick Stevedores No 2 Pty Ltd v Proceeds of the Sale of the Vessel MV Skulptor Konenkov* (1998) 160 ALR 132 (Federal Court of Australia) (where it was held to encompass a claim characterized as one for unjust enrichment); *The Alexandrea* [2002] 3 SLR 56 (High Court of Singapore).

[188] *Gatoil International Inc v Arkwright-Boston Manufacturers Mutual Insurance Co* [1985] AC 255, 264, [1985] 1 Lloyd's Rep 181, 183.

called 'a claim in respect of goods and materials supplied to a ship for her operation and maintenance' therefore encompasses:

> ... whatever is fit and proper for the service on which a vessel is engaged, whatever the owner of that vessel, as a prudent man, would have ordered if present at the time ... as applied to those repairs or things provided for the ship by order of the master, for which the owners are liable.[189]

It includes the provision of stevedoring services[190] and claims for the provision of services of officers and crew, or the payment of wages in that respect.[191]

No distinction is drawn between a claim by the person who actually supplied the goods to a ship and a claim by the person who paid for the supply. A person who pays for necessaries, or who advances money to the person who pays for the goods, has as good a claim against the ship and her owners as does the actual supplier.[192] **5.67**

It was an essential ingredient of any claim brought under para (vii) of s 22(1)(a) of the 1925 Act that the claim should relate to necessaries supplied to a particular ship, the identity of which had either been specified in the contract of supply or at least notified to the supplier by the time when the necessaries came to be delivered under such a contract. Since specification of the identity of the particular ship to which necessaries were supplied was an essential ingredient of such a claim, it can be inferred that it was also intended to be an essential ingredient of a claim under art 1(1)(k) of the Arrest Convention, which was derived from the earlier English provision.[193] Thus, para (m) encompasses a contract of supply, whether by way of sale or hire, where the contract expressly provides that the goods or materials are required for the use of a particular ship, the identity of which is specified in the contract or will be specified by the time when the contract comes to be performed.[194] It was held in *The River Rima* that a claim arising out of an agreement for the hire of containers, which contained no provision that the containers should be used for the carriage of cargo by any particular ship, did not fall within this head of jurisdiction.[195] **5.68**

The River Rima was distinguished in the Scots case of *Oceaneering International AG, Petitioners*.[196] In that case, remotely operated vehicle (ROV) equipment, systems, services, and personnel were supplied to the vessel *Sarah*. The *Sarah* was the only **5.69**

189 *The Riga* (1872) LR 3 A&E 516, 522.

190 *The Equator* (1921) 9 Ll L Rep 1.

191 *The Edinburgh Castle* [1999] 2 Lloyd's Rep 362 (a case containing useful illustrations of what may be encompassed within this head of jurisdiction); *The Nore Challenger and the Nore Commander* [2001] 2 Lloyd's Rep 103.

192 *The Henrich Björn* (1885) 10 PD 44, 50; *Foong Tai v Buchheister* [1908] AC 458, 466; *The Kommunar* [1997] 1 Lloyd's Rep 1.

193 *The River Rima* [1988] 1 WLR 758, [1988] 2 All ER 641, [1988] 2 Lloyd's Rep 193.

194 Ibid 763, 645,196, per Lord Brandon; *The Alexandrea* [2002] 3 SLR 56 (High Court of Singapore).

195 *The River Rima* [1988] 1 WLR 758, [1988] 2 All ER 641, [1988] 2 Lloyd's Rep 193.

196 *Oceaneering International AG, Petitioners* [2010] CSOH 161, [2011] 1 Lloyd's Rep 546.

vessel connected with the parties' agreement and, unlike *The River Rima*, the ROV equipment and services had only been supplied for the *Sarah* and for no other vessel. The vessel was always deployed with one or two ROVs and required ROV systems in order to operative effectively, whereas the containers in *The River Rima* were 'merely a form of cargo'. Lord Emslie found that the relevant provision in the Administration of Justice Act 1956,[197] which referred to 'the supply of goods or materials to a ship for her operation or maintenance', covered the ROV equipment and services. The installation, maintenance, and operation of the ROVs and associated systems on board were properly viewed as 'enhancing her operational capabilities'.[198]

5.70 Article 1(1)(l) of the 1999 Arrest Convention provides for jurisdiction in respect of 'goods, materials, provisions, bunkers, equipment (including containers) supplied or services rendered to the ship for its operation, management, preservation or maintenance'. The Article will not resolve the questions as to whether containers themselves are part of the ship's equipment that may be subject to arrest, or whether and to what extent claims in relation to contracts for the supply of containers fall within the *in rem* jurisdiction.[199] It is submitted that the realities of modern commercial practice require that a claim such as that brought in *The River Rima* should be capable of being the subject of an action *in rem*, provided that the ship ultimately made the subject of the action *in rem* is indeed the ship in connection with which the claim ultimately arose or a sister-ship. However, whether this result can be achieved in practice may depend upon the wording of the implementing legislation if and when the 1999 Arrest Convention comes into force.

5.71 There is an equivalent head of jurisdiction in Canada,[200] Hong Kong,[201] New Zealand,[202] Singapore,[203] South Africa,[204] and Australia.[205]

5.72 The Australian provision is, however, wider than s 20(2)(m) in that it includes 'services (including stevedoring and lighterage services) supplied to a ship'. The Federal Court of Australia considered the ambit of this head of jurisdiction in a case involving claims in respect of the lease of land adjoining the berth on which a cargo handling facility had been constructed and licence agreements giving priority berthing rights.[206] The

[197] s 5(2)(k) was equivalent to s 20(2)(m) of the Senior Courts Act and provided for the arrest of a ship on the dependence of an action for claims in relation to 'the supply of goods or materials to a ship for her operation or maintenance'. Section 5(2)(l) referred to claims in relation to 'the construction, repair or equipment of any ship'.

[198] *Oceaneering International AG, Petitioners* [2010] CSOH 161, [2011] 1 Lloyd's Rep 546, 549, [15].

[199] For a discussion of the nature of a container see P J Bordahandy, 'Containers: a Conundrum or a Concept?' (2005) 11 *Journal of International Maritime Law* 342.

[200] Federal Courts Act, s 22(2)(m).

[201] High Court Ordinance s 12A(2)(l).

[202] Admiralty Act 1973, s 4(1)(l).

[203] High Court (Admiralty Jurisdiction) Act, s 3(1)(l).

[204] Admiralty Jurisdiction Regulation Act 105 of 1983, s 1(1)(m), read with (n) and (o).

[205] Admiralty Act 1988, s 4(3)(m).

[206] *Port of Geelong Authority v The Ship Bass Reefer* (1992) 109 ALR 505; followed in *FNP Catalano Nominees Pty Ltd v The Ship FV Comet* [2000] WASC 76, (2000) 155 FLR 115 (Supreme Court of Western Australia).

Court distinguished the decision in *The River Rima*,[207] holding that it was not authority for the wide proposition that there can be no supply to a ship unless the contract of supply specifies and nominates the vessel.[208] Consequently, that decision was no bar to the argument that there was supply of facilities to the ship notwithstanding that the contracts did not specifically refer to the ship. Nevertheless, it was accepted that whatever services were provided, they must be provided 'to the ship for its operation'. It was held that the lease rental referable to a sea-terminal storage area for a ship's cargo was not sufficiently proximate to the operation of the ship as such to warrant its falling within the head of claim.[209] By contrast, the licence fees in respect of the priority berthing services were supplied to the ship for its operation and so could legitimately be the subject of an action *in rem* within s 4(3)(m).[210] A more recent decision has confirmed s 4(3)(m) is to be interpreted broadly and therefore covers the supply of masters and crews pursuant to the terms of a demise charter.[211]

The Canadian provision is in similar terms to the Australian, but the Canadian courts **5.73**
have adopted an even wider construction. In *Hamilton Harbour Commissioners v The Wenchita*,[212] it was held that the provision of a dock and warehouse for a ship to come alongside and discharge into was within the concept of 'necessaries' under the previous legislation.[213]

In *The Alexandrea*,[214] the High Court of Singapore held that this head of jurisdiction **5.74**
would be wide enough to cover claims framed in tort but only where the wrongdoing relates to or is referable to the primary ship supplied with goods or materials for her operation or maintenance. The types of claims posited included claims in tort against the shipowning interest of the primary ship as bailee of goods or materials supplied, or claims for malicious or injurious falsehood to protect the claimant's interests in his property or trade or economic interest generally.[215] In *The Golden Petroleum*,[216] the High Court of Singapore held that the goods supplied to the ship, to which the claim related, must be sufficiently and directly connected with the operation of the ship and must link the user of the goods with the defendant's ship. 'Operation of the ship' could not be equated with the business activities of the owner and could not cover goods loaded onto the vessel simply to be sold on to third parties.

---

207 *The River Rima* [1988] 1 WLR 758, [1988] 2 All ER 641, [1988] 2 Lloyd's Rep 193.

208 *Port of Geelong Authority v The Ship Bass Reefer* (1992) 109 ALR 505, 516, (1992) 37 FCR 374, 385.

209 Ibid 517, 386.

210 Ibid 519, 388.

211 *Programmed Total Marine Services Pty Ltd v The Ship 'Hako Fortress'* [2012] FCA 805, (2012) 293 ALR 139 upheld on this point on appeal: *The Ships 'Hako Endeavour', 'Hako Excel', 'Hako Esteem' and 'Hako Fortress' v Programmed Total Marine Services Pty Ltd* [2013] FCAFC 21, (2013) 211 FCR 369.

212 *Hamilton Harbour Commissioners v The Wenchita* [1927] Ex CR 176.

213 See also *Bell (Charles R) Ltd v The Stephanie Colleen* (1990) 36 FTR 210; *Aldershot Contractors Equipment Rental v The Protostatis* (1968) 67 DLR (2d) 174.

214 *The Alexandrea* [2003] 3 SLR 56.

215 Ibid 62.

216 *The Golden Petroleum* [1994] 1 SLR 92.

5.75 The equivalent South African provision, s 1(1)(i) of the Admiralty Jurisdiction Regulation Act 105 of 1983, was amended in 1992 following the decision of the House of Lords in *The River Rima*[217] to grant jurisdiction *in rem* in respect of 'any container and any agreement relating to any container'.[218] 'Container' is defined in s 1(1) as 'a container for the carriage of goods by sea, including any such container which is empty or otherwise temporarily not being used for such carriage'. Section 3(5)(e) of the Act permits an action *in rem* to be brought against a container. However, despite a perception that the intention of the South African legislature must have been to widen the scope of the Admiralty jurisdiction in relation to claims relating to containers so as to encompass the types of claims made in *The River Rima*,[219] in practice the South African courts have followed the reasoning of the House of Lords and have held that a claim within sub-para (i) is only enforceable *in rem* if the agreement is referable to a specific ship.[220]

5.76 In Hong Kong, the equivalent provision of s 12A(2)(l) has been held to capture not only 'goods or materials' but also services supplied to a ship, even if the contract in question does not specifically refer to the ship.[221] The disbursements must relate to the operational aspect of the ship.

Construction, repair, or equipment of a ship or dock charges or dues

5.77 This head of claim corresponds with art 1(1)(l) of the Arrest Convention except for the use of the narrower phrase 'in respect of' rather than 'arising out of'.[222] A claim for 'construction, repair or equipment' connotes a claim in respect of something of a permanent nature and does not include the supply of consumables.[223] Sheen J is said to have held in an unreported *ex parte* decision[224] that a vessel's classification certificate was part of its equipment, so as to allow the classification society to bring an action *in rem* in respect of its charges for issuing it. Although counter-intuitive, a ship cannot in the modern world operate without such certificates and it is submitted that his decision was correct in principle. The logic of the decision would extend the ambit of this head of jurisdiction to all certificates, whether issued by flag or class, as well as a vessel's SMS and other ISM documentation.

---

217 *The River Rima* [1988] 1 WLR 758, [1988] 2 All ER 641, [1988] 2 Lloyd's Rep 193.

218 *Polar Shipping Inc v Plan Marine AG (The Bugaz)* 31 August 1997, M Stranex, *Shipping Cases of South Africa* (3rd edn, 2000) D 1.

219 *Zygos Corporation v Salen Rederierna AB* 1985 (2) SA 486.

220 *MV Jute Express v Owners of the Cargo lately laden on board the MV Jute Express* 1992 (3) SA 9; *Polar Shipping Inc v Plan Marine AG (The Bugaz)* 31 August 1997, M Stranex, *Shipping Cases of South Africa* (3rd edn, 2000) D 1.

221 *The Oriental Dragon* [2014] 1 HKLRD 649, where management services provided under a contract could have fallen within the ambit of s 12A(2)(l) and (o) of the Hong Kong Ordinance, except that the disbursement part of the management fees did not relate to the vessel's operation or maintenance.

222 s 20(2)(n). 'Any claim in respect of the construction, repair or equipment of a ship or in respect of dock charges or dues.'

223 *The D'Vora* [1953] 1 WLR 34, [1952] 2 All ER 1127, [1952] 2 Lloyd's Rep 404.

224 *The Stinne Peter*, 1986 Fo 171, referred to in the notes to paragraph 2(n) in Volume 2 of Civil Procedure (also known as the White Book), published annually by Sweet & Maxwell.

It should be noted that the claim must be 'in respect of the construction [etc] of a ship'. A claim may arise under a shipbuilding contract which does not fall within that gateway. For example, a buyer may be entitled, if the vessel has not been delivered by the so-called 'drop dead date', to terminate the contract and recover the instalments which it has paid during the course of the vessel's construction. Such a claim would not, it is submitted, fall within s 20(2)(n). The plain purpose of the provision is to protect shipyards who build ships, not disgruntled would-be purchasers of them. Consistently with that view, it may be noted that s 4 of the Admiralty Act 1861 bestowed jurisdiction on the Admiralty Court for claims 'for the building … of any ship'. It is moreover difficult to see why purchasers under shipbuilding contracts should be better placed than buyers of second hand tonnage, who have no right (under the English statute at least) to proceed *in rem*. **5.78**

There is an equivalent head of jurisdiction in Australia,[225] Canada,[226] Hong Kong,[227] New Zealand,[228] Singapore,[229] and South Africa.[230] **5.79**

In *Port of Geelong Authority v The Ship Bass Reefer*, the Federal Court of Australia held that if a charge for berthing a ship arising out of a contract between the shipowner or charterer and the port authority was otherwise sufficiently similar to a charge that might be imposed under a statute or regulation, it could be a 'similar' charge within the meaning of s 4(3)(p), which grants jurisdiction over 'a claim in relation to a liability for port, harbour, canal or light tolls, charges or dues, or tolls, charges or dues of a similar kind, in relation to a ship'.[231] **5.80**

In *Virtu Fast Ferries Ltd v The Ship 'Cape Leveque'*, the same Court held that the sister-ship arrest provision in s 19(a) was not available to support the plaintiff's writ because the words 'first mentioned ship' in s 19(a) do not contemplate a vessel still under construction.[232]

Wages

Except for the words in parentheses, this head of claim[233] corresponds with art 1(1)(m) of the Arrest Convention. A claim by a master or member of the crew for wages gives rise to a maritime lien and is discussed above.[234] **5.81**

---

[225] Admiralty Act 1988, s 4(3)(n), (o), and (p). Note that the ability to arrest a surrogate ship under s 19(a) is not available where the cause of action arose while the ship the subject of the action was under construction: *Virtu Fast Ferries Ltd v The Ship 'Cape Leveque'* [2015] FCAFC 58.

[226] Federal Courts Act, s 22(2)(n) and (s).

[227] High Court Ordinance s 12A(2)(m).

[228] Admiralty Act 1973, s 4(1)(m).

[229] High Court (Admiralty Jurisdiction) Act, s 3(1)(m).

[230] Admiralty Jurisdiction Regulation Act 105 of 1983, s 1(1)(q) and (r).

[231] *Port of Geelong Authority v The Ship Bass Reefer* (1992) 109 ALR 505.

[232] *Virtu Fast Ferries Ltd v The Ship 'Cape Leveque'* [2015] FCAFC 58, [24]–[28]. See para 5.21 above. Note that the Australian legislation specifically excludes from the definition of 'ship' 'a vessel under construction that has not been launched' (s 3(1) of the Admiralty Act 1988).

[233] s 20(2)(o). 'Any claim by a master or member of the crew of a ship for wages (including any sum allotted out of wages or adjudged by a superintendent to be due by way of wages).'

[234] Chapter 4, esp paras 4.31 and following.

5.82 Equivalent statutory provisions granting general jurisdiction *in rem* in respect of wages are found in Australia,[235] Canada,[236] Hong Kong,[237] New Zealand,[238] Singapore,[239] and South Africa.[240]

Disbursements made on account of a ship

5.83 This head of claim[241] corresponds with art 1(1)(n) of the Arrest Convention except for the use of the narrower phrase 'in respect of' rather than 'arising out of'. Whilst a claim by a master for disbursements made on behalf of a ship gives rise to a maritime lien,[242] no lien is created in relation to such a claim by a shipper, charterer, or agent.

5.84 A claim under this head must relate to disbursements made in respect of a particular ship (or a sister-ship)[243] and the disbursement must be related to the operational aspects of the ship. Similarly, in *Bain Clarkson Ltd v the Owners of the Ship Sea Friends*,[244] it was held that an insurance premium in respect of the hull was not concerned with the operational aspects of the ship's life but rather was concerned with protecting the owner's financial interests and so was not a 'disbursement' within sub-para (p).[245]

5.85 Equivalent statutory provisions granting a general jurisdiction *in rem* in respect of disbursements are found in Australia,[246] Canada,[247] Hong Kong,[248] New Zealand,[249] Singapore,[250] and South Africa.[251]

5.86 In *Clifford Chance v The Owners of the Atlantic Trader*,[252] the High Court of Hong Kong adopted a broad construction of the equivalent provision and held that the plaintiff's fees for professional services[253] came within the Admiralty jurisdiction

235 Admiralty Act 1988, s 4(3)(t).
236 Federal Courts Act, s 22(2)(o).
237 High Court Ordinance s 12A(2)(n).
238 Admiralty Act 1973, s 4(1)(o).
239 High Court (Admiralty Jurisdiction) Act, s 3(1)(n).
240 Admiralty Jurisdiction Regulation Act 105 of 1983, s 1(1)(s).
241 s 20(2)(p). 'Any claim by a master, shipper, charterer or agent in respect of disbursements made on account of a ship.'
242 Chapter 4, paras 4.41 and following.
243 *The Lloyd Pacifico* [1995] 1 Lloyd's Rep 54, 57.
244 *Bain Clarkson Ltd v the Owners of the Ship Sea Friends* [1991] 2 Lloyd's Rep 322.
245 In *The Oriental Dragon* [2014] 1 HKLRD 649, the Hong Kong Court of First Instance similarly held that insurance premiums or the expenses of procuring insurance for a ship did not fall within s 12A(2)(o) of the Hong Kong Ordinance.
246 Admiralty Act 1988, s 4(3)(r).
247 Federal Courts Act, s 22(2)(p).
248 High Court Ordinance s 12A(2)(o).
249 Admiralty Act 1973, s 4(1)(p).
250 High Court (Admiralty Jurisdiction) Act s 3(1)(o); *The Ohm Mariana ex Peony*[1993] 2 SLR 698.
251 Admiralty Jurisdiction Regulation Act 105 of 1983 s 1(1)(o).
252 *Clifford Chance v The Owners of the Atlantic Trader* [1991] 2 Lloyd's Rep 324.
253 In *The Westport (No 3)* [1966] 1 Lloyd's Rep 342, a ship's agent's agency fees were held to be within the phrase 'any claim by' an 'agent in respect of disbursements made on account of a ship'.

of the Court on the basis that there was no reason to exclude barristers or solicitors from the class of agents referred to in the paragraph, provided that their services were referable to the ship in question.

General average

This head of claim[254] is if anything wider than art 1(1)(g) of the Arrest Convention, which refers simply to a claim 'arising out of general average'. Hong Kong[255], New Zealand[256], Singapore,[257] and South Africa[258] have enacted the same broad wording as contained in the SCA 1981. However, Australia and Canada use narrower wording: 'in respect of general average'[259] and 'in respect of a general average contribution'.[260] **5.87**

Bottomry

This head of claim[261] corresponds with art 1(1)(h) of the Arrest Convention. As observed above,[262] bottomry bonds are obsolete in modern commerce and it is unlikely that a claim arising out of bottomry will be encountered in modern practice. Nonetheless, all the jurisdictions considered in this work except Australia have retained a claim arising out of bottomry as the basis for an action *in rem*.[263] **5.88**

D. Heads of Claim Recognized in Other Jurisdictions

In addition to the heads of jurisdictions equivalent to s 20(2)(e)–(r) of the SCA 1981, the Australian Admiralty Act confers *in rem* jurisdiction in relation to the following. **5.89**

(1) A claim in respect of a levy in relation to a ship, including one imposed by the Protection of the Sea (Shipping Levy) Act 1981 in relation to which a power to detain the ship is conferred by a law in force in Australia or in part of Australia.[264]

254 s 20(2)(q). 'Any claim arising out of an act which is or is claimed to be a general average act.'
255 High Court Ordinance s 12A(2)(p).
256 Admiralty Act 1973, s 4(1)(q).
257 High Court (Admiralty Jurisdiction) Act, s 3(1)(p).
258 Admiralty Jurisdiction Regulation Act 105 of 1983, s 1(t).
259 Admiralty Act 1988, s 4(3)(h).
260 Federal Courts Act 1985, s 22(2)(q).
261 s 20(2)(r). 'Any claim arising out of bottomry.'
262 Chapter 4, para 4.48.
263 Federal Courts Act 1985, s 22(2)(c) (Canada); High Court Ordinance, s 12A(2)(q) (Hong Kong); Admiralty Act 1973, s 4(1)(r) (New Zealand); High Court (Admiralty Jurisdiction) Act, s 3(1)(q) (Singapore); Admiralty Jurisdiction Regulation Act 105 of 1983, s 1(1)(d) (South Africa).
264 Admiralty Act 1988, s 4(3)(q).

(2) A claim for an insurance premium, or for a mutual insurance call, in relation to a ship.[265] It has been argued unsuccessfully before the English courts that claims for marine insurance fall within existing heads of jurisdiction.[266]
(3) A claim for the satisfaction or enforcement of a judgment given by a court (including a court of a foreign country) against a ship or other property in a proceeding *in rem* in the nature of a proceeding in Admiralty and a claim for the enforcement of, or a claim arising out of, an arbitral award (including a foreign award within the meaning of the Arbitration (Foreign Awards and Agreements) Act 1974) made in respect of a proprietary or general maritime claim.[267] The availability of these heads of claim obviates arguments as to whether an original cause of action has merged with an earlier arbitration award or is barred because the claim is considered to be *res judicata.* The claimant can simply point to the lack of satisfaction of the earlier arbitration award as an independent claim giving rise to its own statutory action *in rem.* Whilst the former head of jurisdiction includes both local and foreign admiralty judgments, it only includes judgments *in rem*, not judgments *in personam.*[268]
(4) A claim for interest in respect of a general maritime claim.[269] The inclusion of this head of jurisdiction was a response to the decision in *The Medina Princess*,[270] in which the parties settled a large admiralty claim just prior to judgment leaving only the claim for interest outstanding; the court held that it did not have jurisdiction over the interest claim as no judgment had been given to which the interest owing could be added. The relevant English legislation has also been amended to allow the courts to award interest from the date on which the cause of action arose to the date on which the substantive claim was settled.[271]

5.90 As noted above,[272] Canada has an open list of maritime claims and therefore any claim relating to any matter coming within the class of subject of navigation and shipping is potentially within the Admiralty jurisdiction.[273] However, in addition to those claims mentioned in s 22(2) and which are largely equivalent to those claims contained in s 20(2) of the SCA 1981, the Federal Courts Act specifically

---

[265] Admiralty Act 1988, s 4(3)(s); this head of jurisdiction is contained in art 1(1)(q) of the 1999 Arrest Convention.

[266] *The Aifanourios* [1980] 2 Lloyd's Rep 403; *Gatoil International Inc v Arkwright-Boston Manufacturers Mutual Insurance Co* [1985] AC 255, [1985] 1 Lloyd's Rep 181.

[267] Admiralty Act 1988, s 4(2)(c) and (3)(u).

[268] Such a claim is not available in English law in relation to arbitration awards: *The Bumbesti* [2000] QB 559, [2000] 2 WLR 533, [1999] 2 Lloyd's Rep 481, at any rate where the *in rem* proceedings are issued after the award has been published, although that decision would not prevent fresh *in rem* proceedings based on the original cause of action: *The Rena K* [1979] QB 377, [1978] 3 WLR 431, [1978] 1 Lloyd's Rep 545. As to whether it is possible to enforce an *in rem* judgment under the Court's residual jurisdiction or CPR 61.5(1)(b), see paras 6.47 and following below.

[269] Admiralty Act 1988, s 4(3)(w).

[270] *The Medina Princess* [1962] 2 Lloyd's Rep 17; ALRC No 33, 1986, para 269.

[271] Senior Courts Act 1981, s 35A(1)(a).

[272] Para 5.04.

[273] Federal Courts Act, s 22(1).

confers jurisdiction in relation to any claim arising out of or in connection with a contract of marine insurance.[274]

Similarly, South Africa has an open list of maritime claims.[275] Nonetheless, jurisdiction is specifically conferred in relation to claims arising out of or relating to the following: **5.91**

(1) The rendering by means of any aircraft, ship, or other means, of services in connection with the carrying of persons or goods to or from a ship, or the provision of medical or other services to or in respect of the persons on being taken to or from a ship.[276]

(2) The remuneration of or payments or disbursements made by, or the acts or omissions of, any person appointed to act or who failed to act
  - (i) as an agent, whether as a ship's clearing, forwarding, or other kind of agent, in respect of any ship or any goods carried or to be carried or which were or ought to have been carried in a ship; or
  - (ii) as a broker in respect of any charter, sale, or other agreement relating to a ship or in connection with the carriage of goods in a ship or in connection with any insurance of a ship or any portion or part thereof or of other property referred to in s 3(5); or
  - (iii) as an attorney or adviser in respect of any matter mentioned in sub-paras (i) and (ii).[277]

(3) Marine insurance or any policy of marine insurance, including the protection and indemnity by any body of persons of its members in respect of marine matters.[278]

(4) The limitation of liability of the owner of a ship or of any other person entitled to any similar limitation of liability.[279]

(5) The distribution of a fund or any portion of a fund held or to be held by, or in accordance with the directions of, any court in the exercise of its Admiralty jurisdiction, or any officer of any court exercising such jurisdiction.[280]

(6) Any judgment or award relating to a maritime claim whether given or made in the Republic or elsewhere.[281] This head of jurisdiction is wider than its Australian counterpart[282] in that it includes the enforcement of any foreign or domestic *in personam* or *in rem* Admiralty judgment.

---

274 Federal Courts Act, s 22(2)(r).

275 Admiralty Jurisdiction Regulation Act 105 of 1983, s 1(1)(ee).

276 Ibid s 1(1)(n).

277 Ibid s 1(1)(p).

278 Ibid s 1(1)(u).

279 Ibid s 1(1)(w); *The Nagos* 1996 (2) SA 261.

280 Admiralty Jurisdiction Regulation Act 105 of 1983, s 1(1)(x).

281 Ibid s 1(1)(aa); *The Mineral Ordaz* 20 April 1999, M Stranex, *Shipping Cases of South Africa* (3rd edn) D 41.

282 Para 5.89(3) above.

(7) Wrongful or malicious proceedings in respect of or involving any property referred to in s 3(5) or the wrongful or malicious arrest, attachment, or detention of any such property, wherever such proceedings, arrest, attachment, or detention took place, and whether in the Republic or elsewhere, and any loss or damage contemplated in s 5(4).[283]

(8) Piracy, sabotage, or terrorism relating to property mentioned in s 3(5) or to persons on any ship.[284]

(9) Any matter not falling under any of the previous paragraphs in respect of which a court of admiralty of the Republic referred to in the Colonial Courts of Admiralty Act, 1890 (53 & 54 Vic c 27) of the United Kingdom, was empowered to exercise Admiralty jurisdiction immediately before the commencement of the Act, or any matter in respect of which a court of the Republic is empowered to exercise Admiralty jurisdiction.[285]

(10) Any contribution, indemnity or damages with regard to or arising out of any claim in respect of any matter mentioned above or any matter ancillary thereto, including the attachment of property to found or confirm jurisdiction,[286] the giving or release of any security, and the payment of interest.[287]

E. Claims Against Aircraft

5.92 An action *in rem* may be brought against an aircraft in the case of a claim in the nature of towage or pilotage relating to that aircraft if, at the time when the action is brought, the aircraft is beneficially owned by the person who would be liable on the claim in an action *in personam*.[288] Although Admiralty jurisdiction extends to any claim under the Salvage Convention 1989, in relation to salvage services, or in the nature of salvage in connection with an aircraft,[289] that jurisdiction can only be exercised *in personam*.

5.93 Hong Kong and Singapore have *in rem* jurisdiction in relation to aircraft to the same extent as England.[290] Canada's *in rem* jurisdiction in relation to aircraft extends to claims for salvage and to claims for towage and pilotage provided the aircraft is waterborne.[291] Neither the Australian, New Zealand, nor South African legislation extends *in rem* jurisdiction to claims relating to aircraft.

---

283 Admiralty Jurisdiction Regulation Act 105 of 1983, s 1(1)(bb).
284 Ibid s 1(1)(cc).
285 Ibid s 1(1)(dd).
286 As to attachment in South African law, see Chapter 2, n 85.
287 Admiralty Jurisdiction Regulation Act 105 of 1983, s 1(1)(ff).
288 s 21(5).
289 Senior Courts Act 1981, s 20(2)(j).
290 See para 5.08 above.
291 See para 5.11 above.

6

ADMIRALTY PROCEDURE AND THE ARREST PROCESS

Claims in admiralty are usually commercial disputes between commercial parties and the practice and procedure of the Admiralty Court is intended to facilitate the resolution of those disputes in a timely and cost-effective manner. It is, however, the availability of the arrest process for many admiralty claims, and the particular procedures relevant to collision and limitation claims, which distinguish the practices and procedures of the Admiralty Court from those in the Commercial Court and which give Admiralty practice its unique features.[1] This chapter is concerned **6.01**

[1] For the need to pay particular attention to those features if one purports to practise in the Admiralty Court see *Owners of the vessel 'Stolt Kestrel' v Owners of the vessel 'Niyazi S'* [2015] EWCA Civ 1035, [38].

primarily with the procedures that relate to a claim *in rem* and to the process of arrest. Matters which arise after the issue of the warrant for arrest are dealt with in the following chapter. The procedures specific to collision and limitation are dealt with separately in the chapters on those topics.

A. Sources of Admiralty Procedure

6.02 The specific procedure for admiralty claims is found in Part 61 of the Civil Procedure Rules (CPR), supplemented by the Practice Direction (PD61) for admiralty claims.[2] Admiralty claims are grouped with commercial matters generally and, therefore, the provisions of Part 58 of the CPR ('Commercial Court') apply to claims in the Admiralty Court unless there is some provision to the contrary in Part 61.[3] Practitioners are expected to follow the Admiralty & Commercial Courts Guide unless there is some inconsistency between it and the relevant Rules of Court or Practice Directions.[4] In addition to Part 61, its accompanying Practice Direction, and the Guide, there is also a small number of Practice Directions in force, some handed down in the pre-CPR era, which remain of occasional relevance in day-to-day practice.[5]

6.03 An 'admiralty claim' is one within the Admiralty jurisdiction of the High Court as set out in s 20 of the Senior Courts Act (SCA) 1981.[6] The scope of those claims is discussed in Chapter 2. Any admiralty claim may be started in the Admiralty Court,[7] but those claims most central to the Admiralty jurisdiction must be started in the Admiralty Court. Those claims are:[8]

---

[2] Similar, although not identical, procedures are used in the other jurisdictions considered in this work: Admiralty Rules 1988 (Admiralty Rules (Cth)); Federal Courts Rules SOR/98–106 (Federal Courts Rules); Rules of the High Court (Cap 4A) Order 75 (Rules of the High Court (HK); High Court Rules Part 25 (Rules of the High Court (NZ)); Rules of Court (Admiralty Proceedings) [Cap 322, R5] [2014 edn] Order 70 (Rules of Court (Sing), and Rules Regulating the Conduct of the Admiralty Proceedings of the Several Provincial and Local Divisions of the Supreme Court of South Africa (Admiralty Proceedings Rules (SAf)).

[3] CPR 61.1(3).

[4] The entirety of the CPR, including its practice directions, and the Admiralty & Commercial Courts Guide, are available online and readily accessed by online search.

[5] They are:

(1) *Practice Direction (Admiralty Court: [Claim Form])* [1979] 1 WLR 426, [1979] 2 All ER 155, [1979] 1 Lloyd's Rep 605, which requires separate claim forms to be used if both *in rem* and *in personam* proceedings are to be commenced. See *Owners of the vessel 'Stolt Kestrel' v Owners of the vessel 'Niyazi S'* [2014] EWHC 1731 (Admlty), [2014] 2 Lloyd's Rep 483, [57] and [76], [2015] EWCA Civ 1035, [15] and [38].
(2) *Practice Direction (Admiralty: Assessors' Remuneration)* [2007] 1 WLR 2508.
(3) *Practice Direction (Adm Ct Practice)* [1996] 1 WLR 127, [1996] 1 All ER 188, which provides that all costs (other than those summarily assessed) will be taxed (ie, assessed) in the Supreme Court Taxing Office (ie, by a costs judge).

These Practice Directions are collated and reproduced in the Admiralty section (2D) of Volume 2 of Civil Procedure (also known as the White Book), published annually by Sweet & Maxwell.

[6] CPR 61.1(2)(a).

[7] CPR 61.2(2).

[8] CPR 61.2(1).

(a) a claim—
  (i) *in rem*;
  (ii) for damage done by a ship;
  (iii) concerning the ownership of a ship;
  (iv) under the Merchant Shipping Act 1995 (MSA);
  (v) for loss of life or personal injury specified in 20(2)(f) of the Senior Courts Act 1981;
  (vi) by a master or member of the crew for wages;
  (vii) in the nature of towage or pilotage;
(b) collision, limitation, and salvage[9] claims.

B. Features of Admiralty Procedure

Several broad observations can be made about the practice and procedure in the Admiralty Court. The first, and perhaps most striking feature, is that the right to arrest a ship or other property is provided for only in the CPR, and not in the 1981 Act. This highlights the fact that the act of arrest is an administrative rather than judicial act. The right to arrest is, therefore, dependent, first, on the establishment of the jurisdiction of the High Court to determine the claim on the merits. **6.04**

Secondly, whilst the arrest process achieves the object of preserving an asset, whether it be a ship or other property, as security for the claim, the arrest process does not share the features of other civil processes that have a similar function, such as a freezing order. In particular, there is no requirement for the claimant to provide cross-undertakings in damages in case the arrest proves to be unjustified,[10] nor is there any requirement to show a risk that the assets might be dissipated, nor indeed even to establish the existence of a *prima facie* case. This has led to criticism of the arrest process as 'draconian' and unduly prejudicial to the interests of shipowners, and to the inclusion in the 1999 Arrest Convention of provision for an arresting party to provide counter-security.[11] **6.05**

Thirdly, and at variance with the procedure in the Commercial Court, many interlocutory applications are heard by the Admiralty Registrar, who is bestowed with all the powers of the Admiralty Judge except where otherwise provided.[12] In **6.06**

[9] Salvage claims are defined even more broadly than in s 20(2)(j) (paras 5.52 above and following) in CPR 61.1(2)(f) to mean claims:

  (i) for or in the nature of salvage;
  (ii) for special compensation under art 14 of the Salvage Convention;
  (iii) for the apportionment of salvage (ie, between co-salvors); and
  (iv) arising out of or connected with any contract for salvage services.

[10] *The Bazias 3 & The Bazias 4* [1993] QB 673.

[11] Arrest Convention 1999, art 6(1).

[12] CPR 61.1(4).

addition, the case management provisions applicable to commercial cases[13] are supplemented in the case of admiralty proceedings by the provision in para 2 of PD61, for the early classification and streaming of cases based on the nature of the issues and the sums in dispute, and the various matters required to be considered under Rule 26.8 of the CPR.[14] This is akin to the 'track-allocation' procedure which takes place elsewhere in the High Court,[15] but not in the Commercial Court.

6.07 A fourth feature of the Admiralty jurisdiction worthy of mention in this connection is the use of assessors. Although provision is made for the use of assessors generally in civil litigation,[16] it is probably safe to say that in Admiralty they are more institutionalized than in any other forum. Assessors are usually[17] mariners with expertise relevant to the particular case.[18] They are most commonly used in collision claims, but the court is permitted to sit with assessors in any claim involving issues of seamanship or navigation,[19] such as some cargo claims. It must be said, however, that the use of assessors outside collision cases is rare.[20] The practice associated with assessors is therefore discussed more fully in Chapter 9. In the meantime, the following points may be noted.

(1) Where assessors are used, the parties are not permitted to call expert evidence on the issues of seamanship and navigation without the leave of the court, because the assessors take the place of expert witnesses.[21]
(2) Provision is made for assessors' remuneration in the CPR[22] and in the relevant Practice Direction,[23] but the court will usually seek an undertaking from the claimant to pay the remuneration on demand after the case has concluded.

6.08 In common with the Commercial Court, the procedures of the Admiralty jurisdiction place considerable reliance on the parties and their legal advisors to facilitate the resolution of the dispute without the need for the court to make orders at every

---

[13] As set out in CPR Part 58, its accompanying Practice Direction, and the Admiralty & Commercial Courts Guide.
[14] PD61 §§2.1–2.3.
[15] CPR Part 26.
[16] CPR 35.15.
[17] There was once a practice of using merchant assessors in references before the Registrar. This is no longer the case, although there is no reason in principle why parties could not request it.
[18] Although little or no opportunity is afforded to the parties to assess the relevance, currency, or level of expertise of the particular assessor.
[19] CPR 61.13.
[20] In *Gard Marine & Energy Ltd v China National Chartering Co Ltd ('The Ocean Victory')* [2013] 4 All ER (Comm) 1058; [2014] 1 Lloyd's Rep 59, Teare J, the Admiralty Judge, observed at [22]: 'It used to be the case that the Commercial Court, when deciding safe port cases, did so with the assistance of an Elder Brother of Trinity House as an assessor (see *Compania Naviera Maropan v Bowater's('the Stork')* [1955] 2 Lloyd's Reports 397, *Leeds Shipping Company v Societe Francaise Bunge (the 'Eastern City')* [1958] 2 Lloyd's Reports 127 and *Tage Berglund v Montoro Shipping Corporation (the 'Dagmar')* [1968] 2 Lloyd's Reports 563) but that practice seems to be in abeyance. In an appropriate case it perhaps ought to be resurrected. It might save expense and time.'
[21] CPR 61.13.
[22] CPR 35.15.
[23] Above, n 5.

step of the proceeding. This reliance can be seen most readily in the procedures for the issue of an arrest warrant, which is done on the basis of a declaration made by the claimant's legal advisor; and in the use of undertakings given both to the court and to other parties interested in the proceedings. These undertakings are given, for example, in the context of seeking the issue of an arrest warrant, requesting a caution against arrest or release, making applications in relation to the vessel whilst under arrest, and making an application for valuation and sale of the vessel.

Finally, mention must be made at slightly greater length of the Admiralty Marshal, a unique feature of Admiralty jurisdiction. **6.09**

C. The Admiralty Marshal

The Admiralty Marshal is integral to the practice and procedure of the Admiralty Court and it is important to understand his role and its attendant responsibilities. The office of the Admiralty Marshal dates back to the earliest days of the Admiralty jurisdiction.[24] It was described in Pritchard's *Digest of Admiralty and Maritime Law* in the following terms:[25] **6.10**

> The Marshal is the executive officer of the court, and performs duties analogous to those of the Sheriff at common law. He is charged with the execution of all process of the court, except writs and subpoenas . . . The Marshal was formerly remunerated by fees but by Admiralty Court Act 1840 3 & 4 Vic c65, ss5–18 (now repealed),[26] a yearly salary was substituted for them, and he was prohibited from taking any fees for his own use. He attends the sittings of the court and carries the silver oar as the emblem of the maritime jurisdiction of the court.

Although the Marshal no longer attends court sittings as a matter of course[27] nor regularly carries around the Admiralty oar,[28] now as then he has a broad responsibility for an arrested vessel while it remains in custody.[29] In *The Hoop* it was said that: **6.11**

> The credit of the Court is concerned in the safe-keeping of the property under its protection. If any such property is lost, it is at least the duty of the Marshal to be prepared to shew that it was not lost by any default of his.[30]

---

[24] Australia refers to the holder of this office as the Admiralty Marshal in the Federal jurisdiction but as the Sheriff in the State jurisdictions; Canada, Singapore, and South Africa describe the office holder as the Sheriff, whilst Hong Kong prefers the term Bailiff, and in New Zealand the office holder is described as the Registrar.

[25] Pritchard, *Digest of Admiralty and Maritime Law* (3rd edn, 1887) 1472.

[26] Following a scandal involving the Admiralty Registrar. For the details, see F L Wiswall, *The Development of Admiralty Jurisdiction and Practice since 1800—An English Study with American Comparisons* (1970).

[27] The Marshal can and does attend court, however, when applications are heard for directions in relation to vessels under arrest, eg, in order to advise the court as to the practicalities involved in keeping a particular vessel under arrest, or as to whether appraisement and sale in the usual way is likely to produce a useful result.

[28] Affectionately known as the 'Admiralty paddle', it is fixed to the judge's bench whenever he is sitting in open court as the Admiralty (rather than as a Commercial Court) Judge.

[29] Although he is not answerable as bailee of the property and is under no obligation to keep it insured: PD61 para 5.7 and para N13 of the Admiralty & Commercial Courts Guide.

[30] *The Hoop* (1801) 4 C Rob 145, 146.

Under CPR Part 61 and PD61, the Marshal has a broad discretion as to the way in which he may exercise his functions and perform his duties. For instance, where a party provides the Marshal with an undertaking other than in prescribed form, it must be given in writing and to the satisfaction of the Marshal (or 'in accordance with such other arrangements as he may require').[31] It is important to bear in mind that the Admiralty Marshal acts as an officer of the court and not as a party to the proceedings. As such, he is entitled to make an application in a proceeding whenever the court can do so of its own motion;[32] there can be no doubt that he may also do so whenever he requires directions from the court.

6.12 Coupled with this responsibility is the need for adequate funds to carry out these functions. Funding of the Marshal's responsibilities in relation to the arrest of a ship is dealt with by the use of the undertakings referred to above which enable the Marshal to obtain or recover funds on demand from the applicants or their solicitors. Occasionally, the Marshal may be left in the unsatisfactory position of being out of pocket while he waits on calls for his fees and expenses to be met.[33]

D. The Procedure Applicable to Claims *In Personam*

6.13 As discussed in Chapter 2, not every claim within the Admiralty jurisdiction of the High Court can be commenced *in rem*. The right to bring an action *in rem* is not available for any claim for damage received by a ship, limitation claims, and applications under the Merchant Shipping Acts; such claims may only be brought *in personam*.

In addition, it will sometimes be desirable or even necessary to bring *in personam* proceedings as well as or instead of *in rem* proceedings, eg, where a vessel has changed ownership between the cause of action arising and the issue of proceedings: even if the claim attracts a maritime lien, the amount recoverable will be limited to (at most) the value of the ship. In addition, service out of the jurisdiction is less restricted in *in personam* than in *in rem* actions, provided of course that the court has subject-matter jurisdiction from another source, a factor which may be important where the vessel seldom if ever calls at a port in the jurisdiction.

[31] PD61 §14.1. A dissatisfied party must apply to the Registrar: §14.2.

[32] In addition to any specific permissions granted by the rules, such as CPR 61.8(9).

[33] Pursuant to the undertaking given in form ADM4 (below, para 6.59). In Australia some attempt has been made to protect the Marshal from such situations. In the Federal Court of Australia, the practice has developed of requiring an applicant for an arrest warrant to tender AUD5,000 on account of the Marshal's expenses at the time of making the application. This practice has been regularized by r 41(2) of the Admiralty Rules which was inserted by para 14 of the Admiralty Amendment Rules 2006 (No 1), Select Legislative Instrument 2006 No 287. See also *The Sheriff of Cape Town v The Argun* 2001 (3) SA 1230 (Supreme Court of Appeal of South Africa) where the Sheriff was forced to bring an application to compel the arresting parties and the owners to fund the costs of the preservation of the ship.

With the exception of limitation actions[34] and collision claims,[35] *in personam* claims[36] proceed largely in accordance with Part 58 of the CPR.[37]

An *in personam* claim commenced in Admiralty is identified as such in the initiating process.[38] The claimant may either be named or described but if the latter, must identify himself by name if requested to do so by any other party.[39] The defendant must be named in the claim form.[40] Any person who acknowledges service or files a defence must identify himself in the defence and, if applicable, supply his date of birth.[41] 6.14

E. The Procedure Applicable to Claims *In Rem*

Commencement of a claim *in rem*

A claim *in rem* is started by the issue of an *in rem* claim form.[42] Where a claim form is issued against more than one vessel, the names of all vessels other than the one served should be struck through by amendment immediately after service.[43] Only one vessel may be proceeded against in an action *in rem*,[44] and multiple actions *in rem* in respect of the same claim are, where the cause of action gives rise only to a statutory right of action *in rem*, prohibited by statute.[45] Where it 6.15

---

34 Chapter 10.

35 Chapter 9. Collision claims may only be brought *in personam* in the limited cases set out in s 22 of the 1981 Act: para 9.05 below.

36 Or, as they are now to be known—with an opacity produced by overzealous application of plain English (para 1.12 above), and notwithstanding the use of the term in the Senior Courts Act 1981—'other claims': PD61 §12.

37 PD61 §§12.1 and 12.2; the chief exception being the early case management scrutiny required by PD61 §2 (para 6.06 above). In practical terms, this may make it more attractive to commence such proceedings in the Commercial Court, rather than the Admiralty Court, since the question of venue for trial is not debated in the Commercial Court (if at all) until the later stage of the case management conference, when there is an opportunity to make oral submissions on the point (to a judge who has not already decided it). CPR Part 58 governs proceedings in the Commercial Court. Commercial Court procedure is not explored further in this work and reference should be made instead to one of the standard practitioners' guides.

38 PD61 §12.3 and Form ADM1A. For a list of the Court's forms and guidance as to where they may be found, see Appendix 7.

39 PD61 §12.4.

40 PD61 §12.5.

41 PD61 §12.6. Provision for this is made in the Acknowledgment of Service form, ADM2.

42 CPR 61.3(2); PD61 §§3.1 and 3.2 and Form ADM1. An Admiralty claim form can be issued when the Registry is closed: Admiralty & Commercial Courts Guide N7.1–7.4 and Appendix 3. An inadvertent use of the *in personam* form (ADM1A), even where the error is culpable, may, at least where the error is clear, be an error of procedure capable of remedy under CPR 3.10: *The Styliani Z* [2015] EWHC 3060 (Admlty). Note that Teare J did not address whether the normal incidents of *in rem* procedure, such as the statutory lien, would apply from the original date of issue or the date of remedy.

43 *The Freccia del Nord* [1989] 1 Lloyd's Rep 388.

44 *The Banco* [1971] P 137, [1971] 2 WLR 335, [1971] 1 All ER 524, [1971] 1 Lloyd's Rep 49.

45 Senior Courts Act 1981, s 21(8).

is possible to do so, therefore, it may be prudent to issue multiple claim forms covering separate claims or groups of claims; this will be possible, for example, where distinct parcels of cargo carried under separate bills of lading have been lost or damaged.

6.16 As with *in personam* proceedings, the claimant may be named or described in the claim form; if the latter, he must identify himself by name if requested to do so by any other party.[46] The defendant, on the other hand, *must* be described[47]—but when acknowledging service must identify himself by name and state the nature of his ownership.[48] Except in collision claims, particulars of claim must be contained in or be served with the claim form or be served on the defendant within seventy-five days after service of the claim form.[49]

6.17 Although as a matter of English domestic law[50] the court is not seised until service of the claim form,[51] that is not to say that issue of the claim form is without wider consequences. In addition to the effect of creating a 'statutory lien' over the *res*,[52] it is the issue of the claim form which amounts to 'suing' for the purposes of arts 2 and 6 of the Brussels and Lugano Conventions.[53] It also creates seisin for the purpose of the *lis pendens* provisions of the European Jurisdiction Regulation[54] and the Lugano II Convention.[55]

---

46 PD61 §3.2.

47 PD61 §3.3.

48 PD61 §§3.4, 3.9.

49 CPR 61.3(3). This is a remarkably long period (fourteen days is the default under CPR 7.4(1)(b)), the purpose of which is presumably to give time for any interlocutory wrangling, eg, over the arrest of the *res*, to have been resolved in good time, so as not to interfere with the service of the particulars of claim.

50 And thus for the purpose of seisin under the Brussels Convention, which has, however, largely been superseded, first by the Brussels I Regulation (Council Regulation (EC) No 44/2001) and more recently by the Brussels I Regulation 'recast' (Regulation (EU) No 1215/2012), which applies to proceedings commenced after 1 January 2015. The Brussels Convention (which itself went through five iterations) still applies to a small number of non-European territories of Member States, to which EU Regulations do not extend. The Lugano Convention, which regulates jurisdiction between EU and EFTA countries, had largely followed the wording and structure of the Brussels Convention. In December 2007, however, its text was replaced by a near-copy of the original Brussels I Regulation. It has different commencement dates, depending on the EFTA country: it applies to proceedings commenced on or after 1 January 2010 (Norway), 1 January 2011 (Switzerland), and 1 May 2011 (Iceland). Seisin under the Lugano II Convention is the same as under the Brussels I Regulation, ie, the date of issue of proceedings (art 30).

51 *Dresser v Falcongate* [1992] QB 502, [1992] 2 WLR 319, [1992] 2 All ER 450, [1991] 2 Lloyd's Rep 557; see also *The Ursus* [2015] SGHCR 07.

52 Para 2.07(1) above.

53 *Canada Trust v Stolzenberg (No 2)* [2002] 1 AC 1, [2000] 3 WLR 1376, [2000] 4 All ER 481. The significance of this is that it is at the date of issue, rather than service, of proceedings that the facts needed to found jurisdiction, such as domicile, are to be looked for. The same would apply under the Brussels I Regulations (art 3 in 44/2001 and art 4 in 1215/2012) and the Lugano II Convention (art 3).

54 Brussels I Regulation 44/2001, art 30. Brussels I Regulation 'recast' 1215/2012, art 32.

55 See n 50 above.

Service of a claim form *in rem*

A claim form *in rem* may be served: 6.18

(1) on property, by fixing a copy of the claim form on the outside of the property in a position which may reasonably be expected to be seen;[56]
(2) on freight, by fixing a copy of the claim form either on the cargo in respect of which the freight was earned or on the ship on which the cargo was carried;[57]
(3) on the fund in court, by filing the claim form at the court.[58]

It must be served within twelve months of the date of its issue,[59] unless its validity is extended by the court.[60] If the property is to be arrested or is already under arrest, the Marshal will serve the claim form.[61] In all other cases, the claimant must serve the claim form[62] and is under a duty to serve the claim form promptly.[63]

Substituted service is not generally appropriate in *in rem* proceedings for two reasons. The first is that the property must be within the jurisdiction to be susceptible to the jurisdiction of the court[64] and substituted service has the potential to subvert that connection. The second reason stems from the traditional view that the *in rem* jurisdiction is not invoked until the writ is served on the ship and the warrant executed.[65] PD61 makes clear the circumstances and ways in which service of a claim form *in rem* is possible: 6.19

(1) Where a person with custody of the property to be served refuses access to that property, the claim form is served by leaving a copy of it with that person.[66]

---

56 PD61 §3.6(1)(a).
57 PD61 §3.6(1)(b).
58 PD61 §3.6(3).
59 CPR 61.3(5)(b).
60 Para 6.20 below.
61 PD61 §3.7.
62 PD61 §3.8.
63 *The Johnny Two* [1992] 2 Lloyd's Rep 257.
64 *The Freccia del Nord* [1989] 1 Lloyd's Rep 388. Under the CPR the position is put beyond doubt by PD61 §3.6(7), which expressly requires 'the property against which the claim is brought or part of it' to be 'within the jurisdiction of the court' if an order for substituted service under CPR 6.15 is to be made. An attempt to argue otherwise was dismissed as 'astonishing' in *The Stolt Kestrel* [2015] EWCA Civ 1035, [95]–[97], where para 6.19 of this work was quoted with approval.
65 *The Banco* [1971] P 137, 153, [1971] 2 WLR 335, 341, [1971] 1 All ER 524, 533, [1971] 1 Lloyd's Rep 49, 53; *The Good Herald* [1987] 1 Lloyd's Rep 236, 238.
66 PD61 §3.6(2); In *BC Ltd v Roger Mills* (unreported Docket T-2587-97, 26 January 1998), the Federal Court of Canada was concerned with a situation where the vessel, the 'Zomby Woof', had been left in the possession of a Rottweiler. As the vessel was clearly within the jurisdiction, the court authorized substituted service of the statement of claim, the affidavit in support of a warrant and the arrest warrant itself in the mailbox of the owner of the vessel so that 'the Sheriff will stand a sporting chance of staying beyond the reach of the jaws of Mr Hill's Rottweiler'. It is not difficult to imagine a similar path being adopted in the English Admiralty Court.

(2) Where there is a caution against arrest,[67] the claim form is served on the person named in the caution as being authorized to accept service.[68]

(3) Alternatively, a solicitor may be authorized to accept service,[69] the parties may make an agreement about the manner in which service is to be effected,[70] or the court may make directions as to the manner of service,[71] provided that the property, or part of it, is within the jurisdiction of the court.[72]

Renewal of a claim form *in rem*

6.20 If a claim form is not served during the initial period of its validity, then an application can be made for it to be extended. Particular considerations apply in the context of collision claims under s 190 Merchant Shipping Act 1995; they are addressed below at paras 9.07 and following. In the general run of cases, the application must be made under CPR 7.6.[73] The considerations relevant to renewal of a writ *in rem* where service had not been effected were outlined by Brandon J in *The Berny*.[74] The applicant was expected to establish:

(1) that none of the ships proceeded against in respect of the same claim, whether in one action or more than one action, had been, or would be, present at a place within the jurisdiction during the currency of the writ; alternatively

(2) that if any of the ships had been, or would be, present at a place within the jurisdiction during the currency of the writ, the length or other circumstances

---

[67] For reasons unknown, in PD61 §3.6(4) and CPR 61.9(6), the term 'notice against arrest' appears where clearly 'caution against arrest' was meant.

[68] PD61 §3.6(4).

[69] PD61 §3.6(5), for example, in an acknowledgment of service filed before service—a counter-intuitive procedural step made possible by CPR 61.3(6), though not of itself obviating the need for service: PD61 §§3.7, 3.8.

[70] PD61 §3.6(6).

[71] Pursuant to CPR 6.15: PD61 §3.6(7).

[72] PD61 §3.6(7).

[73] The application should, as a 'general rule', be made before the time to serve has expired (CPR 7.6(2)(a)); in practical terms, an application made after the expiry of the initial 12 month period, under CPR 7.6(3), will face real difficulties, as the courts are unsympathetic to what are, by definition, late applications. In either case, it must be borne in mind that an extension obtained without notice before service can be challenged by the defendant after service. See generally (in respect of applications under CPR 7.6(2)) *Hashtroodi v Hancock* [2004] 1 WLR 3206 and *Collier v Williams* [2006] EWCA Civ 20, [2006] 1 WLR 1945 and the notes to CPR 7.6 in any practitioners' civil practice guide. See also, by way of example, *F G Hawkes (Western) Ltd v Beli Shipping Co Limited* [2009] EWHC 1740 (Comm), [2010] 1 Lloyd's Rep 449, where the Court declined to grant an extension of time for service of a claim form because the delay in service was due to 'neglect or oversight in getting on with service until too late and for reasons solely attributable to the Claimant or its legal representatives': at 454, [35].

[74] *The Berny* [1979] QB 80, [1978] 2 WLR 387, [1978] 1 All ER 1065, [1977] 2 Lloyd's Rep 533. See also *Dagnell v JL Freedman & Co* [1993] 2 All ER 161, [1993] 1 WLR 388; *Konstantinidis v World Tankers Corp Inc (The World Harmony)* [1967] P 341, [1965] 2 All ER 139; *The Salviscount* [1984] 1 Lloyd's Rep 164. These authorities should be approached with caution: the rules in the CPR governing extension of originating process are not the same as those which prevailed under RSC Order 6 rule 8. In particular, the test of 'good reason' no longer applies, at any rate in quite the same way, under CPR 7.6(2) (see the cases referred to in n 73 above). *The Berny* was cited by Hamblen J

of her visit to or stay at such a place were not, or would not be, such as to afford reasonable opportunity for effecting service on her and arresting her;[75] alternatively

(3) that if any of the ships had been, or would be, present at a place within the jurisdiction during the currency of the writ, the value of such ship was not, or would not be, great enough to provide adequate security for the claim, whereas the value of all or some or one of the ships proceeded against would be sufficient, or anyhow more nearly sufficient, to do so.[76]

These considerations are likely to inform, although not determine, the exercise of the court's discretion under CPR 7.6, the chief component of which is otherwise consideration of the overriding objective set out in CPR Part 1.[77] The evidence in support of an application for an extension will therefore need to condescend to the steps taken by the claimant's solicitors to track the vessel(s),[78] so as to be in a position to serve the claim form when it comes into the jurisdiction. 6.21

The fact that a vessel has been sold after the issue of a writ but before its service has been held to be an 'overwhelming' reason for renewing the writ, as the claimant would be unable to issue a fresh writ *in rem*.[79] However, it is submitted that the court would only renew a claim form in such circumstances if the claimant were otherwise able to satisfy it (on the basis of Brandon J's criteria) that renewal was appropriate. Moreover, sale of the vessel on its own would be insufficient on an application brought *after* expiry of the claim form, as would the third of Brandon J's considerations. That is because the court has no jurisdiction to extend time after the expiry of the claim form unless the court or the claimant has been 'unable' to serve it (in the case of the claimant, having taken all reasonable steps to do so).[80] Only if the claimant is able to satisfy the court in that regard can other matters affecting the exercise of the court's discretion be considered—and matters such as the sale of a ship would have to be balanced against other factors, such as the

---

in *Owners of the vessel 'Stolt Kestrel' v Owners of the vessel 'Niyazi S'* (n 81 below) at [49], but in the limited context of the difficulty of effecting service on a vessel in an anchorage. Hamblen J was moreover considering the availability of the mandatory extension of time under s 190(6) MSA 1995, applicable only in collision cases, not the general power to extend time under the CPR.

[75] In this regard, Hamblen J in the Admiralty Court considered that the claimant in *Owners of the vessel 'Stolt Kestrel' v Owners of the vessel 'Niyazi S'* [2014] EWHC 1731 (Admlty), [2014] 2 Lloyd's Rep 483 had not had a reasonable opportunity to arrest the defendant vessel in circumstances where the vessel had been present in the jurisdiction, at anchorage, only for a further four days following the collision (a finding not challenged on appeal). See, however, n 74 above: this was not a CPR 7.6 case.

[76] *The Berny* [1979] QB 80, 103, [1978] 2 WLR 387, 406, [1978] 1 All ER 1068, 1082, [1977] 2 Lloyd's Rep 533, 546.

[77] See the cases referred to in n 73 above.

[78] A reasonably competent solicitor is expected to be aware of the Lloyd's Maritime Information Service and be able to access the relevant information: *Ministry of Defence v The Owners of the ship Radnes* (unreported, Queen's Bench Division, (Admiralty Court) 20 October 1995 per Rix J).

[79] *The Helene Roth* [1980] 1 All ER 1078, [1980] 1 Lloyd's Rep 477.

[80] CPR 7.6(3).

perceived justice of permitting an action *in rem* to be brought against a vessel no longer owned by the party who would be liable *in personam*,[81] well after, say, the expiry of a Hague Rules time limit.

Acknowledgement of service of a claim *in rem*

Generally

6.22 An acknowledgement of service must be filed[82] within fourteen days after service of the claim form,[83] whether or not the claim form contains particulars of the claim.[84] Any person wishing to defend the claim, regardless of whether or not they have been served with the claim form, may file an acknowledgement of service.[85] A person who acknowledges service must identify himself by his full name,[86] state the nature of his ownership,[87] and provide his date of birth.[88]

In relation to challenges to the jurisdiction

6.23 An acknowledgement of service does not deprive a defendant of any right to dispute the jurisdiction of the court.[89] On the contrary, if a defendant wishes to dispute jurisdiction[90] he must file an acknowledgement of service, and would be well advised to tick the box indicating an intention to contest the jurisdiction. He must then, within the time stipulated by the Rules,[91] make an application pursuant to Part 11 of the CPR. It is not necessary for a defence to be filed before such an application is brought,[92] and since defending the claim on the merits would almost certainly amount to a submission to the jurisdiction, he would be well advised not to do so.

6.24 A defendant who fails to file an acknowledgement of service and who does not make an application disputing the jurisdiction of the court will be treated as having accepted the court's jurisdiction to try the claim.[93] However, if a defendant makes an unsuccessful application under Part 11, his earlier acknowledgement of service ceases to have effect,[94] so that if the Rules require an acknowledgement of

[81] In *The Helene Roth*, the transfer was to another company in the same group, which might not attract the same degree of sympathy as a wholly arm's length transfer: cf *The Tjaskemolen (now named Visvliet)* [1997] 2 Lloyd's Rep 465.
[82] Except in relation to limitation claims (CPR 61.11(6)) as to which see Chapter 10.
[83] CPR 61.3(4); PD61 §3.4 and Form ADM2.
[84] PD61 §3.5
[85] CPR 61.3(6).
[86] PD61 §3.4, 3.9.
[87] PD61 §3.9.
[88] PD16 §10.7. Provision is made for this on the Acknowledgment of Service form (ADM2).
[89] PD61 §3.11; CPR 11(3). The Acknowledgment of Service form (ADM2) makes provision for the party acknowledging service to indicate whether or not jurisdiction is contested.
[90] Below, paras 6.30 and following.
[91] This is usually fourteen days (CPR 11(4)), but two months in collision claims (CPR 61.4(4)).
[92] CPR 11(9).
[93] CPR 11(5).
[94] CPR 11(7)(a).

service[95] a fresh acknowledgement must be filed within fourteen days after (or such other period as the court may direct on) the disposal of the Part 11 application.[96]

In relation to disputes regarding security

Where an *in rem* claim form has been issued and security sought, if there is a dispute between the parties as to the appropriate form and amount in which the security should be provided, any person who has filed an acknowledgement of service may apply for an order specifying the amount and form of the security.[97] **6.25**

Judgment in default

In any claim *in rem*, apart from a collision claim,[98] a claimant may obtain judgment in default of an acknowledgement of service if the defendant has not filed such acknowledgement within fourteen days after service of the claim.[99] Similarly, judgment in default of defence can be obtained where the relevant time limit for so doing has expired;[100] since, in an action *in rem*, an acknowledgement of service will *ex hypothesi* have been filed, the period for serving the defence will be twenty-eight days after the service of the particulars of claim.[101] A claimant who seeks judgment in default must file:[102] **6.26**

(1) an application notice;[103]
(2) a certificate proving service of the claim form;[104] and
(3) evidence proving the claim to the satisfaction of the court.[105]

This material must be served on all those who have entered cautions against release, unless the court otherwise orders.[106]

In addition, judgment in default is also available in default of the provision of security pursuant to the undertaking which must be given when a caution against arrest is entered.[107] Where a party at whose instance a caution against arrest has **6.27**

[95] Which is the case in all *in rem* proceedings: see, generally, CPR 61.3(4) and, in relation to collision actions, CPR 61.4(3).
[96] CPR 11(7)(b).
[97] CPR 61.5(10).
[98] Judgment in default is only available in collision claims for failure to file a collision statement of case (CPR 61.9(2)).
[99] CPR 61.9(1)(a).
[100] CPR 61.9(1)(b).
[101] CPR Part 15.4(1)(b). This may be anything up to 103 days after service of the claim form, if the particulars of claim were not served with it.
[102] CPR 61.9(3)(a).
[103] CPR 61.9(3)(a)(i); PD61 §8.1 and Form ADM13.
[104] CPR 61.9(3)(a)(ii).
[105] CPR 61.9(3)(a)(iii). In this respect the application for default judgment in an *in rem* claim is more closely analogous to a summary judgment application under CPR Part 24 than it is to an application for default judgment under CPR Part 12.
[106] CPR 61.9(4).
[107] Para 6.58 below.

been entered has been served with a claim form, and the sum claimed does not exceed the amount specified in the undertaking given in the request, the claimant may seek judgment in default against that party where the undertaking has not been fulfilled within fourteen days after service of the claim form.[108] No particular procedure or form is prescribed for such an application, which should therefore be made in the usual way under CPR Part 23 and supported by appropriate evidence.

6.28 The court has power to set aside or vary any judgment entered by default.[109] The rules do not themselves prescribe the criteria pursuant to which the court may set aside a default judgment, but in *The Selby Paradigm*[110] it was held that the discretion to set aside a judgment arises when the justice of the matter so requires. David Steel J held that, subject to such matters of delay and prejudice, the threshold is for the applicant to establish clearly that, by reason of the absence of any representations on the part of the defendants (ie, on the application for a default judgment) there was in fact a real prospect of success in defending the claim.[111] In other words, notwithstanding that judgment will (or should) not be granted in the absence of evidence proving the claim 'to the satisfaction of the Court', the test for setting aside a default judgment *in rem* is the same as or functionally indistinguishable from that provided in CPR Part 13 (for setting aside an ordinary default judgment) or that which applies to applications for summary judgment or for permission to appeal, ie, a more than fanciful prospect of success.[112]

Summary judgment

6.29 Summary judgment cannot be ordered against a defendant *in rem*.[113] There is, however, nothing to prevent a defendant applying for summary judgment against a claimant,[114] on the ground that the claim has no reasonable prospect of success.[115]

Challenges to the jurisdiction

6.30 A defendant who wishes to dispute the court's jurisdiction (or its exercise) must make an application pursuant to CPR Part 11 or, where the vessel has been arrested, apply to set aside the arrest pursuant to CPR 61.8(4)(b).[116] Other than where the

[108] CPR 61.9(6).
[109] CPR 61.9(5).
[110] *The Selby Paradigm* [2004] EWHC 1804 (Admlty), [2004] 2 Lloyd's Rep 714.
[111] Ibid 717, [29].
[112] *Swain v Hillman* [2001] 1 All ER 91; *Tanfern Ltd v Cameron-MacDonald (Practice Note)* [2000] 1 WLR 1311, [2000] 2 All ER 801.
[113] CPR 24.3(2)(b); *The Failal* [2000] 1 Lloyd's Rep 473.
[114] CPR 24.3(1).
[115] CPR Part 24.2 (a)(i), as to which, see *Three Rivers District Council v Bank of England (No 3)* [2001] UKHL 16, [2003] 2 AC 1, [2001] 2 All ER 513.
[116] See in this connection para 6.47 below. The sensible course, where both are available, will be to bring the application under both procedural heads.

underlying cause of action is one in respect of which the parties have agreed to arbitration,[117] challenges to the court's *in rem* jurisdiction will be limited to the following, considered briefly in turn below:

(1) Cases where the jurisdiction *in rem* has not been properly invoked, either because of the nature of the claim or because of the identity of the vessel.
(2) Applications under the Brussels or Lugano Conventions or under the EU Jurisdiction Regulations.
(3) Claims arising out of contracts with foreign jurisdiction clauses.
(4) Claims which offend s 34 of the Civil Jurisdiction and Judgments Act (CJJA) 1982.
(5) Claims in respect of which another available forum is clearly more appropriate.

No jurisdiction under sections 20 to 21 of the Senior Courts Act 1981

In other contexts the onus lies on the claimant to establish the factual connecting factors to the standard of good arguable case—which means, where there is a competing jurisdiction under the European Conventions or Regulations, that it must show that it has the better of the argument.[118] The position is different in relation to the *in rem* jurisdiction of the Admiralty Court, in relation to which two distinct aspects must be considered. **6.31**

(1) Is the claim within one of the relevant jurisdictional heads? In most cases the question will be whether the claim is one of those listed in s 20(2) of the SCA 1981, although others may in theory be possible.[119] This question of law must be resolved in the claimant's favour for his claim to proceed and 'for the purpose of determining that question it is necessary to assume, without deciding, that the respondents have an arguable case in law in respect of their claim'.[120]

---

[117] As to which, see paras 11.43 and following below.

[118] *Canada Trust v Stolzenberg (No 2)* [2002] 1 AC 1, [2000] 3 WLR 1376, [2000] 4 All ER 481, in relation to the establishment of domicile for the purpose of the Lugano Convention. *Seaconsar Far East Ltd v Bank Markazi Jomhouri Islami Iran* [1994] 1 AC 438, [1993] 3 WLR 756, [1993] 4 All ER 456, [1994] 1 Lloyd's Rep 1, in relation to cases requiring permission to serve out of the jurisdiction. *Bols Distilleries BV v Superior Yacht Services Ltd* [2006] UKPC 45, [2007] 1 WLR 12, [2007] 1 All ER (Comm) 460, [2007] 1 Lloyd's Rep 683 suggested that the claimant must show 'much the better' of the argument. The requirement for 'much' the better of the argument to be shown was the subject of cogent criticism in Briggs & Rees, *Civil Jurisdiction & Judgments* (6th edn, 2015) at para 2.126, criticism accepted by Aikens LJ in *Joint Stock Company Aeroflot Russian Airlines v Berezovsky* [2013] EWCA Civ 784, [2013] 2 Lloyd's Rep 242, [50]: 'The only point of the word is to emphasise the fact that if the two arguments are equal, then the party asserting … jurisdiction will not succeed.' This was followed by Carr J in *CH Offshore Ltd v PDV Marina SA* [2015] EWHC 595 (Comm), [39]–[40].

[119] Conceivable examples include claims within the residual jurisdiction, as in *The Despina GK* [1983] QB 214, [1982] 2 Lloyd's Rep 555, as to which see para 6.50 below.

[120] *The Antonis P Lemos* [1985] AC 711, 724, [1985] 2 WLR 468, 471, [1985] 1 All ER 695, 698, [1985] 1 Lloyd's Rep 283, 286; *The St Elefterio* [1957] P 179, 185; *The Moschanthy* [1971] 1 Lloyd's Rep 37, 42.

There is no scope, it is submitted, for such questions to be resolved on a 'good arguable case' basis; rather the issue must be finally determined.[121] That is because of the consequences that the establishment of *in rem* jurisdiction carries with it, in terms of the rights over the *res* both as between the particular claimant and the owners and as between each of those parties and others.

(2) Are the requisite factors connecting the 'relevant person' to the vessel established?[122] The burden is on the claimant to establish these on the balance of probabilities.[123] For the same reasons as arise in relation to the first issues, it is submitted that this must be correct in principle. In an appropriate case, this could involve disclosure and cross-examination; in effect, a trial of the issue.

Applications under the European legislation

6.32 Where the party sued in an action *in rem* is domiciled in an EU or European Free Trade Association (EFTA) country (or one of its non-European dominions), then the Brussels or Lugano Conventions or the EU Jurisdiction Regulations may

[121] Insofar as the New Zealand decisions in *The Fua Kavenga* [1987] 1 NZLR 550, 555, and *The Akademik Shokalskiy* [1995] 2 NZLR 743 may suggest that the onus is on the defendant on an application challenging the jurisdiction to establish that the claimant does *not* have an arguable case in law, it is submitted that they are out of step with principle and with the English authorities. Of course, on an application for what is now summary judgment against the claimant (see above, para 6.29), which might previously have been brought as an application to strike out a claim as being frivolous, vexatious, or disclosing no cause of action, the position will be different: see *The Moschanthy* [1971] 1 Lloyd's Rep 37, in which such was the second ground of the application, and in which Brandon J held (at p 42) that the court:

> ... should only stay an action on that ground when the hopelessness of the plaintiff's claim is beyond doubt. If it is not beyond doubt, but, on the contrary, the plaintiff has an arguable, even though difficult, case in fact and law, the action should be allowed to proceed to trial.

This approach holds good today, although the language would nowadays be in terms of 'a more than fanciful prospect of success' (see para 6.28 above).

[122] These will not arise in relation to claims giving rise to maritime liens, since the ownership of the vessel is essentially irrelevant in such cases. In cases within s 21(4) of the 1981 Act, by contrast, the relevant nexus between relevant person and vessel must be established as at the time that the cause of action arose and at the time that the claim form was issued.

[123] *I Congresso del Partido* [1978] QB 500, 535–537; *The Aventicum* [1978] 1 Lloyd's Rep 184, 186; *The Maritime Trader* [1981] 2 Lloyd's Rep 153, 157. This is also the position in Singapore: *The Catur Samudra* [2010] 1 Lloyd's Rep 305; see also *The Bunga Melati 5* [2011] SGHC 195 where the High Court of Singapore analysed s 4(4) of the High Court (Admiralty Jurisdiction) Act and distinguished between 'jurisdictional facts', which must be proved on the balance of probabilities, and 'jurisdictional questions of law', for which a plaintiff need only show a 'good arguable case'. The Court of Appeal largely agreed with this analysis (although it overturned the result) but considered that the plaintiff need only show an 'arguable case' in relation to jurisdictional questions of law: [2012] SGCA 46. In *The Akademik Shokalskiy* [1995] 2 NZLR 743 the New Zealand High Court declined to follow *The Aventicum* and *The Maritime Trader*, and *I Congresso del Partido* was not referred to. That would appear to be out of step with the Australian jurisprudence also: see the helpful and (it is respectfully submitted) correct analysis in *The Owners of the Shin Kobe Maru v Empire Shipping Company Inc* (1994) 181 CLR 404. However, the approach of the Australian High Court was followed in New Zealand in *Baltic Shipping Co Ltd v Pegasus Lines SA* [1996] 3 NZLR 641, where the Australian position was viewed as being consistent with the English approach.

come into play.[124] At the risk of oversimplifying the position,[125] the possibility of founding jurisdiction through *in rem* proceedings in such cases (other than collision actions) is confined to those cases in which the *res* is actually arrested. If it is not, for whatever reason, then jurisdiction is not founded for those purposes. That is because a saving is made for jurisdiction founded by arrest pursuant to the Arrest Convention by art 71 of the Regulation (art 57.1 of the Brussels and Lugano Conventions, art 67.1 of the Lugano II Convention). But in order to take advantage of that facility, an arrest must actually be made.[126] In collision cases, however, an arrest need not have been made, provided it could have been and security was provided.[127] In either case, the claim form will need to have been served, not necessarily on the ship, but otherwise in accordance with the provisions of the CPR, for the English court to take jurisdiction, because that is what English procedural law requires.[128]

The taking of jurisdiction under art 71 is not the end of the story, however: in the event that proceedings are pending in another EU or EFTA State, the *lis pendens* provisions of the Conventions or Regulation are still applicable,[129] and it will still be necessary to investigate the questions of which court was first seised and as to whether the parties, *cause* and *objet* of the two sets of proceedings are the same.[130] If it is determined that the English proceedings should be stayed or dismissed, the court has a discretion to maintain the arrest (or the security provided in order to lift the arrest) pending the outcome of the foreign proceedings.[131] **6.33**

Foreign jurisdiction clauses

Three distinct settings must be considered. **6.34**

[124] See n 50 above.

[125] For a more complete analysis of all these points, see *Dicey & Morris on the Conflict of Laws* (15th edn, 2012), Briggs & Rees, *Civil Jurisdiction & Judgments* (6th edn, 2015) or D C Jackson, *Enforcement of Maritime Claims* (4th edn, 2005).

[126] *The Anna H* [1995] 1 Lloyd's Rep 11; *The Deichland* [1990] 1 QB 361, [1989] 2 All ER 1066, [1989] 2 Lloyd's Rep 113.

[127] *The Po* [1991] 2 Lloyd's Rep 206 CA, applying art 1(1)(b) of the Collision Convention 1952. The aspect of that decision relating to stay of proceedings is probably no longer good law following the decision in *Owusu v Jackson* (n 133 below).

[128] Other potentially relevant conventions in the maritime sphere include: the International Convention on Civil Liability for Oil Pollution Damage 1969 (art IX); the Athens Convention on Passengers and their Luggage 1974 (art 17); and the Hamburg Rules 1978 (art 21).

[129] *The Tatry v The Maciej Rataj* [1994] ECR I-5439, [1999] QB 515, [1995] All ER (EC) 229, [1995] 1 Lloyd's Rep 302. As Briggs & Rees (n 125 above) point out (at para 2.48, n 307), jurisdiction under the Arrest Convention, permitted under what is now art 71 of the 'recast' Brussels I Regulation (1215/2012), is 'derived from the Regulation and subject to its control', citing *Nürnberger Allgemeine Versicherungs AG v Portbridge Transport International BV* [2004] ECR I-10327, [17].

[130] For this purpose at least, the form of the action *in rem* is disregarded and the parties underlying it must be identified: *The Maciej Rataj* (n 129 above). The *cause* of an action is the facts and the rule of law which underlie it; its *objet* is the end in view. See *Briggs & Rees* (n 125 above) at para 2.265.

[131] Civil Jurisdiction and Judgments Act 1982, s 26.

(1) In cases falling within the Brussels I Regulation (44/2001) or the Brussels/Lugano Conventions, ie, where at least one of the parties to the relevant clause is domiciled in a Member State and the clause confers exclusive jurisdiction on the courts of another Member State,[132] then—unless the foreign court was first seised—the *in rem* proceedings will continue unaffected. That is because once jurisdiction has been established under the Conventions or Regulation (which includes establishing it by arrest under the Arrest Convention), then (*lis pendens* apart) the court has no discretion to stay the proceedings.[133]

(2) In cases falling within the 'recast' Brussels I Regulation (1215/2012), the position is different. First, the requirement that at least one of the parties be domiciled in a Member State has been done away with (art 25.1). Second, under art 31.2 the 'court first seised' rule no longer applies to cases involving exclusive jurisdiction clauses. In such a case, if the court agreed to by the parties is seised, any other court, whether seised before or after the first court, must stay its proceedings. Although there has not yet been a case on the point, it seems clear enough that a court becoming seised by means of *in rem* process, typically by an arrest, will have to stay its proceedings if another EU court having exclusive jurisdiction under art 25 is or becomes seised.[134] If the court designated in the agreement declares that it has no jurisdiction, then the stay on the proceedings in the arresting court can be lifted (art 31.2); conversely, if the designated court rules that it does have jurisdiction, then the arresting court must 'decline jurisdiction in favour of that court' (art 31.3). Note, however, that a submission to the jurisdiction of the arresting court will, in effect, override any jurisdiction clause in favour of another court.[135]

(3) In cases outside the ambit of the European instruments, the court has a discretion whether to stay the proceedings. Given that jurisdiction has *ex hypothesi* been founded as of right within the jurisdiction (ie, by service of originating process on the vessel), it will be for the defendant to persuade the court that there is some other, clearly more appropriate jurisdiction for the trial of the action.[136] The existence of the foreign jurisdiction clause will be a powerful, although not necessarily decisive, factor in favour of a stay.

---

[132] Art 23 of the Regulation and the Lugano II Convention, art 17 of the Brussels and Lugano I Conventions.

[133] *Owusu v Jackson* [2005] ECR I-1383, [2005] QB 801, [2005] 2 WLR 942, [2005] 2 All ER (Comm) 577, [2005] 1 Lloyd's Rep 452.

[134] See para 6.33 above.

[135] Arts 26 and 31.2 of the 'recast' Brussels I Regulation (1215/2012). The same result does not necessarily follow under the other European legislation: although there is an equivalent to Art 26 in the earlier Regulation (44/2001) and the Conventions, the usual position is that the court second seised is required to stay its proceedings 'of its own motion', pending resolution of any challenge to the jurisdiction of the court first seised: see, eg, art 29.1 of the 'recast' Regulation; art 27.1 of its predecessor. A submission would not affect that.

[136] See the line of cases commencing with *Spiliada Maritime Corp v Cansulex Ltd, The Spiliada* [1987] AC 460, [1986] 3 WLR 972, [1986] 3 All ER 843, [1987] 1 Lloyd's Rep 1. See also subsequent

Section 34 of the Civil Jurisdiction and Judgments Act 1982

If the proceedings fall foul of s 34 of the 1982 Act, they will have to be dismissed.[137] **6.35**

Forum non conveniens

This ground of objection to the exercise of the court's jurisdiction can only be raised in cases falling outside the scope of the EU Regulations and the Brussels/Lugano Conventions.[138] In non-European cases, the position is the same as that touched upon in para 6.34(3) above, with the exception that, if there is no foreign jurisdiction clause, that factor can obviously not be prayed in aid of a stay. **6.36**

Waiver and submission

It is possible in most circumstances for an otherwise sound objection to the jurisdiction to be defeated by a submission to or waiver of defect in the jurisdiction. It is necessary in this connection to distinguish between two situations.[139] The first arises where an action is brought in respect of a matter which in the ordinary way the court would not have jurisdiction to entertain, but where it is not precluded from doing so if no objection is taken. Thus where, for example, a vessel owned by a party domiciled in the EU is served with *in rem* process (in a non-collision case) without being arrested,[140] the action can properly proceed unless an application is made to set aside the claim and the service of it. Thus, the objection to jurisdiction can be waived and the entry of an unconditional appearance is an example of such a waiver.[141] **6.37**

The second arises where jurisdiction has been withdrawn from the court and conferred on another tribunal. In circumstances where a statute creates a right and in plain language gives a specific remedy or appoints a specific tribunal for its enforcement, a party seeking to enforce the right must resort to this remedy or to this tribunal and not to others. In such a case, it is immaterial whether the parties wish the court to try the action. It must disclaim jurisdiction and entry of an unconditional appearance does not preclude the defendant from raising the objection at a later stage since a party cannot by unilateral act confer on a court jurisdiction which that court does not have.[142] **6.38**

considerations of *Owusu v Jackson* (n 133 above) in the context of foreign parallel proceedings, such as *Catalyst Investment Group Ltd v Lewinsohn* [2009] EWHC 1964 (Ch), [2010] 2 WLR 839, [2010] 1 All ER (Comm) 751.

137 *Republic of India v India Steamship Co Ltd (The Indian Grace) (No 2)* [1997] UKHL 40, [1998] AC 878, [1997] 3 WLR 818, [1997] 4 All ER 380, [1998] 1 Lloyd's Rep 1. See Chapter 2 above, paras 2.35 and following.

138 *Owusu v Jackson*(n 133 above).

139 *Rothmans of Pall Mall (Overseas) Ltd v Saudi Arabian Airlines Corporation* [1981] QB 368, 375, [1980] 3 WLR 642, 649, [1980] 3 All ER 359, 364.

140 Para 6.32 above.

141 Another was debated in *The Indian Grace (No 2)* [1997] UKHL 40, [1998] AC 878, [1997] 3 WLR 818, [1997] 4 All ER 380, [1998] 1 Lloyd's Rep 1, in which the second issue was whether the defendant was estopped from raising the s 34 defence.

142 *Wilkinson v Barking Corporation* [1948] 1 KB 721, 724, [1948] 1 All ER 564, 567. This is not thought to occur frequently in shipping practice.

Preservation of security

6.39 If it is determined that the English proceedings should be stayed or dismissed in favour of another jurisdiction, the court has the power to maintain any arrest, or the security provided in order to lift the arrest, pending the outcome of the foreign proceedings.[143]

Procedure subsequent to acknowledgement of service

6.40 Once an acknowledgement of service has been filed, and provided the Registrar has not allocated the case to some other court or to himself,[144] the exchange of statements of case and pre-trial procedure will, save in collision actions,[145] largely be governed by the procedure applicable to a claim in the Commercial Court,[146] except that the claimant is permitted seventy-five days from the date of service of the claim form in which to serve the particulars of claim.[147] The procedure in relation to matters of exclusively Admiralty interest, on the other hand, such as cautions, arrest, sale, and priorities, are governed by Part 61 and its accompanying Practice Direction.

6.41 There are, however, other features of Admiralty Court proceedings which do not arise in the Commercial Court and which merit special mention.

References to the Registrar

6.42 At any stage in the claim, a question or issue may be referred by the Court to the Registrar for a determination.[148] For example, the determination of quantum following (or even before) a trial on liability in collision cases is almost invariably carried out on a reference. Once a reference has been made, particulars of claim, if not already served, must be filed and served within fourteen days, and any defence must be filed within a further fourteen days.[149] Within seven days after a defence is filed, the claimant must apply for an appointment before the Registrar for a case management conference.[150]

6.43 The term 'reference' is historical. In the time of Lord Stowell, advocates had no right of audience on a reference and it is not difficult to imagine that their course must have been very different. In modern times, however, a reference is no different from any other trial process, and may involve the full panoply of disclosure, witness and expert evidence and oral testimony.

---

[143] Civil Jurisdiction and Judgments Act 1982, s 26.
[144] Pursuant to his case management powers under PD61 §2.1.
[145] Chapter 9.
[146] PD61 §1.1: PD58 applies to Admiralty claims except where inconsistent with Part 61 or PD61.
[147] PD61 §3.10.
[148] PD61 §13.1.
[149] PD61 §13.2.
[150] PD61 §13.3.

Agency

In collision cases, there is a practice of allowing recovery of one per cent of the value of the proved claim in respect of business disruption and expenditure of management time. The practice is rarely, if ever, challenged. As Clarke J said in *The Kumanovo*:[151] 6.44

> I would certainly not encourage a party to challenge the approach in the future because it seems to me to be rooted in good sense. Shipowners' businesses will almost inevitably be disrupted by collision so that there is likely to be an expenditure of management time and cost. It seems to me to be more sensible to adopt the conventional approach of adding one per cent to the damages than to require the shipowners to prove the actual cost.

In *Carisbrooke Shipping CV5 v Bird Port Ltd (The Charlotte C)*[152] Nigel Teare QC, sitting as a Deputy Judge of the Admiralty Court, held that he was unable to distinguish a case involving a ship touching bottom from the collision cases and followed the practice as it had been applied in collision cases.

The practice, which does not appear to have been adopted in other jurisdictions, does not relieve a party of the need to adduce evidence of the loss of management time but in many cases the loss of time will be self-evident. The practice therefore can have the benefit of saving additional costs and expenses in attempting to prove the claim with a fine degree of precision, provided that there is no risk of the practice producing an unjust result.[153] 6.45

Interest

The power of the Admiralty Court, independent of the statutory basis usually relied upon in other courts, to award interest on claims brought within its jurisdiction, is based on equitable principles. In *President of India v La Pintada Compania*, Lord Brandon indicated that the equitable power of the court to award interest on a debt or damages applies to all claims that are now by s 20(2) of the SCA 1981 declared to be within the Admiralty jurisdiction of the High Court of Admiralty, although it was not necessary to decide the point in that case.[154] That power does not extend to the awarding of compound interest;[155] nor does it extend to an award of interest on debts already paid.[156] 6.46

[151] *The Kumanovo* [1998] 2 Lloyd's Rep 301; cf the reference to the practice as 'crude and speculative' in *Carisbrooke Shipping CV5 v Bird Port Ltd* [2005] EWHC 1974, [162] referring to *Tate & Lyle Food and Distribution Ltd v Greater London Council* [1982] 1 WLR 149, a case not concerned with a collision.

[152] *Carisbrooke Shipping CV5 v Bird Port Ltd (The Charlotte C)* [2005] EWHC 1974 (Comm), [2005] 2 Lloyd's Rep 626.

[153] Ibid.

[154] *President of India v La Pintada Compania* [1985] AC 104, 121, [1984] 3 WLR 10, 22, [1984] 2 All ER 773, 783, [1984] 2 Lloyd's Rep 9, 17; *The Aldora* [1975] QB 748, 753.

[155] *President of India v La Pintada Compania* [1985] AC 104, 121, [1984] 3 WLR 10, 22, [1984] 2 All ER 773, 783, [1984] 2 Lloyd's Rep 9, 17.

[156] *The Medina Princess* [1962] 2 Lloyd's Rep 17; *President of India v La Pintada Compania* [1985] AC 104, 121.

F. The Procedure Applicable to Arrest

Entitlement to arrest

6.47 In a claim *in rem*, a claimant or a judgment creditor may apply to have the property proceeded against arrested.[157] Given its association here with 'judgment creditor', it may be surmised that a claimant is one with a claim (i) which, at the time that the claim form was issued, fell within one of the categories which permits the issue of *in rem* process, and (ii) in respect of which no judgment has yet been given. Although the first of these qualifications does not appear in CPR 61.5(1)(a), it is submitted that it is inherent in the restriction of the availability of arrest to 'a claim *in rem*', which is defined in CPR 61.1(2) as meaning 'a claim in an admiralty action *in rem*'. Since the court only has jurisdiction to entertain such a claim in the limited circumstances set out in ss 20–21 of the SCA 1981, it must follow that the availability of arrest for a claimant is similarly circumscribed. This is not just academic: once a defendant has entered an appearance in an action *in rem*, the action continues against him *in personam* without losing its original *in rem* character.[158] A defendant may find it expedient to submit to the jurisdiction in an action which was—but should not have been—commenced *in rem*, but that cannot make the right of arrest available merely because it is no longer possible to contest the jurisdiction of the court.

6.48 More difficult questions arise in relation to the availability of arrest to judgment creditors.[159] Those questions are whether the right of arrest is available:

(1) in existing *in rem* proceedings in which judgment has been given;
(2) where a judgment (*in personam* or *in rem*) has been given on the underlying cause of action in other proceedings in England and Wales;
(3) where such a judgment has been given in foreign proceedings.

These are not easy questions and it is convenient to set out what are submitted to be the answers to them before delving into analysis. They are:

(1) Arrest is possible pursuant to CPR 61.5(1)(b) where the relevant *in rem* judgment was given in the same proceedings. It is possible that the new rule extends no further than this, but—
(2) Logically at least, arrest is also permissible in fresh proceedings brought in respect of domestic judgments (*in rem* or *in personam*) against the vessel's owner, provided that:

---

157 CPR 61.5(1). CJJA 1982, s 25(7) bars arrest in support of proceedings elsewhere in the EU.

158 Para 2.07(3) above.

159 Note that the usual methods of enforcement are available to any judgment creditor who has a judgment enforceable in England and Wales. In particular, a writ of *fieri facias* may be issued to permit the seizure and sale of a ship owned by the judgment debtor: *The Freedom* (1871) LR 3 A&E 495.

(i) the *in rem* proceedings in which arrest is sought to be made were commenced before the judgment was given,[160] or
(ii) the underlying cause of action is one which gives rise to a maritime lien (over the vessel sought to be arrested), or
(iii) the earlier proceedings were undefended *in rem* proceedings.

If either (i) or (ii) applies, there is an existing security interest which can be enforced through the *in rem* process by means of arrest; if (iii) applies, then because the personal liability of the 'relevant person' does not merge in the *in rem* judgment, fresh proceedings are still possible, even against the same *res*.[161] Thus—to state the converse position—where, in earlier proceedings on a claim giving rise only to a statutory right of action *in rem*, judgment was given (other than in default of appearance in *in rem* proceedings) before the commencement of fresh *in rem* proceedings, arrest under CPR 61.5(1)(b) will not be possible, because the court will have no jurisdiction to entertain the fresh proceedings.

(3) The position is slightly more complicated in the case of foreign judgments:
(i) In the case of those foreign judgments which may be enforced by action, the position is the same as in relation to domestic judgments. Section 34 of the Civil Jurisdiction and Judgments Act 1982 does not operate because the claim is not brought on the same cause of action, but on the cause of action created by the judgment, enforceable through the medium of the statutory or maritime lien.
(ii) In the case of foreign judgments which require registration, however, no fresh *in rem* proceedings can be commenced on the judgments (or on the underlying causes of action). Arrest will still be possible, however, in pre-existing *in rem* proceedings that have survived, eg, the operation of the *lis pendens* provisions of the EU Regulations or Brussels/Lugano Conventions.[162]

In order to approach these questions it is necessary first to step back from CPR 61.5(1) and recognize the following parameters which may confine its scope: **6.49**

(1) Proceedings *in rem* can only be issued if the court has jurisdiction to entertain them.
(2) The Admiralty Court's jurisdiction *in rem* is set out in the SCA 1981.
(3) The CPR cannot by itself create new heads of jurisdiction *in rem*.

[160] If the *in rem* proceedings are not commenced until after judgment has been given in such a case, then—unless the judgment was given in default of appearance in earlier *in rem* proceedings, in which case as result of the non-merger doctrine the 'relevant person' is still liable personally—the right to bring a statutory claim *in rem* is lost upon judgment being given.

[161] Above, paras 2.52 and following.

[162] Pursuant to which proceedings between the same parties involving the same cause of action may have to be dismissed in the court seised second. See paras 6.33 and 6.34 above.

(4) Proceedings pursuant to a statutory right of action *in rem* cannot be commenced if the 'relevant person' is no longer liable on the underlying claim,[163] a view which receives some support from the whole tenor of the Arrest Convention, which distinguishes clearly between claims and judgments. It may be noted in this connection that 'Arrest' is defined in the Arrest Convention as:

> ... the detention of a ship by judicial process to secure a maritime claim, but does not include the seizure of a ship in execution or satisfaction of a judgment.

(5) It follows that (other than in relation to judgments *in rem* given in default of appearance) fresh *in rem* proceedings cannot be issued in relation to judgments on claims giving rise only to a statutory right of action *in rem* unless there is some basis for doing so other than s 21(4).

(6) A foreign judgment does not without more take effect in England and Wales. For it to do so it must be capable of recognition, whether at common law, by statute,[164] or under the EU Regulations or Brussels/Lugano Conventions. In general terms,[165] a foreign judgment which is capable of being recognized and which orders the payment of money is enforceable in England and Wales. However, the mechanism by which this can be achieved varies according to the origin of the foreign judgment:

   (i) At common law, a foreign judgment is enforced by bringing an action on the judgment.

   (ii) In cases falling under the 1933 Act[166] or under the EU Regulation or Brussels/Lugano Conventions,[167] however, it is not possible to bring an action on the judgment and it must instead be registered in accordance with the rules of court established for that purpose.[168]

6.50 It must follow from the above that a claim *in rem* cannot in any circumstances be issued to enforce an existing judgment *in personam* on a cause of action giving rise to no more than a statutory right of action *in rem*. Whether the same is true in respect of a judgment *in rem* depends in turn upon whether *The Despina GK* was correctly decided. In that case Sheen J invoked the residual jurisdiction of the Admiralty Court pursuant to s 20(1)(c) of the 1981 Act, in order to permit the arrest of a vessel to enforce a judgment *in rem* of a foreign Admiralty Court.[169]

---

163 Para 2.59 above.

164 Such as s 8 of the Foreign Judgments (Reciprocal Enforcement) Act 1933.

165 The precise criteria vary according to whether enforcement is sought at common law, pursuant to statute, or under the European Regulation or Conventions.

166 s 6 of the 1933 Act.

167 *Dicey & Morris on The Conflict of Laws* (15th edn, 2012) §S14–239, citing *De Wolf v Cox* [1976] ECR 1759, in which the European Court of Justice held that it would be incompatible with the enforcement provisions of the Brussels Convention to permit an action on the original cause of action. The same would seem to be true of an action on the judgment.

168 ie, CPR Part 74.

169 *The Despina GK* [1983] QB 214, [1982] 2 Lloyd's Rep 555.

In order to determine whether he was correct in so doing, it is necessary first to consider the decision relied upon by Sheen J, that of Sir Robert Phillimore in *The City of Mecca*.[170]

In *The City of Mecca*, the arrest of a ship was permitted in order to enforce what was understood to be a judgment *in rem*. Although no precedent was identified for the enforcement of a judgment *in rem* by an action *in rem*,[171] the court's jurisdiction to do so was found to lie in the comity of nations and the duty of civilian admiralty courts to assist each other.[172] That approach, however, for which no remotely contemporary authority was cited, was at odds with a strong and recent line of common law authority as to the basis upon which judgments are accorded recognition at common law.[173] Moreover, it is one thing to uphold the decision *in rem* of a foreign court,[174] but quite another to give effect to the decision of a foreign court by means of *in rem* process. The limits of such a doctrine are undefined,[175] and there is much to be said against it in terms of practice,[176] policy, and law.[177] **6.51**

Furthermore, if the Admiralty Court's jurisdiction prior to the 1840 Act began and ended with claims giving rise to a maritime lien, enforceable by action *in rem*,[178] then it could not have entertained the *in rem* proceedings in *The City of Mecca* unless they were brought to enforce a maritime lien. It is submitted firstly that the basis for the jurisdiction invoked by Sir Robert Phillimore evaporates when this is borne in mind, and secondly that it is in *The Bold Buccleugh* that a sounder basis is to be found for the actual decision reached in *The City of Mecca*. If **6.52**

---

170 *The City of Mecca* (1879) 5 PD 28. The decision was reversed on its facts by the Court of Appeal (1881) 6 PD 106 on the ground that the foreign judgment was not, upon closer inspection, an action *in rem*.

171 Ibid 33.

172 Ibid 30, 34.

173 As *Dicey & Morris* point out (n 167 above) at §14-112, Sir Robert Phillimore's formulation ran directly contrary to the denial by Blackburn J in *Godard v Gray* (1870) LR 6 QB 139, 148 that it was 'an admitted principle of the law of nations that a State is bound to enforce within its territories the judgment of a foreign tribunal'. Blackburn J's approach, alluded to in Sir Robert Phillimore's judgment at p 34, has been approved in recent times: *Dicey & Morris* (n 167 above) §§14-119 to 121 and the cases there cited.

174 As in *Castrique v Imrie* (1870) LR 4 HL 414.

175 For instance, does the doctrine operate following a change of ownership after judgment or in respect of claims which the enforcing court would not but the originating court did recognize as giving rise to a right to proceed *in rem*? What of the judgment of a foreign court against a *res* owned by A in respect of a liability owed by B, pursuant to the wider operation of maritime liens recognized in some jurisdictions (notably the United States of America) but not in England?

176 It is not difficult to imagine, for example, a need for expert evidence in order to determine whether or not the particular foreign judgment is properly to be characterized as *in rem* (as indeed occurred on appeal in *The City of Mecca* itself).

177 Given that an action *in rem* cannot be commenced in order to enforce the judgment of another EU or EFTA court (this *may* arise because the particular judgment is not properly to be classified as being *in rem* and/or *will* arise because such judgments must be recognized and enforced by way of registration rather than by action) there is obvious scope for the doctrine to operate in a discriminatory and thus arguably unlawful fashion.

178 As Sir John Jervis held in *The Bold Buccleugh*; above, para 2.18.

the maritime lien is—as submitted in Chapter 2 above—best viewed as a security right arising at the same time as the cause of action, then there is no reason in principle why it should not (and every reason why it should) survive, enforceable by action *in rem*, until its purpose (ie, to secure the claim) has been satisfied. That analysis, which would not require the invocation of any residual jurisdiction, clearly attracted the Judge in *The City of Mecca*,[179] although it was not the main plank of his reasoning.

6.53 That analysis is not free from difficulties, however. Principal among them is the decision to the contrary of Mocatta J in *The Alletta*,[180] who held that the right to arrest had been lost as a result of an earlier judgment against the former owners. Although nowhere stated in terms, the basis of Mocatta J's judgment was that the underlying cause of action had merged with the earlier judgment. There is no analysis in the judgment, however, as to why or how the *maritime lien* should have suffered the same fate, and the authorities cited by the Judge[181] shed no light upon that issue. In *The Daien Maru No 18*,[182] however, Thean J did give consideration to that question,[183] concluding (rightly, it is submitted) that:

> On these authorities[184] it is clear that a maritime lien gives a right to the ship enforceable by an action in rem. This being the case, it seems to me logical and right that a plaintiff who has instituted an action in rem against a ship to enforce a maritime lien thereon, must be entitled to arrest the ship in the same action even after he has obtained judgment, provided always that in such a case no bail has been previously put up for the ship in that action. If such right of arrest is said to have been lost by virtue of the judgment having been obtained, then it must follow that the lien is extinguished or discharged by such judgment in the same action instituted to enforce it. Such a conclusion in my view is a non sequitur.

Although his decision can in some respects no longer be supported,[185] it is submitted the reasoning and conclusion of Thean J on this point is unimpeachable,[186] and

---

[179] *The City of Mecca* (1879) 5 PD 28, 32–33, 34.

[180] *The Alletta* [1974] 1 Lloyd's Rep 40. It may also be argued that the decision of the Court of Appeal in *The City of Mecca* (1881) 6 PD 106 militates against that conclusion. However, the Court of Appeal approached the matter on the basis that if the foreign judgment did not hold the *ship* to be liable, then it could not be enforced *in rem*; see, eg, per Jessel MR at p 112: 'There is no suggestion from beginning to end that the ship is liable ...' Even if it was correct in 1881, it is submitted that this approach, rooted in the form of the action and (it would appear) the personal responsibility of the ship, cannot survive *The Indian Grace (No 2)*.

[181] *The Point Breeze* [1928] P 135, *The Kalamazoo* (1851) 15 Jur 885, *The Hero* (1865) Br & Lush 447, *The Flora* (1866) LR 1 A&E 45.

[182] *The Daien Maru No 18* [1986] 1 Lloyd's Rep 387 (Sing High Ct).

[183] Ibid 391–392.

[184] *The Bold Buccleugh* (1851) 7 Moo PC 167; *The Two Ellens* (1872) LR 4 PC 161; *The Tolten* [1946] P 135, 145–146.

[185] For example, his view that the action *in rem* was 'an action against the *res*' (p 390 col 1). Such a view is untenable, at least in England, following the decision of the House of Lords in *The Indian Grace (No 2)*.

[186] It has been followed in Hong Kong by Waung J in *Soh v The Owners of the Columbus Caravelle* [2002] HKCFI 563.

anyway to be preferred over the conclusion reached without consideration of the point by Mocatta J in *The Alletta*. It would follow that *The Alletta* is no obstacle to the conclusion that an action *in rem* to enforce a maritime lien is possible after judgment.

Returning, therefore, to *The Despina GK*,[187] if—as submitted above—the residual jurisdiction relied upon by Sheen J did not exist, then the case must have been wrongly decided. That is because, firstly, the underlying cause of action (a cargo claim) did not give rise to a maritime lien, but only to a statutory right of action *in rem* and, secondly, the English proceedings had not been issued until after the foreign judgment had been given. At the date of the issue of proceedings, therefore, no security interest existed to permit the *in rem* jurisdiction of the Admiralty Court to be invoked.[188] **6.54**

Consistent with the analysis advanced above, it is submitted that the questions posed in para 6.48 should be answered as set out in that paragraph—with the consequences discussed in para 6.56 below. **6.55**

A number of points arise from these conclusions. **6.56**

(1) The unintended result of CPR 61.5(1)(b) may be that EU judgments in particular are not enforceable to the same extent (or in the same way)[189] as some English and overseas judgments. Although unobjectionable in the case of a judgment given in the same proceedings as the arrest, it is submitted that this discriminatory consequence means that the provision may require revision in the future.
(2) Another aspect of CPR 61.5(1)(b) which may require consideration is its interaction with CPR 61.10(3), which limits the class of those who may seek payment out of the fund to those 'with a judgment against the property'. Whilst no difficulty will arise where the arresting judgment creditor has an *in rem* judgment against the property (in the same or different proceedings), what of the position where the earlier judgment is *in personam* or *in rem* against a sister-ship? Unless and until these provisions are revised to address these issues head-on, it is submitted that the solution is to view the fresh action as an action on the existing judgment, which can in turn be pursued to judgment; another way of achieving the same object would be for judgment to be entered in the new proceedings for a declaration that the relevant security interest is valid and subsisting and will answer to the earlier judgment.
(3) The final point is to note that, despite having already obtained judgment once, the claimant cannot simply apply for summary judgment based upon

187 Above, para 6.50.
188 Above, paras 2.52 and following.
189 As already noted above, enforcement in the form of, eg, a writ of *fi fa* would still be available.

the earlier judgment (as has traditionally been done where action is brought on a foreign judgment at common law). That is because summary judgment is not available in actions *in rem* (para 6.29 above). Where the judgment debtor is not (or no longer) the owner of the vessel arrested, that may well be only fair. Otherwise, recourse will have to be had to 'cause of action' and 'issue' estoppel if the proceedings are to be any shorter second time around.

Cautions against arrest

6.57 A person who apprehends that a claim *in rem* may be commenced against his ship or property which might lead to the arrest of that ship or property may choose to file a caution against arrest to minimize disruption to his business.[190] The entry of a caution against arrest does not amount to a submission to the jurisdiction of the court,[191] nor does it prevent the arrest of property,[192] but the court may order that any subsequent arrest be discharged and that the arresting party pay compensation to the owner or other persons interested in the arrested property.[193]

6.58 A request for a caution against arrest may be filed by any person,[194] and either constitutes an undertaking to acknowledge service of the claim form and to give security for the claim with interest and costs within three days after receiving notice of a claim, or indicates that a limitation fund has been constituted.[195] On the filing of a request in the appropriate form, a caution against arrest will be entered in the Register.[196] It remains valid for twelve months and may be renewed for a further twelve months by filing a further request.[197]

Procedure for obtaining an arrest warrant

6.59 The party seeking to arrest must first search the Register to determine whether there is a caution against arrest in force.[198] He may then apply for the arrest of the ship or property.[199] An application for arrest includes a personal undertaking by the solicitor for the applicant to pay on demand the fees of the Marshal and all expenses incurred, or to be incurred, by him or on his behalf in respect of:

---

[190] The term 'caution' has replaced the word 'caveat'. In addition, any person may search for any claim form *in rem*, whether or not it has been served: PD61 §3.12.

[191] PD61 §6.1.

[192] For an example (and a good reason for arresting despite the existence of a caution) see para 6.32 above and *The Deichland* [1990] 1 QB 361, [1989] 2 All ER 1066, [1989] 2 Lloyd's Rep 113. Cf. *Stena Bulk AB v Copley* [2015] 1 Lloyd's Rep 280.

[193] CPR 61.7(5).

[194] CPR 61.7(1); PD61 §6.2 and Form ADM7.

[195] CPR 61.7(2).

[196] PD61 §6.3.

[197] CPR 61.7(3) and (4).

[198] CPR 61.5(3)(a); The Register is open for inspection when the Admiralty and Commercial Registry is open, PD61 §6.4.

[199] PD61 §5.1.

(1) the arrest of, or endeavours to arrest, the property; and
(2) the care and custody of it while under arrest; and
(3) the release, or endeavours to release it.[200]

In relation to every claim, the party seeking to arrest must file a declaration,[201] verified by a statement of truth, which states: **6.60**

(1) the nature of the claim or counterclaim and that it has not been satisfied, and, if it arises in connection with a ship, the name of the ship;
(2) the nature of the property to be arrested and, if the property is a ship, the name of the ship and her port of registry; and
(3) the amount of security sought, if any.[202]

In addition to the matters mentioned above, in a claim against a ship pursuant to s 21(4) of the SCA which requires the establishment of a connection between the ship and someone with personal liability in respect of the claim, the declaration must state: **6.61**

(1) the name of the person who would be liable on the claim if it were commenced *in personam*;
(2) that the person referred to above was, when the cause of action arose, the owner or charterer of or in possession or control of the ship in connection with which the claim arose; and
(3) at the time when the claim form was issued, that person was either the beneficial owner of all the shares in the ship in respect of which the warrant is required, or the demise charterer of that ship.[203]

If the claim relates to a ship owned by a State where by any convention or treaty the United Kingdom has undertaken to minimize the possibility of arrest of ships of that State or to a foreign ship belonging to a port of a State in respect of which an order in council has been made under s 4 of the Consular Relations Act 1968,[204] the declaration must state that the relevant notice has been sent or served.[205] **6.62**

If the claim relates to liability incurred under s 153 of the MSA for oil pollution damage, PD61 §5.4(4) must also be observed. **6.63**

---

200 Form ADM4.
201 CPR 61.5(3)(b) and Form ADM5.
202 PD61 §5.3(1).
203 PD61 §5.3(2).
204 CPR 61.5 (5) and (6): Regulations have been made in relation to ships registered in Austria (SI No 1903/1970), Belgium (SI No 1904/1970), Bulgaria (SI No 1918/1970), Czech Republic (SI No 768/1976), Denmark (SI No 1905/1970), Egypt (SI No 217/1986), France (SI No 1970/1906), Germany (SI No 1907/1970 & 1152/1976), Greece (SI No 1970/1908), Hungary (SI No 1971/1846), Italy (SI No 1909/1970), Japan (SI No 1910/1970), Mexico (SI No 1911/1970), Norway (SI No 1912/1970), Poland (SI No 275/1978), Romania (SI No 1920/1970), Slovak Republic (SI No 768/1976), Spain (SI No 1913/1970), Sweden (SI No 1914/1970), and Yugoslavia (SI No 1917/1970).
205 PD61 §5.3(3) and Form ADM6.

6.64 If the application for arrest complies with the CPR and the PD the court will issue an arrest warrant.[206] There is no discretion,[207] other than in cases in which there has, since the issue of the claim form, been a change in the beneficial ownership of the property following a judicial sale by a court exercising admiralty jurisdiction *in rem*.[208]

Validity of arrest warrant

6.65 A warrant of arrest is valid for twelve months but may only be executed if the claim form has been served or remains valid for service at the date of execution.[209]

Service of arrest warrant

6.66 Only the Marshal or his substitute may effect an arrest.[210] As it is convenient to serve the originating process together with the arrest warrant, a claimant may make a request to the court for the Marshal to serve the claim form in circumstances where the property is to be arrested or is already under arrest in current proceedings.[211] The request will usually be made through the Admiralty & Commercial Registry, typically by a solicitor's outdoor clerk. There is no need for a separate application to be made to this end.

Manner of arrest

6.67 Property is arrested by the service on it of an arrest warrant in the same manner as for the service of a claim form *in rem*,[212] namely:

(1) on property, by fixing a copy of the claim form on the outside of the property in a position which may reasonably be expected to be seen;

---

[206] PD61 §5.2 and Form ADM9. However, a warrant will not be issued as of right in the case of property in respect of which the beneficial ownership, as a result of a sale or disposal by any court in any jurisdiction exercising Admiralty jurisdiction *in rem*, has changed since the claim form was issued: CPR 61.5(4).

[207] Similarly, there is no discretion in relation to the issue of an arrest warrant provided the procedural rules have been complied with in Singapore (Rules of Court (Sing) O70r4), New Zealand (High Court Rules (NZ) r 25.35), and South Africa (Admiralty Proceedings Rules (SAf) r 4(2)), but the Registrar may refer the question of whether to issue a warrant to a judge (r 4(2)(b)). Australia (Admiralty Rules (Cth) r 40(1)), Canada (Federal Courts Rules r 481(1)), and Hong Kong (Rules of the High Court (HK) O75r5(1)) retain a discretion in the Registrar to issue the warrant for arrest. In those circumstances, the claimant has an obligation to disclose all information material to the exercise by the court of its discretion: *The Vasso* [1984] QB 477, [1984] 2 WLR 570, [1984] 1 All ER 1126, [1984] 1 Lloyd's Rep 235; *The Varna* [1993] 2 Lloyd's Rep 253; *Lloyds Werft Bremerhaven GmbH v Zoya Kosmodemyanskaya* [1997] FCA 379 (Federal Court of Australia); *The Tat Yau 8* [1998] 4 HKC 108; *The Asian Atlas* [2008] HKLRD 461; *The H156* [1999] 3 SLR 756.

[208] CPR 61.5(4). It is submitted that, in such a case, an application must be made to the court to justify why, notwithstanding the sale, the arrest warrant should be issued.

[209] CPR 61.5(7).

[210] CPR 61.

[211] PD61 §§3.7 and 3.8.

[212] PD61 §5.5(1).

(2) on freight, by fixing a copy of the claim form either on the cargo in respect of which the freight was earned or on the ship on which the cargo was carried.

Where it is not reasonably practicable to serve the warrant, a notice of the issue of the warrant may be served either on the property in the manner set out above, or by giving notice to those in charge of the property.[213] **6.68**

In *The Johnny Two*, Sheen J described the practicalities of the arrest process: **6.69**

> Upon issue of the warrant the Admiralty Marshal telephones the relevant officer of HM Customs and Excise and instructs him to arrest the ship. He tells the Customs Officer his requirements for ensuring the security of the arrest. That is followed up by sending a 'Note of Action' by fax confirming his instructions to arrest the ship and giving the folio number of the action, the name of the plaintiff and the name of the plaintiff's solicitors. An officer of HM then arrests the ship by attaching the Note of Action to the ship. He then carries out the Marshal's instructions for keeping the ship safely under arrest. This can be carried out in a very short space of time.
>
> The warrant of arrest and the writ are then sent by post of HM Customs for execution and service respectively. But frequently, of course, security will have been provided and service of the writ accepted by solicitors so that the ship will have been released before these documents are received by HM Customs.
>
> If a ship is expected to arrive at a known port a warrant of arrest should be issued. A 'Note of Action' instructing a Customs Officer to 'Arrest on arrival' will then be sent to the relevant Customs Office. The ship will then be arrested on arrival by the 'Note of Action' or by execution of the warrant if it has arrived at the Customs Office. In this way a ship may be arrested on a day when the Court Offices are closed.
>
> Arrests in London are effected by the personal attendance of the Marshal's Officer who executes the warrant.
>
> If a caveat against arrest is entered after a warrant is issued but before the arrest is effected, the plaintiff's solicitors will be informed. They will be asked if they still wish to arrest.
>
> If a warrant of arrest is issued in respect of a ship when the port of arrival is not known, the warrant can be left with the Marshal with instructions, endorsed on the undertaking to pay his expenses, to arrest 'at a port to be advised during normal working hours'.
>
> These procedures enable solicitors to arrest a ship at very short notice, particularly when they have taken the precaution of issuing a warrant in advance.[214]

This procedure conceals a trap for the unwary: it can take two days or more for the claim form (sent by post) to catch up with the warrant of arrest and be served. If in the meantime security has been provided by the vessel's P&I Club (say), the temptation will be to allow the ship to sail before the claim form has been served. If the security does not contain an undertaking to appoint solicitors to accept service, the claimant may find that the English court is not yet seised of the action, despite the vessel having been arrested and security provided. Generally speaking, no other vessel can be arrested, partly because the security will usually contain a provision

[213] PD61 §5.5(2).

[214] *The Johnny Two* [1992] 2 Lloyd's Rep 257.

to that effect[215] and partly because of s 21(8) SCA 1981 (discussed below). The claimant may find itself unable in such circumstances to progress its action, at any rate unless and until the vessel arrested returns to an English port for long enough to allow it to be served with the *in rem* claim form.

One claim/one ship

6.70 As a general rule,[216] once a vessel has been arrested and released on security, whether in England or in any other jurisdiction, the court will not normally permit a second arrest of the ship or indeed of any other property of the defendant.[217] The principle underlying the cases[218] is that where security is given and not released it would be vexatious or oppressive to permit an arrest or a second arrest.[219] Moreover, where security to the full value of the vessel has been given, it would be inimical to the *in rem* process to permit further arrest in order to increase that security.[220]

In the Canadian case of *Westshore Terminals Limited Partnership v Leo Ocean, SA*[221] the question arose as to whether the appellant, which had already obtained a warrant for the arrest of the wrongdoing ship, could obtain a warrant in relation to one or more sister-ships. The Federal Court of Appeal held that the appellants could either proceed under s 43(2) of the Federal Courts Act to secure the arrest of the wrongdoing vessel or under s 43(8) to secure the arrest of a sister-ship. Having elected to proceed under s 43(2), the appellants were barred from seeking an arrest under s 43(8).

6.71 The corollary of the general principle against multiple arrests is that it must not of itself be used to create oppression or unfairness. In *The Arctic Star*,[222] subsequent to the provision of adequate security, the vessel's owners took steps which seriously impaired the value of a guarantee. In the circumstances, the Court of Appeal concluded that rearrest was appropriate. Similarly, in *The Hero*,[223] rearrest was

[215] If it does not, then conceivably an application could be made to set aside the arrest and start again (cf *The Silver Athens (No 1)* [1986] 2 Lloyd's Rep 580). It would be necessary to argue (i) that the action had not been 'brought' until service (cf *The Banco*—n 44 above) or (ii) that, on its true construction, s 21(8) does not prevent service where there had only been service (and would not prevent arrest where there had only been service). The arguments are thin, though: the usual view is that suit is brought when the claim form is issued; and it is impossible to see how different ships could be arrested and served within the same action.

[216] See further paras 7.19 to 7.21 and 7.26 to 7.27 below.

[217] *The Arctic Star*, The Times, 5 February 1985 per Lloyd LJ.

[218] *The Kalamazoo* (1851) 15 Jur 885; *The Wild Ranger* (1863) Br & Lush 84, 167 ER 310; *The Christiansborg* (1885) 10 PD 141; *The Joannis Vatis (No 2)* (1922) 10 Ll L Rep 229, [1922] P 213; *The Point Breeze* (1928) 30 Ll L Rep 329, [1928] P 135; *The Alletta* [1974] 1 Lloyd's Rep 40.

[219] *The Tjaskemolen (now named Visvliet) (No 2)* [1997] 2 Lloyd's Rep 476, 479.

[220] And CPR 61.6(3) forbids it.

[221] *Westshore Terminals Limited Partnership v Leo Ocean, SA* [2014] FCA 231, 245 ACWS (3d) 496, 378 DLR (4th) 220.

[222] *The Arctic Star*, The Times, 5 February 1985.

[223] *The Hero* (1865) 13 WR 927, 167 ER 436.

permitted in circumstances where, due to a clerical error, the plaintiff had miscalculated the proper amount of security.

Article 3(3) of the 1952 Arrest Convention recognizes that a ship might be rearrested if the bail or other security has been released before the subsequent arrest.[224] There is nothing in the SCA 1981 which prevents a second arrest if the first arrest has been set aside.[225] **6.72**

Section 21(8) provides: **6.73**

> Where, as regards any such claim as is mentioned in section 20(2)(e) to (r), a ship has been served with a writ or arrest in an action *in rem* brought to enforce that claim, no other ship may be served with a writ or arrested in that or any other action *in rem* brought to enforce that claim: but this subsection does not prevent the issue, in respect of any one such claim, of a writ naming more than one ship or of two or more writs each naming a different ship.

Section 21(8) sets out the general proposition that only one ship (either the ship in connection with which the claim arose or a sister-ship) may be arrested in respect of a general maritime claim. This is consistent with the approach in most of the common law jurisdictions.[226] In South Africa, however, an Admiralty court may order that further property be arrested or attached in order to provide additional security for any claim.[227]

This section does not prevent the commencement of an action *in rem* or the arrest of a ship in circumstances where that ship has already had *in rem* proceedings brought against it in a foreign jurisdiction to enforce the same claim. The wording of s 21(8) restricts its operation to proceedings *in rem* or to a prior arrest in England.[228] **6.74**

A literal reading of s 21(8) could have the effect of preventing the arrest of a ship where another ship has, erroneously, already been arrested in respect of a particular claim. The anomaly created by such a situation can be cured if s 21(8) is interpreted as meaning: 'Where, as regards any such claim as is mentioned in s 20(2)(e) to (r), a ship against which an action *in rem* may be brought has been served with a writ or arrested in an action *in rem* to enforce that claim, no other ship may be served with **6.75**

---

224 Australia has codified the power to permit rearrest in s 21 of the Admiralty Act 1998; see also *Laemthong International Lines Co Ltd as the owners of the ship Laemthong Pride as the surrogate for the vessel Nyanza v BPS Shipping Ltd* (1997) 190 CLR 181 (High Court of Australia); New Zealand courts have an inherent jurisdiction to order the rearrest of a ship, *Det Norske Veritas AS v The Ship Clarabelle* [2002] 3 NZLR 52, [2002] 2 Lloyd's Rep 479; *Baltic Shipping Co Ltd v Pegasus Line SA* [1996] 3 NZLR 641; Canada has not incorporated art 3(3) into the Federal Courts Act but see *The Elecnor SA v The Soren Toubro* (1996) 114 FTR 134 and *Westshore Terminals Limited Partnership v Leo Ocean, SA* [2014] FCA 231, 245 ACWS (3d) 496, 378 DLR (4th) 220.

225 *The Silver Athens (No 1)* [1986] 2 Lloyd's Rep 580.

226 Admiralty Act 1988, s 20 (Australia); Admiralty Act 1973, s 5(2)(b) and Rules of the High Court r 25.34 (New Zealand).

227 Admiralty Jurisdiction Regulation Act 105 of 1983, s 5(2)(d).

228 *The Silver Athens (No 2)* [1986] 2 Lloyd's Rep 583; *Centro Latino Americano de Commercio Exterior SA v The Owners of the Ship Kommunar (No 2)* [1997] 1 Lloyd's Rep 8; *The Tjaskemolen (now named the Visvliet) (No 2)* [1997] 2 Lloyd's Rep 476.

a writ or arrested in that or any other action *in rem* brought to enforce the claim …'. This was the interpretation placed on the section by Sheen J in *The Stephan J*,[229] in a case where a solicitor had received erroneous information from Lloyd's Intelligence Service as to the ownership of the ships 'Stephan J' and 'Herm J' and issued writs *in rem* against both ships. The 'Herm J' was arrested but was released as soon as it was discovered that the information was wrong. When the arrest of the 'Stephan J' was sought subsequently, the Admiralty Registrar refused to issue the arrest warrant on the basis of s 21(8) but his decision was reversed by the Admiralty Judge.

6.76 The essential question in any case is whether the second arrest is an abuse of process. In *The Tjaskemolen (now named Visvliet) (No 2)*,[230] the question was whether the arrest of the 'Visvliet' was vexatious or oppressive having regard to the fact that a Dutch court ordered her release after a hearing on the merits of the claim. Clarke J held that it was not, even though he concluded that the plaintiffs had only themselves to blame for the result reached by the Dutch court, having failed to put all available evidence before that court at the hearing on the merits.[231] Clarke J adopted the approach that the position should be the same as it would have been in Holland had the arrest been maintained, and that it would be oppressive to permit the plaintiffs to retain the security for their claim if to do so would put them in a better position than that in which they would have been in Holland. The requirement of counter security avoided such oppression. Clarke J indicated that he would have reached the same conclusion had art 3(3) of the 1952 Arrest Convention applied and the test had been whether there was 'good cause' to permit an arrest.

Impact of human rights legislation on arrest procedure

6.77 In recent years, litigants have begun to see human rights legislation as an additional means of challenging the arrest process. For example, s 21 of the Bill of Rights Act 1990 (NZ) provides that every person has the right to be secure against unreasonable search or seizure. In *Baltic Shipping Co Ltd v Pegasus Lines SA*, it was argued that the arrest should be set aside on the basis of that section. The argument was given short shift by the New Zealand High Court which observed:

> There is no doubt that the writ *in rem* and the arrest of a vessel is a very strong and effective remedy, but that does not make it unreasonable. It is a seizure by judicial process, to ensure that the ship or some alternative security is available to satisfy a claim which has still to be substantiated. It has been found expedient in international trade as giving some protection to those who give credit or who suffer damage in the course of maritime trade. If a claim is made unreasonably, in the sense of

[229] *The Stephan J* [1985] 2 Lloyd's Rep 344.

[230] *The Tjaskemolen (now named Visvliet) (No 2)* [1997] 2 Lloyd's Rep 476.

[231] It is to be noted, however, that in the unusual circumstances of the case, the court ordered counter security for any loss which the owners might prove they had suffered as a result of arresting the vessel in England if their claim before the arbitrators failed.

being without foundation, the defendant can always move to strike out as well as challenging jurisdiction, as was done in *The Moschanthy*.[232]

While a human rights-based objection to the arrest procedure was rejected in *Baltic Shipping*, it is nevertheless conceivable that such arguments will continue to be pressed in the future. This is particularly so in Canada and England, where human rights legislation impacts more heavily than in some other jurisdictions. **6.78**

G. Proceedings Concerning the International Oil Pollution Compensation Fund

Claims against or concerning the International Oil Pollution Compensation Fund, as provided for in Chapter IV of the MSA, are brought in Admiralty. The Fund may be given notice of proceedings by any party to a claim against an owner or guarantor in respect of liability under ss 153 or 154 of the MSA, or the corresponding provisions of sch 4 to the Act, by serving a notice in writing on the Fund together with copies of the claim form and any statements of case served in the claim.[233] Even if the Fund is not served, it may intervene in any claim brought under ss 153 or 154 of the MSA, or the corresponding provisions of sch 4 to the Act, by serving a notice of intervention on the owner, the guarantor, and the court.[234] **6.79**

When a judgment is given against the Fund in any claim under s 175 of the MSA, or the corresponding provisions of sch 4 to the Act, the Registrar will send a stamped copy of the judgment to the Fund.[235] Notice to the court by the Fund under s 176(3)(b) of the MSA that the amount of the claim is not to be reduced under paras 4 and 5 of art 4 of the Fund Convention, or that it is to be reduced to a specified amount, must be given in writing sent to the court.[236] **6.80**

232 *Baltic Shipping Co Ltd v Pegasus Lines SA* [1996] 3 NZLR 641 (CA) 650.
233 PD61 §11.1.
234 PD61 §11.3.
235 PD61 §11.4.
236 PD61 §11.5.

7

POST-ARREST PROCEDURE

A. The Effect of Arrest

7.01 Immediately upon arrest, a ship becomes security in the custody of the court to await the result of the proceedings giving rise to the arrest. The ship remains in the custody of the court until released upon the provision of alternative security or sale by the court.[1] It is to be noted in this respect that the Marshal has custody but not possession. Any pre-arrest rights and remedies based upon possession are not affected by the arrest.[2]

[1] CPR Part 61.5(9), Admiralty Rules (Cth) r 47(1); Rules of the High Court (NZ) r 25.45; Rules of the High Court (HK) O75 r13; Admiralty Jurisdiction Regulation Act 105 of 1983 (SAf) (AJRA) s 5(3) and Admiralty Proceedings Rules (SAf) r 21; *The Falcon* [1981] 1 Lloyd's Rep 13, 17.

[2] *The Arantzazu Mendi* [1939] AC 256; *Mooloolaba Slipways Pty Ltd v 'The Santa Maria'* [2001] QSC 470.

Once the property has been arrested, the Registrar issues standard directions ordering that the Admiralty Marshal may at any time: **7.02**

(1) take measures to preserve the ship, its machinery, and equipment;
(2) move the ship up to five miles within the limits of the port where it is lying under arrest, either for its safety or to comply with the requirements of the Port Authority;
(3) supply the minimum victuals, domestic fuel,[3] and water necessary to avoid hardship to the crew.[4]

Generally, property under arrest may not be moved unless the court so orders, and the property may be immobilized or prevented from sailing in such manner as the Marshal may consider appropriate.[5] Interference with the arrest process by any party, such as moving the property to be arrested with knowledge that an arrest has been issued, is a contempt of court and is punishable by committal.[6] Interference with the custody of the property under arrest after arrest also amounts to contempt of court.[7] In *The Synova*,[8] Brandon J deprecated the removal of the court's warrant after the debt for which the arrest had been made was paid, but without the permission of the court:[9] **7.03**

> ... it is important that the Court's process of arrest and actions *in rem* should remain inviolate, as far as that can be achieved, and that any violations of that process should be punished appropriately.

In *The Merdeka*,[10] the master of the vessel, knowing her to be under arrest, moved the ship and took her out of the jurisdiction. Sheen J was of the opinion that this was a case of serious contempt and that proceedings to redress contempt were necessary in order to impress on others the consequences of flouting the orders of the court.

---

[3] ie, enough required to keep the generators going, but not to run the main engine.

[4] PD61 §5.6. In Australia, the Marshal is expressly authorized by the Admiralty Rules to take all steps to retain safe custody of and preserve the ship including removing and storing cargo and moving the ship (r 47(2)); in Singapore the Sheriff often applies for an 'omnibus' order authorizing him to take appropriate measures to preserve the ship, her machinery, and equipment, to move the ship within the port limits, and to supply victuals, fuel, and water to the crew: Toh Kian Sing, *Admiralty Law and Practice* (2nd edn, 2007) 210.

[5] CPR 61.5(9).

[6] Rules of the High Court (NZ) r 25.40; *The Seraglio* (1885) 10 PD120; *The Petrel* (1836) 3 Hag Adm 299; *The Harmonie* (1841) 1 Wm Rob 179; *The Synova* [1976] 1 Lloyd's Rep 40.

[7] *The Jarlin* [1965] 1 WLR 1098; *The Mathesis* (1844) 2 W Rob 286; *The Bure* (1850) 14 Jur 1123; *The Merdeka* [1982] 1 Lloyd's Rep 401; *The Abodie Mendi* [1939] P 178.

[8] *The Synova* [1976] 1 Lloyd's Rep 40.

[9] Ibid 41.

[10] *The Merdeka* [1982] 1 Lloyd's Rep 401; the principles established in the English authorities have been followed in the Federal Court of Canada. In *Whyte v The Sandpiper VI* (2002) 112 ACWS (3d) 666, it was held that a show cause order would be issued to the defendants whose dredge and equipment had been arrested. Evidence was led that, subsequent to the arrest, part of the dredge's equipment, the floating dredge spoils pipeline, had been rented out by one of the defendants and moved so that it could be used by a third party.

7.04 The extent of any punishment will depend on the circumstances of the case. The relatively minor contempt that was the subject of *The Synova* attracted a fine of only £100. In *The Merdeka*, the master's written contrite apology, coupled with his voluntary return to London with the vessel, were taken into account in imposing a fine of £350, together with an order for costs.

7.05 An order for the stay of proceedings has no effect on the arrest of property or the provision of security. An arrest remains in force and any security representing the property remains in place.[11]

B. Insurance

7.06 Despite having custody of the property under arrest, the Marshal does not insure the property.[12] Section N13 of the present Admiralty and Commercial Courts Guide confirms the position, which was first adopted on 1 May 1970, that the Marshal will not insure arrested property for the benefit of the parties.[13] Nonetheless, there is authority for the proposition that the Marshal owes a duty to take reasonable care of the vessel whilst it is in his custody and is liable for damage caused by his negligence.[14] The Marshal may therefore insure against his own negligence.

7.07 If the Marshal needs to move the vessel either in accordance with his powers under the standard directions on arrest or pursuant to a specific order of the court, the Marshal will attempt to advise all parties known to him as being on the record in an action *in rem* of his intention to move the vessel or move it beyond the area covered by the usual port risks policy.[15]

[11] CPR 61.12.

[12] PD61 §5.7.

[13] *The Mardina Merchant* [1975] 1 WLR 147, 149, [1974] 3 All ER 749, 750–751, [1974] 2 Lloyd's Rep 424, 425. The Australian Federal Court adopted a similar position: 10 May 1996, Practice Note 12, which was subsequently replaced by Practice Note ADM1, para 7 of which is to the same effect as section N13; see *Den Norske Bank (Luxembourg) SA v Ship 'Martha II'* [2000] FCA 241, 9 March 2000 for a discussion of whether effecting insurance is within the broad powers of the Marshal and as such can be claimed as a cost and expense of the arrest. In New Zealand, the Registrar who effected insurance was held to be entitled to be indemnified for the costs of the insurance by the arresting party: *The Cornelis Verolme* (1996) 9 PRNZ 409.

[14] *The Hoop* (1801) 4 C Rob 145, 165 ER 566; *Auxiliary Schooner 'Leonora'* (No1480) (1920) 2 Ll. L Rep 9; *The Cairnsmore, The Gunda* [1915 Nos 690 and 716] [1920] P 209; *Patrick Stevedores (No 2) Pty Ltd v MV Turakina* (1998) 154 ALR 514 (Federal Court of Australia), (1998) 84 FCR 493; *Weir & Lewisporte Shipyards v Bank of Nova Scotia, Hurley & Maher* [1979] 30 Nfdl & PEIR 223 (Newfoundland Supreme Court).

[15] Admiralty & Commercial Courts Guide N13.2.

C. Joinder of Parties

Any person interested in property under arrest, or in the proceeds of sale of such property, or whose interests are affected by any order sought or made, may be made a party to any claim against the property or proceeds of sale.[16] Such a person will include the owner of cargo on board the arrested vessel, a mortgagee, a charterer, and anyone who may suffer 'not merely financial loss or commercial difficulty, but even danger to persons or property'.[17] **7.08**

D. Subsequent *In Rem* Proceedings

The fact that property is under arrest does not prevent an *in rem* claim form being served upon it or its arrest by any other person claiming to have an *in rem* claim against it.[18] Nor does the sale of the ship prevent an *in rem* claim form being issued against the fund in court.[19] The High Court of Hong Kong has emphasized that the fund in court represents the ship; it is therefore not a valid basis for challenging jurisdiction to suggest that the fact that a ship has been sold and the proceeds of sale used to constitute a fund in court means that the 'ownership' nexus cannot be satisfied by later *in rem* claimants.[20] **7.09**

E. Applications Relating to Undertakings

Where any undertaking is required to be given to the Admiralty Marshal, it must be given in writing to his satisfaction and in accordance with such arrangements as he may require.[21] A court is unlikely to accept a personal undertaking from a solicitor if it is apparent that the amount of the undertaking is beyond the means of the **7.10**

---

[16] CPR 61.8(7).

[17] *The Mardina Merchant* [1975] 1 WLR 147, [1974] 3 All ER 749, [1974] 2 Lloyd's Rep 424.

[18] CPR 61.8(1). Such an arrest may serve either or both of the following purposes: (i) to encourage a shipowner to be more forthcoming in the provision of suitable security; and (ii) to found jurisdiction in cases where the shipowner is domiciled in an EU or European Free Trade Association (EFTA) State: *The Anna H* [1995] 1 Lloyd's Rep 11; *The Deichland* [1990] 1 QB 361, [1989] 2 All ER 1066, [1989] 2 Lloyd's Rep 113 (see para 6.32 above).

[19] *The Leoborg (No 2)* [1963] 2 Lloyd's Rep 441.

[20] *International Transportation Service Inc v The Convenience Container* [2006] 902 HKCU 1 (Hong Kong Court of First Instance).

[21] PD61 §14.1: there does not appear to be any power to tax the Marshal's costs and expenses. The Federal Court of Australia has held that r 78B(1) of the Admiralty Rules (Cth) sets out a *prima facie* position that the Marshal's costs and expenses are not to be taxed. In *Bank of China v Ship 'Hai Shi' (No 3)* [2013] FCA 660, Rares J went so far as to hold that the onus is on the party seeking to displace that *prima facie* position to establish that the Marshal incurred any costs or expenses unreasonably or otherwise than in good faith.

solicitor.[22] It is open to any party to seek a ruling from the Registrar in relation to any requirement relating to an undertaking.[23] Disobedience to any undertaking given to the court can result in committal or, in the case of a solicitor's undertaking, in enforcement of the undertaking pursuant to the court's inherent power over its officers.

7.11 It is the practice of the Admiralty Marshal to divide the expenses of keeping a vessel under arrest equally between all parties who have arrested the vessel. The reasons for this practice are that the Admiralty Marshal is not in a position to determine whether the claimants in the different actions have valid causes of action, nor the amount for which the claimant in any particular action will obtain judgment, nor the order of priorities. It has been suggested that the basis of this rule of thumb is the maxim 'equality is equity'. The application of the equitable maxim however, can produce inequity in circumstances where one party becomes liable to pay some part of the expense of the arrest even though it will be unable to recover its contribution from the funds in court or make any recovery on the claim because a party with higher priority will exhaust the fund.[24]

7.12 In *The Falcon*,[25] Sheen J expressed the view that whilst justice would not necessarily be done by dividing equally between various claimants the expense of maintaining the arrested ship, neither would it necessarily be achieved by dividing the expenses in proportion to the size of the claims. A claimant who had arrested a ship should be required to pay all the expenses of the arrest and maintenance of the arrest until such time as he released his arrest. If a second claimant arrests the ship, the expenses which the first claimant undertook to pay are not thereby increased. Furthermore, if a second arrest is effected, the first arrester can release his arrest and enter a caveat against release. Thereafter, all the expenses of maintaining the arrest will fall on the second arrester. The Judge urged the Marshal to adopt the practice of charging all expenses of custody and sale of the ship to the party who obtains the order for appraisement and sale from the date when he lodges the commission for appraisement and sale, so that each litigant will know the extent of his obligations.

7.13 If there is more than one action and if the ship is appraised and sold by an order in the second or subsequent action, the claimant in the first action should apply to the court for reimbursement of the expenses of preserving the property. The court will so order unless the first claimant has acted in bad faith.[26]

7.14 A party who seeks to be released from an undertaking must make the application for release himself and must show sufficient grounds for the variation or rescission

[22] In *Den Norske Bank (Luxembourg) SA v The Ship Martha II*, unreported No VG70 of 1996, 6 March 1996, the Federal Court of Australia would not accept the personal undertaking of the solicitor where the amount in issue was USD16 million.

[23] PD61 §14.2.

[24] See further Chapter 8 below.

[25] *The Falcon* [1981] 1 Lloyd's Rep 13, 17.

[26] Ibid.

of the undertaking, supported by appropriate evidence.[27] A solicitor who gives an undertaking on an application for an arrest warrant may seek to be released from that undertaking in circumstances where he is no longer able to obtain instructions from his client. In such circumstances, the court may release the solicitor from the undertaking, but usually on condition that the vessel be released immediately and that all the fees and expenses of the Marshal up to and including the release of the vessel first be paid by the solicitor.[28]

F. The Provision of Security

It has been observed above that a claimant with an *in rem* claim may arrest a ship as of right, provided that there is jurisdiction for the claim and the statutory criteria for the issue of an arrest warrant are satisfied. At that point the ship is held as security for the claim or is released upon the provision of adequate security. Once security is provided, the security replaces the ship. **7.15**

Form of security

Originally, bail was given as security for the ship in the same way as bail is provided for an individual under arrest. The security was provided either in the form of a bail bond or cash payment into court. Gradually, in addition to those forms of security, other types of security were provided such as a guarantee to the satisfaction of the claimant or the Marshal, often in the form of a P&I Club letter of undertaking. However, these alternative forms of security were a matter of private arrangement between the parties, and the court had no power to order the provision of security in an alternative form to that to which the plaintiff was entitled under the rules of court, namely, bail or payment into court.[29] The use of bail bonds has become obsolete in modern times and there is no longer any specific provision for bail bonds in the CPR.[30] The court's powers with regard to the form of security **7.16**

---

[27] *Cutler v Wandsworth Stadium Ltd* (1945) 172 LT 207; *The Acrux* [1961] 1 Lloyd's Rep 471.

[28] *Bayside Air Conditioning Pty Ltd v The Cape Don* [1997] 790 FCA, 15 May 1997 (Federal Court of Australia).

[29] *The Alletta* [1974] 1 Lloyd's Rep 40, 50. The Canadian Federal Courts Rules give the court power to order security of four specific types: a bank guarantee (r 486(1)(a); a surety company bond in Form 486A (r 486(1)(b)); a bail bond in Form 486A (r 486(1)(c)); or cash paid into court (r 487(1)). In addition, the plaintiff can consent to release on privately negotiated security terms (r 487(1)(c)). However, the Supreme Court of British Columbia observed that the Court ought not to depart from the type and quality of security contemplated by the Rules unless there is a 'really good reason' for so doing: *North King Lodge Ltd v Owners of the Ship Gowlland Chief* [2003] BCD Civ J 15668, 5 June 2003; see also *Pan Ocean Shipping Co v Breeze Navigation Ltd* [2003] FCJ No 68, 21 January 2003.

[30] Similarly, the South African legislation does not contemplate the use of bail bonds as a form of security, but neither Australia, Canada, Hong Kong, New Zealand, nor Singapore have yet modernized their rules to delete the reference to bail bonds. In South Africa it has been held that the security must be something tangible held or controlled by the Registrar and not a private arrangement: *The*

have been widened considerably by CPR 61.5(10), which gives the court power to specify both the amount and form of security which is to be provided.

7.17 The security most often proffered will take the form of a guarantee or letter of undertaking from a bank, insurance company, or P&I Club, or cash paid into court. The wording of any guarantee or letter of undertaking must be scrutinized carefully to ensure that it deals adequately with substantive rights. It should also contain an appropriate choice of law and forum clause to govern disputes arising from the security itself. Not infrequently, the security includes a submission to the jurisdiction on the part of the defendant.

Amount of security

7.18 The security provided by a defendant for the release of a ship under arrest must be for such sum as represents the claimant's reasonably arguable best case including interest and the claimant's costs of the action.[31] This principle applies also where the release is pursuant to statutory provisions because of a stay or dismissal of proceedings on account of an arbitration agreement or the commencement of litigation in a foreign jurisdiction.[32]

Variation of the security terms

7.19 Where security has been given either to obtain the release of property or to prevent its arrest, the court has power in cases of excessive security to order that the amount of security be reduced and may stay the claim until the order is complied with; in cases where the security proves insufficient, the claimant may arrest or rearrest the property proceeded against in order to obtain further security.[33] However, the power of the court to order, release, or vary the amount of security provided does not involve the exercise of a broad and unfettered discretion. *Prima facie*, the sufficiency of the security is a matter for the parties; if they are unable to agree on the

---

Merak S [2000] 1 Lloyd's Rep 619. Similar observations have been made in Hong Kong: *The Alacrity* [1994] 2 HKC 659. The New Zealand approach is examined in *General Motors New Zealand Ltd v The Ship Pacific Charger* AD135/81, 24 July 1981.

[31] *The Moschanthy* [1971] 1 Lloyd's Rep 37; *The Gulf Venture* [1984] 2 Lloyd's Rep 445; *Freshpac Machinery Pty Ltd v Joana Bonita* (1994) 125 ALR 683 (Federal Court of Australia); *Navios International Inc v The Ship Huang Shan Hai* [2011] FCA 895 (Federal Court of Australia); *Brotchie v The Karey T* (1994) 77 FTR 42; *Amican Navigation Inc v Densan Shipping Co* (1997) 137 FTR 132; *NHM International Inc v FC Yachts Ltd* (2003) 227 FTR 42 (Federal Court of Canada); *Canadian Sub Sea Hydraulic Ltd v The Cormorant* (2006) FC 1050 (Federal Court of Canada); *Schoeller Holidaings Ltd v Owners of Hull CZ007* [2001] 1399 HKCU 1 (High Court of Hong Kong); *Hua Tian Long (No 1)* [2008] 4 HKLRD 719 (Hong Kong Court of First Instance); *Det Norske Veritas AS v The Ship Clarabelle* [2002] NZCA 129, [2002] 2 Lloyd's Rep 479 (New Zealand Court of Appeal).

[32] Civil Jurisdiction and Judgments Act, s 26.

[33] CPR 61.6 (1) and (2). See also paras 6.70 and following above, and paras 7.26–7.27 below.

quantum or form of security, the court cannot impose an agreement upon them.[34] In *The Polo II*, Brandon J described the power in these terms:[35]

> … the power to arrest a ship is a very drastic power. And the power to insist that she shall remain under arrest unless security of a certain amount is given is equally a drastic power, and my view, which I expressed in *The Moschanthy* and which I repeat now, is that that power must not be exercised oppressively, and if it is exercised oppressively then the Court can and should interfere to prevent conduct of that kind. At the same time the Court must make sure that the plaintiff is not left without sufficient security to cover his reasonably best arguable case.

The court may not permit the arrest or rearrest of the property to facilitate further security if the total security would exceed the total value of the property either at the time of the original arrest or when the security was first given.[36] **7.20**

In an application for a reduction in the amount of security sought for the release of a vessel, the conduct of both parties is to be considered in determining who should pay the costs.[37] **7.21**

G. Release from Arrest

Cautions against release

A person who claims to have a right *in rem* against property which is already under arrest and who wishes to be notified of any application in respect of that property or its proceeds of sale can protect his interests[38] by filing a request for a caution against release.[39] On the filing of such a request, a caution against release is entered in the Register.[40] There is provision for the filing of a caution against release even where the Registry is closed.[41] **7.22**

A person who has entered a caution against release which results in delay to the release of the property can be ordered to pay damages for losses suffered by any **7.23**

[34] *The Polo II* [1977] 2 Lloyd's Rep 115; *The Gulf Venture* [1984] 2 Lloyd's Rep 445; *Owners of the Ship Carina v The Owners or Demise Charterers of the Ship MSC Samia* [1997] 1001 FCA, 26 September 1997 (Federal Court of Australia); *Det Norske Veritas AS v The Ship Clarabelle* [2002] NZCA 129, [2002] 2 Lloyd's Rep 479 (New Zealand Court of Appeal).

[35] *The Polo II* [1977] 2 Lloyd's Rep 115, 119.

[36] CPR 61.6 (3).

[37] *The Polo II* [1977] 2 Lloyd's Rep 115.

[38] Or some of them. A caution against release will not found jurisdiction: in the European context, only an arrest, agreement to submit, or a submission to the jurisdiction can have that effect: cf *The Anna H* [1995] 1 Lloyd's Rep 11; *The Deichland* [1990] 1 QB 361, [1989] 2 All ER 1066, [1989] 2 Lloyd's Rep 113.

[39] CPR 61.8(2), PD61 §7.1 and Form ADM11. A caution can be withdrawn; PD61 §7.5 and Form ADM12A.

[40] CPR 61.8 (3), PD61 §7.2.

[41] Admiralty & Commercial Courts Guide N7.4–7.10.

person who has an interest in the property.[42] However, a court will not make an order for damages if there was good reason for the entry and maintenance of the caution.[43]

Release

7.24 Property will be released from arrest if:

(1) it is sold by the court;[44]
(2) the court orders that it be released on an application made by any party;[45]
(3) the arresting party and all other persons who have entered cautions against release file a request for release;[46] or
(4) any party files a request for release containing an undertaking, together with consents to the release of the arresting party and all persons who have entered cautions against release.[47]

As with cautions against arrest, provision has been made for an application for release to be dealt with even when the Registry is closed. It is not automatic that the after-hours process will achieve a release but, if the Admiralty Marshal is contactable and available and there are facilities at the relevant port to assist with a release, it may be possible to proceed after hours.[48]

7.25 Under South African law, a ship is deemed to be released from arrest one year after the giving of a letter of undertaking, whether the undertaking is given by private arrangement between the parties or pursuant to the rules of court.[49]

H. Rearrest

7.26 A vessel which has been arrested and released may be rearrested.[50] However, if security has been provided, rearrest will only be permitted where not to do so would create oppression or unfairness. In *The Arctic Star*,[51] subsequent to the provision of adequate security, the vessel's owners took steps which seriously impaired the value of a guarantee. In the circumstances, the Court of Appeal concluded

[42] CPR 61.8(5).
[43] CPR 61.8(6).
[44] CPR 61.8(4)(a).
[45] CPR 61.8(4)(b).
[46] CPR 61.8(4)(c), PD61 §7.4 and Form ADM12.
[47] CPR 61.8(4)(d), PD61 §7.4 and Form ADM12.
[48] Admiralty and Commercial Courts Guide N11.1–11.4.
[49] *Admiralty Jurisdiction Regulation Act 105* of 1983 s 3(10)(a)(ii), *Tiger Food Industries Ltd v The Ionian Mariner* (30 July 2001), M Stranex, *Shipping Cases of South Africa* (3rd edn, 2000) E 110, E141; *Mediterranean Shipping Co Geneva SA v The Alexandra* CA (13 January 2004), M Stranex, *Shipping Cases of South Africa* (3rd edn, 2000) E 141.
[50] See also Chapter 6, paras 6.70 and following, and paras 7.26 to 7.27.
[51] *The Arctic Star*, The Times, 5 February 1985.

that rearrest was appropriate. Similarly, in *The Hero*,[52] rearrest was permitted in circumstances where, due to a clerical error, the plaintiff had miscalculated the proper amount of security.

The New Zealand Court of Appeal has rejected the proposition that rearrest for the purpose of increased security is only appropriate in exceptional circumstances: **7.27**

> On the one hand there is a rule, or immunity, against rearrest. Its expression is ordinarily couched in terms of the need to avoid oppression or unfairness to a ship's owner who has already provided security and thereby secured the release of the ship in the first place. But, on the other hand, there are clear exceptions to that rule, including in the situation where security was fixed at an inadequate amount initially, or where the actions of the owner have rendered originally adequate security inadequate. In such cases, an application to rearrest may be granted in fairness to the plaintiff.[53]

It is respectfully submitted that the approach of the New Zealand Court of Appeal correctly reflects the authorities. In truth, the 'rule' against rearrest is now no more than a back-stop to a regime driven by a reluctance to see a claimant over- or under-secured.

I. Applications Relating to the Discharge of Cargo

It will often be the case that a ship is arrested but the cargo on board is not. In such circumstances, anyone interested in the cargo who wishes to discharge it may request the Marshal to authorize steps to discharge the cargo.[54] Those making such a request of the Marshal do not become parties to the proceedings. If the Marshal considers the request reasonable,[55] and the applicant gives a written undertaking to pay, on demand, the Marshal's fees and expenses,[56] the Marshal will apply to the court for an order to discharge the cargo. If the applicant is unable or unwilling to give the requisite undertaking, the applicant may be made party to the proceedings and apply to the court for the orders sought and directions as to the Marshal's fees and expenses in relation to the discharge and storage of the cargo.[57] In some circumstances, it may be necessary to seek a declaration as to the ownership of the cargo.[58] **7.28**

---

52 *The Hero* (1865) 13 WR 927.

53 *Det Norske Veritas AS v The Ship Clarabelle* [2002] NZCA 129, [2002] 2 Lloyd's Rep 479, 484, [32] (New Zealand Court of Appeal). See also *Ooo DV Ryboprodukt v UAB Garant* [2008] NZCA 136, [2008] 3 NZLR 326, where the Court permitted the plaintiff to rearrest the vessel three times after the owners reneged on assurances to pay the balance of the claim.

54 CPR 61.8(8)(a)(ii) and (b).

55 CPR 61.8 (9)(a); see also *The Myrto (No 2)* [1984] 2 Lloyd's Rep 341, 347–348.

56 CPR 61.8 (9)(b).

57 CPR 61.8 (10).

58 *Campbell's Meat Market Ltd v The Merak* (2000) 99 ACWS (3d) 5.

7.29 Difficulties arise for those interested in the cargo when the ship is arrested at a port other than the intended port of discharge. Applications have been brought that have amounted, in effect, to applications to continue trading the vessel between the contractual discharge ports. The Court of Appeal considered this type of application in *The Bazias 3 and The Bazias 4*[59] where, at first instance, Saville J had made an order that the vessels should remain under arrest but could return to their employment on their cross-Channel service against certain undertakings given by the defendant owners and the third party freighters. In delivering the judgment of the Court of Appeal, Lloyd LJ commented[60] that the order made by Saville J was a contradiction in terms:

> There is no way in which the vessels could remain within the custody of the Admiralty Marshal, as required by the judge, and yet be allowed to trade outside the jurisdiction.

7.30 Accordingly, if there is indeed any power to permit a ship to trade whilst under arrest, it is unlikely that such a ship would be permitted to trade outside territorial waters. The difficulty with the concept of the ship trading whilst under arrest is that the duty of the Marshal, to keep the ship in safe custody and preserve it, does not extend to managerial control and operation of the ship for the purpose of generating an operational profit for the shipowners and those interested in it. This is clear from the procedures in relation to insurance arrangements in England and Australia for ships under arrest,[61] which specifically provide that the Marshal does not take out indemnity or commercial insurance. The operational control of a ship requires that the master and crew operate the ship in accordance with the owner's or demise charterer's instructions. It is impracticable for the Marshal to exercise a veto in respect of those instructions and the on-board management of the ship unless the Marshal or his nominee is presently on board the ship and supervising its operation. Where the ship is traded, the crew is not engaged by the Marshal.

7.31 The approach taken in Australian cases of the same type was to attempt to distinguish between continuing to trade the ship and moving the ship within the jurisdiction, albeit several hundreds of kilometres, to offload the cargo. Specific power to move a ship that is under arrest is provided in the Admiralty Rules 1988,[62] but as the cases referred to below reveal, the court's use of the provision has become sparing.

7.32 In *Den Norske Bank (Luxembourg) SA v The Ship 'Martha II'*,[63] orders were sought for the ship to be moved to other ports and for the discharge of cargo. The *Martha II*

---

59 *The Bazias 3 and The Bazias 4* [1993] QB 673, [1993] 2 WLR 854, [1993] 1 Lloyd's Rep 101.
60 Ibid 679, 857, 103.
61 PD61 §5.7; Practice Note ADM 1 (2013) (Federal Court of Australia).
62 r 47(2)(d).
63 *Den Norske Bank (Luxembourg) SA v The Ship 'Martha II'*, unreported, Federal Court of Australia (VG 70 of 1996).

was arrested in Melbourne at the behest of the mortgagee. In the expectation that the ship would be refinanced and released, the owner applied to the court for permission to sail the ship to Sydney, and there to load and unload cargo in accordance with its scheduled cargo operations. The application was opposed by the plaintiff mortgagee. The Victorian Deputy Sheriff would not consent to the movement without formal orders of the court. Olney J granted the application subject to certain conditions being fulfilled and undertakings being given by the time charterer, including payment before the ship left Melbourne of the Marshal's costs of supervising the movement and the costs of arrest up to the time of the order. The Marshal and two armed members of the Australian Protective Service were on board. The ship proceeded to Botany Bay, where some cargo was offloaded. On the same day, Sheppard J varied the order of Olney J to direct that no new cargo be loaded on board, the refinancing not having materialized, and ordered the ship to proceed from Botany Bay to Port Jackson to berth or anchor in the custody of the Marshal. The owner and the time charterer then applied for permission for the ship to proceed to Port Botany to offload the balance of the cargo other than mineral sands and then to proceed to Newcastle to discharge the mineral sands, it being alleged there were no suitable discharge facilities anywhere else. Sheppard J made orders for the movement of the ship and discharge of the cargo, but would not allow the ship to sail to Newcastle. He distinguished his earlier decision in *Malaysia Shipyard and Engineering Sdn Bhd v Iron Shortland*,[64] where he had approved orders permitting the arrested vessel to sail between Port Hedland in Western Australia and Port Kembla in New South Wales, on the grounds that the orders in that case were by consent, undertakings were provided by Australian third party charterers, and the case involved 'public interest', namely the potential shortage of iron ore at the Port Kembla steelworks.

A similar application was made in relation to the cargo on board the *Socofl Stream* in *Sovremenniy Kommercheskiy Flot v The Ship 'Socofl Stream'*.[65] The applicant was the consignee of the cargo of steel coils and sought orders permitting the vessel to sail from the port of arrest, Brisbane, to Newcastle in order to discharge the cargo. The arresting party did not oppose the order and the applicant offered cash security to cover the Marshal's expenses of the voyage. There was evidence that it would not be necessary for the vessel to leave the territorial sea in the course of the voyage and so the vessel could, at all times, remain within the jurisdiction of the Federal Court. However, the Marshal strenuously opposed the application on the basis that nothing, not even the presence of security officers on board, could prevent the ship 'turning left' if the master so decided. Kiefel J accepted the Marshal's argument and declined to make the orders. **7.33**

[64] *Malaysia Shipyard and Engineering Sdn Bhd v Iron Shorland* (1995) 131 ALR 738, (1995) 59 FCR 535.

[65] *Sovremenniy Kommercheskiy Flot v The Ship 'Socofl Stream'* [1999] FCA 42.

7.34 It is submitted that the approach of Kiefel J in *The Scofl Stream* and that of Sheppard J in *The Martha II* accords with the underlying rationale of the jurisdiction to arrest. For some time it seemed unlikely that, at least in the Australian context, the orders made by Sheppard J in *The Martha II* and *The Iron Shortland* would again be made. However, in *Commandate Marine Corp v The Boomerang I*[66] Allsop J permitted a vessel to sail whilst under arrest from Fremantle in Western Australia to Sydney. The basis for the decision appears to have been serious doubt as to the legitimacy of the arrest given earlier authority against the proposition that the word 'owner' in s 19(b) of the Admiralty Act included a demise or bare-boat charterer.[67] It is submitted, with respect, that this is wrong in principle. Either the vessel is properly under arrest, in which case—at any rate absent very strong factors making it correspondingly unlikely that the vessel will abscond or significant public policy considerations[68]—obvious practical considerations militate against its being permitted to set sail, even if its ostensible destination is another port within the jurisdiction. Or it is not properly under arrest, in which case it ought to be released. It is difficult to see why the need to resolve a short point of law, even at short notice, should produce a different result.

A more orthodox (and, it is submitted, correct) approach was taken in *Tai Shing Maritime CO SA v The Ship 'Samsun Veritas' as surrogate for the Ship 'Tai Hawk'*,[69] where the Federal Court of Australia made orders permitting a vessel arrested in Port Hedland to sail to the Port of Dampier. The vessel was fully laden with 140,000 tonnes of iron ore and the spring tides meant there was a 'very real likelihood' that the vessel would run aground unless she was moved. The journey involved the vessel leaving Australia's territorial waters for part of the voyage but the Marshal did not oppose the ship going to Dampier provided adequate security arrangements were accommodated. Most importantly, the Court considered that the 'very significant public policy considerations' of safety meant the ship should be permitted to sail to Dampier while under arrest.

7.35 In New Zealand, a passenger vessel was arrested near the start of a week-long voyage. The innocent charterer was threatened with the loss of reputation and the tourists on board with the prospect of a wasted and expensive trip to New Zealand to embark on the voyage. The Court held that it had jurisdiction to authorize the Registrar to permit the vessel to continue with the cruise.[70] Again, it is submitted that this decision is dubious in principle.

---

66 *Commandate Marine Corp v The Boomerang I* [2006] FCA 859.

67 Ibid [5]–[7] citing, inter alia, *The Maria Luisa* (2003) 130 FCR 1; *The Andrea Ursula* [1973] QB 265; *I Congreso del Partido* [1978] QB 500.

68 *Tai Shing Maritime CO SA v The Ship 'Samsun Veritas' as surrogate for the Ship 'Tai Hawk'* [2008] FCA 1546.

69 Ibid.

70 *Marine Expeditions Inc v The Ship Akademik Shuleykin* (unreported, Wellington AD 294, 3 March 1995).

J. Applications Relating to the Loading of Cargo

When a trading vessel is placed under arrest, issues will inevitably arise as to whether the loading of cargo should continue, with the obvious risk that the arrest will not be lifted and the cargo will have to be unloaded again. A degree of common sense is to be applied in such cases. In *The Myrto (No 2)*,[71] Sheen J remarked *obiter*: **7.36**

> If the Marshal arrests a ship which is in the process of loading cargo, he will, as a matter of practice, warn the ship's agent not to continue loading if the writ in the action has been issued by mortgagees. He gives this warning because of the high probability that there will be an order for the sale of the ship. But in other cases the Marshal will not suggest that loading is discontinued because the probability is that security for the claim will be given.

While Sheen J was, with respect, undoubtedly right to differentiate between an arrest by mortgagees and a more run-of-the-mill cargo claim arrest, the risk that the anticipated security will not materialize must be evaluated in the round, if innocent commercial parties are not to be seriously inconvenienced and the Marshal potentially[72] exposed to liability for reducing the value of the security.[73] Whilst some Australian judges have permitted vessels to load while under arrest,[74] in *News Maritime Co Ltd v 'Hyundai Cosmos'*[75] Tamberlin J indicated that substantial and persuasive evidence to justify the loading of additional cargo (73,000 tonnes of coal) would be required before it was permitted: **7.37**

> If the loading of cargo were permitted in this case, problems could arise should it become necessary to offload the cargo in order to carry out a possible sale of the vessel. There could also be complications in relation to liability for any incidents occurring during the on-loading of cargo and also in relation to contracts entered into in connection with the remaining cargo.

K. Applications Relating to the Discharge of the Ship when the Cargo is Arrested

As with requests for the discharge of cargo, a shipowner can, without becoming a party to the proceeding, request the Marshal to discharge the ship in circumstances where only the cargo on board has been arrested.[76] If the Marshal considers **7.38**

[71] *The Myrto (No 2)* [1984] 2 Lloyd's Rep 341, 347–348.
[72] In some jurisdictions at least.
[73] Indeed, the very fact that an application has come before the court for permission to continue loading while the vessel is still under arrest is not an auspicious starting point for the suggestion that security is bound to be provided in the near future.
[74] *Den Norske Bank (Luxembourg) SA v The Ship 'Martha II'*, unreported, Federal Court of Australia (VG 70 of 1996).
[75] *News Maritime Co Ltd v 'Hyundai Cosmos'* [2002] FCA 1164, (2002) 121 FCR 77, 80, [14].
[76] CPR 61.8(8).

the request reasonable[77] and the applicant gives a written undertaking to pay, on demand, the Marshal's fees and expenses,[78] the Marshal will apply to the court for an order to discharge the ship. If the applicant is unable or unwilling to give the requisite undertaking, the applicant may be made party to the proceedings and apply to the court for the orders sought and directions as to the Marshal's fees and expenses.[79]

L. Applications Relating to the Crew

7.39 The arresting party will not normally be concerned about the crew on board the arrested vessel because trading ships will usually provide a P&I Club letter of undertaking or post other security to secure release. If they do not, however, and particularly if it becomes necessary to remove the crew from the ship so that it can be sold, the position of the crew may become a lively and intractable issue— and can seriously delay the process of sale.

7.40 To take a fairly extreme example, in *The River Andoni*,[80] the vessel was arrested by bunker suppliers on 20 September 1994 and judgment in default of defence entered and an order for appraisement and sale made on 4 November 1994. By mid-December it had become clear that the position of the crew was not straightforward. Most if not all of the 49-strong crew were Nigerian and could not simply be removed from the vessel, but had to be repatriated; they were, moreover, owed substantial amounts in unpaid wages and lacked the wherewithal on their own to commence proceedings;[81] they also had substantial personal possessions,[82] which they could not afford on their own to repatriate. Eventually contact was established with the ITF and proceedings were issued on 19 January 1995 on behalf of most of the crew. A month later an order was made that the crew vacate the vessel by a date set a week or so later, but that deadline was later extended by nearly a month. It was not until 17 March 1995, nearly six months after the vessel had first been arrested,[83] that the matter was resolved and an order made for the vessel's release.

---

[77] CPR 61.8(9)(a).

[78] CPR 61.8(9)(b).

[79] CPR 61.8(10).

[80] *The River Andoni* 1994 Fo 1579, 1995 Fo 103.

[81] Until proceedings had been commenced and prosecuted to judgment, there could be no certainty as to their entitlement in that regard, which made paying off the crew in return for being subrogated to their claim an unattractive proposition for the trade creditors.

[82] Some impression of this may be gained from an order made shortly after the crew had commenced proceedings that:

> The Admiralty Marshal to be at liberty to treat as his expenses the reasonable cost of the repatriation of the Master, Officers and Crew, including not more than two (2) 40 foot containers for personal effects (which for the avoidance of doubt do not include cars or other motor vehicles).

In addition to cars, one of the crew had apparently procured a mobile library during the vessel's stay on Merseyside.

[83] During which time the vessel and the predicament of her crew had been raised in the House of Commons: *Hansard*, HC 28 February 1995, col 851.

The court, faced with an impasse such as that which occurred with regard to *The River Andoni*, is faced with a delicate situation. No judge in the modern era would wish to be the author of an order which resulted in riot police—no doubt on live television—storming a freighter and carrying off her unpaid crew for the benefit of substantial commercial interests owed a few tens of thousands of dollars for fuel or lubricants. Indeed, it would run entirely contrary to the long and, indeed, noble tradition of the Admiralty Court of protecting the seaman for such an order to be made without giving the crew every opportunity to present their legitimate concerns, and without the court making every effort to accommodate them. Although, therefore, the court will be prepared to order a recalcitrant crew to vacate a vessel, and to back that order with a penal notice,[84] it is difficult to imagine Clarke J—who as the then Admiralty Judge dealt with the saga of *The River Andoni*—expressing himself in quite the terms chosen by his predecessor, Hewson J, in *The Fairport*:[85] **7.41**

> One thing I can say and that is that if there is anybody left on board 24 hours from now he will get nothing thereafter ... There has been quite enough nonsense. This Court is here to help, but it is not going to be humbugged ... They prayed this Court's aid and, having prayed its aid, they must abide its decision ...

It follows that a claimant faced with a situation in which an owner has become insolvent, leaving an unpaid crew on board the vessel, will be well advised to take steps to address the crew's position sooner rather than later. **7.42**

The Marshal's position

The Marshal owes no duty to the crew on board an arrested vessel, but his approach to crew issues may depend on the extent to which the crew's continued presence on board the ship impacts on his duty to ensure the safe custody and preservation of the ship. Where a ship can be safely locked up as a dead ship, as would be the case, for example, if a yacht or a trawler could be stored on a hardstand or a permanent slipway, it may be unnecessary for even a ship's keeper to be appointed,[86] let alone for the crew to remain on board. **7.43**

The Marshal will incur no liability for crew wages until such time as there is an agreement between the Marshal and the crew that the latter will provide services as and when requested by the Marshal.[87] That may arise if, for example, the Marshal **7.44**

---

[84] Such an order was made several times in the course of *The River Andoni*. The order also required the claimants to deliver sufficient copies of the order to the vessel's master for each crew member to be given his own.

[85] *The Fairport* [1965] 2 Lloyd's Rep 183, 185.

[86] *Clausen v The Ship 'Om Alqora' (No 2)* (1985) 38 SASR 494, 499–500; *Mooloolaba Slipways Pty Ltd v The 'Santa Maria'* [2001] QSC 470.

[87] *Patrick Stevedores (No 2) Pty Ltd v MV Turakina (No 1)* (1998) 84 FCR 493, 502, (1998) 154 ALR 514, 523. See also the more recent Singapore decision of *The 'Makassar Caraka Jaya Niaga III-39'* [2012] SGHC 175.

is required to move the arrested ship because it is adversely affecting the operation of the port or berth, posing a risk to safety in the position where it was arrested, or if it is incurring substantial wharfage charges where arrested.[88] In such circumstances, the Marshal may engage such crew members as are necessary to achieve the purpose and to maintain the crew at a prudent level consistent with the discharge of his duty.[89]

7.45 In *Patrick Stevedores No 2 Pty Ltd v Ship MV Turakina (No 1)*,[90] the Marshal appointed the master of the ship as the ship's keeper. At the time of appointment, the Marshal made it clear to the master that he had no intention of entering into any contractual obligation in relation to the wages and entitlements of the crew. The appointment of the master as ship's keeper did not authorize the master, as agent of the Marshal, to engage the crew on behalf of the Marshal. The crew sought to argue that while on board the ship after arrest, and to the knowledge of the Marshal, the crew performed daily tasks in respect of the ship which contributed to its preservation and safe custody. As the Marshal was duty bound to ensure the safety and preservation of the ship, the crew argued that the work was directed at assisting the Marshal in the discharge of his duty. For that reason, the crew submitted that their wages for performing the work should be treated as part of the Marshal's costs of arrest. Tamberlin J rejected that argument:[91]

> The payment of the wages and other employment entitlements of the crew after arrest and up to sale or repatriation is, generally speaking, not the responsibility of the Marshal unless the Marshal considers it appropriate or necessary to enter into an agreement to engage such crew. The number and nature of the crew to be engaged by the Marshal will vary from time to time depending on the status of particular vessels, such as, for example, whether they are laid up. In many cases the vessels will be carrying cargo. Where this is so the number of crew necessary to man the ship will reflect the need to preserve and exercise custody over the cargo. The appropriate crew number may also depend on whether it was necessary to move the vessel in order to effect discharge of cargo or to berth at a suitable location which may vary from time to time as a result of exigencies at the port of arrest. What is necessary or appropriate in any particular case will depend to a large extent on the nature and quantity of the cargo.

7.46 If the crew on board refuses to assist in the movement of the ship, the Marshal may determine to tow the ship to a new location as a dead ship.[92]

---

[88] *The Mardina Merchant* [1975] 1 WLR 147, 149, [1974] 3 All ER 749, 750–751, [1974] 2 Lloyd's Rep 424, 425.

[89] See *Gulf Azov Shipping Co Ltd v Idisi* [2001] 1 Lloyd's Rep 727, 735, [38] where the Court of Appeal observed that no vessel under arrest needed 27 crew to look after her.

[90] *Patrick Stevedores No 2 Pty Ltd v Ship MV Turakina (No 1)* (1998) 84 FCR 493, (1998) 154 ALR 514.

[91] Ibid 502, 523.

[92] *The Myrto (No 2)* [1984] 2 Lloyd's Rep 341.

The employment relationship

The arrest of the ship does not determine the employment relationship between the owners or demise charterers and the master and crew. Nor will the issue of a claim form against the ship by the master or crew to recover outstanding wages automatically determine this relationship. It will be a question to be ascertained on the facts of each case whether or not the employment contracts of the master and crew have come to an end.[93] Even if the employment relationship has been terminated, then crew members may seek to recover wages accrued up until the termination and, thereafter, damages for breach of contract calculated by reference to the wages lost, the cost of sustenance for a reasonable time at the place of termination pending repatriation to their home port, and the cost of repatriation.[94] **7.47**

The consequence of the continued employment of the crew after arrest will be the *pro tanto* reduction in the value of the ship or proceeds of sale by the amount of the accruing liability for wages—in other words, a reduction in the overall amount available to satisfy those claims which have a lesser priority than the claims of the master and crew.[95] Although the continued engagement of the crew by the owner will give the former rights to wages and entitlements, such as accommodation on board and the right to sustenance, those rights are not enforceable against the Marshal. However, the Marshal may, if he considers it necessary for the safety of the ship or to preserve it, pay wages and provide accommodation and sustenance to the crew on board.[96] **7.48**

The continued presence of the crew on board

The presence of the crew on board is justifiable only for so long as it does not interfere with the ship or the Marshal's custody of it, and does not increase the Marshal's costs of maintaining custody of the ship and preserving it. If a ship can conveniently be laid up as a dead ship pending trial or the provision of security, a crew will not, all else being equal, be permitted to remain on board where that would involve, for example, unnecessary expense in providing power or access to the ship to enable the crew to live on board. Giles J of the New Zealand High Court observed in this connection that it was unnecessary for the crew to remain on board either to assert or protect their rights; just as a mortgagee would not be allowed to enter into possession or exercise powers adverse to the Marshal's custody or, a trade creditor **7.49**

---

[93] *The Fairport (No 2)* [1966] 3 WLR 426, 435, [1966] 2 All ER 1026, 1034, [1966] 2 Lloyd's Rep 7, 14. In some cases, it may be that the contractual relationship is actually between the crew and a crewing agency rather than the vessel: *Ship Hako Endeavour & Ors v Programmed Total Marine Services Pty Ltd* [2013] FCAFC 21.

[94] *United States Trust Company of New York v Master and Crew of the Ship 'Ionian Mariner'* (1997) 77 FCR 563, (1997) 149 ALR 200.

[95] See Chapter 8 in relation to the priority of the master's and crew's claims for wages.

[96] *Clausen v The Ship 'Om Alqora' (No 2)* (1985) 38 SASR 494, 500.

asserting a retention of title clause would not be permitted to unbolt the ship's equipment pending determination of its claims, so it seemed wrong in principle that seafarers should be permitted to remain on board to try and force acceptance of their claims.[97] Without disagreeing with Giles J's observations in principle, it is submitted that much may depend on the particular facts of the case. It may be, as in *The River Andoni*,[98] that disembarking the crew is simply not a practical proposition until arrangements have been put in place to meet their legitimate claims[99] and to secure their orderly repatriation together with their belongings.

7.50 If the crew refuses to leave a ship, the manner of resolving the situation can have significant consequences for the fund which is ultimately available to satisfy the claimant's claim and costs and the claims of others against the ship. The practice of treating wages paid by the claimant after the issue of the writ as the claimant's costs in the action, and thus recoverable, as the costs of the producer of the fund, in priority to other claimants,[100] was disapproved by Cairns J, who said:[101]

> ... if wages continue to accrue I think it must follow that they are recoverable by action and not merely as part of the costs of an action.

7.51 The result is that, in the ordinary course, a claimant will receive no advantage by paying out the claim of the crew, including the payment of repatriation costs, unless it receives the leave of the court to make the payment and to stand in the shoes of the crew in respect of any sums so paid.[102] Where a party stands in the shoes of the crew after payment, the right to recover monies so paid is postponed until after satisfaction of the Marshal's costs and expenses, and also until after satisfaction of the costs of the producer of the fund. Payment of the monies without the leave of the court gives the payer no right to subrogation.[103]

7.52 Nonetheless, in some circumstances, the court will be prepared to treat payments to the crew as part of the costs of the sale, and therefore the costs of the action, if it is appropriate to do so in the interests of all the parties and of justice on the facts of the particular case.[104] In *The Guiseppe di Vittorio (No 2)*, it was necessary for

---

[97] *Partenreederei MS Takitimu v The Ship Takitimu* (unreported, AD No 882, Auckland Registry, 23 March 1998).

[98] Para 7.40 above.

[99] That may require the commencement of proceedings by them and the prosecution of those proceedings to judgment. Only when judgment has been entered is a trade creditor, for example, likely to feel sufficiently confident to offer to pay the crew the amount of their outstanding wages in the first instance, in return for being subrogated to their claims against the fund eventually produced upon sale of the vessel.

[100] *The Fairport (No 2)* [1966] 3 WLR 426, [1966] 2 All ER 1026, [1966] 2 Lloyd's Rep 7.

[101] Ibid 435, 1034, 14.

[102] *Borneo Company v 'Mogileff'* (1921) 7 Ll LR 130; *The Guiseppe di Vittorio (No 2)* [1998] 1 Lloyd's Rep 661.

[103] *The Petone* [1917] P 198. See the *obiter* comments of Siopis J in *Ship Hako Endeavour & Ors v Programmed Total Marine Services Pty Ltd* [2013] FCAFC 21 [3].

[104] *The Guiseppe di Vittorio (No 2)* [1998] 1 Lloyd's Rep 661.

the crew to leave the vessel in order for it to be sold, the crew having commenced proceedings for the payment of their wages. By a previous application brought by the claimant trade creditors, the court had determined the amount of wages owed to the crew as at that date, had ordered that the claimants be at liberty to pay the crew, and had declared that, on payment, the claimants would be subrogated to the crew's maritime lien provided that any sum so paid was paid following the crew's departure from the ship. Clarke J held:[105]

> Although the Court would never permit the crew to stand in the way of a sale, it was nevertheless reasonable for the plaintiffs to incur these expenses and to pay the crew after the crew had left the vessel. In these circumstances I can see no reason why, on the facts of the instant case, the amounts so paid should not be treated as part of the plaintiffs' costs like their other costs of arrest and sale.

Alternatively, where no claimant is prepared or able to pay off the crew in order to **7.53** obtain vacant possession of the ship, the court may order that the Marshal pay the crew's repatriation expenses and, if necessary, the claim for wages. Such expenses may then be rationalized as payments made to realize the ship on a Marshal's sale to best advantage. If so ordered, the expenses will form part of the Marshal's expenses.[106]

These two approaches both result in the payment of the crew's claim. However, the **7.54** order in which the outlay is reimbursed from the fund arising from the sale of the ship is dependent upon who has made the payment. When paid by a party other than by the Marshal, the costs will rank after the Marshal's costs and expenses of the arrest, the costs and expenses of appraisement and sale, and the costs of the producer of the fund. When paid by the Marshal, the crew will obtain a priority unavailable on a proper distribution because its claim will have been met in priority to the costs and expenses of the arresting party and the judgment creditor.

M. Appraisement and Sale

A party may apply to the court at any time during the proceeding of a claim, **7.55** including prior to the determination of the claimant's claim, for an order for the survey, appraisement, and/or sale of a ship.[107] The word 'party' does not include a person who has done no more than file a caution against release, but such a person will be given notice of any application concerning the sale of the ship.[108] It is not expressly provided in the rules that the property must be under arrest at the time when an order for sale is made, but the Practice Direction envisages that, at least in

---

[105] Ibid 672.

[106] *The General Serret* (1925) 23 Ll L Rep 14, 15; *The Myrto (No 2)* [1984] 2 Lloyd's Rep 341, 348; *The Guiseppe di Vittorio (No 2)* [1998] 1 Lloyd's Rep 661.

[107] CPR 61.10(1).

[108] PD61 §9.1(2)(b).

relation to an order for sale, the property will be under arrest.[109] This is consistent with earlier practice.[110]

7.56 The sale of a 'ship' extends to her appurtenances.[111] The ordinary meaning of 'appurtenance' is a mechanical accessory or some apparatus or gear which appertains or belongs to the ship.[112] It does not include fuel oil.[113]

7.57 The practice relating to the sale of the ship was described by Sheen J in *The Silia*:[114]

> When this court orders that a ship is to be sold it is the duty of the Admiralty Marshal to realize the highest price, and it is his practice to sell the ship and her contents, other than those articles which are the personal property of someone other than the owner of that ship. He permits the removal of the personal effects of the crew and equipment which is on hire; he destroys perishable food or other food which might attract vermin. In order to realize the highest price it was the practice in the past for the Marshal to sell separately from the ship such things as tinned food, stores, barometers and chronometers. The manner in which such items are sold is left to the discretion of the Marshal. Barometers and chronometers are now sold with the ship. Unbroached drums of oil are usually sold separately. But the oil in a ship's tanks must, for practical reasons, be sold with the ship. Those reasons are as follows. In some parts of this country the removal of fuel oil from a ship's tanks is prohibited because of the hazards involved. But even where that operation is permitted the oil would have to be pumped out of the tanks. In the case of a ship under arrest the need to remove the oil would be likely to occur at a time when pumps are not in operation and when no engine-room personnel are available. The oil would have to be pumped into a barge or land tanker, and the cost of the operation would have to be paid for. The quantity of oil might be too small to justify the cost of removing it. Furthermore, if the oil were to be removed from the ship it would be likely to attract import duty. On the other hand, that oil will realize the current market price if it is sold in the ship. If anyone other than the owner of the ship asserts a right of property in the oil the Marshal refers that question to this court, as was done, for example, in *The Saint Anna* [1980] 1 Lloyd's Rep 180. In that case it was not contended by the charterers that the Court has no power to sell their fuel oil. The charterers only sought to recover the proceeds of its sale. It is the practice of the Admiralty Marshal to account separately for the proceeds of sale of fuel and lubricating oil sold with the ship because the brokers are entitled to commission on the price of the ship, but not on the price of the oil.

7.58 An application for appraisement or sale contains a personal undertaking by the solicitors for the party making the application to pay on demand the fees and

109 PD61 §9.1(1).

110 *The Wexford* (1888) 13 PD 10; *The Berris* (1905) Fo 497.

111 *The Eurosun and Eurostar* [1993] 1 Lloyd's Rep 106; *The Silia* [1981] 2 Lloyd's Rep 534; *Morelines Maritime Agency Ltd v The Ship Skulptor Vuchetich* (1996) 62 FCR 602, (1996) 136 ALR 206.

112 *The Eurosun and Eurostar* [1993] 1 Lloyd's Rep 106.

113 *The Honshu Gloria* [1986] 2 Lloyd's Rep 63; *The Pan Oak* [1992] 2 Lloyd's Rep 36; *The Eurosun and Eurostar* [1993] 1 Lloyd's Rep 106.

114 *The Silia* [1981] 2 Lloyd's Rep 534, 535.

expenses of the Marshal incurred by him or on his behalf in respect of the appraisement and sale of the property, or of endeavours to appraise or sell the property.[115] Any person interested in property under arrest or the proceeds of sale or whose interests are affected by any order sought may be made a party to the proceedings.[116] Any such application will be heard in public and notice of the application must be served on all parties to the claim, all persons who have requested cautions against release, and the Marshal.[117] If the application for appraisement and sale is made by the Marshal himself in the exercise of his general powers in respect of property under arrest, it would appear that the Marshal will have to fund the costs of the sale himself until those costs can be recovered from the proceeds on completion of the sale.[118]

Sale *pendente lite*

The rules clearly contemplate that an order for sale may be made before judgment. **7.59** Such an order may, however, only be made by the Admiralty Judge and not by the Registrar.[119] A court should not make an order for the appraisement or sale of a ship *pendente lite*, whether or not the action is defended, except for good reason.[120] The principles applicable to such an order were identified by Brandon J in *The Myrto*.[121] Normally an order for sale before judgment will be sought only where there is a default of acknowledgement of service or defence. In such circumstances, it is common practice for the court to make an order on the basis that the security for the claim will be diminished by the continuing costs of maintaining the arrest

---

115 Form ADM14: the undertaking is given by the 'Solicitors on behalf of the claimant'. Presumably this means the firm which is acting for the relevant party and not merely an individual solicitor. In Australia, the Admiralty Rules provide that an application for the valuation and sale of a vessel constitutes an undertaking to pay the Marshal's costs and expenses by 'the party' who made the application (r 69). Other provisions require undertakings by legal practitioners in relation to a caveat against arrest (r 7), an application for arrest (r 41), the discharge of cargo or vessel arrested (r 49), and the release from arrest of a ship or other property (r 53). There are specific provisions dealing with when an undertaking may be given by a law practice rather than an individual legal practitioner (r 75A). Disclosure of matters affecting safety is also required (r 39A).

116 CPR 61.8(7); *The Saint Anna* [1980] 1 Lloyd's Rep 180.

117 PD61 §9.1.

118 Unless the undertaking of the arresting party extends this far. In Australia, an application for the valuation and sale of a vessel constitutes an undertaking by the party who made the application to pay the costs and expenses of the Marshal (r 69); see also Tamberlin J in *The Rangitata* [1998] FCA 244 (Federal Court of Australia). In South Africa there is no requirement that the Sheriff must conduct the sale of a ship. Rule 21(4) of the Admiralty Proceedings Rules provides that 'any interested party' is entitled to apply for the sale of a ship. See *Credit Commerce de France v The Lady Muriel* (21 November 1995) M Stranex, *Shipping Cases of South Africa* (3rd edn, 2000) E 34.

119 PD61 §9.3.

120 *The Myrto* [1977] 2 Lloyd's Rep 243, 260; *The Guiseppe di Vittorio* [1998] 1 Lloyd's Rep 661 (where, in addition, there was no objection); *MT Tigr v Bouygues Offshore* 1998 (4) SA 206; *Farocean Marine (Pty) Ltd v Summit One* 2003 (6) SA 94.

121 *The Myrto* [1977] 2 Lloyd's Rep 243: followed in Hong Kong in *The Athenian Zoe (No 2)* [1985] 1 HKC 367; and New Zealand in *Bank of Nakhodka v The Ship Abruka* (1997) 10 PRNZ 326.

to the disadvantage of all those interested in the ship. If the action is defended, then the court will examine the question of whether there is good reason for making the order more critically, and a significant factor influencing that decision will be the effect of maintaining the arrest on the value of the claimant's security.[122] Where a vessel is sold *pendente lite*, it is still the Marshal that must appraise the vessel and advertise and invite offers for the sale of the vessel. Except in special circumstances, the court will not order the Marshal to sell to a purchaser found by the arresting party, even if the proposed price appears to be at or around the market value for the vessel.[123] This is because a private sale by the arresting party would tend to undermine the impartiality of the Marshal.[124]

7.60 The decision in *The Union Gold* reflects sentiments voiced by Waung J in the earlier Hong Kong case of *The Margo L*.[125] The Singapore High Court followed *The Union Gold* and *The Margo L* (and an even earlier Canadian case)[126] in *The Turtle Bay*[127] and *The Sea Urchin*.[128] Belinda Ang J held that the court would only permit what it termed a 'direct judicial sale' in 'special circumstances' or where 'powerful special features' required it. In *The Sea Urchin*, even the presence of a perishable (and perishing) cargo, with mounting daily costs, was insufficient to qualify.

7.61 Evidence in support of an application for sale *pendente lite* might include:

(1) the overall value of the claim;
(2) the number of cautions against release and other claims against the ship and their likely value;
(3) the value of the ship and its likely diminution in value during the course of the arrest;
(4) the costs of maintaining the vessel's arrest, including such costs as port and berth charges, ship's keeper, crew wages and emoluments, supply of domestic fuel to the vessel, and so on, and the consequent diminution in the claimant's security;
(5) any (prospect of) deterioration in the condition of the ship;

---

122 *The Gulf Venture* [1985] 1 Lloyd's Rep 131; *Bank of Scotland v Nel* (1997) 149 FTR 271; *Neves v Kristina Logos* (1999) 173 FTR 31 (Federal Court of Canada); *Marinis Ship Suppliers Pty Limited v The Ship Ionian Mariner* (1995) 59 FCR 245; *Bayside Air Conditioning Pty Ltd v The Owners of the Ship Cape Don* [1997] FCA 690, 15 May 1997 (Federal Court of Australia); *The Beluga Notification* [2011] FCA 665 (Federal Court of Australia); *UAB Garant v The Ship Aleksandr Ksenefontov* (unreported, High Court of New Zealand 21 December 2007); *Yang Ming Marie Transport Corporation v the Owners of the Ship Dong Yun 419* [2002] 817 HKCU 1 (High Court of Hong Kong); *Dias Compania Naviera SA v Al Kaziemah* 1994 (1) SA 570 (D).

123 *Bank of Scotland Plc v Owners of the Union Gold* [2014] 1 Lloyd's Rep 53.

124 Ibid.

125 *Den Norske Bank ASA v Owners of the ship 'Margo L'* [1997] HKEC 767.

126 *International Marine Banking Co v Dora (No 2)* [1977] FC 603.

127 *The Turtle Bay* [2013] 4 SLR 615.

128 *The Sea Urchin* [2014] SGHC 24.

(6) any necessary work to be done on the ship either to keep it afloat or to enable it to be moved;
(7) the unwillingness of the shipowner to contribute to the costs of the arrest;
(8) the financial position of the shipowner and his unwillingness or inability to provide security for the ship's release;
(9) the likely intervention of claimants with higher priority;
(10) humanitarian considerations in relation to the crew;
(11) whether, if the claimant obtains judgment in his favour, the judgment can be satisfied by the defendant without the need to sell the ship in any event.

Private sale before order

At any time up until an order for sale is made, the shipowner is at liberty to arrange for its sale. Even if such a sale is made, the ship will remain under arrest and subject to the claim upon it.[129] Once an order for sale has been made, however, it is a contempt of court for the owner to attempt to sell the ship.[130] **7.62**

The sale process

Once the court has made an order for sale[131] it will usually set a time within which notice of claims against the proceeds must be filed and the time and manner in which the notice must be advertised.[132] Unless the court otherwise orders, the Marshal is required to have the ship appraised by an experienced valuer[133] who will certify the value of the ship, and the Marshal is required to sell the ship for the highest price he can obtain,[134] which—absent a special order—must not be less than the certified value of the ship. If the Marshal conducts the sale of a vessel negligently, he may be liable for loss suffered in the same way as he is liable for loss or damage suffered by the vessel whilst in his custody.[135] There is no provision in the rules relating to the manner in which a sale must be conducted by the Marshal, but it will most commonly be by private treaty following reasonable advertisement of the ship for sale.[136] **7.63**

---

[129] In *The Monmouth Coast* (1922) 12 Ll L Rep 22, the court approved a private sale but on condition that the proceeds of sale be paid to the Marshal on account of his expenses.

[130] *The Ruth Kayser* (1925) 23 Ll Rep 95; *The Jarvis Brake* [1976] 2 Lloyd's Rep 320, [1976] 2 All ER 886; *The APJ Shalin* [1991] 2 Lloyd's Rep 62.

[131] Form ADM14, PD61 §9.2.

[132] CPR 61.10(2).

[133] The expertise of a broker appointed by the Registrar was challenged in *Mobil Oil NZ Ltd v Ship Rangiora* (unreported, Auckland AD 877, 881, 882, 21 August 1998).

[134] *The Silia* [1981] 2 Lloyd's Rep 534, 535; *Armco Pacific Ltd v Lim Juliano* [1989] 2 HKC 237 (High Court of Hong Kong).

[135] In New Zealand it has been held that a creditor who is dissatisfied with the price achieved by the Registrar has no standing to seek a declaration challenging the validity of the contract; *All Weather Investments Ltd v Sealord Charters Ltd* (1997) 10 PRNZ 320.

[136] Any advertisement in relation to the vessel which might have the effect of detracting from the vessel and hence from the Marshal's ability to achieve full market price could be treated as contempt of court: *The Cerro Colorado* [1993] 1 Lloyd's Rep 58.

Stopping the sale process

7.64 In the event that circumstances change between the making of an order for appraisement and sale and the completion of a sale, a party may apply to the court for the order to be suspended[137] or even set aside. The suspension of an order for sale will only be made on confirmation that there are, or will within a specified and short period be,[138] sufficient funds within the jurisdiction[139] to satisfy all the claims before the court. Such an order will not be made lightly, particularly when the Admiralty Marshal has commenced negotiations with third parties for the sale of the vessel.

The proceeds of sale and the determination of priorities

7.65 The proceeds of sale are paid into court by the Marshal. The Marshal may sell in a foreign currency, in which case, the funds are placed on one day call in an interest bearing account unless the court otherwise orders.[140] An application may be made to the Registrar to place foreign currency on longer term deposit.[141] In any event, notice of the placement of foreign currency in an interest bearing account must be given to all parties interested in the fund,[142] and any party who objects to the mode of investment can apply to the Registrar for directions.[143]

7.66 After the time prescribed for the filing and advertising of claims against the proceeds of sale, any party with a judgment against the property or the proceeds of sale may apply to the court for the determination of priorities.[144] Such an application must be served on all persons who have filed claims against the property.[145] The determination of priorities may only be made by the Admiralty Judge, unless the Judge otherwise orders.[146] The principles relating to the determination of the order of priorities are considered in Chapter 8. Once a determination of the order of priorities has been made, payment out of the proceeds of sale is made to the judgment creditors in order of that determination or as the court otherwise orders.[147]

The effect of judicial sale

7.67 Judicial sale as a step in the enforcement of a claim *in rem* extinguishes the maritime lien or the statutory claim *in rem* in respect of the ship, and transfers it to the

---

137 *The Acrux* [1961] 1 Lloyd's Rep 471.
138 Such an order was made in *The River Andoni* (above, para 7.40).
139 Or even in court.
140 PD61 §9.5.
141 PD61 §9.6.
142 PD61 §9.7.
143 PD61 §9.8.
144 CPR 61.10(3).
145 CPR 61.10(4).
146 PD61 §9.4.
147 CPR 61.10(5).

fund in court. A purchaser from the Admiralty Marshal, therefore, gains clear title to the ship free from any claims, liens, or encumbrances.[148] Despite this well-established principle, it depends for its recognition upon courts in other jurisdictions. In some circumstances, it may not be possible in fact to relieve a ship of all encumbrances and liens if the courts of another country refuse to recognize the judicial sale as having such effect.[149] Difficulties can also arise where a third party, who is neither a party to the arrest proceedings nor amenable to the jurisdiction of the court, is required to facilitate or cooperate in the removal of the registration of an encumbrance on a ship.[150] There is little that a buyer can do to remedy such a situation, and this risk must be taken into account when considering entering into a sale agreement with the Admiralty Marshal.

A conflict may arise between the Marshal's power with respect to the sale of an **7.68** arrested vessel in Admiralty proceedings and the entitlement of statutory authorities under other legislation empowering detention and forfeiture of the same ship. It has been held that the court cannot make an order for the sale and delivery of a ship to a purchaser which would deprive a dock authority, without its consent, of its statutory right of detention.[151] Brandon J appeared to consider himself bound by these authorities in *Corps v Owners of the Paddle Steamer 'Queen of the South'*, although he would have preferred to treat the statutory possessory lien of a dock or harbour authority in the same way as the common law possessory lien of a repairer, and the statutory right of sale of such an authority in the same way as a contractual or statutory right of sale of a mortgagee:[152]

> I should have thought that the court should have power, in an action against a ship, to sell her free of both rights, while transferring equivalent rights with equivalent priority to the proceeds of sale in court, and further should have power to do this whether the dock or harbour authority consents or not. If the court does not have such power it is extremely inconvenient for it means that, in any case where a dock or harbour authority has a right of detention or sale, the court cannot transfer the ship to a purchaser free of encumbrances, with all the disadvantages arising from such a situation ...

The inconvenience was resolved in that case by authorizing the Marshal to pay off the rates owed to the authority and include the expenditure in the Marshal's expenses of sale.[153]

---

[148] *The Tremont* (1841) 1 W Rob 163, 166 ER 534; *The Acrux* [1962] 1 Lloyd's Rep 405; *The Cerro Colorado* [1993] 1 Lloyd's Rep 58.

[149] In *The Acrux* [1962] 1 Lloyd's Rep 405, for example, an order for sale by the Admiralty Court in England was not recognized in Italy; a similar situation arose in relation to the Turkish courts in *The Emre II* [1989] 2 Lloyd's Rep 182 and in *The Cerro Colorado* [1993] 1 Lloyd's Rep 58, it was doubted that the Spanish courts would give effect to a judicial sale by the English Admiralty Court.

[150] *Palm Compania Naviera SA v Federal Government of Brazil* (2 July 1993) M Stranex, *South African Shipping Cases* (3rd edn, 2000) E40.

[151] *The Emilie Millon* [1905] 2 KB 817; *The Spermina* (1923) 17 Ll L Rep 17.

[152] *Corps v Owners of the Paddle Steamer 'Queen of the South'* [1968] P 449, 461, [1968] 1 Lloyd's Rep 182, 192.

[153] Relying on the decisions in *The Parita* [1964] 1 Lloyd's Rep 199; *The Westport (No 2)* [1965] 1 WLR 871, [1965] 2 All ER 447, [1965] 1 Lloyd's Rep 549.

7.69 The Federal Court of Australia considered a similar conflict arising out of the detention of an illegal fishing vessel by the Australian Fisheries Management Authority (AFMA) pursuant to the Fisheries Management Act 1991 (Cth) and the subsequent arrest of the vessel by mortgagees.[154] The question considered by the court was whether the rights asserted by the AFMA constituted a defect of title to the ship which a purchaser would acquire upon the sale of the ship in the proceedings *in rem* by the Admiralty Marshal. So far as any conflict between the Admiralty jurisdiction and civil powers of detention are concerned, the conflict has been resolved by s 36 of the Admiralty Act 1988, which provides that the court's power of arrest prevails, but the claim which is the subject of the statutory power of detention is converted into a claim against the ship having an appropriately high priority.[155] In the case before the court, the right of detention claimed was in aid of a forfeiture by way of penalty and had no relation to a civil claim. Thus, s 36 of the Admiralty Act was of no application. In the light of the provisions made in relation to civil claims, Ryan J considered that the legislature intended to leave to the Court of Admiralty the adjustment of competing rights of the authorized officer under the Fisheries Management Act on the one hand and the plaintiff in an action on the other.

7.70 The case was significant in that it emphasized the broad discretion of the court to resolve the competing interests of a statutory authority and the powers of the court following an arrest. Following the decision, however, the Fisheries Management Act was amended to provide expressly that the seizure, detention, or forfeiture of a boat under that Act has effect despite any arrest pursuant to the Admiralty Act 1988, or the sale or order for sale of the boat pursuant to the provisions of the Admiralty Act 1988.[156] The Full Federal Court considered the application of s 108A in *Scandinavian Bunkering AS v The Bunkers on Board The Ship FV Taruman and Others*.[157] The Court confirmed that s 108A of the Fisheries Management Act prevailed over any valid arrest of a vessel under the Admiralty Act, with the effect that the arrested vessel, including her bunkers, was automatically forfeited to the Commonwealth under s 106A of the Act.

N. Applications Relating to Wrongful Arrest

7.71 There is no provision in the CPR which makes provision for an aggrieved shipowner to claim damages for wrongful arrest. Damages will, however, be awarded where the arresting party had no honest belief in his entitlement to arrest the vessel

[154] *Readhead, Phillip & Ors v Admiralty Marshall, Western Australia District Registry* [1998] FCA 1173.

[155] Admiralty Act 1988, s 36(5).

[156] *Fisheries Management Act* 1991, s 108A.

[157] *Scandinavian Bunkering AS v The Bunkers on Board The Ship FV Taruman* (2006) 151 FCR 126, [2006] FCAFC 75.

or acted without any serious regard to whether there were adequate grounds for the arrest.[158] A defendant shipowner may also be awarded special or indemnity costs in defending such a claim.[159] In *The Kommunar (No 3)*,[160] Colman J observed that it is in the latter sense that the traditional formulation of the requirements for damages, *crassa negligentia* or gross negligence,[161] are used, as implying malice or being equivalent to it. The traditional formulation was stated by the Privy Council in *The Evangelismos*:[162]

> Their Lordships think that there is no reason for distinguishing this case, or giving damages. Undoubtedly, there may be cases in which there is either *mala fides*, or that *crassa negligentia*, which implies malice, which would justify a Court of Admiralty giving damages, as in an action brought at Common law damages may be obtained ... The real question in this case, following the principles laid down with regard to actions of this description, comes to this: is there or is there not, reason to say that the action was so unwarrantably brought, or brought with so little colour, or so little foundation, that it implies malice on the part of the Plaintiff, or that gross negligence which is equivalent to it?

The justification for the principle is that, in an admiralty action *in rem*, the arrest of the *res* is the necessary foundation of the action.[163] If the *res* is arrested under a mistake of fact or law, but *bona fide*, the court will not punish the arresting party. However, if a malicious intention to punish the owner of the *res* by the use of arrest is proved, damages will follow.[164] A claim for damages for wrongful arrest can be brought in the main action.[165] Proof of actual damage is not necessary and nominal damages will be awarded in the absence of proof of special damage.[166] **7.72**

In *Gulf Azov Shipping Co Ltd v Idisi*,[167] the Court of Appeal described Colman J's formulation in *The Kommunar (No 3)*[168] as 'this exposition of the modern law',[169] in holding that the defendants had, at the very least, acted without any serious regard as to whether there were adequate grounds for continuing the arrest in respect of a claim in the sum of USD17 million once it had been decided by Sanyaolu J in the **7.73**

158 *The Kommunar (No 3)* [1997] 1 Lloyd's Rep 22, 30.

159 *Morecorp Holdings Ltd v Island Tug & Barge Ltd* [2009] BCSC 1692 (Supreme Court of British Columbia).

160 *The Kommunar (No 3)* [1997] 1 Lloyd's Rep 22, 30.

161 *The Evangelismos* (1858) 12 Moo PC 352, 166 ER 1174; *The Strathnaver* (1875) 1 App Cas 58; *The Cathcart* (1867) LR 1 A & E 314; *The Walter D Wallett* [1893] P 202; *The Margaret Jane* (1869) LR 2 A & E 345; *Astro VencedorCompania Naviera SA v Mabanaft GmbH* [1971] 2 QB 588.

162 *The Evangelismos* (1858) 12 Moo PC 352, 359–360, 14 ER 945, 948.

163 *The Volant* (1864) 22 Br MC 321, Br & Lush 321, 167 ER 385.

164 *The Victor* [1866] 167 ER 38; *The Glasgow* (1855) 166 ER 1065; *The Nautilus* (1856) 166 ER 1043; *The Margaret Jane* (1869) LR 2 A & E 345.

165 *The Evangelismos* (1858) 12 Moo PC 352, 166 ER 1174; *Lloyd Werft Bremerhaven GmbH v The Owners of the Ship Zoya Kosmodemyanskaya* [1997] 1162 FCA (unreported).

166 *The Walter D Wallett* [1893] P 202.

167 *Gulf Azov Shipping Co Ltd v Idisi* [2001] 1 Lloyd's Rep 727.

168 *The Kommunar (No 3)* [1997] 1 Lloyd's Rep 22.

169 *Gulf Aza Shipping Co Ltd v Idisi* [2001] 1 Lloyd's Rep 727, 735, [40].

High Court in Lagos that the reasonably arguable best case was a claim in the sum of USD1 million. Following the decision of Sanyaolu J, it was alleged that the first defendant, Chief Idisi, had exercised improper influence in preventing the vessel leaving after the release order had been issued; that Chief Idisi had orchestrated the forcible boarding of the vessel to force it to move to a berth adjacent to the second defendant's premises where it was blocked; that Chief Idisi was responsible for the use of gunfire and men boarding the vessel when she was legitimately trying to leave, and that Chief Idisi exercised improper influence over the judiciary in Benin. The Court of Appeal held that, on a summary judgment application, it could not be satisfied that the persons preventing the vessel from leaving were under Chief Idisi's orders, but that it was satisfied that Chief Idisi must have been aware that his claims were not sustainable in the sum of USD17 million. There was thus no arguable defence to the claim for unlawful detention of the vessel and damages were awarded.

7.74 In *The Nicholas M*,[170] the owners had commenced proceedings against the charterers and obtained a maritime attachment of the charterers' assets under New York law. The charterers counterclaimed for the tort of wrongful attachment, which they argued was analogous to the doctrine of wrongful arrest. The Court considered the charterers had a 'good arguable case' that there was a cause of action for wrongful attachment under US federal law. The Court also remarked, *obiter*, that had English law applied, then wrongful attachment of a person's assets would probably have fallen within the scope of the existing tort of wrongful arrest such that the charterer would have been entitled to relief.[171] These remarks suggest English courts are not averse to widening the application of the doctrine of wrongful arrest in appropriate circumstances.

7.75 In *The Fearless I*,[172] a wrongful arrestor argued it was entitled to reimbursement of its costs in arresting and maintaining two vessels in priority to all others except the Chief Bailiff. The wrongful arrestor's earlier claims had been dismissed partly on the basis that the claims did not fall within the admiralty jurisdiction of the High Court. The vessels were subsequently rearrested by two other claimants, whose claims against the vessels succeeded. The Hong Kong Court of First Instance roundly dismissed the wrongful arrestor's claim and distinguished between costs incurred by a wrongful arrestor and those incurred by a lawful arrestor. It was not inequitable for a wrongful arrestor to bear the legal and financial consequences of its own actions and to hold otherwise 'would only serve as a judicial encouragement for wrongful arrests'.[173]

[170] *Congentra AG v Sixteen Thirteen Marine SA (The Nicholas M)* [2008] EWHC 1615 (Comm), [2008] 2 Lloyd's Rep 602. The application before the Court was for the discharge of the charterers' freezing injunction.

[171] Ibid 608, [22]–[23].

[172] *The Fearless I* [2013] 5 HKLRD 48, [2014] Lloyd's Rep Plus 21.

[173] Ibid [43].

The principle established in *The Evangelismos* continues to be applied in several other common law jurisdictions.[174] South Africa and Australia are, however, notable exceptions. The former's Admiralty Jurisdiction Regulation Act 105 of 1983 provides:[175] **7.76**

> Any person who makes an excessive claim or requires excessive security or without reasonable and probable cause obtains the arrest of property or an order of the court, shall be liable to any person suffering loss or damage as a result thereof for that loss or damage.

It has been held that a lack of honest belief will negative 'reasonable and probable cause' in this context,[176] although it is, with respect, a little hard to understand how. 'Reasonable and probable cause' is, to English eyes at least, an objective test, in which the subjective *mens rea* of the arresting party is irrelevant. Of course, the absence of an objectively reasonable and probable cause may point to a lack of honest belief, but it would be unnecessary to go that far in order to hold that the test was not satisfied. Moreover, it may be far harder to establish a lack of honest belief, which would ordinarily require cross-examination, than it would to show that the arresting party had no 'reasonable and probable cause' for doing so. **7.77**

This provision was used as the basis for the Australian provision now contained in the Admiralty Act 1988. However, there had been criticism of the breadth and vagueness of the language in the South African provision and thus the Australian provision is said to be an attempt 'to strike a more precise balance between plaintiff and defendant'.[177] Further, unlike the South African provision, the Australian provision restricts the right to recover to those parties (or persons with an interest in the property) who have suffered loss or damage as a direct result of the arrest. Thus, s 34 of the Admiralty Act provides: **7.78**

(1) Where, in relation to a proceeding commenced under this Act:
  (a) a party unreasonably and without good cause:
    (i) demands excessive security in relation to the proceeding; or
    (ii) obtains the arrest of a ship or other property under this Act; or

---

[174] *Mondel Transport Inc v Afram Lines Ltd* [1990] 3 FC 684 (TD); *The Rhone v The Peter AB Widener* [1993] 1 SCR 497; *Armada Lines Ltd v Chaleur Fertilizers Ltd* [1997] 2 SCR 617; *Li Seng Yee v SS Hai Jye* [1961] HKLR 567; *Victory Star Shipping Co SA v The Owners of the Ship Amigo and World Happy Shipping Ltd* [1994] HKEC 231; *Banque Worms v The Owners of the Ship or Vessel Maule and Compagnia Sud* [1995] 2 HKC 769; *Mobil Oil New Zealand Ltd v The Ship Rangiora* [2000] 1 NZLR 49; *Tomita v The Unnamed Vessel* (unreported, High Court of New Zealand, Auckland, 6 May 2003); *The Ohm Mariana 'Ex Peony'*; *Pacific Navigation Co Pte Ltd v The Owners of the Ship or Vessel Ohm Mariana 'Ex Peony'* [1992] 2 SLR 623; *The AA V* [2001] 1 SLR 207; *Sumitomo Corp (Singapore) Pte Ltd v Owners of the Ship or Vessel Alexandrea* [2002] 3 SLR 56; *Kiku Pacific* [1999] 2 SLR 595; *The Inai Selashi (Ex Geopotes X)* [2005] 4 SLR 1.

[175] Act 105 of 1983, s 5(4).

[176] *MV Cape Athos Shipping v Blue Emerald Shipping Ltd* 2000 (2) SA 327, 336.

[177] Civil Admiralty Jurisdiction, ALRC 33 (1986) para 302.

(b) a party or other person unreasonably and without good cause[178] fails to give a consent required under this Act for the release from arrest of a ship or other property;

the party or person is liable in damages to a party to the proceeding, or to a person who has an interest in the ship or property, being a party or person who has suffered loss or damage as a direct result.

(2) The jurisdiction of a court in which a proceeding was commenced under this Act extends to determining a claim arising under subsection (1) in relation to the proceeding.

7.79 The need for a statutory provision was said to be that wrongful arrest is otherwise very difficult to prove and, in practice, the vexatious or frivolous plaintiff will seldom need to be concerned with the risk of having to pay damages.[179] Despite the legislative interventions, however, it may be noted that there appear so far to have been no decided case in which a shipowner has successfully sought damages for wrongful arrest in Australia and no more than a handful in South Africa.[180]

7.80 In the absence of such an express legislative provision, the courts have been reluctant to depart from the principle in *The Evangelismos*. In *Armada Lines Ltd v Chaleur Fertilizers Ltd*,[181] the Supreme Court of Canada upheld an appeal against an award of damages, which comprised loss of use of working capital, for wrongful arrest of the respondent's cargo. The respondent argued that the disparity between the liability of a plaintiff who obtains a Mareva injunction and the liability of a plaintiff who arrests property in the Admiralty jurisdiction operates unfairly against defendants in Admiralty law actions. The respondent argued for the creation of a new rule, pursuant to which a plaintiff who effects a maritime arrest and then has his claim dismissed will be liable for all damages caused by the arrest. This position was said to find support amongst academic writers.[182] In delivering the judgment of the court, Iacobucci J said:[183]

> While I have some sympathy with this argument, in my view, any such change in the law falls not to the courts, but rather to the legislature to carry out. As noted above, the rule in *The Evangelismos* is of long standing. Whether it does or does not

[178] The equivalent provision in the Arrest Convention 1999, art 6, is 'wrongful or unjustified', a formula which is probably wider than the Australian provision.

[179] Civil Admiralty Jurisdiction, ALRC 33 (1986) para 302.

[180] *RD Summers Fisheries CC v Viking Fishing Co Pty Ltd (MFV Logan Ora)* (1999) 4 SA 1081; *Cape Athos Shipping v Blue Emerald Shipping Ltd (MV Cape Athos)* 2000 (2) SA 327, cf: *Guangzhou Maritime Group Co v Dry Bulk SA (The Yu Long Shan)* (1997) 2 SA 454; *MV Rizcun Trader v Manley Appeldore Shipping Ltd* (2000) 3 SA 776; *Belfry Marine Ltd v Palm Base Maritime (MV Heavy Metal)* (2000) 1 SA 286; *The Sandokan (No 2)*, (28 October 2002). M Stranex, *Shipping Cases of South Africa* (3rd edn, 2000) B 171; cf *The owners of the MV Silver Star v Hilane Ltd* (A2282/2013) [2013] ZAECPEHC 40 (28 August 2013).

[181] *Armada Lines Ltd v Chaleur Fertilizers Ltd* [1997] 2 SCR 617; see also *The Rhone v The Peter AB Widener* [1993] 1 SCR 497, (1993) 101 DLR (4th) 188, (1993) 58 FTR 239, [1993] 1 Lloyd's Rep 600.

[182] S Nossal, 'Damages for the Wrongful Arrest of a Vessel' [1996] LMCLQ 368.

[183] *Armada Lines Ltd v Chaleur Fertilizers Ltd* [1997] 2 SCR 617, 627, [26]–[27].

operate harshly upon defendants is a question best resolved by the legislature ... In this regard, I note that, apparently alone among the common law jurisdictions, Australia has departed from the rule in *The Evangelismos* ... As pointed out by counsel for the appellant, this change was effected not through judicial means, but rather by specific legislative enactment. In my opinion, any analogous change in Canadian law must originate in the legislative branch of government.

A similar argument was raised before the High Court of New Zealand in *Mobil Oil New Zealand Ltd v The Ship Rangiora*[184] by the owners of three arrested vessels who sought to set aside the arrests on the basis that the court's *in rem* jurisdiction had not been properly invoked. Giles J observed:[185] 7.81

In my view, the situation is rather unsatisfactory for ship-owning or chartering interests. In this jurisdiction, unlike our Australian counterparts, a plaintiff arresting a ship has little real vulnerability for the economic consequences visited upon an owner. Damages for wrongful arrest may only be recovered where the arrest has been procured with malice. If the claim can meet the subject-matter test established in the Admiralty Act and the jurisdictional fact test established in *The Akademik Shokalskiy* and *Efem Gorbenko*, then the prospect of exposure to a claim in malice is obviously limited. The owner must post security and contest a claim (even a weak claim), on the merits but in the event of ultimate success, receives no compensation for the cost of the security bond[186] or the loss of use of security funds or for the loss of revenue whilst detained. The situation for an owner is not so bleak in Australia where, as noted, the federal admiralty legislation imposes a liability for damages for unreasonable arrest on parties procuring the arrest of a ship. The test of unreasonableness is a much lesser burden than the test of malice. In my view, a case can be made out for a legislative rebalancing of odds which disproportionately favour plaintiffs in this jurisdiction. In making these observations I acknowledge that our jurisdiction is modelled on the English system which has an ancient heritage. Arrest has always been a very powerful remedy recognized in most jurisdictions—malice is the measurement of English law in wrongful arrest actions. The need for international consistency is ... deserving of consideration. But in my view, we ought not to allow that factor to deter reform where the interests of justice so require.

More recently, the Court of Appeal in Singapore in *The Vasiliy Golovnin*[187] was highly critical of the test in *The Evangelismos*, noting that the high threshold had no doubt deterred many shipowners, probably including deserving ones, from pursuing claims for wrongful arrest. Even where such claims were pursued, the 'one-sidedness of the Evangelismos test' was particularly harsh in light of the fact that a ship arrest can result in substantial disruption and financial losses for which shipowners will rarely receive sufficient compensation from the arresting 7.82

[184] *Mobil Oil New Zealand Ltd v The Ship Rangiora* [2000] 1 NZLR 49.

[185] Ibid 65.

[186] But see *The St Elefterio* [1957] P 179, 187 (plaintiff liable for costs including costs of furnishing bail); *Antares Shipping Corp v The Ship Capricorn* [1977] 2 FC 274 (CA), 279 (expense of giving bail forms part of the taxable costs for which security may be ordered).

[187] *The Vasiliy Golovnin* [2008] 4 SLR 994, [2008] SGCA 39.

party.[188] The Court also questioned whether the historical rationale for the test continued to be relevant, given claimants could now commence *in rem* proceedings through the service of a claim form, without the arrest of the *res*.[189] The Court concluded:

> We would agree with the views of both Iacobucci J[190] and Giles J[191] to the extent that the Evangelismos test is longstanding, and should not be departed from lightly, without good reasons and due consideration. However, it is always open to this court to depart from this judicially created test if the day comes when it no longer serves any relevant purpose.[192] [footnotes added]

Apparently on the brink of rejecting the test in *The Evangelismos*, the Court of Appeal then retreated and instead decided 'to leave this issue to be addressed more fully at a more appropriate juncture' after it had received full arguments from counsel and submissions from those in the maritime industry.[193]

7.83 In fact it was not necessary for the Court to determine the issue because the Court found that the threshold was satisfied on the facts and that the two secured banks had wrongfully arrested *The Vasiliy Golovnin*. This was said to be for three reasons. First, Crédit Agricole, one of the two banks, had 'unreasonably persisted' with the arrest of *The Vasiliy Golovnin* (a sister-ship) in Singapore after its claim had been disposed of in Lomé, Togo, even though the Lomé court had held that sufficient security had already been provided. Second, the banks' breach of contract claim against the shipowner under the relevant bills of lading was without substance. Third, the banks had failed to disclose material facts at the *ex parte* hearing at which the primary Judge had ordered the arrest of *The Vasiliy Golovnin*. The Court of Appeal concluded:

> It appears clear to us that the Banks' conduct in initiating the arrest could not, after taking account all the circumstances, be fairly said to be the result of an honest belief that they had valid claims, but rather arose from an ill-conceived and reckless attempt to steal a march on FESCO [the shipowner] and to force its hand in providing additional security for their claims. If the Banks felt that the security provided was insufficient, the Banks ought, in the prevailing circumstances, to have appealed this issue in Lomé rather than to open up a second, costly and inherently vexatious, front in Singapore.[194]

For now, therefore, the test in *The Evangelismos* remains the law of Singapore but it seems that the Court of Appeal would be receptive to arguments that the threshold should be lowered, should the issue arise again.

---

188 Ibid [120].
189 Ibid [124]–[125].
190 In *Armada Lines Ltd v Chaleur Fertilizers Ltd* [1997] 2 SCR 617.
191 In *Mobil Oil New Zealand Ltd v The Ship Rangiora* [2000] 1 NZLR 49.
192 *The Vasiliy Golovnin* [2008] 4 SLR 994, [2008] SGCA 39, [134].
193 Ibid.
194 Ibid [141].

8

DISTRIBUTION OF THE FUND

A. Priorities

The establishment of the order of priority or the ranking of claims against the fund generated by the sale of the ship or other property by the Admiralty Marshal at the conclusion of Admiralty proceedings is one of the most important features of the Admiralty jurisdiction. The ranking of claims is necessary, or at least of greatest practical importance, where the fund is insufficient to meet all the judgments obtained against the ship. Whilst the Admiralty jurisdiction itself is governed by statute, the law as to the establishment of priorities is not.[1] The ranking of priorities by the Admiralty Court is an exercise of a long-standing equitable jurisdiction. In this respect, it is clear that the equitable doctrines and principles which apply to determine priority are those generally applicable by a court of equity to the determination of priorities. This includes the application of the maxims of equity[2] and **8.01**

[1] South Africa is the exception with specific ranking rules contained in s 11 of the Admiralty Jurisdiction Regulation Act 105 of 1983.

[2] *The Falcon* [1981] 1 Lloyd's Rep 13.

the principle that any party seeking to invoke the equitable jurisdiction of the court should put before it all relevant facts and circumstances.[3]

8.02 One consequence of the way in which the law of priorities has developed is that there is often a lack of certainty as to the way in which a claim might in fact be ranked at the conclusion of the proceedings. This uncertainty is exacerbated by the absence of international uniformity as to the law of priorities and of any likelihood of achieving such uniformity given the lack of interest in the International Convention on Maritime Liens and Mortgages 1993 and its predecessors.[4] This means that a claimant can achieve a very different outcome with respect to the recoverability of his claim depending upon the jurisdiction in which he arrests a vessel and the priority which that particular jurisdiction accords to the particular type of claim in the given circumstances.[5] Two examples suffice to illustrate this point.

(1) In *The Halcyon Isle*,[6] the ship was arrested in Singapore, claims *in rem* having been commenced against her by both the mortgagees and shiprepairers who had carried out repairs to the ship in New York. The ship was sold for USD1,380,000. The mortgagees obtained judgment for USD14,413,000 and the shiprepairers for USD237,011. Under the law of Singapore, a shiprepairer's claim does not have the character of a maritime lien. Thus, applying the law of Singapore as to priorities, the mortgagees exhausted the fund and the shiprepairers recovered nothing. Had the ship been arrested in the United States of America, or even in Canada, the shiprepairer's claim would have had the character of a maritime lien and would have ranked ahead of the claim by the mortgagees.
(2) In *The Betty Ott v General Bills Ltd*,[7] the Court of Appeal of New Zealand was required to determine the priority between a ship's mortgage registered in Australia and an earlier equitable charge over the vessel created in New Zealand. The Court of Appeal treated the mortgage as an equitable mortgage because it was not registered on the New Zealand register.[8] Thus, applying ordinary equitable principles, the Court was faced with two competing equities and thus the first in time, the equitable charge, prevailed. Had the ship been arrested in Australia, the registered mortgage, being a legal interest, would have prevailed over the equitable charge.

[3] *The Leoborg (No 2)* [1964] 1 Lloyd's Rep 380, 383.

[4] Convention on Maritime Liens and Mortgages 1926 and 1967. Under the 1993 Convention, the ranking order is wages, injury, salvage, pilotage, collision. Time affects the salvage claims *inter se* and they rank in inverse order to the time of their creation. Otherwise, all other claims of the same nature rank *pari passu*.

[5] Whether or not a particular claim is recognized as a maritime lien under English law is discussed in Chapter 4.

[6] *Bankers Trust International Ltd v Todd Shipyards Corporation (The Halcyon Isle)* [1981] AC 221.

[7] *The Ship Betty Ott v General Bills Ltd* [1992] 1 NZLR 655.

[8] A dubious conclusion considered further below, para 8.41.

Consequently, it is important for maritime claimants that their claim is classified correctly and that they have some guidance as to where that claim will rank in the jurisdiction in which proceedings have been commenced. In some circumstances it will become clear very early on that there is nothing to be gained, but only significant costs to be incurred, by proceeding in a jurisdiction where their claim will be accorded a relatively lowly ranking.[9] **8.03**

Most commonly, although by no means invariably, disputes about the ranking of claims arise between the mortgagee, the crew, the cargo interests, and necessaries men. That is because, in practice: **8.04**

(1) claims by the holders of possessory liens tend to be dealt with early in a dispute so that the lien is often relinquished before any question of priority arises;
(2) claims arising out of collision damage are usually secured by a P&I letter of undertaking and so do not often feature in a priority dispute;
(3) similarly, salvage claims are often secured at an early stage, before being dealt with, eg, by arbitration under the terms of the Lloyd's Open Form (LOF).

Nevertheless, issues can and do arise involving these types of claim also, and so the respective priority of each type of maritime claim is considered in this chapter.

The priority ranking of maritime claims

There is in general terms a well-recognized order for the ranking of claims following the sale of the vessel.[10] This order has given rise to what are described as 'ranking rules'. The 'ranking rules' attempt to provide a coherent ordering not only of the priority of classes of claims made against the ship or property but also of the priority *inter se* of claims of the same class and type (for example, one wages claim with another), and the ranking *inter se* of claims of the same class but of different types (for example, a maritime lien for seaman's wages with a maritime lien for salvage). Further, the rules must cater for claims outside the normal scope of admiralty such as possessory liens and statutory powers of detention and sale. **8.05**

It would be erroneous, however, to apply the ranking rules slavishly in order to determine the precise manner in which the fund should be distributed. That would be to ignore the equitable foundations of the determination of priorities and that **8.06**

---

[9] See, for example, *Fraser Shipyard and Industrial Centre Ltd v Expedient Maritime Co Ltd (The Atlantis Two)* (1999) 170 FTR 1 in which many of the suppliers of necessaries withdrew from the proceedings upon realizing that their claims would be categorized merely as statutory claims *in rem* and that the fund was likely to be insufficient to meet claims of that character.

[10] *The Ruta* [2000] 1 WLR 2068, [2001] 1 All ER 450, [2000] 1 Lloyd's Rep 359; *Patrick Stevedores No 2 Pty Ltd v The MV Skulptor Konenkov* (1997) 75 FCR 47, (1997) 144 ALR 394 (Federal Court of Australia); *Governor & Company of the Bank of Scotland v The Nel* [2001] 1 FC 408, 189 FTR 230 (Federal Court of Canada); *Fournier v the Ship Margaret Z* [1999] 3 NZLR 111 (High Court of New Zealand).

the so-called ranking rules are merely a *prima facie* order that can in the particular circumstances of the individual case be displaced by equitable principles and considerations of public policy. A broad discretionary approach exists in relation to rival claims ranked by reference to considerations of equity, public policy, and commercial expediency, with the objective of doing justice between the parties.[11]

8.07 The importance of the application of equitable principles in relation to the ranking of maritime claims was reaffirmed by David Steel J in *The Ruta*.[12] The vessel had been involved in a collision with three anchored yachts. The question arose as to the priority between the crew's claim for wages and the three claims for collision damage. Contrary to the traditional rule, the Judge ranked the wages claim ahead of the collision claims:[13]

> I spoke at the beginning of this section of my judgment of the suggestion in some of the text books that there is a rule whereby the damage lien has priority over a wages' lien. It is clear even from the restricted citation of authority set out above that questions of priority are not capable of being compartmentalised in the form of strict rules of ranking. The general approach is accurately summarised in *Thomas, Maritime Liens,* (1980), p. 234, para 418:
>
> 'The Admiralty and appellate courts have adopted a broad discretionary approach with rival claims ranked by reference to considerations of equity, public policy and commercial expediency, with the ultimate aim of doing that which is just in the circumstance of each case.'

In circumstances where the owners of the vessel were insolvent and the only remedy open to the wage claimants was recovery against the proceeds of sale, David Steel J held that considerations of public policy justified according them a very high level of priority. Those factors of public policy were said to include the general concern for mariners' interests traditionally exhibited by the Admiralty Court and the practical reality that it would be rare for outstanding wages to amount to more than a fraction of the value of the vessel compared with the 'value' of the damage lien.

8.08 The fact that a general discretion exists in relation to the ranking of priorities does not mean, however, that there are no guiding principles as to the manner in which such discretion ought to be exercised. On the contrary, the cases reveal clear trends in the application of equitable principles to the determination of priorities. First, it is clear that the highest priority after the costs and expenses of the Admiralty Marshal is accorded to the costs of the party who preserves the *res* for the benefit of all claimants, in other words, the costs of the producer of the fund. Secondly, principles of public policy dictate that the next highest priority will

[11] D R Thomas, *Maritime Liens* (1980), para 418; *The Ruta* [2000] 1 WLR 2068, 2075–2076, [2001] 1 All ER 450, 458, [2000] 1 Lloyd's Rep 359, 364, [21]; *Bajpayee v The Estancia* [2003] FCA 1640 (Federal Court of Australia); *Metaxas v The Galaxias (No 2)* [1989] 1 FC 386 (Federal Court of Canada); *The Offi Gloria* [1993] 3 NZLR 576 (High Court of New Zealand).

[12] *The Ruta* [2000] 1 WLR 2068, [2001] 1 All ER 450, [2000] 1 Lloyd's Rep 359.

[13] Ibid 2075–2076, 458, 364, [21].

be determined as amongst the claimants for wages, for salvage, and for damage. The rationale behind the priority accorded to this group of claimants is that it is generally considered desirable that seamen are protected, that salvors are encouraged, and that safe navigation is promoted. It is also apparent that, as regards the ranking of those claims *inter se*, a distinction is sometimes drawn between those arising out of relationships voluntarily entered into, and those arising outside of any such relationship. Regard may also be had to whether or not alternative remedies are available to the claimant. Finally, and consistently with the application of equitable principles more generally, the conduct of (including delay by) the party who is seeking the application by the court of equitable principles may be relevant.

The *prima facie* ranking

Any court faced with a dispute as to the appropriate ranking of priorities will commence its determination with the *prima facie* ranking which is as follows. **8.09**

(1) The Admiralty Marshal's costs and expenses connected with the arrest of the vessel and its appraisement and sale.
(2) (i) The costs of the arresting party up to and including the arrest of the vessel concerned,[14] and
    (ii) The costs of the party who obtained the order for the appraisement and sale of the vessel, for the period up to and including the order itself.[15]
(3) Maritime liens.
(4) Possessory liens.
(5) Mortgages.
(6) Other statutory actions *in rem*.
(7) *In personam* claims.

If there is anything left in the fund once the above claims have been satisfied, the owner of the *res* is entitled to the balance.

The same *prima facie* order is accepted in Australia,[16] Canada,[17] Hong Kong,[18] and Singapore.[19] The position in New Zealand and South Africa is outlined below.[20] **8.10**

[14] *The Rana* (1921) 8 Ll L Rep 369; *The Athena* (1921) 8 Ll L Rep 482.
[15] *The Immacolata Concezione* (1883) 8 PD 34; *The Rana* (1921) 8 Ll L Rep 369; *The Athena* (1921) 8 Ll L Rep 482; *The Reina (No 2)* [1963] 2 Lloyd's Rep 513.
[16] *Patrick Stevedores No 2 Pty Ltd v The MV Skulptor Konenkov* (1997) 75 FCR 47, (1997) 144 ALR 394 (Federal Court of Australia).
[17] *Fraser Shipyard and Industrial Centre Ltd v Expedient Maritime Co Ltd (The Atlantis Two)* (1999) 170 FTR 1, subject to some minor differences particularly relating to the recognition accorded to foreign liens.
[18] *The Sparti* [2000] 3 HKC 323.
[19] *Bankers Trust International Ltd v Todd Shipyards Corporation (The Halcyon Isle)* [1981] AC 221, [1980] 3 WLR 400, [1980] 3 All ER 197, [1980] 2 Lloyd's Rep 325.
[20] Paras 8.12 and 8.13.

8.11 Any party seeking to challenge the *prima facie* ranking will bear the onus of establishing that there is some basis, equitable or otherwise, for disturbing the *prima facie* order. Whilst David Steel J highlighted the 'broad discretionary approach' adopted by the courts, it is clear nonetheless that courts will be slow to depart from the usual order of priorities unless the application of the *prima facie* order produces a plainly unjust result.[21] In Canada, consistently with this approach, it has been held that the usual order is not to be departed from unless 'it is necessary to prevent an obvious injustice'[22] as opposed to 'merely an unfortunate result of a business decision, a result to some degree unfair'.[23] Similarly, in Hong Kong, it has been held that it is not sufficient to complain about injustice—a party must be able to point to some 'recognized and established principle of equity', such as unconscionability,[24] although this may, in view of the reasoning in *The Ruta*, be to put the point too strongly.

New Zealand

8.12 New Zealand generally applies the same broad equitable approach to the ranking of maritime claims although there is case law to suggest that there is a rather more stringent *prima facie* ranking than applies in England.[25] The authority of those cases has been superseded by the provisions of the Maritime Transport Act 1994 which do not replicate the previous statutory ranking provided for in the now repealed *Shipping and Seamen Act* 1952, except to the extent of preserving the priority of life salvage over property salvage.[26]

South Africa

8.13 South Africa, by contrast, has codified the order in which claims are paid and there does not appear to be any residual discretion in the court to reorder the statutory ranking. The ranking order provided for is as follows:[27]

(1) costs and expenses incurred to maintain, keep custody of, and preserve the property sold or to procure its sale and in respect of the distribution of the proceeds of sale whether the sale results from claims against an associated ship or not;

---

21 *The Pickaninny* [1960] 1 Lloyd's Rep 533, 537; *The Lyrma (No 2)* [1978] 2 Lloyd's Rep 30, 33.

22 *Montreal Dry Docks Co v Halifax Shipyards* (1920) 60 SCR 359; *Osborn Refrigeration Sales & Service Inc, The Atlantean I* [1979] 2 FC 661; *Metaxas v The Galaxias (No 2)* [1989] 1 FC 386; *Scott Steel Ltd v Ship Alarissa (The Edmonton Queen)* (1997) 125 FTR 284.

23 *Fraser Shipyard and Industrial Centre Ltd v Expedient Maritime Co Ltd (The Atlantis Two)* (1999) 170 FTR 1, [201].

24 *The CC Orient* [1985] 1 HKC 115.

25 *Fournier v The Ship Margaret Z* [1999] 3 NZLR 111, 117; *Hill v the Ship James Cook* [1997] 3 NZLR 752; *Turners and Growers Exporters Ltd* v *The Ship Cornelis Verolme* [1997] 2 NZLR 110.

26 Maritime Transport Act 1994 (NZ), s 219A(2).

27 Admiralty Jurisdiction Regulation Act 105 of 1983 and J Hare, *Shipping Law and Admiralty Jurisdiction in South Africa* (1999) 108.

(2) claims to a preference based on possession of the property sold, whether by way of a right of retention or otherwise, provided that such claims have arisen before any other claim except preservation and sale costs;
(3) claims for salvage, wreck, or general average;
(4) claims for master's and seamen's wages and remuneration;
(5) port, canal, other waterways, or pilotage dues;
(6) claims for loss of life or personal injury;
(7) claims for loss of or damage to property arising from delict;
(8) claims for the repair of the ship or supply of goods or the rendering of services to or in relation to a ship for the employment, maintenance, protection, or preservation thereof;
(9) premia owing under any policy of marine insurance;
(10) claims to contribution from a P&I Club;
(11) claims relating to any mortgage, hypothecation, or right of retention of, and any other charge on, the ship, effected or valid in accordance with the law of the flag of the ship and in respect of any lien for payments or disbursements by any master, shipper, charterer, agent, or any other person for or on behalf or on account of a ship or the owner or charterer of a ship;
(12) claims arising out of any other maritime lien;
(13) any other maritime claims ranked in their order of preference according to the law of insolvency, and if the sale be of an associated ship, arising from or related directly to the operation of and including the carriage of goods in the ship;
(14) any other maritime claims ranked in their order of preference according to the law of insolvency, not arising from or related directly to the operation of and including the carriage of goods in the ship;
(15) any residue remaining shall be paid to the owner of the ship or to a trustee, liquidator, or judicial manager.

Actions on judgments and awards

Both Australia and South Africa permit an action *in rem* to be brought in relation to a judgment or arbitral award.[28] In South Africa, the Admiralty Jurisdiction Regulation Act 105 of 1983, s 11(9) provides that a judgment or arbitral award shall rank in accordance with the claim in respect of which it was given or made. The Australian legislation is silent as to the ranking of such a claim but it is submitted that the South African approach accords with the equitable principles which govern priorities generally, and that it would be inequitable for a claimant to lose his priority simply on the basis that he had taken steps to enforce the claim. It is submitted that the same will apply in England and Wales where an arrest has been made by a judgment creditor pursuant to CPR 61.5(1)(b).[29] **8.14**

[28] See Chapter 5, paras 5.89(3) and 5.91(6).
[29] As to which, see paras 6.48 and following.

The classes in detail

The Admiralty Marshal's costs and expenses

8.15 The proceeds of sale of a ship which has been sold by order of the court should be used first to pay the Admiralty Marshal's charges and expenses.[30] The nature of such expenses is varied. For example, they may extend to costs related to the crew.[31] Where a party is unable to pay off the crew in order to obtain vacant possession of the ship, the court may order that the Marshal pay the crew's repatriation expenses and, if necessary, any claim for wages. Such expenses may then be rationalized as payments made to realize the ship on a Marshal's sale to best advantage. If so ordered, the expenses will form part of the Marshal's expenses.[32]

8.16 The ship may need to be repaired in order to achieve the best possible sale price and the costs of such repairs will form part of the Marshal's expenses.[33] Similarly, it may be necessary for classification society fees to be paid and such fees have been considered properly recoverable as part of the Marshal's expenses.[34] However, in more recent times, the Admiralty Marshal has reached an understanding with the major classification societies pursuant to which, in return for the societies retaining the vessel in class and making her records available for inspection, he will consider making an application for payment of their outstanding fees from the proceeds of sale.[35] This arrangement has the obvious benefit of not wasting funds on classification fees should the ship not realize more than its scrap price on sale. There does not, however, seem to be any good reason why the practice endorsed in *The Parita* would not continue to apply in relation to a classification society with which the Marshal had not reached such an understanding, thereby enabling fees paid to be treated as part of the Marshal's expenses.

8.17 It has also been accepted, at least in Australia, that the cost of liability insurances, including legal advice to the Marshal as to the need for such insurances, in relation to potential claims for environmental damage, clean-up costs, and wreck removal are to be treated as part of the Marshal's expenses.[36]

8.18 Further, the Marshal may need to pay outstanding port charges and the like which are also recoverable as part of his expenses.[37]

---

30 *The Falcon* [1981] 1 Lloyd's Rep 13, 17; *The World Star* [1987] 1 Lloyd's Rep 452.

31 See generally above, paras 7.39 and following.

32 *The 'General Serret'* (1925) 23 Ll L Rep 14,15; *The Myrto (No 2)* [1984] 2 Lloyd's Rep 341, 348; *The Guiseppe di Vittorio (No 2)* [1998] 1 Lloyd's Rep 661; *Keppel Corporation v Chemical Bank* [1994] 1 SLR 346; *The Aquarius III* [2002] 4 SLR 202 (High Court of Singapore).

33 *The Westport (No 2)* [1965] 1 WLR 871, [1965] 2 All ER 447, [1965] 1 Lloyd's Rep 549.

34 *The Parita* [1964] 1 Lloyd's Rep 199.

35 *The Honshu Gloria* [1986] 2 Lloyd's Rep 63, 65.

36 *Bank of China v The Ship 'Hai Shi'* (No 3) [2013] FCA 660. In England and Wales, the Marshal does not insure property under arrest: PD61 para 5.7 and Admiralty & Commercial Courts Guide N13.

37 *The Freightline One* [1986] 1 Lloyd's Rep 266, 272; followed by the High Court of Singapore in *SINWA (Singapore) Pty Ltd v Owners of the Ship Hurst* [1999] 1 SLR 237.

Where the Marshal is required to remove cargo prior to the sale of the vessel, such costs are not included in the Marshal's costs of sale and arrest, the rationale being that the cargo owners must bear the expense of removal for which they would then have a claim against the shipowner which would rank in priority along with the other substantive claims.[38] **8.19**

Costs of the producers of the fund

The rationale for the priority accorded to the costs of the arresting party is that those costs will have been incurred in producing the fund that is for the benefit of all claimants against the vessel that has been arrested and then, eventually, sold.[39] The costs are limited to those relating to the arrest or the appraisement and sale and do not extend to the costs incurred in prosecuting the substantive claim,[40] which have the same priority as that accorded to the substantive claim. The arresting party is also entitled to interest on the sums paid to the Admiralty Marshal for the purpose of maintaining the arrest.[41] **8.20**

In exceptional circumstances, an arresting party may also be entitled to claim, as costs of the arrest, costs incurred in the administration of the fund that has been held in court.[42] Whether the court permits such costs to have priority is a matter of discretion taking into account whether: **8.21**

(1) the costs were reasonably incurred;
(2) the costs were aimed at producing or preserving the fund for the general benefit of all the creditors; and
(3) the costs were incurred because the party incurring them was uniquely able to do something that did or might be for the benefit of all creditors.

It is not, however, necessary to prove an actual benefit to the fund in incurring the costs.[43] Such costs were accorded priority in *The Leoborg (No 2)*,[44] having arisen out of correspondence between the solicitors for the arresting party and the Admiralty Registry in relation to the investment of the fund and the movement of the vessel. However, in *The Ocean Glory*,[45] it was held that costs incurred in relation to the removal of the crew from the vessel and maintaining the arrest were incurred in connection with working out the arresting party's own position in relation to

---

[38] *The Jogoo* [1981] 1 WLR 1376, [1981] 3 All ER 634, [1981] 1 Lloyd's Rep 513; *The Myrto (No 2)* [1984] 2 Lloyd's Rep 341.

[39] *The Ocean Glory* [2002] 1 Lloyd's Rep 679, 680, [3]; *The Falcon* [1981] 1 Lloyd's Rep 13; *The Rubi Sea* [1992] 1 Lloyd's Rep 634.

[40] *The Margaret* (1835) 3 Hag Adm 238, 166 ER 394; *The William F Safford* (1860) Lush 69, 167 ER 37; *The World Star* [1987] 1 Lloyd's Rep 452; *Patrick Stevedores (No 2) Pty Ltd v MV Skulptor Konenkov* (1997) 75 FCR 47, (1997) 144 ALR 394.

[41] *The World Star* [1987] 1 Lloyd's Rep 452.

[42] *The Leoborg (No 2)* [1964] 1 Lloyd's Rep 380; *The Ocean Glory* [2002] 1 Lloyd's Rep 679.

[43] *The Ocean Glory* [2002] 1 Lloyd's Rep 679, 680, [4].

[44] *The Leoborg (No 2)* [1964] 1 Lloyd's Rep 380.

[45] *The Ocean Glory* [2002] 1 Lloyd's Rep 679.

the repatriation of the crew, and in deciding how long it would or could afford to maintain the arrest. Such costs did not benefit the claimants as a whole.

8.22 In some circumstances, the court will be prepared to treat payments to the crew as part of the costs of the sale and therefore the costs of the action, if it is appropriate to do so in the interests of all the parties and of justice on the facts of the particular case.[46] This will most likely occur where the expenses have been incurred to repatriate the crew. Repatriation expenses, or *viaticum*, have traditionally been accorded high priority on the basis that, otherwise, the expenses of the crew's maintenance may fall on the taxpayer.[47] Where, however, the payment of wages is made by the claimant with the leave of the court or pursuant to a court order, the claimant will normally stand in the shoes of the crew in respect of sums so paid and will be able to claim against the proceeds of the sale of the ship with the same priority that the crew would have had.[48] Thus, crew's wages are treated differently from the costs of repatriation.

Maritime liens

8.23 English law, in modern times, recognizes four main categories of maritime lien: claims for salvage, claims for damage done by a ship, claims for seamen's wages, and claims for master's wages and disbursements.[49] Where several liens of different character are attached to the one ship, there is a *prima facie inter se* ranking of maritime liens. While subject to many variations and exceptions, the generally recognized order is:

(1) damage and salvage liens. As between such liens, they rank interchangeably in inverse order of attachment,[50] save that where no salvage lien has attached between them, damage liens *inter se* rank *pari passu;*[51]
(2) the wages' lien;
(3) the lien for master's disbursements.

8.24 **The salvage lien** As explained by Brandon J in *The Lyrma (No 2)*,[52] it is a long standing principle that a maritime lien on a ship for salvage has priority over all other liens which attached before the salvage services were rendered. The basis for the principle is that the salvage services preserved the property to which the earlier liens attached and out of which, if of course it is sufficient, the claims to which such liens relate can be satisfied.[53]

[46] *The Guiseppe di Vittorio (No 2)* [1998] 1 Lloyd's Rep 661.
[47] *The Constanzia* (1866) 15 WR 183; *The World Star* [1987] 1 Lloyd's Rep 452.
[48] *The World Star* [1987] 1 Lloyd's Rep 452, 455.
[49] See generally above, Chapter 4.
[50] *The Veritas* [1901] P 304; *The Inna* [1938] P 148, (1938) 60 Ll L Rep 414.
[51] *The Stream Fisher* [1927] P 73, (1926) 17 Asp MLC, 26 L1 L Rep 4; *The Ruta* [2000] 1 WLR 2068, [2001] 1 All ER 450, [2000] 1 Lloyd's Rep 359.
[52] *The Lyrma (No 2)* [1978] 2 Lloyd's Rep 30.
[53] *The Veritas* [1901] P 304; *The Mons* [1932] P 109, (1932) 43 Ll L Rep 151; *The Inna* [1938] P 148, (1938) 60 Ll L Rep 414.

Where there are competing salvage liens, it is usual that they will rank in inverse order of attachment on the basis that the latest salvor has succeeded in preserving the *res*.[54] Where there are multiple salvors involved in a common salvage purpose, the *in rem* claims will rank *pari passu*.[55] **8.25**

The exposition of the principles relating to the priority accorded to the claimant who has preserved the *res* arises mainly in the context of cases relating to salvage and, in particular, to competition between the earlier damage lien and the later claim for salvage. In *The Veritas*, Gorell Barnes J said:[56] **8.26**

> It would seem clear that maritime liens may be divided into two classes—first, liens arising ex delicto; and secondly liens arising ex contractu or quasi ex contractu. It is almost obvious that liens of the latter class must in general rank against the fund in the inverse order of their attachment on the res. They are liens in respect of claims for services rendered, and it is reasonable that services which operate for the protection of prior interests should be privileged above those interests. Thus in the present case … the second set of salvors are preferred to the first because the first share in the later benefit conferred on the common subject of the liens.

In *The Lyrma (No 2)*[57] Brandon J applied the same principle in granting a salvor a higher priority than the crew, in respect of wages earned both before and after the salvage.

The question is whether this principle is restricted to salvage cases or whether it should be of broader application. By way of example, consider the facts of *The Halcyon Isle* discussed above.[58] Without the repairs to the vessel which were conducted in New York, the ship could not have sailed to Singapore and therefore could not have been arrested in that jurisdiction by the mortgagee. It is arguable that, without the repairs, the ship could never have reached Singapore so as to be realized for a high price by the Singapore Court; and thus that the repairer preserved the *res* for all lien holders and, as such, deserved to rank more highly. Such a contention was explored by the Federal Court in Canada in *The Atlantis Two*.[59] In considering a claim by Canadian necessaries men, the court concluded that the unjust result which would occur if their claim was not accorded any altered priority was that the increased value of the ship would benefit, or unjustly enrich, American necessaries men, some of whom had 'slept on their claims'. Thus, to avoid the unfairness, the court was prepared to permit a portion of the Canadian necessaries men's claim to rank *pari passu* with the claim of the American necessaries men.[60] **8.27**

---

[54] *The Lyrma (No 2)* [1978] 2 Lloyd's Rep 30, 34.
[55] *The Russland* [1924] P 55, 60.
[56] *The Veritas* [1901] P 304, 312–313.
[57] *The Lyrma (No 2)* [1978] 2 Lloyd's Rep 30.
[58] Para 8.02(1).
[59] *Fraser Shipyard and Industrial Centre Ltd v Expedient Maritime Co Ltd (The Atlantis Two)* (1999) 170 FTR 1.
[60] See para 4.50 above for an account of the approach in Canada regarding the classification of maritime liens according to their *lex causae*.

8.28 **The damage lien** The damage lien is accorded high priority so as to be seen 'somewhat quaintly, as a potent weapon in the promotion of safe navigation'.[61] It will usually rank behind a salvage lien which has preserved the *res* and may take priority over a wages' lien. The presumption that a damage lien takes priority over a wages' lien may be displaced where:

(1) the wage claimants have no alternative remedy;
(2) the damage lien would exhaust the fund;
(3) the damage lien is not attributable to the negligence of the wage claimants.

8.29 The rationale for the relative priority between a damage lien and a wages' lien can be traced back to the decision of Dr Lushington in *The Aline*,[62] in which the non-availability of an alternative remedy for the injured party, as compared to the redress available to the mortgagee and bottomry bond holder, was considered to be a significant factor in the grant of priority to the damage lien.

8.30 This reasoning was adopted in *The Benares*[63] and *The Chimera*,[64] in which cases the damage lien was accorded priority over the wages' lien on the basis that the wage claimants were able on the particular facts to bring an *in personam* claim against their employers. Similarly in *The Duna*,[65] the wages' lien was postponed to the damage lien on the 'well known principle of equity, where one party has several and the other but one remedy, it inflicts no hardship upon those seamen sending them to their personal action against an owner who is not stated to be bankrupt or insolvent'.[66] The Court of Appeal affirmed the equitable basis for these decisions in *The Ehn*[67] in holding that it would be inequitable to permit the owner of the vessel who caused the damage to withhold part of the fund for the payment of wages.

8.31 In *The Veritas*,[68] a distinction was drawn between liens arising *ex delicto* and those arising *ex contractu*. That distinction, and the preference accorded to the former, were justified on the basis that the person having the right arising *ex contractu* has chosen to enter into a relationship with the vessel (owner) for his own interests. That rationalization cannot be carried too far, however. In *The Ruta*, David Steel J commented that:

> The contrast between the voluntary nature of the wages lien and the involuntary nature of the damage lien might afford some justification for giving priority to the damage lien. But the contrast would, on the face of it, be more significant in

[61] *The Ruta* [2000] 1 WLR 2068, 2076, [2001] 1 All ER 450, 458, [2000] 1 Lloyd's Rep 359, 364, [22].
[62] *The Aline* (1839) 1 W Rob 111, 166 ER 514.
[63] *The Benares* (1850) 1 Not Cas Supp 50, 14 Jur 581.
[64] *The Chimera* (1852) 11 LT 113, 8 PD 131.
[65] *The Duna* (1861) 5 LT 217.
[66] Ibid; *The Linda Flor* (1857) Swab 308, 166 ER 1150.
[67] *The Ehn* (1883) 8 PD 130.
[68] *The Veritas* [1901] P 304.

resolving the ranking between a damage lien and an earlier salvage lien. Once engaged the seaman has no option but to continue to volunteer his services.[69]

It was conceded in *The Mons*[70] that wages earned subsequent to the salvage services took priority over the salvage claim. However, that view was rejected in *The Lyrma (No 2)*,[71] where it was held that no distinction could be drawn between wages earned before and after a salvage service; they were all subordinate on the basis that the salvage services had preserved the *res*. **8.32**

As between themselves, damage liens rank equally and are dealt with *pari passu*.[72] **8.33**

Wages' lien The public policy considerations relating to the protection of mariners provides the basis for the high priority accorded to the lien for master's and seamen's wages. As against other liens, there is no distinction drawn between the lien in respect of the master's wages and that relating to the crew's claims. **8.34**

Whilst the wages' lien will generally be subordinated to a salvage lien and a damage lien, the application of the equitable principles discussed above may displace the *prima facie* ranking. **8.35**

As between themselves, master's and seamen's claims rank *pari passu*.[73] **8.36**

Disbursements' lien The lien for master's disbursements is generally treated in the same manner as the lien for master's wages and, as between disbursement liens themselves, they are treated *pari passu*.[74] **8.37**

Mortgages

The high priority accorded, *prima facie*, to mortgages is a particular feature of English law and has been followed in Australia, Canada, Hong Kong, New Zealand, and Singapore. By contrast, South Africa accords mortgages a very low priority and even the 1993 Convention places mortgages lower in the order than does English law. International banking interests are, of course, opposed to any lower ranking of the mortgage than it currently has under English law, and their opposition explains, in part, the reluctance of the international community to embrace the Conventions on this topic. **8.38**

The ranking of mortgages *inter se*[75] Registered mortgages take priority over unregistered mortgages, even if the registered mortgagee had notice of the unregistered **8.39**

69 *The Ruta* [2000] 1 WLR 2068, 2076, [2001] 1 All ER 450, 458, [2000] 1 Lloyd's Rep 359, 364, [22].

70 *The Mons* [1932] P 109, (1932) 43 Ll L Rep 151.

71 *The Lyrma (No 2)* [1978] 2 Lloyd's Rep 30.

72 *The Stream Fisher* [1927] P 73, (1926) 17 Asp MLC, 26 Ll L Rep 4; *The Ruta* [2000] 1 WLR 2068, [2001] 1 All ER 450, [2000] 1 Lloyd's Rep 359.

73 *The Royal Wells* [1985] QB 86, [1984] 3 WLR 698, [1984] 3 All ER 193, [1984] 2 Lloyd's Rep 255.

74 *The Mons* [1932] P 109.

75 For a different view, see DC Jackson, *Enforcement of Maritime Claims* (4th edn, 2005) §§23.125 and following.

mortgage.[76] Similarly, a registered mortgage takes priority over an equitable charge, with or without notice.[77] Where there are competing registered mortgages, the first in time will prevail. The Merchant Shipping Act 1995 (MSA) provides:[78]

> (1) Where two or more mortgages are registered in respect of the same ship or share, the priority of the mortgagees between themselves shall, subject to paragraph (2) below, be determined by the order in which the mortgages were registered (and not by any other matter).
> (2) Registration regulations may provide for the giving to the registrar by intending mortgagees of 'priority notices' in a form prescribed by or approved under the regulations which, when recorded in the register, determine the priority of the interest to which the notice relates.[79]

8.40 The difficulty of determining the priority between two registered mortgages where one is registered in a foreign State is highlighted by the decision of the New Zealand Court of Appeal in *The Ship Betty Ott v General Bills* referred to above.[80] The Court of Appeal cited the following dictum of Lord Diplock in *The Halcyon Isle* in support of its conclusion that a foreign registered mortgage, for the purpose of a priorities dispute, was to be treated only as an equitable mortgage:

> ... it is also relevant to note that for the purpose of priority of ranking inter se mortgages fall into two classes: (1) British registered mortgages (which can only be upon British ships) and (2) other mortgages, British or foreign (which can be upon either British or foreign ships). British registered mortgages rank in priority to all other mortgages and rank inter se in order of date of registration. All other mortgages regardless of whether they are British or foreign rank inter se in order of date of creation.[81]

8.41 The Court of Appeal considered that this dictum meant that all foreign mortgages rank together with domestic unregistered mortgages and other equitable charges in order of date of creation, and that foreign registration is not recognized as creating a legal as distinct from an equitable charge.[82] It is submitted that Paul Myburgh's comment, that it is difficult to accept such a conclusion and that the better interpretation of Lord Diplock's dictum is that it does not set out a priority regime for registered foreign mortgages of foreign vessels, is well made.[83] It is clear

---

[76] *Coombes v Mansfield* (1855) 24 LJ Ch 513; see also *The Ship Betty Ott v General Bills* [1992] 1 NZLR 655.

[77] *Black v Williams* [1895] 1 Ch 408; see also *The Ship Betty Ott v General Bills* [1992] 1 NZLR 655.

[78] Strictly speaking, the provision is of application only to British-registered mortgages. It is submitted that in the case of competing foreign registered mortgages, the same result will follow, unless they are both governed by a law which is to different effect.

[79] Similar provisions exist in Australia, Personal Property Securities Act 2009, s 55; Canada, Canada Shipping Act 2001, c 26, s 67; Hong Kong, Merchant Shipping (Registration) Ordinance Cap 415, s 45; New Zealand, Shipping Registration Act 1992, s 40; Singapore, Merchant Shipping Act Chapter 179, s 28; South Africa, Shipping Registration Act 58 of 1998, sch 1, s 10.

[80] Para 8.02(2).

[81] *Bankers Trust Ltd v Todd Shipyards Corporation (The Halcyon Isle)* [1981] AC 221, 233.

[82] *The Ship Betty Ott v General Bills* [1992] 1 NZLR 655, 666

[83] P Myburgh, 'Recognition and Priority of Foreign Ship Mortgages' [1993] LMCLQ 155, 159.

that, in English law, the validity of a foreign mortgage on a ship is determined by the law of the State of registration of the ship.[84] If a foreign mortgage is determined to be valid, there can be no rationale for according it a lesser status than a mortgage which is registered in the forum, particularly if the legal consequences of the relevant foreign registration scheme coincide exactly with those of the *lex fori*, as was the case in *The Betty Ott*.[85] As Myburgh observes, the decision deprives holders of registered ship mortgages of adequate security in all jurisdictions save that in which the ship is registered.[86]

Statutory rights of action in rem

Statutory claims *in rem*, both as between different claims *in rem* or as between claims of the same type, are ranked equally and share in the fund *pari passu*.[87] **8.42**

Effect of contractual security on priority

In the ordinary case, where a claimant has already obtained adequate security for its claim upon the release of the vessel from arrest, questions as to whether his claim still has the same priority will not arise. In practice, therefore, such questions will only arise in circumstances in which the security has proved insufficient in amount or wholly or partially illusory and the availability of proceeding against the proceeds of sale by writ of *fi fa* is unattractive, because of the insufficiency of the fund and the fact that the claim will thereby rank as merely personal, postponed to any claim supported by a maritime or statutory lien. On a doctrinal level, the issue would be whether the release (or non-arrest) of the vessel in return for the contractual security had caused any maritime or statutory lien over the *res* to be lost. **8.43**

However, the law of Admiralty does not resolve such issues by reference solely to doctrine. Rather, the question is to be resolved by reference to the equitable principles which guide the determination of priorities in general and by reference to the analogous theoretical question whether the claimant would have been entitled to rearrest the vessel despite already having obtained security.[88] Thus in *The Ruta*,[89] it was held by David Steel J that claimants who had obtained security, which was both at risk of being dishonoured and anyway substantially less than their claim, should rank equally with the other two claimants in circumstances where all three vessels had been involved in a collision with The Ruta arising out of the same incident. **8.44**

---

84 *The Arosa Kulm* [1959] 1 Lloyd's Rep 212; *The Pacific Challenger* [1960] 1 Lloyd's Rep 99; *The Angel Bell* [1979] 2 Lloyd's Rep 491.

85 Art 2 of the 1993 Convention on Maritime Liens and Mortgages provides that if a mortgage is registered in accordance with the law of the State in which the vessel is registered the mortgage ranks in accordance with the law of the State of registration.

86 P Myburgh, 'Recognition and Priority of Foreign Ship Mortgages' [1993] LMCLQ 155, 160.

87 *The Africano* [1894] P 141.

88 Above, paras 6.70 and following, and paras 7.26 to 7.27.

89 *The Ruta* [2000] 1 WLR 2068, [2001] 1 All ER 450, [2000] 1 Lloyd's Rep 359.

8.45 Similarly, a party who voluntarily satisfies the claim of the holder of a maritime lien does not, absent an order of the court, thereby acquire the priority of the maritime lien, although it may be that priority will be accorded to the contractual assignee of a debt supported by a maritime lien.[90]

Ranking of claims where sister-ship arrest

8.46 Does the priority which a claim would have possessed in relation to the wrongdoing ship carry over to the sister-ship or should the claim rank differently on the sister-ship? It appears that when the claim is pursued against the sister-ship it enjoys the same priority as a statutory right *in rem*. In *The Leoborg (No 2)*,[91] one of the competing claims against the sister-ship was for wages earned aboard the wrongdoing ship. Whilst this would have ranked as a maritime lien had the claim been brought against the wrongdoing ship, it ranked as a statutory right *in rem* against the sister-ship, although Hewson J observed (in the particular procedural circumstance which confronted him)[92] that the point:

> ... raises matters which might have very far-reaching consequences. With these things in mind, I find it impossible for me in this motion to decide the point, which must expressly be left open for some future occasion in some other case.[93]

Counsel opposing the seamen's claim for priority of a maritime lien on the surrogate ship[94] suggested that there would be no injustice to the seaman because, to the extent that he failed to recover from the sister-ship, he would still have a lien over the wrongdoing ship.[95] Further, it was suggested that the downgrading of the maritime lien to a statutory action *in rem* when brought against a sister-ship was consistent with the policy of the English courts against the extension of maritime liens.

8.47 Two distinct questions are involved when considering the ranking of claims in relation to sister-ships: the ranking of transferred claims *inter se* and the ranking of transferred claims vis à vis claims which originated against the sister-ship. It is relevant to both questions that a claim pursued against a sister-ship is by definition a statutory action *in rem*. There is no right to proceed on a maritime lien against a

---

[90] *The Petone* [1917] P 198, 208; *The Leoborg (No 2)* [1964] 1 Lloyd's Rep 380, 383; see also Chapter 4, paras 4.12 and following in relation to the assignment and transfer of maritime liens.

[91] *The Leoborg (No 2)* [1964] 1 Lloyd's Rep 380.

[92] The relevant seaman had died, and opposing counsel did not have instructions from his widow.

[93] *The Leoborg (No 2)* [1964] 1 Lloyd's Rep 380, 382.

[94] The future Lord Hobhouse.

[95] It is submitted that this analysis is correct, being consistent with the instrumental analysis of the action *in rem* set forth in Chapter 2 above and with the discussion in Chapter 6 above regarding the availability of arrest to a judgment creditor. It is, however, wholly inconsistent with the conclusion reached by Mocatta J in *The Alletta* [1974] 1 Lloyd's Rep 40, discussed at para 6.53.

sister-ship. A consideration of the principles which apply to the determination of priorities reveals that it cannot be right to accord a claim which would be classified as a maritime lien in relation to the wrongdoing ship priority in relation to claims against sister-ships. For example, there can be no justification for giving priority to the salvor of ship A over the mortgagee of ship B in respect of a fund constituted by the sale of ship B when the salvor has done nothing to preserve the *res*, ie, ship B. Thus, transferred claims should have the status of statutory rights *in rem* against the sister-ship and maritime liens and mortgages over the sister-ship should take priority over all transferred claims.

On that basis, it would seem that all statutory claims *in rem*, whether transferred or relating specifically to the sister-ship should rank equally *inter se* on the basis that they all arise on the basis of the liability of the relevant person. This is consistent with the approach in *The Leoborg (No 2)*.[96] Such an approach has been enshrined in the Australian legislation.[97] **8.48**

In South Africa all claims in respect of associated ships are met in the order stipulated in s 11 of the Admiralty Jurisdiction Regulation Act 105 of 1983.[98] This produces a worse result for the claimant pursuing an associated ship than the position followed in *The Leoborg (No 2)*.[99] **8.49**

Ranking of claims where there is a possessory lien

Thomas notes that:[100] **8.50**

> . . . the evolved position has been to recognise the superior claim of the Admiralty Marshal subject to an effective judicial protection of the interest of the possessory lienee. It is the duty of the possessory lienee to surrender his possession of the *res* to the Admiralty Marshal whereupon the court undertakes to protect both his interest and priority against the *res* or any fund in the hands of the court which represents the *res*. The possessory lienee is thereby in no way prejudiced by being compelled to part with possession.

A possessory lienee has priority over all claims except maritime liens which have attached before the possessory lien.[101] Therefore, it has priority over a mortgage even if the mortgage was executed before possession.[102] **8.51**

---

96 *The Leoborg (No 2)* [1964] 1 Lloyd's Rep 380.
97 Admiralty Act 1988, s 35(1).
98 Above, para 8.13.
99 *The Leoborg (No 2)* [1964] 1 Lloyd's Rep 380.
100 D R Thomas, *Maritime Liens* (1980), para 453.
101 For possessory liens generally, see D C Jackson, *Enforcement of Maritime Claims* (4th edn, 2005), Chapter 20.
102 *The Immacolata Concezione* (1883) 9 PD 37; *The Tergeste* [1903] P 26; *The Acacia* (1880) 4 Asp MC 254; *Fraser Shipyard and Industrial Centre Ltd v Expedient Maritime Co Ltd (The Atlantis Two)* (1999) 170 FTR 1; *Hill v The Ship James Cook* [1997] 3 NZLR 752.

8.52 A holder of a possessory lien who arrests the vessel does not thereby lose the benefit of the possessory lien unless he surrenders possession and elects to proceed solely on the basis of an action *in rem*.[103]

Ranking of claims where there is a statutory power of detention

8.53 A statutory power of detention is likely strictly speaking to fall outside the usual Admiralty ranking of competing claims and unlikely to be such as to rank other than in priority to all other claims. In practice, much may depend upon whether on the construction of the particular statute it is possible for the court to bypass the problem at an earlier stage, as in *Corps v Owners of the Paddle Steamer 'Queen of the South'*.[104] That will not be possible where, for example, the statutory power of detention is preliminary to the forfeiture of the vessel under customs legislation.

8.54 In Australia, the Admiralty Act 1988 provides that where a ship that has been detained under a statutory power of detention in relation to a civil claim is arrested and sold under the Admiralty Act, the civil claim is payable in priority to any claim against the ship other than the claim of the Marshal for expenses.[105]

Reopening the question of priorities

8.55 The court may reopen the question of priorities where an order for payment out of a fund has been made, but usually only before payment has been made.[106] In *Textainer Equipment Management BV v Baltic Shipping Co*,[107] the Federal Court of Canada, whilst agreeing with the general thrust of the English authorities, was nevertheless prepared to vary an order for payment out of the fund in circumstances where the court had parted with only a portion of the fund and where the creditors who had received payment were still before the court, not yet having obtained judgment, but having given undertakings in respect of the funds they had received. The court acknowledged that the position might have been different had final judgment been entered in favour of those creditors so that they were no longer subject to the jurisdiction of the court.

B. Insolvency Issues

8.56 This section does no more than dip a toe into the waters of insolvency law. Those waters are tricky enough to navigate in the context of domestic insolvency

[103] *The Honey I* [1987] 1 SLR 282 (High Court of Singapore) citing with approval *The Acacia* (1880) 4 Asp MC 254 and *The Immacolata Concezione* (1883) 9 PD 37; *Babcock Fitzroy Ltd v The Ship 'The M/V Southern Pasifika'* [2012] 2 NZLR 652, [2012] NZHC 1245, [2012] 2 Lloyd's Rep 423.

[104] *Corps v Owners of the Paddle Steamer 'Queen of the South'* [1968] P 449, above para 7.68.

[105] Admiralty Act 1988, s 36(5).

[106] *The Markland* (1872) LR 3 A & E 340; *The Stream Fisher* [1927] P 73, (1926) 17 Asp MLC 117, 26 Ll L Rep 4; *The Fairport (No 4)* [1967] 1 WLR 964, [1967] 2 All ER 914, [1967] 1 Lloyd's Rep 602; *The CC Orient* [1985] 1 HKC 115.

[107] *Textainer Equipment Management BV v Baltic Shipping Co* (1995) 92 FTR 267, [1995] 2 FC 609.

proceedings brought against companies registered and operating in the forum. Where foreign companies or windings-up are involved, they are murky and treacherous and must be navigated with care.[108] However, it is impossible to ignore the interaction between the admiralty process and insolvency proceedings, however underdeveloped that interaction may be—as to which Thomas put the position aptly:[109]

> The law of [insolvency] seems to have developed with little regard to the Admiralty proceeding *in rem*.[110] Certainly it is difficult to fit the Admiralty proceeding into the legislative language of the relevant statutes which regulate [insolvency proceedings]. Yet the need for the latter to accommodate the action *in rem* and the potential conflict between the two processes is plain. A *res* may concurrently be the subject of an arrest in the Admiralty Court and an asset capable of liquidation in [insolvency proceedings]. In such a circumstance it is important for a maritime claimant to be able to ascertain whether it is the jurisdiction of the Admiralty Court or some other court which prevails and which mode of legal process is available for the satisfaction of the claim.

Where both sets of proceedings are brought in the same jurisdiction,[111] two situations need to be considered: **8.57**

(1) where *in rem* claimants have issued proceedings in the Admiralty Court prior to the date of the presentation of a petition for a winding-up order;
(2) where *in rem* claimants have issued proceedings in the Admiralty Court between the date of the presentation of a petition for the winding-up and the date of the winding-up order.

---

108 And with the aid of specialist texts, such as Sheldon (ed), *Cross-Border Insolvency* (4th edn, 2015), I F Fletcher, *Insolvency in Private International Law* (2nd edn, 2005), G Moss QC, I Fletcher, & S Isaacs QC, *The EC Regulation on Insolvency Proceedings* (2nd end, 2009), J Marshall, *European Cross Border Insolvency* (2004).

109 D R Thomas, *Maritime Liens* (1980), para 99.

110 The converse observation might be made with equal force.

111 Note that it is possible, given (in very broad terms) sufficient connecting factors to make it expedient to do so, to wind up foreign companies in England, unless their 'centre of main interest' (COMI) is in another EU country, in which case only that country will have jurisdiction to do so under the European Insolvency Regulation (Council Regulation (EC) 1346/2000). The recast European Regulation on Insolvency (Reg 2015/848 of 20 May 2015) entered into force from 26 June 2015 and will apply to insolvency proceedings from 26 June 2017. Its principal areas of impact will be: an adjustment of the rules on COMI, so as to make it harder to forum shop in advance of insolvency; an extension of the scope of main and secondary proceedings; a reduction in the need for secondary proceedings; and enhanced cooperation between insolvency office holders and the court.

The other international insolvency regime which may operate in admiralty cases is the UNCITRAL Model Law on Cross-Border Insolvency, given the force of law in Great Britain by SI No 2006/1030. See para 8.74 below. For an example of its operation in the shipping arena, see *Cosco Bulk Carrier Co Ltd v Armada Shipping SA* [2011] EWHC 216 (Ch), [2011] 2 All ER (Comm) 481.

Note further that, as a matter of English law, foreign companies are 'unregistered companies' for the purpose of the 1986 Insolvency Act: *Stocznia Gdanska v Latreefers Inc (No 2)* [2001] 2 BCLC 116 and, as such, are addressed in Part V and may be wound up under s 221(1) of that Act. By s 229, the provisions of Part IV of the Act (which include those set out under para 8.58 below) apply to the liquidation of unregistered companies.

8.58 The following provisions of the Insolvency Act 1986 are relevant in this connection.[112]

(1) Section 126, which enables a company, creditor, or contributory to apply at any time between the presentation of a winding-up petition to any court in which an action is pending against the company for a stay of the action.
(2) Section 127, which provides that, in a winding-up by the court, any disposition of the company's property made after the commencement of the winding-up is, unless the court otherwise orders, void. However, this does not affect anything done by an administrator while the winding-up petition is suspended under para 40 of Schedule B1.[113]
(3) Section 128, the effect of which is that any attachment, sequestration, distress, or execution put in force within the jurisdiction against the estate or effects of a UK-registered company after the commencement of the winding-up, is void where that company is being wound up by the court.
(4) Section 129, the effect of which is that the winding-up is deemed to commence at the earlier time of the presentation of the petition for winding-up and the passing of a resolution for a voluntary winding-up,[114] unless the winding-up order is made under para 13(1)(e) of Schedule B1, in which case the winding-up is deemed to commence on the date of the order.[115]
(5) Section 130(2), which provides for an automatic stay of proceedings against the company or its property from the time of the winding-up order. The court's permission is required in order for the proceedings to continue or for new proceedings to be commenced.
(6) Section 183, which disentitles a creditor, as against a liquidator, from retaining the benefit of any execution or attachment against the land or goods of a company which has not been perfected by the commencement of the winding-up.

8.59 It is at the outset important to bear in mind the difference in security terms between a maritime lien and a statutory action *in rem*. In the former case, the lien attaches to the ship as soon as the claim arises; in the latter, the security interest created by s 20 of the Senior Courts Act 1981 does not arise until the claim form is issued.

Issue of proceedings prior to petition for winding-up

8.60 Where *in rem* proceedings have been commenced before presentation of a petition for winding-up, they will initially be stayed once the winding-up order is

---

[112] There are comparable provisions in Australia (Bankruptcy Act 1966 (Cth) and Corporations Law 2001 (Cth)); Canada (Bankruptcy and Insolvency Act RCS 1985 B-3); Hong Kong (Bankruptcy Ordinance Cap 6, Companies Ordinance Cap 32, and Companies (Winding-Up) Rules Cap 32H); New Zealand (Companies Act 1993); Singapore (Bankruptcy Act 1995, Cap 20 and Companies Act 1967, Cap 50); South Africa (Companies Act No 71 of 2008).

[113] Insolvency Act 1986, s 126(2).

[114] In the case of a resolution for a voluntary winding-up, the court has power, in the case of fraud or mistake, to direct otherwise.

[115] Insolvency Act 1986, s 129(1A).

granted, and an application to the court seised with the winding-up for permission to proceed will be necessary.[116] That permission should ordinarily be forthcoming, however, because an *in rem* creditor who has issued his writ *in rem* before presentation of the winding-up petition has already acquired the status of secured creditor.[117]

The court also has a broad discretion under s 130(2) to do 'what is right and fair according to the circumstances of each case'.[118] In *In re Aro*, the Court of Appeal considered this 'alternative approach' and, in that connection, was troubled by the practical implications of concluding, as Oliver J had at first instance, that it was arrest and not issue which rendered the *in rem* claimant a secured creditor.[119] Logically, this reasoning might suggest that the court would have permitted the *in rem* action to continue even if it had agreed with Oliver J. In the result, however, it gave essentially the same reason for granting permission on this basis as it had on the first, which was that '[t]he service of the writ adds nothing to the status of the claimant vis-à-vis the vessel sued'.[120] It is not therefore clear from *In re Aro* what, if anything, this 'alternative approach' adds in the context of *in rem* proceedings, although the case of *Re Lineas Navieras Bolivianas*,[121] considered below,[122] may have taken the reasoning a stage further. **8.61**

Issue of proceedings after petition for winding-up

Although the court's permission would be required in order to commence it (whether as an action against the company or its property),[123] the same result will obtain in an action *in rem* to enforce a maritime lien or a proprietary claim brought after presentation of the winding-up petition or even the making of a winding-up **8.62**

[116] Pursuant to s 130(2) of the 1986 Act. A foreign liquidation will not have that (automatic) effect, even where it has been commenced in another EU country: *Mazur Media Ltd v Mazur Media GmbH* [2004] EWHC 1566, [69]–[70], [2004] 1 WLR 2966, [2005] 1 Lloyd's Rep 41, [2005] 1 BCLC 305.

[117] *The Zafiro* [1960] P 1, [1959] 3 WLR 123, [1959] 2 All ER 537, [1959] 1 Lloyd's Rep 359; *In re Aro Co Ltd* [1980] Ch 196; *In re Lineas Navieras Bolivianas SAM* [1995] BCC 666. *In re Aro* was followed by the Court of Appeal in Singapore in *Kuo Fen Ching v Dauphin Offshore Engineering & Trading Pte Ltd* [1999] 3 SLR 721. In Canada, by contrast, a claimant does not become a secured creditor by enforcing a statutory right *in rem*: *Benson Bros Shipbuilding Co (1960) Ltd v The Ship Miss Donna* [1978] 1 FC 379, 387. In South Africa, s 10 of the Admiralty Jurisdiction Regulation Act provides that any property arrested or attached, or security furnished, or the proceeds of any property sold in execution or under an order of the court in the exercise of its admiralty jurisdiction, will not vest in a trustee or form part of the assets to be administered by a liquidator or insolvency practitioner.

[118] *In re Aro Co Ltd* [1980] Ch 196, 209E–H; *Cosco Bulk Carrier Co Ltd v Armada Shipping SA* [2011] EWHC 216 (Ch), [2011] 2 All ER (Comm) 481, [47]; *In re Grosvenor Metal Co Ltd* [1950] Ch 63, 65; *Re B+B Construction Co Ltd* [2003] HKCFI 33, [5].

[119] *In re Aro Co Ltd* [1980] Ch 196, 210A–211A.

[120] Ibid 211B.

[121] *Re Lineas Navieras Bolivianas* [1995] BCC 666.

[122] Paras 8.64 and following.

[123] Cf *In re Australian Direct Steam Navigation Co* (1875) LR 20 Eq 325; *The Constellation* [1965] 2 Lloyd's Rep 538.

order.[124] The court's permission ought therefore to be readily forthcoming to, for example, the mortgagee or the holder of a maritime lien in order to permit him to realize his security.[125] It is possible that the same may in some circumstances apply under the EU Insolvency Regulation, art 5.1,[126] which provides that:

> The opening of insolvency proceedings shall not affect the rights in rem of creditors or third parties in respect of tangible or intangible, moveable or immoveable assets ... belonging to the debtor which are situated within the territory of another Member State at the time of the opening of proceedings.

However, it will be noted that this provision only operates where the relevant asset is elsewhere within the EU when the (winding-up) proceedings are commenced, which may very well not be the case in relation to a ship. In any other case, the ranking of claims is a matter for the law of the court in which the liquidation is proceeding.[127]

8.63 The position is less certain in relation to claims which attract only a statutory right of action *in rem*, particularly where the claimant must establish that the beneficial ownership of the ship to be arrested is vested in the 'relevant person' at the time when the proceedings are commenced.[128] That is because, in *Ayerst v C & K (Construction) Ltd*,[129] a case concerned with the construction of the Finance Act 1954, the House of Lords held that when a company was ordered to be wound up, the effect was to divest it of the 'beneficial ownership' of its assets within the meaning of s 17(6)(a) of the 1954 Act. Lord Diplock, with whom the other members of the Appellate Committee agreed, derived his authority for this proposition from the decision a century earlier in *In re Oriental Inland Steam Co*,[130] observing that:

> The authority of this case for the proposition that the property of the company ceases upon the winding up to belong beneficially to the company has now stood unchallenged for a hundred years.[131]

This would seem to be a formidable obstacle to the proposition that proceedings can be commenced *in rem* on a general maritime claim once a winding-up has commenced. However, both the High Court of Australia and the High Court of Hong Kong have declined to adopt the reasoning of Lord Diplock in *Ayerst*. Before turning to those authorities,[132] it is necessary first to consider the difficult case of

---

124 *In re Rio Grande do Sul Steamship Company* (1877) 5 Ch D 282.

125 The case of *In re Australian Direct Steam Navigation Co* (1875) LR 20 Eq 325 is not to contrary effect. That case is best understood as one of procedural convenience, as Arden J (on this point, correctly) indicated in *In re Lineas Navieras Bolivianas* [1995] BCC 666, 677H.

126 Art 8 of the recast European Regulation on Insolvency is in the same terms.

127 Art 4.2(i); Art 7(2)(i) of the recast European Regulation on Insolvency is in the same terms.

128 See Chapter 5, para 5.13.

129 *Ayerst v C & K (Construction) Ltd* [1976] AC 167, [1975] 2 All ER 537.

130 *In re Oriental Inland Steam Co* (1874) 9 Ch App 557.

131 *Ayerst v C & K (Construction) Ltd* [1976] AC 167, 180, [1975] 2 All ER 537, 546 per Lord Diplock.

132 Below, para 8.67.

Re Lineas Navieras Bolivianas SAM,[133] on the assumption that the rule in *Ayerst* is indeed applicable in the Admiralty context.[134]

The relevant facts in *Re Lineas Navieras Bolivianas SAM* were as follows. Prior to presentation of the winding-up petition, the vessel had already been arrested by one creditor, and others had issued writs *in rem* against her. Between the presentation of the winding-up petition and the making of the winding-up order, (1) five further writs *in rem* were issued by the applicants, none of whose claims was such as to give rise to a maritime lien, and (2) the Admiralty Court made an order for the appraisement and sale of the ship, subject to the leave of the Companies Court, which leave was later granted. The applicants applied for permission to continue with their actions in the Admiralty Court. Arden J, as she then was, drew the distinction between claims brought to enforce maritime liens, and those brought pursuant to the statutory right of action *in rem*:[135] **8.64**

> First there is the claim of a maritime lienor. In his case the lien attaches to the ship as soon as the circumstances occur which gave rise to the lien. In contradistinction a statutory lien granted by s 20 of the Supreme Court Act 1981 does not affect the ship until the writ is issued.

Counsel for the liquidator sought to draw the obvious conclusion from this distinction, ie, that:[136]

> Upon commencement of the winding up the assets passed into the statutory scheme for dealing with the assets for the benefit of all creditors. Therefore there was not the necessary unity of ownership of the vessel between the time the claim arose and the time the claim was asserted by issue of the writ in rem (see *The Monica S* [1968] P 741). If the liquidator as opposed to the Admiralty Marshal sold the vessel, it would be encumbered by the claims of those who issued their writs in rem prior to the commencement of winding up when the vessel was still owned by [the relevant person], but it would not be encumbered by the claims of these applicants.

It is respectfully submitted that that analysis is, if *Ayerst* is to be followed, plainly correct. However, the Judge did not adopt it. Instead, having quoted from Lord Diplock's speech in *Ayerst*, Arden J continued:[137]

> ... a critical feature of this case was [the] ... order for the sale of the ship. Once that happened, the proceeds of sale were held by the Admiralty Court to be applied in accordance with its procedures ... The effect of the order for sale ... on the assets of the company must have been to convert the company's interest in the ship into a right to receive the balance of the proceeds of sale remaining after satisfaction of the prior claimants. As a result of conversion [*sic*] it would appear that the present

[133] *Re Lineas Navieras Bolivianas SAM* [1995] BCC 666.
[134] Noting para 5.25 above where it is submitted that the assumption is not well made.
[135] Ibid 669G.
[136] Ibid 675C–D.
[137] Ibid 676D.

applicants do not in fact require leave under s 130(2) because they are not proceeding against either the company or the company's property.

8.65 It is respectfully submitted that that reasoning (which does not appear to have been advanced in argument) is flawed. The procedures of the Admiralty Court allow—indeed, in effect require—actions *in rem* which could have been brought against a vessel which has meanwhile been sold in accordance with its procedures, to be brought against the fund in court which has been generated by that sale.[138] If the sale (or, worse still, the order for sale) had the effect of transferring the beneficial ownership of the vessel or of the fund generated by its sale away from the owning company (query to whom), then it would be quite impossible for any claim *in rem* to be issued after the date of the sale or order. Whilst it is of course right in one sense that the proceeds of sale are 'held by the Admiralty Court', there is no reason in principle or practice to treat that holding as equivalent to the vesting of a company's property in a liquidator.

8.66 That is not to say, however, that Arden J was necessarily wrong on the facts of the case to grant the relief sought by the applicants. The third ground cited by her in support of her conclusion, echoing the 'alternative approach' in *In re Aro*[139] was that:

> ... refusal of leave would amount to preventing the applicants from enforcing security and would enable some only of the claimants on the proceeds of sale to scoop the pool.[140]

Leaving to one side that the applicants had no security to enforce, it may well have been 'right and fair according to the circumstances of [the] case' to have granted leave to permit the proceedings to proceed. That is difficult to assess on the facts of *Re Lineas Navieras Bolivianas SAM*, because it was not necessary for Arden J to explain why, on the hypothesis that she was wrong about the existence of the applicants' 'security', it might nevertheless have been right and fair to grant leave. But it is certainly possible to conceive of a case in which the grant of permission might well be 'just and fair'. An obvious example would be where a claimant *in rem*, immediately following issue of the claim form, presented a winding-up petition, with the object of ensuring, in effect, that his claim would be accorded a higher priority than other would-be statutory claimants *in rem*. It is not difficult to imagine a court looking askance at such an attempt to 'steal a march' on other *in rem* creditors.[141]

---

[138] Para 2.07(8) above and the cases there cited. Note also in this connection CPR 61.10(2) and (3); PD61 §3.6(3).

[139] Para 8.61 above.

[140] *In re Aro* [1995] BCC 666, 677A.

[141] In *Re Lineas Navieras Bolivianas SAM*, the petition had been presented by one of the earlier *in rem* claimants, although that claimant had some claims which were purely personal and could not be brought *in rem*: [1995] BCC 666, 667H, 673E.

8.67 Returning to the question of whether the rule in *Ayerst* is correct or should be followed in Admiralty proceedings,[142] the Australian case, *Commissioner of Taxation v Linter Textiles Australia Ltd (in liquidation) (Linter)*,[143] concerned a taxation statute, as did *Ayerst*. The relevant question before the court for present purposes was whether, as a consequence of the winding-up of the Linter Group, the shares in Linter Textiles had ceased to be beneficially owned by the Linter Group, thus making it ineligible to claim a sought-after tax deduction pursuant to s 80A of the Income Tax Assessment Act 1936 (Cth). The majority of the High Court of Australia,[144] which included at least three equity and trusts specialists, held that the winding-up of a limited company does not have the effect of divesting the company of beneficial ownership of its assets. In their joint reasons, Gleeson CJ, Gummow, Hayne, Callinan, and Heydon JJ approved the decision of Menzies J in *Franklin's Selfserve v Commissioner of Taxation*[145] and declined to accept Lord Diplock's suggestion that 'upon going into liquidation a company ceases to be the "beneficial owner" of its assets as that expression has been used as a term of legal art since 1874'.[146] The majority suggested that the continued acceptance of *Ayerst* appears to stem from the use of the term 'trustee' in circumstances where, at best, it was being used in a metaphorical or analogical sense,[147] noting that that very point had been made a few years after the decision in *In re Oriental Inland Steam Co* by Romer J in *Knowles v Scott*:[148]

> In my judgment the liquidator is not a trustee in the strict sense,[149] with such liability affecting his position as has been contended by the Plaintiff. The consequences would be very serious if such a doctrine were to be upheld. If a liquidator were held to be a trustee for each creditor or contributory of the company, his liability would indeed be onerous, and would render the position of a liquidator one which few persons would care to occupy.

The High Court held instead that:[150]

> The critical point is that the change in the control of affairs of the company has no impact upon its beneficial ownership of its assets.

---

[142] Above, para 8.63.
[143] *Commissioner of Taxation v Linter Textiles Australia Ltd (in liquidation)* [2005] HCA 20, (2005) 220 CLR 592.
[144] Gleeson CJ, McHugh, Gummow, Hayne, Callinan, and Heydon JJ.
[145] *Franklin's Selfserve v Commissioner of Taxation* (1970) 125 CLR 52.
[146] *Commissioner of Taxation v Linter Textiles Australia Ltd (in liquidation)* [2005] HCA 20, (2005) 220 CLR 592, 604, [24].
[147] Ibid 607, [32].
[148] *Knowles v Scott* [1891] 1 Ch 717, 721–722.
[149] That is of course correct. In *Buchler v Talbot* [2004] 2 AC 298, 309A, [28], Lord Hoffmann, having cited *Ayerst*, went on (in a passage noted by Kirby J, who was in the minority in *Linter*) to explain: 'It is a special kind of trust because neither the creditors nor anyone else have a proprietary interest in the fund. The creditors have only a right to have the assets administered by the liquidator in accordance with the provisions of the [1986 Act] ...'
[150] *Commissioner of Taxation v Linter Textiles Australia Ltd (in liquidation)* [2005] HCA 20, (2005) 220 CLR 592, 612–613, [54]–[55].

> By analogy with the general law, the circumscribing or suspension by reason of the appointment of the liquidator of the exercise by the usual organs of the company of the incidents of ownership of the assets of the company does not mean that the company itself has ceased to own beneficially its assets within the meaning of s 80A(1). Power to deal with an asset and matters of ownership or title are not interchangeable concepts.

8.68 The High Court of Hong Kong was confronted with circumstances which relate directly to the interaction between the Admiralty jurisdiction and the insolvency provisions. In *International Transportation Service Inc v The Convenience Container*,[151] the owner of four vessels which had been arrested on the basis of general maritime claims sought to have the arrests set aside on the basis that the 'ownership' nexus required by s 12B of the High Court Ordinance[152] was not satisfied. The reason given was that, at the time when the writs *in rem* were issued, the owner had already entered into voluntary winding-up (in Singapore), the effect of which was to render the beneficial owner of the vessels a different person from their owner at the time when the causes of action arose. Rejecting that submission, Waung J held that the key to the reasoning in *Linter* was that there was no trust that a court of equity could recognize and that power or control of assets has no direct bearing on their ownership.[153] This, he observed, was consistent with the reasoning in *I Congresso del Partido*[154] in which Goff J explained that beneficial ownership in the context of the predecessor to s 21(4) of the *Senior Courts Act* 1981 was concerned with title and not possession or control or use or benefit.[155] Waung J's view was that:

> ... when the legal principle is properly understood then all the common law jurisdiction [*sic*] earlier mentioned, whether Hong Kong, Singapore,[156] New Zealand or England should and would hold *Linter* to be the correct principle.[157]

It is submitted, however, that the better view is that of the Court of Appeal of Hong Kong, which is that *Ayerst* and *Linter* are to be understood in their proper

---

151 *International Transportation Service Inc v The Convenience Container* [2006] 902 HKCU 1 (Hong Kong Court of First Instance).

152 Section 12B of the High Court Ordinance is *in pari materia* with s 21(4) of the Senior Courts Act 1981.

153 *International Transportation Service Inc v The Convenience Container* [2006] 902 HKCU 1, [2006] 3 HKLRD 610, 624–627, [34] (Hong Kong Court of First Instance).

154 *I Congresso del Partido* [1978] 1 QB 501, 538.

155 *International Transportation Service Inc v The Convenience Container* [2006] 902 HKCU 1, [2006] 3 HKLRD 610, 620–621, [22] (Hong Kong Court of First Instance).

156 Three Singapore authorities had been cited. In *Low Gim Har v Low Gim Siah* [1992] 2 SLR 593 Chan J had examined the decisions in *Ayerst, Franklin* and *CSD v* Livingstone [1956] AC 694 and observed that, 'it is possible for me to conclude that it is still the general rule that in a winding-up of a company, the company retains the legal ownership (and no differentiation needs to be made with respect to its equitable ownership) of all its assets ...'. In *Ng Wei Teck v Overseas-Chinese Banking Corp* [1998] 2 SLR 1 there was no reference to *Ayerst* nor to the central proposition under consideration. In *Kuock v CSD* [2003] 4 SLR 43, *Ayesrt* was cited but nothing said as to whether it was correctly decided.

157 *International Transportation Service Inc v The Convenience Container* [2006] 902 HKCU 1, [2006] 3 HKLRD 610, 627–628, [35] (Hong Kong Court of First Instance).

context, ie, revenue law, and shed no light on the position in *in rem* procedure.[158] If that is not right, however, the approach of the Australian and first instance Hong Kong courts is unlikely to prevail in the English courts over that of Lord Diplock in *Ayerst*.

Moreover, even if *Linter* were to be preferred over *Ayerst* in the context of s 21(4) of the 1981 Act, that would mean only that the Admiralty Court had jurisdiction to entertain the claim. The court seised with the winding-up will still need to give permission for the action to be brought, and—assuming for present purposes that such permission were forthcoming—it is difficult to see how the general maritime claimant could thereby be put in a better position than the personal creditors of the owning company. That is because, whilst the issue and service of a writ *in rem* may not—unlike an arrest[159]—amount to a sequestration, the coming into effect of a statutory lien would surely amount to a 'disposition' of the company's property[160] and thus be void under s 127 of the 1986 Act.[161] Even if that is not right, its effect is sufficiently akin to a disposition for the court on an application for permission to look askance at securing one creditor (or class of creditors) at the expense of the remainder.[162] The grant of permission, if forthcoming, would therefore be liable to be subject to conditions, pursuant to s 130(2) of the 1986 Act, that the commencement of the *in rem* proceedings would not have that effect. **8.69**

That is not to say that the court would necessarily refuse to grant permission. It is well recognized that the Admiralty Court is far better placed than the Chancery Division to arrest and sell a ship for the benefit of all creditors.[163] There may be much to be gained, therefore, by permitting an action *in rem* to be commenced (subject to conditions), in order to maximize the recovery for the liquidation as a **8.70**

---

158 *International Transportation Service Inc v The Convenience Container* [2007] HKCA 305, [2007] 3 HKLRD 575; [2007] 4 HKC 484 [77].

159 *In re Australian Direct Steam Navigation Co* (1875) LR 20 Eq 325; *The Constellation* [1966] 1 WLR 272, 274, [1965] 2 Lloyd's Rep 538, 541.

160 Cf *Re Wiltshire Iron Co* (1868) LR 3 Ch App 443; *Re Park Ward & Co Ltd* [1926] Ch 828; *Re Liverpool Civil Service Association* (1874) 9 Ch App 511. It could be argued to the contrary that the lien arises by operation of law rather than as a result of any disposition by the company, but it is difficult to see why that should affect the operation of the clear words of s 127.

161 In *Re Lineas Navieras Bolivianas SAM*, however, Arden J did not consider s 127 affected the writs issued after presentation of the winding-up petition: [1995] BCC 666, 676H. She did not explain why, however, and it is respectfully submitted that on this point also she was wrong.

162 In *Re Lineas Navieras Bolivianas SAM* [1995] BCC 666 it was argued (p 673D) that:

> ... it was not right and fair that a party that does not itself have a valid action in rem should be able by the commencement of the winding-up proceedings to pre-empt and prejudice the rights of those who do have arguable statutory rights in rem simply because the latter have not yet issued proceedings, although they would have done so in the ordinary course of Admiralty procedure.

That argument was not adopted in terms by Arden J and it is submitted that she was right not to do so. Timing is frequently critical in cases of insolvency, and it is difficult to see why an *ex hypothesi* unsecured maritime claimant should be in a better position than other unsecured creditors, merely because he had but did not in time avail himself of an opportunity not available to those others.

163 *The Constellation* [1996] 1 WLR 272, [1965] 2 Lloyd's Rep 538; *In re Lineas Navieras Bolivianas SAM* [1995] BCC 666.

whole. Perhaps, if the claim were modest and the *in rem* claimant would not otherwise be enthusiastic about pursuing at some expense an action for little benefit to itself, the court would permit the claim to attract its usual priority, but it is submitted that that is unlikely to be the case as a matter of course.

8.71 The consequence of s 128 of the 1986 Act is that, once winding-up proceedings have been commenced, any order for sale is likely, as in *Re Lineas Navieras Bolivianas SAM*,[164] to be made subject to the permission of the Companies Court to proceed with it. As indicated above, however, that permission may be expected in the usual case to be readily obtained.

Recognition of foreign insolvency proceedings

8.72 The interaction between the admiralty process and foreign insolvency proceedings requires reference to four main sources of law: the European Insolvency Regulation,[165] the Cross-Border Insolvency Regulations 2006,[166] s426 of the Insolvency Act 1986, and the common law.

The European Insolvency Regulation

8.73 Insolvency proceedings commenced in another EU country are to be accorded recognition under art 16.1 and given effect to automatically under art 17.1.[167] The effect of such proceedings on an admiralty action commenced thereafter will be for the law governing the liquidation to resolve; that is, the law of the Member State where the debtor has its 'centre of main interests', the 'main insolvency proceedings'.[168] Where a debtor has assets in another Member State, 'secondary proceedings' can be opened in that other State if the debtor possesses an 'establishment' within the territory of that other Member State.[169]

Where the *in rem* proceedings were commenced first, they will be unaffected, in the first instance at least, by the liquidation.[170]

---

[164] *Re Lineas Navieras Bolivianas SAM* [1995] BCC 666

[165] 1346/2000 and the recast European Regulation on Insolvency (Reg 2015/848 of 20 May 2015).

[166] Which gives effect to the UNCITRAL Model Law on Cross-Border Insolvency. Amongst the other jurisdictions considered in this work, Australia, Canada, New Zealand, and South Africa have also enacted legislation giving effect to the Model Law: The Cross-Border Insolvency Act 2008 (Cth); Bankruptcy & Insolvency Act RSC 1985 B-3 Part XIII and Companies & Creditors Arrangement Act RSC 1985 C-36 Part IV; Insolvency (Cross-border) Act 2006 (NZ); Cross-border Insolvency Act 42 of 2000 (SAf).

[167] Art 19.1 and 20.1 of the recast European Regulation on Insolvency.

[168] Art 3.1 of both the original and the recast European Insolvency Regulations.

[169] Art 3.2–3.3 of both the original and the recast European Insolvency Regulations.

[170] *Mazur Media Ltd v Mazur Media GmbH* [2004] 1 WLR 2966, [2005] 1 Lloyd's Rep 41, [2005] 1 BCLC 305. It remains to be definitively established whether the rights *in rem* referred to in Art 5 of the original (Art 8 of the recast) Insolvency Regulation encompass admiralty rights *in rem*. (Some guidance may be had from paras 102–104 of the Virgos-Schmit Report (3 May 1996,

The Cross-Border Insolvency Regulations

8.74 The effect of the Cross-Border Insolvency Regulations (CBIR) is that foreign insolvency proceedings will be recognized by the courts of Great Britain without the need for reciprocal treaty arrangements. However, the European Insolvency Regulation prevails if both States are EU Member States.[171] Broadly, a foreign representative administering foreign insolvency proceedings can apply to a British court both to commence proceedings (or to participate in proceedings) where the provisions of British insolvency law would otherwise apply in relation to the debtor[172] and for recognition of the foreign proceedings in which the foreign representative has been appointed.[173]

Art 1 of the Model Law (as implemented in Great Britain) provides that it applies where:

(a) assistance is sought in Great Britain by a foreign court or a foreign representative in connection with a foreign proceeding; or
(b) assistance is sought in a foreign State in connection with a proceeding under British insolvency law;[174] or
(c) a foreign proceeding and a proceeding under British insolvency law in respect of the same debtor are taking place concurrently; or
(d) creditors or other interested persons in a foreign State have an interest in requesting the commencement of, or participating in, a proceeding under British insolvency law.

The recognition of foreign insolvency proceedings as 'main proceedings' gives rise to an automatic stay which will apply to certain types of creditor actions including: the commencement of proceedings concerning the debtor company's assets, rights, obligations, or liabilities; execution against its assets and/or the transfer or

---

OJL 6500/96), described by the Supreme Court in *Trustees of the Olympic Airlines SA Pension & Life Assurance Scheme v Olympic Airlines SA* [2015] UKSC 27, [2015] 1 WLR 2399, [2015] 1 BCLC 589, [9]–[10] as 'much the most useful source of guidance' on the interpretation of the Regulation.) If they do, then these provisions provide further support for the proposition advanced in the text, at any rate where neither main nor secondary insolvency proceedings are afoot in the same jurisdiction as the *in rem* action.

[171] This is the effect of art 3 of the European Insolvency Regulation and the recast Regulation.

[172] Arts 11 and 12.

[173] Art 15.

[174] Art 2(a) defines 'British insolvency law' as:

(i) in relation to England and Wales, provision extending to England and Wales and made by or under the Insolvency Act 1986 (with the exception of Part 3 of that Act) or by or under that Act as extended or applied by or under any other enactment (excluding these Regulations); and
(ii) in relation to Scotland, provision extending to Scotland and made by or under the Insolvency Act 1986 (with the exception of Part 3 of that Act), the Bankruptcy (Scotland) Act 1985 or by or under those Acts as extended or applied by or under any other enactment (excluding these Regulations).

disposal of its assets.[175] The CBIR makes no specific reference to admiralty claims; however, art 32 preserves, to some extent, the position of secured claims or rights *in rem*.[176]

8.75 So far as the CBIR is concerned, the logical order of enquiry as to its impact, if any, on *in rem* proceedings afoot in England is as follows:

(1) Whether there is a foreign proceeding or a foreign main proceeding.
A foreign proceeding is a judicial or administrative proceeding pursuant to a law relating to insolvency; a foreign main proceeding means a foreign proceeding taking place where the debtor has the centre of its main interests.[177] This would normally be the place of its registered office although the term is not defined.

(2) Whether an application has been made to the court for recognition of the foreign proceedings in which the foreign representative has been appointed.
A foreign representative means a person or body, including one appointed on an interim basis, authorized in a foreign proceeding to administer the reorganization or the liquidation of the debtor's assets or affairs or to act as a representative of the foreign proceedings.[178]

(3) Whether the application has been brought in accordance with art 15(2).
Prior to the CBIR, the relevant question was whether the forum where the *in rem* action was proceeding would recognize the foreign liquidation.[179] In general terms, a foreign liquidation would be recognized if the shipowner was

---

[175] Art 20; *Bank of Tokyo-Mitsubishi UFJ Ltd v The Owners of the MV Sanko Mineral* [2014] EWHC 3927 (Admlty), [2015] 1 Lloyd's Rep 247. For the development of that case, see *sub nom Tabitha v Glencore* [2015] EWHC 1031 (Ch). For further commentary on the case, see Emma Park, 'Claim against Proceeds of Judicial Ship Sale' (2015) 4 *Shipping & Trade Law* 3.

[176] As with the reference in the European Insolvency Regulations to rights *in rem*, however, it is not wholly certain (and should not be assumed) that this term of art encompasses the rights *in rem* with which admiralty process is concerned.

[177] Art 2.

[178] Ibid. Where proceedings *in rem* have been commenced in Australia, one difficulty seems to arise from the definition of the courts that are deemed competent to entertain such an application. Section 10 of the Cross-Border Insolvency Act 2006 (Cth), provides that the functions referred to in the Model Law relating to recognition of foreign proceedings and cooperation with foreign courts shall be performed by:

(a) if the functions relate to a proceeding involving a debtor who is an individual—the Federal Court of Australia;
(b) if the function relates to a proceeding involving a debtor other than an individual:
  (i) the Federal Court of Australia; and
  (ii) the Supreme Court of a State or Territory.

It would appear that if the shipowner whose vessel has been arrested in Australia is an individual subject to foreign insolvency proceedings, then the Federal Court only is competent to deal with an application brought pursuant to art 15. This could create some tension if the *in rem* proceedings have been commenced in a Supreme Court of a State.

[179] *Felixstowe Dock & Rly Co v United States Line Inc* [1989] QB 360; *Banque Indosuez SA v Ferromet Resources Inc* [1993] BCC 112; *Fournier v The Ship Margaret Z* [1997] NZLR 629; *Turners & Growers Exporters Ltd v the Ship Cornelis Verolme* [1997] 2 NZLR 110.

incorporated or traded in the jurisdiction in which the liquidation was being conducted (or if the law of its incorporation would recognize the liquidation), or (perhaps) if it had submitted to the jurisdiction of the foreign court.[180] There is now little room left for the exercise of any discretion as to whether or not to recognize the foreign proceedings: in broad terms, unless the court considers it manifestly contrary to public policy to do so,[181] it must recognize foreign main proceedings taking place in the State where the debtor has its COMI and foreign secondary proceedings taking place in a State where the debtor has an establishment.[182]

(4) The consequences of recognition.[183]
Art 20 provides that upon recognition of a foreign proceeding that is a foreign main proceeding, subject to para 2 of the article:[184]
   (a) commencement or continuation of individual actions or individual proceedings concerning the debtor's assets, rights, obligations, or liabilities is stayed;
   (b) execution against the debtor's assets is stayed;
   (c) the right to transfer, encumber, or otherwise dispose of any assets of the debtor is suspended.

The operation of art 20(2) was explored by the New Zealand High Court in *Kim v STX Pan Ocean Co Ltd*.[185] STX had applied to the bankruptcy court in Korea for an order commencing rehabilitation proceedings and had obtained an interim moratorium pending determination of the proceedings. A week later, the ship *New Giant* was arrested in New Zealand. Three days later, the Korean court ordered STX be placed in rehabilitation and appointed administrators. The administrators applied for recognition in New Zealand of the Korean rehabilitation proceedings as foreign main proceedings under the Insolvency (Cross-border) Act 2006 (NZ). The Korean proceedings were duly recognized, triggering a stay of all New Zealand proceedings pursuant to Art 20(1). The question became whether, notwithstanding the automatic stay, the court should exercise its discretion under Art 20(2) to permit the admiralty proceedings in New Zealand to continue. Applying the reasoning in *In Re Aro Co Ltd*,[186] Gilbert J concluded that the claimants had obtained

[180] Sheldon, *Cross-Border Insolvency*, (4th edn, 2015), 255–284. See, too, Dicey, Morris & Collins, *The Conflict of Laws*, (15th edn, 2015) § 30R-100f.

[181] Art 6.

[182] Art 17. 'Establishment' is defined in art 2(e).

[183] Arts 20–21.

[184] Which—as enacted in Great Britain—provides, broadly, that any stay or suspension shall be of the same scope and effect as under British insolvency law and subject to the same powers of the court and the same prohibitions, limitations, exceptions, and conditions as would apply under British law.

[185] *Kim v STX Pan Ocean Co Ltd* [2014] NZHC 845. See also *Cosco Bulk Carrier Co Ltd v Armada Shipping SA* [2011] EWHC 216 (Ch), [2011] 2 All ER (Comm) 481.

[186] *In Re Aro Co Ltd* [1980] Ch 196, above paras 8.60–8.61. As did Briggs J in *Cosco v Armada* (n 184 above), [47] and [50].

a security interest against *New Giant* immediately upon the issue of the admiralty proceedings, which predated the commencement of the rehabilitation proceedings in Korea. He observed that the *Insolvency (Cross-border) Act* is procedural in nature and is designed to facilitate the management or realization of the debtor's assets in a single jurisdiction in accordance with the *pari passu* principle. It is not intended to deprive creditors of their substantive rights or interests. Gilbert J declined to conclude that the interim moratorium order[187] purported to restrict creditors with maritime liens or statutory rights *in rem* from pursuing *in rem* claims and drew attention specifically to its lack of extraterritorial reach. Leave was granted to continue the *in rem* proceedings in New Zealand.

The 'beguiling' nature of para 2 of art 20 has led the Federal Court of Australia to develop a practice, where foreign insolvency proceedings are invoked, of making special orders to ensure that, before an arrest warrant is issued in a proceeding *in rem* under the Admiralty Act, a judge, rather than a registrar, considers whether the plaintiff's claim against the ship is based on an existing secured interest.[188] As Rares J observed in *Kim v Daebo International Shipping Co Ltd*:[189]

> It may be thought unlikely that the *Model Law* was understood or intended by either its creators or by the Parliament when giving it the force of law in Australia ... to supervene or impliedly repeal the domestic statutory remedies provided in States Parties, ... in respect of maritime creditors' rights to proceed *in rem* on a secured or proprietary claim that pre-existed any interim or final orders recognising a foreign proceeding under Arts 19 or 20 of the *Model Law*.
>
> That is why it is appropriate that, once a foreign proceeding has been recognised or an interim stay granted under Arts 19 or 20, and before any arrest warrant is issued, a judge (preferably one familiar with the principles of Admiralty and maritime law as well as insolvency law) consider the nature of the plaintiff's proceeding *in rem*, including where a general maritime claim is asserted when that proceeding was filed, to determine whether the arrest ought to occur.

8.76 Neither the Model Law nor the CBIR defines the term 'execution'. It has been held, in *Danny Morris v The Ship 'Kiama'*,[190] that the arrest and subsequent sale of a ship pursuant to the judicial order of an admiralty court does not amount to a process of execution. The English authority on this precise issue is unsettled. It was held in *In re Australian Direct Steam Navigation Company*[191] and *The Constellation*[192] that a sale following an arrest is the equivalent of execution within the meaning of the Insolvency Act. The contrary view was reached in *TheZafiro*[193] and it was the latter

[187] Made pursuant to art 45.

[188] *Atlasnavios Navegacao LDA v The Ship Xin Tai Hai (No 2)* (2012) 215 FCR 265; *Yu v STX Pan Ocean Co Ltd* (2013) 223 FCR 189; *Kim v Daebo International Shipping Co Ltd* [2015] FCA 684.

[189] *Kim v Daebo International Shipping Co Ltd* [2015] FCA 684, [14]–[15].

[190] *Danny Morris v The Ship 'Kiama'* [1998] FCA 256.

[191] *In re Australian Direct Steam Navigation Company* (1875) LR 20 Eq 325.

[192] *The Constellation* [1966] 1 WLR 272.

[193] *TheZafiro* [1960] P 1.

view that found favour with Carr J in *The Kiama* on the basis that '... as a matter of law, the arrest of the ship did not occur as part of a process of execution. It came about at the behest of the plaintiffs in accordance with the Admiralty Rules'.

Where, however, no security has been obtained over a ship at the time when a foreign winding-up order is made, the result is likely to be that the maritime claimant will be unable to bring *in rem* proceedings, and—unless the foreign court grants permission to sue *in rem*—will be limited to proving in the foreign liquidation.[194] This is, in part, because a court exercising admiralty jurisdiction will not be a court exercising jurisdiction pursuant to a law relating to insolvency and so admiralty proceedings, of themselves, cannot be 'foreign proceedings' within the definition of art 2 of the Model Law. The Model Law does not include a provision along the lines of art 5.1 of the European Regulation on Insolvency.[195]

Section 426

Section 426 of the Insolvency Act 1986 makes provision for the cooperation between courts in the United Kingdom and courts in the Channel Islands, Isle of Man, and certain other countries[196] in relation to insolvency proceedings.[197] Assistance can be requested pursuant to a letter of request from the court of a designated country and the type of assistance that can be given is broad. The UK court can apply either UK insolvency law or that of the relevant foreign country. **8.77**

Despite the development of judicial practice by which some degree of international cooperation in corporate insolvency matters had been achieved by reference to a principle of 'modified universalism', in *Re HIH Casualty and General Insurance Ltd* there was disagreement in the House of Lords whether, but for s 426, the court would have any inherent jurisdiction to accede to a request for cooperation from a foreign court whose insolvency scheme was not in accordance with English law.[198]

---

[194] See, for example, *Harms Offshore AHT 'Taurus' GmbH & Co KG v Bloom* [2009] EWCA Civ 632; [2009] All ER (D) 276.

[195] Above, para 8.62.

[196] Anguilla, Australia, the Bahamas, Bermuda, Botswana, Brunei, Canada, Cayman Island, Falkland Islands, Guernsey, Gibraltar, Hong Kong, the Republic of Ireland, Malaysia, Montserrat, New Zealand, South Africa, St Helena, Turks and Caicos Islands, Tuvalu, and the Virgin Islands.

[197] Similar provisions exist in Australia (Corporations Act 2001, s 591) and New Zealand (Insolvency (Cross-border) Act 2006, s 8).

[198] *Re HIH Casualty and General Insurance Ltd* [2008] UKHL 21, [2008] 1 WLR 852, [2008] Bus LR 905, [2008] 3 All ER 869, [2008] Lloyd's Rep IR 756, [2008] BCC 349. Lords Scott and Neuberger thought that it would not; Lords Hoffmann and Walker took the opposite view. See *McGrath as Liquidators of HIH Insurance Ltd* (2008) 26 ACLC 921, [2008] NSWSC 881; *De Akers v Deputy Commissioner of Taxation* (2014) 223 FCR 8, [2014] FCAFC 57 (for the similar Australian approach); *William v Simpson* [2011] 2 NZLR 380 (for the similar New Zealand approach) and *Re Pioneer Iron and Steel Group Co Ltd* [2013] HKCFI 324 (for the position in Hong Kong).

Common law

8.78 So far as a foreign liquidation governed neither by the European Insolvency Regulation nor the CBIR is concerned, the logical order of enquiry as to its impact, if any, on *in rem* proceedings is as follows.

(1) *Whether the forum where the in rem action is proceeding will recognize the foreign liquidation.* In general terms, the foreign liquidation will be recognized if the shipowner was incorporated or traded in the jurisdiction in which the liquidation is being conducted (or if the law of its incorporation would recognize the liquidation), or if it submitted to the jurisdiction of the foreign court.[199]
(2) Whether there are any *bars to recognition*,[200] such as considerations of public policy, fraud, or natural justice.
(3) *The consequences (if any) of recognition.*[201] That will in turn involve consideration of whether, as a matter of the law governing the foreign liquidation, the making of the order constituting those proceedings has extraterritorial effect.[202] Assuming that it does, and that its effect under that law is to vest title to the company's moveables in the foreign liquidator, the foreign winding-up order will result in a 'consequential and instantaneous' vesting of the property in the vessel in the foreign liquidator, subject to any prior attachment in (or recognized in) England.[203]

8.79 Thus where security over a ship has been established, either by maritime lien or by commencing an action *in rem*, before the making of the foreign winding-up order, the right of the foreign liquidator to receive the vessel or the funds generated by its sale will be recognized, once those claims have been satisfied or secured.

8.80 The decision of the High Court of New Zealand in *Turners & Growers Exporters Ltd v The Ship Cornelis Verolme*,[204] is consistent with these principles. In that case the shipowner had been made bankrupt pursuant to an order of the Commercial Court of Antwerp. An application was made by the trustees in bankruptcy for its release from arrest. The application was resisted by the master and crew, who feared losing their security in New Zealand and their priority under New Zealand law. The High Court held, following English authority,[205] that the liquidation

---

[199] Sheldon, *Cross-Border Insolvency*, (4th edn, 2015), 254–284. See, too, Dicey, Morris & Collins *The Conflict of Laws*, (15th edn, 2015) §30R-100f.

[200] See generally Sheldon (n 198 above), Chapter 11.

[201] Ibid Chapter 10.

[202] Ibid 419.

[203] Ibid 420. See also, in relation to the effect of the restraining order of a foreign court: *Felixstowe Dock & Rly Co v United States Lines Inc* [1989] QB 360, [1989] 2 WLR 109, [1988] 2 All ER 77, [1987] 2 Lloyd's Rep 76; *Banque Indosuez SA v Ferromet Resources Inc* [1993] BLC 112; *Fournier v The Margaret Z* [1997] NZLR 629.

[204] *Turners & Growers Exporters Ltd v The Ship Cornelis Verolme* [1997] 2 NZLR 110.

[205] *Bank of Ethiopia v National Bank of Egypt and Liguori* [1937] 1 Ch 513, 524.

of a foreign company in its place of incorporation and the appointment of a foreign administrator would be recognized by New Zealand law unless the foreign proceedings were not final, contrary to public policy or breached natural justice, subject to the provisions of any positive law in the local jurisdiction in which the assets of the company were located.[206] The Court noted that recognition of foreign insolvency at common law does not merely oblige the court to acknowledge it, but 'carries with it the active assistance of the Court'.[207] When assessing the competing interests of the master and crew against the applications by the trustees in bankruptcy and other interested parties, the court highlighted the following considerations.

(1) Whether it was necessary for the master and crew to have direct recourse to the vessel herself, if an alternative source to secure that payment could be found.[208]
(2) The need of the trustees, who were best placed to reposition the vessel for sale at the best possible price, to manage the liquidation from a global standpoint.
(3) Solutions to legal problems created by international transactions and cross-border insolvencies in particular should reflect modern commercial international practice and not be anachronistically encumbered by dictates from another age derived from different circumstances.[209]

The court held in the circumstances that the Belgian liquidation should be recognized and that its obligation to give 'active assistance' would be satisfied if the vessel was released against adequate security for the master and crew to ensure that any judgment ultimately given would be met, with such security to be held in New Zealand rather than Belgium.

Where, however, no security has been obtained over the ship at the time that the foreign winding-up order is made, the result is likely to be that the maritime claimant will be unable to bring *in rem* proceedings, and—unless the foreign court grants permission to sue *in rem*—will be limited to proving in the foreign liquidation. That is not necessarily so, however. If an ancillary winding-up is commenced in England, for example, it may be possible to seek permission from the English court to commence *in rem* proceedings along the lines indicated above.[210] **8.81**

---

206 *Re Alfred Shaw & Co* (1897) 8 QLJ 93; *Macauley v Guaranty Trust Co of New York* (1927) 44 TLR 99.

207 *Re African Farms Ltd* (1906) TS 373, 377.

208 An approach consistent with authority going back at least as far as *The Aline* (1839) 1 Wm Rob 111, 166 ER 514: see *The Ruta* [2000] 1 WLR 2068, [2001] 1 All ER 450, [2000] 1 Lloyd's Rep 359 and above, paras 8.06 and following.

209 The view taken by the High Court of New Zealand is broadly consistent with the approach of the Superior Court in Bankruptcy of Quebec; *Antwerp Bulkcarriers NV v van Doosselaere and de Roy Montreal* (5000 11 004112 963, 28 June 1996).

210 Para 8.70.

9

PROCEDURE IN COLLISION CASES

A. Procedure

9.01 Traditionally, collision claims have been treated differently from other claims arising in the Admiralty jurisdiction. This tradition is continued by the Civil Procedure Rules (CPR) which make special provision for collision claims in part 61.4. A collision claim may be commenced either *in rem* or *in personam*.[1] If it is commenced *in personam*, the procedure applicable to claims proceeding in the Commercial List applies, subject to the particular provisions contained in rule 61.4 of the CPR.

9.02 A 'collision claim' is defined as a claim within s 20(3)(b) of the Senior Courts Act (SCA) 1981.[2] Section 20 confers Admiralty jurisdiction on the High Court in relation to:

---

[1] But see para 9.05 below.
[2] CPR 61.1(2)(d).

(3) (b) any action to enforce a claim for damage, loss of life or personal injury arising out of—
(i) a collision between two ships; or
(ii) the carrying out of or omission to carry out a manoeuvre in the case of one or more of two or more ships; or
(iii) non-compliance, on the part of one or more of two or more ships, with the collision regulations;

Thus, in order to qualify as a 'collision claim', at least two ships must be involved in the occurrence which gives rise to the claim. A ship hitting a jetty, for example, does not give rise to a 'collision claim'—and, as a pedant would point out, is not a collision but an allision—but a 'putting-by', where the vessels do not even come into contact,does.

Commencement of a collision claim

A collision claim must be started in the Admiralty Court.[3] It will be started by a claim form in the same manner as any other claim commenced in the Admiralty jurisdiction of the High Court. However, a claim form relating to a collision claim need not contain and should not be followed by particulars of claim as is required in all other claims.[4] **9.03**

The claim form in a collision action may not be served out of the jurisdiction unless: **9.04**

(1) the defendant has his habitual residence or a place of business within England or Wales; or
(2) the cause of action arose within inland waters of England or Wales within the limits of a port of England or Wales; or
(3) an action arising out of the same incident or series of incidents is proceeding in the court or has been heard and determined; or
(4) the defendant has submitted to or agreed to submit to the jurisdiction;

and the court gives permission in accordance with s III of Part 6.[5] Where the court grants permission, the court will specify the period within which the defendant may file an acknowledgement of service[6] and, where appropriate, a collision statement of case.[7]

---

[3] CPR 61.2(1)(b).

[4] CPR 61.4(2) which states that r 7.4 does not apply.

[5] CPR 61.4 (7) and s 22(2)(a), (b), and (c) of the SCA 1981. As with CPR 61.11(5) (see below, para 10.165) the draftsman of this rule appears to have overlooked that permission is neither required nor, in all probability, allowed in cases falling within the EU Regulation or the Brussels/Lugano Conventions. Until this anomaly has been ironed out by the framers of the rules, it is suggested that the safe course in such cases will be to apply for permission anyway (while drawing attention to this anomaly); permission may be expected to be granted 'on the nod'.

[6] Which will be derived from the Table of periods set out in the Appendix to PD6B.

[7] CPR 61.4(8). The period for filing the collision statement of case will be two months after filing acknowledgment of service (CPR 61.4(5)(a)).

9.05 The restriction on service out of the jurisdiction mirrors SCA 1981, s 22(2), which restricts the basis on which the High Court may entertain collision actions *in personam*, be it brought as a claim or (unless arising out of the same incident) by way of counterclaim.[8] Thus the section prohibits the commencement of a claim *in personam* unless the defendant has his habitual residence or a place of business within England or Wales; or the cause of action arises within inland waters of England or Wales within the limits of a port of England or Wales; or the action arises out of the same incident or series of incidents which is proceeding in the court or has been heard and determined,[9] unless the defendant has submitted to or agreed to submit to the jurisdiction of the court.[10]

9.06 Whilst these provisions merely restrict the exercise of jurisdiction which the court would (presumably) otherwise have, s 22(6) provides that the court 'shall have jurisdiction' in such cases, except that it must not entertain an *in personam* collision action until any proceedings brought by the plaintiff in any court outside England and Wales against the same defendant in respect of the same incident or series of incidents have been discontinued or otherwise come to an end.[11] The following points arise in this connection.

(1) There is no difficulty in founding jurisdiction on the section in cases falling outside the EU Regulation or the Brussels/Lugano Conventions. Although theoretically the exercise of the jurisdiction will be subject to *forum conveniens* considerations, it will—given the connecting factors which must be present in order to found jurisdiction in the first place—be a rare case indeed which is within s 22(2) but where the court nevertheless declines to exercise its jurisdiction on such grounds.

(2) Matters may be more difficult in relation to cases within the EU Regulation and the Brussels/Lugano Conventions, albeit in a relatively narrow band of cases. It should be noted first that it is inconceivable that, where there is a conflict between the provisions of the Regulation/Conventions and of the 1981 Act, the former will not prevail. That being so, the first and second grounds of jurisdiction in s 22(2) present no problem, as they effectively echo arts 4 and 7.2 of the recast Regulation (and their equivalent under the Conventions) respectively. However, s 22(2)(c) is without direct equivalent under the Regulation/ Conventions; art 8(3)[12] comes close, but is narrower than s 22(2)(c). It is therefore submitted that, to the extent that the scope of the latter provision exceeds art 8(3), jurisdiction cannot be founded upon it.

---

8 SCA 1981, s 22(4).

9 Ibid s 22(2)(a)–(c).

10 Ibid s 22(5).

11 Ibid s 22(3).

12 'A person domiciled in a Member State may also be sued ... on a counter-claim arising from the same ... facts on which the original claim was based, in the court in which the original claim is pending.'

Time limit for commencement of action

The time limit for commencing collision actions in England[13] is two years.[14] However, that is subject to potential extension: **9.07**

(1) As a matter of discretion, 'in accordance with rules of court';[15] and
(2) Mandatorily, if there has not been, within the two-year period, 'any reasonable opportunity of arresting the defendant ship' either within the jurisdiction of the court or (if different) within 'the territorial sea of the country to which the plaintiff's ship belongs or in which the plaintiff resides or has his principal place of business'.[16]

This provision can also be prayed in aid when it comes to extending the validity of the claim form. Thus in *Owners of the vessel 'Stolt Kestrel' v Owners of the vessel 'Niyazi S'*,[17] *in rem* proceedings were issued (just) within the initial two-year period. Shortly before the expiry of the twelve-month validity of the claim form, the claimant applied for an order extending its validity for a further eight months. It was common ground that s 190 MSA 1995, rather than CPR 7.6, informed the exercise of the court's jurisdiction to extend time. Hamblen J held on the facts that there had been no reasonable opportunity to arrest the defendant vessel and that it was therefore a case to which s 190(6) applied, so that a mandatory extension of time was required. **9.08**

Where the extension is sought under s 190(5), a two-stage test is required:[18] **9.09**

> At stage one the Court must consider whether good reason for an extension has been demonstrated by the plaintiff, which is essentially a question of fact. If, and only if, the plaintiff succeeds at stage one in establishing good reason does the

---

13 More specifically: 'any proceedings to enforce any claim or lien against a ship or her owners-
(a) in respect of damage or loss caused by the fault of that ship to another ship, its cargo or freight or any property on board it; or
(b) for damages for loss of life or personal injury caused by the fault of that ship to any person on board another ship.'

14 Merchant Shipping Act 1995 (MSA 1995), s 190. Similar provisions are enacted in Canada, Marine Liability Act 2001 c6, s 23; Hong Kong, Merchant Shipping (Collision Damage Liability and Salvage) Ordinance, s 7; Singapore, Maritime Conventions Act 1911, s 8; and South Africa, Merchant Shipping Act 1951, s 344(1).

15 MSA 1995, s 190(5).

16 MSA 1995, s 190(6). Note that s 190(6) applies only to *in rem* proceedings: *The Stolt Kestrel* [2015] EWCA Civ 1035, [48]–[49].

17 *Owners of the vessel 'Stolt Kestrel' v Owners of the vessel 'Niyazi S'* [2014] EWHC 1731 (Admlty), [2014] 2 Lloyd's Rep 483, unchallenged on this point on appeal: [2015] EWCA Civ 1035.

18 *The Al Tabith* [1995] 2 Lloyd's Rep 336 CA, 342 col 1. It has been common ground in several cases (including *The Stolt Kestrel* and *MIOM 1 Limited v Sea Echo ENE (No 2)* [2011] EWHC 2715 (Admlty), [54], [2012] 1 Lloyd's Rep 140) that this is the appropriate test. Although it echoes the test which applied, pre-CPR, to the renewal of writs (following cases such as *The Myrto (No 3)* [1987] AC 597), an attempt to argue that the regime under CPR 7.6(2) and (3) (as applicable) should apply was rejected in *The Stolt Kestrel* [2015] EWCA Civ 1035, [72]–[92].

> Court proceed to stage two, which is a discretionary exercise involving value judgments including, where appropriate the balance of hardship, which then enters the arena for the first and only time.

A 'good reason' requires the claimant to show that the failure to serve 'was not merely due to [its] own mistake ...'.[19] What is a good reason cannot be defined and must depend on all the circumstances of the case.[20]

9.10 It is possible to contract out of the two-year time limit. Whether that is the effect of the parties' agreement is a matter of construction. For a recent example see *The Pamela*,[21] where Teare J analysed the particular agreement in the light of the well-known English authorities on the point.[22]

9.11 Until 2012, s 396 of the now repealed Navigation Act (Cth) (1912) mirrored s 190 of the MSA 1995 and the Australian courts took a similar approach to the question of extensions of time.[23] A similar provision was apparently inadvertently omitted from the Navigation Act (Cth) 2012[24] and it is now necessary to look to each individual State or Territory limitation statute,[25] in conjunction with the limitation period provided for in s 37 of the Admiralty Act 1988, in order to determine the relevant limitation period. Section 37 provides:

> (1) A proceeding may be brought under this Act on a maritime claim, or on a claim on a maritime lien or other charge, at any time before the end of:
> (a) the limitation period that would have been applicable in relation to the claim if a proceeding on the claim had been brought otherwise than under this Act; or
> (b) if no proceeding on the claim could have been so brought—a period of three years after the cause of action arose.

---

[19] *The Al Tabith* [1993] 2 Lloyd's Rep 214, 219 col 1 per Sheen J, approved by Hirst LJ in the Court of Appeal at [1995] 2 Lloyd's Rep 336, 342 col 1.

[20] *The Pearl of Jebel Ali and The Pride of Al Salam 95* [2009] EWHC 1365 (Admlty), [2009] 2 Lloyd's Rep 484, [37]. In that case, a non-culpable misunderstanding of an agreement in 'unusual and clumsy terms' was, even if a 'mistake', held to be a good reason. Compare and contrast the Court of Appeal's scathing characterization of the attempt to issue a hybrid *in rem* and *in personam* claim form in *The Stolt Kestrel* [2015] EWCA Civ 1035, [38].

[21] *Owners of the ship 'Theresa Libra' v Owners of the ship MSC 'Pamela'* [2013] EWHC 2792 (Admlty), [2013] 2 Lloyd's Rep 596.

[22] *Wright v John Bagnall & Sons Ltd* [1900] 2 QB 240; *Lubovsky v Snelling* [1944] 1 KB 44, [1943] 2 All ER 577, (1943) 77 Ll L Rep 57; *The Sauria and the Trent* [1957] 1 Lloyd's Rep 396.

[23] *Ling v Owners of the ship 'Longevity'* [1995] FCA 1564; *Loucas G Mastas Salvage v The 'Ionian Mariner'* [1997] FCA 1633; *Engert v Sydney Ferries Corporation* [2009] NSWSC 1400; *Balnaves v Smith* [2011] Qd R 17, [2010] QSC 39.

[24] It is anticipated there will be an amendment in due course.

[25] The Limitation Act 1969 (NSW) s 22, the Limitation Act 1985 (ACT) s 19, the Limitation Act 1981 (NT) s 20, and the Limitation Act 1974 (Tas) s 8 are in terms similar to s 190 MSA 1995. The Limitation of Actions Act 1974 (Qld), Limitation of Actions Act 1936 (SA), the Limitation of Actions Act 1958 (Vic), and the Limitation Act 2005 (WA) make no specific provision for actions to enforce a claim or lien against a vessel or her owners in respect of loss or damage to life or property, for personal injury or salvage, and thus regard must be had to the general limitation periods for claims in tort or contract, generally three years in respect of personal injury claims and otherwise six years.

(2) Subsection (1) does not apply if a limitation period is fixed in relation to the claim by an Act, an Imperial Act, an Act of a State or an Act or Ordinance of a Territory including such an Act or Ordinance in its application in a part of Australia.

Subsection (3) grants power to a court to grant an extension of time.[26]

Section 37 is 'not easy to understand'[27] and its 'effect is not entirely clear'.[28] In *Geraldton Port Authority v The Ship 'Kim Heng 1988' (No 2)*,[29] it was contended that the effect of s 37(1) was that para (a) should apply to *in personam* proceedings in the Admiralty jurisdiction conferred by the Admiralty Act and that para (b) should apply to actions *in rem*. Proceedings had been commenced *in rem* (outside the three-year limitation period) to recover damages in respect of the collision of each of three vessels with berths in the Geraldton Port. Separate proceedings were commenced *in personam* against the charterers.[30] Although he did not consider it necessary to decide the point at an interlocutory stage of the proceedings, McKerracher J declined to accept the contention of the defendants in the *in rem* proceedings that dismissing the *in rem* claim by virtue of it being out of time would also have the effect of dismissing the *in personam* proceeding.[31] McKerracher J did not consider that it was the legislative intent that a plaintiff would lose the benefit of a six-year limitation period for an *in personam* claim just because a very similar claim was first issued *in rem*. Given that the Admiralty Act does not require a claim *in personam* to be brought pursuant to that Act,[32] that conclusion must be correct.

The Maritime Transport Act 1994 (NZ) is in similar terms to s 190 of the MSA 1995 and provides for a two-year limitation period in relation to collision claims.[33] This time limit prevails[34] over that contained in the Limitation Act 2010 (NZ), which otherwise applies a six-year limitation to all money claims based on acts or omissions occurring after 31 December 2010 and which has removed the previous **9.12**

---

26 Where:

(a) but for this subsection, a court would not have power to extend a limitation period in respect of a maritime claim or a claim of a particular kind on a maritime lien or other charge; and

(b) the court has power to extend a limitation period in respect of a claim of the same kind;

then, by force of this subsection, the court has power, exercisable in the same way, and in the same kinds of circumstances, as the power referred to in paragraph (b) to extend the period fixed by subsection (1) in respect of maritime claims, or claims on maritime liens or other charges, of a kind referred to in that subsection.

27 *Geraldton Port Authority v The Ship 'Kim Heng 1988' (No 2)* (2012) 291 ALR 471, [2012] FCA 353 [25] per McKerracher J.

28 Davies & Dickey, *Shipping Law in Australia* (3rd edn, 2004) 446.

29 (2012) 291 ALR 471, [2012] FCA 353.

30 As is permitted by r 18 of the Admiralty Rules (Cth).

31 (2012) 291 ALR 471, [2012] FCA 353, [7].

32 As compared with an action *in rem*, Admiralty Act 1988, s 14.

33 Maritime Transport Act 1994 (NZ), s 97.

34 Ibid s 40.

general exception for causes of action falling within the Admiralty jurisdiction of the High Court which are enforceable *in rem*.[35]

Service and arrest

9.13 As noted above,[36] it is not strictly necessary in collision actions to arrest a vessel for the service of the claim form to 'count' for the purposes of the 'recast' Brussels 1 Regulation (1215/2012) and its siblings.

Acknowledgement of service

9.14 An acknowledgement of service in form ADM2 must be filed once the claim form has been served.[37]

Objections to jurisdiction

9.15 If the defendant wishes to dispute the court's jurisdiction, he must make an application under Part 11 within two months after filing his acknowledgement of service.[38]

Collision statements of case (Preliminary Acts)

9.16 A significant feature of collision cases, whether commenced *in rem* or *in personam*, is that all parties must file and prepare a collision statement of case.[39] Collision statements of case were previously known as preliminary acts and PD61 makes clear that the law relating to preliminary acts continues to apply to collision statements of case.[40] Preliminary acts continue to be required in similar actions in Australia, Canada, Hong Kong, New Zealand, and Singapore.[41]

9.17 Although it is not explicit in the CPR,[42] a collision statement of case is required only where there is a collision between two or more ships.[43] That does not mean, however, that only the ship-owning parties to the action are required to file a collision statement of case. On the contrary: 'Every party must ... file ... a completed collision statement of case.'[44] In *The Beaverford*, Hewson J said:

> I know of no case where preliminary acts have been ordered in respect of parties other than vessels, but the fact that there is no reported case does not, in

[35] For an example of the application of the predecessor to the Limitation Act 2010 see *Ladd v Carr* [2010] NZHC 1602.
[36] Para 6.32, text accompanying n 127.
[37] CPR 61.4(3).
[38] CPR 61.4(4).
[39] CPR 61.4(5). Form ADM3.
[40] PD61 §4.5
[41] Admiralty Rules (Cth), rr 24–28; Federal Courts Rules, r 498; Rules of the High Court (HK), O75 rr 18–20; Rules of the High Court (NZ), rr 25.22–25.24; Rules of Court (Sing), O70 rr 17–19.
[42] Cf the Admiralty Rules (Cth), r 24(1), Federal Courts Rules, r 498(1); Rules of the High Court (HK), O75 rr 18(1); Rules of the High Court (NZ), r 25.23(1); Rules of Court (Sing), O70 rr 17(1).
[43] *The El Oso* (1925) 133 LT 269; 16 Asp MLC 530.
[44] CPR 61.4(5).

> my opinion, bind me to restrict the application of preliminary acts to vessels in some way or another interested in or connected with the collision. The words of [the rule] are plain ... I feel in no way constrained by those words to restrict the filing of preliminary acts to vessels provided there is a collision between two vessels ...[45]

The Port of London Authority, whose employees had been actively engaged in both the movement of a barge and the direction of the ship at the relevant time, was therefore ordered to file a preliminary act.

Purpose

Traditionally, the practice of collision statements of case has been thought to serve three functions: **9.18**

(1) to force the parties to state their version of the facts while still fresh in their recollection;[46]
(2) to force the parties to 'plead blind', so as to prevent them from shaping their case to meet the facts put forward by the other party;[47]
(3) statements made in the collision statement of case are admissions of fact binding on the party making them.[48]

To these points may be added the utility of obliging each party to provide answers to certain set questions, which have presumably been found by the courts over the years to be useful ones.

Form

A collision statement of case must be in the form set out in the Practice Direction.[49] **9.19**
That form is in two parts.[50] Part 1 comprises a list of questions which relate to matters such as the description of the vessel, the speed, course, weather, tide, distance of first sighting the colliding vessel, alterations to course made and observed, lights and signals showing, and so forth. Parties are required to provide as full and complete answers as possible to these questions and the answers should descend to a reasonable level of particularity.[51]

---

45 *The Beaverford, Owners of the Dumb Barge Sunweld v Canadian Pacific Railway Co* [1961] 1 WLR 793, 797, [1960] 3 All ER 612, 615, [1960] 2 Lloyd's Rep 216, 219.

46 *The Frankland* (1872) LR 3 A&E 511. A point whose significance is capable of exaggeration, when it is borne in mind that a collision action need not be brought until two years after the collision (even without extensions of time), and that the same is not demonstrably more true of a preliminary act than it is of any other statement of case.

47 *The Vortigern* (1859) Swab 518, 166 ER 1242.

48 *The Lady Belle* [1933] P 275, [1933] All ER 881, (1933) 46 Ll L Rep 342; *Owners of the Steamship Devonshire v Owners of the Barge Leslie (The 'Devonshire')* [1912] P 21; see also *Goldman v The Ferry Kameruka* [1971] NSWLR 393, 395 per Macfarlan J who described a preliminary act as a 'solemn' document which should be given 'greater weight as an admission than the usual kinds of admission that are more often seen in the courts'.

49 CPR 61.4(6)(a).

50 PD61 §4.2 and ADM3.

51 Admiralty & Commercial Courts Guide, N5.6.

9.20 Part 2 requires a statement of any other facts and matters on which the party relies, of any allegations of negligence or fault relied upon, and of the remedy sought. The Admiralty & Commercial Courts Guide indicates that the provisions of Appendix 4 to that Guide apply to Part 2 of a collision statement of case.[52] That means that the principles applicable to the drafting of a statement of case apply equally to the preparation of a collision statement of case. As with any other statement of case, a collision statement of case must be verified by a statement of truth.[53]

Filing and service

9.21 A collision statement of case must be filed by every party within two months after the defendant has filed an acknowledgement of service or, where the defendant challenges jurisdiction, within two months after the defendant files the further acknowledgement of service.[54] Upon filing a collision statement of case, notice must be given to every other party that the document has been filed but the collision statements of case are not served until all have been filed.[55] This preserves the integrity of the documents and has the effect of requiring the parties to 'plead blind' with the aim of ascertaining the true state of affairs at the time of the collision.

Amendment

9.22 The significance which attaches to collision statements of case means that they must be prepared with particular care, not least because amendment of Part 1 is not readily available. Statements in a preliminary act have in the past been described as 'solemn admissions' of 'high evidential value', and thus (presumably) of greater force than ordinary admissions.[56] To that end, evidence was not normally admissible to contradict the statements made in the preliminary act.[57] Leave to amend preliminary acts was similarly not lightly given, because any amendment involved a departure from a formal admission and was likely to be made with knowledge of the opposing party's case. Effect is still given to this principle. The Admiralty & Commercial Courts Guide makes clear that the answers to the question contained in Part 1 of the collision statement of case will be treated as admissions made by the party answering the questions, and leave to amend such answers will be granted only in exceptional circumstances.[58] As Gross J indicated in *The Topaz and Irapua*,[59] there is no greater willingness to permit amendments to Part 1 of a

52 Ibid N5.5.
53 CPR 61.4(6)(b).
54 CPR 61.4(5).
55 PD61 §4.4; fourteen days is permitted for the service of collision statements of case after the last has been filed.
56 *The Winona* (1944) 77 Ll L Rep 156, 158. And see n 48 above.
57 *The Lady Belle* [1933] P 275, [1933] All ER 881, (1933) 46 Ll L Rep 342.
58 Admiralty & Commercial Courts Guide, N5.7.
59 *The Topaz and Irapua* [2003] EWHC 320 (Admlty), [2003] 2 Lloyd's Rep 19. The judgment contains a useful summary of the applicable principles at 22, [13].

collision statement of case than there was in relation to preliminary acts although, in practical terms, a refusal to grant leave is unlikely to be the end of the matter. That is because, whilst the party concerned will be held to the admissions contained in the collision statement of case, the court is not similarly bound and must, regardless, proceed on the evidence which 'it deems most accurate and trustworthy'.[60] By contrast, Part 2 of a collision statement of case is the equivalent of a pleading and so the usual rules as to amendments to pleadings apply.[61]

Dispensing with collision statements of case

The requirement to file and serve a collision statement of case is not one that is lightly dispensed with by a court. In *The Beaverford*, Hewson J said: **9.23**

> I have in mind that for, I think, over a hundred years now it has been the practice in this division for vessels in collisions to file preliminary acts so that there may be on record admissions binding on the parties, but not on the court, which are set down at the earliest possible moment after the collision. It is a practice which should not be departed from except in very exceptional circumstances.[62]

For that reason, the parties cannot simply agree to dispense with collision statements of case. The appropriate course, where it makes obvious sense to do so, will be for the parties to write jointly to the court to explain the position. If the court is not (or is unlikely to be) persuaded in this manner, then it will be necessary to attend before the Registrar or the Judge in order to argue the point.

A party may encounter difficulties in completing a collision statement of case, but that is not a reason for failing to comply with the requirement. The overriding principle is that of mutuality so that where one party has complied with the requirement, the other party similarly ought to be required to do so.[63] A party should therefore attempt to answer as many of the questions as possible and, if that party is unable to answer any question, a reason ought to be given for the inability to do so.[64] **9.24**

A similar approach was adopted by the High Court of Hong Kong which held that it would not be right to dispense with the need to file a preliminary act, even though, being filed late and after pleadings, it would not have the weight and usefulness of a preliminary act filed within the time limited by the rules.[65] **9.25**

---

60 *The Geo W McKnight* (1947) 80 Ll L Rep 419, 423; see also *The Teng He* [2000] 3 SLR 114 (High Court of Singapore).

61 CPR Part 17.

62 *The Beaverford, Owners of the Dumb Barge Sunweld v Canadian Pacific Railway Co* [1961] 1 WLR 793, 796, [1960] 3 All ER 612, 615, [1960] 2 Lloyd's Rep 216, 219; followed in *The Graingers (No 4) The British Oil and Cake Mills Ltd v John H Whitaker (Tankers) Ltd* [1964] 1 WLR 1474, [1964] 3 All ER 705, [1964] 2 Lloyd's Rep 415.

63 *The El Oso* (1925) 133 LT 269, 16 Asp MLC 530.

64 *The Beaverford, Owners of the Dumb Barge Sunweld v Canadian Pacific Railway Co* [1961] 1 WLR 793, 795, [1960] 3 All ER 612, 615, [1960] 2 Lloyd's Rep 216, 218.

65 *Wong Wai Fong (Administratrix of the Estate of Wong Fok, deceased) v Leung Cho Sze* [1982] 1 HKC 263, [7].

Judgment in default

9.26 Where a party fails to file a collision statement of case within the requisite time period, judgment in default may be sought against that party.[66]

Agency

9.27 See above, paras 6.44 and following.

Counterclaims and security

9.28 A party who brings a counterclaim pursuant to Part 20 of the CPR or a cross claim *in rem* arising out of the same collision or occurrence may apply to the court to stay the original claim until sufficient security is given to satisfy any judgment that may be given in favour of that party.[67]

Costs in collision cases

The default position

9.29 As with all questions of costs, it is essential to bear in mind that they remain in the discretion of the court. This can have particular significance in the context of collision actions, where traditionally and today[68] the trial Judge may mark the court's displeasure at, for example, any attempt to alter original evidence by disallowing costs which would otherwise have been recoverable. Subject to that, the default position in relation to costs in collision cases where there is a counterclaim is as follows[69]: where a party is held 100 per cent to blame, he will bear all the costs of the action. Where, however, the blame for the collision is apportioned between the parties, then a party will be liable for the same proportion of the other side's costs as he has been found to be to blame, and will recover that proportion of his own costs from the other side that that party has been found to be to blame.

Offers to settle

9.30 It is of course possible and indeed almost invariable for the parties to attempt to protect their position by making offers 'without prejudice save as to costs'. Such offers cannot and do not affect the apportionment of costs incurred before they are made. Indeed, under the provisions which regulate such offers in the particular

---

66 CPR 61.9(2) and (3)(b).

67 CPR 61.4(9).

68 In *The Global Mariner v The Atlantic Crusader* [2005] EWHC 380, [2005] 1 Lloyd's Rep 699, the trial Judge gave effect to this principle by disallowing some of the Atlantic Crusader's costs in view, in part, of the matters set out at 705, [28] of the judgment. For this and other examples, see Gault, Hazelwood, Tettenborn, and Cole (eds), *Marsden on Collisions at Sea* (14th edn, January 2016).

69 In non-counterclaim cases, there is no automatic apportionment of costs. See: *The Antares II and Victory* [1996] 2 Lloyd's Rep 482; *Krysia Maritime Inc v Intership Ltd* [2008] EWHC 1880 (Admlty), [2009] 1 All ER (Comm) 292, [2008] 2 Lloyd's Rep 707; *The Western Neptune* [2009] EWHC 1522 (Admlty), [2010] 1 Lloyd's Rep 172.

context of collision actions, CPR 61.4(10)–(12), their effect (if any) is limited to costs incurred after the date twenty-one days after the offer was made.[70] In relation to costs incurred thereafter, a party to a collision claim involving only property damage[71] may attempt to gain a costs advantage by making an offer to settle in accordance with rule 61.4(12) of the CPR. Such an offer must be in writing and must contain:

(1) an offer to settle liability at stated percentages;
(2) an offer to pay costs in accordance with the same percentages;
(3) a term that the offer remains open for twenty-one days after the date it is made; and
(4) a term that, unless the court orders otherwise, on expiry of that period the offer remains open on the same terms except that the offeree should pay all the costs from that date until acceptance.[72]

If such an offer is made not less than twenty-one days before the start of trial, but is not accepted, and the ultimate judgment is equal to or more favourable than the offer, then subject to the court's overriding discretion to vary them if it considers them to be unjust in the circumstances, the following costs consequences ensue.[73] **9.31**

(1) The maker of the offer is entitled to all his costs from twenty-one days after the offer was made and his costs prior to that time in the percentage to which he would have been entitled had the offer been accepted.
(2) All other parties to whom the offer was made are entitled to their costs up to twenty-one days after the offer was made in the percentage to which they would have been entitled had the offer been accepted but not to any costs thereafter.[74]

On appeal

An offer made before trial will generally have no effect on appeal.[75] Moreover, the provisions contained in CPR 61.4(10)–(12) are by their terms not directly applicable in the case of an appeal, and considerable difficulty may arise in applying them even by analogy where, for example, there has been disallowance at trial of part of an otherwise successful party's costs at trial, or where that party had made an earlier offer which overlaps or coincides with the offer now made by the party which wishes to appeal. Whilst those provisions may well still be relevant, it should also be borne in mind that (i) the issues on appeal are rarely the same as at trial, **9.32**

70 CPR 61.4(11)(a)(i).
71 CPR 61.4(10).
72 CPR 61.4(12) and see *MIOM 1 Ltd v Sea Echo ENE (No 2)* [2011] EWHC 2715 (Admlty), [2012] 1 Lloyd's Rep 140.
73 CPR 61.4(10).
74 CPR 61.4(11). For the consequences where an offer is withdrawn see *The Samco Europe v MSC Prestige* [2011] EWHC 1656 (Admlty), [2011] 2 Lloyd's Rep 579.
75 Cf *East West Corporation v DKBS 1912 and AKTS Svendborg* [2003] 1 Lloyd's Rep 265.

(ii) that the court has an overriding discretion in matters of costs, and (iii) that CPR 44.3(4) requires a court, 'in deciding what order (if any) to make about costs', to 'have regard to all the circumstances, including … (c) … any admissible offer to settle …'.

B. Assessors

9.33 CPR 61.13 provides that the court may sit with assessors when hearing collision claims or other claims involving issues of navigation and seamanship and that the parties will not be permitted to call expert witnesses unless the court orders otherwise.

9.34 Nautical assessors are usually Elder or (nowadays) Younger Brethren of Trinity House, a charitable organization established by Royal Charter granted by Henry VIII in 1514 to a fraternity of mariners called the 'Guild of the Holy Trinity' for the purpose of regulating the pilotage of ships in the king's streams. The practice of an Admiralty Judge sitting with nautical assessors had become well established by the mid-nineteenth century and Dr Lushington made full use of the Trinity Masters, or Elder Brethren of Trinity House, in preference to receiving expert evidence.[76] In modern times, the Corporation of Trinity House is comprised of a fraternity of approximately 300 Brethren drawn from the Royal and Merchant Navies and leading figures in the shipping industry.[77] Nautical assessors might be considered the original embodiment of the statutory court-appointed expert. Lord Sumner described them in this way:

> In Admiralty practice [assessors] are not only technical advisors: they are sources of evidence as to the facts. In questions of nautical science and skill, relating to the management and movement of ships, a Court, assisted by nautical assessors, obtains the information from them, not from sworn witnesses called by the parties …[78]

9.35 The CPR provides for the disclosure of reports prepared by court-appointed experts[79] whilst still making clear that such an expert will not be called upon to give oral evidence nor to be cross-examined.[80] The practice of using nautical assessors has worked well in Admiralty for many years and the Admiralty Judge has expressed the view that 'the Court will strive to maintain the system, confident that it reflects best practice under the CPR'.[81]

---

[76] See, for example, *The Neptune* (1841) 1 W Rob 297; *The Speed* (1844) 2 W Rob 225; *The Nimrod* 7 Not Cas 570.

[77] <http://www.trinityhouse.co.uk>.

[78] *The Australia* [1927] AC 145, 152, (1926) 25 Ll L Rep 141, 144.

[79] Although, as nautical assessors prepare no report as such, this does not happen in collision cases.

[80] CPR 35.15(4) and PD35 §10.4.

[81] *The Pelopidas and TRSL Concord* [1999] 2 Lloyd's Rep 675.

Assessors and expert evidence

Nautical assessors are used as a matter of course in the Admiralty jurisdiction to advise on matters of navigation and seamanship.[82] The CPR make clear that the practice of not allowing additional expert evidence to be called except in unusual circumstances remains the accepted modern practice, and this position is reiterated in the Admiralty & Commercial Courts Guide.[83] The practice was confirmed by the Admiralty Judge in *The Pelopidas and TRSL Concord* where David Steel J emphasized that expert evidence as to matters of seamanship is not admissible at the instance of either party without the leave of the Court and the costs incurred in obtaining nautical advice are not recoverable in the absence of a court order.[84] **9.36**

Nonetheless, there are many examples of cases where an additional expert has been permitted to be called, most usually where the issues involve matters of nautical science outside the field of expertise of the assessors[85] and, more recently, where computer-based models of the collision are sought to be adduced into evidence.[86] **9.37**

The rule against additional expert evidence has come under criticism from the Supreme Court of Canada in *Porto Seguro Companhia de Seguros Gerais v Belcan SA*.[87] The Court identified four defects in the rule. First, it was said that the prohibition on expert evidence violates the principle of natural justice of the right to be heard *audi alteram partem*. Secondly, the court identified that the rule rests on the mistaken premise that assessors will be masters of all matters of expertise that arise in the trial. The third flaw was that the traditional rule does not permit disclosure to the parties of what passes between the Judge and the assessor. Finally, the court considered that the exclusion of expert evidence may create the impression that it is the assessor, rather than the Judge, who is determining important questions of fact. In light of these criticisms of the rule, the Supreme Court held that the rule should be revised and that, in all cases, the parties are entitled to call expert evidence.[88] **9.38**

The position in England is no longer as painted by the Supreme Court of Canada almost ten years ago, if indeed it ever was in all the respects outlined above. As indicated above, the rule has never been immutable; given the developments in **9.39**

---

82 *Esso Petroleum Co Ltd v Southport Corporation* [1956] AC 218.

83 Admiralty & Commercial Courts Guide, N14.1.

84 *The Pelopidas and TRSL Concord* [1999] 2 Lloyd's Rep 675; see also *The Eleftheria v The Hakki Deval* [2006] EWHC 2809 (Comm) and *The Owners of the Ship 'Kamal XXVI' and Barge 'Kamal XXIV' v The Owners of the Ship Ariela* [2007] EWHC 2434 (Comm) [26].

85 *The Ann and Mary* (1843) 2 Wm Rob 189, 166 ER 725; *The Fritz Thyssen* [1968] P 255, [1967] 3 WLR 990, [1967] 3 All ER 117, [1967] 2 Lloyd's Rep 199; *The St Chad* [1965] 1 Lloyd's Rep 107; *The Neptun (Owners) v Humber Conservancy Board* (1937) 59 Lloyd's Rep 158; *The Antares II and Victory* [1996] 2 Lloyd's Rep 482.

86 *The Golden Polydinamos* [1993] 2 Lloyd's Rep 464; *The Fraternity* [1994] 2 Lloyd's Rep 582; *The Pelopidas and TRSL Concord* [1999] 2 Lloyd's Rep 675. Below, paras 9.45 and following.

87 *Porto Seguro Companhia de Seguros Gerais v Belcan SA* [1997] 3 SCR 1278.

88 Ibid 1299, [40].

modern shipping technologies, leave is likely to be given to call additional expert evidence in particularly complex matters[89] or, conceivably, where some particular local geographical knowledge impacts upon matters of seamanship and navigation. Further, as is discussed below, the English Admiralty Court has provided detailed guidance for both courts and practitioners as to the manner in which assessors' assistance is to be dealt with to ensure compliance with the principles of natural justice. The procedure outlined by the English Admiralty Court also addresses any perception that the assessors rather than the Judge are charged with the ultimate decision-making power.[90]

Assessors on appeal

9.40 Nautical assessors are also normally used on appeal where they have been used at trial. Difficulty can of course arise where the advice tendered by the assessors at trial differs from that which is given to the appellate court. In *The Savina*,[91] the House of Lords accepted Willmer LJ's statement in *The Fina Canada*:

> ... we are just as free to consult our assessors as the Judge was to consult the Elder Brethren. We are not bound to accept their advice, any more than we or the learned judge would be bound to accept the advice tendered by the Elder Brethren below. If there is a divergence of view between the Assessors advising this court and the Elder Brethren who advised the Admiralty Court, those advising us are not to be regarded as speaking with any greater authority because they happen to be advising the Court of Appeal. This, I understand, is what is meant by the phrase that there is no appeal from Assessors to Assessors. If there is such a divergence of view, the position is that this Court must make up its own mind as to which advice ought to be accepted.[92]

However, continued the House of Lords, it should only be in exceptional circumstances that an appellate court should put the same questions to its nautical assessors as were put before the assessors at first instance. Three reasons for this were suggested. First, and perhaps not least, it is inviting embarrassment and complication to do so. Secondly, counsel may not have had the opportunity of addressing the appellate court on all the evidence, and, thirdly, the assessors at the appellate level may not have heard all of the evidence and certainly will not have had the advantage of having heard it delivered orally.[93] Given such difficulties, the words of Viscount Dunedin in *The Australia* were thought salutary:

---

[89] See, for example, *The Global Mariner and The Atlantic Crusader* [2005] EWHC 380, [2005] 1 Lloyd's Rep 699, where in addition to experts on 'reconstruction', reports from photogrammetrists were adduced.

[90] This is, it must be said, not a perception held widely (or perhaps at all) among admiralty practitioners, certainly in respect of any of the last five Admiralty Judges, Teare, David Steel, Clarke, Sheen, and Brandon JJ, or among those such as Gross J, who have also tried collision cases.

[91] *The Savina* [1976] 2 Lloyd's Rep 123.

[92] *The Fina Canda* [1962] 2 Lloyd's Rep 445, 454 referring to *The Australia* [1927] AC 145, (1926) 25 Ll L Rep 141.

[93] *The Savina* [1976] 2 Lloyd's Rep 123, 131.

> ... speaking for myself, except for purposes of explanation, I shall always ask an assessor as little as possible. Certainly to find ... different assessors are at variance is much more of a hindrance than an assistance.[94]

The treatment of assessors' evidence

Traditionally, nautical assessors have neither been sworn nor subject to cross-examination, and the advice given by the assessors has remained confidential between the assessors and the court. More recently, a practice has developed whereby the Judge will seek assistance from counsel in formulating the questions which should be put to the assessors, but the responses of the assessors to those questions remained confidential. This practice was considered by the Court of Appeal in *The Bow Spring and The Manzanillo II.*[95] The Court of Appeal expressed the opinion that the practice was not compatible with art 6 of the European Convention for the Protection of Human Rights and Fundamental Freedoms 1950, and that the principles relevant to the concept of a fair hearing must be adapted to the procedure relating to the use of court-appointed experts.[96] According to the Court of Appeal, this means that any consultation between the assessors and the court should take place openly as part of the assembling of evidence. Thus, in addition to seeking counsels' assistance in formulating the questions to be put to the assessors, any answers should be disclosed to counsel, either orally or in writing, to enable counsel to have the opportunity to make submissions as to whether or not their evidence should be accepted. **9.41**

The proper practice to be adopted in all collision cases involving nautical assessors remains that set out by Gross J, in consultation with the then Admiralty Judge, David Steel J:[97] **9.42**

(i) The range of topics on which advice might be sought from the Assessors should be canvassed with counsel by, latest, the stage of final submissions.
(ii) Ordinarily, the questions asked of the Assessors by the Judge should not stray outside the range previously discussed with counsel; should they do so, however, there are safeguards contained in (iii) and (iv) below.
(iii) The questions ultimately put by the Judge, together with the answers given by the Assessors, should be disclosed to counsel before any draft judgment is handed down.
(iv) Counsel should thereafter be given the opportunity to make submissions[98] to the Judge, as to whether the advice given by the Assessors should be followed.

---

[94] *The Australia* [1927] AC 145, 149, (1926) 25 Ll L Rep 141, 143.

[95] *The Bow Spring and The Manzanillo II* [2004] EWCA Civ 1007, [2005] 1 WLR 144, [2005] 1 Lloyd's Rep 1.

[96] Ibid.

[97] *The Global Mariner and The Atlantic Crusader* [2005] EWHC 380, [2005] 1 Lloyd's Rep 699, 702–703, [14]–[15].

[98] And to propose any supplementary questions: see (v).

Ordinarily, any such submissions should be in writing; but if there is good reason for doing so, an application could be made for an oral hearing. The Judge will consider any such submissions before finalizing his judgment.

(v) Generally speaking, the interests of proportionality and finality will make it unnecessary to repeat the procedure after the Judge and the Assessors have had the opportunity of considering the parties' submissions and any suggested further or revised questions. Accordingly, unless the Judge in his discretion thinks it appropriate to disclose them to counsel before the judgment is finalized, any further or revised answers will simply be recorded in the judgment, together with the Judge's decision as to whether or not to accept the Assessors' advice and his reasons for doing so.

Assessors' remuneration

9.43 See above, para 6.07.

Assessors in other jurisdictions

9.44 Nautical assessors continue to be used in admiralty matters in Canada, Hong Kong, and Singapore but not in Australia,[99] New Zealand, or South Africa. Both the Australian and New Zealand Law Reform Commissions recommended the abolition of all special provisions relating to assessors in admiralty.[100] The Federal Courts Rules in Canada make provision for assessors to be appointed to assist the Court 'in understanding technical evidence' or to 'provide a written opinion'.[101] The rule reflects the decision of the Supreme Court of Canada in *Porto Seguro Companhia de Seguros Gerais v Belcan SA*,[102] which considered whether expert evidence should be permitted in addition to the use of assessors.[103] The Supreme Court held that assessors are permitted to assist judges in understanding technical evidence, and further to advise on matters of fact in dispute between the parties but only on condition of disclosure and a right of response sufficient to comply with the requirements of natural justice.[104]

C. Collision Cases in the Computer Age

9.45 It has been the practice in collision cases for illustrative plotting of tracks of vessels leading up to a collision to be prepared for the court and to be tendered in

[99] *Peters Slip Pty Ltd v Commonwealth of Australia* [1979] Qd R 123.

[100] Civil Admiralty Jurisdiction, ALRC No. 33 (1986) para 291; Special Law Reform Committee on Admiralty Jurisdiction, New Zealand, 1982, Appendix 1, para 12.

[101] Federal Courts Rules r 52.

[102] *Porto Seguro Companhia de Seguros Gerais v Belcan SA* [1997] 3 SCR 1278.

[103] This is now expressly permitted under the Federal Courts Rules r 52.1(1).

[104] These requirements are effected through the Federal Courts Rules rr 52(3)–(5).

argument. This was a task often carried out by or with the assistance of expert mariners who could of course never be called to speak to their plots in evidence. In recent years, however, this practice has become computerized. Such is the sophistication of this modelling software that not only are experts needed in order to prepare these reconstructions—for they have moved well beyond the simple plots of yesterday[105]—but they are invariably accompanied by often extensive explanatory material and/or comment.

Concerns about the practice of tendering computerized plots have been voiced by the Admiralty Judge on two bases. First, that it is or may be expert evidence of seamanship or navigation, and thus should not be adduced without leave of the court. Secondly, that it leads to the duplication or waste of costs. David Steel J suggested instead that the preferable practice would be to use a particular brand of software selected by a single expert who is able to furnish the parties and the court with reconstructions based on their favoured assumptions.[106] Whilst absolutely right in principle, there are real difficulties in giving effect to this *dictum* in practice. **9.46**

(1) In a complex case, it is time-consuming enough for an expert to input just one set of data, let alone both parties'.
(2) The software used is frequently proprietary, and so cannot be used by other experts, at any rate without having first paid a licence fee for the privilege of doing so.
(3) Different software packages have different strengths and weaknesses, which inevitably have a very modest but nevertheless in certain situations significant impact on the output data, which may benefit one party or the other. Where two experts are used, these differences are usually acknowledged and ironed out at the experts' meeting (if not before) and so make no difference to the outcome. This would not be the case where only one expert was used.
(4) By the same token, there may be a temptation to use modelling software to perform tasks for which it is not really suitable. In one recent case, software developed for modelling collisions was used to simulate the actions of a vessel at anchor in a fast-flowing current. It was eventually acknowledged that that software was significantly and materially less suited to that particular task than that which had been deployed by the other side. If a single joint expert had been used, there would have been no opportunity (without incurring the expense of double-checking that expert's methods and analysis) to identify that shortcoming.

[105] At least one of the commonly used programs is capable of generating real-time two-or three-dimensional depictions of the resultant reconstruction, which may (in the case of the three-dimensional variant) be viewed from different physical positions.

[106] *The Pelopidas v The TRSL Concord* [1999] 2 Lloyd's Rep 675, 682. That is because differences can arise not only as a result of the assumptions reflected in the data input into the program, but also as a result of differences in modelling methods adopted by different programs.

9.47 The Admiralty Judge has also been at pains to emphasize the importance of keeping the role of plotting in perspective, even when using a computer program for that purpose and even where that plotting is based on black-box data. In *The Pelopidas*, the evidence was that an error of 0.1° would make 15 metres difference in the lateral position. Thus a tiny margin of error may become potentially highly significant. It is submitted that there is much force in David Steel J's observation that the true probative value of these programs is that they may sometimes enable the court to determine, not what may have happened, but what could not possibly have happened.[107]

9.48 However, even computer plotting programs now seem almost passé. The advent of AIS[108] and VDR[109] in particular has made it possible in many cases to analyse in hitherto undreamed-of detail the manoeuvres made by vessels before, during, and after collision.[110] Whilst there are margins for error and although the data must still be interpreted,[111] the uncertainties are of a different order of magnitude compared even to the relatively recent 'old days' of course recorder traces, bell books, and working charts (all of which continue to exist, but are of ever-decreasing forensic value). It has been rightly observed by the High Court of Singapore that advances in technology have made contemporaneous documentary evidence, usually in digital format, even more important in collision cases than preliminary acts, or collision statements of claim. Evidence contained on the course recorder, the time log, and in minutely detailed recordings and reproductions of non-human events relating to the collision is usually available. This makes it difficult, if not impossible, for witnesses to tailor their evidence (let alone 'flog the log')[112] to present a false case.[113]

---

[107] *The Pelopidas v The TRSL Concord* [1999] 2 Lloyd's Rep 675, 682.

[108] Automatic Identification System, a wireless based system, in which the AIS-equipped vessel transmits position, course over the ground, and speed (and sometimes heading) information derived from its GPS (and electronic gyro, in the case of heading).

[109] Voyage Data Recorder, the marine equivalent of aviation's 'black box'. Very considerable amounts of data, including position, course over the ground, speed, rudder angle, heading, engine setting, etc are recorded. A sound recording is usually also included, but only for a limited period, such as the last 30 minutes, at any one time.

[110] In some cases, particularly in Hong Kong, radar tracker evidence has been used for much the same purpose. See, eg, *Kulemesin v HKSAR* [2013] HKCFA 14, [2013] 2 Lloyd's Rep 367, [145]. Radar tracker data gives a generally less reliable picture of a vessel's manoeuvres than AIS or VDR data, particularly when a vessel is turning. There is scope for fierce forensic battle where data of this sort is relied upon, particularly in high-speed collisions. Just such a battle took place in Hong Kong criminal proceedings arising out of the Lamma Island ferry disaster of 1 October 2012, *HKSAR v Chow Chi Wai & Anr.*

[111] For example, a GPS fix will give the position of the vessel's GPS aerial. It will not on its own shed much light on the whereabouts of the vessel's bow, which could be 200m or more away.

[112] An expression used judicially in *The Marinicki* [2003] 2 Lloyd's Rep 655 at [25].

[113] *The Teng He* [2000] 3 SLR 114.

10

LIMITATION OF LIABILITY FOR MARITIME CLAIMS

A. Introduction

Preliminary considerations

10.01 '*Ships are different ...*'. The 'difference' addressed in the articles which bear that title[1] is the privilege afforded to a shipowner (and others) in certain circumstances to limit liability arising out of a single occurrence in accordance with the tonnage of his ship. In all of the jurisdictions covered in this work, this can be achieved either by way of defence (binding only on the parties to the particular action) or by way of action for a decree (to 'bind the world'),[2] which may or may not (depending on the law of the country in question and/or the decision of the Judge in the particular case) require the constitution of a limitation fund.

10.02 As well as being tendentious, limitation is a difficult and broad subject. This chapter is confined to what might be termed 'plain vanilla' limitation; in other words, to limitation regimes arising from or akin to the well-known Conventions of 1957 and 1976, although brief mention is also made of the Athens Convention, because of the potential for overlap with the 1976 Convention.

[1] Lord Mustill, the title to whose article continues '—or are they?', thought not: [1993] LMCLQ 490. The response of David Steel QC sought to make 'the case for limitation of liability' [1995] LMCLQ 77.

[2] Per Longmore J in *The Happy Fellow* [1997] 1 Lloyd's Rep 130, 132. That may be so in theory, but there are significant obstacles to achieving universality in practice, which is perhaps why Lord Philips MR in *Schiffahrtsgesellschaft Ms 'Merkur Sky' mbH & Co KG v Ms Leerort NTH Schiffahrts GmbH & Co KG, The Leerort* [2001] EWCA Civ 1055, [2001] 2 Lloyd's Rep 291 added the wry caveat at 298: 'at least as far as the Admiralty Court was concerned'. These difficulties are considered further below, in paras 10.204 and following.

But these are not the only conventions concerned with the limitation of shipowners' liability—and nor are they the only ones to which effect is given by the Merchant Shipping Act 1995 (MSA). For example, claims arising in relation to oil pollution[3] are governed by the provisions of the International Convention on Civil Liability for Oil Pollution Damage 1992, which came into force on 30 May 1996; the MSA gives effect to that Convention in Chapter III. Claims relating to hazardous and noxious substances are governed by the provisions of the International Convention on Liability and Compensation for Damage in Connection with the Carriage of Hazardous and Noxious Substances by Sea 1996, contained in sch 5A to the MSA. The International Convention on the Carriage of Passengers and their Luggage 1974 (the Athens Convention) is enacted by s 183 and sch 6 of the MSA.[4] **10.03**

In addition to the provisions relating to limitation of liability, s 186 of the MSA provides, subject to certain conditions, for a total exclusion of liability for Crown ships and owners of United Kingdom ships[5] for loss or damage to property by reason of fire on board the ship[6] and for loss or damage to gold, silver, watches, jewels, or precious stones on board the ship by reason of theft, robbery, or other dishonest conduct if their nature and value were not declared at the time of shipment. This provision, too, is mentioned in passing in order to draw attention to its existence, but is not considered further. **10.04**

It is a common characteristic of limitation regimes that they provide some opportunity for the party claiming against the shipowner to have the limits of liability disapplied in the case at hand. This is known as 'breaking limit'. Under the 1957 Convention and its predecessor regimes, whilst the limits of liability were relatively low, breaking limit was—if not commonplace—certainly a practical proposition in a significant number of cases, not least because the burden lay on the party claiming the right to limit to prove his entitlement to do so. In the 1976 Convention, by contrast, both the limits and the bar to breaking limit were raised significantly;[7] the burden of proof, moreover, was reversed, such that in all but **10.05**

---

[3] Other than pollution caused by the bunkers of non-oil carrying ships. See the definition of 'oil' in art 1.5 of the Convention.

[4] Guidance in relation to these other regimes can be found in specialist texts, such as P Griggs, R Williams, and J Farr, *Limitation of Liability for Maritime Claims* (4th edn, 2005) and the IMO publications relating to the individual conventions.

[5] A United Kingdom ship is one registered in the United Kingdom under pt II of the MSA, s 1(3). The exemption extends to the owner, charterer, manager, or operator of such a ship, and to the master, crew member, or servant of such persons when acting in the course of their employment.

[6] *The Diamond* [1906] P 282; *Tempus Shipping v Louis Dreyfus* [1930] 1 KB 699, 708, (1930) 36 Lloyd's Rep 159, 168; *Morewood v Pollock* (1853) 1 El & Bl 743, 118 ER 614; *The Santa Malta* [1967] 2 Lloyd's Rep 391, 393–394.

[7] See in this connection *The Bowbelle* [1990] 1 WLR 1330, 1335, [1990] 1 Lloyd's Rep 532, 535 cited with approval in *The Leerort* [2001] EWCA Civ 1055, [2001] 2 Lloyd's Rep 291, 294, [10]:

> … [under] the Convention of 1976 … shipowners agreed to a higher limit of liability in exchange for an almost indisputable right to limit their liability.

the most egregious cases (scuttling and suicide, for example), there is no realistic prospect of breaking limit.[8]

10.06 As a result of these changes, the focus of enquiry in limitation cases has moved away from breaking limit to issues such as whether the particular claim is one in respect of which the right to limit arises at all, and questions of jurisdiction. This tendency was exacerbated by the coming into force[9] of the 1996 Protocol to the 1976 Convention, which raised the limits of liability still further in the countries which apply it and, in effect, created a third general limitation regime in widespread international use. The attractions of forum shopping are lent further impetus by the considerable variation in the national implementation of the 1976/1996 regimes, in that countries may decide for themselves whether to implement certain provisions, such as the application of the Convention to cleanup liabilities under art 2.1(d). The 1996 Protocol limits were increased again in 2012 with effect from 8 June 2015 (the '2012 uplift'). It is yet to be seen whether the now greater difference between the 1976 Convention limits and the 2012 uplift will exacerbate these issues.

10.07 One consequence of this shift of attention is that the wording of the 1976 Convention has come under a scrutiny which its framers can never have thought it would have to bear. It is not unfair to say that it has been creaking under the strain.

The exercise and nature of the right to limit

10.08 As regards the exercise of the right to limit, it has already been indicated that limitation may be invoked by way of defence or by way of action. The best introduction to and explanation of the difference between these two methods remains that of Brandon LJ in his dissenting judgment in *The Penelope II*,[10] which remains accurate today:

> ... Where there is only one claim, the question of limitation only needs to be dealt with as between the owner and the single claimant concerned. This can be done in proceedings to which those two persons, and only those two persons, are parties. By contrast, where there are several claims made or apprehended, the question of limitation cannot be dealt with as between the owner and any one of the claimants, but must rather be dealt with as between the owner and all the claimants, and also as between the different claimants inter se.
>
> For this latter purpose it is necessary that special proceedings should be instituted to which the owner on the one hand, and all actual or potential claimants on the other hand, are made parties. In such special proceedings the power of the Court to stay any other proceedings brought by individual claimants against the owner in the same or in any other Court is of the utmost importance, for it provides the means

[8] This is so in the common law jurisdictions at least. The position may be different in some civilian countries. See, for example, the French cases referred to by Longmore J in *The Happy Fellow* [1997] 1 Lloyd's Rep 130, 137–138.

[9] In some but by no means all the countries which are party to the 1976 Convention.

[10] *Afromar Inc v Greek Atlantic Cod Fishing Co, The Penelope II* [1980] 2 Lloyd's Rep 17, 21.

> by which the Court can prevent any one such individual claimant from gaining an advantage over the other claimants, and compel him instead to share rateably with those others in the amount of the owner's limited liability available for distribution. The power to stay just referred to extends not only to staying proceedings before a judgment has been given in them, but, more importantly still, to staying the enforcement of any judgment which may already have been obtained.
>
> The special proceedings which are brought by an owner … are known as a limitation action, and the order made in such an action, if the owner succeeds in establishing his right to limit, is known as a decree of limitation…

By contrast with the carrier's right of limitation under the Hague (Visby) Rules (which is substantive), there is high authority for the view that the nature of the right to limit under the 1976 Convention (and its predecessors) is procedural only. Thus: **10.09**

> The effect of the Convention … is not to qualify the substantive right of the claimant against the shipowner but to limit the extent to which that right can be enforced against the limitation fund.[11]

The procedural nature of the right to limit, being a matter for the *lex fori* alone, has considerable relevance when matters of jurisdiction are considered—particularly *forum conveniens* and anti-suit injunctions, but also the question of related actions for the purpose of the EU Brussels I Regulations and their cousins.[12] **10.10**

Historical outline

In *The Bramley Moore,* Lord Denning MR observed of the shipowner's right to limit his liability in respect of certain claims, 'there is not much justice in this rule; but limitation of liability is not a matter of justice. It is a rule of public policy which has its origins in history and its justification in convenience'.[13] **10.11**

The historical origins of limitation in English law may be traced to 1733 when, in the decision of *Boucher v Lawson,*[14] a shipowner was found liable for the loss of a cargo of gold bullion which had been stolen by the master of his ship. The decision highlighted the disadvantage of English shipowners compared with their continental counterparts, who enjoyed rights to limit their liability in such circumstances, and Parliament was petitioned to remedy the injustice.[15] The result was **10.12**

---

[11] *Caltex Singapore Pte Ltd v BP Shipping Ltd* [1996] 1 Lloyd's Rep 286, 293–294 per Clarke J, approved by Clarke LJ in *Seismic Shipping Inc v Total E & P UK Plc (The Western Regent)* [2005] EWCA Civ 9851, [2005] 2 Lloyd's Rep 359, 370, [52] and by Lord Hoffmann in *Harding v Wealands* [2006] UKHL 32, [47], [2007] 2 AC 1, 19, [2006] 3 WLR 83, 96, [2006] 4 All ER 1, 15.

[12] See below, para 10.158. For the relationship between the Regulations and Conventions, see Chapter 6, n 50.

[13] *The Bramley Moore* [1964] P 200, 220, [1964] 2 WLR 259, 265–266, [1964] 1 All ER 105, 109; [1963] 2 Lloyd's Rep 429, 437.

[14] *Boucher v Lawson* (1733) Cas T H 85, 95 ER 53.

[15] P Griggs, 'Limitation of Liability for Maritime Claims: the Search for International Uniformity' [1997] LMCLQ 369, 370—an article which contains a valuable account of the history

the Responsibility of Shipowners Act 1733, the preamble to which contains the justification for limitation which, convenient or not, still prevails today:[16]

> Whereas it is of the greatest consequence and importance to this kingdom, to promote the increase of the number of ships and vessels, and to prevent any discouragement to merchants and others from being interested and concerned therein ...

10.13 The Merchant Shipping Act 1894 introduced the notion of limiting the owner's liability in respect of loss of life or personal injury or damage to property occurring without his actual fault or privity in accordance with the tonnage, rather than the value, of his ship.[17]

10.14 The drive for international uniformity which marked the opening decades of the twentieth century led, in the case of limitation, to the Limitation Convention of 1924. Its attempt to impose s 503 of the Merchant Shipping Act 1894 internationally and without seeking any compromise with continental approaches to limitation probably marked it out for failure, and it was not widely adopted.

10.15 Three decades later, the 1957 Limitation Convention achieved wider acceptance.[18] It endorsed limitation based on the tonnage (rather than value) of the ship, and extended rights of limitation to charterers, managers, operators, masters and crew members, and their servants or agents. As with s 503 and the 1924 Convention, the right to limit would be defeated if the party claiming the right to limit could not show that the relevant loss occurred without his 'actual fault or privity'.[19]

The 1976 Convention

10.16 On 1 December 1986, the Convention on the Limitation of Liability for Maritime Claims 1976 (the 1976 Convention, also known as the London Convention) entered into force.[20] The limitation amounts were subsequently increased by an amending Protocol of 1996, which entered into force on 13 May 2004.[21] The higher limitation amounts apply to incidents occurring on or after that date. From

---

of the right to limit. See also in that regard per Steel J in *CMA CGM SA v Classica Shipping Co Ltd (The CMA Djakarta)* [2003] EWHC 641 (Comm), [2003] 2 All ER (Comm) 21, 25–27, [2003] 2 Lloyd's Rep 50, 52–54, [14]–[27].

[16] For a more contemporary exposition of those principles, see D Steel QC, 'Ships are Different: the Case for Limitation of Liability' [1995] LMCLQ 77.

[17] Merchant Shipping Act 1894, s 503.

[18] With forty-eight State parties.

[19] For a well-known example of 'breaking the limit' under the 1957 Convention see *The Lady Gwendolen* [1965] P 264, [1965] 3 WLR 91, [1965] 2 All ER 283, [1965] 1 Lloyd's Rep 335 CA.

[20] It has been ratified or acceded to by fifty-three States (as at 1 September 2015; source <http://www.imo.org>).

[21] As at 1 September 2015, fifty-two States had acceded to the 1996 Protocol (source <http://www.imo.org>).

8 June 2015, higher limits apply where the 1996 Protocol is in force as a result of the 2012 uplift agreed by the Legal Committee of the International Maritime Organization (IMO) at its 99th Session in 2012.[22]

The 1976 Convention introduced significant changes to the limitation of liability regime with a view to increasing the fund available, extending the classes of claim in respect of which the shipowner could limit, and ensuring that the right to limit was almost indisputable.[23] In that last regard, whereas under the 1924 and 1957 Conventions the onus lay on the party seeking to limit his liability to prove the absence of 'fault or privity' on his part, under the 1976 Convention the entitlement to limit arises as of right unless the claimant proves that the person liable is guilty of deliberate or reckless conduct. **10.17**

The Athens Convention

There is a regime specific to the limitation of liability for passenger claims. Unlike the other limitation regimes touched on above,[24] the Convention Relating to the Carriage of Passengers and their Luggage by Sea 1974 (the Athens Convention), which came into force internationally on 28 April 1987, overlaps with the ground covered by the 1976 Convention. **10.18**

Since 1974, three Protocols to the Athens Convention have been agreed, two of which have entered into force. The 1976 Protocol[25] made the Special Drawing Right (SDR) the relevant unit of account for the purpose of calculating the limitation amount. The 1990 Protocol adopted on 29 March 1990 did not enter into force and has now been superseded by the 2002 Protocol. The 2002 Protocol raised the limits of liability[26] significantly and introduced both a strict liability regime and a requirement for compulsory insurance. The 2002 Protocol finally entered into force twelve months after being accepted by ten States on 23 April 2014. In those jurisdictions where the 2002 Protocol has been adopted, the Convention has been renamed the Athens Convention relating to the Carriage of Passengers and their Luggage by Sea 2002 (the Athens Convention 2002). **10.19**

The regulation of the overlap between the Athens and the 1976 Conventions differs from country to country. The solution in UK law is discussed in para 10.25 below. **10.20**

---

[22] That increase was agreed and implemented, using the 'tacit acceptance procedure', by a decision of the Legal Committee which comes into force thirty-six months after Contracting States are notified, unless not less than one-fourth of the Contracting States have communicated an objection to the amendment within eighteen months of its notification.

[23] *The Breydon Merchant* [1992] 1 Lloyd's Rep 373, 376.

[24] Para 10.03.

[25] Which entered into force on 30 April 1989.

[26] 250,000 SDR per passenger.

B. The Statutory Regimes

The United Kingdom—the Merchant Shipping Act 1995

10.21 The 1976 Convention was enacted into UK law by s 185 of the MSA, which gives the force of law to those provisions of the 1976 Convention that are set out in sch 7 to the Act. On 17 July 1998, the UK gave effect to the 1996 Protocol[27] and denounced the 1976 Convention.[28] The 2012 uplift has automatically come into force in the UK as from 8 June 2015 by virtue of the tacit acceptance mechanism.[29]

10.22 Art 9(1) of the 1996 Protocol provides that as between parties to the 1996 Protocol, the 1976 Convention and the 1996 Protocol are to be read and interpreted as one single instrument. Thus, the text of the 1976 Convention forms part of the 1996 Protocol. However, the practical effect of the denunciation is that the UK owes no treaty obligations to countries that are party to the 1976 Convention but not the 1996 Protocol. This is primarily of relevance to jurisdictional issues and the effect of the constitution of a limitation fund.[30]

10.23 The United Kingdom made certain reservations pursuant to art 15 of the Convention and so not all of the provisions of the 1976 Convention are reproduced in sch 7; where whole paragraphs have been omitted, the remaining provisions are renumbered.

10.24 The Athens Convention 2002, first given effect in its original form in the United Kingdom by s 14 of the Merchant Shipping Act 1979, is now incorporated into the law of the United Kingdom by s 183 of the MSA.[31]

10.25 In order to resolve any conflict between cases falling within both the 1976 Convention and the Athens Convention, the United Kingdom has exercised its right under art 15.3*bis* of the 1996 Protocol to apply national law to regulate the system of liability to be applied to claims for loss of life or personal injury to passengers of a ship. So far as seagoing ships are concerned, it is the Athens Convention which applies.[32] In the very limited sphere of non-seagoing ships, art 7 of the 1976 Convention continues to apply.

---

[27] By the Merchant Shipping (Convention on Limitation of Liability for Maritime Claims) (Amendment) Order 1998 (SI No 1258) and the Merchant Shipping (Convention on Limitation of Liability for Maritime Claims) (Amendment) Order 2004(SI No 1273) (in force on 13 May 2004).

[28] With effect from 13 May 2004.

[29] Above, para 10.16, n 22.

[30] Below, para 10.181.

[31] It had previously been given limited effect by Carriage of Passengers and their Luggage by Sea (Interim Provisions) Order 1980 (SI 1980/1092). See also Merchant Shipping (Convention Relating to the Carriage of Passengers and their Luggage by Sea) Order 2014 (SI No 1361).

[32] Para 6(1) of pt II of sch 7 1996 to the MSA provides that art 7 shall not apply to seagoing ships. The United Kingdom had previously exercised its power to prescribe higher limits for claims arising in relation to carriers who have their principal place of business in the UK. However, since the commencement of the 2002 Athens Protocol, the limit provided for in the

The Australian limitation of liability regime

Australia has given effect to the 1996 Protocol and the 2012 uplift in the Limitation of Liability for Maritime Claims Act 1989 which came into force on 1 June 1991, as amended by the International Maritime Conventions Legislation Amendment Act 2001[33] and the Limitation of Liability for Maritime Claims Amendment Act 2015.[34] The 1989 Act repealed the provisions giving effect to the 1957 Convention which, in 1979, had been enacted as a schedule to the Navigation Act 1912 by virtue of the Navigation Amendment Act 1979 (the 1979 Act). The provisions of the Navigation Act were the first Australian statutory provisions relating to limitation of liability for shipowners. Limitation of liability in respect of government ships was introduced in 1958 but for non-government ships, the provisions in force in relation to limitation of liability continued, until 1979, to be those contained in the Merchant Shipping Act 1894 (Imp). Australia denounced the 1976 Convention on 21 May 2013.[35] **10.26**

The application of the statutory provisions relating to limitation of liability in Australia is complicated by the original imperial legislation which remained in force in Australia until 1979, and by its application both to the Commonwealth of Australia and to the individual States and Territories. In *Kirmani v Captain Cook Cruises Pty Ltd (No 1)*,[36] the High Court of Australia held that s 104(3) of the Navigation Act 1912 was effective to repeal Part VIII of the Merchant Shipping Act 1894 as part of Australian law, be it federal or state.[37] Despite argument to the contrary, the Full Court of the Supreme Court of South Australia has affirmed that the 1979 Act also repealed the provisions of the Merchant Shipping (Liability of Shipowners and Others) Act 1900 (UK).[38] If still in force, that section would have enabled the State of South Australia to limit its liability to a significantly lower amount than that provided for under the 1976 Convention. In delivering the judgment of the court, Doyle CJ held that, even if he were wrong in his primary conclusion, the enactment of the 1976 Convention was inconsistent with the continued operation of the 1900 Act regardless of whether one applied the test of implied repeal, of repugnancy, or of inconsistency for the purposes of s 109 of the Australian Constitution.[39] The enactment of the 1976 Convention indicated an intention to cover the field in the sense of providing a single scheme for **10.27**

Merchant Shipping (Convention Relating to the Carriage of Passengers and their Luggage by Sea) Order 2014 (SI No 1361) is 400,000SDR, which is the same as that under the Athens Convention 2002.

33 No 149, 2001, sch 1.

34 No 44, 2015, sch 1.

35 With effect from 1 June 2014; see above, para 10.22 for the consequences of denunciation.

36 *Kirmani v Captain Cook Cruises Pty Ltd (No 1)* (1985) 159 CLR 351.

37 Ibid 382 per Mason J, 385 per Murphy J, 404, 418–419 per Brennan J, and 420, 424, 441 per Deane J.

38 *Amarantos Shipping Co Ltd v The State of South Australia* (2004) 89 SASR 438, 447–449, [510].

39 Ibid 448, [52].

shipowners to limit liability, subject only to the exceptions which Parliament itself has permitted.[40]

10.28 Australia has not acceded to the Athens Convention.

The Canadian limitation of liability regime

10.29 Canada is not party to the 1976 Convention but signed the 1996 Protocol on 9 September 1997. Canada has, however, given the force of law to the 1976 Convention, as amended by the 1996 Protocol, with some modifications, through the Marine Liability Act.[41] For the purposes of the application of the 1976 Convention, Canada is deemed to be a State Party.[42]

10.30 Canada has also implemented the Athens Convention in the Marine Liability Act without acceding to it, but has not implemented the 2002 Protocol. Section 35 of the Marine Liability Act enacts the Athens Convention and the 1990 Protocol.[43] An extended definition of ship, to include any vessel or craft designed, used, or capable of being used solely or partly for navigation (but excluding an air cushion vessel), is provided for in s 36(1)(a). The definition of 'contract of carriage' is also extended to embrace any contract of 'carriage by water'.[44] In addition, s 36(2) makes explicit that art 19 of the Convention, which provides that the Athens Convention does not modify the rights or duties provided for in international conventions relating to the limitation of liability of owners of seagoing ships, applies to the owners of all ships whether seagoing or not.

The Hong Kong limitation of liability regime

10.31 Hong Kong acceded to the 1976 Convention in 1993, and the 1996 Protocol in 2015. Subject to certain modifications, which are discussed below, the Merchant Shipping (Limitation of Shipowners Liability) Ordinance gives the force of law to the provisions of the Convention as set out in sch 2.[45] However, as at 1 September 2015, Hong Kong has not incorporated the 2012 uplift into domestic law.

10.32 Hong Kong has acceded to the Athens Convention and to the 1976 Protocol. Subject to certain modifications,[46] the Athens Convention is given the force of

---

[40] Ibid 449, [64].

[41] SC 2001, c 6, pt 3 and sch 1.

[42] Marine Liability Act 2001, s 27.

[43] Ibid sch 2.

[44] Ibid s 36(1)(b)

[45] Merchant Shipping (Limitation of Shipowners Liability) Ordinance (Cap 434) which entered into force on 1 October 1993, s 12. Notice that the Merchant Shipping (Limitation of Shipowners Liability) (Amendment) Ordinance 2005 (1 of 2005) was given by LN 81 of 2015, appointing 3 May 2015 as the date of commencement of the 1996 Protocol.

[46] Notably, Hong Kong extends the provisions of the Athens Convention to regional carriage and to any seagoing vessel including air-cushion vehicles designed to operate on or over water while so operating.

law pursuant to s 3 of the Merchant Shipping (Limitation of Shipowners Liability) Ordinance.

The New Zealand limitation of liability regime

Although it did not accede to that Convention until 1994, New Zealand enacted legislation broadly consistent with the 1976 Convention in 1987. It entered into force on 1 August 1987. That legislation was re-enacted as Part VII of the Maritime Transport Act 1994 (the 1994 Act). In giving effect to the 1976 Convention, the New Zealand Parliament adopted the technique of paraphrasing the Convention in the text of the Statute. The result was that there were inconsistencies between the Convention text and the legislation. However, since the enactment of the Maritime Transport Amendment Act 2013,[47] New Zealand has adopted the 1976 Convention as amended by the 1996 Protocol in its entirety, subject to a small number of changes. **10.33**

The limitation provisions in the 1994 Act include the 2012 uplift limits for passenger liabilities and personal injuries generally. New Zealand has made significant changes to the common law relating to claims for personal injuries or death. All such claims were abolished in 1974 and a compulsory statutory compensation scheme was enacted which applies to New Zealand residents and visitors alike.[48] Section 95 provides that where a person on board a ship is killed or injured through the fault of two or more ships, the liability of the owners is joint and several. The section expressly preserves the right of the owners to rely on any defence that might otherwise be available or to limit their liability.[49] **10.34**

New Zealand has not acceded to the Athens Convention nor enacted any legislation giving effect to it. **10.35**

The Singapore limitation of liability regime

Singapore did not accede to the 1976 Convention until 24 January 2005. Effect is given to the provisions of that Convention in Part VIII of the Merchant Shipping Act 1995 (Chapter 179) as a result of the passage of the Merchant Shipping (Amendment) Act 2004. The amending provisions apply to any occurrence which took place after 1 May 2005. Any occurrence prior to that date remains governed by the provisions of the 1957 Convention as implemented in Singapore by the previous Part VIII of the Merchant Shipping Act 1995.[50] **10.36**

Singapore has not acceded to the Athens Convention, nor given effect to its provisions in domestic legislation. **10.37**

---

47 Public Act 2013 No 84, s 24.
48 Accident Compensation Act 2001.
49 Maritime Transport Act 1994, s 95(2).
50 Merchant Shipping (Amendment) Act 2004, s 3.

The South African limitation of liability regime

10.38 South Africa is not a party to any of the international Conventions relating to the limitation of liability for maritime claims, including the Athens Convention. The limitation regime is provided by s 261 of the Merchant Shipping Act 57 of 1951, which provides for 'tonnage limitation'. Section 261(1) permits the owner of a ship to limit for specified claims caused without the shipowner's 'actual fault or privity'. Section 263(2) extends the right to limit to 'any charterer, and any person interested in or in possession of such ship, and a manager or operator of such ship.'

10.39 South Africa has, by virtue of s 8 of the Admiralty Jurisdiction Regulation Act 105 of 1983, preserved the jurisdiction that existed in South Africa immediately before the commencement of the Act. Thus, English law relating to limitation of liability as at 1983 will apply in respect of claims falling within this jurisdiction to the extent that it is not inconsistent with limitation provisions of the Merchant Shipping Act 1951.[51]

C. The Principles Applicable to Limitation of Liability

Persons entitled to limit liability

10.40 Art 1 of the 1976 Convention provides that:

> Shipowners and salvors, and any person for whose act, neglect or default the shipowner or salvor is responsible, [and their insurers[52]] may limit their liability in accordance with the rules of this Convention for claims set out in Art 2.

The liability of a shipowner includes liability in an action brought against the vessel herself.[53]

Shipowners

10.41 Despite the reference to 'seagoing ships' in the definition of 'shipowner' in art 1(2), the provisions of the MSA extend the application of the 1976 Convention beyond seagoing ships: firstly, the right to limit liability applies to any ship 'whether seagoing or not';[54] secondly, a 'ship' is defined to include references to any structure (whether completed or in the course of completion) launched and intended for use in navigation as a ship or part of a ship;[55] and thirdly, although art 15(5) provides that the Convention shall not apply to 'aircushion vehicles', this provision has not

---

51 G Hofmeyer, *Admiralty Jurisdiction Law and Practice in South Africa* (2nd edn, 2012) III.90.
52 Art 1(6). See para 10.53 below.
53 Art 1(5).
54 Sch 7 pt II art 2.
55 Sch 7 pt II art 12.

been enacted in sch 7 to the MSA and therefore does not have the force of law in the United Kingdom.[56]

The term 'shipowner' is defined in art 1(2) to mean the owner, charterer, manager, or operator of a seagoing ship. Despite this apparently straightforward definition, there can be considerable scope for debate whether a particular party does or does not fall within it. **10.42**

Charterers

A charterer does not have to be acting *qua* owner to bring itself within the provisions of art 1.[57] Prior to the decision of the Court of Appeal in *CMA CGM SA v Classica Shipping Co Ltd ('The CMA Djakarta')*,[58] the view had been taken that a charterer could only limit his liability under the 1976 Convention if he had been acting in the capacity of owner of the vessel.[59] The rationale for such a view was that it could never have been intended that a shipowner, who had suffered loss or damage as a consequence of the charterer's actions, would be obliged to look to the limitation fund and himself have to share in that fund to the detriment of the other claimants on whose behalf the fund had been primarily established. In *The CMA Djakarta*, a claim was brought by the owners against the time charterers for breach of the terms of the charter relating to dangerous cargo in which the charterers sought to limit their liability. It was held by Steel J at first instance that a charterer could only limit his liability when he was acting as if he were the shipowner or, in other words, if he were acting in the management or operation of the vessel.[60] The Court of Appeal rejected this view on the basis that it had been arrived at by an incorrect approach to the interpretation of art 1. Longmore LJ, with whom the other members of the Court agreed, observed that to say that a failure to prevent the loading of a dangerous cargo was not an act of managing or operating a ship under time charter so that the right to limit could not arise was to place a gloss on the word 'charterer' which is by no means apparent from the words used:[61] **10.43**

> ... the mere fact that 'charterer' is part of the definition of the word 'shipowner' cannot of itself mean that a charterer (an expression otherwise unqualified) has to be acting as if he were a shipowner before he can limit his liability. To my mind the

[56] Indeed, certain provisions of the 1976 Convention are made applicable to hovercraft in the United Kingdom through the provisions of the Hovercraft (Civil Liability) Order 1986 (SI 1986/1305), as amended by the Hovercraft (Convention on Limitation of Liability for Maritime Claims (Amendment)) Order 1998 (SI 1998/1257).

[57] *The CMA Djakarta* [2004] EWCA Civ 114, [2004] 1 All ER (Comm) 865, [2004] 1 Lloyd's Rep 460.

[58] Ibid.

[59] *The Aegean Sea* [1998] 2 Lloyd's Rep 39; *The CMA Djakarta* [2003] EWHC 641 (Comm), [2003] 2 All ER (Comm) 21, [2003] 2 Lloyd's Rep 50.

[60] *The CMA Djakarta* [2003] EWHC 641 (Comm), [2003] 2 All ER (Comm) 21, [2003] 2 Lloyd's Rep 50.

[61] *The CMA Djakarta* [2004] EWCA Civ 114, [2004] 1 All ER (Comm) 865, 871, [2004] 1 Lloyd's Rep 460, 465, [13].

ordinary meaning of the word 'charterer' connotes a charterer acting in his capacity as such, not a charterer acting in some other capacity.

10.44 The approach to the interpretation of art 1 taken by the Court of Appeal was thus to apply the 'broad and generally acceptable principles of construction' required when interpreting international conventions.[62] As limitation of liability in English law is governed by an international convention incorporated into United Kingdom law, the task of any court was to construe the Convention without any English law preconceptions.[63] The effect of the decision is that a charterer's ability to limit will depend on the type of claim that is brought against him rather than the capacity in which he was acting when his liability was incurred.

Slot charterers

10.45 Do the words 'charterer … of a seagoing ship' afford the right to limit to a 'slot charterer' (who is neither a charterer nor an operator of the whole ship but only of part of the ship)? Griggs, Williams, and Farr observe that all the other parties referred to in art 1(2) have an interest in the whole ship and the limit of their liability is calculated by reference to the tonnage of the whole ship; there is no provision which allows a slot charterer to limit his liability proportionately to the amount of space which he has chartered.[64] In *The CMA Djakarta*,[65] the Court of Appeal preferred to leave for another day the question of whether 'charterer' means the charterer of the ship as a whole or charterer of part of the ship. A literal reading of the words 'of a … ship' apart, there seems no very compelling reason why it should not mean the latter. As Longmore LJ observed, the Court had already held in *The Tychy*[66] that the word 'charterer' included a 'slot charterer' in the context of the Arrest of Seagoing Ships Convention 1952. It would seem absurd that a charterer of the whole ship should be able to limit his liability in respect of particular damage but to deny that right to a charterer of part of the ship in respect of precisely the same damage—and it is correspondingly difficult to see how a purposive construction of the article should require that conclusion.

[62] *Stag Line Ltd v Foscolo, Mango & Co Ltd* [1932] AC 328, 350, (1931) 41 Ll L Rep 165, 174; *James Buchanan & Co Ltd v Babco Forwarding & Shipping (UK) Ltd* [1978] AC 141, 152, [1977] 3 WLR 907, 911–912, [1977] 3 All ER 1048, 1052–1053, [1978] 1 Lloyd's Rep 119, 122; *Fothergill v Monarch Airlines Ltd* [1981] AC 251, 272, 282, 293, [1980] 3 WLR 209, 214, 223, 233–234, [1980] 2 All ER 696, 699–700, 706, 714–715, [1980] 2 Lloyd's Rep 295, 298, 304, 311; *Morris v KLM Royal Dutch Airlines* [2002] UKHL 7, [2002] 2 AC 628, 656, [78]; Vienna Convention on the Law of Treaties 1969 arts 31 and 32.

[63] *The CMA Djakarta* [2004] EWCA Civ 114, [2004] 1 All ER (Comm) 865, 869, [2004] 1 Lloyd's Rep 460, 463, [9].

[64] P Griggs, R Williams, and J Farr, *Limitation of Liability for Maritime Claims* (4th edn, 2005) 11.

[65] *The CMA Djakarta* [2004] EWCA Civ 114, [2004] 1 All ER (Comm) 865, [2004] 1 Lloyd's Rep 460, 465, [13].

[66] *The Tychy* [1999] 2 Lloyd's Rep 11.

Managers

There is as yet no authority as to the content of the word 'manager' or the circumstances in which such a person might be able to limit its liability. Could, for example, an independent crewing agent limit its liability where its negligent employment of an incompetent officer led to an accident? It has been suggested[67] that if the word 'manager' in art 1(2) is restricted to one who is involved in the operation of the ship, the crewing agent would probably not be covered, and nor would it fall within the scope of cover provided for in art 1(4)—for the reason that, as an independent contractor, it would not be one 'for whose act, neglect or default' the shipowner is vicariously responsible. It is submitted that neither of these propositions is necessarily correct.[68] **10.46**

Some elucidation of the first point has been provided by the Full Federal Court of Australia (albeit in the context of the phrase 'operated by' as used in the now repealed s 10 of the *Navigation Act* 1912 (Cth)), to the effect that the ordinary meaning should be given to the word without infusing it with qualifying notions based on ownership.[69] This approach is consistent with that advocated in *The CMA Djakarta*.[70] The Full Court held that the word encompasses notions of a real, substantial, and direct role in the management and control of the commercial, technical, and crewing operations of the ship. Although the context in that case differed from that of the 1976 Convention, it is submitted that the Australian court's approach is applicable in this connection also, ie, to give the word its ordinary English meaning, influenced by the maritime context of the interrelated practical responsibilities involved in the management and control of a ship.[71] Thus the outcome of the issue will vary from case to case, depending on the intimacy of the connection between the particular 'manager' and the vessel herself. **10.47**

Salvors

The term 'salvor' is defined in art 1(3) to mean any person rendering services in direct connexion with salvage operations which include operations relating to wreck removal,[72] removal, and destruction of cargo,[73] and measures taken by third parties to avert or minimize loss.[74] **10.48**

---

67 P Griggs, R Williams, and J Farr, *Limitation of Liability for Maritime Claims* (4th edn, 2005) 9.

68 As to the second of them, see paras 10.49 and following below.

69 *ASP Ship Management Pty Ltd v AAT* [2006] FCAFC 23; (2006) 149 FCR 261, 288, [105].

70 *The CMA Djakarta* [2004] EWCA Civ 114, [13], [2004] 1 All ER (Comm) 865, 871, [2004] 1 Lloyd's Rep 460, 465.

71 *ASP Ship Management Pty Ltd v AAT* [2006] FCAFC 23, [105]; (2006) 149 FCR 261.

72 Art 2(1)(d).

73 Art 2(1)(e).

74 Art 2(1)(f).

Others

10.49 Art 1(4) extends the right to limit liability to 'any person for whose act, neglect or default the shipowner or salvor is responsible', an extension of uncertain scope. Whilst it seems plain enough that it extends to a shipowner's servants, however unlikely it might be that such individuals could be the target of litigation,[75] its application beyond that limited sphere is more difficult—not least because there may not be precise overlap between on the one hand 'responsibility' for another's 'act, neglect or default' under art 1(4) and, on the other, what the general law would regard as vicarious liability. Indeed, even in the context of a shipowner's employees, the liability of the employer may be personal rather than vicarious,[76] but it would be surprising if a negligent chief officer could not limit his liability in circumstances in which his employer could, simply because the liability of the employer was categorized as direct rather than vicarious.

10.50 The significance of this difficulty should not be exaggerated, of course. It seems unlikely that the draftsmen of the 1976 Convention could have intended that the application of art 1(4) should turn upon precisely how the liability in question was viewed by its governing law. But if a broader construction is to be given to art 1(4), what are its limits? Is it enough, for example, that a party should have been instrumental in bringing about a state of affairs in respect of which both he and the shipowner have attracted civil liability? If so, then the independent repairer whose 'act, neglect or default' resulted in the vessel's unseaworthiness and, consequently, damage to cargo would (assuming liability against it could be established) be able to limit its liability; this seems as surprising a result as the chief officer who could not limit his liability in the previous example.

10.51 The solution, it is submitted, is to focus on the wording of art 1(4) and its requirement that the shipowner be responsible for the 'act, neglect or default' of the other party, rather than its consequences,[77] thus eschewing enquiry into whether the employer's responsibility is categorized under domestic law as direct or vicarious. In the result, the chief officer[78] ought to be able to limit, while the independent repairer could not.

Mortgagees

10.52 Unlike the position under s 3(1) of the 1958 Merchant Shipping (Liability of Shipowners and Others) Act,[79] which gave effect to the 1957 Convention,

---

[75] Although for an example, see *Offshore Nautical (CI) Ltd v Quality Time Training Ltd* [2006] EWHC 347 (Comm).

[76] Although the factual constellation in that case was different, in that the negligent individual was not the employee of the defendant, note the remark of Lord Brandon in *McDermid v Nash Dredging* [1987] AC 906, 919.

[77] Compare and contrast the Civil Liability (Contribution) Act 1978.

[78] Or the director/superintendent in *The Ert Stefanie* [1989] 1 Lloyd's Rep 349, a decision on s 503 of the Merchant Shipping Act 1894.

[79] Section 3(1) provided that the persons entitled to limit liability included 'any charterer and any person interested in or in possession of the ship and, in particular, any manager or operator of the ship'.

a mortgagee in possession does not have the right to limit under the MSA. That is not to say, however, that a mortgagee might not in a given situation be, for example, an 'operator' of the ship.

Insurers

Art 1(6) of the 1976 Convention entitles an insurer to the benefits of the Convention 'to the same extent' as the assured himself. Griggs, Williams, and Farr suggest that the terms of art 1(6) of the 1976 Convention may have inadvertently cut down the liability insurer's rights, in that if the insurer is afforded the right to limit (only) 'to the same extent' as the assured, then he may not be entitled to rely on those provisions of the policy or of the Marine Insurance Act 1906 that would otherwise restrict or remove his liability to the assured,[80] such that he had to meet the third party's claim in full if the assured had forfeited his right to limit liability. Griggs, Williams, and Farr themselves point out a solution to this apparent problem in the provision of s 1(1) of the Third Parties (Rights Against Insurers) Act 1930 that: **10.53**

> ... his (the assured's) rights against the insurer under the contract in respect of the liability shall, notwithstanding anything in any Act or rule of law to the contrary, be transferred to and vest in the third party to whom the liability was so incurred.

They argue that only those limited rights which the assured has against the insurer under the liability policy are transferred to the third party under the 1930 Act. In other words, the 1930 Act defines the liability of the insurer to the third party and art 1(6) of the 1976 Convention only comes into play when that liability has been determined.[81] Without dissenting from this 'solution', it is submitted that the problem is somewhat contrived; the evident purpose of art 1(6) is to extend and not to restrict insurers' rights.

Australia

Australia has not made any reservations under art 15(2) of the 1976 Convention relating to non-seagoing ships. This is significant, given the observation of Gibbs CJ in *Kirmani v Captain Cook Cruises Pty Ltd* that 'no authority is needed for the proposition that a ship which is used entirely within the limits of internal waters, and never goes to sea, is not a seagoing ship'.[82] Thus, the construction placed by the **10.54**

---

[80] As in *The Fanti and The Padre Island* [1990] 2 Lloyd's Rep 191, in which the House of Lords held that a third party claimant stepping into the shoes of the assured under the 1930 Act and thereby taking over the assured's rights under a P&I policy, could not recover from the P&I insurer under that Act unless and until the assured had complied with all the P&I Club's Rules, which included a 'pay to be paid' clause.

[81] P Griggs, R Williams, and J Farr, *Limitation of Liability for Maritime Claims* (4th edn, 2005) 16.

[82] *Kirmani v Captain Cook Cruises Pty Ltd* (1985) 159 CLR 351, 369.

High Court of Australia on the definition of 'shipowner' in art 1 of the Convention means that vessels used only on internal waters are unable to limit their liability. Australia does not apply the provisions of the 1976 Convention to the ships of the naval, military, or air forces of a foreign country.[83]

Canada

10.55 The Marine Liability Act expands the class of persons who may limit their liability by including 'any person who has an interest in or possession of a ship from and including its launching'.[84] Thus, there are two Canadian modifications to the Convention, the person 'in possession of' and the person with 'an interest in' the ship. The meaning of 'in possession' was considered by the Federal Court in *Bayside Towing v Canadian Pacific Railway Co*,[85] which held that a tug owner could not be said to be in possession of the tow during towage on the basis of the so-called 'flotilla principle' or by reference to the public policy rationale for limitation of liability. 'An interest in' the ship may include the holder of a share in a ship or a mortgagee and even, in the Canadian context, the holder of a maritime lien who is deemed to carry a proprietary interest[86] (although it is not easy to conceive of circumstances in which a lienee could have any liability which it would wish to limit).

10.56 Canada has deleted the reference to 'seagoing' in the definition of 'ship' and defines 'carriage' with reference to 'water' rather than 'sea'.[87] The effect is to extend the application of the Convention to all navigable waters.

Hong Kong

10.57 Hong Kong has expanded the definition of 'ship' to include any air-cushion vehicle designed to operate in or over water while so operating and any structure (whether completed or in the course of completion) launched and intended for use in navigation as a ship.[88] It also extends the right to limit to any ship, whether seagoing or not.[89] The meaning of the word 'shipowner' has a correspondingly broader meaning than in art 1(2) of the Convention.[90]

New Zealand

10.58 Prior to the implementation of the 1996 Protocol in New Zealand, the definition of 'owner' in the 1994 Act differed somewhat from the definition in the 1976 Convention. 'Owner':

---

83 Limitation of Liability for Maritime Claims Act 1989, s 7.
84 Marine Liability Act 2001, s 25(1)(b).
85 *Bayside Towing v Canadian Pacific Railway Co* [2001] 2 FC 258 (TD).
86 *Todd Shipyards Corp v Altema Compania Maritima SA (The Ioannis Daskalelis)* (1972) 32 DLR (3d) 571, [1974] SCR 1248; *Marlex Petroleum Inc v Har Rai* (1984) 4 DLR (4th) 739.
87 Marine Liability Act 2001, s 25(1)(b)–(c).
88 Merchant Shipping (Limitation of Shipowners Liability) Ordinance 1997, s 13(a).
89 Ibid s 14.
90 Ibid.

(a) means every person who owns the ship or has any interest in the ownership of the ship;
(b) in any case where the ship has been chartered, means the charterer;
(c) in any case where the owner or charterer is not responsible for the navigation and management of the ship, includes every person who is responsible for the navigation and management of the ship.[91]

An attempt to argue that this section excluded time and voyage charterers from the right to limit liability, contrary to the accepted position in English law as to the interpretation of 'charterer' in the 1976 Convention, was rejected in *Tasman Orient Line CV v Alliance Group Ltd*, where the Court refused to narrow the definition of 'owner' for the purposes of the New Zealand Act and held that 'owner' includes time charterers and sub-time charterers, at least in relation to claims brought by cargo owners against the sub-time charterer as carrier.[92] Although the decision was based squarely on the reasoning of Steel J at first instance in *The CMA Djakarta*,[93] subsequently reversed by the Court of Appeal,[94] the New Zealand Court's ruling in *Tasman Orient Line* was closer in spirit to and not inconsistent with the Court of Appeal's. There was no reason to suppose, therefore, that the law of New Zealand required a charterer to be acting *qua* owner in order to invoke limitation. This would seemingly have been resolved now in favour of the English position, as s 84 of the 1994 Act now simply incorporates the definitions in the 1976 Convention, other than with respect to the meaning of 'ship'. As the court expressly left open the question of whether the sub-time charterer would have been entitled to maintain its right to limit in the event of a claim brought against it by the registered owner of the vessel, it now seems more likely that the decision in *The CMA Djakarta* will be followed, so that it will be unlikely that it could.[95] **10.59**

A 'ship' is defined in s 84 as follows: **10.60**

In the LLMC Convention and the LLMC Protocol, ship or seagoing ship—
(a) means every description of vessel (including barges, lighters and like vessels) used or intended to be used in navigation, however propelled; and
(b) includes any structure (whether completed or nor) launched and intended for use as a ship or part of a ship; and
(c) includes any ship used by or set aside for the New Zealand Defence Force.

It is clear that there is no requirement that the relevant 'ship' be seagoing, but the definition would not appear to extend the benefits of limitation to hovercraft.[96]

---

[91] Maritime Transport Act 1994, s 84.
[92] *Tasman Orient Line CV v Alliance Group Ltd* [2004] 1 NZLR 650, 659, [30].
[93] *The CMA Djakarta* [2003] EWHC 641 (Comm), [2003] 2 All ER (Comm) 21, [2003] 2 Lloyd's Rep 50.
[94] *The CMA Djakarta* [2004] EWCA Civ 114, [2004] 1 All ER (Comm) 865, [2004] 1 Lloyd's Rep 460.
[95] *Tasman Orient Line CV v Alliance Group Ltd* [2004] 1 NZLR 650, 660 [34].
[96] Compare the definition in the Admiralty Act 1973, s 2, which expressly 'includes hovercraft'.

In *Birkenfeld v Yachting New Zealand Inc*,[97] the Court of Appeal held that a rigid inflatable boat (RIB) was a 'ship' for the purposes of s 84.

Singapore

10.61 Section 136(3) of the 1995 Act extends the provisions of the Convention to non-seagoing ships.[98]

South Africa

10.62 Section 261 of the 1951 Act provides that 'the owner of a ship' is entitled to limit liability and s 2 defines 'owner' to mean any person to whom a ship or a share in a ship belongs. Section 261(2) extends the application of sub-s (1) to 'owners, builders or other persons interested in any ship built at any port or place in the Republic, from and including the launching of such ship until the registration thereof . . .'. Section 263(2) provides further that 'owner' includes 'any charterer, any person interested in or in possession of such ship, and a manager or operator of such ship'. Thus, unlike the provisions of the MSA currently applicable in the United Kingdom, the master and crew are excluded from the limitation provisions; conversely, the South African regime permits a mortgagee in possession to limit.

10.63 It is not necessary that the ship be registered in South Africa and the provisions of s 261(1) apply 'from and including the launching of such a ship until the registration thereof'—as well as thereafter.[99] A 'ship' is defined in s 2 of the 1951 Act to mean 'any vessel used for transportation or for any other purpose on or under the surface of the water' and a 'vessel' is defined as including 'any ship, or any boat, small vessel or other description of a vessel used or designed to be used in navigation, but excludes any dynamically supported craft'. This definition is narrower than that contained in s 1(1) of the Admiralty Jurisdiction Regulation Act 105 of 1983 which confers jurisdiction on the Admiralty Court in relation to claims for limitation of liability, so that not all ships within the jurisdiction of the Admiralty Court enjoy the right to limit derived from the 1951 Act.[100]

Claims subject to limitation of liability

10.64 Art 2 lists the claims which may be subject to limitation of liability under the Convention, provided that the basis for the particular claim is not exempt under art 3 and provided that the claim has not arisen due to conduct barring limitation

[97] [2006] NZCA 434, [2007] 1 NZLR 596.
[98] Merchant Shipping Act 1995, s 136(3).
[99] Merchant Shipping Act 57 of 1951, s 261(2).
[100] 'Ship' in the Admiralty Jurisdiction Regulation Act 105 of 1983 means any vessel used or capable of being used on the sea or internal waters, and includes any hovercraft, powerboat, yacht, fishing boat, submarine vessel, barge, crane barge, floating crane, floating dock, oil or other floating rig, floating mooring installation or similar floating installation, whether self-propelled or not.

within the meaning of art 4. It provides that the claims listed may be subject to limitation 'whatever the basis of liability may be'. Thus, for example, claims in the nature of indemnity under a contract, for breach of statutory duty, or for contribution under the Civil Liability (Contribution) Act 1978 (or equivalent) can all be the subject of limitation.

Art 2(1)(a) contemplates four types of claims: **10.65**

(1) claims in respect of loss of life or personal injury occurring on board or in direct connexion with the operation of the ship;
(2) claims in respect of loss or damage to property occurring on board the ship;
(3) claims in respect of loss of or damage to property (including damage to harbour works, basins and waterways, and aids to navigation) occurring in direct connexion with the operation of the ship. This category caters for cases of collision with another ship or structure;
(4) claims in respect of loss of or damage to property occurring in direct connexion with salvage operations,

and consequential loss resulting therefrom.

'... consequential loss ...'

There are two possible meanings which could be ascribed to the phrase 'and consequential loss resulting therefrom'.[101] They could relate to further loss (or damage) resulting from, eg, the loss of property (such as bunkers), such as pollution of beaches and resulting clean-up costs;[102] alternatively, they may be confined to 'consequential loss' in the narrow sense, ie, losses caused to the property owner consequential upon the loss of or damage to his property, such as loss of profits.[103] **10.66**

The point is a significant one. Consider, for example, a claim by an owner against a charterer for breach of a safe port warranty, which breach results in the holing of a bunker tank and loss of bunker oil which in turn causes environmental damage. It is not possible for the charterer to limit in relation to the damage to the ship itself **10.67**

[101] A third is put forward in J Reeder (ed), *Brice on Salvage* (5th edn, 2012) at §7-106 and by P Griggs, R Williams, and J Farr, *Limitation of Liability for Maritime Claims* (4th edn, 2005) 16, namely that the phrase refers back to claims 'occurring on board or in direction connection with salvage operations'. That cannot be correct; the phrase 'occurring on board or in direct connection with salvage operations' is adjectival and governs 'loss of life or personal injury or loss of or damage to property': *Bouygues Offshore SA v Caspian Shipping (Nos 1, 3, 4 and 5)* [1998] 2 Lloyd's Rep 461, 473. The phrase 'and consequential loss resulting therefrom' refers back to 'loss of life or personal injury or loss of or damage to property'.

[102] A view which found favour with Thomas J in *Aegean Sea Traders Corp v Repsol Petroleo SA, The Aegean Sea* [1998] 2 Lloyd's Rep 39, 52. Note that limitation in respect of clean-up costs is not available under English law (because art 2(1)(d) is of no application in the UK), where such liability is incurred outside the UK; liability incurred inside the UK is brought within the limitation of liability regime by s 168 of the 1995 Act.

[103] Indirect support for this view may be furnished by s 168 of the MSA 1995, which deems liability incurred under s 154 (liability for damage caused by and clean-up of bunker oil escaping other than from oil tankers) 'to be a liability to damages in respect of such damage to property as is

(see para 10.70 below), and there is clearly no need for him to do so in relation to the loss of his own oil; but can the charterer limit his liability in respect of the owner's claim to be indemnified against *his* liability to the littoral State (or other public or private interests) for environmental damage? The answer is that he may do so only if (i) the environmental damage is '[a] damage to property ...[b] occurring ... in direct connection with the operation of the ship',[104] or (ii) if the environmental damage (or the owner's liability in respect of it) is 'consequential loss arising from' the 'loss of ... property' (ie the bunker) from the ship.

10.68 The view was expressed in the previous edition of this work that the narrower construction was to be preferred on the basis that, although particular weight should not be attached to s 168 of the 1995 Act, the absence of the words 'or damage' and the difficulty of applying any notion of 'consequential loss' (in the wider sense) to loss of life (to which the phrase also applies) tip the scales in favour of the narrow reading of the words.

10.69 The contrary view was, however, preferred by Finkelstein J in the Federal Court of Australia when considering whether a claim for pure economic loss was within the meaning of consequential loss.[105] Relying primarily on *obiter* remarks in the decision of Thomas J, referred to above, and *The Breydon Merchant*, Finkelstein J also expressed reservation as to the construction advocated above, both on the basis that the UK and some continental jurisdictions are familiar with economic claims arising out of the loss of life, and that it is 'impermissible to base a construction of the Article ... by looking at [it] with a grammar in one hand and a dictionary in the other'.[106] Despite having commenced the task of construction by analysing the context of the Convention and the purpose and object for which it was made, the reasons advanced by Finkelstein J with respect fail to engage with the point that the context of the adoption of Art 2 in 1976 was such that a claim for economic loss not contingent on damage to property is most unlikely to have even been contemplated,[107] and was certainly not referred to in the *travaux préparatoires*. Further, *The Breydon Merchant* does not in terms support a claim for pure economic loss. Although correctly decided, the decision should be confined to its facts, in that it deals with the diminution in value of cargo, not property more generally. The basis of the right to recovery was not stated in that case to be pure economic loss, but the diminution in the value of cargo which has historically been the measure of damage in a claim for damage to cargo. For these reasons, it is contended that the

mentioned in' art 2.1(a). There would be no need for such a deeming provision if such liability were clearly encompassed within the phrase 'or consequential loss resulting therefrom'. More direct support, perhaps, is afforded by the absence from the phrase of the words 'or damage'.

104 A contention which also appealed to Thomas J in *The Aegean Sea* [1998] 2 Lloyd's Rep 39.

105 *Qenos Pty Ltd v The Ship APL Sydney* [2009] FCA 1090, (2009) 187 FCR 282.

106 Ibid 289–290. For *The Breydon Merchant* see n 23 above.

107 Ibid 288, 292.

narrower view remains preferable. There was no opportunity for the Full Federal Court to consider the judgment at first instance as no appeal was filed.

Damage to the vessel

The claims in respect of which an owner or charterer can limit do not include claims for loss or damage to the ship relied on to calculate the limit; that is because the property damaged cannot be the same as the thing whose operation caused the damage. The 'property' envisaged in art 2(1) must be the property of a third party either on board or external to the vessel.[108] It is submitted that it can extend to the littoral environment, being property of a public (if not private) nature. **10.70**

Where salvage services have been rendered to a vessel resulting in salvors obtaining a lien upon the cargo for their reward, the amount due to the salvors by cargo owners in respect of each parcel is damage to that cargo within the meaning of the Convention, and a claim for damages against the shipowner brought by cargo owners falls within art 2(1)(a).[109] However, a claim for amounts paid to salve the very ship relied on to calculate the limit cannot be within art 2(1)(a). Such a claim is one for consequential loss resulting from the damage to the ship and cannot be brought within art 2(1)(a) or (f) (ie, claims in respect of steps taken to minimize loss).[110] **10.71**

The same principle applies to a shipowner's claim to be indemnified against liability to contribute in general average. Any contribution made by the shipowner will be made as a result of the damage to the vessel and does not therefore fall within art 2(1)(a).[111] **10.72**

Art 2(1)(b) permits liability for claims in respect of loss resulting from delay in the carriage by sea of cargo, passengers, or their luggage to be limited. **10.73**

Art 2(1)(c) permits the limitation of liability for claims in respect of other loss resulting from infringement of rights other than contractual rights, occurring in direct connexion with the operation of the ship or salvage operations. In Australia, this has also been held to include claims for pure economic loss.[112] **10.74**

---

108 *The CMA Djakarta* [2004] EWCA Civ 114, [25]–[26], [2004] 1 All ER (Comm) 865, 875–876, [2004] 1 Lloyd's Rep 460, 467–468. The House of Lords gave permission to appeal against the Court of Appeal's decision, but the case was compromised before it came on for hearing. The Supreme Court has given permission, in effect, to pick up where *The CMA Djakarta* left off on this point in *Gard Marine v China National Chartering Co Ltd. ('The Ocean Victory')* [2015] EWCA Civ 16, [2015] 1 Lloyd's Rep 381. The point was not considered at first instance or in the Court of Appeal, all parties recognizing that *The CMA Djakarta* was binding. The Supreme Court is expected to hear the appeal in 2016.

109 *The Breydon Merchant* [1992] 1 Lloyd's Rep 373.

110 *The CMA Djakarta* [2004] EWCA Civ 114, [29], [2004] 1 All ER (Comm) 865, 877, [2004] 1 Lloyd's Rep 460, 469.

111 Ibid 878, 469, [30].

112 *Qenos Pty Ltd v The Ship APL Sydney* [2009] FCA 1090, (2009) 187 FCR 282. See para 10.69 above.

10.75 Art 2(1)(d) confers the right to limit on claims in respect of the raising, removal, destruction, or the rendering harmless of a ship which is sunk, wrecked, stranded, or abandoned, including anything that is or has been on board such ship. This article is, however, of no application in the United Kingdom.[113]

10.76 Art 2(1)(e) allows claims in respect of the removal, destruction, or rendering harmless of the cargo of the ship to be limited.

10.77 Art 2(1)(f) permits limitation in relation to claims of a person other than the person liable in respect of measures taken in order to avert or minimize loss for which the person liable may limit his liability in accordance with this Convention, and further loss caused by such measures. *The Breydon Merchant*[114] provides a useful illustration—and illumination—of this wording. In that case the shipowner sought to limit in respect of a claim by cargo owners to recover amounts paid in salvage by way of damages for breach of contract. Sheen J found that if the salvors had not been engaged, the ship and cargo would have suffered further loss and damage. The cargo owners' claim was thus one by a person other than the person liable in respect of measures taken to avert or minimize loss; it was therefore a claim in respect of which the shipowners could limit their liability.

10.78 Art 2(2) provides:

> Claims set out in paragraph 1 shall be subject to limitation of liability even if brought by way of recourse or for indemnity under a contract or otherwise. However, claims set out under paragraph 1(d), (e) and (f) shall not be subject to limitation of liability to the extent that they relate to remuneration under a contract with the person liable.

Thus the claim in *The Breydon Merchant* was within art 2(2) as well as art 2(1)(a) and (f).[115] The combined effect of ss 2(1)(f) and 2(2) can be summarized as follows.

(1) The loss in respect of which the measures to avert or minimize are taken must be one in respect of which the right to limit liability arises.
(2) The claim must be in respect of either (a) expenses incurred by persons other than the shipowner (the person liable) to avert or minimize loss, or (b) further loss caused by the taking of such measures.
(3) Where the claim is brought by a third party by virtue of a contract with the shipowner (the person liable) to carry out such measures, that claim is not subject to limitation.

Costs

10.79 Art 11(1) provides that any fund constituted pursuant to the provisions of the Convention 'shall be available only for the payment of claims in respect of which

---

[113] Sch 7 pt II art 3(1). No such fund as is referred to in that sub-article has yet been established.
[114] *The Breydon Merchant* [1992] 1 Lloyd's Rep 373.
[115] Ibid; see also *Sun Wai Wah Transportation Ltd v Cheung Kee Marine Services Co Ltd* [2009] HKCFI 1098, [2010] 1 HKLRD 833.

limitation of liability can be invoked'. The claims for which liability can be invoked, as provided for in art 2, relate to claims under the substantive law. Limitation cannot therefore be invoked against an order for costs.[116]

Australia

As in the United Kingdom, art 2(1)(d) (wreck removal) does not apply in Australia; nor does art 2(1)(e) (cargo removal/clear-up).[117] **10.80**

In *Newcastle Port Corporation v Pevitt & Ors*,[118] Palmer J of the Supreme Court of New South Wales held that a limitation fund established under art 11 of the 1976 Convention is exclusive of any legal costs which may be incurred in establishing a claim against that fund.[119] This conclusion was directly contrary to that reached by Newman AJ in the same court in *Noferi v Smithers*.[120] However, in the latter case it appears that there was no dispute between the parties that the limitation fund included the costs of the proceedings, and it is submitted that Palmer J was right not to follow it. In reaching his decision, Palmer J adverted to the apparent anomaly created where shipowners' liabilities for legal costs will be left at large, which could be considered inconsistent with the purposes of the 1976 Convention. The Judge noted that the Convention recognizes in art 14 that it could only go so far in limiting claims against shipowners. Calculation of the limits of compensation payable to claimants could be made uniform no matter what national jurisdiction determined those claims. However, the procedures for determining whether or not the claims were established and how they were to be dealt with could not be made uniform without invasive domestic procedural law which would be contentious, inconvenient, and unnecessary.[121] **10.81**

Canada

In contrast to the position in the United Kingdom where unlimited liability for wreck removal has been retained, claims for such expenses in Canada are subject to limitation, and art 2(1)(d) of the 1976 Convention is included in the Marine Liability Act.[122] **10.82**

The Supreme Court of Canada considered the meaning of the phrase 'in direct connection with the operation of the ship' within the context of art 2(1)(a) of the 1976 Convention in *Isen v Simms*,[123] although the case arose under the provisions **10.83**

116 *Thompson v Masterton* [2004] 1 Lloyd's Rep 304 (Royal Court of Guernsey); *Newcastle Port Corporation v Pevitt* [2003] NSWSC 888, (2003) 58 NSWLR 548: cf *Swiss Bank Corp v Brink's-MAT Limited* [1986] 1 QB 853, [1986] 3 WLR 12, [1986] 2 All ER 188, [1986] 2 Lloyd's Rep 99 in the context of the Warsaw–Hague Convention.

117 Limitation of Liability for Maritime Claims Act 1989, s 6.

118 *Newcastle Port Corporation v Pevitt & Ors* [2003] NSWSC 888, (2003) 58 NSWLR 548.

119 Ibid 557, [36].

120 *Noferi v Smithers* [2002] NSWSC 508.

121 *Newcastle Port Corporation v Pevitt* [2003] NSWSC 888, (2003) 58 NSWLR 548, 559, [45].

122 Marine Liability Act 2001, s 24.

123 *Isen v Simms* [2006] 2 SCR 349, (2006) 273 DLR (4th) 752.

of the now repealed Canada Shipping Act 1985. The plaintiff had sustained an injury to his eye from the bungie cord that was being used to secure a boat's engine cover immediately following the use of the boat on a lake. The Supreme Court overturned the decision of the Full Federal Court[124] upholding the owner's right to limit, preferring the view of the dissenting Judge that the fact that the accident involved a boat did not transform the matter into a maritime matter and was therefore not a matter within the jurisdiction of federal Canadian maritime law. Adopting the reasoning of Décary J in the court below, Rothstein J, with whom the other members of the court agreed, said: 'Nothing has happened on water which could be said to be directly or even indirectly related to the accident. There is no issue as to the seaworthiness of the ship, the issue at best being one as to the roadworthiness of a boat being prepared on land for road transportation.'[125]

10.84 The decision of the Supreme Court highlights the importance in Canadian law of determining whether the general grant of maritime jurisdiction to the Federal Court, as prescribed in s 22(2) of the Federal Courts Act, has been properly invoked. Once a particular claim is found to fall within the enumerated headings, there is necessarily substantive maritime law to support the claim.[126] The test for determining whether the subject matter under consideration was one of maritime law was stated by the Supreme Court in *Monk Corp v Island Fertilizers Ltd*[127] to be that the subject matter is 'so integrally connected to maritime matters as to be legitimate Canadian maritime law within federal competence'. In *Siemens Canada Ltd v JD Irving Ltd*,[128] Siemens unsuccessfully appealed the finding of Heneghan J that a claim for damage sustained to two rotors that fell off a barge into the waters of Saint John Harbour during loading fell within the court's jurisdiction and was therefore subject to limitation under the Marine Liability Act.

Hong Kong

10.85 Art 2(1)(d) does not apply in Hong Kong unless an order has been made by the Chief Executive establishing a fund to compensate harbour or conservancy authorities for the reduction in the amount recoverable by them consequent upon the application of art 2(1)(d).[129]

New Zealand

10.86 Section 86 of the 1994 Act, which previously made provision for the types of claims which may be subject to limitation, now merely makes clear that limitation of liability under the 1976 Convention applies in respect of each distinct occasion

---

[124] *Isen v Simms* FCJ No 756, 2005 FCA 161

[125] *Isen v Simms* [2006] 2 SCR 349, (2006) 273 DLR (4th) 752 [28].

[126] *Skaarup Shipping Corp v Hawker Industries Ltd* [1980] 2 FC 746 (CA).

[127] *Monk Corp v Island Fertilizers Ltd* [1991] 1 SCR 779.

[128] *Siemens Canada Ltd v JD Irving Ltd* [2012] FCA 225; see also *Buckley v Buhlman* [2012] FCA 9.

[129] Merchant Shipping (Limitation of Shipowners Liability) Ordinance 1997, s 15. As at 1 September 2015, no such order had been made by the Chief Executive.

without regard to liability arising on any other occasion, and 'applies, subject to subsection (4) of this section, whether the liability arises at common law or under any other enactment, and notwithstanding anything in any other enactment'.[130] This sub-section maintains the clarity that existed before the 1996 Protocol was implemented in New Zealand that claims of the kind contemplated by art 2(2), being those brought by way of recourse, or for an indemnity under a contract, or otherwise, are subject to limitation.

Singapore

Section 136 of the 1995 Act provides that 'the provisions of the Convention, other than paragraph 1(d) and (e) of Art 2 of the Convention, shall have the force of law in Singapore'. Thus claims relating to wreck removal or to the removal and destruction of cargo on the ship, cannot be subject to limitation of liability in Singapore. **10.87**

South Africa

The claims for which liability may be limited are those arising on any single occasion[131] in respect of: **10.88**

(1) loss of life or personal injury to any person;
(2) loss of or damage to any property or rights of any kind, whether movable or immovable.[132]

It is a peculiar feature of the South African provision that there is no reference to the claim having to arise 'on board' or 'in the navigation or management' of a ship. The section therefore includes loss of life, personal injury, or property damage occurring ashore. Section 263 extends the application of the Part to 'any person (other than the owner) who is responsible for the fault of the ship' and to any person who is for the time being responsible for the navigation and management of the ship. A reading of the Part as a whole would therefore suggest that there must be some connection between the navigation and management of the ship and the claim itself. **10.89**

Claims exempt from limitation

Art 3 provides that the rules of the Convention do not apply to: **10.90**

(1) claims for salvage or contribution in general average;
(2) claims for oil pollution damage within the meaning of the International Convention on Civil Liability for Oil Pollution Damage dated 29 November 1969 or of any amendment or Protocol thereto which is in force. As noted above (para 10.03, footnote 3) the 1969 Convention is of limited application,

130 Maritime Transport Act 1994, s 86(3).
131 Merchant Shipping Act 57 of 1951, s 261(3).
132 Merchant Shipping Act 57 of 1951, s 261(1).

applying only to the discharge of oil from ships actually carrying oil in bulk as cargo.[133] Thus other types of pollution claims resulting, for example, from the discharge of bunker fuel from a bulk carrier, are capable of being the subject of limitation if they result in damage to property.

(3) claims subject to any international convention or national legislation governing or prohibiting limitation of liability for nuclear damage;[134]

(4) claims against the shipowner of a nuclear ship for nuclear damage;

(5) claims by servants of the shipowner or salvor whose duties are connected with the ship or the salvage operations, including claims of their heirs, dependants, or other persons entitled to make such claims, if under the law governing the contract of service between the shipowner or salvor and such servants the shipowner or salvor is not entitled to limit his liability in respect to such claims, or if he is by such law only permitted to limit his liability to an amount greater than that provided for in art 6.

In the UK, such a provision is contained in s 185(4) of the MSA.

10.91 In *The Breydon Merchant*,[135] cargo owners brought a claim against the owners of the vessel for damages for breach of the contract of carriage. They contended that the vessel had been unseaworthy at the commencement of the voyage and, as a result, she suffered a serious engine room fire and had required salvage services. Consequently the cargo owners would be obliged to pay the salvors their due proportion of the salvage reward. The shipowners had claimed a decree limiting their liability. The issue between the parties was whether the cargo owners' claim was a claim in respect of which the shipowners were entitled to limit their liability, arising as it did from the necessary provision and performance of salvage services. Sheen J held that the cargo owners' claim was in respect of loss of or damage to property occurring on board the vessel and consequential loss resulting therefrom. The cargo owners were not making, nor of course could they make, a claim for salvage against the shipowners: they were claiming damages for breach of contract. As such, their claim was neither in whole nor in part a claim for salvage and art 3(1) was of no application.

Australia

10.92 Art 3(e) of the 1976 Convention prevents a shipowner or salvor from seeking to limit claims by their employees, or the employees' heirs or dependants, if the law of the jurisdiction so provides. Section 93 of the Navigation Act 2012 does so provide.

---

[133] International Convention on Civil Liability for Oil Pollution Damage dated 29 November 1969, art 1 as amended by art 2 of the 1992 Protocol.

[134] In the UK, the right to limit under the MSA is expressly excluded by the Nuclear Installations Act 1965, which provides a strict liability regime governing the carriage of nuclear matter within the territorial limits of the United Kingdom.

[135] *The Breydon Merchant* [1992] 1 Lloyd's Rep 373.

Canada

Canada has not made any alteration to the provisions of art 3 of the 1976 Convention. **10.93**

Hong Kong

Those claims which are expressed to be excluded from the ambit of the Convention by art 3 are similarly excluded under the Hong Kong legislation. Further, the Merchant Shipping (Limitation of Shipowners Liability) Ordinance 1997 makes express that the matters referred to in art 3(b) and (c) are those claims in respect of any liability incurred under s 6 of the Merchant Shipping (Liability and Compensation for Oil Pollution) Ordinance (Cap 414) and claims made pursuant to ss 3 or 4 of the Nuclear Material (Liability for Carriage) Ordinance (Cap 479).[136] **10.94**

Section 7 of the Control of Exemption Clauses Ordinance (Cap 71) prevents an employer from 'restrict[ing] his liability for death or personal injury resulting from negligence'. In *Fong Yau Hei v Gammon Construction Ltd*, it was held that although the legislation was not specifically directed at art 3(e) of the Convention, the general policy as enshrined in s 7 was sufficient for the purpose of manifesting the requisite intention of excluding the operation of the Convention in relation to claims by employees.[137] **10.95**

New Zealand

The exception in art 3(e) of the 1976 Convention for claims by employees under contracts of service, although included in the Convention as incorporated into the 1994 Act, is of limited effect, as the rights of employees arising out of personal injury claims are specifically covered by the Accident Compensation Act 2001. That Act is expressed not to be limited or affected by s 86 and so claims by employees fall outside the ambit of the 1994 Act altogether. **10.96**

Claims for wreck removal brought by harbour authorities or the Minister for Transport are excluded from limitation.[138] **10.97**

Singapore

Singapore has not made any amendments to the provisions of the Convention relating to exemption from the right to limit. **10.98**

South Africa

There is nothing in the South African legislation which makes any provision for exemptions from the right to limit. **10.99**

---

136 Merchant Shipping (Limitation of Shipowners Liability) Ordinance 1997, s 16.
137 *Fong Yau Hei v Gammon Construction Ltd* [2008] 2 HKCFA 27, (2008) 11 HKCFAR 212.
138 Maritime Transport Act 1994, s 86(4).

Conduct barring limitation

10.100 Art 4 provides:

> A person shall not be entitled to limit his liability if it is proved that the loss resulted from his personal act or omission, committed with the intent to cause such loss, or recklessly and with knowledge that such loss would probably result.

10.101 The test for establishing conduct which would bar limitation is very stringent and is far more difficult to satisfy than that of the 1957 Convention, pursuant to which the owner of a seagoing ship could limit his liability 'unless the occurrence giving rise to the claim resulted from the actual fault or privity of the owner'. The stricter test of the 1976 Convention was a *quid pro quo* for shipowners agreeing to a higher limit of liability in exchange for an almost indisputable right to limit their liability. Indeed, in *Schiffahrtsgesellschaft Ms 'Merkur Sky' mbH & Co KG v Ms Leerort NTH Schiffahrts GmbH & Co KG (The Leerort)*,[139] the Master of the Rolls observed that Counsel had been unable to point to any collision case in any jurisdiction where the right to limit under the 1976 Convention had been successfully challenged.[140]

10.102 The language of art 4 echoes that of art 25 of the Warsaw Convention, as amended in 1955, which provides:

> The limits of liability specified in Article 22 shall not apply if it is proved that the damage resulted from an act or omission of the carrier, his servants or agents, done with intent to cause damage or recklessly and with knowledge that damage would probably result.

As the Master of the Rolls commented in *The Leerort*,[141] the limitation provisions in relation to merchant shipping provide an even greater protection than those in relation to carriage by air, in that only the personal act or omission of a shipowner (or person included within that category) can defeat the right to limit. In the vast majority of cases, it is unlikely to be possible to satisfy the test, which requires firstly the relevant act to have been committed by an individual, whose act may be seen as that of the owner (usually a company), and secondly that it be sufficiently egregious.

10.103 As to the first question, this is traditionally taken to require identification of the 'directing mind and will' of the company,[142] although as Lord Hoffmann pointed

---

139 *The Leerort* [2001] EWCA Civ 1055, [2001] 2 Lloyd's Rep 291, 295, [18].

140 The counsel referred to, now Teare J, informs us that he is not 'convinced' that his inability to refer to such a case had extended expressly to 'any jurisdiction'. At all events, it is clear that such cases do exist: see the two French decisions, *The Heidberg* and *The Johanna Hendrika*, referred to by Longmore J in *The Happy Fellow* [1997] 1 Lloyd's Rep 130, 137–138. Note also *Margolle v Delta Maritime, The Saint Jacques II and The Gudermes* [2003] 1 Lloyd's Rep 203, in which, in view of the particular navigational faults alleged, Gross J refused summary judgment on a claim to limit.

141 *The Leerort* [2001] EWCA Civ 1055, [2001] 2 Lloyd's Rep 291, 294, [13].

142 After the speech of Viscount Haldane LC in *Lennard's Carry Co Ltd v Asiatic Petroleum Co Ltd* [1915] AC 705, 713.

out in *Meridian Global Funds Management (Asia) Ltd v Securities Commission*,[143] this rule of attribution is really a matter of interpretation or construction of the particular substantive rule at issue in the case at hand, rather than one of metaphysics.[144] For the purposes of an attempt to break the limit, it is necessary to identify the individual who is the directing mind and will of the shipowning company for the purpose of the particular aspect of operating the ship which is the subject of the claim,[145] or in other words, the individual(s) within the company hierarchy with duties corresponding with those to be expected of an individual owner and whose (in)actions can be attributed to the company.[146]

The next stage of the enquiry is to establish that the act was done 'recklessly and with knowledge that such loss would probably result'. Short of (attempted) suicide, scuttling, or a deliberate attempt to ram another vessel (by the vessel's owner or 'directing mind'), this is almost impossible to establish. That is because, as the Court of Appeal held in *The Leerort*, this wording 'requires foresight of the very loss that actually occurs, not merely of the type of loss that occurs'.[147] In that case, it had been argued that the words 'such loss' meant loss of the type suffered and that to identify the type of loss, it was necessary to refer back to the various types of loss set out in art 2. Thus the claims advanced for collision damage were in respect of 'loss of or damage to property', so that the only foresight required to defeat the right to limit was the likelihood of loss of or damage to property. However, Lord Phillips MR considered that such an argument ran counter to the clear meaning of the wording of art 4 and that the words 'such loss' clearly referred back to the loss that had actually resulted and was the subject matter of the claim in which the right to limit was asserted.[148] Consequently, where the loss in respect of which a claim is made resulted from a collision between ship A and ship B, the owners of ship A, or of the cargo in ship A, will only defeat the right to limit liability of the owner of ship B if they can prove that the owner of ship B intended that it should collide with ship A (or perhaps intended that it should collide with another ship) or acted recklessly with the knowledge that it was likely so to collide.[149] **10.104**

Australia

The construction placed on the wording of art 4 by the English Court of Appeal in *The Leerort* is consistent with the approach taken in Australia with regard to **10.105**

[143] *Meridian Global Funds Management (Asia) Ltd v Securities Commission* [1995] AC 500, 507G–511C, [1995] 3 NZLR 7, 13–16, [1995] 3 WLR 413, 419–423, [1995] 3 All ER 918, 924–927.

[144] Compare and contrast, to that end, *Tesco Supermarkets v Nattrass* [1972] AC 153, esp per Lord Diplock at 199–200, and *In re Supply of Ready Mixed Concrete (No 2)* [1995] 1 AC 456.

[145] This may be a relatively lowly person in the company's hierarchy, as in *The Lady Gwendolen* [1965] P 294, but may equally be a very senior individual, as in *The Truculent* [1952] P 1.

[146] See further para 10.109 below and the discussion of the New Zealand authorities of *The Pembroke* and *The Tasman Pioneer*.

[147] *The Leerort* [2001] EWCA Civ 1055, [2001] 2 Lloyd's Rep 291, 295, [13]; *The MSC Rosa M* [2000] 2 All ER (Comm) 458, 461–462, [2000] 2 Lloyd's Rep 399, 401, [14].

[148] *The Leerort* [2001] EWCA Civ 1055, [2001] 2 Lloyd's Rep 291, 295, [15].

[149] Ibid 295, [16]–[17].

similar wording in the Marine Pollution Act 1987 (NSW), which implemented the International Convention for the Prevention of Pollution from Ships 1973. In *Morrison v Peacock & Roslyndale Shipping Co Pty Limited*,[150] the New South Wales Court of Appeal held that the phrase 'recklessly and with knowledge that damage would probably result' in s 8(3) required actual advertence to the risk of damage by the owner or master involved; it was not material to inquire what a prudent person would consider might happen.[151] The Court accepted the reasoning applied to the same phrase in art 25 of the Warsaw Convention by the English Court of Appeal in *Goldman v Thai Airways International Ltd*,[152] where Eveleigh LJ held that '... it is not sufficient to show that he deliberately broke a regulation, even one which is designed for safety, unless it is also shown that he had knowledge that injury would probably result'. The same approach is likely to be taken by Australian courts in relation to the identical wording contained in the Limitation of Liability for Maritime Claims Act 1989.

Canada

10.106 The approach of the Canadian Courts echoes that of the English in their approach to the identification of persons whose acts are to be attributed to the shipowning company. In *The Rhone v The Peter A B Widener*,[153] the Supreme Court of Canada considered a claim for limitation by Great Lakes Towing, the owner of two tugs, the master of which had been found to have negligently caused a collision between *The Rhone*, which was moored in Montreal Harbour, and *The Widener*, a dumb barge under tow. In considering the 1957 Convention, the Court held that there was no 'actual fault or privity' on the part of Great Lakes as the negligent tugmaster was not part of the 'directing mind and will' of the company. He exercised no 'decision-making authority on matters of corporate policy' and, despite his functions as 'troubleshooter' and trainer of new tugmasters and his paperwork responsibilities, he remained basically a 'port captain' subject to supervision and direction. Similarly, the approach in *The Leerort*[154] was affirmed by the Supreme Court of Canada in *Peracomo Inc v Telus Communications Co*,[155] a case in which the owner of a fishing vessel cut a fibre-optic submarine cable that had become tangled in the vessel's fishing gear. The Supreme Court found that the owner had acted recklessly when cutting the cable, consulting no charts nor making any enquiries as to the nature and use of the cable, but that since he believed that the cable had been abandoned, 'he did not actually know that his actions would probably result in damaging someone's property who would then have to repair it'.[156]

[150] *Morrison v Peacock & Roslyndale Shipping Co Pty Limited* (2000) 50 NSWLR 1710.
[151] See now the Marine Pollution Act 2012 (NSW) s 5(b).
[152] *Goldman v Thai Airways International Ltd* [1983] 1 WLR 1186, 1199.
[153] *The Rhone v The Peter A B Widener* [1993] 1 SCR 497, (1993) 101 DLR (4th) 188, (1993) 58 FTR 239, [1993] 1 Lloyd's Rep 600.
[154] [2001] EWCA Civ 1055 [15], [2001] 2 Lloyd's Rep 291, 295.
[155] (2014) SCC 29, [2014] 1 SCR 621, [30]–[34].
[156] Ibid [35].

Hong Kong

The approach of the Hong Kong courts is consistent with the English approach.[157] **10.107**

New Zealand

In New Zealand it has been held that where the party seeking to limit liability is a corporation, it must be shown that the functions of the person responsible for the damage were such that they ought to be attributed to the company as if they were its own.[158] **10.108**

There are two conflicting first instance decisions in New Zealand which should be noted, which whilst referring to the now repealed s 85(2) of the Maritime Transport Act 1994, remain relevant given that s 85(2) simply reproduced art 4 without alteration. In *Nelson Pine Industries Ltd v Seatrans New Zealand Ltd (The Pembroke)*[159] the court was concerned with whether Seatrans could rely on the limitation provisions of the Hague-Visby Rules, in light of art IVbis which provides that 'a servant or agent shall not be entitled to avail himself of [the defences and limits of liability] if it is proved that the damage resulted from an act or omission of the servant or agent done with intent to cause damage or recklessly and with knowledge that damage would probably result', in circumstances where a machinery cargo was stowed on deck in breach of contract. The Judge concluded that the carrier, and in particular the master, its agent, knew that damage to some of the machinery was probable and recklessly proceeded to stow the open top containers on deck.[160] His Honour went on to hold that, in order to be prevented from relying on the package limitation provisions in the Hague-Visby Rules, the recklessness and knowledge required to be shown was that of the master, not that of the carrier's management. In the later decision of *Tasman Orient Line CV v Alliance Group Ltd*,[161] the Tasman Pioneer grounded as a consequence of errors of navigation on the part of her master. Williams J was obliged to consider whether the master's actions were to be attributed to Tasman Orient, the sub-time charterer. He concluded that Tasman Orient had no reason to suspect that ship and cargo would not proceed uneventfully to their destination under the control of those employed by the owner or the managers. Accordingly, s 85(2) did not operate to defeat Tasman Orient's claim to be entitled to a decree limiting its liability. The Judge expressly declined to follow the decision in *The Pembroke*, preferring the English and Australian authorities on art 4 of the 1976 Convention.[162] Having regard to the desirability of uniformity in **10.109**

157 *Profit Country Enterprises Ltd v Sea-Land Service Inc* [1998] HKCU 2060.

158 *Meridian Global Funds Management Asia Ltd v Securities Commission* [1995] 2 AC 500 (PC); [1995] 3 NZLR 7; *Yachting NZ Inc v Birkenfeld (No 2)* (unreported, High Court of New Zealand, Civ 2005-404-438, 22 July 2005 per Keane J).

159 *The Pembroke* [1995] 2 Lloyd's Rep 290.

160 Ibid 297.

161 *Tasman Orient Line CV v Alliance Group Ltd* [2004] 1 NZLR 650.

162 *Grand Champion Tankers Ltd v Norpipe A/S (The Marion)* [1984] 1 AC 563; *Meridian Global Funds Management (Asia) Ltd v Securities Commission* [1995] 2 AC 500, [1995] 3 NZLR 7; *MSC Mediterranean Shipping Co SA v Delumar BV BA (The MSC Rosa M)* [2000] 2 Lloyd's Rep 399; *The Leerort* [2001] EWCA Civ 1055, [2001] 2 Lloyd's Rep 291; *Sellers Fabrics Pty Ltd v Hapag-Lloyd AG (The Encounter Bay)* [1998] NSWSC 646.

the construction of international conventions by domestic courts (and because it is plainly correct), it is suggested that Williams J's is the approach to be followed. In a subsequent first instance decision, that was indeed the approach that was followed, although no reference was made to *The Pembroke*.[163]

Singapore

10.110 The English approach to the construction of art 4 of the 1976 Convention would appear to be accepted in Singapore. As regards the construction of the similar wording of art 25 of the Warsaw Convention, the English decision in *Goldman v Thai Airways International Ltd*[164] has been endorsed by the Court of Appeal and has been followed subsequently.[165]

South Africa

10.111 In South Africa the right to limit arises only in the absence of the 'actual fault or privity' of the party seeking to limit liability.[166] This is the wording contained in the predecessors to the 1976 Convention and the test of what amounts to 'actual fault or privity' was described by Lord Denning MR in *The Eurysthenes* as follows:

> ... when the old common lawyers spoke of a man being 'privy' to something being done, or of an act being done 'with his privity', they meant that he knew of it beforehand and concurred in it being done. If it was a wrongful act done by his servant, then he was liable for it if it was done 'by his command or privity', that is, with his express authority or with his knowledge and concurrence. 'Privity' did not mean that there was any wilful misconduct by him, but only that someone else did it and that he knowingly concurred in it. Without his 'actual fault' meant without any actual fault by the owner personally. Without his 'privity' meant without his knowledge or concurrence... When I speak of knowledge, I mean not only positive knowledge but also the sort of knowledge expressed in the phrase 'turning a blind eye'.[167]

In *Atlantic Harvesters of Namibia v Unterweser Reederei (The St Padarn)*,[168] it was held that there was no valid reason for the similar South African provisions not to be construed in accordance with the English authorities on the subject.

The limitation amounts

10.112 The limits applicable in the different jurisdictions considered in this book are set out in the tables below.

---

163 *Daina Shipping Co v Te Runanga O Ngati Awa* [2013] NZHC 500, [2013] 2 NZLR 799.

164 *Goldman v Thai Airways International Ltd* [1983] 1 WLR 1186.

165 *Singapore Airlines v Fujitsu Microelectronics (Malaysia)* [2001] 1 SLR 241; *Clarke Beryl Claire v Silkair (Singapore) Pte Ltd* [2002] 3 SLR 1 (Court of Appeal).

166 Merchant Shipping Act 57 of 1951, s 261(1).

167 *The Eurysthenes* [1976] 2 Lloyd's Rep 171, 179; see also *The Lady Gwendolen* [1965] P 294, *The England* [1973] 1 Lloyd's Rep 373, and *The Marion* [1984] 1 AC 563.

168 *Atlantic Harvesters of Namibia v Unterweser Reederei (The St Padarn)* 1986 (4) SA 865 (C) 875.

Loss of life or PI	UK LLMC 2012 uplift	Aus LLMC 2012 uplift	Can Has not adopted the 1996 Protocol but gives effect to its provisions, including the 2012 uplift	HK Protocol 1996 (without 2012 uplift)	NZ LLMC 2012 uplift	Sing LLMC 76	SA
All ship sizes/ tonne							206.67 SDR
<300gt	1m SDR		C$1,000,000 (other than if carried on board or a passenger)			166,667 SDR	
300–500/ tons						333,000 SDR	
+501–3,000/ tons						500 SDR	
+3001–30,000/ tons						333 SDR	
<2,000gt	3.02m SDR (300-2000gt)	3.02m SDR	3.02m SDR (300-2000gt)	2m SDR	3.02m SDR		
+2,001–30,000gts	1,208 SDR	1,208 SDR	1,208 SDR	800 SDR	1,208 SDR		
+30,001–70,000gts	906 SDR	906 SDR	906 SDR	600 SDR	906 SDR	250 SDR	
+ each gts >70,000	604 SDR	604 SDR	604 SDR	400SDR	604SDR	167 SDR	

10.113

Passenger claims	UK Non-seagoing vessels only	Aus	Canada	HK	NZ	Sing	SA No provision made
	175,000 no of passengers (per capita limit)	175,000 × certificated no of passengers	2,000,000 SDR or 175,000 SDR x certificated no of passengers/ carried on board if no certification required, whichever is greater	175,000 × certificated no of passengers	175,000 × certificated no of passengers	46,666 × certificated no of passengers but maximum 25,000,000 SDR	

10.114

Passenger claims Athens	UK seagoing vessels only	Aus Not party	Canada Not party	HK	NZ Not party	Sing Not party	SA Not party
Personal injury or death per passenger	250,000 SDR strictly, and further liable unless without fault up to 400,000 SDR			46,666 SDR			
Personal injury or death where carrier has principal place of business in UK or HK per passenger	400,000SDR			300,000SDR			
Loss or damage to baggage per passenger/ vehicle	2,250 SDR (excluding luggage in or on a vehicle) 12,700 SDR (per vehicle including luggage therein) 3,375 SDR to other luggage			833 SDR (excluding luggage in or on a vehicle) 3,333 SDR (per vehicle including luggage therein) 1,200 SDR to other luggage			

10.115

Any other claims	UK LLMC 2012 uplift	Aus LLMC 2012 uplift	Can Has not adopted the 1996 Protocol but gives effect to its provisions, including the 2012 uplift	HK Protocol 1996 (without 2012 uplift)	NZ LLMC 2012 uplift	Sing LLMC 76	SA
All ship sizes/tonne							66.67 SDR
<300gt	500,000 SDR		C$500,000			83,333 SDR	
300–500/ tons						167,000 SDR	
+501– 30,000/tons						167 SDR	
<2,000gt	1.51m SDR (300- 2000gt)	1.51m SDR	1.51m SDR (300-2000gt)	1m SDR	1.51m SDR		
+2,001– 30,000gts	604 SDR	604 SDR	604 SDR	400 SDR	604 SDR		
+30,001– 70,000gts	453 SDR	453 SDR	453 SDR	300 SDR	453 SDR	125 SDR	
+ each gts> 70,000	302 SDR	302 SDR	302 SDR	200 SDR	302 SDR	83 SDR	

The limitation amounts, for claims other than those relating to passengers, are set out in art 6(1) which was amended by the 1996 Protocol and then further by the 2012 uplift. It distinguished between personal injury claims and property damage claims, with the limits for the former being significantly higher. **10.116**

'Distinct occasion'

Art 6(1) commences with the following expression: **10.117**

> 1. The limits of liability for claims other than those mentioned in Article 7, **arising on any distinct occasion**, shall be calculated as follows … (emphasis added).

This phrase has become a focus of attention in limitation cases as claimants seek to identify the 'concatenation' of errors that lead to a particular casualty, and thereby to increase the size of the limitation fund.[169]

Early judicial consideration of the phrase is found in *The Schwan*,[170] where the master manoeuvred her in a river so that she collided with two different vessels. Each collision was avoidable had the master not acted negligently and the first collision was determined not to have been the cause of the second, despite the short time interval between the two. Lord Esher MR said that in such a case, the ship could not limit its liability to one fund but was liable to each of the two plaintiffs to the full extent of her statutory liability on the basis that, 'It is not the time which is the substantial thing; but whether both are the result of the same act of want of seamanship'.[171] **10.118**

The Federal Court of Australia gave detailed consideration to the phrase in *The APL Sydney*.[172] On13 December 2008 the *APL Sydney* was ordered to anchor in Port Phillip Bay to await the allocation of a berth before unloading in Melbourne. A gale was blowing and the ship dragged its anchor and ruptured a gas pipeline lying on the bottom of Port Phillip Bay, which was used to transport gas from a refinery on one side of the Bay to factories on the other side of the Bay. The factory owners brought claims in the Federal Court for their losses. The shipowner claimed its rights to limit and constituted a fund in the Federal Court. The claimants argued that there had in fact been four distinct occasions which had caused the loss and thus contended that the fund established was inadequate. The evidence was that the pipeline had stayed intact for 35 minutes and there were three subsequent manoeuvres of the ship using her engine that may have caused new loss or damage. After a trial lasting four weeks, during which the minutiae of the ship's movements and the master's actions were explored in detail, Rares J found that there were two distinct occasions that occurred in direct connection **10.119**

169 *Strongwise Ltd v Esso Australia Resources Ltd (the APL Sydney)* [2010] FCA 240, (2010) 185 FCR 149, [81].

170 [1892] P 419; see also *The Creadon* (1886) 5 Asp MC 585; *The Rajah* (1872) LR 3 A & E 539; *The Lucullite* (1929) 33 Lloyd's L Rep 186.

171 [1892] P 419, 438–439.

172 *Strongwise Ltd v Esso Australia Resources Ltd (the APL Sydney)* [2010] FCA 240, (2010) 185 FCR 149.

with the operation of the APL Sydney that gave rise to the claims for loss of or damage to property and consequential loss resulting therefrom within the meaning of Arts 2(1)(a) and 6(1) of the Convention. The first occasion comprised the events that preceded the actual occasion of the anchor fouling the pipeline (at 15:44 –15:45) when he found that the Master should have weighed anchor and sailed clear despite the contrary instructions of harbour control to await a pilot. The second comprised a chain of events leading to and immediately following the rupture of the pipeline (at 16:20 –16:21) after the windlass had failed, the pilot re-boarded, and the ship's engines were put ahead on the basis that the dragging anchor would be clear.[173] However, the anchor was not clear, with the result that the pipeline then ruptured.

Rares J framed the relevant test thus:

> Where a single act, neglect or default of a shipowner places him in such a relationship that, as a matter of common sense, it is a cause of loss or damage suffered by a third party, that third party will have a claim under Art 2 of the Convention. And, such a claim will be caused by an occurrence and, so, will arise on that distinct occasion for the purposes of Arts 6, 7, 9 and 11.
>
> But where a subsequent act, neglect or default of the same shipowner separately operates to cause different or separately identifiable loss or damage to the same third party, or to others, then a new claim or claims will arise on that later distinct occasion. The latter occasion is distinct because, first there is a new event (the separate act, neglect or default), secondly, there is new loss or damage; and thirdly, the new cause is, as a matter of common sense, not a necessary or inseparable consequence of the earlier act, neglect or default.[174]

10.120 *The APL Sydney* is an illustration of the complicated preliminary skirmishes in which parties may need to engage simply to establish the size of the fund available even before embarking upon a trial of the action—and this is despite the relative simplicity of the text of Art 6(1).[175] It is perhaps also noteworthy that a significant basis of the decision of Finkelstein J in an earlier interlocutory skirmish involving the same incident,[176] was said to be the need to avoid technical interpretation (in favour of a 'bona fide' interpretation) of Art 2. It is respectfully submitted that the technicality which attends the judgment of Rares J, although somewhat in line with the view expressed above regarding the proper interpretation of Art 2, may suffer from the vice which concerned Finkelstein J, in that in this case, the language of Art 6 has been strained far beyond its intended meaning.

---

[173] Ibid [361].

[174] Ibid [78]–[79]. For the reasons for judgment for the final order constituting the two limitation funds see *Strongwise Ltd v Esso Australia Resources Ltd (The APL Sydney)(No 2)* [2010] FCA 575, (2010) 185 FCR 237.

[175] As to whether a claimant is required to plead that the damage arose on multiple distinct occasions, and subsequent disclosure issues, see *Commonwealth of Australia v Shenzhen Energy Transport Co Ltd (The Shen Neng 1)* [2015] FCAFC 116.

[176] *Qenos Pty Ltd v The Ship APL Sydney* (2009) 187 FCR 282; above para 10.69.

Art 6(2) is known as the 'spill-over' provision, the effect of which is to allow personal injury claimants access both to the loss of life and personal injury fund available under art 6(1)(a) and, where that fund is insufficient to pay those claims in full, to the property fund available under art 6(1)(b) even when there are no property claims; if there are property claims, then the unpaid balance of personal injury claims ranks rateably with them. **10.121**

The tonnage figure referred to in the Convention is the gross tonnage, ascertained in accordance with Annex 1 of the *International Convention on Tonnage Measurement of Ships*.[177] **10.122**

Measurement of ships

For States who are members of the International Monetary Fund, the unit of account by reference to which the limitation amount is calculated is the Special Drawing Right (SDR). The monetary liability is determined on the basis of the units of account established or calculated at the relevant liability level and converted into SDR. The value of 1 SDR is calculated daily from the market values of a basket of major currencies and is used to fix the comparative values of other national currencies.[178] Use of the SDR as the unit of account alleviates the previous problem of divergence in national exchange rates. Under the 1957 Convention, the limitation amount was calculated in Poincaré francs, which in turn were converted into the local currency. Under the 1976 Convention, there is a different non-SDR formula for those States who are not members of the IMF which allows conversion into gold and then into the national currency. The underlying requirement is to approximate the real value to the SDR formula. **10.123**

In towage cases, the relevant vessel for limitation purposes will be the one(s) held to have been at fault,[179] generally (although not invariably) the tug, even where tug and tow are in the same ownership.[180] This is so even where the towage is conducted on BIMCO Towhire or Towcon terms; clause 18 of both forms provides for a 'knock-for-knock' arrangement which, regardless of where fault actually lies, shifts any liability to a third party to the owners of the tug in cases where the loss to the third party is caused by reason of contact with the tug, and to the owners of the tow in cases where the loss to the third party is caused by reason of contact with the tow. In *Smit International (Deutschland) GmbH v Joseph Mobius Bau-Gesellschaft GmbH & Co (The Janus)*,[181] the claimant's tug was towing the defendant's barge when the barge struck a vessel owned by a **10.124**

[177] 23 June 1969, 1291 UNTS entered into force on 18 July 1982.

[178] The values are published on the IMF's website at <http://www.imf.org>.

[179] *The Bramley Moore* [1964] P 200, [1963] 2 Lloyd's Rep 429; a decision under the 1958 Convention. The position before 1958 was—as Lord Denning MR observed at 218, 'based on no logical ground'—different where tug and tow were in the same ownership; in those cases the limit was to be found by reference to the tonnage of the two: *The Ran* [1922] P 80.

[180] *London Dredging Co v Greater London Council (The Sir Joseph Rawlinson)* [1973] QB 285, [1972] 3 All ER 590, [1972] 2 Lloyd's Rep 437.

[181] *The Janus* [2001] 2 All ER (Comm) 265.

third party, allegedly due to the negligence of the master of the tug. Morison J rejected an argument that because of the terms of clause 18 the tow rather than the tug should be treated as the ship by reference to which liability should be limited. His decision has been criticized,[182] but it is respectfully submitted that it is correct.

10.125 Where a salvor is seeking to limit, the fund should be calculated by reference to the tonnage of the vessel in relation to which causative negligence is proved. Where the negligent salvor is 'not operating from any ship' or is 'operating solely on the ship to, or in respect of which he is rendering salvage services', the limit of his liability will be calculated on the basis of a deemed tonnage of 1500 tons.[183] Whilst this may be simple enough to operate in a straightforward salvage operation, as Brice points out,[184] larger-scale and more complex operations are likely to present particular challenges in the context of limitation of liability. It is respectfully submitted that the thrust of his conclusion[185] is correct, ie, that the proper approach— consistent with that in towage cases—is to consider each of the salvage units at fault; if they are several, then the limitation fund will be increased by the 'fund' of each such unit.

10.126 The limits of liability relating to hovercraft are contained in art 6 of the Hovercraft (Civil Liability) Order 1986.[186]

10.127 The limit in relation to passenger claims is contained in art 7, which (as noted above)[187] is of very limited application, as it does not apply to seagoing ships. The limit under art 7 is not based on the tonnage of the ship but rather on the number of passengers which the ship is certified to carry and is calculated as:

> 175,000SDR × the number of passengers which the ship is authorized to carry according to her certificate.[188]

---

[182] D Malet, 'Maritime Claims Limitation & Towage' [2002] LMCLQ 177.

[183] Sch 7 pt I art 6(3); art 6(4) of the Convention text.

[184] *Brice on Maritime Law of Salvage* (5th edn, 2012), §7-112.

[185] Ibid §7-115.

[186] As amended by the Hovercraft (Convention on Liability for Maritime Claims (Amendment)) Order 1998, those limits are:

(1) In respect of claims for loss of life or personal injury:
   - (i) £852,085 for craft with a maximum operational weight not exceeding 8,000kgs;
   - (ii) £1,659,605 for craft with a maximum operational weight between 8,001kgs and 13,000kgs;
   - (iii) £25.55 for each additional kg in excess of 13,000kgs

(2) In respect of all other claims:
   - (i) £357,360 for craft with a maximum operational weight not exceeding 8,000kgs
   - (ii) £698,270 for craft with a maximum operational weight between 8,001kgs and 13,000kgs
   - (iii) £10.75 for each additional kg in excess of 13,000kgs.

[187] Para 10.25.

[188] With no global limit; prior to the 1996 Protocol, claims under art 7 were subject to a maximum global limit of 25,000,000 SDR.

Cross claims

The treatment of cross claims is addressed in art 5 of the Convention: **10.128**

> Where a person entitled to limitation of liability under the rules of this Convention has a claim against the claimant arising out of the same occurrence, their respective claims shall be set off against each other and the provisions of this Convention shall only apply to the balance, if any.

Simple though it may appear, this provision is not without its difficulties. Although its operation is straightforward enough, for example, in the case of cross claims between the owners of colliding ships, what of the case where one of the claims falls outside the terms of the Convention, but the other falls within it? The net effect of applying the letter of the article, ie, setting the claims off against each other in full before applying the terms of the Convention, would be to deprive the party with the claim within the Convention of some or all of his entitlement to limit. Consider, for example, a claim for salvage (clearly outside the terms of the Convention: art 3(a)) worth USD100,000, and a USD250,000 cross claim for damage said to have been caused by negligence on the salvor's part,[189] in respect of which the salvor would (absent art 5) be able to limit his liability to USD50,000. If the claims were netted off without regard to limitation, the salvor will lose his remuneration *and* have to pay USD50,000 to the aggrieved property owner; if limitation were taken into account first, however, he would at least recover (on these figures) half his remuneration. **10.129**

It is submitted once again that Brice[190] is correct that the solution is to be found in the stipulation in art 5 itself that limitation will be applied 'to the balance'. Limitation could only be applied 'to the balance' if 'the balance' was a claim in respect of which limitation is available under the terms of the Convention. If the numbers set out in the example above were reversed, such that the salvor's award exceeded that amount of the property owner's (unlimited) counterclaim, there could be no question that the balance of that claim could be the subject of limitation—yet that is precisely what art 5 appears to prescribe. The necessary implication, therefore, is that art 5 operates only where both (or all) the claims in question are within art 2 of the Convention. **10.130**

Australia

Australia is a party to the 1996 Protocol and so the limits of liability are the same as in the United Kingdom. Legislation has been enacted to provide for the 2012 uplift.[191] **10.131**

The calculation of tonnage is made in accordance with Annex 1 to the International Convention on Tonnage Measurement of Ships 1969, which entered into force in **10.132**

189 Such situations are complex enough, even without the intrusion of questions of limitation: see generally *Brice on Maritime Law of Salvage* (5th edn, 2012) §§7-118 and following.

190 Ibid §7-133.

191 Limitation of Liability for Maritime Claims Amendment Act 2015 (Cth), sch 1.

Australia on 21 August 1982. It is given legislative effect by Marine Order 19 (Tonnage measurement) 2014, made under ss 153 and 340 of the Navigation Act 2012.

Canada

10.133 Although not a party to the 1976 Convention, Canada has enacted legislation which provides for the same level of limitation of liability as provided for in the 1996 Protocol and 2012 uplift except in relation to vessels of less than 300 gross tonnes. Vessels of less than 300 gross tonnes have a liability limit for passengers, or persons carried on board otherwise than as passengers, equal to the greater of 2,000,000 SDRs or 175,000 SDRs multiplied by the number of passengers the ship is authorized to carry (or the number of persons on board if no authorization is required under the Canadian Shipping Act 2001).[192] A limit of C$1 million exists in relation to other personal injury or death claims and C$500,000 in relation to all other claims.

10.134 In a case involving a collision between a moored vessel and a dumb barge under tow by a flotilla of four tugs, the Supreme Court of Canada held that, for the purpose of determining the appropriate unit of limitation, only the tonnage of the 'wrongdoing mass', in that case the lead tug from which the tugmaster negligently directed the flotilla, was to be taken into account, rather than the aggregate tonnage of both tugs belonging to the party seeking to limit.[193] In *Bayside Towing v Canadian Pacific Railway Co*,[194] a loaded dumb barge towed by a tug collided with a bridge causing C$5 million worth of damage. The tonnage of the tug produced a limitation fund of C$500,000. The tug and the barge were in separate ownership. It was argued that, although the real ownership was separate, the tug could also be said to be the 'shipowner' for the tow since the tug owners were 'in possession of' the barge during the tow and thus the combined tonnage should be used to determine the amount of the fund. Gibson J rejected this argument and applied the decision in *The Rhone*[195] in calculating liability on the basis of the tug (as the wrongdoing mass) alone. Thus in Canada, as in England, the flotilla principle, whereby aggregate tonnage is used to calculate the limitation fund, applies only when there is commonality both of ownership *and* of causative negligence.

Hong Kong

10.135 Hong Kong has adopted the 1996 Protocol but as at 1 September 2015, has not applied the 2012 uplift limit. Although s 28 of the Merchant Shipping (Limitation of Shipowners Liability) Ordinance 1997 now provides that the Chief Executive in

[192] Maritime Liability Act, SC 2001, c 6, s 28.

[193] *The Rhone v The Peter A B Widener* [1993] 1 SCR 497, (1993) 101 DLR (4th) 188, (1993) 58 FTR 239, [1993] 1 Lloyd's Rep 600.

[194] *Bayside Towing v Canadian Pacific Railway Co* [2001] 2 FC 258 (TD), (2000) 197 FTR 251.

[195] *The Rhone v The Peter A B Widener* [1993] 1 SCR 497, (1993) 101 DLR (4th) 188, (1993) 58 FTR 239, [1993] 1 Lloyd's Rep 600.

Council may by order implement any protocol to the 1976 Convention which may apply to Hong Kong from time to time, no indication has been given of whether the power will be exercised. In the implementation of the 1996 Protocol, Hong Kong removed the special provision for the limitation amounts which applied to ships with a tonnage of less than 300 tons.[196]

The tonnage of a ship is required to be calculated in accordance with the order made by the Chief Executive, and such order must, so far as is practicable, give effect to the regulations in Annex 1 of the International Convention on Tonnage Measurement of Ships 1969.[197] **10.136**

As a result of the implementation of the 1996 Protocol, an unusual circumstance arises where there is a limitation amount of 46,666 SDRs per passenger under the Athens Convention, and 175,000 SDRs per passenger under the 1996 Protocol. Unlike the position in the United Kingdom, discussed above at para 10.25, no clear provision has been made to separate out how and which limitation regime applies. Section 23 of the Merchant Shipping (Limitation of Shipowners Liability) Ordinance 1997, situated in Part III (which deals with the LLMC), expressly provides that 'nothing in this Part relieves a person of any liability imposed on him under Part II'. Section 11, situated in Part II (which deals with the Athens Convention), provides that 'nothing in this Part affects the operation of Part III'. **10.137**

New Zealand

New Zealand has adopted the 1996 Protocol and the 2012 uplift so its limitation amounts accord with those in Australia, no special provision for ships under 300 tons having been made since the 1996 Protocol was adopted.[198] **10.138**

New Zealand implements the International Convention on Tonnage Measurement of Ships 1969 by force of the Maritime Rules Part 48: Tonnage Measurement.[199] Where the tonnage of a ship is unable to be ascertained to calculate the limitation fund, the Director of Maritime New Zealand, New Zealand's maritime regulator, may receive a direction from the court to estimate the tonnage of the ship, and that estimate is taken to be the gross tonnage.[200] **10.139**

---

196 Merchant Shipping (Limitation of Shipowners Liability) (Amendment) Ordinance 2005, s 14.

197 The Merchant Shipping (Liability of Shipowners and Others) (Calculation of Tonnage) (Hong Kong) Order (Chapter 434A), 1987 provides for tonnage to be calculated in accordance with the International Convention on Tonnage Measurement of Ships. Although this order was made under the now repealed Merchant Shipping Act 1979 (Hong Kong) Order 1980, s 29(2) of the Merchant Shipping (Limitation of Shipowners Liability) Ordinance 1997 provides that it continues in force and is deemed to have been made by the Chief Executive under s 17(2) of that Ordinance.

198 Maritime Transport Act 1994, s 84A gives the 1976 Convention as amended by the 1996 Protocol the force of law in New Zealand. Section 87A permits the Governor-General to notify amended limits made in accordance with Art 8 of the 1996 Protocol. The 2012 uplift was notified by the Maritime Transport (Limitation of Liability for Maritime Claims) Order 2015 (LI 2015/111).

199 Maritime Transport Act 1994, s 36 permits the Minister to make rules in relation to tonnage.

200 Maritime Transport Act 1994, s 87(5).

Singapore

10.140 Singapore has not adopted the 1996 Protocol but has made special provision for ships with a tonnage of less than 300 tons.[201] It also modifies the amounts in respect of 'harbour craft' and provides that the aggregate amounts in art 6(1) are replaced by the sum insured under compulsory insurance against third party risks.[202]

10.141 For the purposes of the limitation fund, the tonnage of a ship is determined in accordance with the provisions in the Merchant Shipping (Tonnage) Regulations,[203] which implement the International Convention on Tonnage Measurement of Ships 1969.[204]

South Africa

10.142 The 1997 amendment to s 261 of the 1951 Act introduced Special Drawing Rights for expressing the relevant limitation amounts. Where claims are brought in respect of loss of life or personal injury, the aggregate amount for which the owner is liable is 206.67 SDR per ton.[205] Claims in respect of loss or damage to property are limited to 66.67 SDR per ton.[206] Where claims are brought for both loss of life or personal injury and for damage to property, the aggregate amount for which the owner is liable is 206.67 SDR per ton but the former have priority to the extent of an aggregate amount of 140 SDR per ton. In relation to the balance of the fund, the unsatisfied portion of the loss of life or personal injury claims rank *pari passu* with the property claims.[207]

10.143 The International Convention on Tonnage Measurement of Ships 1969 was given the force of law in s 356*bis* of the 1951 Act and is used to calculate a ship's gross register tonnage for the purpose of limitation of liability.[208] However, calculation of a ship's gross tonnage for the purposes of the limitation amount under South African law will yield a lower tonnage. This is because s 262(2) of the 1951 Act excludes from such tonnage 'any space occupied by seamen or apprentice-officers and appropriated to their use which has been certified by a surveyor to comply in all respects with the requirements of this Act'.

Reservations

10.144 Difficulties can arise in practice from the reservation provisions in the Convention. Art 15(1) provides that the 1976 Convention applies whenever a person entitled

[201] Merchant Shipping Act 1995, s 137(1).
[202] Ibid. 'Harbour craft' are those craft licensed as such under the Maritime and Port Authority of Singapore Act (Cap 170A).
[203] Reg 12, 1990 edn amended by Nos S333/94, S44/96 and S63/96.
[204] Merchant Shipping Act 1995, s 137(2).
[205] Merchant Shipping Act 57 of 1951, s 261(1)(a).
[206] Merchant Shipping Act 57 of 1951, s 261(1)(b).
[207] Merchant Shipping Act 57 of 1951, s 261(1)(c).
[208] Although note that the power to make a notification or declaration to give effect to the International Convention on Tonnage Measurement of Ships 1969 is now contained in s 356(2) of the 1951 Act.

to limit liability seeks to do so before the court of a State which is party to the Convention, or seeks the release of a ship or other property from arrest or the discharge of security within the jurisdiction of a State party. However, art 15(1) further provides that a State party is entitled by its domestic legislation to exclude either wholly or partially from the application of the Convention any person who would otherwise be entitled to limitation if such person is not habitually resident or does not have its principal place of business in a State party at the time when the right to limit is invoked. Similarly, any State party may exclude a ship if it does not fly the flag of a State party at the time when the right to limit is invoked or its release from arrest is sought. The United Kingdom has not made such a reservation.

Art 15(2) entitles a State party to make specific regulation in its national law in relation to the limit of liability of non-seagoing ships. Thus, a State party may regulate by specific provisions of national law the system of limitation of liability to apply to vessels which are according to the law of that State intended for navigation on inland waterways. In the United Kingdom, this right has been exercised and limitation is available to non-seagoing ships. **10.145**

Art 15(2) also permits a State party to regulate by national law the system of limitation to be applied to vessels of less than 300 tons. Art 6 provides that there is a single minimum limitation fund for all ships not exceeding 2,000 tons,[209] ie, the fund is the same for ships of ten tons as it is for ones of 2,000 tons. The reservation in art 15(2) enables a party to make special provisions in relation to vessels of less than 300 tons. If it does, the fund available for compensation may be substantially below the levels specified in art 6. These provisions are of no relevance to passenger claims since, by virtue of art 7, limitation in respect of this type of claim is not regulated by the tonnage of the ship but is calculated by reference to the number of passengers which the ship is certified to carry. In the United Kingdom, there is a minimum level of limitation for ships of less than 300 tons in respect of all claims covered by art 6.[210] **10.146**

Art 15(3) allows a State party to make specific national regulations in relation to the right of limitation where no nationals of other States are involved. In other words, it would be possible for a State to have its own limitation regime in respect of purely domestic accidents involving only nationals of that State. The United Kingdom has not exercised this right and so the 1976 Convention applies regardless of the nationality of those involved. **10.147**

Art 15(4) provides that a party shall not apply the Convention to ships constructed for or adapted to and engaged in drilling, when that State has by its national legislation established a higher limit of liability than that set out in the 1976 Convention **10.148**

---

209 Per amendment via the 1996 Protocol.

210 MSA 1995, sch 7, part II, art 5(1).

or when the State is party to an international convention regulating liability in respect of such ships. No reservation has been made by the United Kingdom in this respect, and it follows that the provisions of the 1976 Convention apply to drilling ships provided they satisfy the definition of 'ship'.

10.149 Art 15(5) specifies that the Convention will not apply to air cushion vessels or floating platforms constructed for the purpose of exploring or exploiting the natural resources of the seabed or the subsoil. Although not framed as such, it has been treated as optional by the United Kingdom and does not appear in the Act. The application of the 1976 Convention to hovercraft is governed by the Hovercraft (Civil Liability) Order 1986.[211]

D. Jurisdiction to Bring a Limitation Claim

Introduction

10.150 As noted in para 10.06 above, now that the limits provided for in the Convention are for practical purposes unbreakable, rather more attention is now paid than perhaps once it was to whether the claim is one in respect of which limitation can be invoked at all. That factor, coupled with the much higher limits available under the 1996 Protocol, which is in force in the United Kingdom and in fifty-one other countries, has also resulted in close attention being paid to questions of the Court's jurisdiction to entertain limitation proceedings at all.

10.151 The Convention does not on its face purport to deal with jurisdiction. However, two of its provisions in particular (arts 10 and 11) have been widely understood to impact on this issue, although precisely what that impact might be remains a matter of debate. The focus of that debate is whether those provisions are to be construed narrowly, so as to prevent a limitation action other than by way of response to proceedings brought to enforce a claim subject to limitation, or more widely, such that the Court's jurisdiction is unaffected by them. The latter construction is presently in the ascendancy, at any rate in the English courts.[212]

Invoking the right to limit

10.152 It is not necessary to admit liability before invoking the right to limit.[213]

---

[211] Liability itself in relation to hovercraft is divided between air-carriage and sea-carriage regimes: see *Halsbury's Laws, Shipping & Navigation*, §331.

[212] *The Western Regent* [2005] EWCA Civ 985, [2005] 2 Lloyd's Rep 359, rejecting the argument that the scheme of the Convention was that limitation should be invoked responsively—and that art 10.3 indicated and art 11.1 provided as much. Permission to appeal was granted by the House of Lords in this case, but it settled before argument was heard.

[213] *Bouygues Offshore SA v Caspian Shipping Co (Nos 1, 3, 4 and 5)* [1998] 2 Lloyd's Rep 461.

Under the 1976 Convention, the right to limit liability can be invoked either without constituting a limitation fund under art 10, or after constituting such a fund under art 11. The Convention distinguishes between those two methods of invoking limitation and treats them differently. As there is no general jurisdiction provision in the Convention stating where the right of limitation must be invoked, a party may seek to limit its liability in any Contracting State which has personal jurisdiction over the defendant.[214] **10.153**

Pursuant to art 10(1), limitation may be invoked without constitution of a fund, and jurisdiction to entertain a claim for a decree limiting liability under the MSA does not depend upon the commencement of legal or arbitral proceedings against the party seeking to limit liability.[215] Art 10(1) provides: **10.154**

> Limitation of liability may be invoked notwithstanding that a limitation fund as mentioned in article 11 has not been constituted. However, a State party may provide in its national law that, where an action is brought in its courts to enforce a claim subject to limitation, a person liable may only invoke the right to limit liability if a limitation fund has been constituted in accordance with the provisions of this convention or is constituted when the right to limit is invoked.

The underlined sentence does not appear in sch 7 to the MSA as the United Kingdom has not adopted such a provision in its national law. It is clear from that sentence, however, that the Convention contemplates that limitation may be invoked even where no action has been brought by a claimant to enforce a claim subject to limitation.[216] In *Caspian Basin v Bouygues (No 4)*,[217] Rix J, as he then was, said:

> There can be nothing surprising or inappropriate about a limitation action being commenced in the same forum as a claimant's action to establish liability; but equally there is nothing unusual about a limitation action taking place in a different forum from that in which liability is being litigated.[218]

The correctness of this was unsuccessfully challenged in the Court of Appeal for Gibraltar, which was expressly invited not to follow the reasoning in the English Court of Appeal supporting this position.[219] The basis for the alternate construction

[214] *The Western Regent* [2005] EWCA Civ 985, [2005] 2 Lloyd's Rep 359, 364, [16]; *Merlin Unternehmensverwaltung GMVH v Zelikov* [2007–09] Gib LR 154. Note that within the EU/EFTA, any court with jurisdiction over liability has jurisdiction over limitation, so that an owner may limit in the courts of his domicile, even absent liability proceedings. *Schlosser Report*, para 128. See art 9 of the 'recast' Brussels I Regulation (1215/2012), art 7 of the Brussel I Regulation (44/2001) and Lugano II Convention, and art 6a of the Brussels/Lugano I Conventions.

[215] *The Western Regent* [2005] EWCA Civ 985, [2005] 2 Lloyd's Rep 359; *The Denise* [2004] EWHC 3305 (Admlty), [2005] 2 All ER 47.

[216] *The Western Regent* [2005] EWCA Civ 985, [2005] 2 Lloyd's Rep 359, 364, [17].

[217] *Caspian Basin v Bouygues* (No 4) [1997] 2 Lloyd's Rep 507, 525.

[218] A passage cited with approval by the Court of Appeal in *The Western Regent* [2005] EWCA Civ 985, [2005] 2 Lloyd's Rep 359, 368, [40].

[219] *Merlin Unternehmensverwaltung GmbH v Zelikov* [2007–09] Gib LR 154. A further attempt in the Isle of Man met with no greater success: *Dominator Ltd v Gilberson SL*, 1 May 2009, digested in the Manx Law Newsletter Issue 1, October–December 2008.

was said to lie in the need for Art 10.1 to be construed responsively, having regard to Arts 10.3 and 11.[220] The Court followed the position in England, holding that the construction of Art 10.1 was clear, particularly where the option not to include the second sentence in national law had been taken up, and that art 11 could not cut down the otherwise clear meaning.[221]

10.155 It follows that there is nothing in the Convention or in the MSA to require a person who wishes to limit his liability to wait until a claimant has started proceedings before invoking his right to limit.[222] That suggests in turn that the regime under art 10 (in permitting limitation to be invoked in the absence of liability proceedings) may differ from that under art 11, if Colman J's understanding of that article in *The ICL Vikraman* is correct—namely that a limitation fund can only be constituted in a jurisdiction in which liability proceedings have been commenced.[223] However, it is submitted that there is no difference, for the reason that the common assumption in *The ICL Vikraman*, that art 11.1 restricts the constitution of a fund to jurisdictions in which liability claims have been brought, was misplaced: art 11.1 is by its terms permissive and does not purport to permit a party claiming a right to limit to bring his claim *only* in a jurisdiction in which he has been sued.

The location of limitation proceedings

10.156 Art 11 confers a right on a person invoking limitation to constitute a fund but does not require that a fund in fact be so constituted. It provides:

> Any person alleged to be liable may constitute a fund with the Court or other competent authority in any State Party in which legal proceedings are instituted in respect of claims subject to limitation. The fund shall be constituted in the sum of such of the amounts set out in arts 6 and 7 as are applicable to claims for which that person may be liable, together with interest thereon from the date of the occurrence giving rise to the liability until the date of the constitution of the fund. Any fund thus constituted shall be available only for the payment of claims in respect of which limitation of liability can be invoked.

10.157 In deciding that limitation proceedings could be commenced under art 10 even in the absence of liability proceedings in the same jurisdiction, the Court of Appeal in *The Western Regent* expressly left open the issue whether art 11 applies only to jurisdictions in which legal proceedings have already been instituted by a claimant, or whether it includes those in which limitation proceedings have been commenced; in other words, whether a party seeking the right to limit must commence

---

[220] This argument had been raised and rejected rejected in *The Western Regent* [2005] EWCA Civ 985, [2005] 2 Lloyd's Rep 359.

[221] *Merlin Unternehmensverwaltung GmbH v Zelikov* [2007–09] Gib LR 154, 164.

[222] *The Western Regent* [2005] EWCA Civ 985, [2005] 2 Lloyd's Rep 359.

[223] *ICL Shipping Ltd v Chin Tai Steel Enterprise Co Ltd ('The ICL Vikraman')* [2003] EWHC 2320 (Comm), [2004] 1 WLR 2254, 2266, [2004] 1 All ER (Comm) 246, 251, [2004] 1 Lloyd's Rep 21, 30, [46]. This point was left open by the Court of Appeal in *The Western Regent*, 364–365, [20]. See further below, para 10.157.

a limitation action and then constitute his fund in the same jurisdiction.[224] On the one hand, it is arguably stretching the natural meaning of the language of art 11 to include limitation proceedings within the phrase 'legal proceedings ... in respect of claims subject to limitation', particularly if in fact no claims have yet been brought against the party claiming the right to limit; on the other:

(1) that expression differs from and is wider than the expression used in Article 10,[225] 'action ... to enforce a claim subject to limitation', and the wider language used in art 11 is apt to include limitation proceedings; and
(2) there is nothing in art 11 which stipulates that a fund can *only* be constituted in such a jurisdiction.

It is submitted that it would be a surprising result if a party could commence limitation proceedings in a jurisdiction but not constitute a fund there.[226] Thus if the Court of Appeal's conclusion in *The Western Regent* is correct—and it is respectfully submitted that it is—then this consideration ought to tip the balance in favour of the broader construction of art 11. That was not the view of Colman J in *The ICL Vikraman*,[227] who at para 49 expressed the view that:

> Article 11 ties the entitlement to constitute a limitation fund to the commencement of legal proceedings in order to provide certainty as to the venue of the fund, rather than leaving it to the shipowner to constitute the fund in a jurisdiction chosen by him. He is to be confined to a state party in which such proceedings have already been commenced.[228]

However, as Clarke LJ pointed out at paras 28–29 of his judgment in *The Western Regent,* the broader construction of art 11 was not contended for in *The ICL Vikraman* (see the account of the arguments advanced at paras 18–42 of Colman J's judgment), in which the issue was whether an arbitration amounted to 'legal proceedings' for the purposes of art 11(1) (which Colman J answered in the affirmative). That said, Colman J's view may derive some support from the decision of the Dutch Supreme Court in *The Sherbro,*[229] in which it was held that the appointment of a court expert was a 'legal proceeding'—without which it appears to have been of the view that a fund could not have been constituted under art 11.

---

224 *The Western Regent* [2005] EWCA Civ 985, [2005] 2 Lloyd's Rep 359, 364–365.

225 In the sentence omitted from sch 7 to the MSA.

226 Although it is fair to say that that argument can work equally well in reverse, in support of a narrow construction of both arts 10 and 11.

227 *The ICL Vikraman.* [2003] EWHC 2320 (Comm), [2004] 1 WLR 2254, [2004] 1 All ER (Comm) 246, [2004] 1 Lloyd's Rep 21. See also to similar effect at 2265–2266, 258, 30, [44]–[46].

228 Note, however, that Colman J appears to have taken the view that it would be possible to commence limitation proceedings in the absence of the constitution of a fund (presumably under art 10): see para 60 of his judgment where, contemplating the issue of limitation proceedings, he remarked: 'Indeed, if a limitation fund has not yet been constituted at the time of issue of the limitation claim form, none of the defendants may yet have launched proceedings in this country.'

229 This 1996 decision on the 1976 Convention (*SCAC Delmas Vieljeux v The Dutch State*, NJ 1998, 489) is not, as suggested at [2004] 1 WLR 2255, reported at (1883) 5 Asp MCL (*sic*) 88.

Lis pendens

10.158 The existence of proceedings in another jurisdiction is relevant in two procedural settings: (i) where the Court is considering an anti-suit injunction (which by definition can arise only in cases falling outside the ambit of the Brussels I Regulations[230] or the Brussels and Lugano Conventions), and (ii) where an application is made to stay proceedings under arts 29 or 30 of the 'recast' Brussels I Regulation (1215/2012) (arts 27 or 28 of the Brussels I Regulation 44/2001 and the Lugano II Convention; arts 21 and 22 of the Brussels and Lugano Conventions).

10.159 The approach of the courts in the former situation, born of the procedural nature of the right to limit, is in general one of tolerance towards the prosecution of liability proceedings in other jurisdictions in which issues of limitation will also be decided, irrespective of whether the applicable limitation regime in the foreign jurisdiction is the same as that applicable here.[231] In *The Western Regent*, Clarke LJ in refusing the grant of an anti-suit injunction was clear that '... the English court should leave the court in Texas to decide what effect to give to the decree granted in this action'.[232]

10.160 For the purposes of the European jurisdiction regimes, a limitation action does not involve the same *cause et objet* as liability proceedings; however, the two sets of proceedings may—depending on the facts—be 'related actions' within the meaning of art 30 of the 'recast' Brussels I Regulation (1215/2012) (art 28 of 44/2001 and the Lugano II Convention; art 22 of the Brussels and Lugano I Conventions).[233]

E. Limitation Procedure

The distinction between limitation as a defence and as a decree

10.161 A distinction must be made between invoking limitation as a right, in order to obtain a general decree of limitation, binding on all the world, and its invocation as a defence or counterclaim for a restricted decree, in which case only the parties to those proceedings will be bound.[234] The expectation is that a general decree will be sought only in separate, free-standing proceedings, which is why a counterclaim for a general decree of limitation may only be made with the permission of the

[230] Council Regulation (EC) No 44/2001 and EU Regulation 1215/2012 (the 'recast' Brussels I Regulation).

[231] *Bouygues Offshore SA v Caspian Shipping Co (Nos 1, 3, 4 and 5)* [1998] 2 Lloyd's Rep 461; *The Western Regent* [2005] EWCA Civ 985, [2005] 2 Lloyd's Rep 359.

[232] *The Western Regent* [2005] EWCA Civ 985 [52], [2005] 2 Lloyd's Rep 359, 370, [52].

[233] *The Happy Fellow* [1997] 1 Lloyd's Rep 130; *Maersk Olie & Gas A/S v Firma M de Haan and W de Boer* (Case C-39/02), [2005] 1 Lloyd's Rep 210 ECJ. In *The Happy Fellow*, art 22 did apply; but it was not applicable in the *Maersk* case.

[234] Note in this connection CPR 61.11(22) and PD61 §§10.5, 10. 7, and 10.18.

Court.[235] It is therefore used as a counterclaim principally where there will be a single (major) claimant against the party seeking to limit.

Commencement of a claim

A limitation claim must be commenced in the Admiralty Court[236] by the issue of a limitation claim form.[237] PD61 §10.1 provides that the claim form must be in form ADM15, accompanied by a declaration setting out the facts on which the claimant relies, stating the names and addresses (if known) of all persons who, to the knowledge of the claimant, have claims against him in respect of the occurrence to which the claim relates (other than named defendants) and verified by a statement of truth; the claimant and at least one defendant must be named in the claim form but all other defendants may be described.[238] **10.162**

Service of the claim form

The claim form must be served on all named defendants and any other defendant who requests service, and may be served on any other defendant.[239] **10.163**

CPR 61.11(5) provides that the claim form may not be served out of the jurisdiction unless: **10.164**

(1) the claim falls within s 22(2)(a),(b), or (c) of the Senior Courts Act (SCA) 1981 (in other words, a collision claim involving a defendant whose habitual residence or place of business is in England or Wales, or where the cause of action arose in England or Wales, or where an action arising out of the same incident or series of incidents is proceeding in the court or has been heard and determined by the court);
(2) the defendant has submitted to or agreed to submit to the jurisdiction of the court; or
(3) the Admiralty Court has jurisdiction over the claim under any applicable Convention; and

the court grants permission in accordance with s IV of Part 6.

In *The ICL Vikraman*,[240] Colman J held that the 1976 Convention was an 'applicable Convention' for the purposes of CPR 61.11(5)(c), that the institution of 'legal proceedings' within the jurisdiction entitled the shipowners to constitute a limitation fund in the UK under art 11, and that once a limitation fund had been so constituted, **10.165**

235 CPR 61.11(22)(b).
236 CPR 61.2(1)(c).
237 CPR 61.11(2).
238 CPR 61.11(3).
239 CPR 61.11(4).
240 *The ICL Vikraman* [2003] EWHC 2320 (Comm), [2004] 1 WLR 2254, [2004] 1 All ER (Comm) 246, [2004] 1 Lloyd's Rep 21.

the court had jurisdiction to grant permission to serve the claim form out of the jurisdiction. There are, as Colman J recognized,[241] difficulties with CPR 61.11(5) and the requirement for permission for service out; those difficulties arise in cases where the court has jurisdiction under art 9 of the 'recast' Brussels I Regulation (1215/2012)[242] (art 7 of the Brussels I Regulation 44/2001 and the Lugano II Convention; art 6A of the Brussels and Lugano I Conventions).[243] That is because under CPR 6.33 no permission is required in such cases for service of the Claim Form out of the jurisdiction. Until this anomaly has been ironed out by the framers of the Rules, the safe course will be to seek permission, which ought to be granted 'on the nod'.

Acknowledgement of service

10.166 An acknowledgement of service is not required[244] unless a defendant wishes to dispute jurisdiction, or argue that the court should not exercise jurisdiction, in which case an acknowledgement of service[245] must be filed within fourteen days of service (or where the claim form is served out of the jurisdiction, within the time specified in rule 6.35).[246]

10.167 A defendant who files an acknowledgement of service under para (7)(b) will be treated as having accepted the court's jurisdiction unless he brings his Part 11 application within fourteen days after filing the acknowledgement of service.[247]

Defence or notice admitting right to limit

10.168 Alternatively, a defendant must file a defence or a notice admitting the right of the claimant to limit liability within twenty-eight days of service.[248] Failure to do so will mean that the claimant has to apply for a general decree of limitation under CPR 61.11(12).

Restricted limitation decree

10.169 Where one or more named defendants admit the right to limit, the claimant may apply for a restricted limitation decree[249] and the court will issue a

[241] Ibid 2271, 262–263, 33, [65].

[242] Which provides that a court with jurisdiction under the Regulation over liability actions also has jurisdiction over limitation actions.

[243] The same would apply, of course, to claims within sub-para (b), at any rate where the case is within the 'recast' Brussels I Regulation (1215/2012): art 25. Under the other European jurisdiction regimes, at least one of the parties must be domiciled in a Regulation or Convention State; in such cases, the Court will have jurisdiction under arts 23 and/or 24 of the Brussels I Regulation (44/2001) and the Lugano II Convention (arts 17 and/or 18 of the Brussels and Lugano I Conventions).

[244] CPR 61.11 (6).

[245] In Form ADM16B; PD61 §10.4.

[246] CPR 61.11 (7)(b).

[247] CPR 11(4)(a).

[248] CPR 61.11(7)(a).

[249] In Form ADM17.

decree[250] limiting liability only against those defendants.[251] A restricted limitation decree may also be obtained against any named defendant who fails to file a defence within the time specified for so doing.[252] It is not necessary to advertise a restricted limitation decree but a copy must be served on any defendant to whom it applies.[253]

General limitation decree

Where all the defendants upon whom the claim form has been served admit the claimant's right to limit liability, the claimant may apply to the Admiralty Registrar for a general limitation decree[254] and the court will issue a limitation decree.[255] **10.170**

Where at least one defendant upon whom the claim form has been served does not admit the claimant's right to limit, the claimant may still apply for a general limitation decree,[256] but in order to do so it must, within seven days of the date of the filing of the defence of the defendant last served or the expiry of the time for doing so, apply to the Registrar for a case management conference.[257] On such application, the Registrar may grant a general limitation decree, or alternatively order service of a defence or disclosure by the claimant or make any other appropriate case management directions.[258] **10.171**

Consequences of—and challenges to—the grant of a limitation decree

Once a limitation decree has been granted, the court may order that any proceedings in relation to any claim arising out of the occurrence be stayed, order the claimant to establish a limitation fund or make such other arrangements for the payment of claims against which liability is limited, or, if the decree is a restricted limitation decree, distribute the fund.[259] **10.172**

Advertisement

If the decree is a general limitation decree, the court will give directions as to the advertising of the decree and set a time within which notice of claims against the fund must be filed or application made to set aside the decree.[260] The claimant is required to advertise the decree as directed by the court and to file **10.173**

250 In Form ADM18.
251 CPR 61.11(9).
252 CPR 61.11(10)(a).
253 CPR 61.11(10)(b).
254 In Form ADM17A; PD61 §10.6.
255 CPR 61.11(11).
256 CPR 61.12; PD61 §10.7(2).
257 PD61 §10.7.
258 PD61 §10.8.
259 CPR 61.11(13)(a).
260 CPR 61.11(13)(b).

a declaration that the decree has been so advertised, together with copies of the advertisements.[261]

Claiming against the fund

10.174 Any defendant to a limitation claim who wishes to assert a claim must file and serve a statement of case containing the particulars of the defendant's claim on the limiting party and on all other defendants within the time period set in the decree.[262] If a defendant is unable to file and serve a statement of case in accordance with the rules, he must file a declaration verified by a statement of truth stating the reason for such inability.[263]

Challenging the decree

10.175 Any person other than a defendant upon whom the claim form has been served may apply to the court within the time fixed in the decree to have a general limitation decree set aside.[264] Such an application must be supported by a declaration stating that the applicant has a claim against the claimant arising out of the occurrence and setting out the grounds for contending that the claimant is not entitled to the decree, either in the amount of limitation or at all.[265]

10.176 No later than seven days after the time for filing claims or declarations (set out in the decree: CPR 61.11(15)) has expired, the Registrar will set a date for a case management conference.[266]

Manner of constitution of the limitation fund

10.177 The Convention does not require the constitution of a limitation fund in order to invoke limitation of liability unless such is required by national law;[267] there is no such requirement in the United Kingdom. A limitation fund may be established before or after a limitation claim has been started[268] and may be constituted by making a payment into court,[269] or by the provision of an 'acceptable' guarantee (even in the absence of legislation specifically providing for the constitution of a fund by guarantee).[270]

10.178 Where a limitation fund is established, it must be the sterling equivalent of the number of special drawing rights to which the claimant claims to be entitled to limit

261 CPR 61.11(14).
262 CPR 61.11(15); PD61 §10.15.
263 PD61 §10.17; and Form ADM21.
264 CPR 61.11(16).
265 CPR 61.11(17).
266 PD61 §10.17.
267 Art 10(1).
268 CPR 61.11(19).
269 CPR 61.11(18).
270 *Kairos Shipping Ltd v Enka & Co LLC (the 'Atlantik Confidence')* [2014] EWCA Civ 217, [2014] 1 WLR 3883, [2014] 1 All ER (Comm) 909, [2014] 1 Lloyd's Rep 586.

his liability together with interest from the date of the occurrence giving rise to the liability to the date of the payment into court.[271] A claimant who does not know the sterling equivalent of the required number of special drawing rights on the date of payment into court may calculate it on the basis of the latest available published sterling equivalent of a special drawing right as fixed by the International Monetary Fund.[272] Upon establishing the fund, the claimant must give written notice to every named defendant specifying the date of payment in, the amount paid in, the amount and rate of interest included, and the period to which it relates.[273]

Where the sterling equivalent on the date of payment into court differs from that used for calculating the amount of that payment into court, the claimant may make up any deficiency by making a further payment into court which, if made within fourteen days after the payment into court, will be treated, except for the rules relating to the accrual of interest on money paid into court, as if made on the date of the original payment into court.[274] Alternatively, the claimant may apply to the court for payment out of any excess amount, together with any accrued interest.[275] Such an application may be made without notice to any other party but must be supported by evidence proving the sterling equivalent of the appropriate number of special drawing rights on the date of payment into court.[276] Written notice must be given to every named defendant of any excess amount which has been paid out to the claimant under para 10.11(2)(b) of PD61.[277] **10.179**

If a limitation claim is not commenced within seventy-five days after the date of the establishment of the fund, the fund will lapse and all money in court, including interest, will be repaid to the person who paid it into court.[278] The lapsing of a fund does not prevent the establishment of a new fund.[279] **10.180**

Effect of constitution of the limitation fund

One advantage of constituting a limitation fund is that it may act as a bar to other actions. Art 13 provides as follows. **10.181**

(1) Where a limitation fund has been constituted in accordance with Art 11, any person having made a claim against the fund shall be barred from exercising any right in respect of such a claim against any other assets of a person by or on behalf of whom the fund has been constituted.

271 PD61 §10.10(2).
272 PD61 §10.11(1).
273 PD61 §10.13(1).
274 PD61 §10.11(2)(a).
275 PD61 §10.11(2)(b).
276 PD61 §10.12.
277 PD61 §10.13(2).
278 CPR 61.11(20).
279 PD61 §10.9.

(2) After a limitation fund has been constituted in accordance with Art 11, any ship or other property, belonging to a person on behalf of whom the fund has been constituted, which has been arrested or attached within the jurisdiction of a State Party for a claim which may be raised against the fund, or any security given, may be released by order of the court or other competent authority of such State. However, such release shall always be ordered if the limitation fund has been constituted:

(a) at the port where the occurrence took place, or, if it took place out of port, at the first port of call thereafter; or

(b) at the port of disembarkation in respect of claims for loss of life or personal injury; or

(c) at the port of discharge in respect of damage to cargo; or

(d) in the State where the arrest is made.

(3) The rules of paragraphs 1 and 2 shall apply only if the claimant may bring a claim against the limitation fund before the court administering that fund, and the fund is actually available and freely transferable in respect of that claim.

10.182 However, there is no scope for the operation of art 13 if the vessel was arrested and security provided in a State not party to the same Convention (in other words, in the case of the UK, the 1996 Protocol). In *The ICL Vikraman*,[280] the ship ICL Vikraman had been involved in a collision with another ship in the Malacca Strait and had sunk with loss of life. A sister-ship, the ICL Raja Mahendra, was arrested in Singapore, which then applied the 1957 Convention, by certain cargo interests. The shipowner's P&I Club issued to those cargo interests a letter of undertaking, which was not limited by reference to the 1976 Convention, as security for the cargo owners' claim, and in return the sister-ship was released from arrest. The cargo owners' claim was heard in arbitration in London, and the shipowner, having commenced his limitation action and constituted the limitation fund in London, sought an order pursuant to art 13(2) of the 1976 Convention for the release of the letter of undertaking. The cargo owners contended that, having arrested and obtained security in Singapore, they were not bound by the 1976 Convention, and the English Court had no jurisdiction over them in relation to limitation under the 1976 Convention. They therefore resisted the making of an order for the release of their security in order that they would be able to enforce the letter of undertaking without regard to the shipowner's right to limit under the 1976 Convention.

10.183 The cargo owners succeeded on this point. Colman J held that the geographical scope of the 1976 Convention, as provided for in art 15, was confined to State parties. Thus, it only applied where a shipowner sought to limit his liability before the court of a State party or where the release was sought of a ship arrested or of security given within a State party. He therefore had to consider where the letter of undertaking

[280] *The ICL Vikraman* [2003] EWHC 2320 (Comm), [2004] 1 WLR 2254, [2004] 1 All ER (Comm) 246, [2004] 1 Lloyd's Rep 21.

in the present case had been 'given'. On the facts, the letter of security had been provided by the P&I Club in order to obtain the release in Singapore of the arrested sister-ship, but the letter of undertaking had been sent by the P&I Club's London office to the agents of the cargo interests in Stanmore, Middlesex. Colman J held that a letter of undertaking was 'given' in the place where a court had immediate control over it, rejecting an argument that a letter of undertaking was 'given' where it was physically delivered. Thus, on the facts of the case before him, the place where the letter of undertaking was 'given' was Singapore because the letter stood in the place of the arrested vessel and the proceedings in Singapore had not been discontinued.

The cargo owners sought also to argue, in reliance upon the earlier Court of Appeal decision in *Polish Steam Ship Co v Atlantic Maritime Co*[281] and an *obiter dictum* of Sir John Knox in *Bouygues Offshore SA v Caspian Shipping Co (Nos 1, 3, 4 and 5)*[282] that the limitation fund was only 'actually available and freely transferable' once a decree of limitation was granted. Colman J rejected that argument, citing the decision of Sheen J in *The Bowbelle*[283] and holding[284] that: **10.184**

> The correct construction of article 13(3) is … that a limitation fund established in this country is actually available to a given claimant notwithstanding there being no limitation decree at the material time. That availability continues unless and until a claimant discharges the burden of proving that the shipowner is not entitled to the decree.

Distribution of the fund

No money paid into court for the establishment of a limitation fund can be paid out except pursuant to an order of the court.[285] Presumably this is so even in respect of a lapsed fund. **10.185**

Art 12(1) provides that the fund is to be distributed among the claimants in proportion to their established claims against the fund. Paragraph 9 of pt II of sch 7 to the MSA provides that no lien or other right in respect of any ship or property shall affect the proportions in which the fund is distributed among several claimants. **10.186**

Interest

Provision is made for the rate of interest to be awarded for the purposes of art 11(1) of the 1976 Convention to be one per cent more than the base rate quoted by the Bank of England.[286] **10.187**

---

[281] *Polish Steam Ship Co v Atlantic Maritime Co* [1985] 1 QB 41, [1984] 2 Lloyd's Rep 37.

[282] *Bouygues Offshore SA v Caspian Shipping Co (Nos 1, 3, 4 and 5)* [1998] 2 Lloyd's Rep 461, 473.

[283] *The Bowbelle* [1990] 1 WLR 1330, [1990] 3 All ER 476, [1990] 1 Lloyd's Rep 532.

[284] *The ICL Vikraman* [2003] EWHC 2320 (Comm) [80], [2004] 1 WLR 2254, 2276–2277, [2004] 1 All ER (Comm) 246, 267, [2004] 1 Lloyd's Rep 21, 37.

[285] CPR 61.11(21); an application must be in form ADM20, PD61 §10.14.

[286] Merchant Shipping (Liability of Shipowners and Others) (New Rate of Interest) Order 2004 (SI No 931).

Costs

10.188 Costs are in the discretion of the court, but the general rule is that costs should follow the event.[287] In a contested limitation claim, it may be expected that the party seeking to limit will be required to pay the costs of proving those matters which he must prove in order to obtain the decree, namely that the claim falls within art 2 of the 1976 Convention. A party opposing the right to limit is likely to be required to pay the costs of investigating and determining the facts which art 4 of the 1976 Convention provides that he must prove if, at the end of the trial, he fails to establish those facts.[288]

Australian procedure

10.189 A party that has been sued in relation to a maritime casualty may invoke limitation proceedings in the same suit. Alternatively, a party which considers that a suit is likely may seize the initiative and commence limitation proceedings itself. If the right to limit is challenged, the court will usually order either that the issue of the right to limit be tried first before the vessel is released from arrest, or, alternatively, that the security cover the total of the maximum amount of the claim, plus interest and costs before the vessel is released.[289]

10.190 Whilst the authorities speak in terms of a limitation action giving rise to a 'defence',[290] as Dixon J observed in *James Patrick & Co Ltd v Union Steamship Co of New Zealand Ltd*[291] 'the statute gives no defence; at best it limits damages'. The Admiralty Act 1988 provides that a person who apprehends a claim for compensation under a law that gives effect to provisions of a Liability Convention may apply to the Federal Court to determine the question of whether the liability may be limited.[292] This section does not affect the jurisdiction of any other court,[293] so that similar proceedings could be commenced in the various State Supreme Courts who are also invested with Admiralty jurisdiction by virtue of s 9 of the Admiralty Act.

10.191 As permitted by the second sentence of art 10(1), Australia has not made any domestic law requiring the constitution of a limitation fund. Thus a party to a marine casualty which seeks to invoke its right to limit liability has a right to decide whether to constitute a fund or not.

10.192 The 1988 Act invests the Supreme Courts of the States with jurisdiction in respect of limitation of liability. It is therefore possible to proceed with a limitation claim in

---

287 CPR 44.2(a).

288 See *The Capitan San Luis* [1994] QB 465, 473, [1994] 2 WLR 299, 306, [1993] 2 Lloyd's Rep 573, 579.

289 *Barde AB v ABB Power Systems (The Barde Team)* (1995) 69 FCR 277, 132 ALR 358; *Victrawl Pty Ltd v AOTC Ltd* (1993) 45 FCR 302; 117 ALR 347.

290 *Podmore v Aquatours Pty Ltd* [1984] 1 NSWLR 111.

291 *James Patrick & Co Ltd v Union Steamship Co of New Zealand Ltd* (1938) 60 CLR 650, 673.

292 Admiralty Act 1988, s 25(1).

293 Admiralty Act 1988, s 25(2).

either the Federal Court of Australia or in one of the Supreme Courts of the States or Territories.[294]

Section 25(3) empowers the Federal Court to determine whether or not liability may be limited and, if so, to determine the amount of that limit; to order the constitution of a limitation fund for the payment of claims; and to make any other orders in respect of the administration and distribution of the fund. The Admiralty Rules 1988 provide for a limitation action to be commenced as an action *in personam*[295] by a statement of claim[296] which names at least one respondent in the initiating process.[297] Other respondents need not be so named in the initiating process but may be identified as respondents by reference to their being members of a specified class of persons. In the latter case, the initiating process need not be served on such respondents. **10.193**

Art 6(3) of the International Convention on Civil Liability for Oil Pollution Damage 1969 gives power to State parties to make provision for priority. Australia has done this in s 8 of the Limitation of Liability for Maritime Claims Act 1989, which provides that claims for damage to harbour works and the like take priority over claims for loss arising from other types of property damage and delay in the carriage of cargo, passengers, or their luggage. **10.194**

Canadian procedure

Admiralty jurisdiction in Canada is exercised by both the Federal Court and the provincial courts. The right to limit liability may be asserted in the filing of a defence, or by way of action or counterclaim for declaratory relief in any court of competent jurisdiction.[298] However, a limitation fund may be constituted only in the Federal Court.[299] Where a claim is made or apprehended against a person in respect of liability limited by ss 28 or 29 of the Marine Liability Act or arts 6(1) or 7(1) of the Convention, s 33 of the Act permits the Federal Court to take any step it considers appropriate with regard to the determination of the amount of the liability, such as providing for the constitution and distribution of the fund, the joinder of parties, the provision of security, the payment of costs, and the enjoining of persons from commencing or continuing proceedings. Section 33 makes no reference to a claim which is limited by s 30, namely one in respect of the liability of an owner of a dock, canal, or port, but s 32(2) specifically provides for such a person to assert the right to limitation of liability in any court of competent jurisdiction in Canada. **10.195**

---

294 Limitation of Liability for Maritime Claims Act 1979, s 9.
295 r 21(1).
296 r 21(2) and Form 7.
297 r 21(3).
298 Marine Liability Act 2001, s 32.
299 Marine Liability Act 2001, s 32(1); Federal Court Rules SOR/98-106, s 496.

10.196 When determining whether or not to release a ship or property under art 13(2) of the Convention, a court in Canada must not have regard to a limitation fund established in a foreign jurisdiction unless that jurisdiction is a State party to the Convention.[300]

Hong Kong procedure

10.197 The procedure relating to limitation claims is set out in O75 rr 37–40 of the Rules of the High Court (Cap 4A). There is no requirement for the constitution of a limitation fund before limitation of liability can be invoked. The rules draw a clear distinction between the role of the registrar and that of the Admiralty Judge in the context of dealing with limitation claims. A limitation decree is only made by a judge on the trial of a contested limitation action,[301] otherwise a summons for a limitation decree is to be brought before a registrar.[302]

10.198 The rate of interest to be prescribed for the purpose of art 11(1) is prescribed by the Merchant Shipping (Limitation of Shipowners Liability)(Rate of Interest) Order and is currently 5.2 per cent.[303]

New Zealand procedure

10.199 Rule 25.25 in Part 25 of the High Court Rules governs the procedure for limitation actions.[304] It provides for limitation proceedings to be commenced in the form of an admiralty action *in personam*[305] and governs the manner in which parties must be named or described in the relevant court documents.[306]
If it appears at the hearing of the application that the plaintiff's right to limit is undisputed, the court must make a decree to that effect fixing the amount of the limit.[307]

Singapore procedure

10.200 Order 70 rr 36–39 of the Rules of Court (Admiralty Proceedings) 1996[308] govern the procedure relating to limitation claims in Singapore. The party seeking to limit his liability must first prove his case in the action before a limitation decree will be granted. There is no requirement for the constitution of a limitation fund before limitation of liability can be invoked.

---

300 Marine Liability Act 2001, s 34(2).

301 O75 r 39(2).

302 O75 r 38, *The Equator Crystal* [1998] 4 HKC 568.

303 Cap 434D as set from 12 December 2008.

304 Part of the reforms to the rules of court in New Zealand, now all located in Schedule 2 to the Judicature Act1908, inserted by the Judicature (High Court Rules) Amendment Act 2008, No 90.

305 Rules of the High Court (NZ), r 25.25(1).

306 Rules of the High Court (NZ), r 25.25(2)–(5).

307 Rules of the High Court (NZ), r 25.6(4).

308 No S71/1997 pursuant to s 80, Supreme Court of Judicature Act (Chapter 322).

The Singapore court has the power to award interest on the claim to be calculated before distribution.[309] Interest is awarded on a claim made against the limitation fund. **10.201**

Art 6(3) provides that, without prejudice to the rights of the 'injury' claims under art 6(2), a State party is at liberty to enact that claims for damage to harbour works, basins, waterways, and navigational aids shall have priority over other claims. Singapore has enacted such a provision.[310] **10.202**

South African procedure

A claim arising out of or relating to the limitation of liability of the owner of a ship or of any other person entitled to any similar limitation of liability is a 'maritime claim' within the meaning of s 1(1) of the Admiralty Jurisdiction Regulation Act 105 of 1983 and, as such, falls within the Admiralty jurisdiction of the Supreme Court of South Africa.[311] The Supreme Court has a wide discretion in the manner in which limitation claims are managed by the Court. The Admiralty Proceeding Rules provide:[312] **10.203**

> Where any person claims to be entitled to a limitation of liability referred to in paragraph (w) of the definition of maritime claim in section 1(1) of the Act, the court may give such directions as it deems fit with regard to the procedure in any such claim, the staying of any other proceedings and the conditions for the consideration of any such claim, which may include a condition that such amount as the court may order be paid to abide the result of the consideration of the said claim, or that the claimant be required to admit liability for all or any claims made against him or her, or any other condition which the court deems fit.

F. The Effect of a Limitation Decree in Other Countries

Preliminary remarks

The effect in country X of a decree given in country Y under a limitation regime to which X is not party is not easy to determine. It is, moreover, quintessentially a matter for country X to determine.[313] It is submitted that, so far as concerns the recognition of overseas limitation decrees within England and Wales (and some if not all of the other jurisdictions covered in this work), that the matter is best approached from first principles, ie, those which govern generally the effect given to foreign judgments. **10.204**

To that end, a clear distinction must be made between the effect of judgments between EU and EFTA Member States (and thus falling for recognition under **10.205**

309 Sch 1, para 6, Supreme Court of Judicature Act (Chapter 322).
310 Merchant Shipping Act 1995, s 136(2).
311 Admiralty Jurisdiction Regulation Act 105 of 1983, s 2(1).
312 Admiralty Proceedings Rules (SAf), r 23(2).
313 As Clarke LJ recognized in *The Western Regent* [2005] EWCA Civ 985, [2005] 2 Lloyd's Rep 359, 370, [51].

the Brussels I Regulations or the Brussels/Lugano Conventions), and those which must be recognized (if at all) at common law.[314]

Within the EU

10.206 A general decree of the right to limit, at any rate once no longer open to challenge, is a judgment capable of recognition and enforcement under the Brussels I Regulations (and/or Brussels/Lugano Conventions), regardless of whether the enforcing/recognizing State is itself a signatory to the particular limitation regime relied upon as the source of the right to limit.[315] This unexpected result follows from the goal of the European jurisdiction regimes:

> ... to prevent parallel proceedings before the courts of different Contracting States and to avoid conflicts between decisions which might result therefrom. Those rules are therefore designed to preclude ... the possibility of ... the non-recognition of a judgment on account of its irreconcilability with a judgment given in proceedings between the same parties in the State in which recognition is sought.[316]

At common law

10.207 In order to be recognized at common law, the foreign judgment must be between the parties or their privies, final and conclusive, on the merits, and the court pronouncing it must have been competent (in English eyes).[317] Each of these requirements is capable of giving rise to difficulties; however, in the context of limitation decrees, the most significant is likely to be the requirement that the foreign judgment has been given 'on the merits'.[318]

10.208 Assuming those requirements to be satisfied in the particular case, the next question is the practical effect of recognition. Is recognition confined to recognizing that the beneficiary of the relevant decree was entitled to limit his liability in country Y under the relevant limitation regime—thus leaving the way clear to the application of country X's own regime? Or does it go further and import country Y's decree into country X? It is tentatively submitted that the former is the better view; the procedural nature of the right to limit means that it does not readily lend itself to a *quasi* form of action estoppel.[319]

---

[314] There can be no question of *enforcement* of such judgments, eg, under the Foreign Judgments (Reciprocal Enforcement) Act 1933, since by its very nature a decree of limitation will not be for a fixed sum of money.

[315] *Maersk Olie & Gas A/S v Firma M de Haan & W de Boer* [2005] 1 Lloyd's Rep 210 ECJ.

[316] Ibid 214, [31].

[317] *Dicey, Morris & Collins on the Conflict of Laws*, (15th edn, 2015), r 35(2).

[318] See in this connection the *dicta* of Lords Diplock and Brandon in *The Sennar* (No 2) [1985] 1 WLR 490, 494, 499 HL.

[319] A view supported by the conclusion reached—albeit in a rather different setting—by the Deputy Judge at first instance in *Good Challenger Navegante v Metalexportimport* [2003] 1 Lloyd's Rep 471, 480, [33]. The point was not pursued on appeal.

Thus, for example, a limitation decree in a 1976 Convention country which does not apply the 1996 Protocol would (all else being equal) be entitled to recognition in a 1996 Protocol country, but the effect of that recognition would be to prevent the reopening, eg, of any argument over entitlement to limit (provided of course that the relevant provisions were the same in both countries), but it would not result in the application of the lower limits of liability in fresh proceedings commenced in the 1996 Protocol country. **10.209**

G. The Effect of the Owner's Insolvency on the Constitution of a Limitation Fund

Section 127 of the Insolvency Act 1986 provides that in a winding-up by the court, any disposition of the company's property made after the commencement of the winding-up is void unless the court otherwise orders. Although the word 'disposition' is not defined in the Insolvency Act, it is given wide meaning in order to achieve the purposes of the section and includes any act which, in reducing or extinguishing the company's rights in an asset, transfers value to another person.[320] The constitution of a limitation fund, even prior to a determination of liability, constitutes a transfer of value to another person. It is suggested that, by analogy with the decision in *Re Flint*, the fact that a fund may be constituted pursuant to a court order will not save it from EU validation.[321] **10.210**

Further, s 128(1) provides, 'Where a company registered in England and Wales is being wound up by the court, any attachment, sequestration, distress or execution put in force against the estate or effects of the company after the commencement of the winding up is void.' It has been held that the arrest of a ship or other property by the Admiralty Marshal in an admiralty claim *in rem* is a 'sequestration' within the meaning of s 128(1) of the Insolvency Act, and that a sale following an arrest is the equivalent of execution within the meaning of s 183(1) of the Insolvency Act.[322] Sir George Jessel said that the term 'sequestration' had no particular technical meaning but simply meant the detention of property by a Court of Justice for the purpose of answering a demand which is made.[323] Thus the arrest of a ship after a petition has been presented for the winding-up of the shipowning company will be void. As the constitution of the limitation fund is essentially a substitution for the arrest of the vessel[324] it can by analogy be argued that the constitution of the fund **10.211**

320 R M Goode, *Principles of Corporate Insolvency Law* (2nd edn, 1997) 424.

321 *Re Flint* [1993] Ch 319.

322 *In re Australian Direct Steam Navigation Company* (1875) LR 20 Eq 325; *The Constellation* [1966] 1 WLR 272.

323 *In re Australian Direct Steam Navigation Company* (1875) LR 20 Eq 325, 326–327.

324 1976 Convention, art 13.

is also a 'sequestration' within the meaning of s 128(1) of the Insolvency Act, and it is submitted that a court would so hold. Thus where a limitation claim has been commenced either before or subsequently to the commencement of the winding-up, application should be made to the Companies Court pursuant to s 130(2) of the Insolvency Act for leave to continue the proceedings.

11

ARBITRATION ISSUES

A. Introduction

Arbitration has long been favoured as a dispute resolution mechanism by parties **11.01** to maritime contracts. There are a number of reasons for this. First, arbitration has a degree of flexibility as to the manner and time in which a dispute may be heard and resolved that is not always available in the court system. Secondly, there is the possibility of choosing an arbitrator with particular expertise in the subject matter of the dispute which may thereby result in a quicker and cheaper resolution of it, particularly if complex expert evidence can be avoided. Thirdly, arbitration has the advantage of confidentiality.

In order to promote the harmonization of the procedures relating to interna- **11.02** tional commercial arbitration, UNCITRAL developed a Model Law governing the arbitration agreement, the composition and jurisdiction of the arbitral tribunal, the conduct of the arbitral proceedings, and the making of and recourse against the award. Enforcement of arbitral awards is facilitated by the New York Convention on the Recognition and Enforcement of Foreign Arbitral Awards 1958 (the New York Convention) to which (among many others) the United Kingdom, Australia, Canada, New Zealand, Hong Kong, Singapore, and South Africa are parties. The law relating to arbitration in England is governed by the Arbitration Act 1996 (the 1996 Act), modelled on the UNCITRAL model law. Similarly, there is legislation governing international commercial arbitration in Australia,[1] Canada,[2] Hong Kong,[3] New Zealand,[4] Singapore,[5] and South Africa.[6]

11.03 The Admiralty procedures described in this work are, in many respects, anathema to the arbitral process. However, as the arrest of a ship is a common method of securing an arbitration claim, the practices and procedures of the admiralty courts remain to that extent relevant to those involved in arbitration, and the interaction between the two processes needs to be understood. That interaction and certain other issues arising in the court/arbitration context are discussed in this chapter. This chapter does not therefore set out to provide a detailed discussion of the law relating to the arbitration of maritime disputes. That task has already been undertaken by others.[7]

B. The Arbitration Act 1996

Overview

11.04 The 1996 Act came into force on 31 January 1997, the progeny of a Report prepared by the then Lord Justice Mustill in 1989,[8] with the express intention to 'restate and improve' the existing statutory and common law rules. The Departmental Advisory Committee on Arbitration Law (DAC), of which Mustill LJ was chairman, had been asked to consider whether the UNCITRAL Model Law should be adopted. The result was the 1996 Act, which aims to restate the basic principles of the English law of arbitration while following the structure and content of the UNCITRAL Model Law as far as possible.[9] It is not, however, intended to be an exhaustive code. Indeed, some aspects which might be expected to be covered by such a statute, such as a statement of the principles of confidentiality relating to arbitration, have been deliberately omitted.[10]

---

1 International Arbitration Act 1974 (Cth), which provides for the UNCITRAL Model Law (except Chapter VIII) to have the force of law in Australia in international commercial arbitrations.

2 Commercial Arbitration Act RSC 1985 c 17 (2d Supp), which incorporates the UNCITRAL Model Law.

3 Cap 609 Arbitration Ordinance, which came into effect on 1 June 2011 and gives the force of law to large parts of the UNICTRAL Model Law. For a detailed commentary see Chief Justice Ma (Editor in Chief) and Dennis Brock (General Editor), *Arbitration in Hong Kong: A Practical Guide* (2nd edn, 2011).

4 Arbitration Act 1996 (NZ), which is based on the UNCITRAL Model Law.

5 Singapore International Arbitration Act (Chapter 143A), which is based on the UNCITRAL Model Law.

6 Arbitration Act 42 of 1965.

7 See, eg, B Harris, R Planterose, and J Tecks, *The Arbitration Act 1996—A Commentary* (3rd edn, 2003); C Ambrose and K Maxwell, *London Maritime Arbitration* (3rd edn, 2009); Lord Mustill and S C Boyd, *Commercial Arbitration* (2nd edn, 1989) and *Companion* (2001).

8 'The 1989 Mustill Report' [1989] 6 Arbitration International 1.

9 Explanatory memorandum accompanying the 1996 Bill and 'The 1989 Mustill Report' [1989] 6 *Arbitration International* 1.

10 See further below, paras 11.23 and following.

Arbitrations to which the 1996 Act applies

Part I of the 1996 Act is headed 'Arbitration pursuant to an arbitration agreement' **11.05** and it is this Part which is relevant to the arbitration of maritime disputes.[11] The 1996 Act applies to arbitral proceedings commenced after 31 January 1997 regardless of when the arbitration agreement was made,[12] where the seat of arbitration is England, Wales, or Northern Ireland.[13] Whilst the seat of arbitration is ordinarily the physical location where the arbitration takes place, it is in fact a reference to the legal place of the arbitration.[14] Thus parties could agree that the 'seat' of the arbitration be London, thereby triggering the application of English law and practice, but for the convenience of the parties and witnesses could if necessary conduct some or all of the arbitration in, for example, Indonesia.[15]

The 1996 Act applies only when the arbitration agreement is in writing.[16] **11.06** Although interesting questions could arise as to whether an agreement reached orally but by reference to a well-known standard form (such as to salvage a vessel in accordance with Lloyd's Open Form) could amount to an agreement in writing,[17] the better view must be that it would not. It is surprisingly easy for an oral agreement to arbitrate to be made, particularly in relation to existing disputes, a circumstance which may come back to haunt a party (or its legal advisor) when it comes to enforcement of an award under the New York Convention since, like the 1996 Act, it applies only to awards made pursuant to written arbitration agreements.

The objects of the Act

The 1996 Act sets forth in s 1 three general principles. **11.07**

(1) The object of arbitration is to obtain the fair resolution of disputes by an impartial tribunal without unnecessary delay or expense.

[11] Part II of the Act relates to matters in the nature of consumer arbitration agreements and Part III relates to the enforcement of foreign arbitral awards.

[12] s 84.

[13] s 2(1).

[14] s 3; *ABB Lummus Global Ltd v Keppel Fels Ltd* [1999] 2 Lloyd's Rep 24; *Dubai Islamic Bank Pjsc v Paymentech Merchant Services Inc* [2001] 1 All ER (Comm) 514, [2001] 1 Lloyd's Rep 65; *Shagang South-Asia (Hong Kong) Trading Co Ltd v Daewoo Logistics* [2015] EWHC 194 (Comm), [2015] 1 All ER (Comm) 545, [2015] 1 Lloyd's Rep 504. See also *PT Garuda Indonesia v Birgen Air* [2002] 1 SLR(R) 401, [2002] 1 SLR 393, [2002] SGCA 12, [2002] 5 LRC 560 and the distinction drawn between the 'place' (ie, seat) and 'venue' of the arbitration. For a discussion of the issue see G Petrochilos, 'On the Juridical Character of the Seat in the Arbitration Act 1996' [2002] LMCLQ 66.

[15] s 34(2)(a); *Naviera Amazonica Peruana SA v Compania Internacional de Seguros del Peru* [1988] 1 Lloyd's Rep 116, 121.

[16] s 5(1).

[17] T Landau, 'The Requirement of a Written Form for an Arbitration Agreement: when "Written" means "Oral"', in Berg (ed), *International Commercial Arbitration: Important Contemporary Questions* (2002) 19.

(2) The parties should be free to agree how their disputes are resolved, subject only to such safeguards as are necessary in the public interest.
(3) In matters governed by Part I the court should not intervene except as provided by the Act.

11.08 The first principle is reflected in s 33, which requires the tribunal 'to adopt procedures suitable to the circumstances of the particular case, avoiding unnecessary delay or expense, so as to provide a fair means for the resolution of the matters falling to be determined'. The 1996 Act then sets out a non-exhaustive list of the measures which a tribunal can adopt in order to carry out this duty.

11.09 The second principle is reflected in the division in the 1996 Act between mandatory and non-mandatory provisions. The mandatory provisions apply notwithstanding any agreement to the contrary[18] and are listed for convenience in sch 1 of the 1996 Act. They relate principally to the general duties of the tribunal and the parties, and the right of the court to supervise. The non-mandatory provisions 'allow the parties to make their own arrangements by agreement but provide rules which apply in the absence of such agreement'.[19]

11.10 The third principle is reflected in the restrictions on the power of the court to intervene in the arbitral process and on the availability of appeal, a deliberate attempt to change 'the widely held suspicion that the English courts were only too ready to interfere in the arbitral process and to impose their own dicta on the parties'.[20]

C. The Objects Explored

Fair resolution of disputes without unnecessary expense or delay

11.11 The relative speed and economy of arbitration has been, historically, its most significant feature. More recent history has, however, shown that modern arbitral proceedings can be at least as time consuming and even more expensive than litigation. Insofar as the balance has been redressed in favour of arbitration in relation to the resolution of commercial disputes, that is due in part to the reduced scope for court intervention under the 1996 Act, and in part to an increase in the sophistication (and thus the cost) of the case management techniques employed in the Commercial and Admiralty Courts, but the difference probably remains marginal. Inordinate delay has largely been consigned to the past in both litigation and arbitration, by a combination of a greater readiness to strike out cases mired in excessive delay[21] and what has become in both fields a culture of more hands-on

---

[18] s 4(1).
[19] s 4(2).
[20] Lord Saville, 'The Arbitration Act 1996' [1997] LMCLQ 502, 511.
[21] For which statutory intervention was necessary in the field of arbitration, in the form of s 13A of the Arbitration Act 1950, now s 41(3) of the 1996 Act.

case management by courts and tribunals. In the latter case, this has been driven largely by the terms and ethos of specialist arbitral bodies.

The London Maritime Arbitrators' Association

Whilst maritime arbitration is subject to the legislation governing commercial arbitrations generally, various specific terms on which maritime arbitrations might be conducted have been developed in jurisdictions around the world for use specifically in the resolution of maritime disputes. In England, the most specialized are those developed by the London Maritime Arbitrators' Association (LMAA). The LMAA, founded in 1960, is an organization comprised of practising arbitrators and users of London maritime arbitration, which supports, promotes, and provides for the arbitration of maritime disputes in London. To that end, the LMAA has drawn up terms pursuant to which various types of arbitration and, more recently, mediation may be conducted. **11.12**

A number of versions of the LMAA Terms have been promulgated since 1984, the most recent being the LMAA Terms (2012) which apply to all references commenced on or after 1 January 2012. The LMAA also publishes a Small Claims Procedure (2012), Mediation Terms (2002), and the LMAA FALCA (fast and low cost arbitration) Rules.[22] The LMAA Terms apply whenever the arbitration clause specifies that they are to do so, where both parties have agreed that the Terms shall apply,[23] or when both parties appoint LMAA arbitrators, who almost invariably accept appointment on the LMAA Terms. Unless the parties agree otherwise, a submission to arbitration on LMAA Terms amounts to an agreement that England is the seat of the arbitration and that English law applies to the arbitration; it also bestows jurisdiction on the tribunal to determine: **11.13**

> ... all disputes arising under or in connection with the transaction the subject of the reference, and each party shall have the right before the tribunal makes its award (or its last award, if more than one is made in a reference) to refer to the tribunal for determination any further dispute(s) arising after the commencement of the arbitral proceedings.[24]

In addition to the powers of the tribunal specified in the Act, the LMAA Terms set out a number of specific powers which are expressed to be 'exercised in a suitable case so as to avoid unnecessary delay or expense, and so as to provide a fair means for the resolution of the matters falling to be determined'. These include: **11.14**

(1) the power to limit the number of expert witnesses or to exclude expert evidence altogether;

---

[22] The terms and a commentary on the terms can be found at <http://www.lmaa.london>, along with the text of the BIMCO/LMAA Arbitration Clause.

[23] Para 5.

[24] Para 10.

(2) the power to direct that arbitrations which raise common issues of fact or law be conducted concurrently and to give appropriate directions in relation to the evidence given in one arbitration as it relates to the other, thus enabling 'chain arbitrations' to be heard together, a measure which undoubtedly results in very considerable costs savings; and
(3) the power to stay a claim for failure to comply with an order to provide security for costs.[25]

For detailed commentary on the LMAA Terms and practice, see *Ambrose & Maxwell on London Maritime Arbitration* (3rd edn, 2009).[26]

Other arbitral organizations

11.15 The LMAA is, of course, far from being the only body through which parties may choose to arbitrate maritime disputes. Also eminent in that regard in England is the London Court of International Arbitration (LCIA), an institution which traces its history back to Victorian times.[27] In addition to case-management by the tribunal in LCIA matters, there is also a secretariat which attends to certain administrative matters. Maritime matters are also arbitrated before the ICC.

11.16 In Australia, the Australian Maritime and Transport Arbitration Commission (AMTAC)[28] was established as a Commission of the Australian Centre for International Commercial Arbitration (ACICA)[29] in 2010. Further, the Maritime Law Association of Australia and New Zealand (MLAANZ) has produced a set of terms with an appropriate MLAANZ Arbitration clause. In addition, the Australian Commercial Disputes Centre (ACDC)[30] acts as the Asia-Pacific Registry for the LCIA. New Zealand does not have a particular institution dedicated to maritime arbitration.

11.17 Canada has two recognized maritime arbitration institutes: the Association of Maritime Arbitrators of Canada (AMAC) and the Vancouver Maritime Arbitrators' Association.[31]

---

[25] Para 14. The only sanction available under the 1996 Act, following failure to comply with a 'peremptory' order to put up security for costs, is the draconian one to dismiss the claim altogether. Although LMAA tribunals are perfectly prepared to exercise that power, the milder alternative of a stay may be more attractive in some cases.

[26] Although this edition does not, by definition, cover the changes made by the LMAA Terms 2012, those changes were not so extensive as to undermine its utility. The changes are summarized on the LMAA website in a page ('Commentary on the LMAA Terms 2012') which prints out on a single side of A4 paper.

[27] <http://www.lcia.org>.

[28] <http://www.amtac.org.au>.

[29] <http://www.acica.org.au>.

[30] <http://www.acdcltd.com.au>.

[31] <http://www.vmaa.org>.

Singapore established the Singapore International Arbitration Centre (SIAC) in 1991.[32] The SIAC Rules for international arbitration and the Singapore Bunker Claims Procedure are based on the UNCITRAL Arbitration Rules and the Rules of the LCIA with some modifications. 11.18

The Hong Kong International Arbitration Centre (HKIAC) was established in 1986.[33] The HKIAC revised its rules in 2013. They are billed (on the HKIAC website) as 'light touch' 'Administered Arbitration Rules', 'a balance between the more hands-off approach of the UNCITRAL Arbitration Rules and the practice of overly regulated administered arbitration'. In January 2015, HKIAC published separate 'Procedures for the Administration of Arbitration under the UNCITRAL Arbitration Rules'. 11.19

South Africa presently has no structured maritime arbitration procedure. 11.20

Party autonomy

Powers of the arbitral tribunal

The overwhelming emphasis of the 1996 Act is on giving the parties the power to control the scope of the tribunal's power whilst providing for the default position in the event that the parties fail to select a particular process or procedure. Thus the 1996 Act provides that, unless otherwise agreed by the parties, an arbitral tribunal has the power: 11.21

(1) and subject to review by the court, to rule on its own jurisdiction;[34]
(2) to decide all procedural and evidential matters[35] including the appointment of assessors;[36]
(3) to order as interim relief security for costs, inspection or preservation of property subject to the proceedings, or the taking of samples from the property and the preservation of evidence;[37]
(4) to make provisional awards;[38]
(5) to dismiss a claim for inordinate and inexcusable delay, or to continue proceedings in the absence of a party and make an award on the evidence before it in the case of failure by a party to attend a hearing or give written evidence after due notice has been given;[39]

---

32 <http://www.siac.org.sg>.
33 <http://www.hkiac.org>.
34 ss 30–32; *LG Caltex Gas Co. Ltd v China National Petroleum Corp* [2001] EWCA Civ 788, [2001] 1 WLR 1892, [2001] 4 All ER 875.
35 ss 34 and 38(5).
36 s 37.
37 s 38.
38 s 39.
39 s 41.

(6) to determine which law governs the dispute in the absence of a choice by the parties;[40]
(7) to make a declaration, to order payment of a monetary sum, to order a final (though not an interlocutory) injunction, to order specific performance (except in relation to a contract relating to land), to order rectification, setting aside, or cancellation of a deed or other document;[41]
(8) to award pre-award and post-award interest,[42] which may be compounded (unlike the usual position in the courts);
(9) to correct an award to remove a clerical mistake or error, or make an additional award in respect of any claim presented to the tribunal but not dealt with in the award;[43]
(10) to withhold an award for non-payment of fees and expenses;[44]
(11) to award costs,[45] to determine the recoverable costs on such basis as it sees fit,[46] and to direct that the recoverable costs be limited to a specified amount.[47]

Powers of the court

11.22 In contrast to the wide powers given to an arbitral tribunal, the powers of the court, although numerous, are narrow and circumscribed by the 1996 Act. The 1996 Act provides that the court has power:

(1) to order a stay of legal proceedings;[48]
(2) to direct an interpleader issue to arbitration;[49]
(3) to order that arrested property be retained as security or that alternative security be provided where Admiralty proceedings are stayed;[50]
(4) to extend time[51] or compute time in accordance with the Limitation Acts;[52]
(5) to give directions as to the making of an appointment of arbitrators or umpires in the event of the parties' failure to agree and to revoke appointments or remove arbitrators;[53]

---

40 s 46.
41 s 48.
42 s 49.
43 s 57.
44 s 56.
45 s 61.
46 s 63.
47 s 65.
48 s 9. This applies only to domestic legal proceedings. Non-EU foreign legal proceedings can be restrained under s 37 of the Senior Courts Act 1981: *AES Ust-Kamenogorsk Hydropower Plant LLP v Ust-Kamenogorsk Hydropower Plant JSC* [2013] UKSC 35, [2013] 1 WLR 1889, [2014] 1 All ER (Comm) 1, [2013] 2 Lloyd's Rep 281, whether or not arbitration proceedings are afoot or contemplated: [47]–[48]. See further at para 11.55 and following below.
49 s 10.
50 s 11
51 s 12.
52 s 13.
53 ss 17, 18, 19, 21, 24, and 25.

(6) to determine questions as to the substantive jurisdiction of the tribunal;[54]
(7) to order compliance with peremptory orders made by the tribunal, unless otherwise agreed by the parties;[55]
(8) to compel the attendance of witnesses or the production of documents,[56] and to make orders in relation to the service of documents;[57]
(9) to make orders in relation to matters of evidence and matters relating to property the subject of the proceedings including for the sale of goods, the grant of an interim injunction, or the appointment of a receiver, unless otherwise agreed by the parties;[58]
(10) to determine a preliminary point of law, unless otherwise agreed by the parties;[59]
(11) to extend time for the making of an award, unless otherwise agreed by the parties;[60]
(12) to make orders in relation to the withholding of an award for non-payment of fees and expenses;[61]
(13) to award costs if the tribunal does not deal with the question of costs;[62]
(14) to grant leave to enforce an award in the same manner as a judgment or order of the court;[63]
(15) to confirm, vary, or set aside an award that has been challenged for lack of substantive jurisdiction,[64] or to remit, set aside, or declare the award to be of no effect on the basis of serious irregularity;[65]
(16) to determine an appeal on a question of law, unless otherwise agreed by the parties.[66]

Confidentiality and privacy

Source Fundamental to the concept of party autonomy is the right of the parties to appoint a private judge to adjudicate a dispute and to make a binding decision. It has long been assumed to be implicit in the choice to arbitrate in England that privacy and confidentiality will be assured throughout the process. The fact that the Act is silent on the question does not detract from this premise, it being explicit in the Departmental Advisory Committee Report of February 1996 that the courts **11.23**

54 s 32.
55 s 42.
56 s 43.
57 s 77.
58 s 44.
59 s 45.
60 s 50.
61 s 56.
62 s 63.
63 s 66.
64 s 67.
65 s 68.
66 ss 69–71.

should be left to work out the ambit of the confidentiality requirements which attached to arbitrations.[67] And indeed, the courts are continuing to grapple with the issues which arise in relation to confidentiality in arbitration. The main issues are threefold: the juridical nature of the obligation of confidentiality; the range of persons bound by the obligation of confidence; and the extent to which the requirement of confidentiality is transposed into court proceedings to challenge the arbitration or some aspect of it.

11.24 **Nature** The obligation of confidence imposes a duty not to use documents obtained in the course of an arbitration 'for any purpose other than the dispute in which they were obtained'.[68] The juridical basis of the obligation of confidentiality in arbitral proceedings is said to arise from an implied term attaching 'as a matter of law' as a necessary incident of the contract to arbitrate and 'an essential corollary of the privacy of arbitration proceedings'.[69] The doctrine rests upon the assumption that the parties have a legitimate interest in privacy which the court will protect. An exception based on the subsequent need to protect the inconsistent interest of one party alone is properly formulated in terms of reasonable necessity rather than mere convenience or advantage.[70]

11.25 The English approach has been accepted in Singapore[71] and tacitly, it would appear, in Hong Kong.[72] The High Court of Australia, however, has taken a view which is contrary to that of the English courts and has concluded that confidentiality is not an essential attribute of a private arbitration imposing an obligation on each party not to disclose the proceedings or documents and information provided in and for the purposes of the arbitration.[73] The Australian approach draws a fundamental distinction between a hearing being conducted in private and one which is in fact confidential. The court drew attention to a number of features of an arbitration proceeding which make confidentiality unachievable.

(1) No obligation of confidence attaches to witnesses. This was conceded before the court, but may not always be so.[74]

---

[67] Departmental Advisory Committee, Report on the Arbitration Bill, February 1996, paras 10–17.

[68] *Dolling-Baker v Merrett* [1990] 1 WLR 1205, 1213, [1991] 2 All ER 890, 899.

[69] Ibid; *Ali Shipping Corp v Shipyard Trogir* [1999] 1 WLR 314, [1998] 2 All ER 136, [1998] 1 Lloyd's Rep 643 per Potter LJ; *Emmott v Michael Wilson & Partners Ltd* [2008] EWCA Civ 184, [2008] Bus LR 1361, [2008] 2 All ER (Comm) 193, [2008] 1 Lloyd's Rep 616.

[70] See *Ali Shipping* and *Emmott* (n 69 above).

[71] *Myanma Yaung Chi OO Co Ltd v Win Win Nu* [2003] 2 SLR 547 and s 22 of the International Arbitration Act 1994 provides that on the application of any party, arbitration proceedings shall be heard 'otherwise than in open court'. See also *AAY & Ors v AAZ* [2009] SGHC 142.

[72] *Oriental Press Group Ltd v Next Magazine Publishing Ltd* [1998] 40 HKCU 1.

[73] *Esso Australia Resources Ltd v Plowman* (1995) 183 CLR 10, 30 per Mason CJ, 34 per Brennan J. A commentary on the Australian position is found in The Hon A Rogers QC and D Miller, 'Non-confidential Arbitration Proceedings' (1997) 71 *Australian Law Journal* 436.

[74] Below, para 11.33.

(2) The various ways in which an award made in an arbitration may come before a court involving disclosure to the court by a party to the arbitration and publication of the court proceedings.

However, documents produced by a party compulsorily pursuant to a direction of the arbitrator were thought to attract the same confidentiality that would attach to them if the parties were litigating their dispute, subject only to the legitimate interest of the public in obtaining information about the affairs of public authorities.[75] The rationale for accepting a similar duty in relation to arbitration as applies in relation to litigation was the acceptance of Colman J's view in *Hassneh Insurance Co v Mew* that because parties to an English law arbitration submit to the possibility that the English discovery procedure will apply to their arbitration, by implication they must be mutually obliged:

> ... to accord to documents disclosed for the purposes of the arbitration the same confidentiality which would attach to those documents if they were litigating their disputes as distinct from arbitrating them.[76]

The Australian approach has not met with universal approbation. The comments of Lord Neill QC make clear the objections to it: 11.26

> If some Machiavelli were to ask me to advise on the best method of driving international arbitration away from England I think that I would say that the best way would be to reintroduce ... all the court interference that was swept away ... The second best method but the two boats are only separated by a canvas would be for the House of Lords to overthrow *Dolling-Baker* and to embrace the majority judgment of the High Court of Australia in *Esso/BHP*. This would be to announce that English law no longer regarded the privacy and confidentiality of arbitration proceedings (using that term in the broadest sense) as a fundamental characteristic of the agreement to arbitrate. Lawyers and businessmen in France, Germany, Switzerland and in the countries of the Commonwealth and elsewhere would take note and there would be a flight of arbitrations from this country to more hospitable climes.[77]

New Zealand was sufficiently concerned to avoid any potential adoption of the Australian approach into its law that it enshrined the duty of confidentiality in legislation.[78] Section 14B of the New Zealand Arbitration Act 1996 provides that every arbitration agreement to which that section applies is deemed to provide that the parties and the arbitral tribunal must not disclose confidential information. Exceptions to confidentiality include: 11.27

(1) where the disclosure is made to a professional or other adviser;

75 *Esso Australia Resources Ltd v Plowman* (1995) 183 CLR 10, 33 per Mason CJ, 47 per Toohey J.
76 *Hassneh Insurance Co v Mew* [1993] 2 Lloyd's Rep 243, 247.
77 Lord Neill QC 'Confidentiality in Arbitration' (1996) 12 *Arbitration International* 287, 316
78 NZLC 83, 2003 Improving the Arbitration Act 1996, para 35.

(2) if disclosure is necessary to ensure a party has a full opportunity to present that party's case and disclosure is no more than what is reasonably necessary to achieve this;
(3) if disclosure is required by law; or
(4) if disclosure is compelled by court order.[79]

The tribunal may also, if requested by one of the parties, make an order allowing disclosure of confidential information.[80]

11.28 Thus the section deems there to be an agreement between the parties not to disclose any information relating to arbitral proceedings, breach of which will be actionable on the basis of breach of contract. The exceptions specified in the Act are narrower than those accepted in English law, and, in particular, will not include disclosures required by law but not made in compliance with section 14C(d) of the Act and disclosures for other legitimate reasons not specified in the Act. The High Court may make an order allowing disclosure if the public interest in permitting disclosure outweighs the public interest in preserving confidentiality, and only if the disclosure is not more than what is reasonably necessary to protect those other public interest considerations.[81]

11.29 It seems that Canadian courts are leaning closer towards the Australian position than to the English/New Zealand position. The Canadian Commercial Arbitration Act does not include provisions on the privacy or confidentiality of arbitral proceedings; nor does the Vancouver Maritime Arbitrators' Association. Recent court decisions have declined to find that documents and information disclosed in arbitral proceedings are confidential.

(1) In *Adesa Corporation v Bob Dickenson Auction Services Ltd*[82] it was stated on a preliminary motion that there is an expectation of privacy in arbitration proceedings that should be fostered to maintain the integrity of the arbitration proceedings. However, Cameron J commented:

> I do not regard confidentiality as essential to the arbitration process... I am not persuaded that the confidentiality of the arbitration process, including the need to encourage the truth of the evidence therein, is so important as to outweigh the need in this court for justice if that requires the disclosure.[83]

(2) However, in a case concerned with whether or not the transcript of the arbitration proceedings and the award were admissible as evidence against the defendant on a summary trial application, the Supreme Court of British Columbia was able to determine the question by reference to the procedural

[79] New Zealand Arbitration Act 1996 s 14C.
[80] New Zealand Arbitration Act 1996 s 14D.
[81] New Zealand Arbitration Act 1996 s 14E.
[82] *Adesa Corporation v Bob Dickenson Auction Service Ltd* (2004) 247 DLR (4th) 730; 73 OR (3d) 787.
[83] Ibid 758, [56].

rules of court, thereby avoiding any decision on the broader question.[84] On the secondary question as to whether the transcript and award could be used in relation to the defendant's application to summarily dismiss the proceedings brought against him, the Court said that it was 'both reasonable and necessary (in the sense used by the English Court of Appeal in *Ali Shipping*) to consider both the Arbitration Award and the portions of the transcript relied on' because the costs of adducing the impugned evidence in summary dismissal proceedings would be excessive, the efficiency of summary dismissal proceedings would be severely impugned, and the transcript puts the claimant's case on the highest possible evidentiary plane, which was essential to the assessment of the legal and factual issues raised in the summary dismissal application. BM Davies J said:

> While it may eventually be necessary for the courts of this province to comprehensively address the contradictory positions taken by the English Court of Appeal in *Ali Shipping* and the Australian High Court in *Esso Australia*, it is not necessary that I do so in this case.[85]

(3) In *Trans-Send Freight Systems Ltd v Markel Insurance Co of Canada*,[86] the insured Trans-Send Freight Systems Ltd engaged in arbitration in Georgia with its customer in relation to a cargo of stolen goods. The insured subsequently brought an action against its insurer, Markel. The insurer and broker sought production of documents over which the insured claimed arbitration privilege. Although the rules of the American Arbitration Association provided that confidential information disclosed during proceedings shall not be divulged by an arbitrator or administrator, Master Birnbaum considered this obligation applied to the arbitrator and administrator alone, not the parties. The Master then considered relevant case law including Cameron J's comments in *Adesa Corporation* but concluded there was no Georgia law requiring the documents to be kept confidential and commented:

> I also note that the courts of appeal in the various jurisdictions cited—England, Hong Kong and Australia—do not agree that documents produced in arbitrations are confidential.[87]

The decision to order the production of the documents was affirmed on appeal,[88] with the appeal court noting the following in relation to confidentiality:

> Counsel for the appellant has urged me to adopt what he described as a growing trend in England and Wales and elsewhere to afford privacy protection to arbitration proceedings in order to bring Ontario into step with other jurisdictions and to foster

[84] *Hi-Seas Marine Ltd v Boelman* [2006] BCJ No. 655, 27 March 2006.
[85] Ibid, [67].
[86] *Trans-Send Freight Systems Ltd v Markel Insurance Co of Canada* (2009) 71 CCLI (4th) 132; 74 CPC (6th) 272.
[87] Ibid, [10].
[88] *Trans-Send Freight Systems Ltd v Markel Insurance Co of Canada* (2010) ONSC 205.

> the development of commercial arbitration in Ontario. While there may be merit in conferring certain privacy rights to parties engaged in commercial arbitration, it is my respectful view that that can be done only by legislative action. I would not be inclined to initiate such a dramatic change in our law by judicial action. There is no basis under the present state of the law to afford such protection on the facts of this case.[89]

It seems that documents and information disclosed in Canadian arbitral proceedings will not necessarily attract confidentiality and may be required to be disclosed in subsequent litigation. In order to keep such material confidential, a party would need to apply for a sealing order[90] and would be well advised to include appropriate confidentiality clauses in any arbitration agreement.

11.30 **Scope** The duty of confidence applies to any document prepared for and used in an arbitration, or disclosed or produced in the course of an arbitration including pleadings, discovery, written and oral evidence, notes and transcripts of evidence, submissions, and the award.[91] There is no requirement that the material have any special quality of confidence about it.[92]

11.31 Although the precise scope of the obligation of confidence has not yet been delineated, the Court of Appeal in *Ali Shipping* identified a number of exceptions which have already been recognized by English courts to the broad rule of confidentiality:

(1) where the disclosure is made with the express or implied consent of the party who originally produced the material;
(2) where the material is ordered by a court to be disclosed;
(3) where the court grants leave to disclose the material, such leave being granted when, and to the extent to which, it is reasonably necessary for the protection of the legitimate interests of an arbitrating party against a third party.[93] The Court of Appeal noted that, to date, this exception has been held to be applicable only to the disclosure of an award but that it was clear that the principle also covers pleadings, written submissions, and proofs of witnesses as well as transcripts and notes of the evidence given in the arbitration.[94] However, it is submitted that there is much force in the observation of Stephen Males QC that there is no obvious reason why the court's power over the implied undertaking which applies to documents compulsorily disclosed in court proceedings can be transposed to a duty of confidence which attached as an implied

[89] Ibid, [7].
[90] A discussion of Canadian courts' approach to sealing orders is found in 'Confidentially Speaking: Commercial Arbitration in Canada's Open Courts' (2011) 28(4) *Journal of International Commercial Arbitration* 355.
[91] *Dolling-Baker v Merrett* [1990] 1 WLR 1205, 1213, [1991] 2 All ER 890, 898.
[92] *Ali Shipping Corp v Shipyard Trogir* [1999] 1 WLR 314, [1998] 2 All ER 136, [1998] 1 Lloyd's Rep 643.
[93] *Hassneh Insurance Co v Mew* [1993] 2 Lloyd's Rep 243; *Glidepath BV v Thompson* [2005] EWHC 818 (Comm); [2005] 2 All ER (Comm) 833, [2005] 2 Lloyd's Rep 549.
[94] *Dolling-Baker v Merrett* [1990] 1 WLR 1205, [1991] 2 All ER 890.

term of an agreement to arbitrate and that the better view is that there is no such exception;[95]

(4) where the interests of justice require disclosure.[96]

In *Ali Shipping*, the Court of Appeal was not prepared to widen the scope of the exceptions simply on the basis that the parties to whom disclosure is contemplated are in the same beneficial ownership and management as the complaining party. Two reasons were given for this refusal; the first being that it is possible to envisage a situation where, despite the feature of common beneficial ownership between them, one entity may wish to keep private from the other the details of materials generated in an earlier arbitration. Secondly, where the problem arises in relation to disclosure in later proceedings, to propound such an exception is to leave out of account that the real interest of the objecting party is to withhold disclosure of such materials from the subsequent decision maker. The Court noted that while such motives may not be 'worthy' in the broad sense, they may be a permissible tactic, and unless the stance of the objecting party can be shown to be fraudulent or in the nature of an abuse of process, then the court should be prepared to grant injunctive relief, subject only to proof of a recognized exception to the rule of confidentiality. **11.32**

The duty of confidence has been said to be owed not merely by the parties to the arbitration but also by the arbitrator and witnesses called in the arbitration.[97] So far as the obligation owed by the arbitrator is concerned, on appointment, the arbitrator becomes a third party to the arbitration agreement which becomes a tri-lateral contract.[98] Thus, in the absence of an express term in the appointment of the arbitrator, an obligation of confidentiality can also be implied as a matter of law into that contract. The juridical basis of the obligation must, however, be different in relation to witnesses who are not parties to the arbitration agreement. If there is any such obligation, it must be founded on the equitable duty of confidence so that it will need to be established that the information has the necessary degree of confidence about it, that it has been imparted in circumstances importing an obligation of confidence and that there has been unauthorized use.[99] **11.33**

[95] S Males QC, 'Confidence in Arbitration' [1998] LMCLQ 245, 252.

[96] In *London and Leeds Estates Ltd v Paribas Ltd (No 2)* [1995] 1 EGLR 102 Mance J held that a party to court proceedings was entitled to call for the proof of an expert witness in a previous arbitration in a situation where it appeared that the views expressed by him in that proof were at odds with his views as expressed in the court proceedings. In *Emmott v Michael Wilson & Partners Ltd* [2008] EWCA Civ 184, [2008] Bus LR 1361, [2008] 2 All ER (Comm) 193, [2008] 1 Lloyd's Rep 616, the Court of Appeal upheld the first instance Judge's decision to permit part disclosure of a defence and counterclaim, which had been served in an earlier arbitration proceeding, to a New South Wales court in subsequent related litigation. Both the primary Judge and the Court of Appeal considered disclosure was in the interests of justice so as to prevent the foreign court from being potentially misled, in circumstances where the cases in the various proceedings involved the same or similar allegations.

[97] *London and Leeds Estates Ltd v Paribas Ltd (No 2)* [1995] 1 EGLR 102, 137.

[98] *Cie Europeene de Cereals SA v Tradax Export SA* [1986] 2 Lloyd's Rep 301.

[99] *Coco v A N Clark (Engineers) Ltd* [1969] RPC 41, 46; *Attorney-General v Observer Ltd* [1990] 1 AC 109, [1988] 3 All ER 545.

11.34 **Related court hearings** So far as the interrelation between the arbitral process and any subsequent court hearing is concerned the general rule in relation to court hearings, as expressed in the Civil Procedure Rules (CPR), is that a hearing is to be in public.[100] In March 2002 rules specific to arbitration claims were promulgated.[101] 'Arbitration claims' are defined in rule 62.2 as follows:

> (1) In this Section of this Part 'arbitration claim' means—
> (a) any application to the court under the 1996 Act;
> (b) a claim to determine—
> (i) whether there is a valid arbitration agreement
> (ii) whether an arbitration tribunal is properly constituted; or what matters have been submitted to arbitration in accordance with an arbitration agreement;
> (c) a claim to declare that an award by an arbitral tribunal is not binding on a party; and
> (d) any other application affecting—
> (i) arbitration proceedings (whether started or not); or
> (ii) an arbitration agreement.

11.35 Rule 62.10 provides that the court may order that an arbitration claim be heard either in public or in private and specifically excludes rule 39.2 from the ambit of the Part. There is a presumption in para 3, however, that the determination of a preliminary point of law under s 45 and that an appeal under s 69 on a question of law will be heard in public, which is unsurprising in view of the terms of s 69(3)(c)(ii). Otherwise all arbitration claims are to be heard in private. Therefore, in relation to appeals the starting point is to treat the public interest in a public hearing as outweighing any desire by the parties for continuing confidentiality; the converse is the case in relation to all other arbitration claims.

11.36 The meaning of 'in private' has been held by the Court of Appeal to be the same in both r 39.2 and r 62.10, and refers to situations in which a hearing would formerly have been described as being *in camera* or in secret and not simply in chambers.[102] Although the starting point of privacy for arbitration claims is contrary to the general principle established in rule 39.2, it rests clearly on the philosophy of party autonomy in modern arbitration law. Mance LJ observed:

> Party autonomy requires the Court so far as possible to respect the parties' choice of arbitration. Their choice of private arbitration constitutes an election for an alternative system of dispute resolution to that provided by the public Courts. The

[100] CPR 39.2(1).

[101] Civil Procedure (Amendment No 5) Rules 2001, SI 2001/4015 Section I of CPR Part 62.

[102] *Department of Economic Policy and Development of the City of Moscow v Bankers Trust Co* [2004] EWCA Civ 314, [2005] QB 207, [2004] 3 WLR 533, [2004] 2 All ER (Comm) 193, [2004] 2 Lloyd's Rep 179.

> same philosophy limits Court intervention to the minimum necessary in the public interest, which must include the public interest in ensuring not that arbitrators necessarily decide cases in a way which a Court would regard as correct, but that they at least decide them in a fundamentally fair way: see s.1 of the 1996 Act. The object of modern arbitration legislation, starting from at least the 1979 Act, has been to offer the international community an attractive framework within which to arbitrate in England.[103]

Rule 62.10 is therefore to be considered the starting point, and if neither the parties nor the Judge raise any question about the appropriateness of a private hearing, the hearing will remain private.[104] Once the question of a public hearing is raised, the Judge will be obliged to consider and weigh all the relevant circumstances. The mere fact that the parties have agreed to arbitrate confidentially and privately cannot dictate the approach to be taken under rule 62.10 because claims commenced under Part 62 are no longer consensual and there may be a public interest in having the matter heard in public.[105] **11.37**

Publication of judgments Rule 62.10 deals only with the question of whether the hearing should be in public or in private. It says nothing about whether the resulting judgment should be published. The distinction between the hearing and the judgment is recognized by the terms of art 6 of the European Convention for the Protection of Human Rights and Fundamental Freedoms 1950.[106] Art 6 purports to impose an absolute requirement to pronounce judgments in public; however, this absolute requirement has been recognized by the European Court of Human Rights to be subject to some qualification to be assessed in the light of the special features of the proceedings in question.[107] In *Hakansson v Sweden*[108] it was held that: **11.38**

> … neither the letter nor the spirit of this provision prevents a person from waiving of his own free will, either expressly or tacitly, the entitlement to have his case heard in public. However, a waiver must be made in an unequivocal manner and must not run counter to any important public interest.

---

103 Ibid 228, 552, 212, 192, [30].

104 *Glidepath BV v Thompson* [2005] EWHC 818 (Comm), [2005] 2 All ER (Comm) 833, 839, [2005] 2 Lloyd's Rep 549, 552, [19].

105 *Department of Economic Policy and Development of the City of Moscow v Bankers Trust Co* [2004] EWCA Civ 314, [2005] QB 207, 229, [2004] 3 WLR 533, 553–554, [2004] 2 All ER (Comm) 193, 213, [2004] 2 Lloyd's Rep 179, 192–193, [34] and the case there referred to, *Television New Zealand Ltd (TVNZ) v Langley Productions* [2000] 2 NZLR 250 in which the New Zealand High Court held that, in the particular circumstances, the proceedings should be subject to 'normal open process' and *Associated Electric and Gas Insurance Services Ltd v European Reinsurance Co of Zurich* [2003] UKPC 11, [2003] 1 WLR 1041, [2003] 1 All ER (Comm) 253.

106 Contained in Schedule 1 to the Human Rights Act 1998.

107 *B v UK* (2002) 34 EHRR 529, 540, [39]; *Pelling v Bruce-Williams (Secretary of State for Constitutional Affairs intervening) W* [2003] EWHC 1541, [2004] Fam 23, [2004] 2 WLR 509, [2003] 4 All ER 1074, upheld on appeal [2004] EWCA Civ 1046, [2004] Fam 155, [2004] 3 WLR 1178, [2004] 3 All ER 875.

108 *Hakansson v Sweden* (1991) 13 EHRR 1, 16, [66].

In particular, it has been held that nothing in Art 6 conflicts with the voluntary waiver by parties of court proceedings in favour of arbitration.[109] Mance LJ considered that the effect of these decisions was that the parties could waive publicity where it does 'not run counter to any important public interest' but that this does not mean that the parties can, by simple agreement, insist on a court restricting publication.[110]

11.39 The Court of Appeal has held that the public interest in ensuring appropriate standards of fairness in the conduct of arbitrations militates in favour of a public judgment in respect of judgments given on applications under s 68 (serious irregularity in the conduct of the arbitral process).[111] There is a legitimate interest in the operation and practice of arbitration given the importance of arbitration to international commercial and financial dealings, and so it is desirable that judgments be public for the guidance of lawyers and commercial parties. Nonetheless, there will be circumstances in which it will be appropriate for the judgment to remain confidential. Such circumstances were found to exist in *Department of Economic Policy and Development of the City of Moscow v Bankers Trust Co*[112] where the Judge at first instance found that the judgment covers 'sensitive matters of greatest confidentiality'.[113]

11.40 A party seeking to maintain the confidentiality of a judgment is not required to establish positive detriment beyond the undermining of its expectation that the matters would remain confidential. Further, the fact of bringing an application before the court cannot, of itself, amount to a waiver of confidentiality. Mance LJ indicated that the Judge at first instance was entitled to balance the absence of any substantial evidence of detriment against a failure by the other party to provide 'any good reason for publication'.[114]

Minimal court interference

Rights of appeal

11.41 Just as the court's supervisory powers are curtailed, so too is its power to interfere with an arbitral award through the avenue of appeal. Prior to the coming into force of the 1996 Act, the right to appeal from an arbitral award was governed by the so-called '*Nema* Guidelines,'[115] pursuant to which the appellant was required to

---

[109] *Suovaniemi v Finland* Appeal No 31737/96, 23 February 1999, European Court of Human Rights.

[110] *Department of Economic Policy and Development of the City of Moscow v Bankers Trust Co* [2004] EWCA Civ 314, [2005] QB 207, 225–227, [2004] 3 WLR 533, 549–551, [2004] 2 All ER (Comm) 193, 209–211 [2004] 2 Lloyd's Rep 179, 190–191, [27].

[111] Ibid 231, 555–556, 215, 194, [39].

[112] Ibid.

[113] Ibid 225–227, 549–551, 209–211, 190–191, [27].

[114] Ibid 233–234, 557–558, 217, 195, [46].

[115] *BTP Tioxide Ltd v Pioneer Shipping Ltd (The Nema)* [1982] AC 724, [1981] 2 Lloyd's Rep 239.

demonstrate that the arbitrator was 'obviously wrong' or, in a case of general public importance, that his conclusion was at least open to serious doubt.

The 1996 Act adopts the *Nema* Guidelines but goes further. Under s 69 of the 1996 Act, an appeal is limited to a point of English law. It is no longer possible to appeal on a point of foreign law. There is a further consideration expressed in s 69(3)(d) which provides: **11.42**

> The court must be satisfied that, despite the agreement of the parties to resolve the matter by arbitration, it is just and proper in all the circumstances for the court to determine the question.

However, it will be a rare case in which the *Nema* Guidelines are satisfied, but the court is unpersuaded that it is just and proper for it to determine the question.

Stay of the proceedings

Interaction between the arbitration process and admiralty procedures occurs most frequently when an attempt is made to combine the security aspects of an action *in rem* with a determination on the merits by an arbitral tribunal. This may arise when the claimant has agreed to arbitration but is concerned that assets may not be available to it when the award is made. The claimant may therefore wish to arrest *in rem* at the outset to preserve the ship or to have security put up in lieu. It is not an abuse of process to arrest a vessel after the commencement of arbitral proceedings for the sole purpose of obtaining security for the claims being arbitrated.[116] Alternatively, the claimant may arrest the ship in support of the admiralty action with every intention of pursuing that action rather than arbitrating. **11.43**

Where the claim in respect of which the vessel is arrested is subject to an arbitration clause, the court will invariably stay the *in rem* proceedings in so far as they raise substantive issues falling within the scope of the arbitration agreement. This approach accords with the Arrest Convention.[117] However, a distinction is to be drawn between suits brought for the purpose of determining the merits of the underlying claim and suits brought solely to obtain security for that claim. A suit commenced solely for the purpose of obtaining security will not breach the arbitration clause,[118] and nor will it amount to a waiver or abandonment of the right to arbitrate.[119] **11.44**

[116] *The Jalamatsya* [1987] 2 Lloyd's Rep 164.

[117] Art 7 provides that where the court of arrest has no jurisdiction on the merits, or where the parties have agreed to submit the dispute to a foreign court or to arbitration, then, provided that the plaintiff brings proceedings in a court which has jurisdiction on the merits, or in the agreed foreign court, or before the agreed arbitration tribunal, within a time allowed by the court of arrest the security will not be released, but will remain in the court of arrest to satisfy any judgment in the other court or any award in the arbitration.

[118] *Petromin SA v Secnav Marine Ltd* [1995] 1 Lloyd's Rep 603; *In re Q's Estate* [1999] 1 Lloyd's Rep 931; *Kallang Shipping SA Panama v AXA Assurances Senegal (The Kallang)* [2008] EWHC 2761 (Comm); [2009] 1 Lloyd's Rep 124.

[119] *Comandate Marine Corp v Pan Australia Shipping Pty Ltd* [2006] FCAFC 192, (2006) 157 FCR 45.

11.45 The court's power to grant a stay on terms is set out in s 11 of the 1996 Act which provides:

> (1) Where Admiralty proceedings are stayed on the ground that the dispute in question should be submitted to arbitration, the court granting the stay may, if in those proceedings property has been arrested or bail or other security has been given to prevent or obtain release from arrest—
> (a) order that the property arrested be retained as security for the satisfaction of any award given in the arbitration in respect of that dispute, or
> (b) order that the stay of those proceedings be conditional on the provision of equivalent security for the satisfaction of any such award.
>
> (2) Subject to any provision made by rules of court and to any necessary modification, the same law and practice shall apply in relation to property retained in pursuance of an order as would apply if it were held for the purposes of proceedings in the court making the order.

11.46 Section 11 reproduces, with one major exception, s 26 of the *Civil Jurisdiction and Judgments Act* 1982. Section 26 came into force on 1 November 1984. Prior to that enactment, courts recognized that there was jurisdiction to continue arrests as security for judgments, but not as security for arbitration awards. As Robert Goff LJ said in *The Andria now renamed Vasso*:[120]

> ... on the law as it stands at present, the court's jurisdiction to arrest a ship in an action in rem should not be exercised for the purpose of providing security for an award which may be made in arbitration proceedings. That is simply because the purpose of the exercise of the jurisdiction is to provide security in respect of the action in rem, and not to provide security in some other proceedings, for example, arbitration proceedings.

11.47 On to that principle was grafted the principle in *The Rena K*, where Brandon J held that:[121]

> There is nothing in section 1(1) of the Arbitration Act 1975 which obliges the court, whenever it grants a stay of an action in rem in which security has been obtained, to make an order for the unconditional release of such security. Nor did section 4(2) of the Arbitration Act 1950, now repealed, impose any such obligation. That being so, I think that it is a matter for the discretion of the court, acting under [RSC, Ord 75, r 13(4)], what order it should make with regard to such security, and that the way in which it exercises that discretion must depend on the circumstances of each particular case.
>
> If, on the one hand, the case is one where in all probability the stay will be final and there will therefore never be any judgment in the action to be satisfied, the court should exercise its discretion by releasing the security unconditionally, as was done in *The Golden Trader* [1975] Q.B. 348. If, on the other hand, the case is one where the stay may well not be final and there may well therefore still be a judgment in the action to be satisfied, the court should exercise its discretion either by refusing to release the security at all, or by only releasing it subject to a term that the defendants shall provide alternative security for payment of any award in the arbitration.

---

[120] *The Andria now renamed Vasso* [1984] QB 477, 490.

[121] *The Rena K* [1979] QB 377, 404–405; approved by the Court of Appeal in *The Tuyuti* [1984] QB 838, 846.

> On this view of the law it is necessary to consider, in relation to the facts of this particular case, whether in all probability the stay will be final and there will therefore never be any judgment in the action to be satisfied, or whether the stay may well not be final and there may well therefore still be a judgment in the action to be satisfied.

Thus, arrests could be continued in respect of claims referred to arbitration only on the theoretical basis that if the respondent was unable to satisfy the award, the claimant would revive the stayed proceedings and obtain a judgment *in rem*. Thus, in considering whether or not to grant a stay, the court was required to consider whether or not the respondent would be able to satisfy any award.[122] This had the consequence that much time was taken up at the early stages of every dispute where a vessel was arrested and where the dispute was subject to arbitration in determining whether an award was likely to be met or not. **11.48**

When s 26 was enacted the effect of it was to assimilate claims in arbitration with *in rem* proceedings in the Admiralty Court so that the discretion is now the same in both classes of case.[123] The only question now is whether the respondent is able to offer any alternative security. **11.49**

Section 26 had permitted the court to impose conditions upon the stay of judicial proceedings, and the power was interpreted as applying only to discretionary stays (ie, in respect of domestic arbitration agreements).[124] However, under the 1996 Act, all stays are mandatory[125] and so the issue does not arise. **11.50**

Australia has adopted a provision which is in similar terms to s 26 of the Civil Jurisdiction and Judgments Act 1986.[126] Singapore[127] and Hong Kong,[128] too, have adopted similar provisions. South Africa has done the same, although its provision has the distinguishing feature that it is not necessary for an action *in rem* in fact to have been commenced; it requires merely that an application for arrest be made.[129] The English, Australian, Hong Kong, and Singapore provisions presuppose that admiralty proceedings are already on foot. No such provision has, however, been enacted in Canada or New Zealand and those jurisdictions have to date continued to apply *The Rena K* principle.[130] **11.51**

---

122 *Gulf Mid-East Lines v The Silver Athens* 1984 Fo 217, 31 July 1984 per Sheen J.

123 *The Bazias 3 and The Bazias 4* [1993] QB 673, [1993] 1 Lloyd's Rep 101.

124 *The World Star* [1986] 2 Lloyd's Rep 274.

125 s 9.

126 Admiralty Act 1988, s 29; *Allonah Pty Ltd v The Ship Amanda N* (1989) 21 FCR 60, 90 ALR 391 (Federal Court of Australia).

127 International Arbitration Act (Chapter 143A), s 7(1); *Front Carriers Ltd v Atlantic & Orient Shipping Corp* [2006] SGHC 127 (High Court of Singapore).

128 Arbitration Ordinance Cap 609, s 20(6) and High Court Ordinance Cap 4, s 12B(6A).

129 Admiralty Jurisdiction Regulation Act 105 of 1983 s 5(3); *Katagum Wholesale Commodities Co Ltd v MV Paz* 1984 (3) SAfLR 261; *Euromarine International of Mauren v The Ship Berg* 1984 (4) SAfLR 647.

130 *Atlantic Lines & Navigation Co v Didymi* [1985] 1 FC 240; *Cyber Sea Technologies Inc v Underwater Harvester Remotely Operated Vehicle* [2002] FCT 794 (Federal Court of Canada); *The Irina Zharkikh and Ksenia Zharkikh* [2001] 2 NZLR 801, [2001] 2 Lloyd's Rep 319 (High Court of New Zealand).

11.52 The continued validity of *The Rena K* principle in those jurisdictions is, however, open to question in light of the decision of the House of Lords in *The Indian Grace (No 2)*.[131] In *The Britannia*,[132] Waung J said:

> In my judgment, the obviously correct analysis in *The Rena K, The Tuyuti* and *The Bazias 3* afford high and good authority against Mr Barlow's submission that the Admiralty Court has no jurisdiction to maintain the arrest of the vessel in the face of the mandatory stay of proceedings under the *Arbitration Ordinance*. I accept of course that it is not legitimate if the arrest was to provide security for the possible foreign arbitration award but it is perfectly legitimate and proper if the arrest is for the purpose of this action when the stay might be lifted because of the defendant's failure to honour the arbitration award or to redeliver the vessel back to the owners. This is precisely the situation here.

This decision has been criticized for its unquestioning acceptance of:

> ... Brandon J's unexplored assumption in *The Rena K*—which was similarly left in abeyance by Robert Goff LJ in both *The Vasso and The Tuyuti*—that an Admiralty action *in rem* was different from an action in personam, and that the doctrines of merger and issue estoppel did not operate to bar a subsequent action *in rem* following on judgment in personam[133]

and for its omission of any apparent consideration of the decision in *The Indian Grace (No 2)*, despite judgment in that case having been delivered three months earlier.[134]

11.53 More recently, and after a detailed consideration of the judgment in *The Indian Grace (No 2)*, Young J of the High Court of New Zealand followed and applied the principles in *The Rena K*.[135] Mr West has criticized that decision also, essentially on the basis that it fails to distinguish between a 'true action *in rem*' founded on a maritime lien and a 'quasi action *in rem*' founded on a statutory basis.[136] However, in the light of the analysis set out in Chapter 2, it is submitted that:

(1) the supposed distinction between an action *in rem* founded on a maritime lien and one founded on a statutory claim *in rem* is illusory;
(2) the decision in *The Indian Grace (No 2)* goes no further than affirming that the substantive rights which underlie an action *in rem* are personal and, for

---

[131] *Republic of India v India Steamship Co Ltd (The Indian Grace) (No 2)* [1997] UKHL 40, [1998] AC 878, [1997] 3 WLR 818, [1997] 4 All ER 380, [1998] 1 Lloyd's Rep 1. Cf the comments of Justice Ng in *Handytankers Ks v The owners and/or demise charterers of the ship or vessel M/V Atlas, subsequently renamed as Kombos* [2009] HCAJ 241.

[132] *The Britannia* [1998] 1 HKC 221.

[133] M West, 'Arbitrations, Admiralty Actions *in rem* and the Arrest of Ships in the Hong Kong SAR; in the Twilight of The Indian Grace (No 2)?' [2002] LMCLQ 259, 265.

[134] Ibid 261.

[135] *The Irina Zharkikh and Ksenia Zharkikh* [2001] 2 NZLR 801, [2001] 2 Lloyd's Rep 319.

[136] A distinction also drawn by Nigel Meeson & John Kimbell, *Admiralty Jurisdiction & Practice*, (4th edn, 2011), Chapter 3.

that reason, an action *in rem* can be regarded as being an action against the owners from the moment the Admiralty Court is seised with jurisdiction;
(3) there is, however, an additional right, and that is the security interest which is created in and attaches to the claim. This security interest arises both in relation to claims which are classed as maritime liens and those which are merely statutory actions *in rem*, provided in the latter case that the *in rem* proceedings have been commenced;
(4) an arbitral tribunal has power only to deal with the substantive rights underlying the actions *in rem*, the personal claim. Jurisdiction *in rem* is vested only the Admiralty Court;
(5) thus, an arbitral tribunal can make no award that affects the security interest created by the action *in rem*; the award can only ever relate to the underlying *in personam* claim. Thus, there is no merger of the action *in rem* with the arbitral award and therefore no reason why the Admiralty Court will not retain jurisdiction over the action *in rem* should the arbitral award not be satisfied.[137]

Whilst the precise question determined in *The Rena K* will no longer arise in English law because of the enactment of s 11(1) of the 1996 Act, the wider issue of the question of merger may well arise again and remains of significance in England and Wales, Hong Kong, New Zealand, and Singapore. By contrast, Australia, Canada, and South Africa have obviated the problem by providing that an action *in rem* can be brought to enforce an arbitral award.[138] **11.54**

Anti-suit injunctions

An anti-suit injunction is an order restraining a party from commencing or pursuing proceedings before a foreign court. Anti-suit injunctions are generally met with consternation by courts of other jurisdictions which see them as an infringement on their sovereignty. The English justification for such an injunction is that it is not directed at a foreign court but, rather, at a party who is amenable to the jurisdiction of the English courts and who has wrongfully commenced litigation or arbitration in a foreign jurisdiction.[139] Whilst the explanation may sound reasonable to English lawyers, it is not widely accepted abroad. Leggatt LJ, in *Phillip Alexander Futures & Securities Ltd v Bamberger*, emphasized the need for caution unless it can truly be said that the defendant is amenable to the jurisdiction of the English courts.[140] If the defendant lives or has assets of substance in England then, **11.55**

[137] See, too, *The Bumbesti* [2000] QB 559, [2000] 2 WLR 533, [2000] 2 All ER 692, [1999] 2 Lloyd's Rep 481.
[138] Admiralty Act 1988 s 4(3)(u) (Australia); Federal Courts Act s 22(1) (Canada); Admiralty Jurisdiction Regulation Act 105 of 1983 s 1(1)(aa) (South Africa).
[139] *Turner v Grovit* [2001] UKHL 65, [2002] 1 WLR 107, 117, [23], [2002] 1 All ER 960.
[140] *Phillip Alexander Futures & Securities Ltd v Bamberger* [1996] CLC 1757.

in reality, it can be said that he is amenable to the jurisdiction. If not then the only way in which the order can be enforced is if a foreign court recognizes the order, and that will militate against the grant of interlocutory relief.

11.56 There is no dispute in principle that an anti-suit injunction may be used to restrain a breach of an arbitration agreement and that courts should not be reticent in granting such an injunction 'on the clear and simple ground that the defendant has promised not to bring [other proceedings]'.[141] Whilst this proposition may be straightforward where the party who is in breach of the contractual obligation to arbitrate is not domiciled in an EU (or EFTA) country and the proceedings pursued are not before the courts of an EU State, it is no longer apposite where an EU party or EU proceedings are involved. Like the Conventions before it, the Regulations exclude arbitration from its ambit,[142] and an English court could previously exercise its jurisdiction to grant an anti-suit injunction against a party domiciled in a Member State to restrain it from pursuing proceedings in that or another Contracting State.[143] However, it is now clear that it is impossible for an English court to grant an anti-suit injunction in such a case. The European Court of Justice has ruled that it is incompatible with the Regulation for a court of a Member State to make an order to restrain a person from commencing or continuing proceedings before the courts of another Member State on the ground that such proceedings would be contrary to an arbitration agreement.[144]

11.57 In *West Tankers*, the charterer commenced arbitration in London against the shipowner claiming damages arising out of a collision. The charterer's insurer paid the charterer up to the policy limits and then commenced proceedings in Italy against the shipowner to recover those sums pursuant to the insurer's rights of subrogation. The English court granted the shipowner an anti-suit injunction, restraining the insurers from continuing the Italian proceedings. The question of whether the Court had jurisdiction to grant that injunction was then referred to the ECJ. The ECJ noted that arbitration was expressly excluded from the scope of the Regulation but held that where the subject matter of the dispute comes within the scope of the Regulation, a preliminary issue such as the applicability of an arbitration agreement also comes within its scope of application. The use of an anti-suit injunction

[141] *Aggeliki Charis Compania Maritima SA v Pagnan SpA (The Angelic Grace)* [1995] 1 Lloyd's Rep 87, 96.

[142] Art 1.2(d) of both Regulations 44/2001 and 1215/2012.

[143] *Navigation Maritime Bulgare v Rustal Trading Ltd (The Ivan Zagubanski)* [2002] 1 Lloyd's Rep 106; *Through Transport Mutual Insurance Association (Eurasia) Ltd v New India Assurance Co Ltd* [2004] EWCA Civ 1598, [2005] 1 All ER (Comm) 715, [2005] 1 Lloyd's Rep 67.

[144] *Allianz SpA, formerly Riunione Adriatica di Sicurtà SpA v West Tankers Inc* (187/07) [2009] ECR 663; [2009] 1 Lloyd's Rep 413. Even before this case was decided, anti-suit injunctions had effectively been outlawed in European cross-border litigation by the European Court's decision in *Turner v Grovit* (n 139 above) [2005] 1 AC 101, [2004] 3 WLR 1193, [2005] ICR 23, [2004] 2 All ER (Comm) 381, [2004] 2 Lloyd's Rep 169.

to prevent the court of a Member State from ruling on the applicability of the Regulation essentially amounted to stripping that court of the power to rule on its own jurisdiction under the Regulation.

While the *West Tankers* matter was pending before the ECJ, the London arbitration continued. The tribunal had to determine two further issues: whether the insurers were liable for the shipowner's legal fees and expenses associated with the Italian proceedings, and whether the insurers were liable to indemnify the owners against an award made against the owners in the Italian proceedings that was greater than the liability of the owners as determined by the tribunal. The arbitral tribunal published an award holding that it lacked jurisdiction to grant equitable damages for breach of the obligation to arbitrate or an indemnity. The Commercial Court allowed the shipowner's appeal from this decision, holding that there was nothing in the reasoning of the ECJ which required the jurisdiction of the arbitrators to be circumscribed by the Regulation. Arbitration fell outside the Regulation and an arbitral tribunal was not bound to give effect to the principle of effective judicial protection. Accordingly, the tribunal was not deprived, by reason of European law, of the jurisdiction to award equitable damages for breach of the obligation to arbitrate.[145]

Since the ECJ decision in *West Tankers*, English courts have considered a number of issues related to anti-suit injunctions in other cases involving London arbitration and foreign parallel proceedings. In *Toyota Tsusho Sugar Trading Ltd v Prolat Srl*, the English Commercial Court ruled that it had jurisdiction to determine an application for a declaration that a binding arbitration clause existed between the parties, even though one of the parties had commenced parallel proceedings concerning the same subject matter in Naples.[146] The Court noted that the Regulation did not apply to arbitration. To determine whether or not there was an arbitration agreement and to make a declaration accordingly was outside the Regulation and the arbitration tribunal was 'free to consider matters relating to arbitration even though the Italian court is also seised with a dispute of identical, similar or related nature'.[147] **11.58**

In *Starlight Shipping Co v Allianz Marine and Aviation Versicherungs Ag and Ors (The Alexandros T)*,[148] the Court held that it had jurisdiction to make an award for specific performance of a promise not to sue under an arbitration agreement. Such an award was 'no more than a determination by the English court of the rights and

[145] *West Tankers Inc v Allianz Spa & Anor (The Front Comor)* [2012] EWHC 854 (Comm), [2012] 2 All ER (Comm) 395, [2012] 2 Lloyd's Rep 103. See also *Starlight Shipping Co v Allianz Marine & Aviation Versicherungs AG (The Alexandros T)* [2014] EWCA Civ 1010, [2014] 2 Lloyd's Rep 544.

[146] *Toyota Tsusho Sugar Trading Ltd v Prolat Srl* [2014] EWHC 3649 (Comm), [2015] 1 Lloyd's Rep 344.

[147] Ibid 347, [17].

[148] *Starlight Shipping Co v Allianz Marine and Aviation Versicherungs Ag and Ors (The Alexandros T)* [2014] EWHC 3068 (Comm), [2014] 2 Lloyd's Rep 579.

obligations under the settlement agreements ... and a determination by the English court of the appropriate remedy in respect of a breach ...'.[149] Such orders were not intended to usurp the jurisdiction of the Greek court (in which the shipowners had subsequently commenced proceedings after settlement agreements had been concluded) but rather to assist the Greek court. As Briggs and Rees remark: 'This seems very challenging indeed, for the consequences of disobedience are practically identical to those which result from disobedience to an injunction.'[150]

11.59 The limitation expressed in *West Tankers* now prevents English courts from enjoining a party within its jurisdiction from commencing or continuing proceedings in a foreign court within the Brussels/Lugano regime, and does not apply to disputes involving proceedings in non-Member States.[151] Even in proceedings involving Member States, it seems English courts will continue to carve out their own capacity to rule on matters of jurisdiction, but will stop short of awarding anti-suit injunctions.

11.60 Finally, it should be noted that, although the text of the operative parts of the Regulations (art 1.2(d)) is identical, the 'recast' Brussels I Regulation (1215/2012) contains a lengthy recital (12) not present in its predecessor (44/2001). The essence of the recital is as follows:

(1) There is nothing to prevent a court examining whether the arbitration agreement is 'null and void, inoperative or incapable of being performed, in accordance with [its] national law'. Rulings on that issue will not be recognized and enforced under the Regulation.
(2) If a court does conclude that the arbitration agreement is 'null and void [etc]', its ruling on the substance of the matter should be capable of recognition and enforcement under the Regulation.[152]
(3) However, that 'should be without prejudice to the competence' of Member State courts 'to decide on the recognition and enforcement of arbitral awards' under the New York Convention, 'which takes precedence over this Regulation'.

The intent of the recital appears to be to allow arbitration to proceed and to limit (without excluding) the opportunity afforded by the Regulation to undermine it. As yet, it is too soon to tell what difference it will make in practice.

---

149 Ibid 595, [75].

150 Adrian Briggs & Peter Rees, *Civil Jurisdiction & Judgments* (6th edn, 2015) at para 2.09, n 60. There is a useful discussion of the interplay between the Regulation and arbitration at paras 2.42–2.44.

151 *AES Ust-Kamenogorsk Hydropower Plant LLP v Ust-Kamengorsk Hydropower Plant JSC* [2013] UKSC 35, [2013] 1 WLR 1889, [2014] 1 All ER (Comm) 1, [2013] 2 Lloyd's Rep 281.

152 Compare the first edition of this work at para 11.57.

APPENDIX 1

Admiralty Court Act, 1840

(3 & 4 Vict c 65)

An Act to Improve the Practice and Extend the Jurisdiction of the High Court of Admiralty of England.

Whereas the jurisdiction of the High Court of Admiralty of England may be in certain respects advantageously extended, and the practice thereof improved:

3. Whenever a vessel shall be arrested, etc., court to have jurisdiction over claims of mortgagees

Whenever any ship or vessel shall be under arrest by process issuing from the said High Court of Admiralty, or the proceeds of any ship or vessel having been so arrested shall have been brought into and be in the registry of the said court, in either such case the said court shall have full jurisdiction to take cognizance of all claims and causes of action of any person in respect of any mortgage of such ship or vessel, and to decide any suit instituted by any such person in respect of any such claims or causes of action respectively.

4. Court to decide questions of title, etc.

The said Court of Admiralty shall have jurisdiction to decide all questions as to the title to or ownership of any ship or vessel, or the proceeds thereof remaining in the registry, arising in any cause of possession, salvage, damage, wages, or bottomry, which shall be instituted in the said court after the passing of this Act.

6. The court in certain cases may adjudicate, etc.

The High Court of Admiralty shall have jurisdiction to decide all claims and demands whatsoever in the nature of salvage for services rendered to or damage received by any ship or sea-going vessel, or in the nature of towage, or for necessaries supplied to any foreign ship or sea-going vessel, and to enforce the payment thereof, whether such ship or vessel may have been within the body of a county, or upon the high seas, at the time when the services were rendered or damage received, or necessaries furnished, in respect of which such claim is made.

22. Jurisdiction to try questions concerning booty of war

The said High Court of Admiralty shall have jurisdiction to decide all matters and questions concerning booty of war, or the distribution thereof, which it shall please her Majesty, Her Heirs and Successors by the advice of her and their Privy Council, to refer to the judgment of the said court; and in all matters so referred the court shall proceed as in cases of prize of war, and the judgment of the court therein shall be binding upon all parties concerned.

23. Jurisdiction of courts of law and equity not taken away

Provided always, that nothing herein contained shall be deemed to preclude any of her Majesty's courts of law or equity now having jurisdiction over the several subject matters and causes of action herein-before mentioned from continuing to exercise such jurisdiction as fully as if this Act had not been passed.

APPENDIX 2

Admiralty Court Act, 1861

[24 Vict c 10]

An Act to Extend the Jurisdiction and Improve the Practice of the High Court of Admiralty

WHEREAS it is expedient to extend the jurisdiction and improve the practice of the High Court of Admiralty of England: Be it therefore enacted. etc. as follows:

1. Short title

This Act may be cited for all purposes as 'The Admiralty Court Act, 1861'.

2. Interpretation of terms

In the interpretation and for the purposes of this Act (if not inconsistent with the context or subject) the following terms shall have the respective meanings hereinafter assigned to them; that is to say, '**Ship**' shall include any description of vessel used in navigation not propelled by oars: '**Cause**' shall include any cause, suit, action, or other proceeding in the Court of Admiralty.

3. Commencement of Act

This Act shall come into operation on the First Day of June One thousand eight hundred and sixty-one.

4. As to claims for building, equipping, or repairing of ships

The High Court of Admiralty shall have jurisdiction over any claim for the building, equipping, or repairing of any ship, if at the time of the institution of the cause the ship or the proceeds thereof are under arrest of the court.

5. As to claims for necessaries supplied to ships

The High Court of Admiralty shall have jurisdiction over any claim for necessaries supplied to any ship elsewhere than in the port to which the ship belongs, unless it is shown to the satisfaction of the court that at the time of the institution of the cause any owner or part owner of the ship is domiciled in England or Wales: Provided always, that if in any such cause the plaintiff do not recover twenty pounds, he shall not be entitled to any costs, charges, or expenses incurred by him therein, unless the judge shall certify that the cause was a fit one to be tried in the said Court.

6. As to claims for damage to cargo imported

The High Court of Admiralty shall have jurisdiction over any claim by the owner or consignee or assignee of any bill of lading of any goods carried into any port in England or Wales in any ship, for damage done to the goods or any part thereof by the negligence or misconduct of or for any breach of duty or breach of contract on the part of the owner, master, or crew of the ship, unless it is shown to the satisfaction of the court that at the time of the institution of the cause any owner or part owner of the ship is domiciled in England or Wales: Provided always, that if in any such cause the plaintiff do not recover twenty pounds, he shall not be entitled to any costs, charges, or expenses incurred by him therein, unless the judge shall certify that the cause was a fit one to be tried in the said court.

7. As to claims for damage done by ships

The High Court of Admiralty shall have jurisdiction over any claim for damage done by any ship.

8. As to questions touching ownership, etc., of ships

The High Court of Admiralty shall have jurisdiction to decide all questions arising between the co-owners, or any of them, touching the ownership, possession, employment, and earnings of any ship registered at any port in England or Wales, or any share thereof, and may settle all accounts outstanding and unsettled between the parties in relation thereto, and may direct the said ship or any share thereof to be sold, and may make such order in the premises as to it shall seem fit.

9. Extending 17 & 18 Vict c 104 as to claims for salvage of life

All the provisions of 'The Merchant Shipping Act 1854' in regard to salvage of life from any ship or boat within the limits of the United Kingdom, shall be extended to the salvage of life from any British ship or boat, wheresoever the services may have been rendered, and from any foreign ship or boat, where the services have been rendered wholly or in part in British waters.

10. As to claims for wages and for disbursements by master of a ship

The High Court of Admiralty shall have jurisdiction over any claim by a seaman of any ship for wages earned by him on board the ship, whether the same be due under a special contract or otherwise, and also over any claim by the master of any ship for wages earned by him on board the ship, and for disbursements made by him on account of the ship: Provided always, that if in any such cause the plaintiff do not recover fifty pounds, he shall not be entitled to any costs, charges, or expenses incurred by him therein, unless the judge shall certify that the cause was a fit one to be tried in the said court.

11. As to claims in respect of registered mortgages

The High Court of Admiralty shall have jurisdiction over any claim in respect of any mortgage duly registered according to the provisions of the Merchant Shipping Act, 1854, whether the ship or the proceeds thereof be under arrest of the said court or not.

12. Sections 62 to 65 of 17 & 18 Vict c 104 extended to Court of Admiralty

The High Court of Admiralty shall have the same powers over any British ship, or any share therein, as are conferred upon the High Court of Chancery in England by the sixty-second, sixty-third, sixty-fourth and sixty-fifth sections of The Merchant Shipping Act, 1854.

13. Part 9 of 17 & 18 Vict c 104, extended to Court of Admiralty

Whenever any ship or vessel, or the proceeds thereof, are under arrest of the High Court of Admiralty, the said court shall have the same powers as are conferred upon the High Court of Chancery in England by the ninth part of the Merchant Shipping Act, 1854.

14. Court to be a court of record

The High Court of Admiralty shall be a Court of record for all intents and purposes.

15. Decrees of Court of Admiralty

All Decrees and Orders of the High Court of Admiralty, whereby any Sum of Money, or any Costs, Charges, or Expenses, shall be payable to any Person, shall have the same Effect as Judgments in the Superior Courts of Common Law, and the Persons to whom such Monies, or Costs, or Charges, or Expenses, shall be payable, shall be deemed Judgment Creditors, and all Powers of enforcing Judgments possessed by the Superior Courts of Common Law, or any Judge thereof, with respect to Matters depending in the same Courts, as well as against the Ships and Goods arrested as against the Person of the Judgment Debtor, shall be possessed by the said Court of Admiralty with respect to matters therein depending; and all Remedies at Common Law possessed by Judgment Creditors shall be in like manner possessed by Persons to whom any Monies, Costs, Charges, or Expenses are by such Orders or Decrees of the said Court of Admiralty directed to be paid.

16. Proceedings where a claim is made to goods taken in execution

If any claim shall be made to any goods or chattels taken in execution under any process of the High Court of Admiralty, or in respect of the seizure thereof, or any act or matter connected therewith, or in respect of the proceeds or value of any such goods or chattels, by any landlord for rent, or by any person not being the party against whom the process has issued, the registrar of the said court may, upon application of the officer charged with the execution of the process, whether before or after any action brought against such officer, issue a summons calling before the said court both the party issuing such process and the party making the claim; and thereupon any action which shall have been brought in any of her Majesty's superior courts of record, or in any local or inferior court, in respect of such claim, seizure, act, or matter as aforesaid, shall be stayed; and the court in which such action shall have been brought, or any judge thereof, on proof of the issue of such summons, and that the goods and chattels were so taken in execution, may order the party bringing the action to pay the costs of all proceedings had upon the action after issue of the summons out of the said Admiralty Court; and the judge of the said Admiralty Court shall adjudicate upon the claim, and make such order between the parties in respect thereof and of the costs of the proceedings, as to him shall seem fit; and such order shall be enforced in like manner as any order made in any suit brought in the said court. Where any such claim shall be made as aforesaid, the claimant may deposit with the officer charged with the execution of the process either the amount or value of the goods claimed, the value to be fixed by appraisement in case of dispute, to be by the officer paid into court to abide the decision of the judge upon the claim, or the sum which the officer shall be allowed to charge as costs for keeping possession of the goods until such decision can be obtained; and in default of the claimant so doing, the officer may sell the goods as if no such claim had been made, and shall pay into court the proceeds of the sale, to abide the decision of the judge.

17. Powers of Superior Courts extended to Court of Admiralty

The Judge of the High Court of Admiralty shall have all such powers as are possessed by any of the Superior Courts of Common Law or any Judge thereof to compel

18. Party in Court of Admiralty may apply for an order for inspection by Trinity Masters

Any party in a cause in the High Court of Admiralty shall be at liberty to apply to the said court for an order for the inspection by the Trinity Masters or others appointed for the trial of the said cause, or by the party himself or his witnesses, of any ship or other personal or real property, the inspection of which may be material to the issue of the cause; and the court may make such order in respect of the costs arising thereout as to it shall seem fit.

...

33. Bail may be taken in the Court of Admiralty for the Court of Appeal, etc.

In any cause in the High Court of Admiralty bail may be taken to answer the judgment as well of the said court as of the Court of Appeal, and the said High Court of Admiralty may withhold the release of any property under its arrest until such bail has been given; and in any appeal from any decree or order of the High Court of Admiralty the Court of Appeal may make and enforce its order against the surety or sureties who may have signed any such bail bond in the same manner as if the bail had been given in the Court of Appeal.

34. Hearing of cross causes

The High Court of Admiralty may, on the application of the defendant in any cause of damage, and on his instituting a cross cause for the damage sustained by him in respect of the same collision, direct that the principal cause and the cross cause be heard at the same time and upon the same evidence; and if in the principal cause the ship of the defendant has been arrested or security given by him to answer judgment, and in the cross cause the ship of the plaintiff cannot be arrested, and security has not been given to answer judgment therein, the court may, if it think fit, suspend the proceedings in the principal cause, until security has been given to answer judgment in the cross cause.

35. Jurisdiction of the court

The jurisdiction conferred by this Act on the High Court of Admiralty may be exercised either by proceedings *in rem* or by proceedings *in personam.*

APPENDIX 3

Supreme Court of Judicature (Consolidation) Act, 1925

(15 & 16 Geo. 5.) CHAPTER 49

PART II

JURISDICTION AND LAW

22.—(1) The High Court shall, in relation to admiralty matters, have the following jurisdiction (in this Act referred to as "admiralty jurisdiction") that is to say— Admiralty jurisdiction of High Court.

(*a*) Jurisdiction to hear and determine any of the following questions or claims:—

(i) Any question as to the title to or ownership of a ship, or the proceeds of sale of a ship remaining in the admiralty registry, arising in an action of possession, salvage, damage, necessaries, wages or bottomry;

(ii) Any question arising between the co-owners of a ship registered at any port in England as to the ownership, possession, employment or earnings of that ship, or any share thereof, with power to settle any account outstanding and unsettled between the parties in relation thereto, and to direct the ship, or any share thereof, to be sold, or to make such order as the court thinks fit;

(iii) Any claim for damage received by a ship, whether received within the body of a county or on the high seas;

(iv) Any claim for damage done by a ship;

(v) Subject to the provisions of section five hundred and forty-seven of the Merchant Shipping Act, 1894, with respect to the summary determination of salvage disputes, any claim in the nature of salvage for services rendered to a ship (including, subject to the provisions of the said Act, services rendered in saving life from a ship), whether rendered on the high seas or within the body of a county, or partly on the high seas and partly within the body of a county, and whether the wreck in respect of which the salvage is claimed is found on the sea or on the land, or partly on the sea and partly on the land; 57 & 58 Vict. c. 60.

(vi) Any claim in the nature of towage, whether the services were rendered within the body of a county or on the high seas;

(vii) Any claim for necessaries supplied to a foreign ship, whether within the body of a county or on the high seas, and, unless it is shown to the court that at the time of the institution of the proceedings any owner or part owner of the ship was domiciled in England, any claim for any necessaries supplied to a ship elsewhere than in the port to which the ship belongs;

(viii) Any claim by a seaman of a ship for wages earned by him on board the ship, whether due under a special contract or otherwise, and any claim by the master of a ship for wages earned by him on board the ship and for disbursements made by him on account of the ship;

(ix) Any claim in respect of a mortgage of any ship, being a mortgage duly registered in accordance with the provisions of the Merchant Shipping Acts, 1894 to 1923, or in respect of any mortgage of a ship which is, or the proceeds whereof are, under the arrest of the court;

(x) Any claim for building, equipping or repairing a ship, if at the time of the institution of the proceedings the ship is, or the proceeds thereof are, under the arrest of the court;

(xi) Any matter concerning booty of war, or the distribution thereof, which may be referred to the court by His Majesty in Council;

(xii) Any claim—

(1) arising out of an agreement relating to the use or hire of a ship; or

(2) relating to the carriage of goods in a ship; or

(3) in tort in respect of goods carried in a ship;

unless it is shown to the court that at the time of the institution of the proceedings any owner or part owner of the ship was domiciled in England:

(*b*) Any other jurisdiction formerly vested in the High Court of Admiralty:

(*c*) All admiralty jurisdiction which, under or by virtue of any enactment which came into force after the commencement of the Act of 1873 and is not repealed by this Act, was immediately before the commencement of this Act vested in or capable of being exercised by the High Court constituted by the Act of 1873.

(2) The provisions of paragraph (*a*) of subsection (1) of this section which confer on the High Court admiralty jurisdiction in respect of claims for damage shall be construed as extending to claims for loss of life or personal injuries.

(3) In this Act, unless the context otherwise requires, the expression "ship" includes any description of vessel used in navigation not propelled by oars.

APPENDIX 4

Administration of Justice Act, 1956

1956 (4 & 5 ELIZ. 2) CHAPTER 46

Part I

Admiralty Jurisdiction and other Provisions as to Ships

1.—(1) The Admiralty jurisdiction of the High Court shall be as follows, that is to say, jurisdiction to hear and determine any of the following questions or claims— Admiralty jurisdiction of the High Court.

(*a*) any claim to the possession or ownership of a ship or to the ownership of any share therein;

(*b*) any question arising between the co-owners of a ship as to possession, employment or earnings of that ship;

(*c*) any claim in respect of a mortgage of or charge on a ship or any share therein;

(*d*) any claim for damage done by a ship;

(*e*) any claim for damage received by a ship;

(*f*) any claim for loss of life or personal injury sustained in consequence of any defect in a ship or in her apparel or equipment, or of the wrongful act, neglect or default of the owners, charterers or persons in possession or control of a ship or of the master or crew thereof or of any other person for whose wrongful acts, neglects or defaults the owners, charterers or persons in possession or control of a ship are responsible, being an act, neglect or default in the navigation or management of the ship, in the loading, carriage or discharge of goods on, in or from the ship or in the embarkation, carriage or disembarkation of persons on, in or from the ship;

(*g*) any claim for loss of or damage to goods carried in a ship;

(*h*) any claim arising out of any agreement relating to the carriage of goods in a ship or to the use or hire of a ship;

(*j*) any claim in the nature of salvage (including any claim arising by virtue of the application, by or under section fifty-one of the Civil Aviation Act, 1949, of the law relating to salvage to aircraft and their apparel and cargo);

(*k*) any claim in the nature of towage in respect of a ship or an aircraft;

(*l*) any claim in the nature of pilotage in respect of a ship or an aircraft;

(*m*) any claim in respect of goods or materials supplied to a ship for her operation or maintenance;

(*n*) any claim in respect of the construction, repair or equipment of a ship or dock charges or dues;

(*o*) any claim by a master or member of the crew of a ship for wages and any claim by or in respect of a master or member of the crew of a ship for any money or property which, under any of the provisions of the Merchant Shipping Acts, 1894 to 1954, is recoverable as wages or in the court and in the manner in which wages may be recovered;

(*p*) any claim by a master, shipper, charterer or agent in respect of disbursements made on account of a ship;

(*q*) any claim arising out of an act which is or is claimed to be a general average act;

(*r*) any claim arising out of bottomry;

(*s*) any claim for the forfeiture or condemnation of a ship or of goods which are being or have been carried, or have been attempted to be carried, in a ship, or for the restoration of a ship or any such goods after seizure, or for droits of Admiralty, together with any other jurisdiction which either was vested in the High Court of Admiralty immediately before the date of the commencement of the Supreme Court of Judicature Act, 1873 (that is to say, the first day of November, eighteen hundred and seventy-five) or is conferred by or under an Act which came into operation on or after that date on the High Court as being a court with Admiralty jurisdiction and any other jurisdiction connected with ships or aircraft vested in the High Court apart from this section which is for the time being assigned by rules of court to the Probate, Divorce and Admiralty Division.

(2) The jurisdiction of the High Court under paragraph (*b*) of subsection (1) of this section includes power to settle any account outstanding and unsettled between the parties in relation to the ship, and to direct that the ship, or any share thereof, shall be sold, and to make such other order as the court thinks fit.

(3) The reference in paragraph (*j*) of subsection (1) of this section to claims in the nature of salvage includes a reference to such claims for services rendered in saving life from a ship or an aircraft or in preserving cargo, apparel or wreck as, under sections five hundred and forty-four to five hundred and forty-six of the Merchant Shipping Act, 1894, or any Order in Council made under section fifty-one of the Civil Aviation Act, 1949, are authorized to be made in connection with a ship or an aircraft.

(4) The preceding provisions of this section apply—

(*a*) in relation to all ships or aircraft, whether British or not and whether registered or not and wherever the residence or domicile of their owners may be;

(*b*) in relation to all claims, wheresoever arising (including, in the case of cargo or wreck salvage, claims in respect of cargo or wreck found on land); and

(*c*) so far as they relate to mortgages and charges, to all mortgages or charges, whether registered or not and whether legal or equitable, including mortgages and charges created under foreign law:

Provided that nothing in this subsection shall be construed as extending the cases in which money or property is recoverable under any of the provisions of the Merchant Shipping Acts, 1894 to 1954.

Mode of exercise of Admiralty jurisdiction.

3.—(1) Subject to the provisions of the next following section, the Admiralty jurisdiction of the High Court, the Liverpool Court of Passage and any county court may in all cases be invoked by an action in personam.

(2) The Admiralty jurisdiction of the High Court may in the cases mentioned in paragraphs (*a*) to (*c*) and (*s*) of subsection (1) of section one of this Act be invoked by an action in rem against the ship or property in question.

(3) In any case in which there is a maritime lien or other charge on any ship, aircraft or other property for the amount claimed, the Admiralty jurisdiction of the High Court, the Liverpool Court of Passage and any county court may be invoked by an action in rem against that ship, aircraft or property.

(4) In the case of any such claim as is mentioned in paragraphs (*d*) to (*r*) of subsection (1) of section one of this Act, being a claim arising in connection with a ship, where the person who would be liable on the claim in an action in personam was, when the cause of action arose, the owner or charterer of, or in possession or in control of, the ship, the Admiralty jurisdiction of the High Court and (where there is such jurisdiction) the Admiralty jurisdiction of the Liverpool Court of Passage or any county court may (whether the claim gives rise to a maritime lien on the ship or not) be invoked by an action in rem against—

(*a*) that ship, if at the time when the action is brought it is beneficially owned as respects all the shares therein by that person; or

(*b*) any other ship which, at the time when the action is brought, is beneficially owned as aforesaid.

(5) In the case of a claim in the nature of towage or pilotage in respect of an aircraft, the Admiralty jurisdiction of the High Court, the Liverpool Court of Passage and any county court may be invoked by an action in rem against that aircraft if at the time when the action is brought it is beneficially owned by the person who would be liable on the claim in an action in personam.

(6) Notwithstanding anything in the preceding provisions of this section, the Admiralty jurisdiction of the High Court, the Liverpool Court of Passage or any county court shall not be invoked by an action in rem in the case of any such claim as is mentioned in paragraph (*o*) of subsection (1) of section one of this Act unless the claim relates wholly or partly to wages (including any sum allotted out of wages or adjudged by a superintendent to be due by way of wages).

(7) Where, in the exercise of its Admiralty jurisdiction, the High Court, the Liverpool Court of Passage or any county court orders any ship, aircraft or other property to be sold, the court shall have jurisdiction to hear and determine any question arising as to the title to the proceeds of sale.

(8) In determining for the purposes of subsections (4) and (5) of this section whether a person would be liable on a claim in an action in personam it shall be assumed that he has his habitual residence or a place of business within England and Wales.

Jurisdiction in personam of courts in collision and other similar cases

4.—(1) No court in England and Wales shall entertain an action in personam to enforce a claim to which this section applies unless—

(*a*) the defendant has his habitual residence or a place of business within England and Wales; or

(*b*) the cause of action arose within inland waters of England and Wales or within the limits of a port of England and Wales; or

(*c*) an action arising out of the same incident or series of incidents is proceeding in the court or has been heard and determined in the court.

In this subsection—

"inland waters" includes any part of the sea adjacent to the coast of the United Kingdom certified by the Secretary of State to be waters falling by international law to be treated as within the territorial sovereignty of Her Majesty apart from the operation of that law in relation to territorial waters;

"port" means any port, harbour, river, estuary, haven, dock, canal or other place so long as a person or body of persons is empowered by or under an Act to make charges in respect of ships entering it or using the facilities therein, and "limits of a port" means the limits thereof as fixed by or under the Act in question or, as the case may be, by the relevant charter or custom;

"charges" means any charges with the exception of light dues, local light dues and any other charges in respect of lighthouses, buoys or beacons and of charges in respect of pilotage.

(2) No court in England and Wales shall entertain an action in personam to enforce a claim to which this section applies until any proceedings previously brought by the plaintiff in any court outside England and Wales against the same defendant in respect of the same incident or series of incidents have been discontinued or otherwise come to an end.

(3) The preceding provisions of this section shall apply to counter-claims (not being counter-claims in proceedings arising out of the same incident or series of incidents) as they apply to actions in personam, but as if the references to the plaintiff and the defendant were respectively references to the plaintiff on the counterclaim and the defendant to the counter-claim.

(4) The preceding provisions of this section shall not apply to any action or counter-claim if the defendant thereto submits or has agreed to submit to the jurisdiction of the court.

(5) Subject to the provisions of subsection (2) of this section, the High Court shall have jurisdiction to entertain an action in personam to enforce a claim to which this section applies whenever any of the conditions specified in paragraphs (*a*) to (*c*) of subsection (1) of this section are satisfied, and the rules of court relating to the service of process outside the jurisdiction shall make such provision as may appear to the rule-making authority to be appropriate having regard to the provisions of this subsection.

(6) Nothing in this section shall prevent an action or counterclaim which is brought in accordance with the provisions of this section in the High Court, the Liverpool Court of Passage or a county court being transferred, in accordance with the enactments in that behalf, to some other court.

(7) The claims to which this section applies are claims for damage, loss of life or personal injury arising out of a collision between ships or out of the carrying out of or omission to carry out a manoeuvre in the case of one or more of two or more ships or out of non-compliance, on the part of one or more of two or more ships, with the collision regulations.

(8) For the avoidance of doubt it is hereby declared that this section applies in relation to the jurisdiction of any court not being Admiralty jurisdiction, as well as in relation to its Admiralty jurisdiction, if any.

Wages

5.—(1) Section one hundred and sixty-five of the Merchant Shipping Act, 1894 (which imposes restrictions on suits for wages), is hereby repealed.

(2) Nothing in this Part of this Act shall be construed as limiting the jurisdiction of the court to refuse to entertain an action for wages by the master or a member of the crew of a ship, not being a British ship.

Court in England and Wales not to have jurisdiction in cases falling within Rhine Convention.

6. No court in England and Wales shall have jurisdiction to determine any claim or question certified by the Secretary of State to be a claim or question which, under the Rhine Navigation Convention, falls to be determined in accordance with the provisions thereof and any proceedings to enforce such a claim which are commenced in any such court shall be set aside.

APPENDIX 5

Senior Courts Act, 1981 (UK) [latest version amended 2005]

An Act to consolidate with amendments the Supreme Court of Judicature (Consolidation) Act 1925 and other enactments relating to the [Senior Courts] in England and Wales and the administration of justice therein; to repeal certain obsolete or unnecessary enactments so relating; to amend Part VIII of the Mental Health Act 1959, the Courts-Martial (Appeals) Act 1968, the Arbitration Act 1979 and the law relating to county courts; and for connected purposes. [28th July 1981]

20 Admiralty jurisdiction of High Court

(1) The Admiralty jurisdiction of the High Court shall be as follows, that is to say—

(a) jurisdiction to hear and determine any of the questions and claims mentioned in subsection (2);

(b) jurisdiction in relation to any of the proceedings mentioned in subsection (3);

(c) any other Admiralty jurisdiction which it had immediately before the commencement of this Act; and

(d) any jurisdiction connected with ships or aircraft which is vested in the High Court apart from this section and is for the time being by rules of court made or coming into force after the commencement of this Act assigned to the Queen's Bench Division and directed by the rules to be exercised by the Admiralty Court.

(2) The questions and claims referred to in subsection (1)(a) are—

(a) any claim to the possession or ownership of a ship or to the ownership of any share therein;

(b) any question arising between the co-owners of a ship as to possession, employment or earnings of that ship;

(c) any claim in respect of a mortgage of or charge on a ship or any share therein;

(d) any claim for damage received by a ship;

(e) any claim for damage done by a ship;

(f) any claim for loss of life or personal injury sustained in consequence of any defect in a ship or in her apparel or equipment, or in consequence of the wrongful act, neglect or default of—

(i) the owners, charterers or persons in possession or control of a ship; or

(ii) the master or crew of a ship, or any other person for whose wrongful acts, neglects or defaults the owners, charterers or persons in possession or control of a ship are responsible,

being an act, neglect or default in the navigation or management of the ship, in the loading, carriage or discharge of goods on, in or from the ship, or in the embarkation, carriage or disembarkation of persons on, in or from the ship;

(g) any claim for loss of or damage to goods carried in a ship;

(h) any claim arising out of any agreement relating to the carriage of goods in a ship or to the use or hire of a ship;

[(j) any claim—

(i) under the Salvage Convention 1989;

(ii) under any contract for or in relation to salvage services; or

(iii) in the nature of salvage not falling within (i) or (ii) above;

or any corresponding claim in connection with an aircraft;]

(k) any claim in the nature of towage in respect of a ship or an aircraft;
(l) any claim in the nature of pilotage in respect of a ship or an aircraft;
(m) any claim in respect of goods or materials supplied to a ship for her operation or maintenance;
(n) any claim in respect of the construction, repair or equipment of a ship or in respect of dock charges or dues;
(o) any claim by a master or member of the crew of a ship for wages (including any sum allotted out of wages or adjudged by a superintendent to be due by way of wages);
(p) any claim by a master, shipper, charterer or agent in respect of disbursements made on account of a ship;
(q) any claim arising out of an act which is or is claimed to be a general average act;
(r) any claim arising out of bottomry;
(s) any claim for the forfeiture or condemnation of a ship or of goods which are being or have been carried, or have been attempted to be carried, in a ship, or for the restoration of a ship or any such goods after seizure, or for droits of Admiralty.

(3) The proceedings referred to in subsection (1)(b) are—

(a) any application to the High Court under the Merchant Shipping Acts 1894 to 1979 other than an application under [the Merchant Shipping Act 1995];
(b) any action to enforce a claim for damage, loss of life or personal injury arising out of—
(i) a collision between ships; or
(ii) the carrying out of or omission to carry out a manoeuvre in the case of one or more of two or more ships; or
(iii) non-compliance, on the part of one or more of two or more ships, with the collision regulations;
(c) any action by shipowners or other persons under the [Merchant Shipping Act 1995] for the limitation of the amount of their liability in connection with a ship or other property.

(4) The jurisdiction of the High Court under subsection (2)(b) includes power to settle any account outstanding and unsettled between the parties in relation to the ship, and to direct that the ship, or any share thereof, shall be sold, and to make such other order as the court thinks fit.

(5) Subsection (2)(e) extends to—

(a) any claim in respect of a liability incurred under the [Chapter III of Part VI of the Merchant Shipping Act 1995]; and
(b) any claim in respect of a liability falling on the [International Oil Pollution Compensation Fund, or on the International Oil Compensation Fund 1984, under Chapter IV of Part VI of the Merchant Shipping Act 1995,][or on the International Oil Pollution Compensation Supplementary Fund 2003,].

[(6) In subsection (2)(j)—

(a) the "Salvage Convention 1989" means the International Convention on Salvage, 1989 as it has effect under [section 224 of the Merchant Shipping Act 1995];
(b) the reference to salvage services includes services rendered in saving life from a ship and the reference to any claim under any contract for or in relation to salvage services includes any claim arising out of such a contract whether or not arising during the provision of the services;
(c) the reference to a corresponding claim in connection with an aircraft is a reference to any claim corresponding to any claim mentioned in sub-paragraph (i) or (ii) of paragraph (j) which is available under section 87 of the Civil Aviation Act 1982.]

(7) The preceding provisions of this section apply—

(a) in relation to all ships or aircraft, whether British or not and whether registered or not and wherever the residence or domicile of their owners may be;

(b) in relation to all claims, wherever arising (including, in the case of cargo or wreck salvage, claims in respect of cargo or wreck found on land); and

(c) so far as they relate to mortgages and charges, to all mortgages or charges, whether registered or not and whether legal or equitable, including mortgages and charges created under foreign law:

Provided that nothing in this subsection shall be construed as extending the cases in which money or property is recoverable under any of the provisions of the [Merchant Shipping Act 1995].

21 Mode of exercise of Admiralty jurisdiction

(1) Subject to section 22, an action in personam may be brought in the High Court in all cases within the Admiralty jurisdiction of that court.

(2) In the case of any such claim as is mentioned in section 20(2)(a), (c) or (s) or any such question as is mentioned in section 20(2)(b), an action in rem may be brought in the High Court against the ship or property in connection with which the claim or question arises.

(3) In any case in which there is a maritime lien or other charge on any ship, aircraft or other property for the amount claimed, an action in rem may be brought in the High Court against that ship, aircraft or property.

(4) In the case of any such claim as is mentioned in section 20(2)(e) to (r), where—

(a) the claim arises in connection with a ship; and

(b) the person who would be liable on the claim in an action in personam ("the relevant person") was, when the cause of action arose, the owner or charterer of, or in possession or in control of, the ship,

an action in rem may (whether or not the claim gives rise to a maritime lien on that ship) be brought in the High Court against—

(i) that ship, if at the time when the action is brought the relevant person is either the beneficial owner of that ship as respects all the shares in it or the charterer of it under a charter by demise; or

(ii) any other ship of which, at the time when the action is brought, the relevant person is the beneficial owner as respects all the shares in it.

(5) In the case of a claim in the nature of towage or pilotage in respect of an aircraft, an action in rem may be brought in the High Court against that aircraft if, at the time when the action is brought, it is beneficially owned by the person who would be liable on the claim in an action in personam.

(6) Where, in the exercise of its Admiralty jurisdiction, the High Court orders any ship, aircraft or other property to be sold, the court shall have jurisdiction to hear and determine any question arising as to the title to the proceeds of sale.

(7) In determining for the purposes of subsections (4) and (5) whether a person would be liable on a claim in an action in personam it shall be assumed that he has his habitual residence or a place of business within England or Wales.

(8) Where, as regards any such claim as is mentioned in section 20(2)(e) to (r), a ship has been served with a writ or arrested in an action in rem brought to enforce that claim, no other ship may be served with a writ or arrested in that or any other action in rem brought to enforce that claim; but this subsection does not prevent the issue, in respect of any one such claim, of a writ naming more than one ship or of two or more writs each naming a different ship.

22 Restrictions on entertainment of actions in personam in collision and other similar cases

(1) This section applies to any claim for damage, loss of life or personal injury arising out of—

(a) a collision between ships; or

(b) the carrying out of, or omission to carry out, a manoeuvre in the case of one or more of two or more ships; or

(c) non-compliance, on the part of one or more of two or more ships, with the collision regulations.

(2) The High Court shall not entertain any action in personam to enforce a claim to which this section applies unless—

(a) the defendant has his habitual residence or a place of business within England or Wales; or
(b) the cause of action arose within inland waters of England or Wales or within the limits of a port of England or Wales; or
(c) an action arising out of the same incident or series of incidents is proceeding in the court or has been heard and determined in the court.

In this subsection—

"inland waters" includes any part of the sea adjacent to the coast of the United Kingdom certified by the Secretary of State to be waters falling by international law to be treated as within the territorial sovereignty of Her Majesty apart from the operation of that law in relation to territorial waters;

"port" means any port, harbour, river, estuary, haven, dock, canal or other place so long as a person or body of persons is empowered by or under an Act to make charges in respect of ships entering it or using the facilities therein, and "limits of a port" means the limits thereof as fixed by or under the Act in question or, as the case may be, by the relevant charter or custom;

"charges" means any charges with the exception of light dues, local light dues and any other charges in respect of lighthouses, buoys or beacons and of charges in respect of pilotage.

(3) The High Court shall not entertain any action in personam to enforce a claim to which this section applies until any proceedings previously brought by the plaintiff in any court outside England and Wales against the same defendant in respect of the same incident or series of incidents have been discontinued or otherwise come to an end.

(4) Subsections (2) and (3) shall apply to counterclaims (except counterclaims in proceedings arising out of the same incident or series of incidents) as they apply to actions, the references to the plaintiff and the defendant being for this purpose read as references to the plaintiff on the counterclaim and the defendant to the counterclaim respectively.

(5) Subsections (2) and (3) shall not apply to any action or counterclaim if the defendant thereto submits or has agreed to submit to the jurisdiction of the court.

(6) Subject to the provisions of subsection (3), the High Court shall have jurisdiction to entertain an action in personam to enforce a claim to which this section applies whenever any of the conditions specified in subsection (2)(a) to (c) is satisfied, and the rules of court relating to the service of process outside the jurisdiction shall make such provision as may appear to the rule-making authority to be appropriate having regard to the provisions of this subsection.

(7) Nothing in this section shall prevent an action which is brought in accordance with the provisions of this section in the High Court being transferred, in accordance with the enactments in that behalf, to some other court.

(8) For the avoidance of doubt it is hereby declared that this section applies in relation to the jurisdiction of the High Court not being Admiralty jurisdiction, as well as in relation to its Admiralty jurisdiction.

23 High Court not to have jurisdiction in cases within Rhine Convention

The High Court shall not have jurisdiction to determine any claim or question certified by the Secretary of State to be a claim or question which, under the Rhine Navigation Convention, falls to be determined in accordance with the provisions of that Convention; and any proceedings to enforce such a claim which are commenced in the High Court shall be set aside.

24 Supplementary provisions as to Admiralty jurisdiction

(1) In sections 20 to 23 and this section, unless the context otherwise requires—

"collision regulations" means [safety regulations under section 85 of the Merchant Shipping Act 1995];

"goods" includes baggage;
"master" has the same meaning as in the [Merchant Shipping Act 1995], and accordingly includes every person (except a pilot) having command or charge of a ship;
"the Rhine Navigation Convention" means the Convention of the 7th October 1868 as revised by any subsequent Convention;
"ship" includes any description of vessel used in navigation and (except in the definition of "port" in section 22(2) and in subsection (2)(c) of this section) includes, subject to section 2(3) of the Hovercraft Act 1968, a hovercraft;
"towage" and "pilotage", in relation to an aircraft, mean towage and pilotage while the aircraft is waterborne.

(2) Nothing in sections 20 to 23 shall—

(a) be construed as limiting the jurisdiction of the High Court to refuse to entertain an action for wages by the master or a member of the crew of a ship, not being a British ship;
(b) affect the provisions of section [226 of the Merchant Shipping Act 1995] (power of a receiver of wreck to detain a ship in respect of a salvage claim); or
(c) authorise proceedings in rem in respect of any claim against the Crown, or the arrest, detention or sale of any of Her Majesty's ships or Her Majesty's aircraft, or, subject to section 2(3) of the Hovercraft Act 1968, Her Majesty's hovercraft, or of any cargo or other property belonging to the Crown.

(3) In this section—

"Her Majesty's ships" and "Her Majesty's aircraft" have the meanings given by section 38(2) of the Crown Proceedings Act 1947;
"Her Majesty's hovercraft" means hovercraft belonging to the Crown in right of Her Majesty's Government in the United Kingdom or Her Majesty's Government in Northern Ireland.

Other particular fields of jurisdiction

25 Probate jurisdiction of High Court

(1) Subject to the provisions of Part V, the High Court shall, in accordance with section 19(2), have the following probate jurisdiction, that is to say all such jurisdiction in relation to probates and letters of administration as it had immediately before the commencement of this Act, and in particular all such contentious and non-contentious jurisdiction as it then had in relation to—

(a) testamentary causes or matters;
(b) the grant, amendment or revocation of probates and letters of administration; and
(c) the real and personal estate of deceased persons.

(2) Subject to the provisions of Part V, the High Court shall, in the exercise of its probate jurisdiction, perform all such duties with respect to the estates of deceased persons as fell to be performed by it immediately before the commencement of this Act.

26 Matrimonial jurisdiction of High Court

The High Court shall, in accordance with section 19(2), have all such jurisdiction in relation to matrimonial causes and matters as was immediately before the commencement of the [M8]Matrimonial Causes Act 1857 vested in or exercisable by any ecclesiastical court or person in England or Wales in respect of—

(a) divorce a mensa et thoro (renamed judicial separation by that Act);
(b) nullity of marriage ... [F108]; and
(c) any matrimonial cause or matter except marriage licences.

27 Prize jurisdiction of High Court

The High Court shall, in accordance with section 19(2), have as a prize court—

(a) all such jurisdiction as is conferred on it by the Prize Acts 1864 to 1944 (in which references to the High Court of Admiralty are by virtue of paragraph 1 of Schedule 4 to this Act to be construed as references to the High Court); and

(b) all such other jurisdiction on the high seas and elsewhere as it had as a prize court immediately before the commencement of this Act.

APPENDIX 6

Web Addresses for Non-UK Admiralty Statutes

The URLs given below, linking to official government legislation sites, were correct at the time of going to press.

All the jurisdictions examined in this book, with the exception of Singapore, have 'Legal Information Institutes', accessible through worldlii.org. The respective 'LII' will usually provide access to the legislation in the relevant jurisdiction. Alternatively, a simple web search is usually effective in locating legislation and other information.

Australia

Admiralty Act 1988 bit.ly/AU_AA88

Canada

Federal Courts Act 1985 bit.ly/CA_FCA85

Hong Kong

High Court Ordinance Cap 4 bit.ly/HK_HCO

New Zealand

Admiralty Act 1973 bit.ly/NZ_AA73

Singapore

High Court (Admiralty Jurisdiction) Act (Cap 123) bit.ly/SG_HCAJA

South Africa

Admiralty Jurisdiction Regulation Act 105 of 1983[1] bit.ly/ZA_AJRA

---

[1] Amended by the Admiralty Jurisdiction Regulation Amendment Act 87 of 1992. No consolidated version is available on the government website, but one is reproduced in Appendix 11 of the first edition of this work.

APPENDIX 7

Admiralty Court Forms

Although it is hoped that practitioners will find this list of the Court's forms helpful, the text of those forms has deliberately not been reproduced in this work. The forms themselves are available free of charge on the internet. At the time of writing, they are to be found at www.justice.gov.uk> Courts > Procedure rules > Civil procedure rules > Forms > Admiralty. All the following should appear.

Form	Title
ADM1	Claim Form (Admiralty claim *in rem*).
ADM1A	Claim Form (Admiralty claim).
ADM1C	Notes for defendant on replying to an admiralty claim form.
ADM2	Acknowledgment of Service (Admiralty claim).
ADM3	Collision statement of case.
ADM4	Application and undertaking for arrest and custody.
ADM5	Declaration in support of application for warrant of arrest.
ADM6	Notice to Consular Officer of intention to apply for warrant of arrest.
ADM7	Request for caution against arrest.
ADM9	Warrant of Arrest.
ADM10	Standard Directions to the Admiralty Marshal.
ADM11	Request for caution against Release.
ADM12	Request and undertaking for release.
ADM12A	Request for withdrawal of caution against Release.
ADM13	Application for judgment in default of filing an acknowledgment of service and/or defence or collision statement of case.
ADM14	Order for sale of a ship.
ADM15	Claim Form (Admiralty limitation claim).
ADM15B	Notes for defendant (Admiralty limitation claim).
ADM16	Notice of admission of right of claimant to limit liability.
ADM16A	Defence to admiralty limitation claim.
ADM16B	Acknowledgment of Service (Admiralty limitation claim).
ADM17	Application for restricted limitation decree.
ADM17A	Application for general limitation decree.
ADM18	Restricted limitation decree.
ADM19	General limitation decree.
ADM20	Defendant's claim in a limitation claim.
ADM21	Declaration as to inability of a defendant to file and serve statement of case under a decree of limitation.

APPENDIX 8

The Arrest Conventions of 1952 and 1999

The International Convention for the Unification of Certain Rules Relating to the Arrest of Seagoing Ships was done at Brussels on 10 May 1952 (the Arrest Convention). The primary purpose of the Arrest Convention was to protect the interests of both ship and cargo in avoiding interruption of the voyage by arrest for claims without any relationship to the operation of the ship.[1] It was ratified or acceded to by 63 countries. The United Kingdom ratified the Arrest Convention on 18 March 1959.[2] Given that the United Kingdom has given effect to the Arrest Convention, the English courts may look at the terms of the Convention to assist in the construction of the statute which currently gives effect to that Convention, namely the Supreme Court Act 1981.[3] **0.1**

Australia has not ratified the Arrest Convention, however the provisions of the Admiralty Act 1988 are largely consistent with the provisions of the Convention. Canada has not ratified the Arrest Convention but has adopted some of its provisions into Canadian domestic law, notably the concept of sister-ship arrest.[4] Hong Kong became a party to the Arrest Convention in 1963 and its provisions are given effect to by Sections 12A and B of the High Court Ordinance (Cap 4). New Zealand has not ratified the Arrest Convention but, like Australia, has given effect to most of its provisions in the Admiralty Act 1973. Singapore has not ratified the Arrest Convention but it is largely given effect to in the High Court (Admiralty Jurisdiction) Act, which confers admiralty jurisdiction on the High Court of Singapore.[5] South Africa has not ratified the 1952 Convention and, in the Admiralty Jurisdiction Regulation Act 105 of 1983, has adopted a much broader admiralty jurisdiction than is provided for in the Arrest Convention. **0.2**

During the debates leading up to the Arrest Convention, it had emerged that there were two fundamental differences between the common law and the civil law systems with respect to arrest. In civil law countries a vessel could be arrested as security for any claim, whether or not it was of a maritime nature. The arrest of a vessel was merely one element of a general power to arrest a debtor's property. For example, the *saisie conservatoire* in the French system was applied to property other than ships. By contrast, in the common law systems a vessel could only be arrested in those limited number of circumstances where the claim gave rise to the right to proceed *in rem*. The second important difference between the two systems was the approach taken to wrongful arrest. In civil law systems, the arresting party could be held liable for damages suffered by the owner as a consequence of the arrest. The common law systems, however, restricted the owner to the cost of the security.[6] The Arrest Convention was a compromise between the differing approaches in the common law and civilian systems to the arrest of ships. It also introduced the previously unknown concept of 'sister-ship' arrest. **0.3**

---

[1] Report of the Chairman of the CMI International Sub-Committee to the Lisbon Conference; The Travaux Préparatoires to the 1999 Convention in F Berlingieri, *Berlingieri on Arrest of Ships* (3rd edn, 2000) 385.

[2] Neither Australia, Canada, New Zealand, Singapore nor South Africa have ratified the 1952 Convention. Hong Kong ratified it on 29 March 1963.

[3] *The Banco* [1971] 1 All ER 524, 532, [1971] P 137, 152; *The Eschersheim* [1976] 1 All ER 920, [1976] 1 WLR 430, [1976] 2 Lloyd's Rep 1; *The Deichland* [1990] 1 QB 361, [1989] 2 All ER 1066, [1989] 2 Lloyd's Rep 113.

[4] Federal Courts Act RSC 1985, c.F-7, ss 22 and 43; Supreme Court Act RSBC 1996 c.443.

[5] Chapter 123, 15 January 1962 as amended.

[6] F Berlingieri, *Berlingieri on Arrest of Ships* (5th edn, 2011) 1.11.

0.4 The Arrest Convention sets out a number of so-called 'maritime claims'[7] and provides that arrest may be made in respect of such claims but no others.[8] The list of maritime claims included in the Arrest Convention is based on those contained in s 22 of the Supreme Court of Judicature (Consolidation) Act 1925. There is no general definition of what constitutes a 'maritime claim' and it appears that there was no discussion of the conceptual nature of a maritime claim in the conferences preceding the adoption of the Arrest Convention. The English position was simply adopted even without the inclusion of all the claims secured by a maritime lien under the Convention on Maritime Liens and Mortgages 1926.[9] The distinction between the two Conventions needs to be understood. The Convention on Maritime Liens and Mortgages 1926, to which the United Kingdom has never become a party, deals with the privileged character of certain claims and provides that certain claims shall be paid with priority.[10] By contrast, the Arrest Convention was designed to establish in respect of which claims it was possible to effect an arrest whilst saying nothing about the ultimate priority of those claims. The remarks of the French delegate, Mr de Grandmaison, are helpful in illuminating the difference between maritime liens and statutory actions *in rem*. He said:

> ... the Maritime Liens and Mortgages Conventions dealt with the privileged character of certain claims and stated that certain claims shall be paid with priority over certain other claims. But today that is not the question. The question is to know for which claim it will be permitted to the Court to effect the conservative arrest of a ship, and that simply gives to the claimant a security for the future. Therefore one has here not to look for a privileged claim but for a maritime claim, since the sacrifice that the continentals make is to waive the right of arrest for non maritime claims.[11]

0.5 The Arrest Convention provides that either the ship in respect of which the maritime claim arose or other ships in the same ownership may be subject to arrest. Where a ship is bare-boat chartered, or in other cases where the owner is not liable for the claim, other ships in the same ownership as the bareboat charterer or other person liable may be arrested.[12] The Arrest Convention provides that ships cannot be arrested twice.[13] It also provides that ships may only be arrested under judicial authority[14] and makes provision for the release of ships on provision of security.[15] All matters of procedure and questions concerning liability for wrongful arrest are required to be dealt with according to the law of the State in which the ship is arrested.[16] The Arrest Convention makes provision for rules relating to jurisdiction in respect of the merits of the case and the recognition of foreign judgments with respect to any security given to obtain the release of the ship.[17] Significantly, the Arrest Convention provides expressly that it is not to be construed as creating rights of action or maritime liens which do not exist under the laws of the forum in which the ship is arrested.[18]

---

[7] Art 1.

[8] Art 2.

[9] *The Deichland* [1990] 1 QB 361, [1989] 2 All ER 1066, [1989] 2 Lloyd's Rep 113; F Berlingieri, *Berlingieri on Arrest of Ships* (5th edn, 2011) 3.01.

[10] The 1926 Convention had been updated by the Convention on Maritime Liens and Mortgages 1967 but this Convention never achieved the requisite number of ratifications and never entered into force. A further attempt was made and the Convention on Maritime Liens and Mortgages 1993 was done at Geneva on 6 May 1993. It entered into force on 5 September 2004. The following countries are parties to that Convention: Ecuador, Estonia, Monaco, Nigeria, Russian Federation, Saint Vincent and the Grenadines, Spain, Syrian Arab Republic, Tunisia, Ukraine, and Vanuatu.

[11] CMI Bulletin No 105, p 225; Travaux Préparatoires p 282 in F Berlingieri, *Berlingieri on Arrest of Ships* (5th edn, 2011) 3.01, fn 8.

[12] Art 3.

[13] Art 3.

[14] Art 4.

[15] Art 5.

[16] Art 6.

[17] Art 7.

[18] Art 9.

The International Convention on the Arrest of Ships 1999 (the 1999 Convention) was done at Geneva on 12 March 1999. The purpose of the Convention was to update and refine the Arrest Convention, partly as a consequence of the adoption of the new Convention on Maritime Liens and Mortgages in 1993. It entered into force on 14 September 2014, the date by which ten States had expressed their consent to be bound by it. At the date of writing, only eleven States have become party to the Arrest Convention 1999.[19] **0.6**

It is argued that the 1999 Convention has clarified a number of problems of interpretation with the Arrest Convention and so it is difficult to understand why the 1999 Convention is not attracting additional ratifications.[20] One reason for the lack of ratifications from European States, however, may be that, following the transfer by the Treaty of Nice of authority to the European Union in matters of private international law, this is a Convention to which they can no longer subscribe individually. Generally, the scope of application of the 1999 Convention is broader than that of its predecessor. The list of maritime claims in the 1999 Convention is significantly wider and incorporates claims for environmental damage under art 1(d) of the Salvage Convention,[21] wreck removal, ship management services, insurance premia and calls, commissions and brokerages, ship sale contracts. Further, it expands the scope of certain existing heads of claim so as to embrace claims for 'special compensation' in relation to salvage claims, agreements relating to the carriage of passengers, claims for 'provisions, bunkers, equipment (including containers) supplied or services rendered to the ship for its operation, management, preservation or maintenance' in the context of 'goods and material claims', claims for 'port canal, dock, harbour and other waterway dues' within the scope of claims for 'port dues', 'costs of repatriation and social insurance contributions' within claims for wages and claims for construction, reconstruction, repairs, equipping or converting the ship. The definition of 'arrest' has been expanded to include 'a restriction on removal of a ship'. Further, art 8 expands the provisions of the Convention from seagoing ships to all ships regardless of whether the ship arrested is flying the flag of a State Party. **0.7**

Article 2 of the 1999 Convention makes clear that only court authorized arrest is possible and that a choice of law or forum clause is of no effect in relation to the jurisdiction where the arrest occurs. Pursuant to art 3, the link required between a maritime claim and the person owning, operating or demise chartering the ship is emphasized so as to ensure that a ship is not arrested in relation to a claim that is not enforceable against that ship. However, the time at which ownership is relevant pursuant to the Convention differs from the time at which it is relevant in English law. Article 3(1) provides that arrest is permissible if the person who owned the ship at the time when the maritime claim arose is the owner of the ship when the arrest is affected. In English law, the relevant time is when the action *in rem* is brought. The sister-ship provision remained the same as in the Arrest Convention despite support from the United Kingdom, Australia, Canada, Japan, The Netherlands and the Comité Maritime International that the South African concept of 'associate-ship arrest' be adopted.[22] **0.8**

Article 4 mandates release of a ship where 'sufficient security has been provided in a satisfactory form' and provides that the State courts will determine whether or not the security is sufficient. Article 5 allows for rearrest of the same ship or other ships to supplement security already provided where the security proves inadequate, where the guarantor is unlikely to fulfil its obligations or where the vessel is released in circumstances effectively outside the control of the claimant. **0.9**

Article 6 gives the court discretion as to whether to require security from the claimant as a condition for arrest in case it be determined subsequently that the arrest was 'wrongful or unjustified' or that excessive security was demanded and provided. These latter two provisions represent a significant departure from the existing position in the law of the United Kingdom. Article 7 provides that the arresting court has jurisdiction on the merits unless there is a valid jurisdiction or arbitration clause and that the arresting State is obliged to recognize a final decision on the merits by another State by releasing the security to the successful claimant. **0.10**

---

[19] Albania, Algeria, Benin, Bulgaria, Congo, Ecuador, Estonia, Latvia, Liberia, Spain, and the Syrian Arab Republic.

[20] F Berlingieri, 'The 1952 Arrest Convention Revisited' [2005] LMCLQ 327, 337.

[21] International Convention on Salvage 1989.

[22] Travaux Préparatoires in F Berlingieri, *Berlingieri on Arrest of Ships* (5th edn, 2011) Appendix VII.

A Comparison between the 1952 and 1999 Conventions

Definitions

1952 Article 1	1999 Article 1
1. "Maritime Claim"	1. "Maritime Claim"
(a) damage caused by any ship either in collision or otherwise;	(a) loss or damage caused by the operation of the ship;
(b) loss of life or personal injury occurring caused by any ship or occurring in connexion with the operation of any ship;	(b) loss of life or personal injury occurring, whether on land or on water, in direct connection with the operation of the ship;
(c) salvage;	(c) salvage operations or any salvage agreement, including, if applicable, special compensation relating to salvage operations in respect of a ship which by itself or its cargo threatened damage to the environment;
	(d) damage or threat of damage caused by the ship to the environment, coastline or related interests; measures taken to prevent, minimize, or remove such damage; compensation for such damage; costs of reasonable measures of reinstatement of the environment actually undertaken or to be undertaken; loss incurred or likely to be incurred by third parties in connection with such damage; and damage, costs, or loss of a similar nature to those identified in this subparagraph (d);
	(e) costs or expenses relating to the raising, removal, recovery, destruction or the rendering harmless of a ship which is sunk, wrecked, stranded or abandoned, including anything that is or has been on board such ship, and costs or expenses relating to the preservation of an abandoned ship and maintenance of its crew;
(d) any agreement relating to the use or hire of the ship, whether by charter party or otherwise;	(f) any agreement relating to the use or hire of the ship, whether contained in a charter party or otherwise;
(e) any agreement relating to the carriage of goods in any ship whether by charter party or otherwise;	(g) any agreement relating to the carriage of goods or passengers on board the ship, whether contained in a charter party or otherwise;
(f) loss of or damage to goods including baggage carried in any ship; board a ship;	(h) loss of or damage to or in connection with goods (including luggage) carried on board the ship;
(g) general average;	(i) general average;
(h) bottomry;	

(*Continued*)

1952 **Article 1**	**1999** **Article 1**
(i) towage;	(j) towage;
(j) pilotage;	(k) pilotage;
(k) goods or materials wherever supplied to a ship for her operation or maintenance;	(l) goods, materials, provisions, bunkers, equipment (including containers) supplied or services rendered to the ship for its operation, management, preservation or maintenance;
(l) construction, repair, or equipment of any ship or dock charges and dues;	(m) construction, reconstruction, repair, converting or equipping of the ship;
	(n) port, canal, dock, harbour and other waterway dues and charges;
(m) wages of Masters, Officers, or crew;	(o) wages and other sums due to the master, officers and other members of the ship's complement in respect of their employment on the ship, including costs of repatriation and social insurance contributions payable on their behalf;
	(p) disbursements incurred on behalf of the ship or its owners;
(n) Master's disbursements, including disbursements made by shippers, charterers or agents on behalf of a ship or her owner;	
	(q) insurance premiums (including mutual insurance calls) in respect of the ship, payable by or on behalf of the shipowner or demise charterer;
	(r) any commissions, brokerages or agency fees payable in respect of the ship by or on behalf of the shipowner or demise charterer;
(o) disputes as to the title or ownership of any ship;	(s) any dispute as to ownership or possession of the ship;
(p) disputes between co-owners of any ship as to the ownership, possession, employment or earnings of that ship;	(t) any dispute between co-owners of the ship as to the employment or earnings of the ship;
(q) the mortgage or hypothecation of any ship;	(u) a mortgage or a "hypothèque" or a charge of the same nature on the ship;
	(v) any dispute arising out of a contract for the sale of the ship.
2. "Arrest"	2. "Arrest"
The detention of a ship by judicial process to secure a maritime claim, but does not include the seizure of a ship in execution or satisfaction of a judgment.	Any detention or restriction on removal of a ship by order of a Court to secure a maritime claim, but does not include the seizure of a ship in execution or satisfaction of a judgment or other enforceable instrument.

(*Continued*)

1952 Article 1	1999 Article 1
3. "Person" Includes individuals, partnerships and bodies corporate, Governments, their Departments, and Public Authorities.	3. "Person" Means any individual or partnership or any public or private body, whether corporate or not, including a State or any of its constituent subdivisions.
4. "Claimant" A person who alleges that a maritime claim exists in his favour.	4. "Claimant" Any person asserting a maritime claim.
	5. "Court" Any competent judicial authority of a State.

Powers of arrest

1952 Article 4 & 2	1999 Article 2
A ship may only be arrested under the authority of a Court or of the appropriate judicial authority of the Contracting State in which the arrest is made. A ship flying the flag of one of the Contracting States may be arrested in the jurisdiction of any of the Contracting States in respect of any maritime claim, but in respect of no other claim; but nothing in this Convention shall be deemed to extend or restrict any right or Powers vested in any Governments or their Departments, Public Authorities, or Dock or Harbour Authorities under their existing domestic laws or regulations to arrest, detain or otherwise prevent the sailing of vessels within their jurisdiction.	1. A ship may be arrested or released from arrest only under the authority of a Court of the State Party in which the arrest is effected. 2. A ship may only be arrested in respect of a maritime claim but in respect of no other claim. 3. A ship may be arrested for the purpose of obtaining security notwithstanding that, by virtue of a jurisdiction clause or arbitration clause in any relevant contract, or otherwise, the maritime claim in respect of which the arrest is effected is to be adjudicated in a State other than the State where the arrest is effected, or is to be arbitrated, or is to be adjudicated subject to the law of another State. 4. Subject to the provisions of this Convention, the procedure relating to the arrest of a ship or its release shall be governed by the law of the State in which the arrest was effected or applied for.

Exercise of right of arrest

1952 Article 3	1999 Article 3
1. Subject to the provisions of § 4 of this Article and of Article 10, a claimant may arrest either the particular ship in respect of which the maritime claim arose, or any other ship which is owned by the person who was, at the time when the maritime claim arose, the owner of the particular ship, even though the ship arrested be ready to sail; but no ship, other than the particular ship in respect of which the claim arose, may be arrested in respect of any of the maritime claims enumerated in Article (1)(o) (p) or (q). 2. Ships shall be deemed to be in the same ownership when all the shares therein are owned by the same person or persons. 3. **[see below under Right of Rearrest and Multiple Arrest]**	1. Arrest is permissible of any ship in respect of which a maritime claim is asserted if: (a) the person who owned the ship at the time when the maritime claim arose is liable for the claim and is owner of the ship when the arrest is effected; or (b) the demise charterer of the ship at the time when the maritime claim arose is liable for the claim and is demise charterer or owner of the ship when the arrest is effected; or (c) the claim is based upon a mortgage or a "hypothèque" or a charge of the same nature on the ship; or (d) the claim relates to the ownership or possession of the ship; or (e) the claim is against the owner, demise charterer, manager or operator of the ship and is secured by a maritime lien which is granted or arises under the law of the State where the arrest is applied for.
4. When in the case of a charter by demise of a ship the charterer and not the registered owner is liable in respect of a maritime claim relating to that ship, the claimant may arrest such a ship or any other ship in the ownership of the charterer by demise, subject to the provisions of this Convention, but no other ship in the ownership of the registered owner shall be liable to arrest in respect of such maritime claims. The provisions of this paragraph shall apply to any case in which a person other than the registered owner of a ship is liable in respect of a maritime claim relating to that ship. This provision does not apply to claims in respect of ownership or possession of a ship.	2. Arrest is also permissible of any other ship or ships which, when the arrest is effected, is or are owned by the person who is liable for the maritime claim and who was, when the claim arose: (a) owner of the ship in respect of which the maritime claim arose; or (b) demise charterer, time charterer or voyage charterer of that ship. This does not apply to claims in respect of ownership or possession of a ship. 3. Notwithstanding the provisions of paragraphs 1 and 2 of this article, the arrest of a ship which is not owned by the person liable for the claim shall be permissible only if, under the law of the State where the arrest is applied for, a judgment in respect of that claim can be enforced against that ship by judicial or forced sale of that ship.

Release from arrest

1952 Article 5	1999 Article 4
The Court or other appropriate judicial authority within whose jurisdiction the ship has been arrested shall permit the release of the ship upon sufficient bail or other security being furnished, save in cases in which a ship has been arrested in respect of any of the maritime claims enumerated in Article 1(1)(0) and (p). In such cases the Court or other appropriate judicial authority may permit the person in possession of the ship to continue trading the ship, upon such person furnishing sufficient bail or other security, or may otherwise deal with the operation of the ship during the period of arrest.	1. A ship which has been arrested shall be released when sufficient security has been provided in a satisfactory form, save in cases in which a ship has been arrested in respect of any of the maritime claims enumerated in article 1, paragraphs 1(s) and (t). In such cases, the Court may permit the person in possession of the ship to continue trading the ship, upon such person providing sufficient security, or may otherwise deal with the operation of the ship during the period of the arrest.
In default of agreement between the Parties as to the sufficiency of the bail or other security, the Court or other appropriate judicial authority shall determine the nature and amount thereof.	2. In the absence of agreement between the parties as to the sufficiency and form of the security, the Court shall determine its nature and the amount thereof, not exceeding the value of the arrested ship.
The request to release the ship against such security shall not be construed as an acknowledgment of liability or as a waiver of the benefit of the legal limitation of liability of the owner of the ship.	3. Any request for the ship to be released upon security being provided shall not be construed as an acknowledgment of liability nor as a waiver of any defence or any right to limit liability.
	4. If a ship has been arrested in a non-party State and is not released although security in respect of that ship has been provided in a State Party in respect of the same claim, that security shall be ordered to be released on application to the Court in the State Party.
	5. If in a non-party State the ship is released upon satisfactory security in respect of that ship being provided, any security provided in a State Party in respect of the same claim shall be ordered to be released to the extent that the total amount of security provided in the two States exceeds: (a) the claim for which the ship has been arrested, or (b) the value of the ship, whichever is the lower. Such release shall, however, not be ordered unless the security provided in the non-party State will actually be available to the claimant and will be freely transferable.

(*Continued*)

1952 Article 5	1999 Article 4
	6. Where, pursuant to paragraph 1 of this article, security has been provided, the person providing such security may at any time apply to the Court to have that security reduced, modified, or cancelled.

Right of rearrest and multiple arrest

1952 Article 3 (3)	1999 Article 5
3. A ship shall not be arrested, nor shall bail or other security be given more than once in any one or more of the jurisdictions of any of the Contracting States in respect of the same maritime claim by the same claimant: and, if a ship has been arrested in any one of such jurisdictions, or bail or other security has been given in such jurisdiction either to release the ship or to avoid a threatened arrest, any subsequent arrest of the ship or any ship in the same ownership by the same claimant for the same maritime claim shall be set aside, and the ship released by the Court or other appropriate judicial authority of that State, unless the claimant can satisfy the Court or other appropriate judicial authority that the bail or other security had been finally released before the subsequent arrest or that there is other good cause for maintaining that arrest.	1. Where in any State a ship has already been arrested and released or security in respect of that ship has already been provided to secure a maritime claim, that ship shall not thereafter be rearrested or arrested respect of the same maritime claim unless: (a) the nature or amount of the security in respect of that ship already provided in respect of the same claim is inadequate, on condition that the aggregate amount of security may not exceed the value of the ship; or (b) the person who has already provided the security is not, or is unlikely to be, able to fulfil some or all of that person's obligations; or (c) the ship arrested or the security previously provided was released either: (i) upon the application or with the consent of the claimant acting on reasonable grounds, or (ii) because the claimant could not by taking reasonable steps prevent the release. 2. Any other ship which would otherwise be subject to arrest in respect of the same maritime claim shall not be arrested unless: (a) the nature or amount of the security already provided in respect of the same claim is inadequate; or (b) the provisions of paragraph 1(b) or (c) of this article are applicable. 3. "Release" for the purpose of this article shall not include any unlawful release or escape from arrest.

Protection of owners and demise charterers of arrested ships

1952 Article 6	1999 Article 6
	1. The Court may as a condition of the arrest of a ship, or of permitting an arrest already effected to be maintained, impose upon the claimant who seeks to arrest or who has procured the arrest of the ship the obligation to provide security of a kind and for an amount, and upon such terms, as may be determined by that Court for any loss which may be incurred by the defendant as a result of the arrest, and for which the claimant may be found liable, including but not restricted to such loss or damage as may be incurred by that defendant in consequence of: (a) the arrest having been wrongful or unjustified; or (b) excessive security having been demanded and provided.
All questions whether in any case the claimant is liable in damages for the arrest of a ship or for the costs of the bail or other security furnished to release or prevent the arrest of a ship, shall be determined by the law of the Contracting State in whose jurisdiction the arrest was made or applied for.	2. The Courts of the State in which an arrest has been effected shall have jurisdiction to determine the extent of the liability, if any, of the claimant for loss or damage caused by the arrest of a ship, including but not restricted to such loss or damage as may be caused in consequence of: (a) the arrest having been wrongful or unjustified; or (b) excessive security having been demanded and provided.
The rules of procedure relating to the arrest of a ship, to the application for obtaining the authority referred to in Article 4, and all matters of procedure which the arrest may entail, shall be governed by the law of the Contracting State in which the arrest was made or applied for.	3. The liability, if any, of the claimant in accordance with paragraph 2 of this article shall be determined by application of the law of the State where the arrest was effected. 4. If a Court in another State or an arbitral tribunal is to determine the merits of the case in accordance with the provisions of article 7, then proceedings relating to the liability of the claimant in accordance with paragraph 2 of this article may be stayed pending that decision. 5. Where pursuant to paragraph 1 of this article security has been provided, the person providing such security may at any time apply to the Court to have that security reduced, modified or cancelled.

Jurisdiction on the merits of the case

1952

Article 7

1. The Courts of the country in which the arrest was made shall have jurisdiction to determine the case upon its merits:
   .. if the domestic law of the country in which the arrest is made gives jurisdiction to such Courts;
   .. or in any of the following cases namely:
   (a) if the claimant has his habitual place of residence or principal place of business in the country in which the arrest was made;
   (b) if the claim arose in the country in which the arrest was made;
   (c) if the claim concerns the voyage of the ship during which the arrest was made;
   (d) if the claim arose out of a collision or in circumstances covered by Article 13 of the International Convention for the unification of certain rules of law with respect to collisions between vessels, signed at Brussels on 23 September 1910;
   (e) if the claim is for salvage;
   (f) if the claim is upon a mortgage or hypothecation of the ship arrested.
2. If the Court within whose jurisdiction the ship was arrested has not jurisdiction to decide upon the merits, the bail or other security given in accordance with Article 5 to procure the release of the ship shall specifically provide that it is given as security for the satisfaction of any judgment which may eventually be pronounced by a Court having jurisdiction so to decide; and the Court or other appropriate judicial authority of the country in which the arrest is made shall fix a time within which the claimant shall bring an action before a Court having such jurisdiction.
3. If the parties have agreed to submit the dispute to the jurisdiction of a particular Court other than that within whose jurisdiction the arrest was made or to arbitration, the Court

1999

Article 7

1. The Courts of the State in which an arrest has been effected or security provided to obtain the release of the ship shall have jurisdiction to determine the case upon its merits, unless the parties validly agree or have validly agreed to submit the dispute to a Court of another State which accepts jurisdiction, or to arbitration.
2. Notwithstanding the provisions of paragraph 1 of this article, the Courts of the State in which an arrest has been effected, or security provided to obtain the release of the ship, may refuse to exercise that jurisdiction where that refusal is permitted by the law of that State and a Court of another State accepts jurisdiction.
3. In cases where a Court of the State where an arrest has been effected or security provided to obtain the release of the ship:
   (a) does not have jurisdiction to determine the case upon its merits; or
   (b) has refused to exercise jurisdiction in accordance with the provisions of paragraph 2 of this article,

   such a Court may, and upon request shall, order a period of time within which the claimant shall bring proceedings before a competent Court or arbitral tribunal.

(*Continued*)

1952 Article 7	1999 Article 7
or other appropriate judicial authority within whose jurisdiction the arrest was made may fix the time within which the claimant shall bring proceedings.	
4. If, in any of the cases mentioned in the two preceding paragraphs, the action or proceedings are not brought within the time so fixed, the defendant may apply for the release of the ship or of the bail or other security.	
5. This Article shall not apply in cases covered by the provisions of the revised Rhine Navigation Convention of 17 October 1868.	
	4. If proceedings are not brought within the period of time ordered in accordance with paragraph 3 of this article then the ship arrested or the security provided shall, upon request, be ordered to be released.
	5. If proceedings are brought within the period of time ordered in accordance with paragraph 3 of this article, or if proceedings before a competent Court or arbitral tribunal in another State are brought in the absence of such order, any final decision resulting therefrom shall be recognized and given effect with respect to the arrested ship or to the security provided in order to obtain its release, on condition that: (a) the defendant has been given reasonable notice of such proceedings and a reasonable opportunity to present the case for the defence; and (b) such recognition is not against public policy (*ordre public*).
	6. Nothing contained in the provisions of paragraph 5 of this article shall restrict any further effect given to a foreign judgment or arbitral award under the law of the State where the arrest of the ship was effected or security provided to obtain its release.

Application

1952 Article 8	1999 Article 8
1. The provisions of this Convention shall apply to any vessel flying the flag of a Contracting State in the jurisdiction of any Contracting State. 2. A ship flying the flag of a non-contracting State may be arrested in the jurisdiction of any Contracting State in respect of any of the maritime claims enumerated in Article 1 or of any other claim for which the law of the Contracting State permits arrest. 3. Nevertheless any Contracting State shall be entitled wholly or partly to exclude from the benefits of this Convention any Government of a non-contracting State or any person who has not, at the time of the arrest, his habitual residence or principal place of business in one of the Contracting States.	1. This Convention shall apply to any ship within the jurisdiction of any State Party, whether or not that ship is flying the flag of a State Party.
	2. This Convention shall not apply to any warship, naval auxiliary or other ships owned or operated by a State or used, for the time being, only on government non-commercial service. 3. This Convention does not affect any rights or powers vested in any Government or its departments, or in any public authority, or in any dock or harbour authority, under any international convention or under any domestic law or regulation, to detain or otherwise prevent from sailing any ship within their jurisdiction. 4. This Convention shall not affect the power of any State or Court to make orders affecting the totality of a debtor's assets. 5. Nothing in this Convention shall affect the application of an international convention providing for limitation of liability, or domestic law giving effect thereto, in the State where an arrest is effected. 6. Nothing in this Convention shall modify or affect the rules of law in force in the States Parties relating to the arrest of any ship physically within the jurisdiction of the State of its flag procured by a person whose habitual residence or principal place of business is in that State, or by any other person who has acquired a claim from such person by subrogation, assignment or otherwise.

(*Continued*)

1952 **Article 8**	1999 **Article 8**
4. Nothing in this Convention shall modify or affect the rules of law in force in the respective Contracting States relating to the arrest of any ship within the jurisdiction of the state of her flag by a person who has his habitual or principal place of business in that State. 5. When a maritime claim is asserted by a third party other than the original claimant, whether by subrogation, assignment or otherwise, such third party shall, for the purposes of this Convention, be deemed to have the same habitual residence or principal place of business as the original claimant.	

Non-creation of maritime liens

1952 **Article 9**	1999 **Article 9**
Nothing in this Convention shall be construed as creating a right of action, which, apart from the provisions of this Convention, would not arise under the law applied by the Court which has seisin of the case, nor as creating any maritime liens which do not exist under such law or under the Convention on Maritime Liens and Mortgages, if the latter is applicable.	Nothing in this Convention shall be construed as creating a maritime lien.

Reservations

1952 **Article 10**	1999 **Article 10**
The High Contracting Parties may at the time of signature, deposit of ratification or accession, reserve (a) the right not to apply this Convention to the arrest of a ship for any of the claims enumerated in paragraphs (o) and (p) of Article 1, but to apply their domestic laws to such claims;	1. Any State may, at the time of signature, ratification, acceptance, approval, or accession, or at any time thereafter, reserve the right to exclude the application of this Convention to any or all of the following: (a) ships which are not seagoing; (b) ships not flying the flag of a State Party;

(*Continued*)

1952 Article 10	1999 Article 10
(b) the right not to apply the first paragraph of article 3 to the arrest of a ship, within their jurisdiction, for claims set out in Article 1, paragraph (q).	(c) claims under article 1, paragraph 1(s). 2. A State may, when it is also a State Party to a specified treaty on navigation on inland waterways, declare when signing, ratifying, accepting, approving or acceding to this Convention, that rules on jurisdiction, recognition and execution of court decisions provided for in such treaties shall prevail over the rules contained in article 7 of this Convention.

Depositary

	1999 Article 11
	This Convention shall be deposited with the Secretary-General of the United Nations.

Signature, ratification, acceptance, approval and accession

1952 Article 12	1999 Article 12
	1. This Convention shall be open for signature by any State at the Headquarters of the United Nations, New York, from 1 September 1999 to 31 August 2000 and shall thereafter remain open for accession. 2. States may express their consent to be bound by this Convention by: (a) signature without reservation as to ratification, acceptance or approval; or (b) signature subject to ratification, acceptance or approval, followed by ratification, acceptance or approval; or (c) accession. 3. Ratification, acceptance, approval or accession shall be effected by the deposit of an instrument to that effect with the depositary.

States with more than one system of law

1999

Article 13

1. If a State has two or more territorial units in which different systems of law are applicable in relation to matters dealt with in this Convention, it may at the time of signature, ratification, approval or accession declare that this Convention shall extend to all its territorial units or only to one or more of them and may modify this declaration by submitting another declaration at any time.
2. Any such declaration shall be notified to the depositary and shall state expressly the territorial units to which the Convention applies.
3. In relation to a State Party which has two or more systems of law with regard to arrest of ships applicable in different territorial units, references in this Convention to the Court of a State and the law of a State shall be respectively construed as referring to the Court of the relevant territorial unit within that State and the law of the relevant territorial unit of that State.

Entry into force

1999

Article 14

1. This Convention shall enter into force six months following the date on which 10 States have expressed their consent to be bound by it.
2. For a State which expresses its consent to be bound by this Convention after the conditions for entry into force thereof have been met, such consent shall take effect three months after the date of expression of such consent.

Revision and amendment

	1999 Article 15
	1. A conference of State Parties for the purpose of revising or amending this Convention shall be convened by the Secretary-General of the United Nations at the request of one-third of the State Parties. 2. Any consent to be bound by this Convention, expressed after the date of entry into force of an amendment to this Convention, shall be deemed to apply to the Convention, as amended.

Denunciation

	1999 Article 16
	1. This Convention may be denounced by any State Party at any time after the date on which this Convention enters into force for that State. 2. Denunciation shall be effected by deposit of an instrument of denunciation with the depositary. 3. A denunciation shall take effect one year, or such longer period as may be specified in the instrument of denunciation, after the receipt of the instrument of denunciation by the depositary.

Languages

	1999 Article 17
	This Convention is established in a single original in the Arabic, Chinese, English, French, Russian and Spanish languages, each text being equally authentic.

INDEX

Please see under entries for individual countries for specific topics relating to that country